# Samuel Palmer
1805–1881

*Vision and Landscape*

Tom Butler
a 70th birthday present
from Sally Lloyd, at
St Olave's Church, EC3
15th February 2006

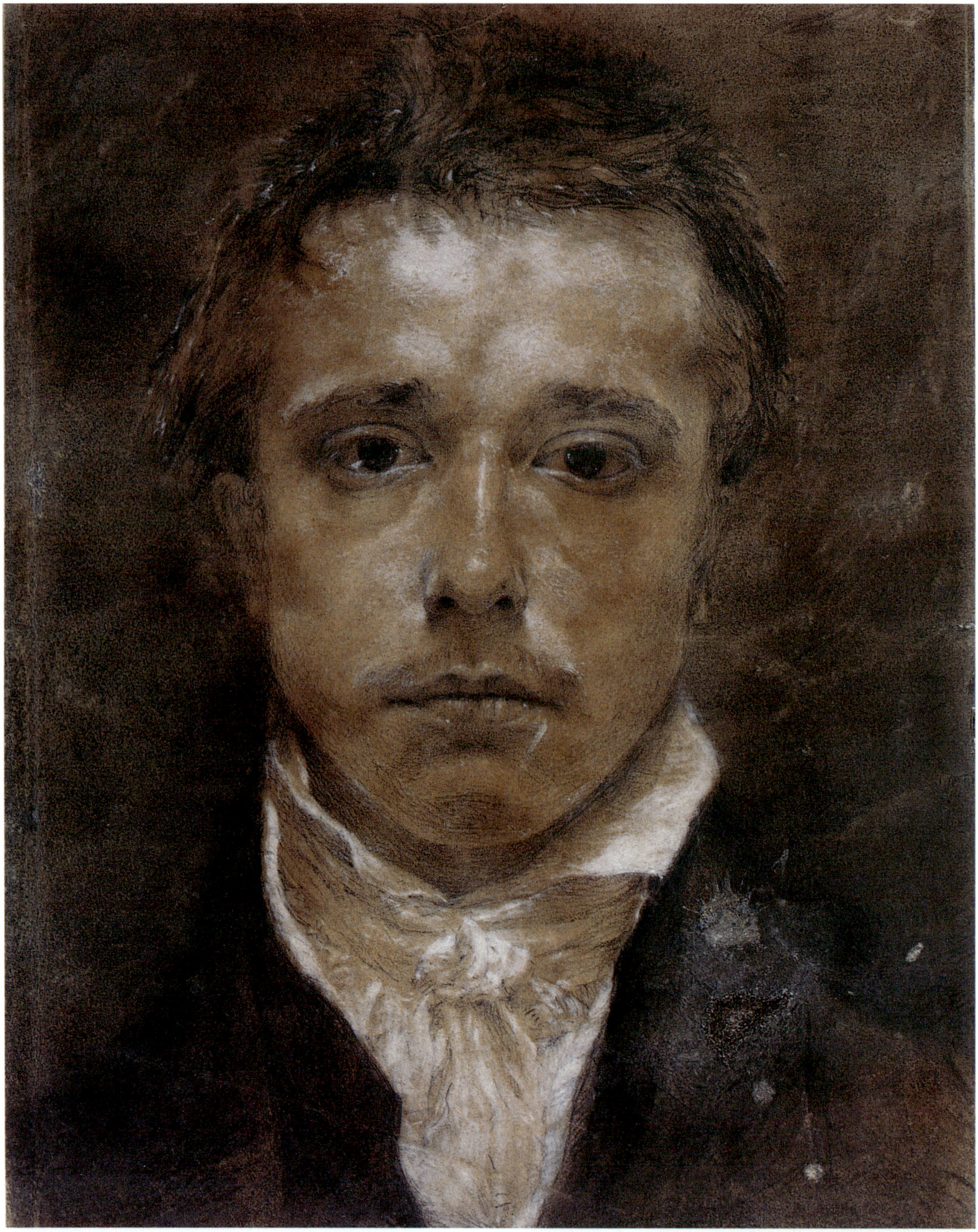

# Samuel Palmer
## 1805–1881

## *Vision and Landscape*

William Vaughan
Elizabeth E. Barker
Colin Harrison

*with contributions by*
David Bindman, David Blayney Brown,
Alexandra Greathead, Marjorie Shelley and
Scott Wilcox

THE BRITISH MUSEUM PRESS

The Metropolitan Museum of Art, New York

This catalogue is published to accompany an exhibition shown at the British Museum from 21 October 2005 to 22 January 2006 and at The Metropolitan Museum of Art, New York, from 7 March 2006 to 28 May 2006.

In London the exhibition is made possible by the American Friends of the British Museum and its supporters. Generous support was also provided by James Fairfax, The Paul Mellon Centre for British Art and The Essick Foundation.

In New York, the exhibition is made possible by Gilbert and Ildiko Butler.

Additional support has been provided by William G. and Grace Brantley Anderson; The Horace W. Goldsmith Foundation; and The Schiff Foundation.

The exhibition was organized by the British Museum and The Metropolitan Museum of Art, New York.

Frontispiece: Samuel Palmer, *Self-Portrait*, *c.*1834–5 (cat. 1)


First published in 2005 by The British Museum Press
A division of The British Museum Company Ltd
38 Russell Square, London WC1B 3QQ

www.britishmuseum.co.uk

Reprinted with corrections 2005

A catalogue record for this book is available from the British Library

ISBN-13: 978-0-7141-2641-8

ISBN-10: 0-7141-2641-1

Designed and typeset in Monotype Baskerville by James Shurmer

Printed in Spain by Grafos SA, Barcelona

# Contents

# Directors' Foreword

This exhibition continues a series of fruitful and friendly collaborations between the Department of Prints and Drawings at the British Museum and the Department of Drawings and Prints at The Metropolitan Museum of Art. We are delighted to add *Samuel Palmer (1805–1881): Vision and Landscape* to a series which already includes *Correggio and Parmigianino* (2000) and *Clouet to Seurat: French Drawings from the British Museum* (2005).

It seems fitting to mark the year 2005, the bicentenary of Samuel Palmer's birth, with a major retrospective of this British Romantic's work. Although various smaller exhibitions have brought Palmer before the public eye in recent decades, nearly eighty years have passed since the last comprehensive survey of his entire career. The Victoria and Albert's groundbreaking 1926 *Exhibition of Drawings, Etchings & Woodcuts by Samuel Palmer and other Disciples of William Blake* had profound influence on British art, inspiring a generation of Neo-Romantic painters and printmakers. The present retrospective seeks to introduce the full range of Palmer's genius – in watercolours, drawings, etchings, temperas and oils – to a new generation. We hope the visitors to our exhibition will find Palmer's work at all stages – from youthful vision to mature naturalism to late pastoral – as compelling as we do.

We have been extraordinarily fortunate in securing unprecedented loans for the exhibition from both sides of the Atlantic and indeed further afield. The project could not have been undertaken without the generous participation of the Ashmolean Museum, which has generously made available its unrivalled holdings of the artist's work, and whose curator, Colin Harrison, has played a major role in preparing this catalogue. We are also deeply indebted to the Fitzwilliam Museum, the Victoria and Albert Museum, the Tate, the Yale Center for British Art, the Rijksmuseum, and the other lenders institutional and private for making this retrospective possible.

The exhibition was selected and organized by William Vaughan, Guest Curator for the British Museum, in collaboration with Elizabeth E. Barker, Director of the Picker Art Gallery at Colgate University (formerly of The Metropolitan Museum of Art). Constance McPhee, Associate Curator of Drawings and Prints at the Met, took up the reins in the project's final stages, and steered it ably to its conclusion in New York.

The exhibition is made possible in London by the American Friends of the British Museum and its supporters. Generous support was also provided by James Fairfax, The Paul Mellon Centre for British Art and The Essick Foundation.

The Metropolitan Museum is indebted to Gilbert and Ildiko Butler, whose support of the exhibition has greatly enriched this project. The Metropolitan is also grateful to William G. and Grace Brantley Anderson, The Horace W. Goldsmith Foundation and The Schiff Foundation for their crucial assistance toward the realization of this exhibition.

NEIL MACGREGOR
*Director*
The British Museum

PHILIPPE DE MONTEBELLO
*Director*
The Metropolitan Museum of Art

# Authors' Acknowledgements

In assembling this retrospective of Palmer's art we are deeply aware of the debt that we owe those generations of scholars before us whose work has contributed so much to the task of identifying and assessing the achievements of this major artist. Raymond Lister's catalogue raisonné of 1988 remains the most detailed and comprehensive overview of Palmer's oeuvre, and we have used it as the principal reference point in our catalogue entries, while adding amendments and revisions in the light of more recent research.

An exhibition of this nature is dependent on the assistance and goodwill of very many people. Principal among these are the lenders, who are listed on p. 250. We are particularly fortunate that so many owners of Palmer's works have responded to our requests for loans with such generosity.

During the course of the preparation of this exhibition the curators have received advice and assistance from a huge number of experts, well-wishers and enthusiasts – too many, alas, to be able to mention all. We would, however, like to give a special thanks to the following: Brien Allen, Graham Allen, Thomas Andrews, Caroline Bacon, Saretta Barnet, Phillip Basner, Shelley M. Bennett, Jeffrey Berenson, Richard Beresford, David Bindman, David Blayney Brown, Calvin Brown, Christopher Brown, Gilbert and Ildiko Butler, Martin Butlin, Michael Campbell, Andrew Clayton-Payne, John Commander, Katherine Coombs, Mark Cummings, Jan Debbaut, Stephen Deuchar, Harriet Drummond, Rhoda Eitel-Porter, Robert N. Essick, Theresa Fairbanks, Sir James Fairfax, Richard Feigen, Gillian Forrester, David Franklin, Peter Gilbert, Laura M. Giles, Sir Nicholas Grimshaw, Ann Guite, Ruth Hibbard, Simon and Gayle Jenkins, Mark Jones, Revd Stephen Laird, Ronald de Leeuw, Lowell Libson, Tim Linnell, Andrew Loukes, Ger Luijten, James MacGregor, Amy Meyers, Jane Munro, Sandy Nairne, Richard Nathanson, Charles Nugent, Edward J. Nygren, Ursula Overbury, Russell Panczenko, Lucy Pelz, Charles E. Pierce Jr., Mark Pomeroy, Martin Postle, Earl A. Powell III, Ann Pyne, Peter Raissis, Duncan Robinson, Andrew Robison, Frank Salmon, Susan Schulman, David Scrase, Sir Nicholas Serota, Tessa Sidey, Janet Skidmore, Susan Sloman, Alistair Smith, Michael and Judy Steinhart, Andrew Stevens, MaryAnn Stevens, Victoria Tandy, Susan M. Taylor, Pierre Théberge, Roberta Thompson, Jennifer Tonkovitch, Henry Wemyss, Malcolm H. and Carolyn Wiener, Scott Wilcox, Timothy Wilcox, Phillippa Wood and Andrew Wyld. Dr Roberta J.M. Olson, Associate Curator of Drawings, The New-York Historical Society, kindly reviewed the entry for *The Comet of 1858* (cat. 138) and shared her expert knowledge of the subject.

At the British Museum there has been most generous support on all sides. As Director, Neil MacGregor has been a constant promoter and enthusiast. Particular thanks are due to Frances Carey, who as Deputy Keeper of the Department of Prints and Drawings secured the exhibition for the British Museum and was central to its development in the initial stages. Both at that time and later Antony Griffiths, Keeper of the Department of Prints and Drawings, has been unfailing in his support. Kim Sloan has been invaluable in her advice and guidance. Special thanks to Janice Reading for her constant helpfulness and painstaking administration of the complex loan arrangements. Charles Collinson has done a tremendous job with the framing – a particularly demanding task in this case. Thanks, too, to the Western Pictorial Art paper conservators and mounters for their work. John Williams, Ivor Kerslake and Kevin Lovelock have been helpful well beyond the call of duty in the photography they have provided for the exhibition. Mark McDonald was immensely helpful, in particular in connection with the selection of Old Master prints for the exhibition; Carol Blackett-Ord provided invaluable assistance at critical moments, and Caroline Arno has contributed a splendid photograph of the Sleeping Endymion. In addition, Will Vaughan would like to thank all members of the

Department of Prints and Drawings for their support and for making his time among them so pleasurable.

The staging of the exhibition at the British Museum has been expertly overseen by Carolyn Marsden-Smith, Head of Exhibitions, ably assisted by Elizabeth Morgan, the project manager. Sam Moorhead has been a constant support and made crucial contributions to conceptualization and presentation. Special thanks to Hannah Payne for her excellent and sympathetic design of the exhibition, to Nicholas Newbery for his fine graphic work and Claire Edwards for expert editing of the labels and texts. Many thanks to Sukie Hemmings, Hannah Boulton and Ann Lumley for their essential help in the promotion, sponsorship and marketing of the exhibition; and to Hilary Williams for developing the excellent and wide-ranging education programme that is accompanying the exhibition.

We would also like to express our gratitude to the British Museum Press, in particular Andrew Thatcher and Rosemary Bradley, for making possible the publication of such a handsome, richly illustrated catalogue. Teresa Francis, Managing Editor, has overseen the catalogue in all its stages and provided exemplary editorial support. Colin Grant has been an expert and ever-watchful copy-editor and saved the text from many blemishes. James Shurmer has enriched the whole with a truly beautiful design.

At the Metropolitan Museum Philippe de Montebello, Director and Chief Executive Officer, and Mahrukh Tarapor, Associate Director for Exhibitions, have lent their full support to the exhibition, assisted by the tireless efforts of Martha Deese. The exhibition in New York would not have been possible without the encouragement of George R. Goldner, Drue Heinz Chairman, Department of Drawings and Prints, and of Constance McPhee, Associate Curator, Department of Drawing and Prints, who capably steered the exhibition through its final stages in New York. Kit Basquin, David del Gaizo, Jeff Guerrier, Ricky Luna, Nadine Orenstein, Samantha Rippner, Perrin Stein, Liz Zanis and Mary Zuber in that department also deserve particular mention. Special thanks are due to Wendy Thompson for identifying an Italian engraving in the Ionides album and to Carmen Bambach for guiding our research on John Linnell's so-called Michelangelo drawings. Special thanks are also due to Kate Kooistra Niedermeyer, an intern whose intelligence, hard work and good humour improved all aspects of the exhibition, and to Claire Nicholl, Taube Greenspan and Allison Stagg, volunteers whose generous assistance helped ensure the timely completion of this catalogue.

Malcolm Daniel, Curator in Charge of the Department of Photographs, provided vital information on the Fairy Glen and nineteenth-century photography, a topic on which Roger Taylor offered further insight. In the Department of Paper Conservation Marjorie Shelley, Curator in Charge, and Rachel Mustalish and Margaret Lawson, Associate Conservators, enhanced our understanding of Palmer's materials and techniques. Special thanks are due to Gary Tinterow, Engelhard Curator in Charge, Nineteenth-Century, Modern and Contemporary Art, and to Lisa Messinger, Associate Curator in that department. Barbara Bridgers, General Manager for Imaging, the staff of the Photograph Studio, and Deanna Cross and Carol Lekarew in the Photograph and Slide Library provided crucial assistance in obtaining images for the catalogue.

Linda M. Sylling, Manager for Special Exhibitions and Gallery Installations, masterfully coordinated the presentation of the exhibition at the Metropolitan Museum. Herbert M. Moskowitz, Nina S. Maruca, Aileen K. Chuk and Anne Moore Goslin in the Department of the Registrar managed the complicated loan and shipment arrangements with consummate professionalism. Michael Batista, Exhibition Designer, Connie Norkin, Graphic Designer, and Clint Coller and Rich Lichte, Lighting Designers, brought their remarkable skills to the New York installation. Further thanks are due to Emily Kernan Rafferty, President; John P. O'Neill, Editor in Chief and General Manager of Publications; Rebecca Noonan; Elizabeth Hammer; Rebecca McGinnis; Valerie Troyansky; Marilyn Jensen; Elyse Topalian; Sabina Potaczek; Kenneth Soehner and the staff of the Thomas J. Watson Library; Rosayn D. Anderson, Kathleen Arffmann, Christine S. Begley, Eti Bonn-Muller, Nina Diefenbach, Brooke Horowitz, Andrea Kann and Karen Usdan.

A very special thanks from Will Vaughan to his wife Pek Peppin for constant help and encouragement during the Palmer years. Finally, to all the colleagues, friends and family members not named here we wish to acknowledge our sincere gratitude for their assistance and support.

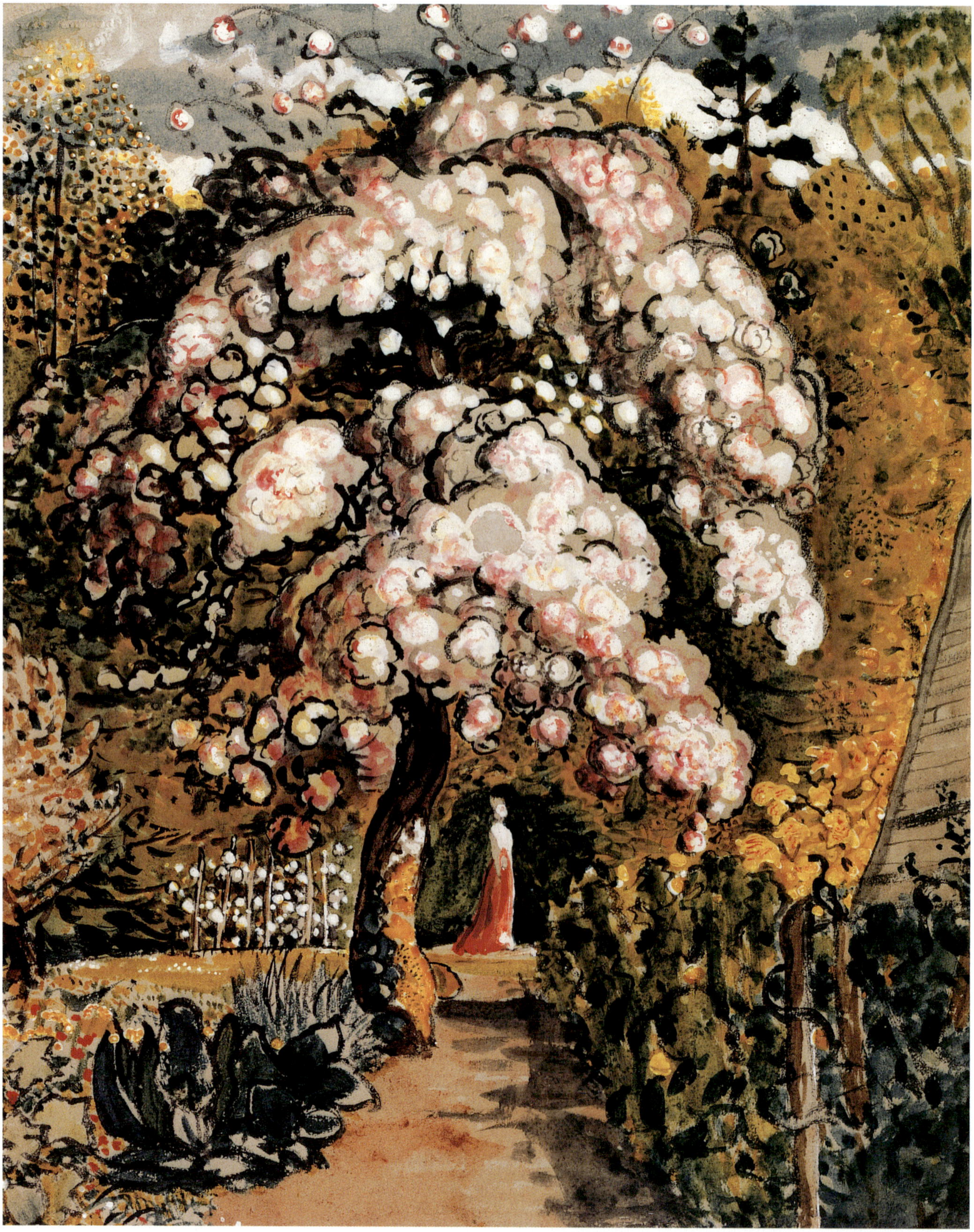

Samuel Palmer, *In a Shoreham Garden*, *c.*1829 (cat. 66).

# Introduction

*William Vaughan*

There are some artists who give us a new way of seeing: Samuel Palmer is one of them. He painted familiar scenes – trees, sheep, villages, the night sky, fields with ripened crops – but in a way that had never been done before. Subsequently, his rich forms and vivid colours have inspired other artists. Many are surprised that works that look so bold and modern can have been painted nearly two centuries ago.

While Palmer was undoubtedly a major innovator he was also very much a child of his time. Born in 1805, he came to maturity when the Romantic movement was at its height in Britain. Wordsworth, Coleridge and Byron were the dominant poets of the day, and Turner was the acknowledged master of landscape painting. An avid reader, Palmer was steeped in the poetry both of his own and former ages. He was also a great admirer of Turner and was certainly inspired by that painter to bring a comparable originality to his own landscapes. But the contemporary who meant most for him was the artist who combined both painting and poetry: William Blake. Palmer was a young man when he met Blake, who was in the last years of his life. Blake is now known as one of the most powerful creative forces in British art and literature. At the time, however, he was living in obscurity, having endured a lifetime of poverty and neglect. Yet he had remained faithful to his own remarkable vision, and the sight of this courage in adversity had a profound impact on Palmer. Most important of all, however, Blake exemplified the concept of the artist promoted by the Romantics: the creative genius valued above all for the uniqueness of his vision, a quality quite different from the everyday perceptions of most people, even those skilled in learning.

Blake's art was centred around an inner world, a mythology of his own creating. Palmer, by contrast, was a painter of the outer world, of visible nature. Yet, despite being distinct from each other, the two practices were not as far apart in those days as they might now seem. While venerating individual genius, the Romantics had also given a new significance to landscape. In an age rife with revolution and technological change they had come to see nature as the repository of a primal state that was being threatened by the material advances of mankind. They were, in a sense, the first ecologists, struggling to preserve both natural scenery and traditional ways of life from the onslaughts of modern civilization. They saw such a mission in religious terms, revering nature as the product of divine creation. As the poet William Cowper put it, 'God made the country and men made the town'.[1] Nobody typified this attitude more strongly in Palmer's day than the poet Wordsworth, who – as is clear in his epic autobiographical poem *The Prelude* – saw nature as providing man with intimations of immortality and a sense of moral worth that could help to guide and sustain his contemporaries in the struggle against the corrupting effects of the modern man-made world. Undoubtedly such thinking played a major part in the vogue for landscape painting at the time. 'View painting' became a major industry and it was quite natural for a young ambitious artist to see it as a promising career.

Palmer had a long career spanning more than sixty years, ending with his death in 1881 in the later Victorian era. During that period his style and practice went through many changes. The young artist painting with visionary fervour became the diligent producer of carefully crafted watercolours and etchings. Finally, in his last years he recaptured a sense of vision, though in a darker, more meditative mood. The stages of this career are described in the catalogue section of this book, but it may be helpful to review the main points of its development here.

Unlike many artists, Palmer did not have to struggle to start on his chosen path. The son of a dreamy bookseller, he had been brought up in a protective environment. His first inclination had been to follow a literary career, but his precocious talent as a painter led his parents to encourage him to become an artist. Already in 1819, when only fourteen, he was exhibiting and selling work. As is shown in the first section of the catalogue and exhibition (see cat. 8), such work was conventional in style, though already showing evidence of a spirited manner of working.

Despite such early success, Palmer was himself dissatisfied with his mode of working. In 1822 he was encouraged to go in a different direction through his meeting with the artist John Linnell. 'It pleased God', wrote Palmer, 'to send Mr. Linnell as a good angel from Heaven to pluck me from the pit of modern art.'[2] Linnell was at that time a painter of sharply observed landscapes that tore aside the conventions of picturesque composition then in vogue (see cat. 21). A fervent Baptist, he saw the direct recording of nature as a religious duty, revealing the workings of the divine. Yet, while Palmer experienced a sharpening of perception under the tutelage of Linnell, he did not share his mentor's faith in the ability of raw observation on its own to communicate a vision of divine creation. It was his second and even greater mentor, William Blake, who encouraged him to believe that a deeper perception was to be gained through the resources of the imagination. His first meeting with Blake – brought about by Linnell – took place in the autumn of 1824. However, Palmer undoubtedly already had knowledge of Blake's art before that time and had already profited in particular from the sight of the wood engravings to Thornton's *Pastorals of Virgil* (cat. 19). These works, together with Blake's *Illustrations of the Book of Job* (cat. 18), acted as talismen for Palmer, providing a guide to how he might himself now perceive the divine in nature.

At this time the word 'vision' began to figure prominently in Palmer's writings. Vision is an ambiguous word. On the one hand, it can refer to a physiological process – the means by which we shape an image of the world in our minds based on the sense data we receive through the eye. On the other, it can mean a special kind of seeing – the perception of that which lies beyond the natural world and which is not visible under normal circumstances. It is the common belief of all religions that there is a higher reality – an eternity, a heaven – beyond the world in which we live. In the western world such beliefs have been further strengthened by the idealist writings of the Greek philosopher Plato, who held that the forms we perceive on earth are but the imperfect copies or imitations of ideal forms in heaven. For most adherents of such doctrines knowledge of this higher world is taken on trust. It is believed in but not directly experienced. However, there are those who feel that they do experience it at times – either within their own imaginations or as a tangible, externally visible presence. Most religions venerate such people as prophets or 'seers', though their claims are usually viewed with scepticism by the more rationally minded.

William Blake experienced visions in this sense. As a child, he saw the face of God peering in at him through an upstairs window of his home, and angels sitting in a tree on Peckham Rye. He continued to have visions in adult life, although equally importantly he believed the rich visualizations of his imagination to be a product of the same process. Palmer was certainly a believer in visions and fascinated by Blake's powers. He believed, moreover, that they were relevant for landscape. Accepting – like Wordsworth and Linnell – that nature provided the visible proof of divine creation, he felt that it could be further used to provide an intimation of the 'higher reality' beyond it, if viewed with the transforming powers of the visionary. As he wrote in 1825, 'the visions of the soul being perfect, are the only true standard by which nature must be tried'.[3] It was this conviction that encouraged him to develop such striking and inventive ways of representing natural scenery in the mid-1820s.

Yet Palmer was never a visionary in the sense that Blake was. Vision appears to have come to Blake as a natural, intuitive process. Though highly imaginative, Palmer did not experience vision in this way. He had to simulate the process through an effort of will. Much of the enthusiastic writing in his drawings and sketches – particularly those in his remarkable sketchbook of 1824 (cat. 9) – show him trying to work himself up to see phenomena such as trees becoming princesses or moons standing tiptoe on the hills. Similarly, when visually aiming to communicate such experiences, he is constantly testing and experimenting with ways of achieving the sense of visionary transformation. This might make him less of a genuine visionary, but it does not make him any less of an artist. On the contrary, it is what gives his work its fascination, sensitivity and richness.

As well as sharpening his perception of nature and introducing him to Blake, Linnell was important to Palmer for encouraging him to study the art of the fifteenth and sixteenth centuries. Such artists were regarded as 'primitives' at the time, as they were less sophisticated in their naturalism than contemporary painters. Yet, just as the Romantics looked to nature as an example of creation unspoiled by the modern world, so they looked to the 'Gothic' artists as possessing a simplicity, directness and spirituality that had become lost in the modern world. Such a view was appropriate for Linnell with his own direct and sharp-eyed approach to landscape painting.

Adulation of medieval art was not new in the 1820s. It had been prevalent on the continent for almost a generation before and had led, among other things, to a group of artists achieving international fame through emulating the art of the 'age of faith'. The Nazarenes – as they became known – had achieved great success in Rome with their work and by the 1820s they were the talk of Europe. The Nazarenes were one of the earliest examples of an artistic practice that became common in the nineteenth century and has had reverberations ever since: the artistic brotherhood that turns its back on the materialism of the present and seeks to revive the spirituality of the past, often in a separate, breakaway community. Other famous examples are the Pre-Raphaelite Brotherhood in Britain in the 1840s and the Nabis in France in the 1890s. In 1824 Palmer sought to set up a similar community with a group of like-minded fellow artists. 'The Ancients', as they called themselves, looked to the art of the later Middle Ages for both technical and spiritual inspiration. For a time they formed a breakaway community in the Kent village of Shoreham, where they caused some consternation to the locals on account of their eccentricities (see pp. 17–21).

As is shown in the third section of the catalogue, the Ancients formed for a time a remarkable group with an intense primitivistic style of great originality, particularly in the cases of George Richmond and Edward Calvert. It was the first time that Britain had experienced the effects of one of those avant-garde groups of artists that have become commonplace in the history of art since the mid-nineteenth century. Yet, despite the achievement, the story was in a sense a sad one, since the communal effort all but broke down within a few years of its initiation. Unlike the Nazarenes before them, and the Pre-Raphaelites after them, the Ancients failed to win critical acclaim for their innovative pictures and all gradually abandoned these for more conventional work. The main reason for this was financial: without being able to sell their works, few could afford to continue in this vein. Palmer, who had a small legacy, was able to hold out longer than most. He remained attached to Shoreham and to a 'visionary' style of painting until 1835, whereas most had left by 1830.

Emulating both the Nazarenes and artists of the fifteenth century, the Ancients produced religious paintings as well as pure landscapes, but the latter were also religious in a sense, for they celebrated the divine in nature. In his pure landscape Palmer came close at times to his older contemporary, the German landscape painter Caspar David Friedrich (see fig. 1). Although the two almost certainly knew nothing of each other's work, both can be seen to be responding to the Romantics' religious approach to nature. Technically, however, their methods were different, Friedrich working in a minute and meticulous manner, Palmer being more given to bravura and boldness. Friedrich, moreover, was more melancholy in his approach. He stressed the isolation of the spiritual man yearning for eternity – a tendency that has helped keep him in vogue in recent times, since it has affinities with modern alienation. Palmer's approach, on the other hand, was more ecstatic. He celebrated the wonder of nature, though he also indicated a sense of mystery and a mood of contemplation.

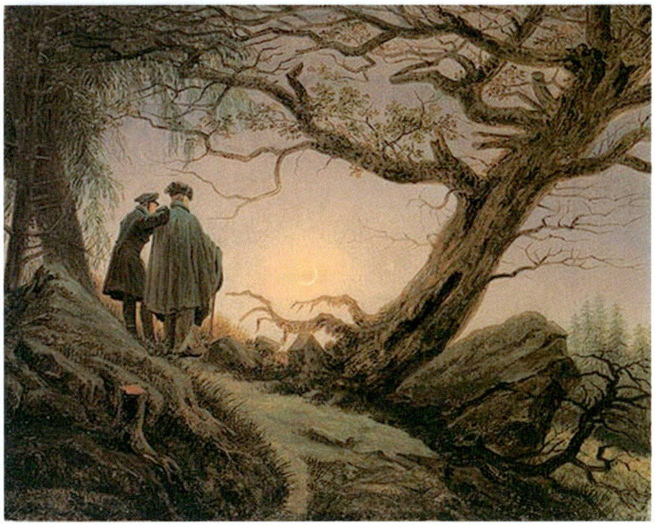

Fig. 1 Caspar David Friederich, *Two Men Contemplating the Moon*, *c.*1830, oil on canvas, The Metropolitan Museum of Art, New York, Wrightsman Fund.

Palmer's idyllic view of nature can be related to a broad artistic type: that of the pastoral. The pastoral was originally a literary genre, though since the early Renaissance it has also been a pictorial one. Rooted in classical antiquity, where its most celebrated treatment was by the Latin poet Virgil, it also took on spiritual dimensions in association with Christianity, where Christ is presented as the Good Shepherd. In English literature the most famous exponent of this Christianized pastoral was John Milton, though Blake also subscribed to the form in his *Songs of Innocence and Experience*. As is made clear in David Brown's essay on Palmer and literature (pp. 23–7), such writing was critical for Palmer. His Shoreham paintings are in the tradition of the spiritual pastoral, showing shepherds and sheep and rural communities protected by enfolding hills. It has frequently been pointed out that such imagery is far from the reality of rural communities in Britain in the 1820s. The period was one of increasing exploitation of the labourers by rich landowners, an exploitation that led at times to uprisings, including the rick-burning of the 'Captain Swing' riots around 1830. Palmer was well aware of such events and it might be asked how he could have turned his back on them in his art. The answer is that he was not trying to depict a literal present in his art. He was aiming to evoke the qualities of a lost or dying way of life. Politically, Palmer was a High Tory and believed that the old traditional masters had cared for the communities in their charge in the way that modern landowners did not. He felt so intensely on the matter that he even attempted to intervene on the part of the Tories in the critical elections of 1832 (see pp. 29–32).

However, in spite of these political concerns Palmer's art was more centrally involved, as has already been indicated, with the intimation of a higher reality. Such a higher reality was mysterious and only partly to be perceived. It is perhaps for this reason that shadows play such an important part in his work. As the absence of light, shadows might seem to be the converse of vision. Yet shadows make things look mysterious, as well as emphasize transience. It is no accident that Palmer should have identified the appearance of a shadow as providing his first creative insight. In his autobiographical letter of 1871 Palmer related the experience that has been repeated in every biography of him ever since: 'when less than four years old', while standing with his nurse Mary Ward, 'watching the shadows on the wall from branches of elm behind which the moon had risen, she transferred and fixed the fleeting image in my memory by repeating the couplet, – "Vain man, the vision of a moment made, / Dream of a dream and shadow of a shade."' 'I never forgot those shadows', Palmer concluded, 'and am often trying to paint them.'[4] It is consistent with Palmer's fascination with shadow that his favourite engraver should have been the Renaissance master Bonasone, whom – as he said in a letter of 1872 to P.G. Hamerton – he admired as 'the greatest master of shadowing upon copper'.[5]

Related to Palmer's interest in shadows was his fascination with all kinds of transformation. Again, this suggests deliberate control rather than some kind of zombie-like transference of 'vision'. His fascination with miniaturization has often been remarked upon, as has the contrary magnifying of individual forms. Even his development of intense colour effects can be seen as a product of this fascination with changes in scale. It is as though everywhere he is looking for means to intensify experience and thereby communicate a sense of the visionary.

Palmer's uncertainties are seen in the way he frequently sent up his own visionary endeavours. He joked about his glasses, which in a note from his now lost sketchbook of 1823–4 he felt were mocking him with their alternative vision: 'The least bit of natural scenery reflected from one of my spectacle glasses laughs me to scorn and hisses at me.'[6] Such humour reminds one that there is also a very earthy side to Palmer. Erotic feelings are frankly expressed in letters to his close friend Richmond (see cat. 52, for example). As might be expected from his rich landscapes, sensuality for him is an essential part of art. Its supposed absence in antique art (a supposition more related to contemporary Neoclassical theory than to an actual absence) was one of the reasons he turned against the classical ideal. As he wrote to Linnell in 1829,

> The chastity of the Antique is too mild and pure for my gross appetite to relish thoroughly – I dare say people have a very refin'd pleasure in a boild chicken, but give me the '*rich experience*' of a roasted goose, which is to chicken what Mike [Michelangelo] is to the Antique.[7]

He was very much a modern, too, in his perception of beauty as dependent on strangeness. His comment on this to Richmond in 1834 seems almost to prefigure Baudelaire's celebrated aphorism, 'le beau est toujours bizarre':[8]

> I believe in my very heart … [t]hat all the very finest original pictures and topping things in nature have a certain quaintness by which they partially affect us – not the quaintness of bungling – the queer doing of a common thought – but a curiousness in their beauty – a salt on their tails by which the imagination catches hold on them while the sublime eagles and big birds of the French academy fly up far beyond the sphere of our affections – one of the very deepest sayings I have met with in Lord Bacon seems to me to be 'There is no excellent beauty without some strangeness in the proportion'.[9]

By the time he wrote this Palmer was already paying the price for such individualism. Despite exhibiting frequently at the Royal Academy in the early 1830s, he sold little and after 1835 this seems to have encouraged him to return to more conventional modes of topographical painting. He travelled to famous beauty spots, such as North Devon and Wales, in the hope of producing more saleable works (see catalogue, section 5). Even with these more conventional works, he found little success and turned to teaching to augment his income.

In 1837 he married Linnell's eldest daughter Hannah, and the couple set off to Italy (see catalogue, section 6). Although they were on their honeymoon, this was no period of leisure. Hannah was herself a gifted and aspiring artist and both worked hard to build up a repertoire of Italian subjects from which they hoped to develop profitable practices on their return. They were also kept busy by a commission from Linnell himself to colour prints that he had made after Michelangelo's work in the Sistine Chapel. Surviving letters from the time reveal that relations with Linnell, his erstwhile saviour and hero, had worsened. This was to set a melancholy pattern that overshadowed the whole of the rest of Palmer's life. Linnell – materially successful in a way that Palmer never was – had a dictatorial personality and constantly subjected his new son-in-law to criticism. This was the period when, as Palmer put it, 'Real life began' (see catalogue, section 7).[10] On their return the couple settled in London. A growing family added to their troubles, causing Hannah to abandon her painting career and Palmer to rely increasingly on teaching and humiliating handouts from Linnell to survive.

Yet, while life was hard, Palmer was not without some professional success. In 1843 he was elected an associate of the Old Water-Colour Society. From that time watercolour painting became the mainstay of his painting activity. For a study of cypresses made in Italy he had the pleasure of receiving lavish praise from the up-and-coming critic John Ruskin, who in his groundbreaking *Modern Painters* said that Palmer was 'deserving of the very highest place among faithful followers of nature' (see cat. 108).[11] With great percipience Ruskin saw Palmer's intensive mode of sketching as providing a new direction for British art, although he equally perceptively said that the artist had not yet worked out how to profit from such work in his finished paintings. Clearly Ruskin never did think Palmer worked it out, for he never mentioned him again. A few years later he was championing the proponents of another style of intensive nature painting: the Pre-Raphaelites.

Palmer's wonderful sketches – so full of vigour and acuity of perception – show how at all stages of his career he was an artist with a very special vision. While his finished watercolours of the middle period at times do fall into relatively unexciting conventional modes, they can often be enthralling, as in his stormy scenes at Tintagel in Cornwall (cats 121–2). Such works show that Palmer had a real gift for dramatic landscape, as do some of his powerful studies of seas and waves (cat. 137). This feeling for the elemental fits in with Palmer's intensive sense of vision and also bears witness to his great admiration for Turner.

Yet it was for quieter work that he gained ultimate acclaim. In 1850 he was elected a member of the Etching Club and was soon building a reputation for fine and highly worked, etched landscape idylls (see pp. 47–52). A few years later, in 1854, he became a full member of the Old Water-Colour Society. By this time he was becoming increasingly noticed, gaining a niche reputation as a painter of poetic idyllic scenes of a somewhat severe kind – what the critic F.G. Stephens referred to as being in the 'Dorian' mood (see pp. 45, 192). To some extent times were moving in his favour. The success of the Pre-Raphaelites had heralded a return to a more poetic kind of painting that fitted in with Palmer's anti-naturalist inclinations. Palmer profited, too, from the parallel revival of interest in Blake, which led in 1863 to the publication of the first major study of this artist: Alexander Gilchrist's *Life of William Blake*. Palmer was one of the principal informants quoted in Gilchrist's book.

In private life Palmer had continued to suffer hardships, the most bitter being the death of his favourite son Thomas More Palmer in 1861. After that he lived the life of the recluse, moving to a house on the outskirts of Reigate. Whatever the personal circumstances, isolation seems to have nurtured his vision, for it was there that he developed his last great watercolours in which something of the visionary intensity of his youth returned (see catalogue, section 8). The greatest of these were the illustrations to Milton's 'L'Allegro' and 'Il Penseroso' (cats 145–53). This series was commissioned, but Palmer's patron (Ruskin's solicitor L.R. Valpy) gave him a free choice of subject and Palmer chose Milton because of the close involvement he had had with the poet's work all his life. So in this last great cycle – as in his finest Shoreham work – Palmer was painting what he wanted in the manner that he wanted. At the time of his death Palmer's reputation was high. It is a sign of this that he was accorded the honour of a special exhibition of his work at the Fine Art Society in the year of his death (1881), in which the Milton watercolours were given pride of place.

Palmer's reputation at that time rested largely on his later etchings and watercolours. This was the kind of art praised by the poet W.B. Yeats in 'The Phases of the Moon' (1919), when he talked of an 'image of mysterious wisdom won by toil'.[12] Yet a discerning few were already aware of the more radical exciting early work that was still at that time largely in the possession of Palmer's own family and the descendants of his friends. Gradually the interest in such work grew, particularly as the taste for a new kind of primitivizing art – christened Post-Impressionism by the critic Roger Fry in the early twentieth century – became avant-garde chic. Eventually, this led to the great retrospective held at the Victoria and Albert Museum in 1926. The enthusiasm felt by its chief organizer, Martin Hardie, for one such work, *In a Shoreham Garden* (cat. 66 and p. 10), sent him by Palmer's son expresses the mood:

> The blossoms are fifty times the size of life, but what does that matter when the blaze of colour or of sunshine has been so wonderfully grasped and portrayed. This is, I think, the most fascinating drawing by Samuel Palmer that I have seen and its interest again is all the greater because it has so many of the so-called post-impressionist qualities about which our critics have raved so much.[13]

Palmer's Shoreham work seemed to be the answer to a prayer for a generation of artists that was, in the words of the painter Paul Nash, seeking to reconcile 'Going Modern' with 'Being British' (see pp. 55–61).[14] For here was a painter of the English countryside interpreting his native scenery with a boldness and vision unprecedented before the twentieth century. 'I shared with Samuel Palmer an appetite for

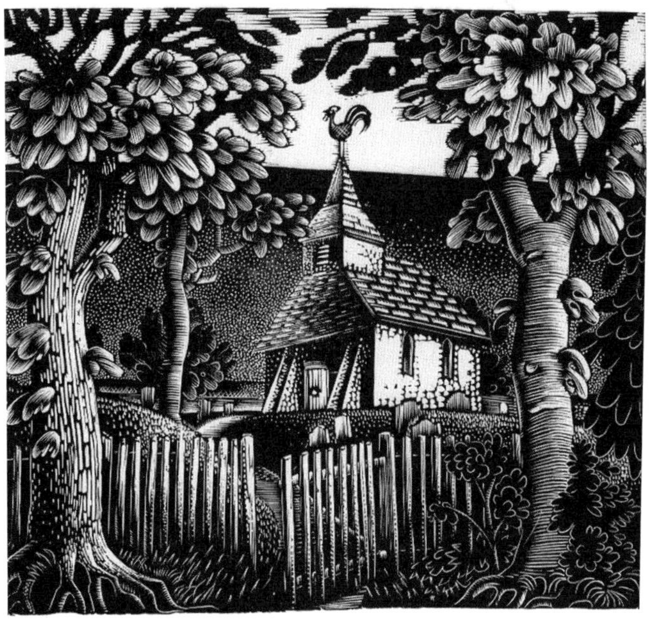

Fig. 2 Eric Ravilious, *Sussex Church*, *c.*1926, wood engraving, private collection.

monstrous moons, exuberance of stars', Nash later wrote, describing his own artistic development.[15] Palmer became the hero of the British Neo-Romantics in the 1930s, a household deity for the likes of Eric Ravilious (fig. 2),[16] Graham Sutherland, John Piper and even Henry Moore. His work was richly praised by influential critics, notably Kenneth Clark and Herbert Read.[17] Not only did his radical imagery fit in with the modernist aesthetic, but the story of his life – the defiant isolated individual – fitted in exactly with the avant-garde notion of the struggling genius pitted against society. His story also became another chapter in that history of modernity expressed in the very different struggles of figures such as John Constable and the Impressionists.

Yet this very claim for visionary integrity has been the reason for his undoing in certain circles in recent times. Palmer has lost none of his revelatory visual appeal for those who encounter him with an open mind, but he is not much in vogue in modish critical and academic circles. As pundits began to turn against modernism in the 1970s, so they found less virtue in an art valued for intense pictorial effects. Worse still, Palmer's enthusiastic celebration of the visionary in nature seemed an irrelevance to a new generation of historians who sought to interpret art principally in terms of its social dimensions. It is striking that, whereas histories of landscape prior to this time would give pride of place to Palmer, he has all but disappeared from those written subsequently. There is no engagement with Palmer, for example, in John Barrell's seminal *The Dark Side of the Landscape*,[18] a work in which Constable is famously taken to task for failing to bear witness to the rural misery of his own day. Whereas there was a *succès de scandale* to be obtained from claiming that the so-called 'natural painter' was in fact promoting an establishment myth about the countryside, there was hardly the same mileage to be made from an artist who was, by his own admission, paying more attention to the inner than the outer world. Palmer's High Toryism, too, made him unattractive to those seeking to align creative achievement with political radicalism. It was difficult to defend him as a counter-cultural hero in the way that Blake, his visionary mentor, could be. It is a sign of the decline of academic interest in Palmer that he should have failed to merit an entry in the reference section of the much praised recent *Oxford Companion to the Romantic Age*, a work that advertises itself as including 'all the significant figures' of the period.[19]

Such a fall in the critical fortunes of the 'visionary' Palmer has been accompanied by a shift of a different kind. This is the revisionist view of Palmer that gives new emphasis to his largely non-visionary later career. Over the past two decades there has been a gradual rehabilitation of the later watercolours and etchings, which can be seen, at their best, to possess a genuine lyricism and be based on an observation of nature that is at times breathtaking. Cynics may point to the strong dealer involvement in this revival (later Palmer is still readily available for sale whereas most of the work of the 'visionary' years has already passed out of private hands). Yet there is no doubting that this later work has a very special quality and that it also has historical importance as a distinctive part of the Victorian art world with interesting connections to both Pre-Raphaelitism and the Aesthetic movement.

Such a history only charts – as most histories of taste do – the surface fashions. Beneath the undulations of Palmer's critical fortunes in recent years a bedrock of interest and affection has remained. Not only has he retained a dedicated public, but he has continued to act as an inspiration for writers and artists as varied as Susan Hill, Sally Vickers, Iain Sinclair, Gilbert and George, Lucian Freud, John Virtue and Andy Goldsworthy. It is hoped that this book and exhibition, encompassing all aspects of his work, will confirm the scale of his achievement and bring it to an even wider audience.

1 William Cowper, *The Task* (1784).
2 *L&L*, p. 8.
3 *L&L*, p. 16.
4 *Letters*, p. 823.
5 *Letters*, p. 862. For further commentary on Palmer and Bonasone see cat. 26.
6 *L&L*, p. 13.
7 *Letters*, p. 54.
8 Charles Baudelaire, 'Exposition Universelle de 1855', *Curiosités esthétiques*, Paris, 1962, p. 215.
9 *Letters*, p. 67.
10 *Letters*, p. 824.
11 Ruskin 1846, p. 402.
12 For reference see p. 27 note 36.
13 Martin Hardie to A.H. Palmer, 15 May 1826: V&A Archive SF 814. 27/7936.
14 Paul Nash, '"Going Modern" and "Being British"', *Week-End Review*, vol. 5, no. 109, 9 April 1932, pp. 443–4.
15 Paul Nash, *Writings on Art*, ed. Andrew Causey, Oxford, 2000, p. 157.
16 Ravilious's wood engraving *Sussex Church* (fig. 2) would appear to be closely related to Palmer's *Hilly Scene* (cat. 17).
17 See for example Kenneth Clark, *Landscape into Art*, London, 1949, pp. 71–2.
18 John Barrell, *The Dark Side of the Landscape: The Rural Poor in English Painting 1730–1840*, Cambridge, 1980.
19 Iain McCalman (ed.), *An Oxford Companion to the Romantic Age: British Culture 1776–1832*, Oxford, 1999; see back cover. The reference section does, by contrast, have an entry on Linnell. There is, it is true, a brief piece on what are called the 'Shoreham Ancients'. However this is so casually written that the author manages to describe the group founded in 1824 as 'Early Victorian'. He ignores the art of the Ancients utterly and appears only to have chosen to mention the group at all in order to castigate its members for 'canonizing Blake by muffling his eighteenth century artisan origins' (pp. 704–5).

# ‘Brothers in art, brothers in love’: The Ancients as an Artistic Community

*William Vaughan*

‘We were brothers in art, brothers in love, and brothers in that for which art and love subsist – the Ideal – the Kingdom within.’[1] This heartfelt endorsement by Edward Calvert of the community of artists that he belonged to points to one of the major circumstances for which Samuel Palmer is remembered. For, as well as being celebrated for his unique form of ‘visionary’ landscape, Palmer has a place in the history of art as the dominating figure in an artistic brotherhood. The Ancients – as they called themselves – were the first clear manifestation in Britain of a highly characteristic form of artistic organization that played a leading role in art and art politics in Europe in the nineteenth century. There had, indeed, been earlier examples on the continent – notably the breakaway group, the Barbus, who emerged from Jacques-Louis David’s Paris studio in the 1790s,[2] and the German Lukasbund, or ‘Brotherhood of St Luke’, set up in 1808 by a group of students at the Vienna Academy, who later achieved international fame after they had moved to Rome in 1810, where they became known as the Nazarenes.[3] Later brotherhoods were to include the Pre-Raphaelite Brotherhood in Britain (1848) and the Nabis in Paris in the 1890s.

All these groups shared a set of key features, of which the most striking were the intention to set up a community of ‘equals’ in opposition to hierarchical authority (usually represented by an art academy); the adulation of the past (usually, though not exclusively, the Middle Ages) as a time of spiritual and artistic excellence in contrast to the morally

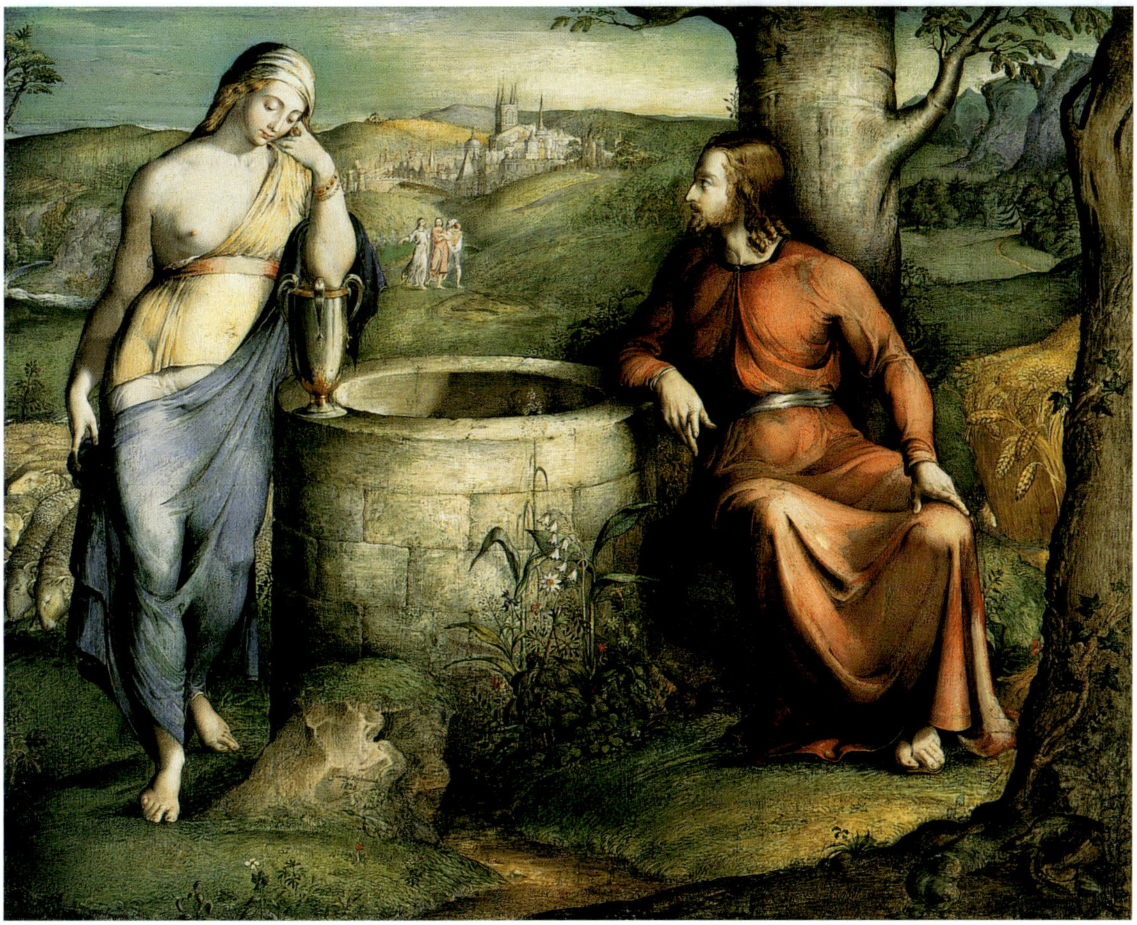

George Richmond, *Christ and the Woman of Samaria*, 1828 (cat. 57).

degraded present; the signalling of difference by means of 'cognitive dressing', i.e. wearing a particular and distinctive costume; and the attempt to break through prevailing systems of patronage to appeal directly to the public. These brotherhoods have largely been perceived as part of the challenge to authority by an artistic avant-garde, and their struggles as part of a fight for modernity in art. Yet, while these breakaway groups constitute an element in the process of criticism and protest that encouraged artistic innovation in the nineteenth and twentieth centuries, they cannot simply be subsumed within a triumphalist account of the progress of art towards some modernist state of perfection – a parallel to the pattern of political revolutions aimed at cleansing society of privilege and ushering in the earthly paradise. The critique mounted by early artistic brotherhoods, in particular, was less focused and homogenous than this. Although they opposed authority, their opposition was as likely to be manifested in terms of extreme conservatism as extreme radicalism. This is certainly true of the Ancients, who tended to be High Tory in their politics and viewed the progressive tendencies of radicals and liberals with aversion.

Rather than lining brotherhoods up with some specific political or artistic agenda, it is perhaps more helpful to view them as a manifestation of a new kind of agency that had widespread application throughout society. As M.A. Clawson has shown, the habit of forming brotherhoods with political and/or social aims became a common practice at the time of the French Revolution and remained thereafter a significant means whereby protest was made and power was negotiated.[4] Considered from this perspective, artistic brotherhoods can be seen as part of a widespread social phenomenon. This viewpoint also helps to focus on the pragmatic nature of the strategies adopted by artistic brotherhoods. For, however much they turned their backs on society and denounced the degraded nature of the age in which they lived, they still sought to achieve fame and material success in the very world that they criticized.

In this essay I wish to situate the activities of the Ancients within this context, considering how their practices might accord with patterns of behaviour common to other artistic brotherhoods and how their aims might relate to other critiques of society in Britain at the time they were established in the mid-1820s. Before doing this, however, it is necessary to consider in more detail what the Ancients actually did. This is not as easy to establish as it might seem. Unlike the most successful artistic brotherhoods of the nineteenth century – notably the Nazarenes and the Pre-Raphaelites – the Ancients left behind very few records of their activities. What documentation there is, moreover, usually comes from reminiscences and second-hand accounts written up to half a century later. The few contemporary references that can be found are oblique ones, mainly coming from surviving letters written by members of the group.[5]

Despite this, we can be certain of some things. There is no doubting that the group really did exist or (as the quotation at the beginning of this article attests) that it had a real hold on its members (see p. 105 for names of the principal figures). Like other brotherhoods, the group was as much concerned to establish a way of life as to develop a particular type of art. It is a sign of this that the 'hub of the fraternity', according to A.H. Palmer, was not an artist at all but Samuel Palmer's cousin, the stockbroker John Giles. The very name 'Ancients' appears to have been precipitated by Giles's 'repeated claim that ancient man was superior to modern man'.[6] More widely educated than the young artists with whom he consorted, Giles seems to have been party to the conservative intellectual movement of the 1820s that was arguing for a reassertion of traditional values to counter the detrimental social effects of 'progress'. Such voices became all the more urgent as the conservative government of the day moved slowly towards the painful concession of reformist measures known as Liberal Toryism.[7]

While the exact date of the founding of the Ancients is not known, there is evidence that they were already in existence by September 1824, when Samuel Palmer wrote to Linnell ending his letter with a greeting to Linnell's children as 'little ancients'.[8] The date of the formation of the Ancients around 1824 raises the question of the extent to which such a grouping was modelled on a knowledge of previous artistic brotherhoods. None of the records make any references to such a debt. They only mention admiration for Blake as a prophetic father figure (they named him 'The Interpreter' after the figure of that name in Bunyan's *Pilgrim's Progress*)[9] and the discovery of the richness and spiritual beauty of medieval art. Yet it is hard to believe that the Ancients were unaware of the most successful breakaway group of the period, the German Nazarenes. This group had leapt to fame at the end of the Napoleonic Wars when they decorated the Prussian consul's reception room in Rome with archaizing frescoes, further making their presence visible to those living in Rome by their distinctive manner of dress (see fig. 3). The activities of the Nazarenes were widely reported by travellers to Italy and had been the subject of several articles in the London press by the mid-1820s.[10] An even more tangible connection was provided by the German merchant Charles Aders, whose collection of early Northern art provided a stimulus for the Ancients' primitivist interests (see cat. 23). It was at Aders's house that Palmer had direct contact with a member of the Nazarenes' circle, meeting Jacob Götzenberger, a pupil of the leading

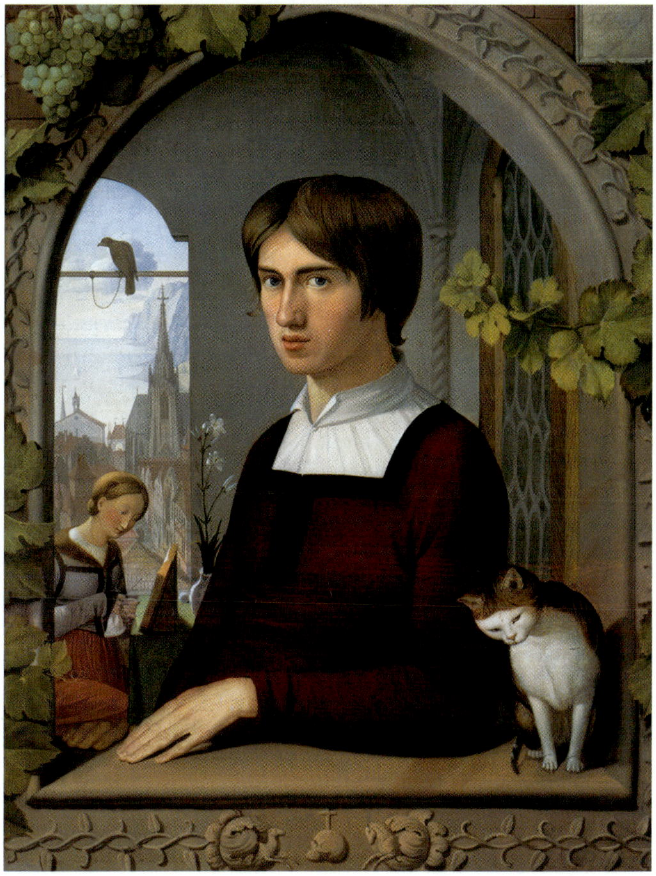

Fig. 3 Friedrich Overbeck, *Franz Pforr*, 1810, oil, National Gallery, Berlin.

Nazarene Peter Cornelius, there in 1827, at least three years after the formation of the Ancients. However, it seems unlikely that Aders would not have talked about his knowledge of the Nazarenes to enthusiasts for early art long before this time.[11]

Like the Nazarenes – and indeed most brotherhoods of the period – the Ancients were formed from of a set of disaffected art students. With the exception of Palmer all the artists in the group were students at the Royal Academy. They appeared to follow a well-established pattern, too, when they established a separate community outside London in the village of Shoreham, Kent. The Barbus had left David's studio to live communally in an abandoned monastery at Chaillot. The Nazarenes moved from Vienna to Rome, where they also inhabited a disused monastery, that of S. Isidoro. Yet, while the Ancients spent much time in Shoreham, they never formed a community as fully as their continental predecessors. In 1827 Palmer wrote to Richmond of 'a room, formerly occupied by the Ancients, 3/6 a week'.[12] But a room is hardly a monastery, and all the indications are that the only member who lived in Shoreham on a more or less permanent basis was Palmer himself. There were practical reasons for this. Most of the Ancients were struggling young artists who wished to maintain a presence in London to build up their clientele and reputation. One of the advantages offered by Shoreham was that it was close enough to the city for brief excursions to be made to it. Visits by most of the group were fleeting, lasting typically not more than a few weeks or even days. This was particularly the case with Richmond (the painter closest to Palmer personally and artistically), who was only able to come to Shoreham for several weeks in the autumn of 1827 after he had made some money from a portrait commission.[13] Palmer's position was somewhat different to most of the other members of the group in that he had recently come into a legacy from his grandfather, which meant that he could live for a time without having to sell his work. The only other major artistic member of the group who had this level of economic independence was Calvert. He, however, was already married and established with a family in Brixton. His visits therefore were also brief. The only members of the Ancients who resided on a more permanent basis for a time at Shoreham were the marginal figures of Palmer's brother William (who also had a legacy and was trying at the time to succeed as a sculptor) and Welby Sherman, an indigent and failing engraver who seems to have lived off the Palmers, eventually cheating the weak-minded William of the remains of his inheritance.[14]

If residence at Shoreham hardly matched the communal intensity of other well-known brotherhoods of the time, other forms of group identity among the Ancients seem to have been similarly weak. One of the strongest features of brotherhoods is 'cognitive dressing' – the adoption of a distinctive costume to signal difference. The hairstyles and archaic costumes sported by both the Barbus and the Nazarenes proved to be one of their most effective ways of drawing attention to themselves. It is often claimed that the Ancients adopted a similar strategy. This would appear to be borne out by portraits of Palmer by Richmond such as fig. 4 and cat. 54 (exhibited at the Academy in 1830), in which he is seen in comparable attire. The title of the work, *Portrait of an Artist*, seems to assert defiantly the alternative lifestyle of the creative individual. However, while it is true that Palmer did indeed dress eccentrically, there is no evidence that any of his associates did likewise. Certainly Richmond's self-portrait shows him in entirely conventional attire (cat. 56), as do other extant portraits of members of the group.

Later accounts do suggest that the Ancients drew attention to themselves in Shoreham by their peculiar behaviour, in particular by the penchant for nocturnal rambles and the reciting of Macbeth and 'gothick' novels such as Mrs Radcliffe's *Mysteries of Udolfo*. They became known –

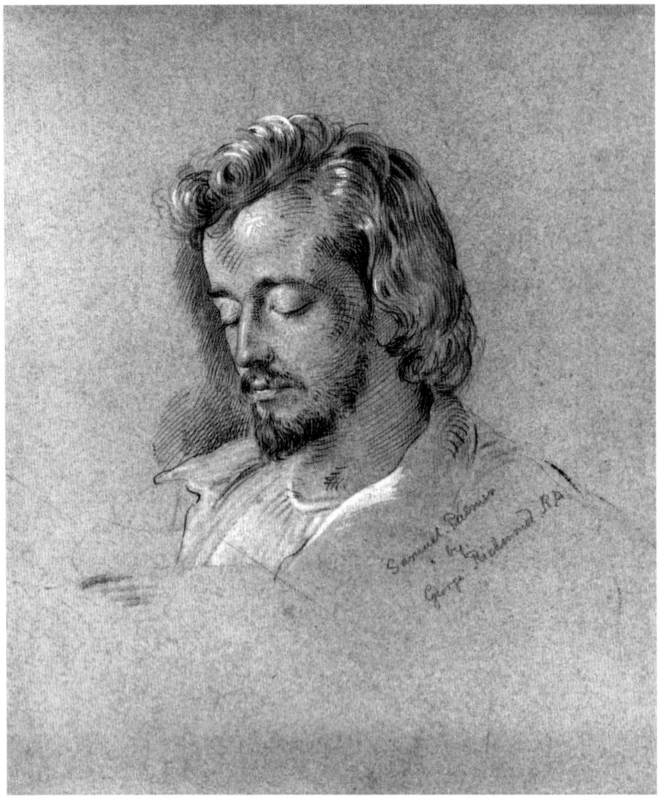

Fig. 4 George Richmond, *Samuel Palmer*, *c.*1829, chalk, National Portrait Gallery, London.

according to Palmer – as 'extollagers' (a rustic stab at 'astrologers').[15] But even then they seem to have been treated as essentially harmless, and relations between them and the locals were on the whole good-natured. Palmer himself became a local landlord, acquiring several properties in the village, which he continued to rent out for the rest of his life. Such normative behaviour contrasts strongly with that of most breakaway communities.

Nevertheless, there may have been more covert activities going on. According to the Ancients' own accounts, they never touched anything stronger than cider, though the character of some of Palmer's letters might imply otherwise (see cat. 52). There is also the question of their personal relations. It is one of the features of breakaway artistic communities of the period that they reveal strong same-sex bonding.[16] Understandably, such matters are played down in subsequent accounts, yet there are hints of strong emotions in surviving manuscripts. A.H. Palmer darkly remarked of certain early notebooks by his father that they showed 'a mental condition which, in many respects is uninviting. It is a condition full of danger, and neither sufficiently masculine nor sufficiently reticent.'[17] These were among the works by Palmer that he later destroyed.

Perhaps the most striking deviation of the Ancients from the normal pattern of breakaway brotherhoods is the lack of a developed manifesto or programme. 'Poetry and sentiment' appear to have been their watchwords,[18] but this hardly amounts to a definite artistic programme, such as can be found expressed by the Barbus, the Nazarenes, the Pre-Raphaelites and the Nabis. However, if there was no shared programme, there does seem to have been some commonality of practice. There is a connecting strain of primitivism to be found in the work of Palmer, Richmond and Calvert during the period of *c.*1825 to 1832 when the Ancients were most active as a group. But even here appearances can be deceptive. With the exception of Welby Sherman – who was employed by Palmer directly to make engravings after his works – the other Ancients show no signs of stylistic primitivism in their work. Indeed, the only other artist who might be said to share some of the primitivistic tendencies of the Ancients was Linnell. He, however, maintained a critical distance from the group and never pursued primitivism to the extent that Palmer, Richmond and Calvert did. Finally, while these three artists might be felt to constitute a group, it should be remembered that two of them were no more than sporadic visitors to Shoreham.

If claims for the consideration of the Ancients as an artistic brotherhood are weak, then they also fall short of successful versions of such organizations in their failure to win financial support and critical acclaim for their way of working. Successful brotherhoods survived usually because they attracted support among critics and patrons. Friedrich Schlegel's defence of the Nazarenes[19] and Ruskin's of the Pre-Raphaelites[20] are cases in point. The Ancients were signally unsuccessful in this. Like other brotherhoods, their main avenue for drawing attention to themselves was via public exhibition. All regularly sent in works to the Academy and quite a number were exhibited (see cats 54, 57). Yet these stimulated no critical enthusiasm and were evidently not considered sufficiently threatening to provoke outrage, as the Pre-Raphaelites were to do a generation later. The only published response (in the *European Magazine*) was that of astonished amusement (see p. 87).

It would seem that the Ancients did try to operate some kind of communal assistance among themselves. When Palmer was trying to promote Sherman's career, he appealed to the group to provide support for the sale of a print, suggesting selling the engraving *Samson and the Lion* in a letter to Richmond of 4 June 1828: 'Could not some means be devised among the "Blessed" in council assembled for selling some impressions of samson?'[21]

Lack of patronage was undoubtedly a key reason for the abandonment of the Ancients' style. None of the works exhibited by the group appear to have sold. In 1834 Palmer described himself in a letter to Richmond as 'at present pinched by a most unpoetical and unpastoral kind of poverty' and bewailed his lack of commissions.[22] Richmond by this time was flourishing. This was not, however, for his work as an Ancient, but for his skilled and flattering portraits. Nevertheless, it was not just financial necessity that caused the Ancients to abandon their ways. Calvert – who had no need to sell work to survive – seems to have lost faith in the manner as much as anyone else, his last work in the style of the Ancients being *The Chamber Idyll* of 1831 (cat. 61). All seemed to regard the manner as a youthful enthusiasm that had been to some extent misguided. When in Italy a few years later, Palmer felt that the experience of High Renaissance art and idyllic scenery had opened his eyes to new possibilities. Reviewing the studies that he made in Italy, he was 'conscious of a real advance in art'.[23] Richmond, similarly enthused by his own Italian experiences, wrote in the same year disparagingly of the earlier endeavours of the Ancients: 'We all wanted thumping when we thought in a dream of sentiment we were learning art.'[24]

As a means for spearheading a new direction in the art world of their time, the Ancients must be deemed to have failed. They would undoubtedly not have been remembered at all, had it not been for developments in the later nineteenth century. The most important was the rise of Pre-Raphaelitism, which gave a new cachet to the medieval idealism that they had espoused. The most significant event for them in connection with this was the rediscovery of Blake and the opportunity which that gave Palmer and others to go into print about their 'brotherhood'. The first published account of the Ancients' activities occurred in fact in Gilchrist's *Life of Blake* (1863),[25] a work produced with the support of W.M. Rossetti and with published reminiscences and letters by Calvert, Richmond, Palmer and Linnell. Pre-Raphaelitism saved the Ancients from oblivion, but it might also have shaped the group's identity. The colourful descriptions of the Ancients' behaviour by the members were published subsequently by them – often after having been repeated endlessly to family and friends and doubtless grown much in the telling. We shall probably now never be able to find out about the activities of this group except through that filter or to know what the 'brothers in art, brothers in love' actually did get up to in those brief, heady days together in Shoreham.

1 Calvert, p. 17.
2 The classic study of this group is G. Levitine, *The Dawn of Bohemianism: The 'Barbu' Rebellion and Primitivism in Neoclassical France*, University Park, PA, 1978. For a more recent account see W. Vaughan, 'The first artistic brotherhood: *fraternité* in the Age of Revolution', in Morowitz and Vaughan, pp. 32–47.
3 K. Andrews, *The Nazarenes*, Oxford, 1964. See also M. Frank, 'The Nazarene *Gemeinschaft*: Overbeck and Cornelius', in Morowitz and Vaughan, pp. 48–66.
4 M.A. Clawson, *Constructing Brotherhood: Class, Gender, and Fraternalism*, Princeton, 1989.
5 The most celebrated accounts of the Ancients can be found in Finch, pp. 45–6; *L&L*, pp. 25–7; Calvert, pp. 17–19, 48–50; and *Richmond Papers*, pp. 14–15, 100. See Bibliography for further details.
6 Lister 1974, p. 52.
7 E.J. Evans, *Britain before the Reform Act: Politics and Society 1815–32*, London, 1989, pp. 19–23.
8 *Letters*, p. 9.
9 Gilchrist 1863, vol. 1, p. 344.
10 For an account of knowledge of the Nazarenes in London in the 1820s see Vaughan 1979 esp. pp. 20–23, 36–8.
11 Vaughan, 1979, pp. 20–23.
12 Letter to Richmond, 10 May 1827: *Letters*, p. 11.
13 *Richmond Papers*, p. 16.
14 Lister 1974, p. 86.
15 Abley, p. 230.
16 Morowitz and Vaughan, pp. 18–19.
17 *L&L*, p. 18.
18 Calvert, p. 18.
19 Andrews 1964, pp. 42–3.
20 Hilton, pp. 11–17.
21 *Letters*, p. 23.
22 *Letters*, p. 62.
23 Letter to Linnell, 16 December 1838: *Letters*, p. 255.
24 28 September 1838; quoted by A.H. Palmer in a letter to Martin Hardie of 11 January 1926 (V&A Archive SF 814-27/7936).
25 Gilchrist 1863; vol. 1, pp. 344–6.

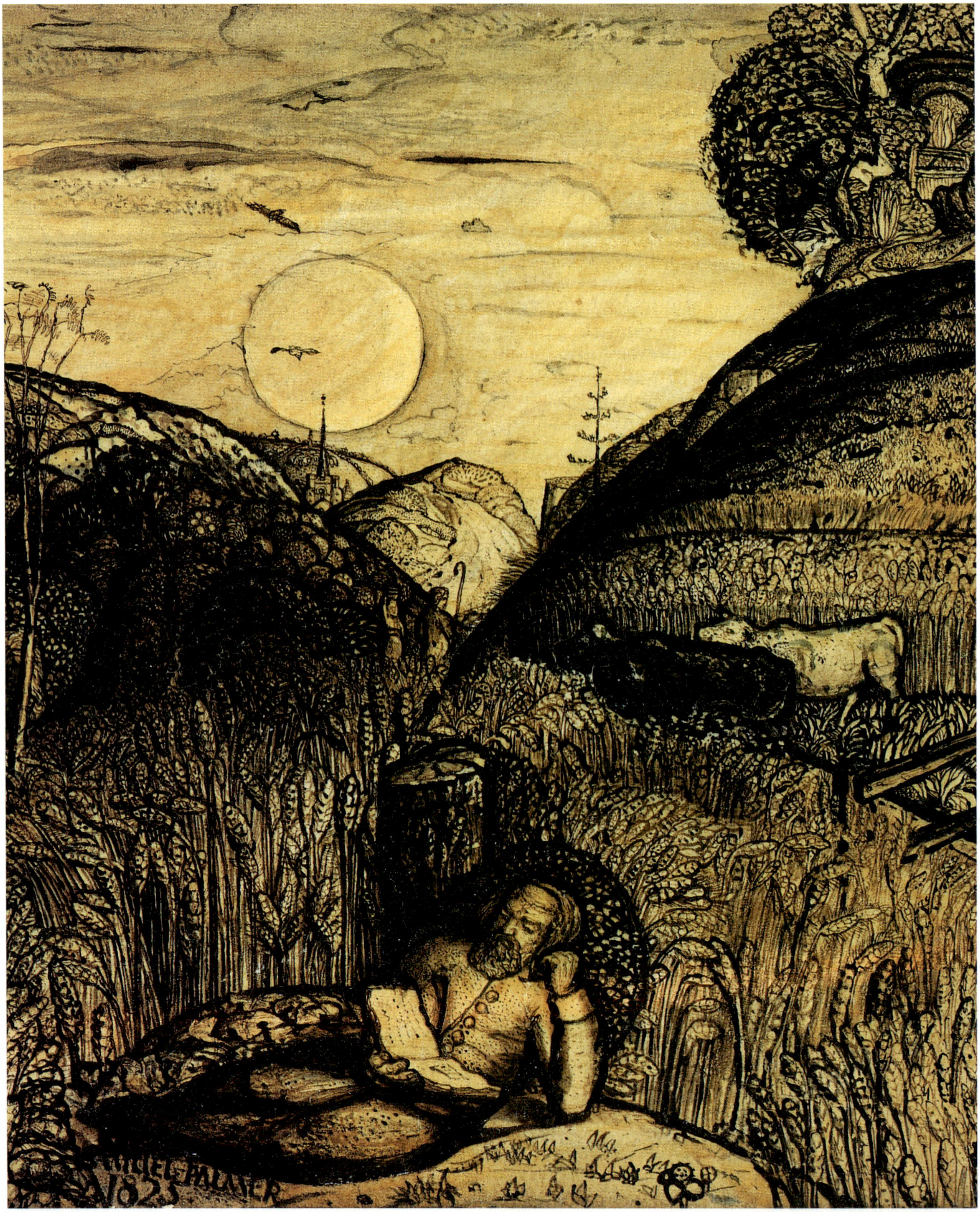

Samuel Palmer, *The Valley Thick with Corn*, 1825 (detail, cat. 15).

# ‘To fancy what is lost to sight’: Palmer and Literature

*David Blayney Brown*

‘I have been working very hard at art which I now love more than ever, and recreating myself with good books … a most comfortable and blessed cordial in this cold heartless and Godless age.’[1] Palmer’s letter to George Richmond in 1832 proclaims his trust in the regenerative power of books, and his twin devotions to image and word. A.H. Palmer said that his father painted with one hand and wrote with the other; he took his reading for granted. Literature was, just as one commentator has described, his ‘screen against the raw, wayward extravagance of the world’.[2] The writings of early divines – as likely to be martyrs to their faith as Palmer felt he was to his art – formed part of this screen’s fabric; another – which he considered as true an expression of goodness and was of greater significance for his work – was pastoral poetry. Neither quite prepared him for Blake, the third great influence on his literary life.

Like Blake, Palmer was steeped in literature from an early age. The son of a bookseller and preacher, he grew up surrounded by the classics and improving works. Even his nurse Mary Ward was a lover of Milton and bequeathed him her copy of Jacob Tonson’s edition of Milton’s poems. The images they gave him – the skylark, the lonely tower, the poet by a haunted stream – stayed with him always. Palmer would recall, of his years at Shoreham, ‘cultivating, among good books, a fastidious and unpopular taste’,[3] but the pattern set in childhood left a lifelong impression. ‘I lost much time formerly’, he told Elizabeth Linnell, ‘but am really glad I had a dose and glut of reading … some savour of which is yet within me like the relish of wine in an empty cask.’ He went on to ‘*entreat* those who are younger than myself to get plenty of reading while they can and that kind of reading which forms a *Taste* … till we come to seek in anything which calls itself a book – not stale notions … but IDEAS made pictorial by imagery and musical by melody and rhythm.’ He recommended ‘our early classics’ in poetry and prose – Milton, Sir Thomas Browne – then Swift, Burke and Dr Johnson; needless to say, he had no use ‘for the books ladies get hold of now’, nor for ‘the literary impudence dandyism and materialism with which most [of] our modern periodicals tend imperceptibly to imbue the mind’.[4]

Palmer did read his contemporaries. He subscribed to Dickens’s *All the Year Round* for its instalments of Wilkie Collins’s *Woman in White*, and to the *Cornhill* or *Nineteenth Century* for Ruskin; he was not above illustrating Dickens or Samuel Rogers; and one of his last projects was the reproduction of his watercolour of Keats’s grave in Rome for a forthcoming edition of the poet.[5] Byron and Wordsworth made occasional appearances in his letters, the latter as much for his qualified admiration for Blake (especially *Songs of Innocence*) as for his own work, but one never feels they were constant companions for Palmer in the way that Virgil, Milton, Shakespeare, Spenser or Bunyan were. These were timeless; they filled his thoughts and letters, and inured him to literary fashion. Making ‘a few assertions *a la mode*’ to another young lady, Richmond’s daughter Laura, in 1862, he recommended the classics as subjects for modern art, ‘for their freshness, being the freshness of first-rate poetry, is eternal … If you tell such a man [of imagination] that they are obsolete, he will smile at you with a peculiar smile; for, by the very constitution of his mind, he and they are contemporaneous.’ More pithily, he added: ‘The Past for Poets. The Present for Pigs.’[6]

Palmer had been busy with Virgil and was soon to return to Milton at the time when he wrote this letter. But the sentiments expressed in it were no less relevant to his frame of mind at Shoreham forty years before. The classics were never just the ‘great Gorge of old poetry to get up the dreaming’ that he described in 1872.[7] They were revealed truth, the measure of experience. ‘Poetry and Sentiment’ constituted the Ancients’ motto as they roamed the Kent countryside, and Palmer’s inner life of faith and books decided what he saw and how he saw it. The Ashmolean’s set of sepias of 1825 (cats 10–15) are intensely literary works, with inscriptions from Virgil, Shakespeare, the Bible and John Lydgate – the last mistaken for Chaucer. But they do more than illustrate these texts: multiple literary themes trail across their landscapes, mingling and building meaning. Probably no particular individual or author is represented by the reclining reader in *The Valley Thick with Corn* (cat. 15 and opposite). The figure is more likely to be a composite portrait of an Ancient who has taken his book into the fields. In his archaic clothes he embodies a shared heritage. Perhaps he is Milton or Bunyan’s Christian, who, together with his creator, may also appear in *Late Twilight* (cat. 13). But this design, which took its cue from *Macbeth*, is also rich in associations with Blake, whom Palmer had met the previous year.

Blake had illustrated *Pilgrim's Progress*, while the motif of the sleeping poet/shepherd can be traced to Blake's *America* and the paradisaical setting to his descriptions of Beulah.[8]

Blake – called the 'Interpreter' by Palmer and the Ancients after the seer who guided Christian in Bunyan's *Pilgrim's Progress* – fostered Palmer's literary tastes and his habits of composite allusion. Blake was at that time being supported by Palmer's own mentor, John Linnell. Palmer studied the designs for the book of Job that Blake made for Linnell (cat. 18) and watched him at work on his 'sublimest' designs for Dante's *Divine Comedy*, while his passionate response to Blake's wood engravings for the edition of Virgil's *Eclogues* prepared by the Linnell family doctor, Robert Thornton – 'the exquisitest pitch of intense poetry'[9] – is legendary (cat. 19). However, Palmer did not follow the rigorous critique of his great predecessors with which Blake hoped to rally 'Young Men of the New Age' like him. He did not engage with the criticisms that Blake made of the great Italian poet Dante for what he saw as the subjugation of his imagination to the doctrines of the Roman Church. Nor did Palmer accept Blake's unconventional treatment of Britain's own epic poet, Milton. Blake's poem *Milton* (1804) had viewed its hero not as a moral teacher but as a fallible and conflicted spirit whose acknowledgement of error and rejection of selfhood allowed him 'to cast aside from Poetry, all that is not Inspiration' – the task of all true artists and one that enabled Blake to identify with his subject.

Blake's *Milton* had been written as if with Milton's intervention, to correct mistaken ideas in *Paradise Lost*. Palmer would in due course apply the same process to Blake himself, transforming Blake's conception of the pastoral even as his art came closest to the outward appearance of Blake's work. The rich landscape imagery of Blake's Dante and Job illustrations serves to expose human failings. Palmer's *Skirts of a Wood* (cat. 14) creates rustic contentment from two of Blake's most telling images of the fallen intellect: his Dante design, *Homer and the Ancient Poets* (fig. 5), in which Dante and Virgil discover Homer, Horace, Ovid and Lucan clustered in a grove whose dense branches cut them off from the flying Daughters of the Imagination; and the ominous frontispiece to *Job* (cat. 18a), in which Job and his family leave their instruments unplayed and observe a passive, bookish religion. They, too, shelter beneath a tree. Blake's view of the natural world was typically equivocal: for all its beauty, it belonged to the material plane from which imagination must be released. For Palmer, however, it was imagination's source, and while borrowing Blake's tree, he replaced his bankrupts of mind and soul with a piping shepherd so at ease with his surroundings as to be almost an emanation from them.

Palmer's response to Blake's plates for Virgil's *Eclogues* involved a similar inversion of meaning. In these Blake was supposed to be enthusing new schoolboy readers – all the more so since he had honoured Virgil's imagination in his Dante series – but it is striking that he gave his prints a negative undertone. Far from sustaining their rustic inhabitants, the little landscapes are the background to an unsettling psychodrama involving Thenot's cynicism and Colinet's lapse into depression (fig. 6). In fact, this showed Blake's empathy with Virgil, who had composed the *Eclogues*

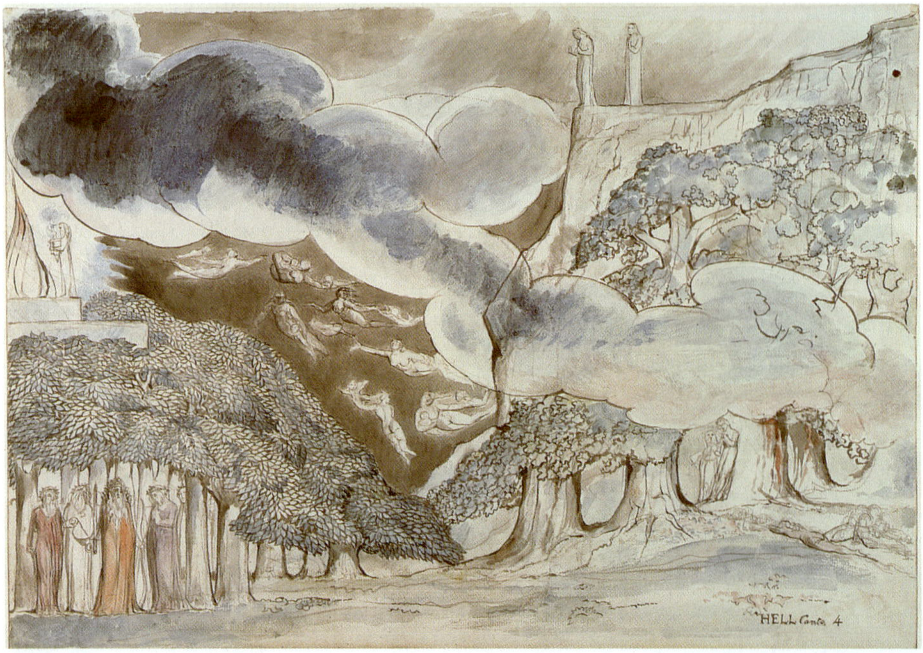


Fig. 5 William Blake, *Homer and the Ancient Poets*, 1824–7, ink and watercolour, Tate.

in the city, following the loss of his country estates in civil war. But while Thornton was sufficiently disturbed to publish Blake's images with a disclaimer, Palmer saw their 'misty and dreamy glimmer' – partly the result of Blake's inexperience with the medium – as a 'glimpse which all the most holy saints and sages have enjoyed, of that rest which remaineth to the people of God'.[10] This reading can seem naïve, a fall into the second-hand thinking that Blake condemned in *Job*. But Palmer's *Shepherds under a Full Moon* (cat. 31) is precise in allowing Blake's bucolics to restore communication with their surroundings, thus saving Blake's imagery from itself and directing the redemptive forces that Blake envisioned to their own creator. And who is to say that vision was not as brightly revealed to Palmer in the fields as to Blake in London? While Blake had considered the ancient poets compromised by their warlike age, Palmer saw how Virgil had used his art to rise above it. Could his own art now reclaim the 'Virgilian muse' banished by the railway whistle?[11]

Palmer wrote to his younger son Alfred Herbert in 1866 that Virgil's *Georgics* 'teach the wisdom of all life and the mysteries of intellectual discipline under the veil of agriculture … so that the veil itself is glorious – the diamond is set in gold'.[12] This beautiful image tells us all we need to know about why Palmer avoided contemporary reportage in his landscape painting, and preferred to symbolize eternal harmonies. Forty-one years before, he had turned to the *Georgics* for the epigraph to the *Rustic Scene* (cat. 10), describing ploughing and sowing at the autumn equinox. The only image of labour among the 1825 sepias, it responds to Virgil's message in these more mature and didactic poems about good husbandry as the link between man and nature, the means of individual and national revival. The motif may also owe something (as Raymond Lister has suggested of all Palmer's ploughmen[13]) to a passage in a favourite book of the Ancients at Shoreham, John Flavel's *Husbandry Spiritualized* (1669): 'Souls are the soyl, conviction is the plow'. Palmer saw a spiritual side to Virgil himself, telling Anne Gilchrist that in Eclogue IV Virgil had 'struck his immortal lyre in prophecy' of the birth of Christ.[14] Virgil remained important to Palmer throughout his life. In Italy, for instance, 'the oxen of Theocritus and Virgil' appeared before him,[15] and later, after the death of his elder son Thomas More, a promising Latinist, he (with the classically minded Edward Calvert) made his own translation of the *Eclogues*, which appeared posthumously in 1883 (cat. 163). Palmer had seen this work as his principal literary achievement and had originally intended to publish it as a text in its own right without illustrations. He changed his mind when, to his disappointment, the critic P.G. Hamerton advised him that the text would not succeed on its own and suggested that he should illustrate it.

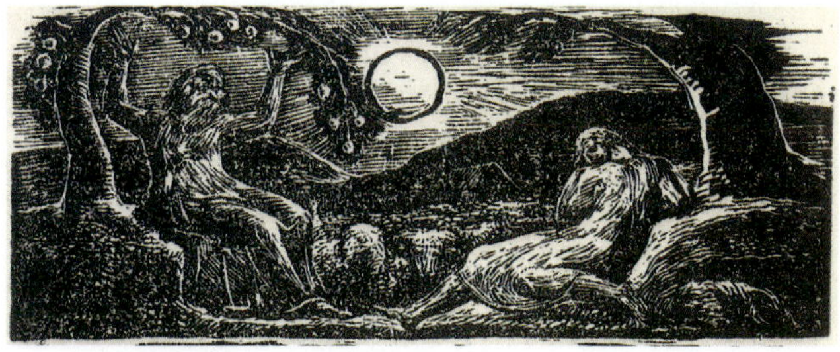

Fig. 6 William Blake, *Thenot and Colinet*, 1820, wood engraving (see cat. 19).

The translation is in fact agreeable enough but dated (Palmer, for example, changed the gender of one protagonist in the tale of male love in Eclogue II in order not to shock his Victorian readers). Today it is certainly his illustrations that have the greater interest.

Palmer made numerous designs for the project (see cats 154–6), but he only completed one etching, *Opening the Fold* (cat. 162), before he died. His surviving son finished four others (see cat. 163). Entering Virgil's poetic landscape and envisioning his prospect of a returning golden age helped Palmer recover his own lost Arcadia. But at least as revealing is the related essay '… On the Country and on Rural Poetry', which he tinkered with for years and appeared as the preface to the book.[16] In some respects a late counterpart to his early address to the Kentish electors (see pp. 29–32 and cat. 95), it expresses similarly conservative ideas and shows how little his view of rural life had changed or engaged with realities. This is an artistic manifesto – or apologia. Palmer scorns the city and those sophisticates who think poetry a waste of time, along with the lesser Augustans – 'Strephons and Chloes of the coffee house' – who had given its pastoral mode a bad name. But even as he asserts the moral benefits of country air and good books, he accepts the inevitability of urban life and that this will bring new readers for whom rural poetry 'presents to fancy what is lost to sight'. He goes on to redefine fancy in its purer form as imagination, whose 'language' is poetry in which 'sacred aspiration and secular wisdom have found their noblest utterance'.

While writing his essay, Palmer read Ruskin's 'Fictions – Fair and Foul' (1880), which lamented the poisoning effect of the city on literary taste.[17] His own manner of resistance was never as isolated as is sometimes thought,[18] though it has certainly contributed to his neglect by recent historians of landscape art. Early in the century the Sketching Society had promoted the illustration of 'poetic passages', and these had inspired Turner to produce works ranging from exhibition canvases to literary vignettes, as well as the 'Pastoral', 'Epic' or 'Elevated Pastoral' categories of his compendium of landscape, the *Liber Studiorum*; he even attempted poetry himself. By mid-century new trends were appearing to vindicate Palmer's poetic instincts. One was the revival of etching, which he considered unique among the arts in its 'compatibility with authorship'.[19] Another was the emergence of the Pre-Raphaelites, whose modern moral subjects did not compromise their poetic impetus and who were rediscovering Blake. In 1862 Palmer read D.G. Rossetti's first volume of poetry, his set of translations *The Early Italian Poets* (1861). Most importantly, within the extended Pre-Raphaelite circle Palmer found new admirers to hear his memories or collect his work. Rossetti's Chelsea neighbour Alexander Gilchrist and his wife Anne turned to him for their pioneering biography of Blake, while Ruskin's solicitor, Leonard Rowe Valpy, encouraged him to produce subjects that affected his 'inner sympathies'. For the ensuing commission he chose his first love, Milton. Hardly surprising, then, that Palmer should think more than ever about poetry and poetic art at this time.

One consequence was a more complete view of Blake's imaginative universe. Since Blake was so little regarded by the Romantic generation of writers, it was certainly Palmer's greatest service to literature to get Victorians to take Blake seriously as an artist, writer and thinker by means of the first-hand information he communicated, so patiently and generously, to the Gilchrists – even if he did recommend editing passages where Blake had turned 'peculiar'. Approving Virgil's reluctance to write about his friends' exploits, Palmer said that 'many years must elapse before events are seen in their just proportion'.[20] Poetic synthesis and understanding are products of time and distance, for 'the mind of a great poet is thrown back into antiquity, whence he symbolises the present'.[21] It was certainly with the benefit of years of reading and thinking that Palmer produced his Milton subjects for Valpy, and the fact that his remark on Virgil echoed Reynolds on Poussin[22] helps explain why the Milton series assimilated the classical as much as the picturesque or Gothic of his earlier style, and why he now distinguished the 'pseudo-classical, which I hate',[23] from the Elysian spirit of Claude or of the Claudean plates of Turner's *Liber* (fig. 7). He loved to tell Valpy – who had feared that he would mount 'the classical Pegasus' to tackle Milton[24] – how the Marquess of Stafford's maid had leant awestruck on her broom in front of Stafford's Claudes thinking she was in heaven.[25] Their luminous prospects gave her what he now sought himself, space – 'essential for Milton' – and 'Romantic sentiment, remoteness of time and place, just the opposite of that preference for the present, which certain critics say is the mark of genius'.[26]

Valpy's commission, leading to eight large watercolours (cats 146–53), began in 1864. In returning to Milton, Palmer addressed the poet not of the sublime – Blake's Milton – but of nature. His subjects from Milton's pagan masque *Comus* had appeared at the Old Water-Colour Society in 1855–6. Now he chose the pastoral poems 'L'Allegro' and 'Il Penseroso'. It is easy to see why he loved them, for in the highest original poetry they realize the 'English version' of Virgil that he had attempted in translation. Rural scenes by day and night are described in the spirits of mirth and melancholy – each, in its way, delightful. For Palmer the duality was propitious. As he said, 'the work of a poet where more is meant than meets the ear would I think suggest

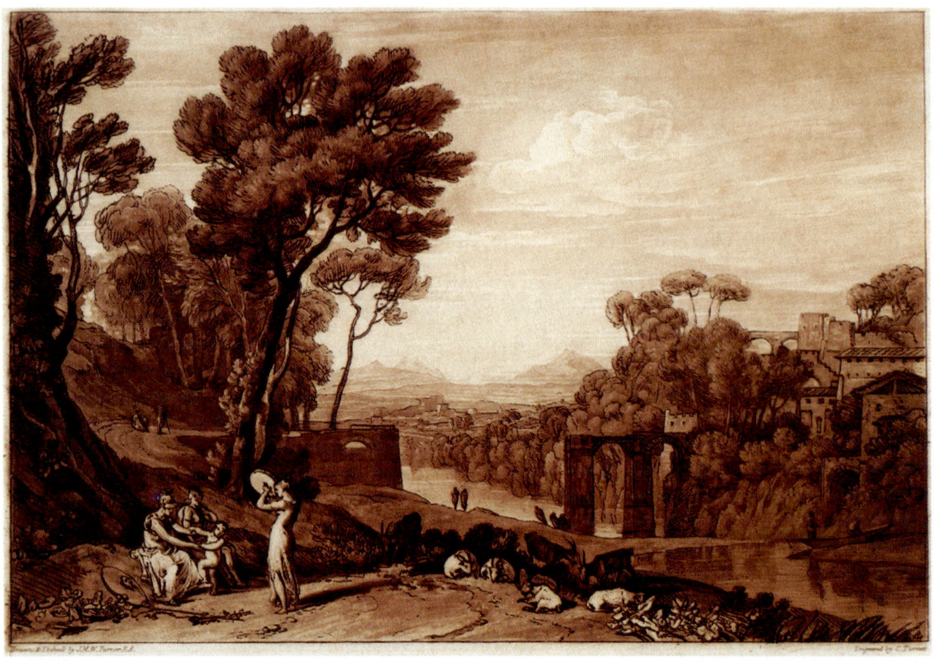

Fig. 7 Charles Turner, after J.M.W. Turner, *Woman with Tambourine*, 1807, mezzotint published in Turner's *Liber Studiorum*, part 1, Tate.

picture work where more is meant than meets the eye'.[27] He did not aim at literal illustration, but to convey the wider psychological terrain of the poems. His table of their attributes (see p. 225) was not textually related but cast in abstract terms,[28] and it was usually Valpy who suggested appropriate epigraphs as the subjects developed. Palmer knew what all lovers of poetry know, that 'select and precious passages gain somewhat by social sympathetic love'.[29] Conceived as pairs, the images are complementary rather than confrontational. In scenes expansive and secluded they take us from morning to night as if through life itself, and saw Palmer's own to its end. He finished the splendid *Prospect* from 'L'Allegro' (cat. 146) in his last months, working in bed, as Blake had on Dante.

The final pair of scenes,[30] *The Bellman* (cat. 159) and *The Lonely Tower* (cat. 161) – the first, 'a breaking out of village fever long after contact',[31] and the second, a vision of Milton's star-gazing scholar mystic – are both from 'Il Penseroso' but embrace the spirit of both poems. Of the former, Palmer said that gloom, by releasing the imagination, 'enforces the sentiment of exuberance',[32] while the latter aspired to 'poetic loneliness – not the loneliness of the desert'.[33] Its glimpse of distant standing stones recalls Blake's use of Stonehenge in his mythology, and the dualism of the whole series is Blakean, too. Since Palmer's settings are rural, the contraries are not as harsh as those of Innocence and Experience or of *The Marriage of Heaven and Hell*, which was doubtless among those works of Blake that Palmer told Valpy 'savour of Manicheism'.[34] But in so uniting the active and contemplative life, memory and imagination, Palmer reconciled his own impulses as painter and writer, reader and dreamer. The Milton project was his last reinvention of himself by means of the literary works that he prized so highly, and it was in truth a resurrection. He hoped that an etched series, of which the final pair alone was completed, would 'live when I am with the fallen leaves'.[35] Decades later Yeats, when referring to one of these etchings, *The Lonely Tower*, wrote of a 'mysterious wisdom won by toil'.[36] This is proof indeed that Palmer spoke to poets as they had to him.

1 Letter to George Richmond, 21 September 1832: *Letters*, pp. 57–8.
2 Abley, p. 9.
3 Letter to P.G. Hamerton, 4 August 1879: *Letters*, p. 970.
4 Letter to Elizabeth Linnell, 14 July 1838: *Letters*, pp. 156–7.
5 Charles Dickens, *Pictures from Italy*, London 1846; Samuel Rogers, *The Pleasures of Memory*, London, n.d. [1865]; *The Burial Place of Keats*, etched by Arthur Evershed in *The Poetical Works and Other Writings of John Keats*, ed. Harry Buxton Forman, London 1883, I, facing p. 106.
6 Letter to Laura Richmond, December 1862 (?): *Letters*, pp. 671–2.
7 Letter to P.G. Hamerton, 9 November 1872: *Letters*, p. 866.
8 *America: A Prophecy*, pl. 7, *'In thunders ends the voice'*; for Beulah, see *inter alia* the MS poem *Vala* or *The Four Zoas*. Linnell owned copies of both works.
9 Notebooks, 1824–35: *L&L*, pp. 15–16.
10 *L&L*, p. 16.
11 'Ah where is the Virgilian muse? At the railway whistle she fled for ever': letter to William Linnell, 29 January 1862: *Letters*, p. 636.
12 Letter to A.H. Palmer, 14 October 1866: *Letters*, pp. 749–50.
13 *Samuel Palmer and 'The Ancients'*, exh. cat., Fitzwilliam Museum, Cambridge, 1984, p. 68, under no. 93.
14 Letter to Anne Gilchrist, 2 February 1862: *Letters*, p. 639.
15 Letter to John Linnell and family, 8 April 1839: *Letters*, p. 321.
16 *An English Version of the Pastorals of Virgil*, London 1883 (cat. 163): reprinted in Abley, pp. 151–66.
17 *Nineteenth Century*, June 1880, pp. 941–62; see Palmer's letter to the Revd John Preston Wright, 26 July 1880: *Letters*, p. 1015.
18 For an excellent summary of the wider background of English Pastoral and Arcadianism see Graham Reynolds, 'Samuel Palmer, Milton and Virgil', in *A Vision Recaptured*, pp. 33–44.
19 Palmer to P.G. Hamerton, 9 November 1872: *Letters*, p. 865.
20 Note to Eclogue VIII; reprinted in Abley, p. 166.
21 Abley, p. 166.
22 '... a mind thrown back two thousand years, and as it were naturalized in antiquity, like that of Nicolo Poussin' (Discourse XIV, in *Sir Joshua Reynolds: Discourses on Art*, ed. Robert R. Wark, New Haven and London 1975, p. 256).
23 Letter to L.R. Valpy, 20 October 1864: *Letters*, p. 712.
24 Letter to L.R. Valpy, July 1864: *Letters*, p. 695.
25 Letter to L.R. Valpy, 1 February 1875: *Letters*, p. 904.
26 Letter to L.R. Valpy, July 1864: *Letters*, p. 695.
27 Quoted by A.H. Palmer: *L&L*, p. 154.
28 Set out in a letter to L.R. Valpy, September 1864: *Letters*, p. 703.
29 Letter to L.R. Valpy, July 1864: *Letters*, p. 694.
30 While Palmer originally conceived of the series as a set of paired subjects, there is some controversy about the extent to which this scheme was fully carried out (see p. 225). The interpretation given by Graham Reynolds in *A Vision Recaptured* (pp. 33–44) is followed here.
31 Letter to P.G. Hamerton, 4 August 1879: *Letters*, p. 970.
32 Letter to L.R. Valpy, July 1864: *Letters*, p. 699.
33 *Letters*, p. 695.
34 Letter to L.R. Valpy, June 1864: *Letters*, p. 691.
35 Letter to L.R. Valpy, 20 October 1864: *Letters*, p. 712.
36 W.B. Yeats, 'The Phases of the Moon', from *The Wild Swans at Coole*, 1919, in *W.B. Yeats: The Poems*, ed. R.J. Finneran, London 1984, p. 163.

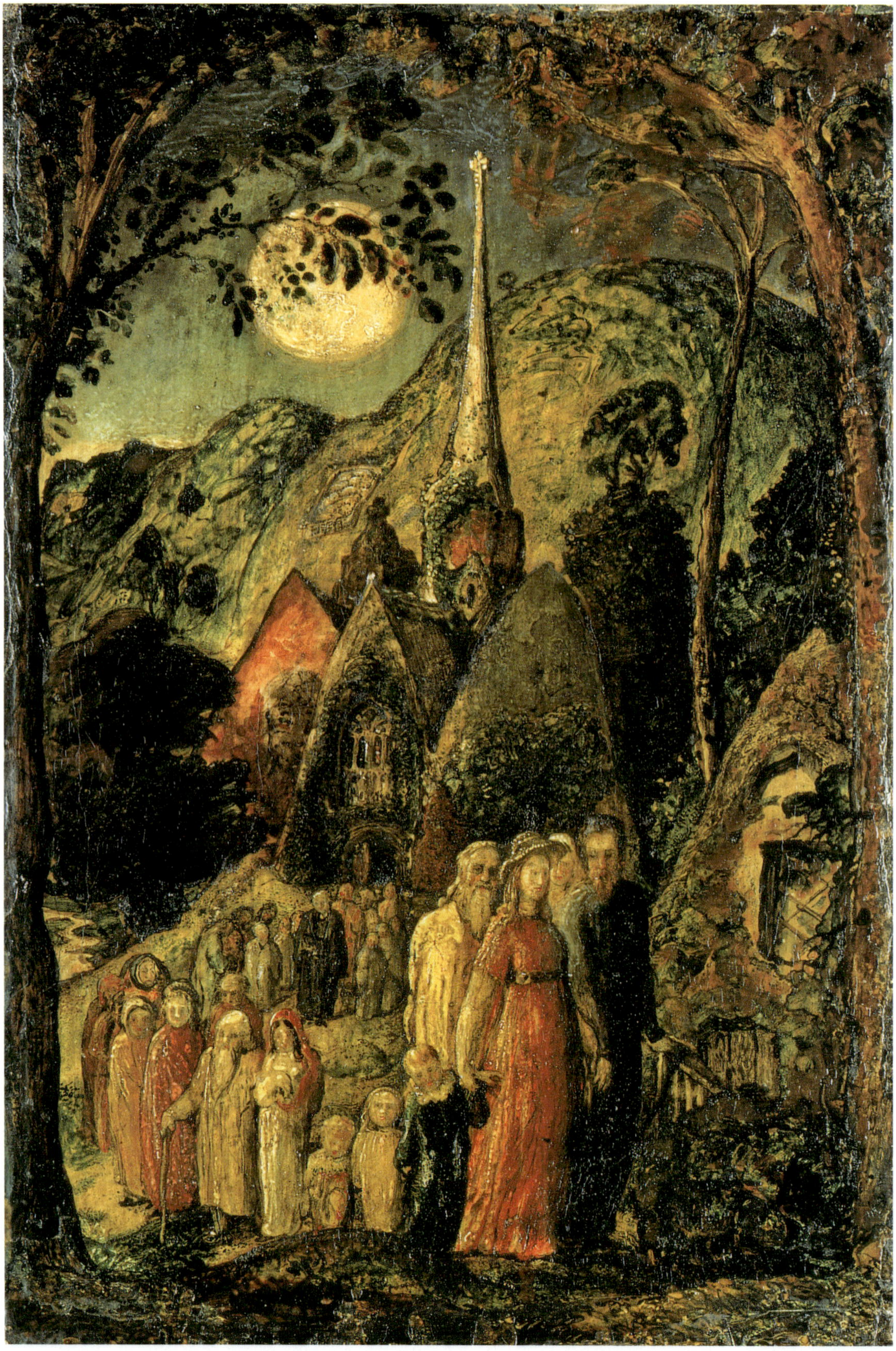

Samuel Palmer, *Coming from Evening Church*, 1830 (cat. 48).

# The Politics of Vision: Palmer's *Address to the Electors of West Kent*, 1832

*David Bindman*

Geoffrey Grigson in his classic book on Palmer of 1947[1] noted that the artist had written an electoral pamphlet towards the end of his period in Shoreham, in support of the Tory candidate Sir William Geary during the election that followed the passage of the Reform Act in 1832. Grigson connected the strong feelings expressed in the pamphlet with Palmer's gradual retreat from Shoreham to London in the years before his final departure in 1834. Grigson, however, knew the pamphlet only from extracts held up for derision in the reforming *Maidstone Gazette* of 11 December 1832, where (attributed to 'the pen of a Reverend Divine') it was described as 'the ravings of a maniac'.[2] In 1985 Michael Collinge, then of the London University Institute of Historical Research, tracked down a copy of the pamphlet in the Maidstone Public Record Office, and I was able to publish the complete text for the first time in the same year in a specialist journal, *Blake: An Illustrated Quarterly*.[3]

The *Maidstone Gazette* complained of the pamphlet's 'gross invectives and foul vituperation', and it does indeed contain ferocious attacks on supporters of the Reform Act, or as Palmer called them 'Jacobinical hyenas'.[4] The 'Men of Kent', who had resisted tyranny from William the Conqueror to Napoleon, are called upon to rise up and fight the proponents of reform, 'the most heartless, the most bloody, most obscene, profane, and atrocious faction, which ever defied God and insulted humanity'. It is claimed that the present reform did not spring from 'the stock of ancient British Whiggism', but 'it is the importation of Yesterday, from poor, degraded, dishonoured, Atheistical France'. Palmer thus employed, with little mitigating humour or irony, imagery associated with Edmund Burke's anti-Revolution pamphlets of the later 1790s, the *Anti-Jacobin Review*, and the loyalist caricatures of Gillray in the 1790s.[5]

The passion and intolerance of the pamphlet might seem hard to reconcile with Palmer's contemplative visionary art. The *Address* can be partly explained as an anguished response to Palmer's experience of rural unrest in the Kent countryside, but the ideological content of the pamphlet is not alien to that of his more sober letters of the late 1820s and early 1830s or, as I will argue, to his art of that period. The Church of England was faced then with calls for reform that seemed to its more conservative supporters like Palmer to threaten both its existence as a national Church and the social order that maintained and was maintained by it.[6] On the other hand his allegiance to the Church of England as the true Apostolic Church did not affect his devotion to the fiercely anti-Anglican William Blake, nor did it prevent him from having friendly if boisterous arguments over religion with his future father-in-law John Linnell, who was from a Dissenting background.

In a long and rambling letter to George Richmond from Shoreham in September 1828 Palmer describes such discussions:

> Our conversation is an entertaining medley not unmix'd with Theology ... Politics we dabble in: Mr. L[innell] though of no party magnifies the peasants; I, also, as you know, of no party, as I love our fine British peasantry, think best of the old high tories, because I find they gave most liberty to the poor, and were not morose, sullen and blood-thirsty like the whigs, liberty jacks and dissenters; whose cruelty when they reign'd, was as bad as that of the worst times of the worst papists; only more sly and smoothlier varnish'd over with a thin shew of reason. On Theology, and church government, we keep up a perpetual running fight: I am for high church and the less of state expediency and money mix'd up with it the better.[7]

The year 1828 was a worrying one for 'old high tories' for it saw the final repeal of the Test and Corporation Acts, which removed the statutory bar on non-Anglicans from holding public and municipal offices. The person who spoke their thoughts most eloquently was William Wordsworth, who, from being a fervent radical in the 1790s, had by the second decade of the nineteenth century become an equally fervent conservative or, as Lord Byron put it more pungently, 'the converted Jacobin [has] long subsided into the clownish sycophant of the worst prejudices of aristocracy'.[8] Despite the dismay that his later poetry caused among his fellow Romantics and his descent into what Shelley called 'ultra-legitimate dulness', it was often invoked in the 1820s in defence of the old political and religious order in the face of mounting pressure from the radicals, who challenged the immemorial right of the Church to collect tithes in the countryside and the right of the state to continue denying the vote to the vast majority of the population.

Wordsworth's 'late period' began in 1814 with *The Excursion*, which among other things offered a myth that owed much to Burke's writings about an England (not Britain) facing from reformers of church and parliament a threat as grave as that offered by the French Revolutionary *sans-culottes* in the Terror of the mid-1790s. Wordsworth describes a uniquely English countryside defined by history and religion, which through the Anglican Church continued to exert a benign and unifying effect on the social and natural order and act as a bulwark against the modern world of materialism in all its godless forms. The essence of the English landscape lay for Wordsworth in a mystical connection between nature, man and God, utterly opposed to the nation created by the 'new' Whigs, utilitarians and radicals. He pictured a benign (and Burkean) polity matured over centuries, in which 'human Charity and social love' were the bonds of society, not abstract justice or the rewards of productivity.

The linchpin of this mythical England was the 'Pastor', the country vicar who brought civility and godliness to the countryside, binding the immemorial past with the present. The bond between God and man is represented by the omnipresent church spire, making an organic connection between church and village, and between the village and 'the swelling hills and spacious plains' around it. In Book VI of *The Excursion* a vicar celebrates this vision of an ideal England:

Hail to the state of England and conjoin
With this a salutation as devout
Made to the spiritual fabric of her church,
Founded in truth; by blood of martyrdom
Cemented; by the hands of wisdom reared
In beauty of holiness, with ordered pomp,
Decent and unreproved …
And O, ye swelling hills and spacious plains,
Besprent from shore to shore with steeple towers
And spires, whose silent finger points to heaven –
Nor wanting at wide intervals, the bulk
Of ancient minster, lifted above the cloud
Of the dense air which town or city breeds,
To intercept the sun's glad beams – may ne'er
That true succession fail of English hearts,
Who with ancestral feeling can perceive
What in those holy structures ye possess
Of ornamental interest, and the charm
Of pious sentiment diffused afar,
And human charity and social love.
Thus never shall the indignities of time
Approach their reverend graces unopposed;
Nor shall the elements be free to hurt
Their fair proportions; nor the blinder rage
Of bigot zeal, madly to overturn;
And if the desolating hand of war
Spare them, they shall continue to bestow
Upon the thronged abodes of busy men
(Depraved, and ever prone to fill their minds
Exclusively with transitory things,)
An air and mien of dignified pursuit,
Of sweet civility, on rustic wilds.

A similarly theocratic vision of the English countryside under threat from modernity may be discerned not only in Palmer's letters but in the most important painting of the later Shoreham years, entitled by Palmer *Coming from Evening Church*, 1830 (cat. 48 and p. 28). It shows all ages and generations of the village from small children to old men leaving the church set in a valley beneath the moon;[9] towards the end of the line of people, the pivot of the group, is the vicar. The Gothic nave of the church is in the centre of a series of echoing forms, of trees, hills behind and the cottage on the right. Village and parishioners are embraced by a continuous ridge, and two foreground trees join to form a protective arbour. The spire is rooted in the church and hillside but is the one element to break out of this enclosed world, precisely representing Wordsworth's 'silent finger [which] points to heaven', though in actuality Shoreham Church was unusual in Kent in *not* having a spire. We can thus read the painting as strongly Wordsworthian, representing the village and its community of young and old as part of the continuity of life through the ages, a natural order under the benevolent dominion of the Old English Church, which knits together an indivisible harmony of nature, nation and religion, protecting it from the world of 'busy men'.

At a more mundane level the painting can be read, like the *Address*, as an answer to those who wished to abolish tithes,

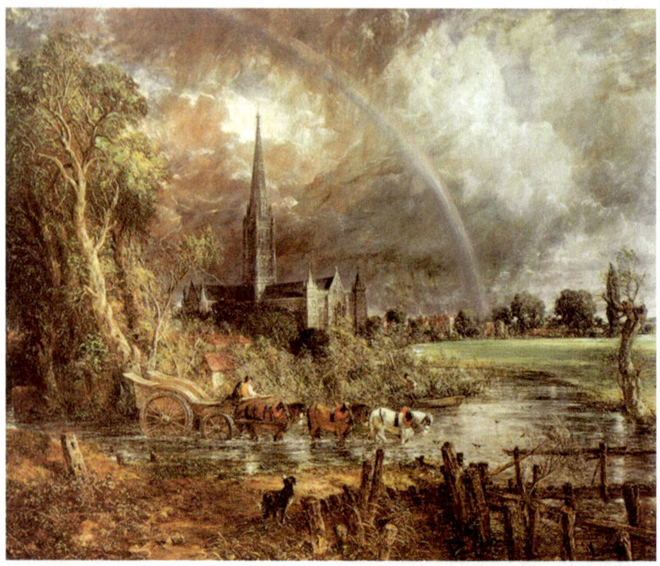

Fig. 8 John Constable, *Salisbury Cathedral from the Meadows*, 1831, oil on canvas, private collection, on loan to the National Gallery, London.

the traditional method of paying the clergy whereby a farmer was obliged to give one tenth of produce either in cash or kind to the local parish. For Palmer tithes were part of the sacramental unity between clergy and people, but they had long been the cause of bitter dissent in rural areas, particularly when there was a poor harvest. Opposition to tithes united Dissenters, who regarded the Church of England as an 'unscriptural institution', with farmers and farm labourers in common cause against the Church and by implication the unified polity represented by Wordsworth's and Palmer's ideal of village life.

Palmer's response to the Church crisis of the late 1820s, though always expressed more pungently, may be compared to that of John Constable who, with his ecclesiastical connections through the Fishers of Salisbury Cathedral, shared a deep apprehension of the threat to the countryside, and was equally prone to attribute a diabolical agency to 'agitators'. In a painting that predates the crisis, *Salisbury Cathedral from the South West* of 1820 (National Gallery of Art, Washington), the needle-like spire seems to grow naturally from the prosperity and civility of its setting, but the 1831 *Salisbury Cathedral from the Meadows* (fig. 8) is, by contrast, deeply agitated in both its surface and underlying sentiment. John Fisher himself described it as representing 'the Church under a cloud',[10] and though Constable resisted allegorical readings of his paintings, it is hard to see the painting as anything other than an image of the Church of England in crisis. If Palmer's Shoreham places the ideal England in a golden age that lingers on in embattled corners of the countryside and in the collective imagination, Constable evokes the forbidding isolation of the cathedral, its grandeur diminished by the broiling sky and the arc of the rainbow.

Palmer's reaction in his letters and art to the social and religious crisis of 1828–30, though passionately expressed, is still far from the unsparing and desperate dogmatism of the *Address to the Electors of West Kent*. In a letter to Richmond of 21 September 1832 he himself notes the change in his view over the previous few years:

> If people knew how deeply the whole world lieth in wickedness, and how totally it is estranged & set in opposition against God; they would I cannot help thinking, no longer wonder why all kinds of sects & schisms may not equally be term'd the Churches of Christ ... Once I was full of this lightness and folly – yea even to the present time my old Adam can see no reason why the sleek & sober Quaker or the meek & moral Unitarian should be beholden to the Church, claiming the power of the keys of the kingdom of Heaven – But blessed be to God. *I am changed ever since you saw me* – I am a free thinker in art in literature in music in poetry – but as I read of but one way to Heaven & that a narrow one it is not for me to chuse which way, I will be saved & make it a pretty speculation or matter of taste, & run to seek my Saviour in holes and corners, but go at once where He is ever to be found, at the Apostolic altar of the Melchisedekian priesthood.[11]

This letter then expresses disdain for his former self when he could disagree vigorously but still courteously with 'respectable' Dissenters like John Linnell. What caused this change? Grigson noted astutely that the early 1830s were the time of the 'Captain Swing' riots when unemployed and hungry farm labourers terrorized farmers in Kent and other counties by setting fire to hayricks, destroying threshing machines and leaving threatening letters. Thanks to the painstaking work of Eric Hobsbawm and George Rudé we can track the spread of such 'incidents' around the Kent countryside.[12] By the end of the 1820s more than a third of the population of the Kentish Weald was unemployed following the agricultural recession after Waterloo, and by 1828 'pauperism, degradation, desperation, and sullen discontent were thus almost universal',[13] although there is no mention of it in Palmer's surviving letters to his London friends. In 1829 a disastrous harvest was followed by a cruel winter, and misery increased even further, especially in Kent. By 1830 open revolt had broken out in the form of rick-burning and later the destruction of threshing machines, sometimes accompanied by sinister letters in the name of 'Captain Swing'.

Palmer in a letter to Linnell of 21 December 1828 fantasizes about being a country vicar himself, living in 'a little thatch'd parsonage and a little quiet, simple evangelical flock in a primitive village where none of the King-choppers had set up business'.[14] It is ironical, therefore, that Shoreham should have been right in the middle of the first wave of the Captain Swing uprisings. The preferred method of dissent in West Kent was arson, followed by threatening letters, often signed by 'Captain Swing'. The very first incident of arson in southern England was recorded at Orpington, just a short distance away, on 1 June 1830, and in early September arson had reached Shoreham itself, and the nearest village Otford, after passing through several nearby towns like Bromley and Sevenoaks and the villages of Brasted, Cowden and Ide Hill;[15] according to Hobsbawm and Rudé, 'By the end of September, a total of twenty incendiary fires had been reported in the district around Bromley, Sevenoaks and Orpington'. There was another outbreak in Otford on 17 October, and many other villages in the area of Sevenoaks and Maidstone were attacked or threatened before the end of the year.

The first week of September saw the worst of the attacks in the area of Shoreham: according to *The Times* of 17 September, 'scarcely a night passes without some farmer having a corn stack or barn set fire to. It is really dreadful.'[16] The farmer in Shoreham whose farm was attacked, a Mr

Love, was, it turns out, well known to Palmer, who described him in a letter to Linnell of 10 October 1827 as 'one of the best farmers hereabout, and a large grower, of whom several of the villagers have what they want for growing'.[17] This was in response to an enquiry by Palmer's father about buying hops. Mr Love, whose two daughters were amateur painters, lived at Filston Hall Farm on the road to Otford where a Mr Jessop also suffered.

The revolt was suppressed by the end of the year, but it might be supposed that the fires consumed not only Palmer's hopes of a peaceful rural retreat from the city but his faith in the 'fine old English peasantry'. However, in the *Address* he does not blame the farm labourers at any point but only the radicals whom he claims had raised the question of tithes as a way of destroying the old order. This implies that the rick-burning labourers had become alienated from the traditional rural compact between landowners and tenants, who could be relied upon to repel foreign ideas. In fact, as Hobsbawm and Rudé make clear, although radicals were involved in the disturbances at certain times, the troubles in West Kent were localized and desperate, the economic conditions of 1828–30 affecting particularly hop production in the Shoreham area. In the *Address* radicals and reformers, under the direct influence of French Jacobin and revolutionary principles, are the people to be feared. In the one reference to the Swing riots in the pamphlet the radicals are described as 'the wretched leaders of this wretched faction, who, during the late dreadful fires, strenuously encouraged the incendiaries! Some of the most abandoned of them published cheap tracts for distribution among the poor, stimulating them to fire their master's property.'[18] Like John Bull in Gillray's caricatures of the 1790s they are led astray by agitators or, to put it cynically, manipulated by the wrong people.[19]

It is hard to believe that Palmer, who may have witnessed the flames erupting from Farmer Love's barns, would have been unaffected by the immediate proximity of rural agitation, but the pamphlet responds primarily to the 1830 revolution in France and the Reform Act. His account of the 1830 revolution follows closely the language of Burke's hysterical anti-French Revolution pamphlets of the later 1790s, like *Thoughts on a Regicide Peace* of 1796. The reformers are 'the whole Radical and Atheistical party of England [which] is now marshaled against the constitutional and religious', and they can only be fought off by the rallying by 'every Christian man in West Kent' in a renewed patriotism and affirmation of the God-given social order.

There is something 'proto-Victorian' in Palmer's (and Wordsworth's) eliding of patriotism and Anglican religion, but there is also an intriguing connection with German landscape painters of the years 1806–20, who, in the period of the patriotic war against France and its aftermath, also invoked the national past in opposition to the present. In Caspar David Friedrich's *Tombs of Ancient Heroes*, 1812,[20] ancient Germanic heroes will, it is hinted, have risen or will rise again to expel the atheistic French from the sacred soil of Germany, and the same artist's *Chasseur in the Woods*, 1814, is full of intimations that bind patriotism inextricably to the spirit; the defeated French soldier is overwhelmed by the spiritual power of Germanic nature.[21] Of course the political situation of the two artists was completely different, but Palmer's *Address to the Electors of West Kent* emphasizes the fact, not always fully appreciated, that a highly politicized sacramental nationalism, rooted in a landscape imbued with a legendary history, was as much part of British as it was of German Romantic art.

1 Grigson 1947, pp. 103–6; and also Geoffrey Grigson, 'Samuel Palmer: The Politics of an Artist', *Horizon*, 1944, pp. 314–28.
2 Grigson 1947, p. 105.
3 Bindman 1985.
4 *An Address*, p. 6.
5 See D. Bindman, *The Shadow of the Guillotine*, London, 1989, esp. pp. 188–9.
6 See anon. article in *Quarterly Review*, 1830, pp. 105–47, and E.J. Evans, 'Some reasons for the growth of English Rural Anti-Clericalism', *Past and Present*, February 1975.
7 *Letters*, p. 37.
8 Cited in Alison Hickey, *Impure Conceits: Rhetoric and Ideology in Wordsworth's 'Excursion'*, Stanford, 1997, p. 4.
9 For the moon in Palmer's art see Grigson, 1947, p. 93.
10 Michael Rosenthal, *Constable: The Painter and his Landscape*, New Haven and London, 1983, p. 230.
11 *Letters*, pp. 58–9.
12 Hobsbawm and Rudé, pp. 172–90.
13 Hobsbawm and Rudé, p. 81.
14 *Letters*, p. 51.
15 See the invaluable table of incidents in Appendix III of Hobsbawm and Rudé, pp. 311–58.
16 Hobsbawm and Rudé, p. 99. Remarkably, we know from the Maidstone Gaol calendar for 1833–51 the names of those who set fire to the corn stacks of Mr Love and others at Shoreham: B. Skinner, aged forty-four, and S. Iggledon, aged thirty (White and Saynor, p. 134).
17 *Letters*, p. 14.
18 *Address*, p. 15.
19 See, for example, *The Tree of Liberty,– with, the Devil tempting John Bull*, 1798, in which Charles James Fox as the serpent in Eden offers John Bull a half-eaten apple inscribed 'Reform' from the Tree of Knowledge.
20 Werner Hofmann, *Caspar David Friedrich*, London, 2000, pp. 88–9, pl. 51.
21 Ibid., pp. 85f., pl. 53.

# Samuel Palmer's Materials and Techniques: The Early Years

*Alexandra Greathead*

Little has been written about the materials and techniques used by Samuel Palmer in the execution of his works in the early part of his life.[1] In Palmer's letters, essays and few remaining sketchbooks from the period[2] the majority of references relate to the aesthetics of the image. This initial investigation into the materials and techniques used by Samuel Palmer in his early works on paper,[3] before his departure to Italy in 1837, focuses on those in the collection of the Ashmolean Museum: in particular, the six sepia drawings (hereafter referred to as the 'sepias') that were executed in 1825 shortly before Palmer settled in Shoreham (cats 10–15).[4] All observations were carried out using a combination of the naked eye, a binocular microscope (×10, ×20 and ×30 magnification), transmitted light and ultraviolet light (UV). Although some of the works are flaked and cracking, none of the losses have been collected, so there were no samples for further analysis.

For many of his works from the early period Palmer used supports very common to the time, such as grey and white Bristol board.[5] Bristol board was a glazed pasteboard made of good quality, wove drawing paper, which appears to have been the product of stationers and paper merchants rather than paper manufacturers. Its composition was therefore the same as pasteboard with the addition of a 'smooth' surface on one or both sides,[6] and was usually blind-stamped 'Bristol Paper'. The smooth surface would have been particularly attractive to Palmer as an artist using it for watercolour paintings and sketches. Palmer complained that in Shoreham he was unable to purchase the 'stiff, cool grey Bristol Board' and could only get 'a light blue which scarcely shows the white heightenings'.[7]

A few of the landscape sketches of Shoreham and its surroundings are executed on a grey/brown lightweight board. In the early nineteenth century this paper was referred to as 'middle-tint paper' and later as 'crayon paper',[8] due to its intended use. On the support used for *Barn in a Valley*, 'Crayon Paper' is blind-stamped in the top left corner. Though of a very similar finish to Bristol board, the surface of crayon paper is not as smooth. With its hard surface, crayon paper was ideal for Palmer's sketching

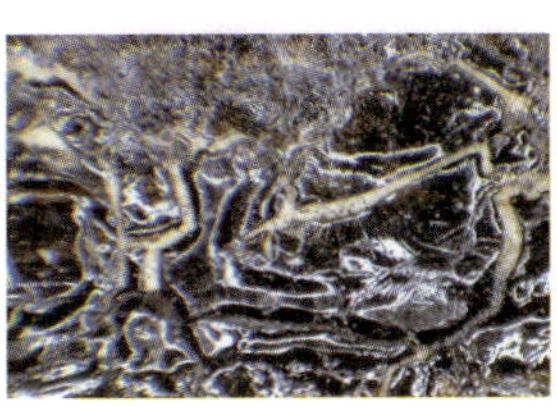

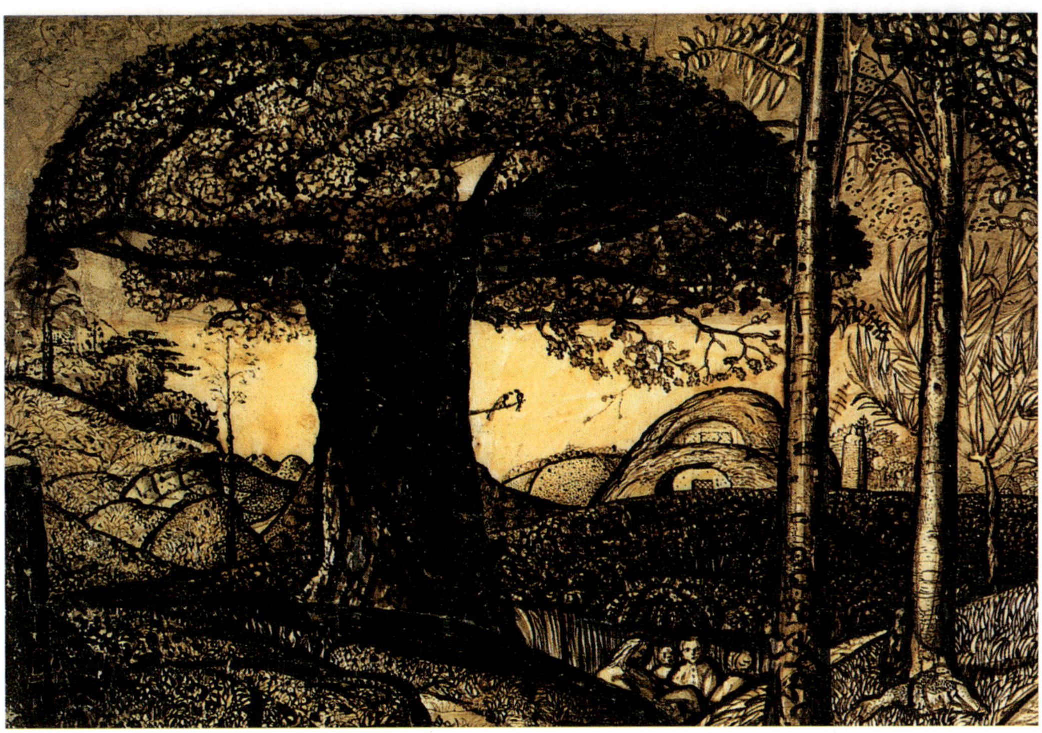

Fig. 9 A ×30 magnification, above, of the right side of the tree trunk from *Early Morning*, 1825, right (detail, cat. 12).

purposes and its well-sized finish ensured that washes did not penetrate deep into the support.

The first impression one has of the six sepias is their print-like appearance. They were produced at a time when Palmer had no practical experience of printmaking but had certainly started to admire it. Palmer began the sepias within a year of meeting William Blake, and it was said that 'many details in these drawings are reminiscent of Blake's woodcuts to Thornton's edition of the *Pastoral of Virgil*'.[9] Palmer also referred to a technique that appears similar to the one he adopted for the six sepias:[10]

> Then presently begin to insert those masses of little forms like the leaves of a near tree, which *serve of shadows* and *themselves make a tint* all this while fattening up the outline, till as near as you can get it you make it like the prints of the Georgics,[11] getting in the minutenesses too ere the colour be begun.

It is unclear, however, why Palmer did not learn the art of printmaking at this stage in his career if the images produced so fascinated him.

Sepia was readily available and commonly used in water-colours and for sketching during this period. The sepia used by Palmer is most likely to have come from cuttlefish of the English Channel or Mediterranean.[12] When first applied, sepia appears almost black but with time turns brown, which is the colour now to be seen on many Palmers, particularly the six sepias.

The sepias are all on off-white, wove paper, which appears to have been cut to size before work was carried out on it.[13] It is possible to view the versos of three of the works that have previously been lifted from their mounts and inlaid.[14] On closer inspection and with transmitted light, it became obvious that the inlaid works are lined. The versos (linings) of these works all have sketches and lines on them, though it is unclear when and by whom the marks were made, but they are consistently in sepia. There are no visible signs of graphite underdrawing, though this is not unusual in sketches. It would appear that the whole drawing was carried out in sepia using both brush and pen. Some areas of the sketches were worked up: washes were applied at a similar time, the 'varnish' layer was applied next, and finally the lines intended to be most dense had a final layer of media applied.

When the sepias were examined with the naked eye it was difficult to establish exactly how Palmer built up the denser lines or indeed if they were built up at all. Whatever he did, it produced a broad, dense, dark line resembling the lines of deeply etched prints. The broadest lines are wide, very proud of the support and predominantly cracked across, rather than along, their length. Without sample analysis, it was unclear whether Palmer had created a highly viscous ink by mixing the sepia with excessive gum arabic and other unknowns, or had laid layer upon layer of sepia until he achieved the desired effect. The cracking was important and potentially indicative of two possibilities: either the works had been handled and flexed too much for the dense media or there were differing drying times in the component layers. Initial inspections with the naked eye and low magnification (× 10) showed that the cracking pattern in one work in particular resembled that of Indian ink.[15] Under magnification (× 30) it was immediately obvious that different drying times were responsible for the cracking, because the top layer of the wide lines was a heavy application of Indian ink, with gum arabic below and an underlayer that was often one or more sepia washes. The higher magnification also showed how other dense areas, such as the front of the smock and the far side of the ox in *A Rustic Scene* (cat. 10), have expanded to form peaks. Cracks have formed along the crests of these areas leaving them very vulnerable to damage, and, indeed, they have already suffered losses. Under magnification it also became apparent that there are areas of wash both under and over the Indian ink.

Many of the light areas in the sepias are 'untoned', i.e. they have no media on them. An example of one of the untoned areas is the quarter moon in *Late Twilight* (cat. 13), where Palmer simply applied a thin layer of 'varnish' to the support. This method of using the support colour was a common technique by the mid-eighteenth century. There was little evidence of lead white in the sepias, although on further investigation it became clear that Palmer had used it in small areas as a deleting medium.

Examination of the layer referred to as 'varnish' with the naked eye, magnification (× 20 and × 35) and UV indicated that it was consistent with gum arabic. Palmer applied the 'varnish' in a very uneven manner with heavier applications in media-rich areas and thinner applications in non-image areas. It is probable that Palmer made several applications to each of the drawings. The thick lines of gum also suggest that they were built up layer by layer, with each layer being allowed to dry before the next was added. It is likely that Palmer was aware of the yellowing of gum arabic, as this was not a new phenomenon. His decision to cover the sepias with gum arabic suggests that he foresaw the ultimate appearance of the works.

The sepias contain great detail in their backgrounds, and on examination it was clear that this was as carefully applied as the main image. In order to create such finely detailed images and lines, the artist needed to use materials and techniques in which the smallest of these would not be lost or appear as a 'blob' in the background. It is possible therefore that this is one of the reasons why Palmer built up the image layer upon layer. It would appear that even at this early stage in his career Palmer would return to a work several times, applying the media and 'varnish' in layers. In the later works referred to as the 'blacks', changes during the execution are very obvious and again suggest some limited reworking.

The Ashmolean Museum possesses four (cats 31, 72, 74 and 77) of the seven works believed to be among the 'blacks' that Palmer referred to in a letter to George Richmond, dated 1832,[16] and that were possibly displayed at the Royal Academy the same year. It is thought that these works were produced in the years following the 1825 sepias. They are predominantly executed in Indian ink and lead white, with areas of the support again left untoned to form part of the image. The lead white has begun to tarnish in several places, such as the figure on the right side of *Shepherds under a Full Moon* (cat. 31). Lead white was one of the most commonly used pigments and in watercolour was well known to tarnish; no doubt Palmer, too, was aware of this.

Three of the blacks have light underdrawing in sepia, but in *Shepherds under a Full Moon* there is significantly more sepia visible, with some areas appearing to be underdrawing and other areas, such as the sky, appearing to be part of the image itself. In these works Palmer used three techniques to create the light areas: exposure of the support colour,[17] 'scratching out'[18] and lead white.[19] These works have fewer of the dense lines and heavy Indian ink applications evident in the sepias, and there is not as much of the 'layering' technique.

As with all Palmer's early works, it was not so much the materials that were unusual, but the way in which he used them. By Palmer's time watercolours were readily available as pre-prepared products. In two highly finished watercolours, *Pastoral with a Horse Chestnut Tree* (cat. 70) and *Ivy Cottage, Shoreham* (cat. 71), which Palmer worked and reworked, there is evidence of both graphite and ink underdrawing. Ink was also used in the later stages over some areas of watercolour to make outlines, such as those forming the windows in *Ivy Cottage*. Palmer's fascination with light and shade is well known, and in his watercolours he handled this in numerous ways, in particular building his works up with areas of underpaint to provide density. Palmer also 'muddied' colours, such as those used in painting the leaves of the chestnut tree in *Pastoral with a Horse Chestnut Tree*, and in doing so imparted an intensity to the yellow/brown leaves without allowing them to become garish and unreal. When creating the area of lawn in the same painting, he used gum arabic in combination with the watercolours to create an area of intense light, which gives the bright green of a lawn in the sun. In both these paintings Palmer painted the clothes of the figures in the mid-ground in single bold colours, for example red or blue. These watercolours are opaque and have had no additional gum added beyond what was used in their manufacture. This serves to provide small, very matt areas, which are also extremely striking. Unfortunately, at times Palmer used too much gum and the consequences are now becoming visible in the form of flaking and some cracking.

Two paintings apparently produced *in situ* were *A Study at Tintern* (cat. 99)[20] and *Study of Trees*.[21] Both these works are quite sketch-like, with visible graphite underdrawing, less layering and none of the heavy applications of gum. There is flaking, particularly in the lead white areas of *Study of Trees*, due mostly to insufficient binding medium for an area of such heavy application. For *A Study at Tintern* the support has been toned, possibly in a colour similar to that visible today, although this painting has suffered from significant fading of the predominant green.

Palmer is both an interesting and a challenging artist from the point of view of the paper conservator. His works pose many technical questions that appear to stem directly from his limited formal training. Equally, however, Palmer's novel techniques and use of materials suggest that he felt none of the constraints to conform that his trained contemporaries may have felt. Although much has become clearer with the examination of some of his works, there is still a great deal more to learn about the materials and techniques that Palmer used during his early years.

1 An exception is the article by Sarah Herring, 'Samuel Palmer's Shoreham Drawings in Indian Ink', *Apollo*, CXLVIII, 441, November 1998, pp. 37–42.
2 Many of Palmer's sketchbooks and other sources were destroyed by his son A.H. Palmer. See Harrison, p. 14.
3 The paper has been written prior to any conservation work carried out on the objects under discussion.
4 These works are *A Rustic Scene*, *The Valley with a Bright Cloud*, *Early Morning*, *Late Twilight*, *The Skirts of a Wood* and *The Valley Thick with Corn*.
5 Krill 1987, p. 139.
6 Ibid.
7 *Letters*, p. 30.
8 Krill 1987, p. 136.
9 *Letters*, p. 21.
10 Abley, p. 107.
11 Blake's woodcuts in Thornton's *Pastorals of Virgil*. See cat. 19.
12 Rutherford J. Gettens and George L. Stout, *Painting Materials: A Short Encyclopaedia*, New York, 1966, p. 155.
13 It is hoped that this will become clearer after conservation.
14 A false border is formed around the work with a window exposing the verso of the object.
15 *The Valley with a Bright Cloud* (cat. 11), in the lower area of the log.
16 *Letters*, p. 57.
17 The sun in *Young Man Yoking an Ox* (cat. 74).
18 The star in *The Flock and the Star* (cat. 72).
19 Part of the smock in *Young Man Yoking an Ox*.
20 The inscription written by Palmer states 'A Study at Tintern drawn on the spot'.
21 Harrison, no. 22.

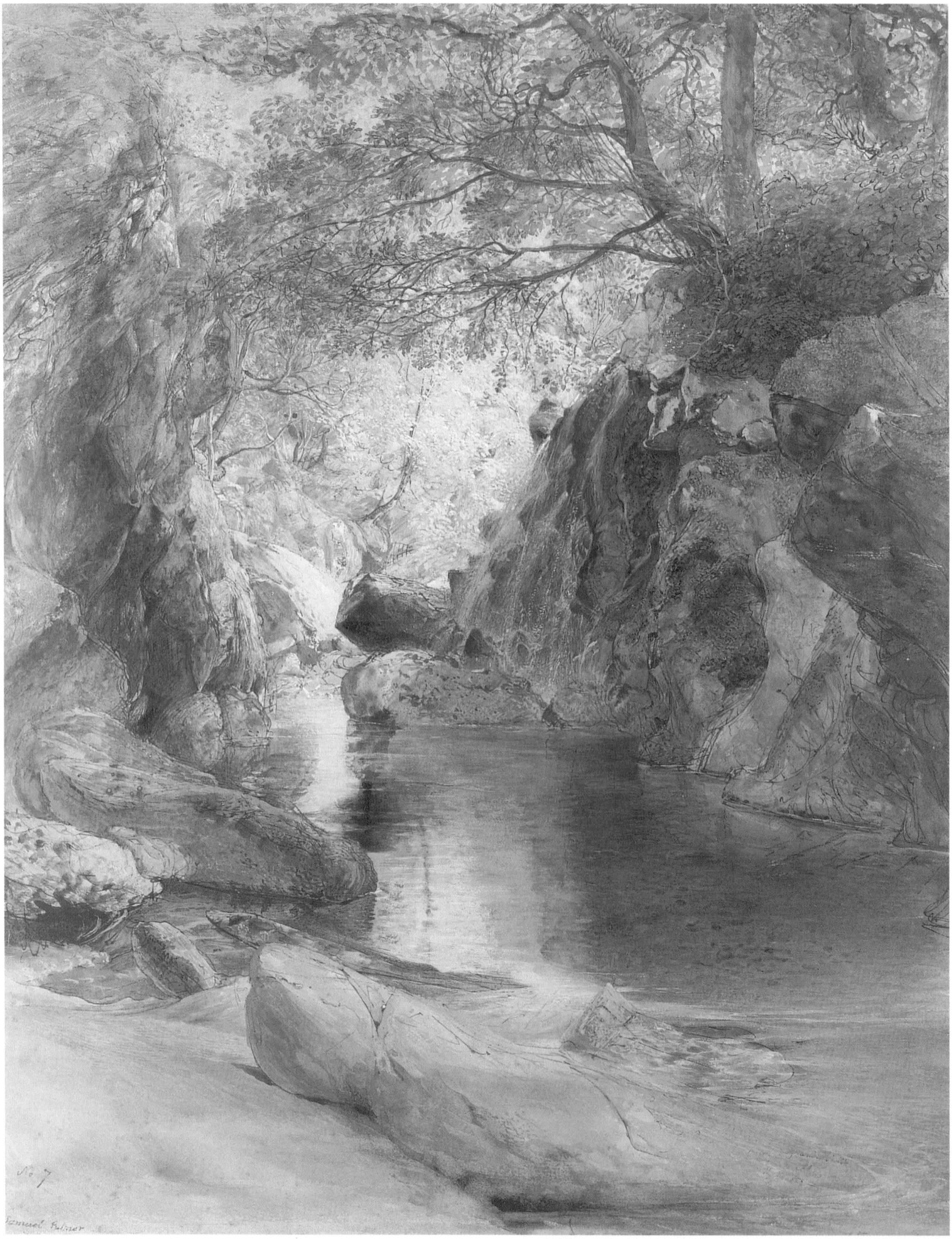

Samuel Palmer, *A Cascade in Shadow*, 1836? (cat. 103).

# Samuel Palmer's Materials and Techniques: The Later Years

*Marjorie Shelley*

From the time Samuel Palmer moved to Lisson Grove in 1833 through to his final years, his artistic practices showed a penchant for the old fashioned and unpretentious. His disdain for the modern is attested to by descriptions of his various dimly lit and 'shabby' painting rooms,[1] and his bizarre *plein air* sketching attire.[2] Some of his materials, such as shell gold, evoke an age of miniature painting and manuscripts. His mechanical aids were time tested: the diminishing mirror for condensing broad vistas;[3] opera glasses, 'which brings close and makes evident the most minute work';[4] and thread, a transferring device for copying.[5] Many of his preferences underscore his eccentricities: white, oil-primed, wooden palettes and porcelain gallipots[6] in an era of Japanned, tinned paint boxes and collapsible containers; and the 'dreamy delicacies' of the quill pen,[7] rather than the 'disagreeable' steel nib.[8] Yet, Palmer also drew on the many innovations of his own era: his pigments, paints, papers and media were neither esoteric nor of his invention but mainstream products readily available for purchase. His economic struggles notwithstanding, he continually sought the finest and often the most costly supplies, and relied upon select colourmen for them.[9]

Setting him apart from his contemporaries are his technical sources and methods. He periodically re-evaluated his aims in order to define a style acceptable to a public whom he found to be of unrefined sensibility, and he drew upon various traditions to do this. Foremost were the transparent wash manner that prevailed throughout the century – the way he was trained and the way he taught[10] – and the more modern technique of opaque watercolour. Persisting from Shoreham were tempera-like painting and finely hatched brushwork. Equally important was his attraction to oil painting, a medium that he had wished to pursue throughout his life, once claiming to be 'a water worker by accident'.[11] This conflict is reflected in his unusual combinations of media, inconsistent methods and a technically varied oeuvre, made more complex by the fact that few of his drawings were finished and were intended for development on separate sheets with body colour, sgrafitto, gums and glazes.

For his papers Palmer's drawings and letters testify to his preferences in texture, colour, thickness and dimensions.[12] His range was confined to subtle-grained, machine-made wove supports, 'hot-pressed thickest Whatman, and extra thick imperial',[13] these having the substance, sizing and surface regularity to make them receptive to the variations in moisture in his watercolour and body-colour washes and to layers of dry media, while being sufficiently strong to withstand the manipulations of his fingers, brush handle and knife. From his early experiences Palmer knew that coloured sheets would best emphasize the diffuse light of opaque paint.[14] Soft buffs, greys, greens or blues, as in *A Study at Tintern* (cat. 99) or *The Cypresses at the Villa d'Este* (cat. 108), provided a unifying middle tone. He claimed that such papers would save time in registering transitory effects,[15] hence his intention that these works should serve as studies for completed compositions on white paper. From the 1860s his most distinctive supports were Bristol and London pasteboards made from as many as six sheets of fine, glazed paper,[16] which he would coat with a zinc white wash.[17] Comparable to his fine hot-pressed papers, their smooth tablet-like quality, 'between paper and ivory', evoked the polish of medieval painting supports, as in *The Prospect* (cat. 146).[18] Possibly these were inspired by the commercially prepared academy boards and millboards used by *plein air* oil painters since the turn of the century, or even the double-layered, lead- and zinc-white, oil-primed coatings of the Pre-Raphaelites.[19]

Many of Palmer's compositions were conceived as studies; thus direct media such as graphite, black chalk, charcoal and pastel, and pen and ink were fundamental to the construction of his finished works. Always emphasizing form and line, he was above all a colourist and his paint box was replete with the most brilliant hues. Among them were traditional pigments from the earths to ultramarine,[20] and numerous artificial colours introduced since the first half of the century. The latter – such as cadmium yellow and zinc white – allowed for chromatic intensity and technical possibilities never before available.[21] His writings reveal his awareness of their properties: the subtle differences in hue; which of them would wash well; which were best suited for the foreground or distance, for layering or for local colour; their appearance when varnished; and which were safe to use.[22] Such issues were of aesthetic importance,[23] but yet were informed by widespread concern about the 'chemical complexity' of painting,[24] and allude to Palmer's knowledge of the wealth of research provided by George

Field's renowned *Chromatography*.[25] Particularly troubling were colours adversely affected by gas lighting recently introduced to the small dark galleries, rooms so 'viley lighted, that you cannot see what is in the pictures by any straining of the eye'.[26] Inequities between natural and artificial illumination undoubtedly prompted Palmer's habit of painting at night by candlelight, as well as that of the Pre-Raphaelites,[27] in order to produce chromatic effects similar to those under exhibition conditions.

Palmer used his exhaustive range of colours in the many forms currently available to watercolourists. That he was occasionally grinding his own pigments with admixtures of honey, and perhaps doing so as late as 1856, was atypical in this era,[28] yet it recalls Blake's methods[29] and advice often voiced early in the century as a means of avoiding the adulterations of colourmen.[30] He also turned to commercially produced paints, 'soft colours in tins',[31] and by inference he seems to have used 'moist' colours in porcelain pans introduced in 1841.The latter were bound with glycerin and tended to be sticky, thus explaining his carefully wrapped 'brights',[32] which required protection from dust so that washes were not sullied. His desire to safeguard the purity of his tints is similarly revealed in his insistence that palettes (his being painted white or, in another case, made of ivory[33]) should be kept scrupulously clean – a concern of many artists in order to see the true colour of their washes before transferring them to white paper.[34] From about mid-century Palmer would also have used watercolour in collapsible metal tubes. Especially convenient for sketching out of doors, they would have appealed to him for their oil-like properties: a viscosity suitable for impasted effects and colour delivered at full saturation.[35]

Palmer's watercolours characteristically begin with a graphite drawing. During his middle years he made little effort to obscure their visibility beneath his washes.[36] Notable in the Italian drawings – for example *The Colosseum and Arch of Constantine from the Palatine, Rome* (cat. 104) – is the pencil work that is precise at the focal point but becomes scribbled toward the margins, an effect possibly inspired by the distortion at the perimeter of the diminishing mirror.[37] Also distinguishing these watercolours is the use of pen and brown ink or black India ink, and 'black chalk' for the prominent lines strengthening the pencil work, as in *Conwy Castle* (cat. 101). The richness of the latter, the tenacity of its particles and lack of crystalinity reveal that it is Conté, a modern fabricated medium.[38]

During his Welsh sketching tours and through the 1840s Palmer's watercolour technique generally reflected widespread practices.[39] His primary means of tonal gradation – superimposing chromatically pure washes of opposite or related colour to modify hues that were too bright and enrich ones that were too dull – reflected his ideas on the relativity of colour.[40] Working wet over dry ensured 'sharpness and decision',[41] rather than the seamless effects produced by painting on a damp sheet or by sponging. Apart from some touches of the latter, the boldness of his strokes resulted from this purposeful manipulation of paint and use of the new flat metal ferrule brush that allowed effects imitating oil.[42] Despite his determination not to mix pigments,[43] touches of compounded colour are invariably present: in *On the North Coast of Devon, Lundy Island in the Distance* (cat. 98), for example, the slightly thickened green dabs are composed of emerald green and barium sulphate (constant white), and the purple of cobalt and alizarin. Though comparatively few of his landscapes are pure wash drawings,[44] such filmy passages are enhanced by the luminosity inherent in the watercolour process, which results from the glow of white paper suffusing through the thinly layered paints. To Palmer 'preserving a blaze of bright colour underneath' was 'the great secret' of this medium.[45] This effect would continually preoccupy him, and surely provoked his search to find a viscous oil-like medium with comparable transparency. It also accounts for his use of white or white-washed papers for his finished works, as this was a crucial element in producing the dramatic lighting that he would pursue during these years.

Characteristically, Palmer enhanced this construct of colour, stroke and light with emphatic accents. Rejecting the range of reductive methods integral to pure wash practices,[46] he sought the particular 'glitter of white that was always present in Turner's landscapes',[47] applying small skips of reserve between his brush strokes, and 'sharp bits of white' incised into the sheet for birds, branches, the moon or reflections, as in *King Arthur's Castle, Tintagel* (cat. 122) or *The Haunted Stream* (cat. 149). Though continually employing these techniques, his preferred means of heightening was body colour. As he and Hannah discovered while in Italy, opaque paint in washes, in solid dabs or dragged dry across paper brought a diffuse fresco-like effect to plumes of smoke, enveloping mists or atmospheric blue skies.[48] 'The glorious sunshine which fuses rocks and trees'[49] results from the reflection of scattered light off the matt surface of this paint – an effect unlike the saturated tonality of transparent washes. For watercolourists this was facilitated in 1834 by the introduction of Chinese white.[50] This viscous non-blackening zinc oxide was a welcome addition to their palette, as calcium carbonate, barium sulphate and lead white had various technical limitations.[51] Analysis of several opaque passages in compositions executed after 1834 – *A Cascade in Shadow* (cat. 103 and p. 36), for example – revealed that he persisted in using calcium carbonate white as he had in earlier works. Representing a very small sample of his extensive oeuvre, these findings, nonetheless, suggest that he chose to ignore the advantages of the new zinc oxide and persisted with the traditional choice. Possibly he, as other artists, found zinc oxide objectionable because of its slightly bluish hue when viewed under daylight,[52] and in 1873 he would claim that his 'tempera' watercolours were 'safely free' of this pigment.[53] Despite this he would also advise his students to use zinc white and employed it himself to prime the supports for his late works.

Palmer's continuing need to find a viable style that conveyed textural diversity and dramatic contrasts of light and dark underscored his resolutions of 1859, in which he sought a new manner of painting and which in effect served to justify his experiments with thickened paint and mixed media that he had been carrying out from 1833.[54] Since that time he had employed varied techniques for enriching his watercolours, adding dabs of surface lustre, gold or ink, layering washes, or gouache and gum with incising and impasto, or creating a range of textures and reflections with paints of different viscosities. In, for example, *A Cascade in Shadow* (cat. 103 and fig. 10) broad passages of body colour in the sky, rocks and pool of water dissolve into transparent veils. The smooth surfaces of the cliffs and water play against the tactile details: the heavily gummed gamboge, the sgrafitto, the scumbled brushwork of the flowing cascade and the meticulously impasted foliage in the distant clearing. The last, made up of brilliant dots of white and yellow, is enhanced by actual reflections of light on the cameo-like relief of paint, a surface possibly inspired by his casts of antique gems.[55] Resolving in 1843 to produce 'more fresco-like treatments' by 'not spreading juicy colour too widely',[56] Palmer had by the late 1850s abandoned compositions largely executed in thin washes, eventually describing his highly elaborated finished landscapes on white card as a 'kind of tempera'.[57] These works from the early 1860s to his last years assumed a new complexity in their range of brushwork: broad sweeps narrowing to stipples and minute strokes of ink, thickened highlights and matt scumbles, solid luminous paint and rich dark glazes.

The binders and additives that Palmer used to transform his water-based paint into oil-like material and produce these effects remain to be explored. The lack of non-destructive techniques prevents their analysis; however, documentary information concerning water-soluble media used by nineteenth-century artists allows his experiments to be put into context. That he was using glue in 1838[58] is revealed by Linnell's letter suggesting that he instead employ egg yolk and sugar.[59] This, the medium of 'tempera and old missals' and the only watercolour genre Palmer professed to know,[60] was long acknowledged to enhance colour and add body; in 1856 he claimed to have 'no difficulties about the egg, which seems material exactly suited to me'.[61] But his gallipots were also filled with other vehicles,[62] agents that would have readily combined with cake paints, gouache and powdered pigment to produce his 'clots of thickened colour' that he pushed around with his fingers and artists' tools.[63] Many types of proteinaceous and vegetable gums were available for aqueous paint: those cited above, and others, such as glair, isinglass, alum, borax, starches, gums arabic and tragacanth, ox gall, and watercolour megilp.[64] Palmer could have chosen any that agreed with the properties of his pigments and were responsive to his brush.

More significantly, his desire to bring his watercolours closer to oil reflects artistic currents throughout the century that favoured the use of such vehicles to modify viscosity, alter translucency and transform surface gloss. The justification for this was a common belief in the inherent connection between watercolour, tempera and fresco – media held to be the route by which 'the Old Masters came to oil painting'.[65] This concept had been voiced by his mentor William Blake, who had used a range of media for his water-based frescos.[66] It also found support among writers and practitioners who both expounded on this theory and advocated varnishing watercolours to enrich their hues.[67] A lustrous surface was held to give these works the stature of oil painting and was an important component of the exhibition watercolour, the standard to which Palmer aspired. The connection between watercolour and egg tempera was also promoted by the 1844 translation of Cennino Cennini's *Il Libro dell'Arte*.[68]

Technical innovations at mid-century encouraging this approach included a 'glass' medium for increasing transparency both in oil and watercolour.[69] The availability of a satisfactory opaque white in 1834 and of watercolour in tubes in the next decade was also part of this trend. These paints found a receptive audience among watercolourists desiring to work in the manner of oil, many of whom adopted coloured paper, which, as with oil, required painting from dark to light. Ruskin's advocacy of opaque paint,[70] the watercolours of the Pre-Raphaelites and later the tempera revivalists testify to this long-lasting fashion among artists.[71] Although Palmer's own distinctive methods were informed by his knowledge of other living artists, the old masters and Blake's practices, his ambition to paint in a thickened and

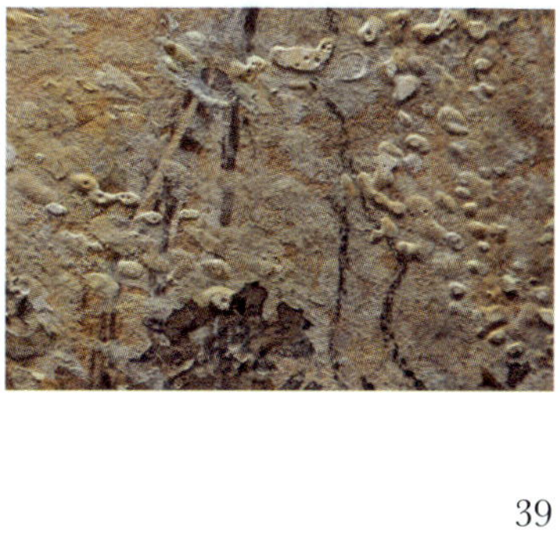

Fig. 10 Detail of *A Cascade in Shadow* (cat. 103) showing impasted body colour applied in small dots, its thick surface reflecting light.

lustrous aqueous paint as very much attuned to popular trends even while he claimed to dismiss them.

'Excess had become a virtue in the imitation of oil painting',[72] and Palmer's late technical explorations exemplify this approach. A drawing 'could not be too much finished',[73] and his employment of substances to attain the perfection required of the exhibition watercolour reflected his desire 'to make the getting in exactly resemble OIL painting'.[74] The complex handling involved in achieving such effects also reveals his struggles in attaining this goal. His palette now regularly encompassed high-pitched garish yellows, oranges and magentas and intensely saturated darks, for example in *A Towered City* (cat. 150). Despite claiming to only layer pigments, he often mixed them, producing sombre hues, especially evident in the foreground of many of his highly wrought compositions, such as *The Prospect* (cat. 146). Because of drying differences among the components a craquelure often developed, and due to the presence of gums and additives localized areas became murky, provoking him to augment their tone with thick glazing and thus further clouding the underlying paint. Yet, notable in these works is the meticulous stippling in the figures and transparent expanses of sky (fig. 11). For this brushwork Palmer may have found inspiration in portrait miniatures and medieval painting, or turned to Field's colour theory or its popular revival among the Pre-Raphaelites, prompted by Ruskin's concept of placing 'atoms of colour in juxtaposition' to increase their intensity.[75] But, unlike others seeking oil-like results, Palmer relied in his late compositions on the brilliant zinc-white priming of the underlying support to achieve his distinctive luminosity, an optical effect resulting from the highly reflective properties of this pigment. Although it was used by other artists to brighten their palettes,[76] in his vision its radiance was equated with light seen through a stained-glass window.[77]

The management of light, reflection and texture and the production of astonishingly vibrant colour[78] found their theoretical source in Palmer's invention, 'chiaroscuro as animator'.[79] The dramatic contrasts this concept demanded – bursts of light and indecipherable shadow, the glow of transmitted light against the glare of reflected light, the 'glitter of white' and 'holes of dark' (fig. 12)[80] – served as foils for his edifying subject matter and sublime topography. These exaggerated elements and the techniques and materials he used for their realization had their greatest impact when viewed at night or under the low illumination of the exhibition gallery. Ironically, they also evoked the variable lighting and staging of the widely embraced shows and spectacles of contemporary London,[81] popular entertainment that Palmer surely scorned.

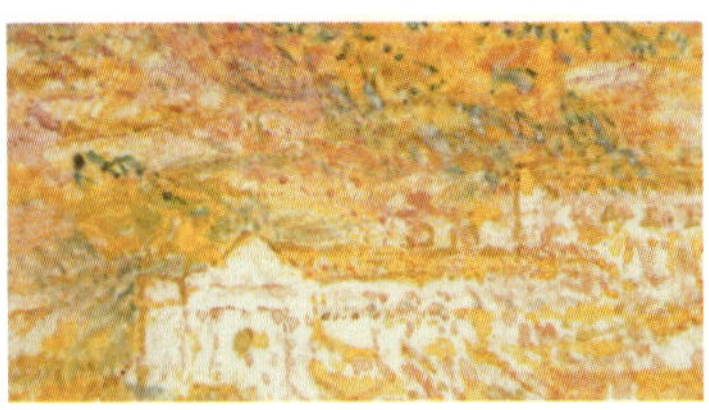

Fig. 11 Detail of *The Prospect* (cat. 146) showing areas of the zinc-white primed ground left in reserve, which contribute to the intense brightness of the hues. Colour and contour are applied with stippled brush strokes.

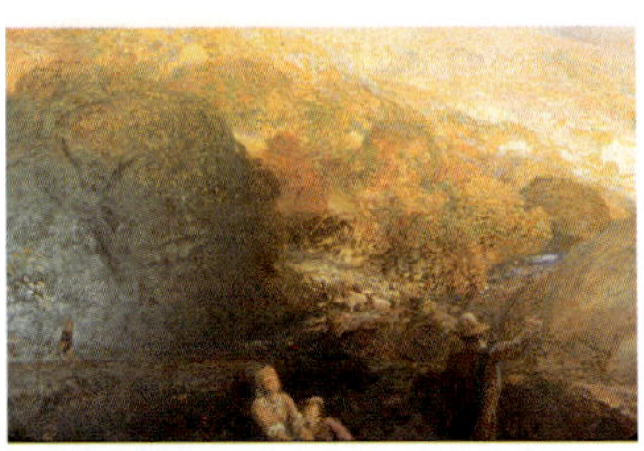

Fig. 12 The lower left foreground of *The Prospect*. Both the dark and glossy passages were produced with multiple layers of gums and additives mixed in or applied to the surface of the paint.

*Acknowledgements*

I wish to thank Colin Harrison for making the Louisa Twining manuscript available to me; Silvia Centeno, Research Scientist, and Lisa Barro, Research Fellow, Metropolitan Museum of Art, New York, for their analysis of pigments; Alison Gilchrest for infrared reflectography; and Jenene Geary for her untiring assistance.

1 *Letters*, p. 649, n. 1; *L&L*, pp. 138, 145–53.
2 *L&L*, p. 75, 114, 131–2.
3 *L&L*, p. 75.
4 *Letters*, p. 292.
5 *Letters*, p. 718.
6 AHP, op. cit., pp. 75–6, 145.
7 On quill pens: *L&L*, p. 265; *Letters*, p. 863.
8 On steel: *Letters*, p. 898.
9 Among the colourmen cited in his letters are Smith and Warner, Roberson and Miller, Newman, and George Field.
10 As is indicated by letters to students and transcriptions of his lessons recorded by Louisa Twining in 1856 (Ashmolean, 'LT ms'). See cat. 131.
11 *Letters*, p. 820; *L&L*, p. 89.
12 Among them, *Letters*, pp. 29, 832, 858, 864.
13 LT ms p. 4; *Letters*, pp. 717–22.
14 Palmer rejected a light blue Bristol, 'which scarcely shows the white heightening' (*Letters*, p. 30), but often used dark grey Crewick crayon papers.
15 *L&L*, p. 76.
16 *Letters*, pp. 864–9, 735.
17 *Letters*, p. 717.
18 *Letters*, pp. 717, 735, 736.
19 Palmer acknowledged that other artists worked on zinc-primed boards: *Letters*, p. 736.
20 Shell gold, made of powdered gold in an aqueous binder, was also a traditional painting material and was used, for example, in *Christian Descending into the Valley of Humiliation* (cat. 120).

21 For this study non-destructive analysis of pigments was undertaken using X-ray fluorescence and Raman spectroscopy by Silvia Centeno, Research Scientist, and Lisa Barro, Research Associate, both of the Metropolitan Museum of Art.
22 On the properties of pigments: *Letters*, pp. 927–8, 884–9.
23 LT ms, p. 14: 'to Paint from Nature one must have knowledge of the colours and their various combinations.'
24 *Letters*, p. 884.
25 *Letters*, p. 888.
26 *Letters*, p. 723.
27 Stephen Hackney, Joyce H. Townsend and Jacqueline Ridge, 'Pre-Raphaelite Methods and Materials', in *Pre-Raphaelite Painting Techniques, 1848–56*, London, 2004, p. 67.
28 On grinding pigments: *Letters*, pp. 242, 1838; *L&L*, p. 66.
29 Gilchrist, 1863, pp. 69–70.
30 Among them, Francis Nicholson, *The Practice of Drawing and Painting Landscape from Nature*, London, 2nd edn 1823, p. 53.
31 These were possibly compounded with honey or sugar to facilitate working up washes with the brush. See *Letters*, p. 119.
32 *L&L*, p. 144.
33 *L&L*, p. 75.
34 *Letters*, pp. 521, 717.
35 *Letters*, pp. 717, 718.
36 This effect was purposeful, for he would describe 'black lead' as being 'brown on the blue distance and gray on the brown foreground' (LT ms, p. 10).
37 These effects are often explained as recalling ideas on 'how the eye sees', generated by the optic device of Cornelius Varley: Jane Bayard, *The Exhibition Watercolour, 1770–1870*, Yale, 1981, p. 78. For Palmer's use of the mirror, see *L&L*, p. 75.
38 At the time Conté was generally referred to as 'black chalk'.
39 As he articulated it, this was based on three methods of making a tint: mixing colour at once, layering over a previously dry colour or hatching (LT ms, p. 3).
40 LT ms, p. 11. For, to him, 'what we think pure colour is not really so'.
41 LT ms, p. 7.
42 For his flat camel hair brushes see *L&L*, p. 113.
43 *Letters*, p. 886.
44 For example, *Trees*, *c.*1846 (Lister 425).
45 LT ms, p. 19.
46 These reductive devices, traditionally held to be innovations of Turner, included rubbing, stopping-out, sponging, blotting, dissolving and lifting.
47 LT ms, p. 19.
48 *Letters*, p. 120, 121.
49 *Letters*, p. 106.
50 Winsor and Newton catalogue, 1851, pp. 5, 12, bound in Thomas Rowbotham, *The Art of Landscape Painting in Water Colours*, London, 1850, pp. 7–17. The pigment was first introduced as a liquid in bottles.
51 Field considered zinc white to be the only satisfactory white for watercolour because of its permanence, body and covering power. George Field, *Chromatography: A Treatise on Colours and Pigments and their Powers in Painting*, rev. T.W. Salter, London, 1869.
52 Hackney, p. 58. Palmer's stated rejection of zinc white may have been inspired by oil painting practices.
53 *Letters*, pp. 715, 886, 1873 (14). The presence of zinc white was confirmed by x-ray fluorescence in the preparation Palmer applied to the Bristol board in *The Prospect* (cat. 146).
54 *L&L*, pp. 55, 113.
55 *L&L*, p. 144.
56 *L&L*, p. 82.
57 *Letters*, pp. 684, 886.
58 A technique he may have learned from Blake: Ormsby 2004, p. 138.
59 *L&L*, p. 66.
60 *Letters*, p. 820.
61 *Letters*, p. 517.
62 *L&L*, p. 145.
63 *L&L*, p. 113–14.
64 See Ormsby 2004, pp. 138–41, on the varied media used for water-based paint.
65 *Letters*, p. 864.
66 Ormsby 2004, pp. 138–41.
67 Among them, Francis Nicholson, *The Practice of Drawing and Painting Landscape from Nature*, London, 2nd edn, 1823, pp. 112–17.
68 Mary P. Merrifield, *A Treatise on Painting Written by Cennino Cennini in the year 1437*[*sic*], London, 1844.
69 John Gage, *George Field and his Circle: From Romanticism to the Pre-Raphaelite Brotherhood*, exh. cat., Fitzwilliam Museum, Cambridge, 1989, p. 59. This silica-based medium was promoted by Thomas Miller, the former partner of Roberson, and was supported by George Field, who sought to develop transparent pigments for both media. It was marketed under the name of 'Van Eyck's Glass Medium for Oil Painting'.
70 And his dismissive attitude toward transparent washes: see John Ruskin, *The Elements of Drawing*, London, 1857, pp. 205–6.
71 Towards the end of the century the same premise would be expounded in John Lewis Roget, *A History of the Old Water-colour Society*, London 1891, vol. 1, pp. 3–4.
72 Marjorie B.Cohen, *Wash and Gouache: A Study of the Development of the Materials of Watercolour*, exh. cat., Fogg Art Museum, Cambridge, Mass., 1977, p. 57.
73 *Letters*, p. 650.
74 *L&L*, p. 113.
75 William Henry Hunt, Birket Foster and J.F. Lewis were also practising the stipple technique; for Merrifield on Cennini see Gage, *George Field*, p. 80.
76 *Letters*, pp. 735–6, 1865 (12).
77 *Letters*, p. 890.
78 For Palmer's reference to his brilliant colours: *L&L*, pp. 290, 291.
79 *L&L*, pp. 78–82.
80 *L&L*, p. 78.
81 Richard D. Altick, *The Shows of London*, Harvard, 1978, chs 12–14, 17 *passim*.

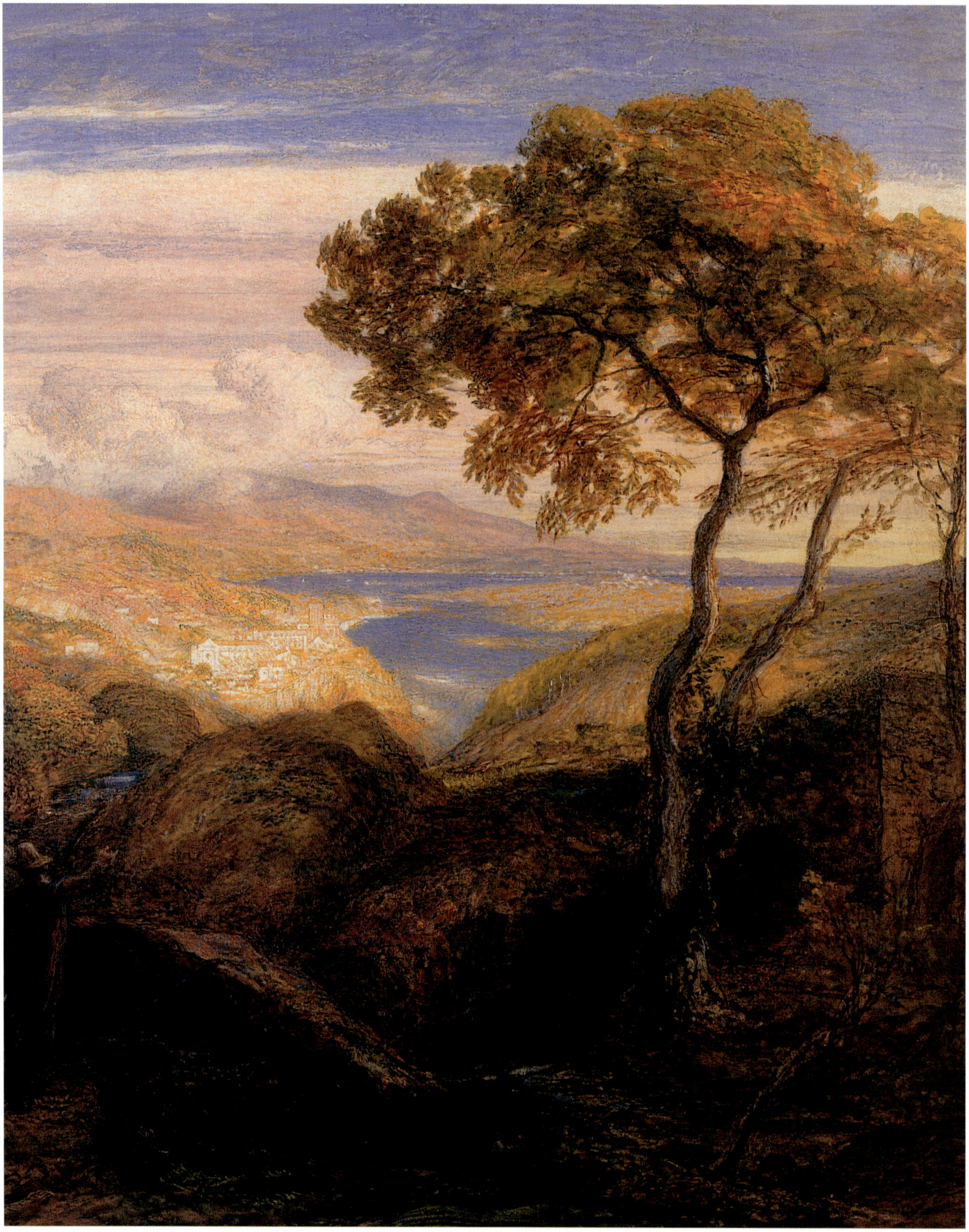

Samuel Palmer, *The Prospect*, 1881 (detail, cat. 146).

# Poetic Feeling and Chromatic Madness: Palmer and Victorian Watercolour Painting

*Scott Wilcox*

Samuel Palmer was elected an associate of the Society of Painters in Water-Colours (Old Water-Colour Society) on 13 February 1843, along with two fellow landscapists: Thomas Miles Richardson Jr. and William Collingswood Smith. In the area of landscape, which had been recognized as the society's particular strength since its inauguration in 1804, the leading lights were Peter De Wint, David Cox Sr. and the president Anthony Vandyke Copley Fielding. For the thirty-eight-year-old Palmer election to the society came as a welcome mark of professional recognition. It marked both an end to his ambitions as a painter in oils – after 1842 he stopped exhibiting oils at the Royal Academy – and a new public phase in his practice as a watercolourist, in which his work in the medium was regularly seen and judged against that of his fellow watercolourists.

In his first decade of exhibiting with the society Palmer garnered little critical attention, unlike Richardson and Smith or George Arthur Fripp, who had become an associate two years before.[1] Eventually, the unchanging picturesque formulae employed by Richardson and Smith wearied the critics, whose commentary on their contributions either turned disdainful or withered away. Fripp, on the other hand, passed easily from promising novice to stalwart of the landscape wing of the society. He was elected a full member in 1845; Smith became a member in 1849 and Richardson in 1851. Palmer had to wait until 1854 to obtain full membership, by which time, as he wrote to George Richmond, 'the appearance of my name year after year in the lower list had become a sort of public annual stigma'.[2]

The infrequent mentions of Palmer in the reviews of the society's exhibitions of the 1840s and early 1850s focused on the brilliance of his effects of light and colour, but also on the inadequacies of his technique. At his first appearance with the society the reviewer for *The Spectator* wrote: 'S. Palmer's fiery sunsets are so crude that we must wait to see what he will do next year.'[3] The verdict the following year was that 'Samuel Palmer is ambitious, and has an eye for colour: his sunsets are radiantly bright; but the sky is the only good part of the picture.'[4] The critic concluded that to achieve the poetical subjects at which he aimed, Palmer 'requires a more intimate knowledge of nature and higher skill in painting than he yet possesses'. Although in succeeding years Palmer's exhibited watercolours were characterized as 'dazzling' and 'too clever and original-looking to be overlooked',[5] overlooked is what they tended to be.

His work was, however, noticed by John Ruskin, who added to his third edition of *Modern Painters*, vol. 1, in 1846:

> S. Palmer, lately admitted a member of the Old Water-Colour Society, is deserving of the very highest place among faithful followers of nature. His studies of foreign foliage especially are beyond all praise for care and fullness. I have never seen a stone-pine or a cypress drawn except by him, and his feeling is as pure and grand as his fidelity is exemplary. He has not, however, yet, I think, discovered what is necessary in a great picture; and his works, sent to the Society's rooms, have been most unfavourable examples of his power, and have been generally, as yet, in places where all that is best in them is out of sight. I look to him, nevertheless, unless he lose himself in over reverence for certain conventionalisms of the older schools, as one of the probable renovators and correctors of whatever is failing or erroneous in the practice of English art.[6]

Ruskin made no further published reference to Palmer's work. Clearly, he was disappointed in his hopes for the artist, and we may surmise that the grounds for his disappointment lay in that 'over reverence' for 'conventionalisms of the older schools'. For Ruskin it scarcely mattered that in Palmer's case it was not an easy reliance on the picturesque clichés deployed by Richardson and Smith but a serious engagement with the principles of Claude and Poussin. Increasingly in his watercolours Palmer attempted to unite the probing and restless naturalism, to which Ruskin responded, with the great compositional and poetic truths embodied in the classical landscape tradition. In this he was perhaps quite consciously assuming the mantle within the society of George Barrett Jr. and John Varley, both of whom died in the year that Palmer became an associate. The only other exponent of that strand of old-fashioned landscape painting within the society was Palmer's fellow Ancient, Francis Oliver Finch, who had joined the society as far back as 1822 (becoming a member in 1827); however, from the 1840s to his death in 1862 Finch attracted even less critical attention than his friend Palmer.

With the passing of the Society of Painters in Water-Colours' old guard – De Wint died in 1849, Copley Fielding in 1855 and Cox in 1859 – along with the death of Turner in 1851, there was a sense, frequently expressed in the critical literature of the period, that a great era in both landscape painting and watercolour was ending and that the future was uncertain. The appearance of Alfred William Hunt and George Price Boyce in the society in the early 1860s, and then of William Holman Hunt, John William North and Albert Goodwin in the early 1870s, seemed to offer some hope for a reinvigoration of the watercolour landscape within the society. Against the work of these progressive new artists, with their Pre-Raphaelite affiliations and their Ruskinian adherence to a more detailed, unconventional naturalism, Palmer's watercolours seemed a hangover from an earlier age. In the words of a critic writing of Palmer's contributions to a survey of British watercolours at the Grosvenor Gallery in 1879,

> His work belongs to a past generation, one where he was overshadowed by the glory of Turner, on the one hand, and buried beneath the rough naturalism of Cox and De Wint, on the other. In his works may be seen the last fading rays of the classical ideal of landscape, the remembrance of the Grand School.[7]

If the forms and subjects of Palmer's landscapes stood out against the work of the new men, in his seemingly radical treatment of colour and light Palmer could be seen as part of that 'school of polychromatic landscape'[8] to which A.W. Hunt, Goodwin and Holman Hunt belonged. From his earliest appearance at the society Palmer had attracted attention and criticism for his 'fiery sunsets'. By 1850, when critical notice of Palmer's work was on the rise, one reviewer asked: 'What shall we say to Mr. Palmer, who, with certain evidences of talent and a dream of truth, offers us such eccentricities of prismatic colour run mad?'[9] Of the two landscapes from *Comus* that Palmer exhibited in 1856, the critic for *The Spectator* wrote: 'The blazing sun in one of them is among the most ambitious and telling effects with which we are acquainted; but it is an effect beyond the reach of art.'[10]

By the later 1860s Palmer could still be derided for the 'rankness and violence' of his colours and 'the intemperance of [his] paint-box',[11] but the tenor of critical comment on the effects of light and colour in his work had become more admiring:

> Mr. Palmer is another artist from whom it is always safe to expect a sensation ... This artist sees visions, and paints Nature in gorgeous robes, which it must be confessed surprise the eye with unwonted effulgence. Yet are the fire and fury of intensest colours so attempered as to reconcile the mind even to excess. Mr. Palmer may rush into chromatic regions where other artists fear even to breathe. But still in the midst of madness there is a method which reconciles the spectator to the result.

The review passed from colour in Palmer's work to the comparably challenging treatment of colour by A.W. Hunt, going on to describe Hunt's watercolours as seeming 'to try, and sometimes to solve, the most recondite of chromatic experiments'.[12]

Four years later *The Art-Journal* again suggested a connection between Palmer's colouristic excesses and the 'experiments' of the new men. When Holman Hunt sent his watercolours, *Sunset at Chimalditi* (present location unknown) and *Festa at Fiesole* (fig. 13), to the society's exhibition in 1870, *The Art-Journal* considered the two works 'as extraordinary phenomena both in Nature and Art'. *Sunset at Chimalditi* was

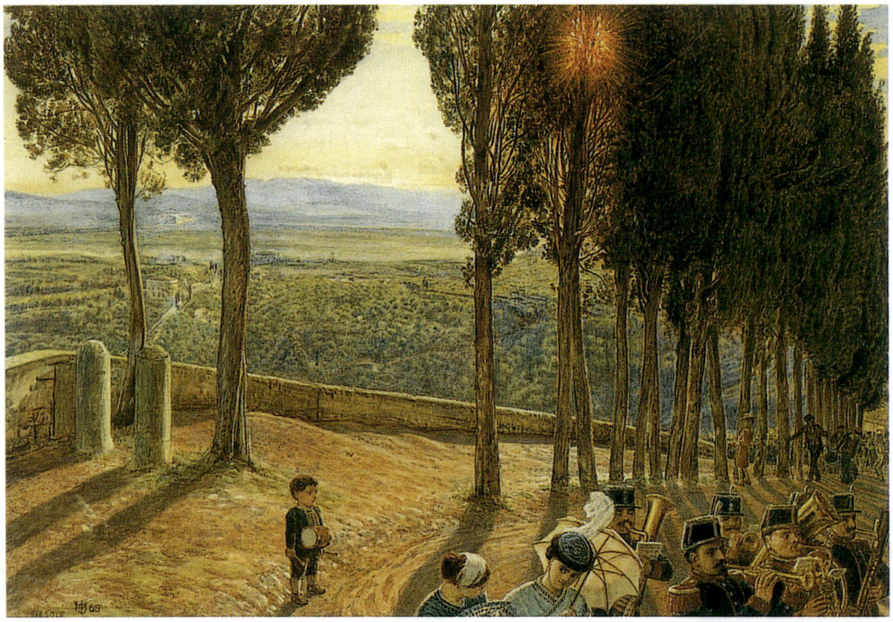

Fig. 13 William Holman Hunt, *Festa at Fiesole*, 1868, watercolour, private collection.

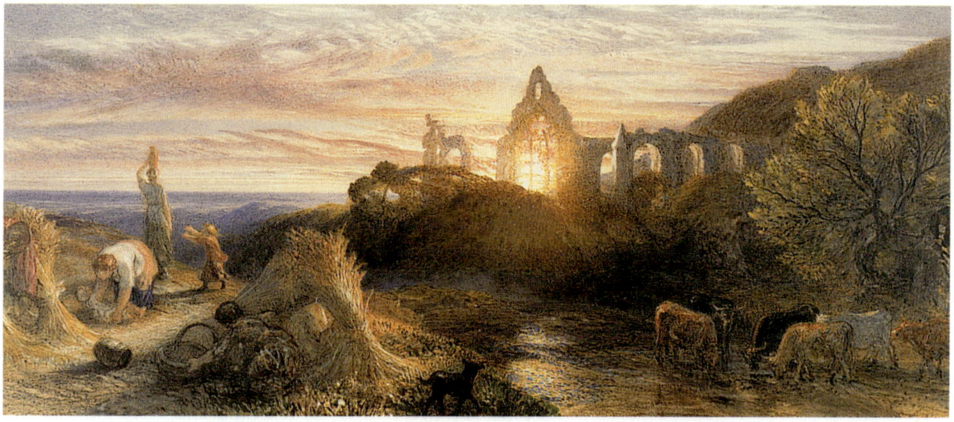

Fig. 14 Samuel Palmer, *Harvesting*, 1863, watercolour, Aberdeen Art Gallery and Museums Collection.

'an earnest endeavour to paint what is unpaintable'. The critic continued in terms very like those in which Palmer's sunset effects had been described in earlier years:

> We do not regard the effect depicted as true to outward nature, it is rather the result of frenzied vision; the eye when dazzled by excess of light sees colours which do not exist outwardly and physically, but only inwardly and within the mind's consciousness. It is an interesting question, not easy of solution, how far a painter is justified in throwing into his picture a poetic cast of thought, a frenzy of colour, which correspond not to nature, but to his individual idiosyncrasies.

Turning to *Festa at Fiesole*, the critic pointed to

> the blazing sun which has burnt a round hole in a tree, and bursts through upon the spectator as fireworks.[13]

This very effect of the rays of a rising or setting sun biting into the forms of foliage, mountainside or masonry had been explored by Palmer again and again in watercolours such as *Harvesting* (fig. 14), exhibited in 1863. After its lengthy treatment of Holman Hunt's landscapes, the 1870 *Art-Journal* review continued:

> From the above problems in polychrome we may pass to somewhat analogous experiments exhibited by Mr. Samuel Palmer, an artist whom we rejoice to find once again upon these walls.

The critic, however, made no further mention of Palmer's colour, concentrating instead on the character of his work that

> carries the mind back not only to past times in history but to prior epochs in Art: this style of landscape may be accounted traditional. As in the pictures of Claude and Poussin, as in the drawings of some of our early watercolour painters, this composition of trees, waters, figures, cattle, has balanced symmetry, and the sentiment glows under poetic ardour. It is good in these days of literal prose to see an Arcadian shepherd, lute in hand, whiling away the weary hours with plaintive melody.[14]

Although Palmer's highly individual handling of colour and the intensity of his sunrise and sunset effects remained focal points for critics, they seemed less exceptional and eccentric in the context of similar chromatic experiments by Holman Hunt and A.W. Hunt.

Colour was one of the recurrent themes in the critical commentary on Palmer's watercolours through the 1870s; the poetry of his conceptions was another. The term 'poetry' was so broadly and indiscriminately applied to landscapes in the criticism of the period as to have only the vaguest of meanings. It could be attached to any work that seemed to have aspirations beyond Pre-Raphaelite literalness. Yet the persistence with which 'poetic' and related terms such as 'idyllic' or 'Dorian' were associated with Palmer's work suggests that he was perceived as being uniquely a poet of landscape and his works a particular embodiment of the concept of poetic landscape. It should be noted that while it was common for society watercolourists to embellish their landscape paintings with quotations from poetry, it was rare for a landscape in this period to embody or illustrate a poetic text as Palmer's works, such as *Tityrus Restored to his Patrimony* (cat. 157), routinely did.

Perhaps to suggest some more specific sense of the works' poetic character, critics reached for the term 'idyllic', which seems to have been as inextricably linked with Palmer's name in the later nineteenth century as 'visionary' was in the twentieth. But 'idyllic' was also applied to the very different rustic subjects of Fred Walker, George Pinwell and Helen Allingham. F.G. Stephens was able to characterize the nature of Palmer's poetic landscape more precisely by calling him 'the painter of the Dorian mood'.[15] This conveyed just the right combination of simplicity, solemnity and antiquity.

Acknowledgement of Palmer's unique position within the ranks of the Society of Painters in Water-Colours and critical reaction to his exhibited work both reached their apogee with the two great Miltonic subjects, *The Eastern Gate* (fig. 15) and *The Prospect* (cat. 146), the last submissions before

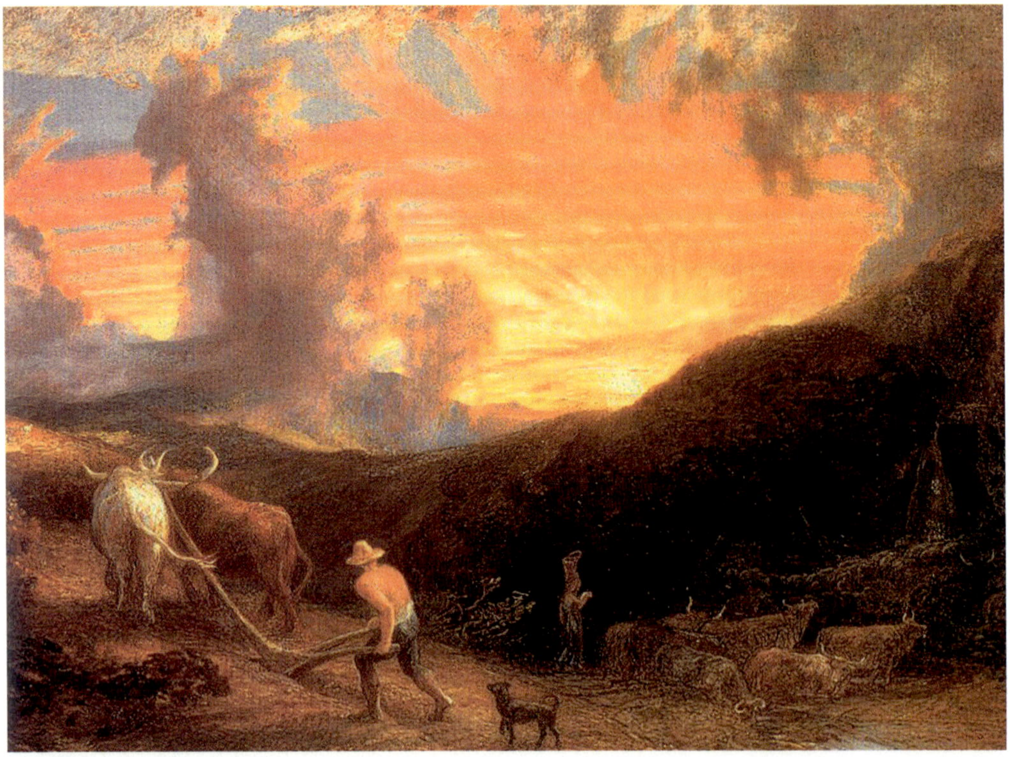

Fig. 15 Samuel Palmer, *The Eastern Gate*, 1881, watercolour, private collection.

his death in 1881.[16] The hanging committee accorded the works places of honour, and *The Times*, *The Athenaeum*, *The Spectator* and *The Art Journal* all included lengthy and laudatory coverage of them in their reviews of the exhibition. According to F.G. Stephens in *The Athenaeum*, these were 'epoch-making pictures'.[17] Both Stephens and *The Art Journal* reviewer compared *The Eastern Gate* with Turner's *Ulysses Deriding Polyphemus* (1829; National Gallery, London), *The Art Journal* calling Palmer's watercolour 'probably the most successful attempt to paint the full glories of sunrise' since Turner's painting.[18] As *The Times* put it, 'the sublimity of the grandest typical phenomenon, never found nobler expression'.[19]

As the splendour of the representation of natural phenomena called to mind Turner's painting, so did Palmer's linking of such phenomena with literary subject matter and with classical landscape traditions, an allegiance to which he shared with Turner but of which he was now almost the sole adherent. *The Spectator* commented: 'No doubt the method is conventional to a high degree, as conventional as Claude's, but it is a convention of Mr. Palmer's own origin; and if it surrenders frankly some natural truths, it seizes others, and very worthy ones, with almost unequalled intensity.'[20] It was the intensity and the originality with which Palmer interpreted both nature and the traditional principles of landscape painting that kept his art relevant up to the time of his death and beyond.

1 The comments in this essay on Palmer's critical fortunes are based on a survey of the reviews of the Society of Painters in Water-Colours' exhibitions in the following: *The Athenaeum*, *The Art-Union* (later *The Art-Journal*), *The Saturday Review*, *The Spectator* and *The Times*.
2 *Letters*, p. 497.
3 *The Spectator*, 6 May 1843, p. 427.
4 *The Spectator*, 4 May 1844, p. 426.
5 *The Athenaeum*, 1 May 1847, p. 471, and 15 May 1847, p. 528.
6 *The Works of John Ruskin*, ed. E.T. Cook and Alexander Wedderburn, London, 1903–12, vol. 3, pp. 604–5 note.
7 *The Spectator*, 25 January 1879, p. 114.
8 *The Art-Journal*, 1 June 1867, p. 147.
9 *The Athenaeum*, 11 May 1850, p. 510.
10 *The Spectator*, 3 May 1856, p. 490.
11 *The Spectator*, 20 June 1868, p. 736.
12 *The Art-Journal*, 1 June 1866, p. 174.
13 *The Art-Journal*, 1 June 1870, p. 174.
14 Ibid.
15 Stephens refers to Palmer as 'the painter of the Dorian mood' in an article in *The Portfolio*, vol. 3, 1872, p. 162, and in his Society of Painters in Water-Colours reviews in *The Athenaeum* in 1874 (25 April, p. 567) and 1880 (11 December, p. 785).
16 *Eventide* (present location unknown) was shown at the winter exhibition later that year, and *The Bellman* (Trustees of the Chatsworth Settlement) was shown in the following spring's exhibition.
17 *The Athenaeum*, 16 April 1881, p. 532.
18 *The Art Journal*, June 1881, p. 190.
19 *The Times*, 13 April 1881, p. 14.
20 *The Spectator*, 16 April 1881, p. 505.

# ‘The excitement of gambling, without its guilt and its ruin’: Palmer and Printmaking

*Elizabeth E. Barker*

‘O! the joy,’ Palmer exclaimed, imagining a well-heeled collector of original artists’ etchings:

> colours and brushes pitched out of the window; plates the *Liber Studiorum* size got out of the dear, little etching-cupboard where they have long reposed; great needles sharpened three-corner-wise like bayonets; opodeldoc rubbed into the forehead to wake the brain up; and a Great Gorge of old poetry to get up the dreaming.[1]

For Palmer the ‘teazing, temper-trying, yet fascinating copper’ offered endless delight; had the work proved remunerative, he would have been content ‘to do nothing else’.[2] Instead, etching remained a largely private passion for Palmer, appreciated by a small but loyal following during the artist’s lifetime and inspiring a group of Neo-Romantic printmakers in the century after his death (see pp. 55–61).

Although Palmer would not take up etching until middle age, his familiarity with prints and printmakers was long-standing. Advice from Linnell and Blake and repeated visits to the British Museum shaped his unorthodox taste.[3] Palmer admired and collected engravings by Giulio Bonasone (fig. 16) , Titian and Claude for their ‘textureless’ and ‘neutral’ shadows; Rembrandt for his exquisite finish; and Turner and Dürer (cat. 24) for their vigorous lines.[4] Palmer grew up and came of age among printmakers: Uwins, Stothard, Wate, Cooke, Linnell, Richmond, Calvert, Sherman and Blake.

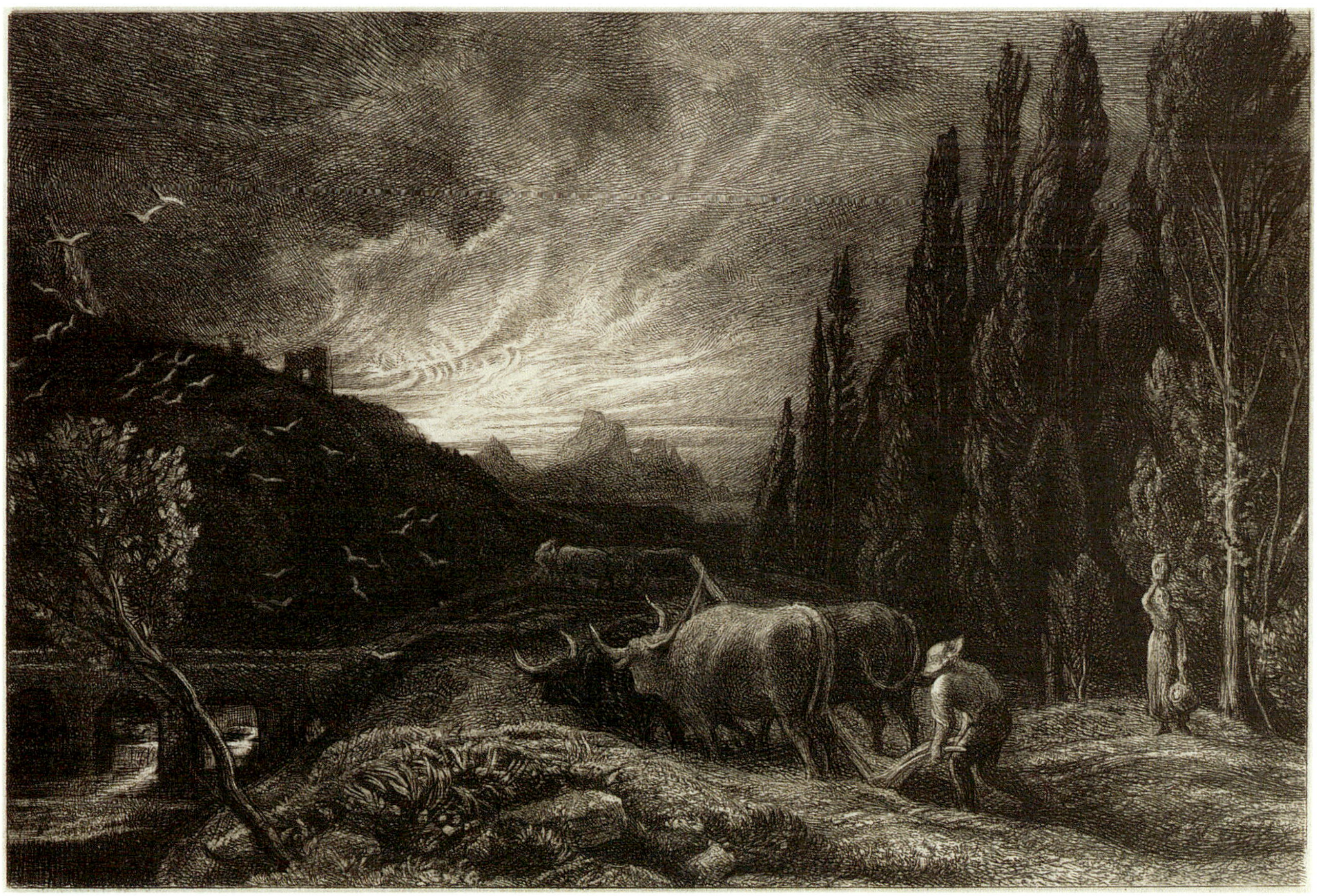

Samuel Palmer, *The Early Ploughman*, begun before 1861 (cat. 140).

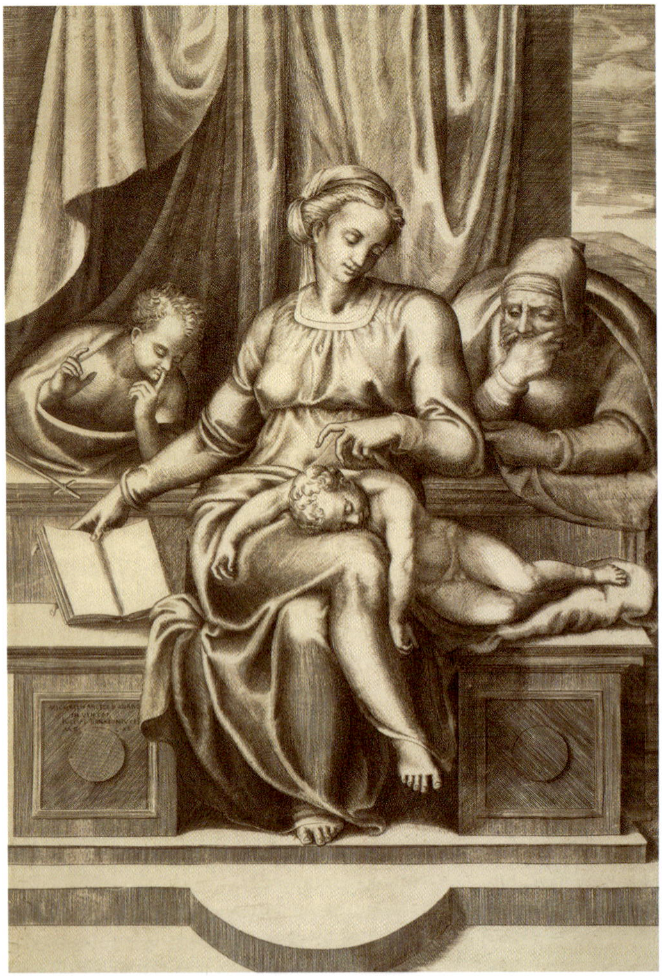

Fig. 16 Giulio di Antonio Bonasone (1500/10–after 1574), after Michelangelo Buonarroti (1475–1564), *The Holy Family*, c.1545, engraving, British Museum (see cat. 26).

When the nineteen-year-old Palmer first met Blake, the sixty-six-year-old artist was engaged in engraving *Illustrations of the Book of Job* (cat. 18): 'the copper of the first plate – "Thus did Job continually" – was lying on the table where he had been working at it. How lovely it looked by the lamplight, strained through the tissue paper!'[5] Another Blake series, the seventeen wood-engraved illustrations to Ambrose Philips's 'Imitation of Eclogue I' in Thornton's *Pastorals of Virgil* (cat. 19), struck Palmer as 'perhaps the most intense gems of bucolic sentiment in the whole range of art'.[6]

Inspired by Blake – and presumably instructed by Calvert[7] – Palmer began to engrave 'a few rough blocks',[8] but he appears soon to have abandoned the attempt. By 3 January 1828 he had entrusted Welby Sherman to 'complete the cutting' of a woodblock (presumably *The Harvest under a Crescent Moon*, cat. 62) 'without obliterating the drawings' on the block.[9]

Intriguingly, however, Evans has attributed to Palmer seven wood engravings recently discovered in an album that descended in the family of Calvert's friend, pupil and patron, Alexander Constantine Ionides (cat. 63).[10] Certain images – a shepherd and his flock, a primitive hut, fruit trees, stars, and the full and crescent moon – do recall Palmer's drawings of the 1820s. Yet the majority of the figures – nude and draped young women and bearded old men fig. 17) – display a frank eroticism typical of Calvert (cats 58, 60, 61), and it seems more likely that he, rather than Palmer, made these prints. Though far cruder in execution than Calvert's signed and dated wood engravings (cats 59–61), the Ionides album prints may record Calvert's earliest attempts in the medium, treasured by his admiring student long after the teacher had come to disdain such imperfect work (and perhaps to destroy other copies of it).

The technique, as Palmer discovered, is not easy to master. To make a wood engraving, the artist draws, then cuts away (using a sharp-pointed tool such as a burin – cat. 127b, c) a design drawn on a polished block of hardwood (usually boxwood) that has been cut across the grain.[11] When the block is inked and printed, the resulting image typically shows white lines against a field of black.

Palmer does not appear to have made any prints during the following two decades. Then, at some time in the late 1840s, possibly as late as 1849, he took up etching, an intaglio (recessed-line) method of printmaking favoured by painters for its autographic qualities.[12] To make an etching, the artist first coats a steel or copper plate with a protective 'ground', or varnish, made of waxes, asphalt and resins. Next, the artist uses a steel-pointed tool (an etching needle or burin) to draw a design onto this ground, thereby revealing the metal beneath. Whereas later nineteenth-century etchers such as Whistler would exploit the medium's capacity for rapid, spontaneous sketching on the plate, Palmer shunned such hurried work and disdained *plein air* etching.[13] Instead, he proceeded from paper studies and pondered each line 'with thoughtful deliberation' until all were as 'faultless as learning bought of old experience, could make them'.[14] Progressing in this painstaking manner, Palmer might take days or even weeks to complete his initial design.[15]

When the design is finished, the artist protects the back and sides of the plate with varnish, then immerses it in the 'mordant', or acid bath. Palmer bit his plates (in mordants of increasing dilution) for periods of an hour.[16] The acid 'bites in', or chemically dissolves, the exposed areas of the plate – the lines of the design – while the surfaces covered by the ground and/or the varnish remain intact.[17] Next, the artist 'stops out', or paints over with varnish, any lines to be protected from further biting before re-immersing the plate. For Palmer, this part of the process was essential, and might be repeated as many as fourteen times, following his favourite maxim:[18] 'One day of stopping-out is worth five with the needle.'[19]

When the etched lines have reached the desired depths (the deeper the line, the darker it prints), the artist removes the varnish, and prints the plate. Palmer (as considered below) usually arranged for a professional to print his plates. The printer warms the plate and covers it with ink, then wipes the surface almost clean, so that the ink remains primarily in the incised lines of the design. The plate is then covered with a sheet of dampened paper and protective felts, and run through a rolling press; the pressure forces the paper into the inked grooves.[20]

After examining the resulting 'proof' impressions, the artist might make further changes, by adding new lines with the etching needle, stopping-out passages with protective varnish and re-biting the plate.[21] Palmer typically repeated the process several times: *The Rising Moon* (cat. 134) progressed through nine 'states', or different stages of the plate. He lingered over some etchings for years: his work on *The Early Ploughman* (cat. 140) stretched across two decades. As with his watercolours, Palmer laboured slowly on his etchings – 'not', he explained, 'from any wish to niggle, but because I cannot otherwise get certain shimmerings of light, and mysteries of shadow'.[22] In such exquisite etchings as *The Bellman* (cat. 159) Palmer seems to have realized the motto 'genius is patience'.[23]

Palmer probably learned the rudiments of etching from Charles West Cope, the painter and printmaker whom Palmer called his 'master in etching'.[24] Cope was a founding member of the Etching Club (1838–85), a social and professional association of twelve painter-etchers formed to share expertise and to publish and sell members' works.[25] On

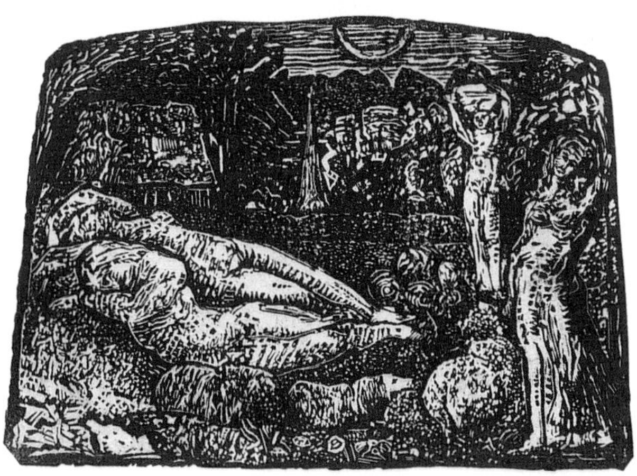

Fig. 17 Attributed to Samuel Palmer, *Naked Women with Attendants*, *c.*1827, wood engraving, folio 15 recto, album of Alexander Constantine Ionides, Victoria and Albert Museum (see cat. 63).

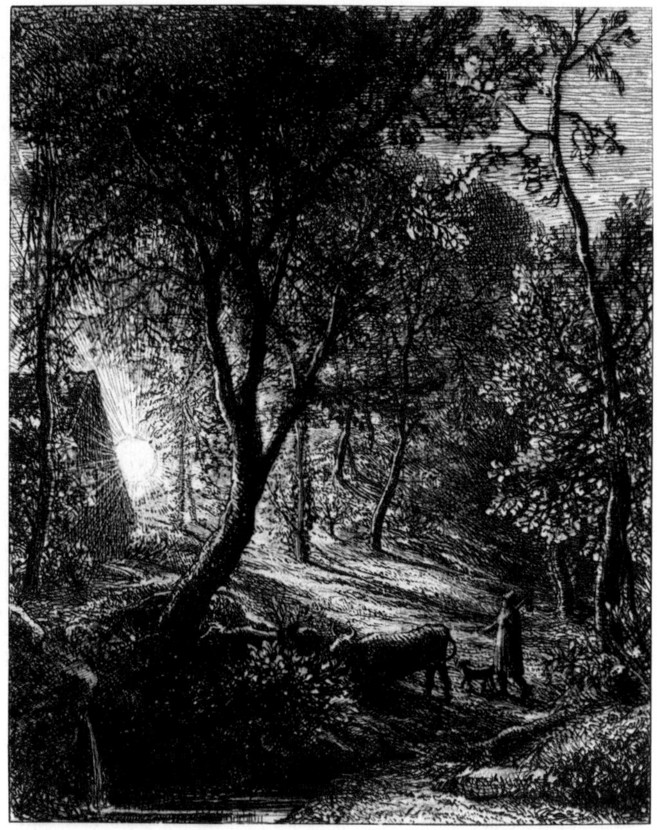

Fig. 18 *The Herdsman's Cottage* or *Sunset*, 1850, etching on off-white laid paper, state 2, The Metropolitan Museum of Art, New York, The Elisha Whittelsey Collection, The Elisha Whittelsey Fund.

29 January 1850 Cope nominated Palmer to membership in the all-male club; on 19 February, at a meeting hosted by Cope, the members received Palmer's probationary plate, *The Willow* (cat. 126), and elected him unanimously to their ranks.

Other members at the time included Thomas Oldham Barlow, Thomas Creswick, John Callcott Horsley and Richard Redgrave; they would later be joined by Richard Ansdell, James Clark Hook, William Holman Hunt, John Everett Millais and Seymour Haden. At monthly supper-meetings held at members' homes or public houses members might examine one another's plates or proofs, print etchings using the club's press, discuss developments abroad and arrange for group publications or submissions to exhibitions.[26] On other occasions, however – such as the meeting held at Palmer's house on 11 June 1860 – 'no business [was] conducted'.

The Etching Club offered more than camaraderie, technical assistance and financial support. As Martin Hardie observed, it also manifested a revolt against the 'artificiality and ugliness' of the early Victorian era, anticipating the Pre-Raphaelite Brotherhood (formed in 1848) in its fight against 'the lethargy, deadness of ideals, and wool-work inanity of the age' and in its admiration for 'the sincerity and truth of old masters of their art'.[27] In this artistic community united by shared ideals, Palmer regained access to the visionary sensibility largely lost to him since the dissolution of the Ancients.

Palmer attended club meetings regularly until his move from London in 1861; afterwards, he supplemented occasional visits with correspondence and contributions to group publications. The other members regarded his work highly: his contribution to the *Songs and Ballads of Shakespeare* (1853) drew the second-highest number of votes in the balloting used to apportion the profits.[28] Palmer seems to have been instrumental in instigating a subsequent publication, *Etchings for the Art Union of London by the Etching Club* (1872).[29]

With the assistance of club members such as Cope, Barlow and Creswick, Palmer's skills as an etcher developed rapidly.[30] Yet, despite the beauty of his work, Palmer never became an assured technician, his etchings remaining 'a scramble of uncertainties from beginning to end'.[31] But he found the process exhilarating:

> The great peculiarity of etching seems to be that its difficulties are not such as excite the mind to 'restless ecstasy', but are an elegant mixture of the manual, chemical and calculative, so that its very mishaps and blunders (usually remediable) are a constant amusement. The tickling sometimes amounts to torture, but on the whole, it raises and keeps alive a speculative curiosity – it has something of the excitement of gambling, without its guilt and its ruin.[32]

Technical mishaps, however happily resolved, only extended Palmer's already prolonged working methods. Seen in this light, his limited production as an etcher is not surprising.

In three decades of work Palmer would complete only thirteen etchings. The earliest, distinguished by their small size, attest to the artist's faith in 'the condensing power of art':[33] *The Willow* (1850, cat. 126), *The Skylark* (1850, cat. 128), *The Herdsman's Cottage* (1850, fig. 18), *Christmas* (1850, cat. 129), *The Vine* (1851–2, fig. 19) and *The Sleeping Shepherd* (*c.*1854–7, cat. 133). The later, larger plates reflect Palmer's search for a 'bold free' style that 'John Bull could see without his spectacles':[34] *The Rising Moon* (*c.*1855–7, cat. 134), *The Weary Ploughman* (1858–65, cat. 139), *The Early Ploughman* (begun before 1861, cat. 140), *The Morning of Life* (begun by 1861, cat. 142), *The Bellman* (1879, cat. 159), *The Lonely Tower* (1879, cat. 161) and *Opening the Fold* (1880, cat. 162). Palmer began, but left unfinished, *The Homeward Star* (begun *c.*1880), *The Cypress Grove* (begun *c.*1880, cat. 163), *The Sepulchre* (begun *c.*1880) and *Moeris and Galatea* (begun *c.*1880). An eighteenth plate, the *Deluge* (apparently in progress in 1871), is unknown.[35]

The idyllic, pastoral subjects of Palmer's etchings (discussed at greater length in the entries) parallel those of his watercolours. P.G. Hamerton found in their entrancing compositions 'a serene spirit inherited from the true and great poets of the old times'.[36] F.G. Stephens characterized their mood as 'Dorian', and likened their articulation to the 'gorgeous ... vivid ... and ... diversified' words of a 'pious, chastened, and severely simple muse'.[37]

Palmer's aims as an etcher are clear. He eschewed straight lines, extensive cross-hatching and simple outlines in favour of more organic forms – entwined, unrepeating, curving marks of various lengths, arranged to evoke tone, texture and mass.[38] The resulting tracery of shimmering lines reveals his tireless efforts to 'make the effect ring'.[39] No etching purist, Palmer sought to unite 'the vigour and texture of old woodcuts' with subtle effects of twilight and sunrise.[40] Ruskin's assertion that chiaroscuro had no place in etching simply bewildered him: 'Is not tone the prerogative of etching,

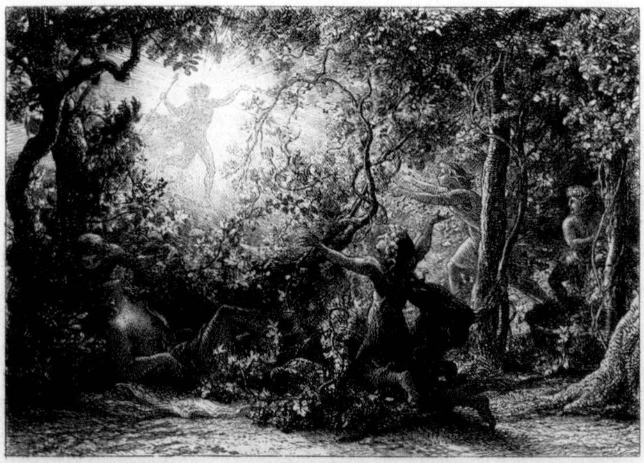

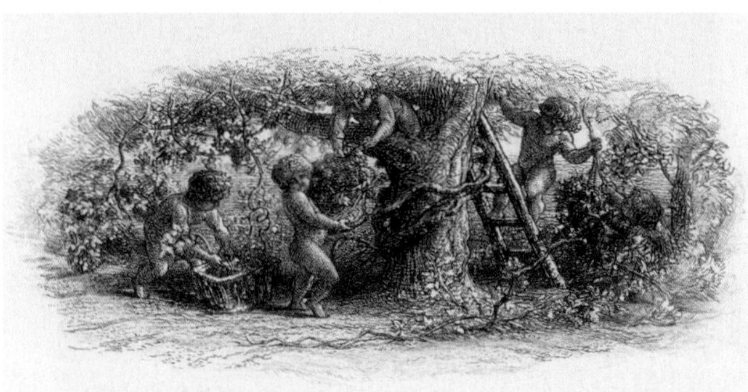

Fig. 19 *Come, Thou Monarch of the Vine!*, or *The Vine*, 1851–2, etchings, from *Songs of Shakespeare Illustrated by the Etching Club* (1853), The Metropolitan Museum of Art, New York, The Elisha Whittelsey Collection, The Elisha Whittelsey Fund.

and chiaroscuro its territory?'[41] Indeed, the very reason that Palmer pursued etching – as opposed to the tonal print-making process of mezzotint – was 'a certain luminousness even in its dark shades'.[42]

In printing Palmer favoured warm white papers (of various hefts), untinged by greys, blues or greens. He preferred deep black inks, or occasionally warm browns, but nothing with a hint of blue.[43] Palmer appears to have coloured one impression of *The Sleeping Shepherd* (National Gallery of Art, Washington, DC, Lessing J. Rosenwald Collection) and planned to colour other etchings.[44] He held admittedly 'fidgetty' ideas about display, advising that frames should 'cut off as little as possible at the top and bottom' and advocating a rabbet (the channel that receives the glass) one-eighth of an inch (3 mm) larger on all sides than the sheet.[45] He recommended 'untinted glass' for framed etchings, and preferred mount boards 'not quite white but of a very delicate hue'.[46] He sent purchasers to the frame-maker Briggs in Marylebone to buy gilded frames of one-and-a-half-inch (38 mm) moulding or three-quarter inch (19 mm) beads of varnished pine with an inlaid black line.[47]

Palmer struggled to find sympathetic printers to realize his ideals. From 1850 until 1863 Gad – of Gad and Keningale, the commercial printers used by the Etching Club – printed Palmer's plates.[48] Palmer described Gad as 'one of the most attentive and obliging men I ever had to do with', but the etcher's son characterized him – like his successor, George Martin Jr., a trade printer who pulled Palmer's plates between 1864 and 1873 – as a mere mechanic.[49] Palmer covered his proofs with notes, diagrams and sketches, and offered further explanations of his intentions in person (cat. 139b). The process tried tempers on both sides: one harried printer reportedly declared that 'he would sooner see the Devil himself than Palmer with a plate to prove'.[50]

Soon, however, circumstances began to change. In the late 1850s in Paris, and in the late 1860s in London, a select group of printers began to specialize in artist's etchings. Their sensitive, creative methods amounted to a veritable collaboration in the finished work. Palmer's etchings would be proved by a pioneer of such 'artistic printing' techniques: Auguste Delâtre, the 'high-priest' of the French etching revival, whose method of painting ink onto the etching plate yielded expressive results.[51] As one of his contemporaries recognized, 'the difference between Delâtre's printing, and that of Gad and Keningale, is something like the difference between Daubigny's manner as a landscape painter, and that of Leader and Vicat Cole'.[52]

On 16 November 1858 Delâtre (invited to London by Whistler) attended a meeting of the Etching Club together with the surgeon, collector and skilled amateur etcher, Seymour Haden (Whistler's brother-in-law).[53] Delâtre thought the members' plates 'capable of much more artistic treatment' and offered to print some, including 'the unappropriated plates on steel by Palmer'.[54] Although no such impressions of Palmer's early steel plates – *The Skylark*, *The Herdsman's Cottage*, *Christmas* and *The Sleeping Shepherd* – are known, Delâtre may have proved *The Weary Ploughman* on the private press that Haden installed in his home around that time (cat. 139).[55] Over the following decade Delâtre would also prove *The Early Ploughman* (*c.*1865–7) and *The Morning of Life* (1869).[56]

After Haden joined the Etching Club (as its last elected member) in 1860, he would prove Palmer's plates as well.[57] At the 9 June 1869 meeting Haden printed *The Morning of Life* on the club's press as a demonstration for the group. Two weeks later he sent Palmer a proof covered with annotations, together with a letter explaining his results.[58] His comments reveal the challenges posed by Palmer's inexpert technique: the plate's excessive margins required time-consuming wiping that allowed the copper to cool, thereby altering the consistency of the ink, before printing; and the combination of etching and engraving created lines of widths and depths so varied that no single ink was suitable for both.[59]

In the 1870s Frederick Goulding – who began to print the Etching Club's works while still a journeyman at Vincent Brooks, Day and Son – printed Palmer's plates.[60] Goulding, who had worked with Whistler and had seen 'plates printed with a tint left on the surface' at the leading Paris firm of Adolphe Goupil, became London's answer to Delâtre:[61] 'with a turn of the wrist, a wave of the muslin, a wreath "of faint smoke curling whitely" from his eternal cigarette, [he] seemed to cast some subtle magic over an etcher's plate'.[62] Palmer came to rely on Goulding as he had on no previous printer. He arranged for him to reprint earlier plates, including *Christmas* (in 1877) and *The Willow* (in about 1879), and to prove new ones, such as *The Lonely Tower* (in 1879).[63]

To assure the sensitive printing of future etchings, Palmer acquired, with Goulding's advice, 'a small, heavy press with a star affording reasonable leverage'.[64] Goulding oversaw its installation at Furze Hill House and instructed Palmer's twenty-year-old son Alfred Herbert Palmer, in its use, proving to be 'a teacher of such zeal, kindness, and efficiency, that in future all the proofs required, were able to be taken at the private press'.[65]

Using the plate *Christmas*, Goulding instructed A.H. Palmer in *retroussage*, the practice of drawing ink gently from the etched lines with a cloth before printing to create an effect of softened edges.[66] The results could be stunning, but struck some artists as dissembling – or simply too dark. Palmer held strong views on the subject:

> I doubt whether etching in the old sense of the word is not almost superseded by the new art of *retroussage* added by the printer upon a comparatively slight fabric. Sometimes it has been very effective, but, in most instances, is so inferior to linear etching as to become quite another art ... It seems to me that the charm of etching is the glimmering through of the white paper even in the shadows; so that almost everything either sparkles, or suggests sparkle ... *Retroussage*, if not kept within narrow bounds, extinguishes those thousand little luminous eyes which peer through a finished linear etching.[67]

Intrigued by Goulding's demonstration, but aware of his father's feelings on the topic, A.H. Palmer tried to navigate a middle course, half-way between the 'cut and dried' printing 'of the early days of the Etching Club' and Goulding's extensive use of *retroussage*.[68] Using his own manner of 'common sense, not extravagant, retroussage', A.H. Palmer followed *Christmas* with reprintings of other plates, such as *The Willow* and *The Early Ploughman*.[69] The results proved successful: P.G. Hamerton praised A.H. Palmer's *Early Ploughman* for revealing the plate's 'full beauty', and Samuel Palmer rebit the copper in an attempt to etch those inked effects into permanency.[70] As A.H. Palmer became more confident in his abilities, he began to print for other artists (such as Cope and Hook) and set up a second 'much more powerful geared press ... made to order from Goulding's specification' in his London studio on Newman Street in November 1880.[71] There he would print the great etchings of his father's last years.

Palmer's final, frenetic period as an etcher – he finished the two Milton plates in 1879, the first Virgil plate in 1880, and began four more Virgil plates at the same time – was cut short by his death in May 1881. In the previous two years he had wholly or partially completed seven of his thirteen total etchings. His son would finish and publish the four unfinished plates, and arrange for photogravures to be made of nine preparatory designs for other Virgil etchings (cat. 163).

In November 1926 the Cotswold Gallery issued a 'Final Edition' of *The Willow*, *Christmas*, *The Early Ploughman*, *The Bellman* and *Opening the Fold*, printed by three admirers of Palmer: Sir Frank Short, the etcher and master printer trained by Goulding; Martin Hardie, the art historian, curator and printmaker who had studied with Short; and F.L. Griggs, the etcher, watercolour painter and teacher of Graham Sutherland.[72]

Since that time Palmer's reputation as an etcher has continued to rise. While some critics, such as Joseph Pennell, regarded Palmer's 'overloading' of his plates as a violation of the form, most believed that his poetic ends justified his unconventional means.[73] Palmer's 'eclectic' method – which united the chiaroscuro of mezzotint, the expressiveness of etching, the sparkle of woodcut and the linear purity of engraving – has never been repeated.[74] Walter Sickert succinctly characterized Palmer's etchings as 'rich, concentrated, indefatigable and intense'.[75] But perhaps the artist's own musings on Blake's wood engravings provide the most fitting description of all:

> Intense depth, solemnity, and vivid brilliancy only coldly and partially describe them. There is in all such a mystic and dreamy glimmer as penetrates and kindles the inmost soul, and gives complete and unreserved delight, unlike the gaudy daylight of this world. They are like all that wonderful artist's works the drawing aside of the fleshly curtain, and the glimpse which all the most holy, studious saints and sages have enjoyed ...[76]

1 *Letters* 1872 (21), p. 866. The etched and mezzotinted plates of J.M.W. Turner's *Liber Studiorum*, or 'Book of Studies' (1807–19), measured approximately 7¼ by 10¼ in (18.4 × 26 cm) each (Forrester 1996). 'Opodeldoc' is an alcoholic solution or ointment containing soap, camphor, oils of marjoram and rosemary and sometimes laudanum.
2 *Letters* 1871 (4), p. 819.
3 Palmer considered the British Museum his academy: 'Mr. Carpenter [Keeper of Prints] is the chancellor of *our* university; our Bodleian is that quiet printroom at the Museum' (*Letters* 1864 [12], p. 706).
4 *Letters* 1872 (20), p. 862. For other engravers admired by Palmer, see *Letters* 1865 (5), pp. 727–8.
5 Gilchrist 1863, vol. 1, p. 297.
6 *Letters* 1872 (1), p. 835.
7 Calvert may well have learned wood engraving from Blake, with whom he experimented in etching, once accidentally setting a chimney ablaze in the process (Calvert 1893, p. 23).
8 *Memoir*, p. 19.
9 *Letters* 1828 (1), p. 18.
10 Evans 2002.
11 Woodcut blocks, by contrast, are sawn longitudinally, along the grain.
12 See Palmer's references to 'plate-paper' as a sketching material, and to the months as a suitable subject for a book of etchings; *Letters* 1849 (8), p. 473; (10), p. 474. A.H. Palmer stated that his father was unlikely to have been 'a mere tyro when he etched ... *The Willow*'; V&A 1926, Introduction, p. 14.
13 'I am no great believer in etching direct from nature; or in doing anything but through the medium of studies' (*Letters* 1871 [6], p. 821).
14 *Memoir*, p. 16.
15 *L&L*, p. 93. Hamerton 1868, p. 350.
16 Inscriptions on the verso of Palmer's preparatory design for Eclogue VIII (Princeton University Art Gallery) indicate that he bit the corresponding plate with increasingly dilute mordants (applied according to a grid pattern) on four hour-long occasions in February and March of 1876 (Lister V19).
17 As a result of this chemical action, etched lines exhibit a coarseness distinct from the smooth quality of engraved lines.
18 *The Bellman* (cat. 8.14) received thirteen bitings, *The Lonely Tower* (cat. 8.16), fourteen (V&A 1926, p. 83).

19 *Letters* 1871 (4), p. 819. Amid notes taken in 1858, Palmer attributed this rule, which he had learned from Thomas Oldham Barlow, to George Cooke (V&A 1926, Appendix, p. 77).
20 As a result of this process, etchings, like other intaglio prints, exhibit raised lines of ink and 'platemarks', or impressions left by the edges of the plate upon the sheet of paper.
21 Hamerton was incorrect in stating in *Etching and Etchers* (1876) that 'Mr. Palmer never once had recourse to re-biting' (V&A 1926, p. 78).
22 *Letters* 1879 (12), p. 970. Palmer had previously written, 'where tone is aimed at, copper bites into time as greedily as acid into copper' (*Letters* 1871 [5], p. 820).
23 *Letters* 1859 (7), p. 557. As Lister notes, Palmer wrongly attributed this saying – actually by Georges-Louis Leclerc de Buffon – to Ralph Waldo Emerson (*Letters* 1857 [2], p. 528 note 4).
24 *Memoir*, p. 16. The two met in 1843, and had become close friends by 1848 (Redgrave 1891, p. 51; *Letters* 1848 [6], p. 463). Palmer may have received assistance from his wife Hannah, who seems to have known etching (*Letters* 1838 [11], p. 179), or from her father John Linnell.
25 Fredericksen 2002; Chambers 1999. A related organization, the Junior Etching Club (1857–64), formed to accommodate additional painter-etchers, counted Whistler, Henry Moore, Sir John Tenniel and Charles Samuel Keene among its members.
26 Between 1854 and 1856 the club met at the King's Arms, Kensington, a setting for scenes in Thackeray's *Book of Snobs* (1848) and *History of Henry Esmond* (1852).
27 Hardie 1910, p. 151.
28 Palmer received 62 votes at the 15 January 1867 meeting, second in a range from 65 (Hook) to 46 (Horsley). This profit-sharing method later became a source of contention among the members, when, on 20 April 1872, the club voted to divide profits equally among contributors, regardless of the time expended in the production of their plates; the measure (opposed by Hook, Cope and Palmer) was reversed on 13 November 1876 (Minutes; *Letters* 1872 [14], p. 855; Chambers 1999, pp. 52–3).
29 A letter from Palmer read at the 19 January 1869 club meeting stated that 'the art-union will be glad to have another set of Etchings by the Club'.
30 *L&L*, pp. 99–100. A.H. Palmer recorded that Creswick's 'timely admonition' of the ruled lines in *The Willow* led Palmer to 'study of the sky of that superb masterpiece *Evening on the Common*'; since that etching was not made until 1857, however, Palmer may have previously studied other etchings by Creswick.
31 *Letters* 1858 (9), p. 546.
32 *Letters* 1872 (21), p. 865.
33 *Memoir*, p. 49; *L&L*, p. 162.
34 Minutes of the Etching Club meeting, 11 November 1862; *Letters* 1869 (6), p. 802.
35 *Letters* 1871 (10), p. 828.
36 Hamerton 1872, p. 162.
37 Stephens 1872, p. 162. For more on Stephens's description of Palmer as 'the painter of the Dorian mood', see pp. 45, 192 and 224 in the present volume.
38 For Palmer's consideration of cloud-shadowing in these terms, see *Letters* 1871 (4), p. 819.
39 *Letters* 1872 (8), p. 844.
40 V&A 1926, Appendix, p. 77.
41 *Letters* 1874 (1), p. 893. Ruskin's letter appeared in *The Architect* (27 December 1873). For Palmer, etchings were essentially studies in 'tone, and mystery, and intricacy' (*Letters* 1872 [12], p. 852).
42 *Letters* 1874 (1), p. 893.
43 *Letters* 1872 (17), p. 858; 1878 (10), p. 960. For Palmer's request that the ink used for *The Morning of Life* contain '*No Blue*' and that only 'white or the very lightest straw color' paper be used and '*dark* India' paper be avoided, see his unpublished letter to Goulding of 12 September 1871, Correspondence. A trial progressive proof of state 7 of *The Morning of Life* in the V&A, made before the completion of the letters and inscribed with Goulding's name and a note that it was printed 'to test the colour of ink', is presumably related to Palmer's request (*A Vision Recaptured*, p. 53, no. 10c).
44 Lister E6. Although no other coloured etchings are known, a working proof of *Christmas* (formerly in the collection of A.H. Palmer) bears the inscription 'Printed for Colouring', and A.H. Palmer recorded several counter-proofs of *The Rising Moon* taken 'in brownish ink, and on drawing paper, with a view of colouring them' (V&A 1926, 170 and 188).
45 *Letters* 1874 (5), p. 901; here, Palmer refers to a watercolour (which Lister identifies as his cat. 187), but Palmer elsewhere expresses similar ideas about framing in relation to etchings. *Letters* 1873 (6), p. 877.
46 *Letters* 1873 (6), p. 877; 1871 (14), p. 833.
47 *Letters* 1873 (6), p. 877; 1873 (12), p. 883.
48 Little is known of these printers. From 1838 the club made regular payments to 'Messrs. Gad & Co.' or 'Messrs. Gad and Keningale' of 9 Sauls Row (off Hampstead Road and 'nearly opposite the reservoir', according to Palmer) for printing their plates. The minutes of the club's 17 March 1863 meeting include the resolution that Hook 'on taking upon himself all the charges of removal from Gad's, may till further arranged, have the custody and use of the club press, slab, muller, &c.' The minutes of the 9 February 1864 meeting formally announced Gad's retirement and arranged to conclude any outstanding club business with him; in a marginal note the printer is named 'W. Gad'.
49 *Letters* 1854 (8), p. 500. Martin, of 83 Hampstead Road, had trained with Gad and succeeded to Gad and Keningale's business (Hamerton 1868, p. 349). A.H. Palmer recalled his father overseeing 'Gad or Martin, striving in vain to make himself understood in a language which, to them, might just as well have been Hebrew' (V&A 1926, Appendix, p. 80).
50 V&A 1926, Introduction, p. 19.
51 Hardie 1910, p. 147. For the etching revival in England and further references to the subject, see Chambers 1999, pp. 1–12.
52 Hamerton 1868, p. 350. Daubigny, a 'serious' French realist painter, is being compared here with two Victorian popularizers of landscape.
53 Delâtre printed Whistler's *Douze eaux-fortes d'apres nature* (*Twelve Etchings from Nature*) in Paris, where the first twenty sets were issued in early November 1858; he brought another fifty sets of the 'French set' to London, where they were published (with a dedication to Haden) several weeks later (Lochnan 1984, p. 58).
54 *Christmas* was 'one of a set of four, nearly alike in size and executed on steel' (*Memoir*, p. 17 note). The others were *The Skylark*, *The Herdsman's Cottage* and *The Sleeping Shepherd*.
55 A signed impression of *The Weary Ploughman* in its fourth state (The Metropolitan Museum of Art, Gift of Theodore de Witt, 1923) is inscribed 'At M^r Haden's prep by Delatre'. In March 1861 Palmer informed Samuel Redgrave: 'Only three impressions of any kind have gone out of the club, unless I reckon two experimental proofs which were taken at Mr. Haydon's' (*Letters* 1861 [3], p. 588). Lister identified the unnamed print as *The Morning of Life* (later proved by Delâtre in July 1869), but it seems more likely to have been *The*

*Weary Ploughman*. Delâtre certainly printed some etchings for the club: the members resolved to thank him at their 9 July 1859 meeting. For Haden's installation of his private press, see Lochnan 1984, p. 59.

56 Alexander 1937, p. 46, cat. no. 9. The plate for *The Early Ploughman* was still in its third state when a proof dated 'Thursday June 8', indicating the year 1865, was pulled (V&A 1926, 197). Delâtre presumably pulled his proof of it before the summer of 1867, when Palmer sent the plate in its fourth state to Hamerton for publication in *Etching and Etchers* (1868) (V&A 1926, p. 79). For *The Morning of Life* proved by Delâtre, see V&A 1926, 206.

57 An impression of *The Morning of Life* in its fourth state (The Metropolitan Museum of Art, Gift of Theodore de Witt, 1923) is signed in graphite beneath the image, 'S.H.', and inscribed on the verso in another hand, 'very early proof printed by S. Haden'. Garton records a number of impressions printed by Haden at the Art Institute of Chicago (Garton 1992, p. 55). Although Haden's relations with Palmer appear to have been cordial, A.H. Palmer credited the successful amateur, who would be instrumental in founding the professional successor to the Etching Club, the Society of Painter-Etchers (now the Royal Society of Painter-Printmakers), in 1880, with leading 'the joyous task of wrecking the old Etching Club for his own advantage' (V&A 1926, Introduction, p. 19). A.H. Palmer further blamed Haden 'for a very considerably reduced output in S.P. ['s] plates', although he noted 'how much can be said on his [Haden's] side of the question, & from his point of view' (Correspondence).

58 For the proof, now in the Princeton University Art Museum, see Pressly 1970, pp. 25–8, cat. 13.

59 In an unpublished letter to Goulding dated 12 September 1871 Palmer further explained that 'before the margin was cut off… [the plate] used to warp very much, & Mr. Haden … had to put a graduated padding of slips of paper at the back' (Correspondence).

60 At the 3 June 1870 meeting the club 'Resolved that Mr. Vincent Brooks (late Day & Co.) be recommended to the art-union to print the work – on condition that the printing shall be exclusively entrusted to Goulding a [*sic*] inkman in his employ, who under the instructions of the Club has produced many successful impressions of their plates for the art-union'.

61 Hardie 1910, pp. 24, 30. Goulding later taught at the National Art Training School (now the Royal College of Art) and the Slade School (beginning in 1876), and became first Master Printer to the Royal Society of Painter-Etchers (1890).

62 Hardie 1913, p. 215. Goulding set up an independent press in 1877 and established his business as an independent printer in 1881, becoming the accepted printer for virtually all the leading engravers and etchers of the day (Hardie 1910, p. 68).

63 For Christmas, see V&A 1926, 174. For *The Willow*, see V&A 1926, 158. For *The Lonely Tower*, see Minutes: at the 9 December 1878 meeting of the Etching Club Palmer's request for the return of his 'trial plate belonging to the Club and not published' – presumably made so that Goulding might reprint it – had been agreed; at the Etching Club meeting of 18 March 1879 Goulding proved *The Lonely Tower*, then in its fourth state (cat. 161).

64 Hardie 1910, p. 124. Ironically, it may have been Goulding's own careless printing of *The Morning of Life* for the Etching Club publication of 1872 that prompted Palmer's desire to train A.H. Palmer.

65 *Memoir*, p. 35.

66 V&A 1926, p. 75.

67 *Letters* 1876 (5), pp. 931–2.

68 Hardie 1910, pp. 121–2.

69 Hardie 1910, p. 125.

70 Alexander 1937, p. 41, cat. no. 1; V&A 1926, Appendix, p. 79.

71 Hardie 1910, p. 121; *Letters* 1880 (33), p. 1034; 1879 (28) p. 989 note; V&A 1926, p. 80. The quotation is from Hardie 1910, p. 124. A.H. Palmer informed Hardie (somewhat petulantly, considering that he was a grown man when his father died, and might have pursued any career he pleased): 'When my father compelled me to give up printing because it was a trade, just when I had bright prospects and plenty of work to do … Goulding bought it.' *Letters*, pp. 765–6 note 2.

72 The edition of seventy-five was printed on old paper and designated by a triangle (symbolizing the trio of printers) etched in the lower margin.

73 Pennell 1925, pp. 139, 176; Wedmore 1911, pp. 133–5; Sparrow 1926, p. 183; Grant 1952, p. 156.

74 Hamerton 1880, pp. 253–4.

75 Sickert 1915, p. 229.

76 *L&L*, pp. 15–16.

# The Artistic Rediscovery of Samuel Palmer

*Colin Harrison*

As with many artists, Palmer's reputation did not long survive his death. Yet by 1949, in his celebrated and much reprinted essay, *Landscape into Art*, Kenneth Clark could write that Palmer had 'had almost too pervasive an influence on recent English painting'.[1] The rehabilitation of Palmer's fame, especially the new recognition of his early work, is one of the most remarkable artistic rediscoveries in modern times. It was brought about by a combination of circumstances: the reprinting of some of his late etchings, the first full retrospective of his work and the independent discovery by a group of young printmakers of his etchings.

Palmer's reputation in the years following his death depended very heavily on the writings of his second and only surviving son, Alfred Herbert. His first attempt at a biography, *Samuel Palmer: A Memoir*, was published to accompany the retrospective exhibition at the Fine Art Society in 1882. It was followed ten years later by the much fuller *Life and Letters*, which is still an invaluable source of information, despite the author's prejudices. Apart from these writings, Palmer was largely unknown to the general public. There was no studio sale, and few important works came on the market: the largest groups were the late Milton watercolours

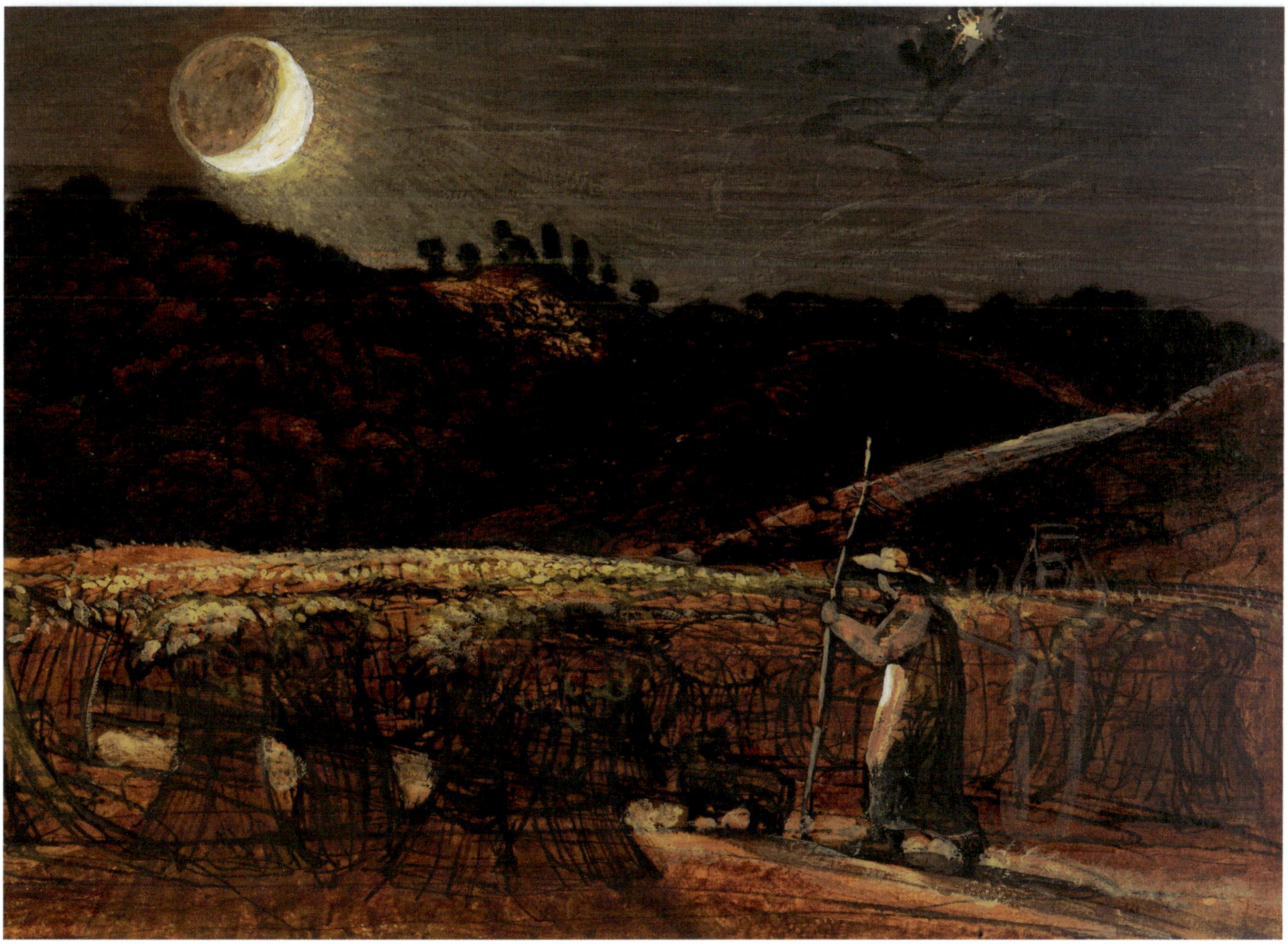

Samuel Palmer, *Cornfield by Moonlight*, c.1830 (cat. 49).

sold by Leonard Rowe Valpy in 1888, and the collection belonging to Palmer's cousin and fellow Ancient, John Giles, in 1881, which included four oil paintings and numerous drawings and watercolours. The only museum with significant holdings of Palmer's works was the Tate Gallery, which acquired a version of *The Bright Cloud* in 1917 and an important group of Shoreham works purchased in 1922, among them *Coming from Evening Church* (cat. 48).[2] Even his etchings, which might have had widespread currency, were comparatively little known and unfashionable: Palmer was hardly mentioned in one of the standard histories of the period, A.M. Hind's *History of Etching and Engraving* (1913). Among Palmer's few admirers was, perhaps unexpectedly, Walter Sickert, who saw in him a champion of the opposition to the authority of the Etching Club and whose 'respect for him and his attitude must remain complete'.[3]

In 1909 A.H. Palmer left England to settle in Canada, where he remained for the rest of his life. Shortly before leaving, he sold a group of his father's works at Christie's, retaining only his favourite drawings and paintings and a collection of etchings and related studies. From his home in Vancouver A.H. Palmer continued to exert a dominant effect on Palmer studies. It was not until the 1920s, however, that his plans for an exhibition of his father's work began to develop seriously. Since 1910 he had been in touch with Martin Hardie, an Assistant Keeper at the Victoria and Albert Museum, amateur etcher and great admirer of Palmer's work. Although the plan to reprint from some of the etching plates was mentioned as early as 1913, the war years were not propitious for their endeavours. In 1920, however, A.H. Palmer sent the block of Palmer's only known wood engraving, *Harvest under a Crescent Moon* (cat. 62), to Hardie, who arranged to have impressions taken from it by A.K. Sabin.[4]

The success of this enterprise encouraged Palmer to send the etching plates remaining in his possession. The most prominent printmaker of the day, and long-serving President of the Society of Painter-Etchers, Sir Frank Short, was the first to take new impressions from two of the plates, but it was another etcher, F.L. Griggs, whose involvement was decisive. As well as being the most brilliant technician alive, he had absorbed Palmer's artistic ideals from his childhood.[5] Negotiations were protracted, partly because of the difficulties in communicating with A.H. Palmer in Vancouver, but, according to the terms of the agreement finally drawn up on 30 March 1926, the five plates were to be printed in an edition by Sir Frank Short, Martin Hardie and F.L. Griggs, after which they were to be defaced and distributed to the V&A and the British Museum, save one for Griggs, at A.H. Palmer's request. A.J. Finberg of the Cotswold Gallery was to sell two-thirds of the impressions through the Cotswold Gallery, and the remainder were reserved by A.H. Palmer. In the event sales were so successful that many of A.H. Palmer's impressions also sold through the Cotswold Gallery. Palmer himself was delighted with the results, declaring that 'only the great, poetic etcher of beautiful old Campden [Griggs] has fully succeeded in imagining what these conceptions of the Virgil etchings are'.[6]

Concurrent with these plans was a related project, also instigated by A.H. Palmer and enthusiastically supported by Hardie, to hold an exhibition of Samuel Palmer's work at the V&A. At first, it was to have been an exhibition of 'S.P.'s own picked impressions of the etchings',[7] together with their preparatory drawings, which A.H. Palmer agreed to lend for two years, 'if possible for exhibition in a group'.[8] Gradually, the scope of the exhibition grew, and A.H. Palmer eventually sent Hardie most of his remaining works by his father. To these were added works by Blake and the other Ancients, together with documents and memorabilia from Palmer and other sources. After long and occasionally difficult negotiations the exhibition opened on 20 October 1926 and continued until the end of the year. Few exhibitions have had such a decisive impact, both on the history of a single artist, or an artistic movement, and on the creative impulses of living artists. Visitors flocked to see this wholly new artist, and the exhibition was an enormous success. As Sir Eric Maclagan, the Director of the V&A, wrote to A.H. Palmer, 'the early watercolours in particular are an absolute revelation both in conception and in technique' (2 November 1926), for, astonishingly, this was the first time that a significant number of the Shoreham works had been exhibited – most had been painted for the artist's own portfolio.

One of the few accounts of a visitor to the exhibition is that of the etcher Robin Tanner, who wrote that he 'positively haunted' it:

> The first item – the self-portrait of Samuel Palmer as a
> young man, which his son had lent and which is now in the
> Ashmolean – I found strangely poignant: never before,
> I thought, had a man's portrait so mirrored his work.
> I knew that the Shoreham drawings, so heavily charged with
> feeling, could only have emerged from such a poet.[9]

Tanner was on the fringe of a group of young printmakers studying at Goldsmiths' College who had already discovered Palmer for themselves two years earlier. The most prominent, Graham Sutherland, remembered: 'The day on which one of our band, William Larkins, brought a small Palmer etching [*The Herdsman's Cottage*, fig. 18] which he had found in Charing Cross Road was a turning point.' Palmer's etching offered the group a wholly new beginning, and they seized it wholeheartedly. Sutherland elsewhere recalled:

> My feeling for this was partly a bid for independence from the stereotyped Seymour Haden etc. engraving tradition of the school, which caused in me a bias towards heavily worked plates – partly also, since I liked Palmer drawings of the early years ... because as a young man I was drawn to a strongly romantic and, so it seemed, independent approach to nature from which I was always drawing.[10]

It was not so much the subject that intrigued them as 'its completeness, both emotional and technical'.[11] The group, which also included Edward Bouverie Houghton and Paul Drury, quickly began to read all they could about Palmer, went on expeditions to Shoreham and adopted the singular costume of the Ancients, cloaks and wide-brimmed hats. More importantly, they sought out his work in public and private collections. Sutherland, for example, visited the Tate, where he was struck by the Shoreham watercolours acquired in 1922: 'The best of the Shoreham drawings, the very best, were unsentimental. The landscapes were daring, and were drawn from unexpected viewpoints: *The Girl in the Ploughed Field* [cat. 32] astonished me with its total disregard for conventional composition. The drawing is almost what we today call naif.'[12]

The lessons Sutherland learnt from Palmer are evident in a series of etchings dating from 1924 to 1930. The earliest, *Number Forty-Nine*, of 1924, shows a barn with a dilapidated roof strongly reminiscent of Palmer's drawings of thatched barns, which Sutherland must surely have seen in Martin Hardie's collection (see cat. 40). *Village*, of the following year, adapts the composition of Palmer's *Girl in a Ploughed Field*, while in *Cray Fields* 'there is less drama but greater magic: the bewitching atmosphere of Palmer, now also to be found in the paintings and watercolours, is clearly in the ascendant here, as we can see from the stars, the tall spires, and the line of hop-poles'.[13] And in *Lammas*, even Palmer's son felt the great affinity of 'sentiment' between Sutherland and his father as he looked at it, 'each time with greater pleasure'.[14] Indeed, the sky in this print might have been etched by Palmer himself: in the first state it is the cobbled clouds of the Shoreham period (fig. 20), while in the last it is a sunset from one of the late etchings.

Among Sutherland's contemporaries, Palmer's influence can be seen most in the etchings of Paul Drury. Although primarily interested in the portrait, during the 1920s he, too, made landscapes inspired by Palmer. Drury later wrote that Palmer's plates 'reflect too those aspects of English genius which have their sources in profound love of poetry, spiritual values, and significant romanticism, as distinct from the more superficial literary and factual facets of our Art'. Drury's *September* (fig. 21) shows a village church, cottages, oasthouses and figures gathering apples under a tree, and is full of the sentiment of Palmer's Shoreham.

The admiration of Sutherland and Drury for Palmer also brought them into contact with F.L. Griggs, whom they visited at Campden, and from whom they learnt invaluable lessons in printing. Unfortunately, the flowering of landscape etching was brief, for the Wall Street Crash in 1929 brought as a consequence a collapse in the market for etchings. Sutherland was, in any case, moving away from printmaking

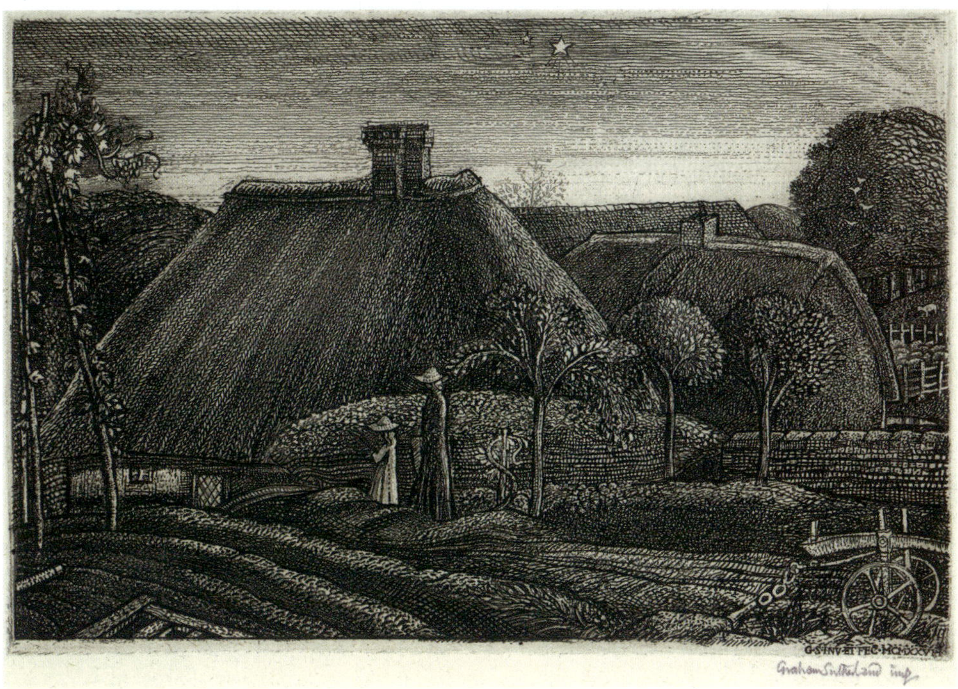

Fig. 20 Graham Sutherland, *Lammas*, *c.*1925, etching, British Museum.

towards drawing and painting, and travelling beyond Kent seeking new subjects, as Palmer had done before him. It is not true, however, as is usually argued, that by the end of the decade Sutherland 'seems to have shaken off the Palmer-inspired mysticism'[15] and that *Pastoral* of 1930 was 'his first genuinely individual work. No trace of Samuel Palmer remains.'[16] Certainly, *Wood Interior* (1929–30) and *Pastoral* (1930) are more individual than the previous etchings, but they still reveal some of the exuberance and feeling for nature that Sutherland found in Palmer, even if, in the latter print, there is now an atmosphere of sinister foreboding that Palmer never attempted. Yet, even in Wales, which Sutherland first visited in 1934, Palmer's example was not forgotten: in writing of 'the exultant strangeness of this place ... the whole setting is one of exuberance – of darkness and light – of decay and life', he wrote in much the same terms as Palmer had of Shoreham. Sutherland painted this clearly constructed landscape, whose essence was both 'intellectual and emotional', not in conventional greens and browns but in blazing colours, red, egg yellow and intense black, just as Palmer had painted Kent.

During the 1930s Palmer's reputation grew steadily among artists. Sutherland was delighted to share his discovery – Henry Moore, for example, remembered: 'When I first met Graham, his big influence, his pace maker was Samuel Palmer.'[17] Although primarily a figurative artist, Moore recognized that 'the few people who thought they were being experimental, modern or whatever you would like to call it ... were all following the same bent, the same route'.[18] Sutherland and Moore were two of the artists described as 'Neo-Romantic' by Raymond Mortimer in a review in the *New Statesman* in 1942; among others were John Piper and Frances Hodgkins.[19] Mortimer characterized the group as making art that appealed to 'mystics and particularly to pantheists who feel a fraternity, or even a unity, with all living things, to those with the "sense sublime of something far more deeply interfused"'.[20] For a later follower, however, they were simply 'the Blake, Palmer, Sutherland movement'.[21]

John Piper, born in the same year as Sutherland and the son of 'a most English person',[22] became a champion of the English landscape and of the English Romantic tradition. In a curious article on 'England's Climate' published in the mouthpiece of the abstract movement in England, *Axis*, he reproduced Palmer's *Barn at Shoreham* and, by implication rather than by specific mention, fitted Palmer into the English Romantic tradition.[23] In his volume *British Romantic Artists* (1942), written in the dark days of the war, Piper went further, arguing that 'in his Shoreham landscapes his consciousness of the past is never absent', and used Kenneth Clark's *Cornfield by Moonlight* (cat. 49) to characterize the

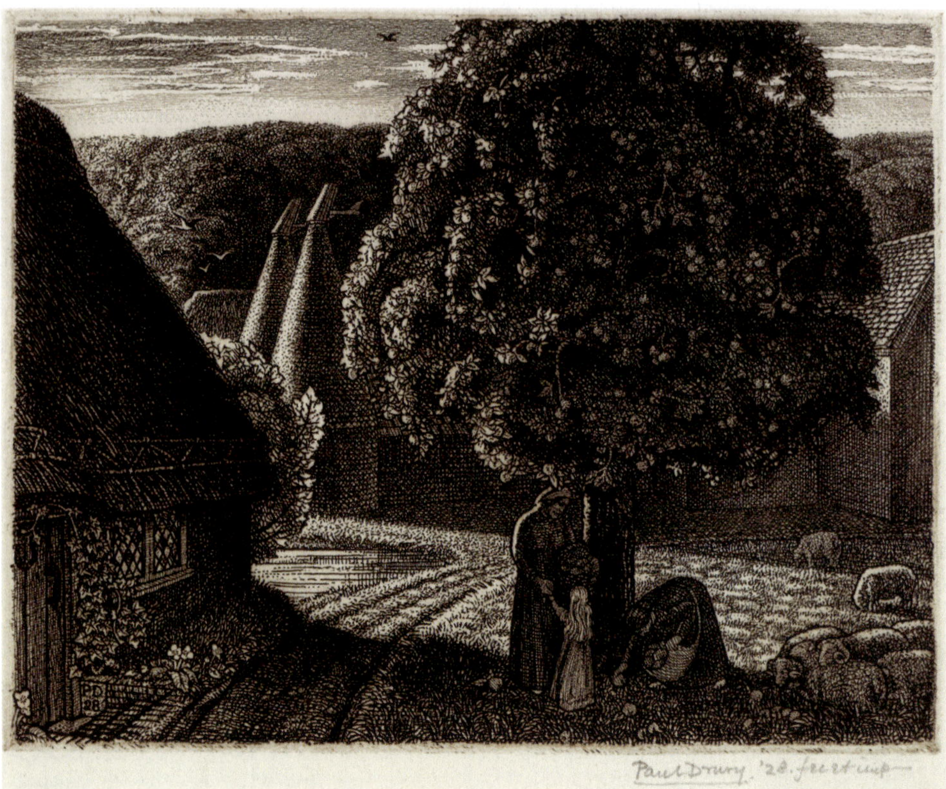

Fig. 21 Paul Drury, *September*, 1928, etching, British Museum.

visionary quality of Palmer's work: 'Mysterious shadows shortening before the rising full moon, the cut edge of the standing corn, fruit trees lolling to the ground under their weight of fruit. These were the realities that gave substance to his visions.'[24] Piper's familiarity with Palmer's Shoreham period showed itself in his own art in a series of 'ruined cottages' between 1941 and 1943, 'painted in the rich brunette of Palmer's gummy watercolours'.[25] Indeed, many of Piper's works during the war share the intensity of feeling and elaborate technique of Palmer's Shoreham watercolours.

The progress of the so-called Neo-Romantics was mirrored by the growing recognition of Palmer's importance in museums. While a Keeper at the Ashmolean between 1931 and 1933, Kenneth Clark had bought from A.H. Palmer's collection the haunting *Self-Portrait* (cat. 1) and the early *Holy Family* (cat. 28) for the Ashmolean, and three works for his own private collection, among them *Cornfield by Moonlight.* In the great exhibition of British Art at the Royal Academy in 1934 Palmer was represented by twelve works, all but one of the Shoreham period and including both *In a Shoreham Garden* (cat. 66) and *The Magic Apple Tree* (cat. 69).[26] Palmer's new place in the history of British art was reflected in a number of articles, some, like Piper's, in progressive periodicals, but others in mainstream journals. Thomas Sturge Moore's rediscovery of the sepia drawings of 1825 was published in *Apollo* in 1936, which also reproduced them for the first time; and Geoffrey Grigson explored aspects of Palmer's life and work in a number of articles in the late 1930s and early 1940s, notably in *Horizon*, a magazine as influential with artists as the cultivated reader.

During the same period, the middle years of the Second World War, Palmer's influence reached its height with a new generation of Neo-Romantic artists.[27] They were a closely knit group, for several of whom the discovery of Palmer's Shoreham works came at formative moments in their careers. Among them were Keith Vaughan, John Minton, Michael Ayrton and John Craxton. Vaughan, who was the oldest, wrote some of the most perceptive lines on the artist in his 'A View of English Painting', first published in 1944,[28] although his art owed the least to Palmer. Ayrton wrote a volume on *British Drawings* in a series of books celebrating the British character published by Collins. There, he noted:

> Of Palmer so much has been recently written that I will not retell the tale of his shortlived period of supreme excellence. Suffice that it is Palmer, more than any other individual draughtsman, who influences the landscape drawing of the younger generation today. He was an artist in whose best work may be found the complete expression, in landscape, of Blake's teaching and example.[29]

Ayrton recognized that the artist whose work most readily displayed first-hand knowledge of Palmer was John Minton: 'Minton is English and Palmer shines through him, but his work is personal none the less.'[30] It was only after experimenting with various styles in London and with the fashionable Surrealism of Pavel Tchelitchew and his associates in Paris that Minton found his own voice. The catalyst came while he was stationed with the Pioneer Corps at

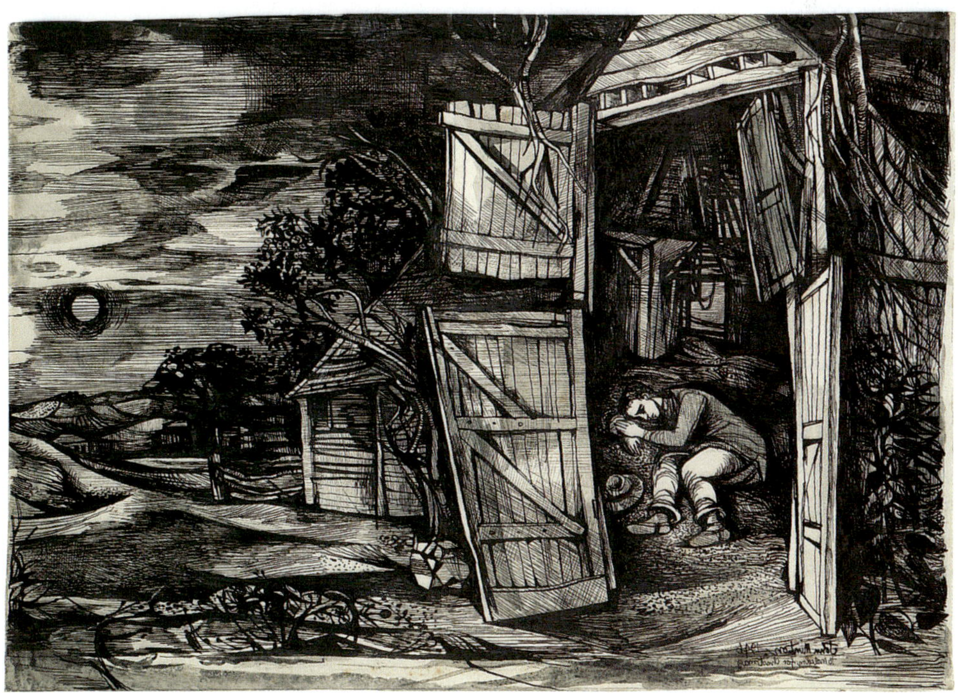

Fig. 22 John Minton, *Young Man Asleep in a Barn*, 1946, pen and ink wash, Ashmolean Museum, Oxford, bequeathed by A.L. Rowse, 1988.

Barmouth in north-west Wales. He was already familiar with Sutherland's interpretation of the Welsh landscape, having been 'very caught up with' the essay 'Welsh Sketchbook' in *Horizon*. In the summer of 1943 he was discharged from the army and resumed his career. During the next three years he worked in an almost exclusively Palmer-inspired mood, drawing closely wrought landscapes, often with timeless figures, in thick Indian ink (fig. 22). He would joke that moons were 'in' and half-moons selling fast. Like his contemporaries, Minton soon progressed beyond the mood of intense pastoralism inspired by Palmer; he became increasingly interested in the urban landscape and the docklands, and the spell was broken when he visited Corsica in 1947. But while it lasted, Palmer's influence was liberating and decisive.

Palmer's work played a similar role in the development of the youngest of the Neo-Romantic artists, John Craxton. He was a friend and protégé of Peter Watson, the proprietor of *Horizon* magazine. Craxton's first major drawings were two landscapes (fig. 23), which were directly inspired by the reproduction in *Horizon* of two of Palmer's sepia drawings of 1825, then newly acquired by the Ashmolean, and were themselves reproduced in *Horizon*.[31] The landscapes in these drawings and in the sequence that followed were imaginary, and derived from Palmer and Blake. Craxton later remembered that 'They were my means of escape and a sort of self-protection ... I wanted to safeguard a world of private mystery, and I was drawn to the idea of bucolic calm as a kind of refuge.'[32]

Also during these years a much older artist, Paul Nash, renewed his acquaintance with Palmer. Nash has always been difficult to classify as an artist, because he restlessly experimented with different styles, and never seemed to be confident enough to settle into his own. As a young man, he shared with Palmer a predilection for nocturnal scenes, 'an appetite for monstrous moons, exuberance of stars', but 'oddly enough, I did not set eyes upon Palmer's designs until five or six years later'.[33] It was only in 1914 that Nash saw the Palmers belonging to Gordon Bottomley, which were not among the artist's best. However, Philip Hendy has argued that Nash had in common with Palmer a 'mystical appreciation of the eerie moods of Nature', a sympathy that he believed to be characteristically English.[34] Certainly, Nash was eager to share his enthusiasm for Palmer with his pupils at the Royal College of Art, as Edward Bawden remembered. In the early 1940s, when Nash was living near Oxford, Nash and Bottomley corresponded about the Palmers in the Ashmolean, and Nash read the biographies of both Palmer and Calvert – 'what a couple of pets they were'.[35] By then, however, Palmer had become a symbol of Romantic escapism, and of the embodiment of rural values increasingly threatened by mechanization and urbanization.

Scholarship had not kept pace with appreciation, but the publication of Geoffrey Grigson's *Samuel Palmer: The Visionary Years* in 1947 effectively established a canon of Palmer's early work and a view of Palmer as a genius who burnt himself out by the time he was thirty that has prevailed until recently. In spite of Grigson's achievement, Palmer has come to be taken for granted. It was for this reason alone that during the 1970s the unscrupulous East End artist, Tom Keating, was able to foist his forgeries on collectors and dealers. The affair, extensively reported in *The Times*, did no harm to Palmer's reputation but severely damaged the London art market. It is now difficult to understand how anybody was taken in by his

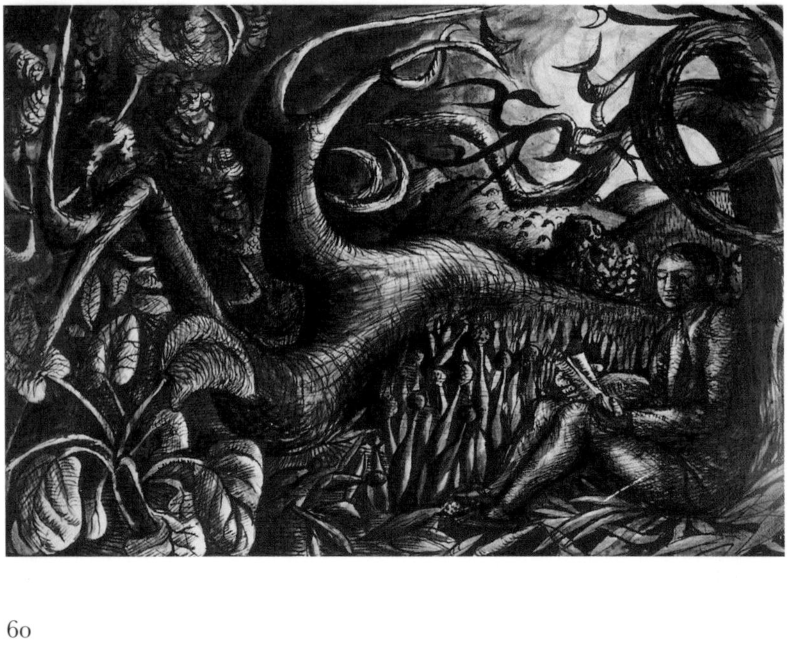

Fig. 23 John Craxton, *Poet in Landscape*, 1941, pen and ink wash, collection of the artist.

poorly painted pastiches, which generally did nothing more than incorporate elements from individual Palmer compositions and reconstitute them into something slightly unfamiliar. Nobody with any deep knowledge of Palmer was taken in – Sir Karl Parker of the Ashmolean denounced one of the fakes four years before the scandal became public – but many optimistic collectors were deceived. The most convincing, and categorical, assessment of the whole affair came, as might have been expected, from the two artists on whom the exhibition in 1926 had made such a profound impression, Graham Sutherland and Paul Drury. In a letter to *The Times* of 3 August 1976 they wrote:

> It is not too much to say that we were shocked at what we saw. It was as if an old friend – long dead – had been impersonated with the aid of liberally and clumsily applied 'make up'. We are neither historians nor 'experts' but painters, and we have known, admired and studied the works of the 'Shoreham Palmer' for 52 years and we have eyes; we also know the terrain.

They concluded that the works in question 'seem to us to be poor versions of his technique and subject ingredients, but bearing no comparable qualities of mind and sensibility'.

Palmer's 'qualities of mind and sensibility' have always attracted artists, from the Pre-Raphaelites F.G. Stephens and Rossetti, who recognized the unique quality of Palmer's 'manifestation of spiritual force absolutely present',[36] to the radical young printmakers of the 1920s, whom Palmer liberated from convention, and the Neo-Romantics, for whom he became associated with an intensely English pastoral vision threatened by the Second World War. Graham Sutherland described Palmer as 'essentially the English Van Gogh', a comparison also made by Kenneth Clark.[37] Palmer has always been an artist's artist.

1 Kenneth Clark, *Landscape into Art*, London, 1949, p. 71.
2 Lister 123, 115, 143, 64, 138, the first four from the sale of John Giles in 1881 and bought from Mrs John Richmond in 1922. In addition, a conventional late watercolour had been acquired by the Whitworth Institute, Manchester, in 1905 (Lister 607), and a group of later works by the V&A (V&A 1926, 117–33).
3 Walter Sickert, 'The Future of Engraving', *Burlington Magazine*, September 1915, reprinted in *Walter Sickert: The Complete Writings on Art*, ed. Anna Gruetzner Robins, Oxford, 2000, pp. 389–95 (p. 391).
4 A.H. Palmer to Martin Hardie, 20 July 1920 (V&A National Art Library).
5 See Jerrold Northrop Moore, *F.L. Griggs: The Architecture of Dreams*, Oxford, 1999, pp. 14–15, 55.
6 V&A 1926, pp. 18–19.
7 A.H. Palmer to Martin Hardie, 9 April 1922 (V&A National Art Library).
8 A.H. Palmer to Martin Hardie, 1 October 1922 (V&A National Art Library).
9 Robin Tanner, *Double Harness: An Autobiography*, London, 1987, p. 41.
10 Douglas Cooper, *The Work of Graham Sutherland*, London, 1961, p. 7.
11 Graham Sutherland, 'The Visionaries: A personal and nostalgic impression', in *The Visionaries*, exh. cat. William Weston Gallery, London, 1973.
12 Letter to Berthoud, quoted in Berthoud 1982, p. 52.
13 Tassi, n.d., p. 20.
14 A.H. Palmer to F.L. Griggs, 23 April 1927 (Ashmolean Museum, Dept of Western Art, Griggs Archive).
15 Tassi, *n.d.*, p. 20.
16 Berthoud 1982, p. 65.
17 Henry Moore in a conversation with Roger Berthoud, 24 July 1979, transcribed in Wilkinson 2002, p. 184.
18 From a talk entitled 'Graham Sutherland: The Last Romantic', 3 May 1982, quoted in Wilkinson 2002, p. 228.
19 On the Neo-Romantics, see *A Paradise Lost: The Neo-Romantic Imagination in Britain, 1935–55*, ed. David Mellor, exh. cat., Barbican Gallery, London, 1987; and Yorke 1988.
20 Quoted in Yorke 1990, p. 89.
21 Keith Vaughan, diary, 24 Feb 1948, quoted in Yorke 1990, p. 125.
22 John Betjeman, *John Piper*, Harmondsworth, 1944, p. 6.
23 See Alan Powers, 'The Reluctant Romantics: *Axis* Magazine 1935–37', in Corbett *et al.* 2002, pp. 249–74.
24 John Piper, *British Romantic Artists*, London, 1942, p. 32.
25 David Fraser Jenkins, *John Piper: The Forties*, exh. cat., Imperial War Museum, London, 2000, p. 42.
26 Andrew Causey, 'English Art and "The National Character", 1933–34,' in Corbett *et al.* 2002, pp. 275–302.
27 See Margaret Garlake, *New Art, New World: British Art in Postwar Society*, New Haven and London, 1998, ch. 5.
28 Published in *New World Unity and Daylight* (1943–4), but more widely accessible in *The Penguin New Writing* 31 (1947), pp. 131–45.
29 Michael Ayrton, *British Drawings*, London, 1946, p. 34.
30 Ibid., p. 47.
31 'Poet in a Landscape, Dreamer in a Landscape', *Horizon* v (1942), pp. 188–9.
32 Yorke 1988, p. 310
33 Paul Nash, 'Aerial Flowers', *Counter Point* 1, 1945, pp. 1–8, reprinted in *Paul Nash: Writings on Art*, ed. Andrew Causey, Oxford, 2000, pp. 155–61 (p. 157).
34 Philip Hendy, 'Paul Nash', *Horizon* VII (*1943*), pp. 413–17 (p. 414).
35 Nash to Bottomley, late August 1941, in Causey 1990, p. 243.
36 D.G. Rossetti in *The Spectator*, 14 February 1883, quoted in V&A 1926, p. vii.
37 Graham Sutherland, 'Landscape and Figures', *The Listener*, 26 July 1962, pp. 132–5, quoted in Yorke 1988, p. 110, and Cooper 1961, p. 7; cf. Clark, *Landscape into Art*, p. 72.

# Chronology

| | | |
|---|---|---|
| 1805 | *27 January* | Born in Newington, south London, the son of a bookseller. |
| 1817 | | Enters Merchant Taylors' School, but leaves after six months. |
| 1818 | *January* | Death of Mother. |
| | | Becomes pupil of the painter William Wate. |
| 1819 | | Exhibits in both the British Institution and the Royal Academy. Sells work for first time from British Institution Exhibition. |
| 1822 | *September* | Meets John Linnell. |
| 1823 | | Meets George Richmond. |
| 1824 | | Forms the artistic brotherhood The Ancients, with Richmond and others. |
| | | Begins 1824 sketchbook. First visits to Shoreham. |
| | | Introduced by Linnell to Blake. |
| 1825 | | Paints the Oxford Sepia cycle. |
| 1826 | | Meets Edward Calvert, who joins the Ancients. |
| | | Moves to the village of Shoreham in Kent, together with father, brother William and nurse Mary Ward. |
| 1828 | | His father rents Water House, a substantial property in Shoreham. |
| 1832 | | Palmer buys a house, 4 Grove Street, Lisson Grove, in London, but continues to spend much time in Shoreham over the next few years. |
| 1835 | | Visits the West Country and Wales. Finally leaves Shoreham. |
| 1836 | | Visits North Wales. |
| 1837 | *18 January* | Death of Mary Ward. |
| | *30 September* | Marries Hannah, the eldest child of John Linnell. |
| | *3 October* | Palmer and Hannah leave England for a journey to Rome, in the company of Richmond and his wife. |
| | *14 November* | They arrive in Rome. |
| 1838 | | Visit Naples. |
| 1839 | *27 November* | Arrive back in England. Over the next few years Palmer makes frequent visits to Wales, Surrey, Kent and Berkshire. |

| | | |
|---|---|---|
| 1842 | *27 January* | Birth of first son, Thomas More. |
| 1843 | | Elected associate of Society of Painters in Water-Colours (Old Water-Colour Society). From this time works principally in watercolour. |
| 1844 | | Birth of daughter Mary Elizabeth. |
| 1846 | | Illustrates Charles Dickens's *Pictures from Italy*. |
| 1847 | *15 September* | Death of Mary Elizabeth. |
| 1848 | | Moves to 1A Victoria Road, Kensington. |
| | *17 December* | Death of father. |
| 1850 | | Election to the Etching Club. Publication of his first four etchings. |
| 1851 | | Moves to 6 Douro Place, Kensington. |
| 1853 | *25 September* | Birth of second son Alfred Herbert. |
| 1854 | | Elected full member of the Old Water-Colour Society. |
| 1859 | | Thomas More taken seriously ill. |
| 1861 | | Takes family to High Ashes Farm, Leith Hill, Surrey, for Thomas More's health. |
| | *11 July* | Death of Thomas More. |
| 1862 | | Moves to Furze Hill House, Mead Vale, Redhill, where he lives for the remainder of his life. |
| 1864 | | Commissioned by Leonard Rowe Valpy to paint series of pictures illustrating Milton's 'L'Allegro' and 'Il Penseroso'. |
| 1872 | | Completes translation of Virgil's *Eclogues*, which he has been working on for several years. On the advice of the art critic P.G. Hamerton decides to produce series of etched illustrations to this before seeking to publish it. |
| 1879 | | Completes the etchings *The Bellman* and *The Lonely Tower* for the Milton poems. |
| 1881 | *24 May* | Dies, with Richmond at his bedside. |
| 1883 | | Publication of *An English Version of the Eclogues of Virgil*. As well as one etching by Palmer, the book contains four others begun by him and completed by A.H. Palmer and facsimile reproductions of designs by Palmer for nine other illustrations. |

# The Catalogue

Palmer's career falls into two parts, here entitled 'The Visionary' (pp. 65–168) and 'The Victorian' (pp. 169–244). In his youth he produced works of startling originality, creating a bold and unprecedented vision of the natural world. In later life he moved away from this style to develop an intricate and highly poetic form of landscape. This book and exhibition aim to show both sides of Palmer's art. Although there are some continuities between the two (particularly in terms of themes), it is felt that each will gain from being viewed as a distinct phenomenon. The first part presents Palmer's earlier achievement, tracing his precocious development, his discovery of the primitive and his masterly progress during the years he spent in the Kent village of Shoreham. In the mid-1830s, at much the same time as he left Shoreham, Palmer's art changed direction. The visionary manner faded and was replaced by a more intricate style, more closely based on naturalistic observation and more elaborate in its design. While never achieving great material success, Palmer gradually won recognition in the Victorian era for his distinguished watercolours and for his steadfast maintenance of an interest in the ideal.

## *Notes on catalogue entries*

Catalogue sections have been written by Elizabeth E. Barker, Colin Harrison and William Vaughan, as shown. Where individual entries are not by the writer of the section this is indicated by initials as follows:

EEB Elizabeth E. Barker

CH Colin Harrison

WV William Vaughan

All works are exhibited at both venues, apart from those with catalogue numbers marked with an asterisk *, indicating works exhibited only at the British Museum, or with a dagger †, indicating works exhibited only at the Metropolitan Museum of Art. Unless otherwise stated, all works are by Samuel Palmer and are executed on paper. Height precedes width in the measurements, which are those of the support (e.g. sheet, canvas or panel), unless otherwise indicated. Citations are abbreviated throughout, and full references are provided in the Bibliography, which also includes material not cited in the texts. Literature and provenance are as given in Lister (see Bibliography) unless otherwise stated; only works published subsequently to, omitted from or substantially different to Lister are supplied in the literature section of each entry.

OPPOSITE
Samuel Palmer,
*The Timber Wain*, *c.*1833–4
(detail, cat. 84).

# Part One: The Visionary

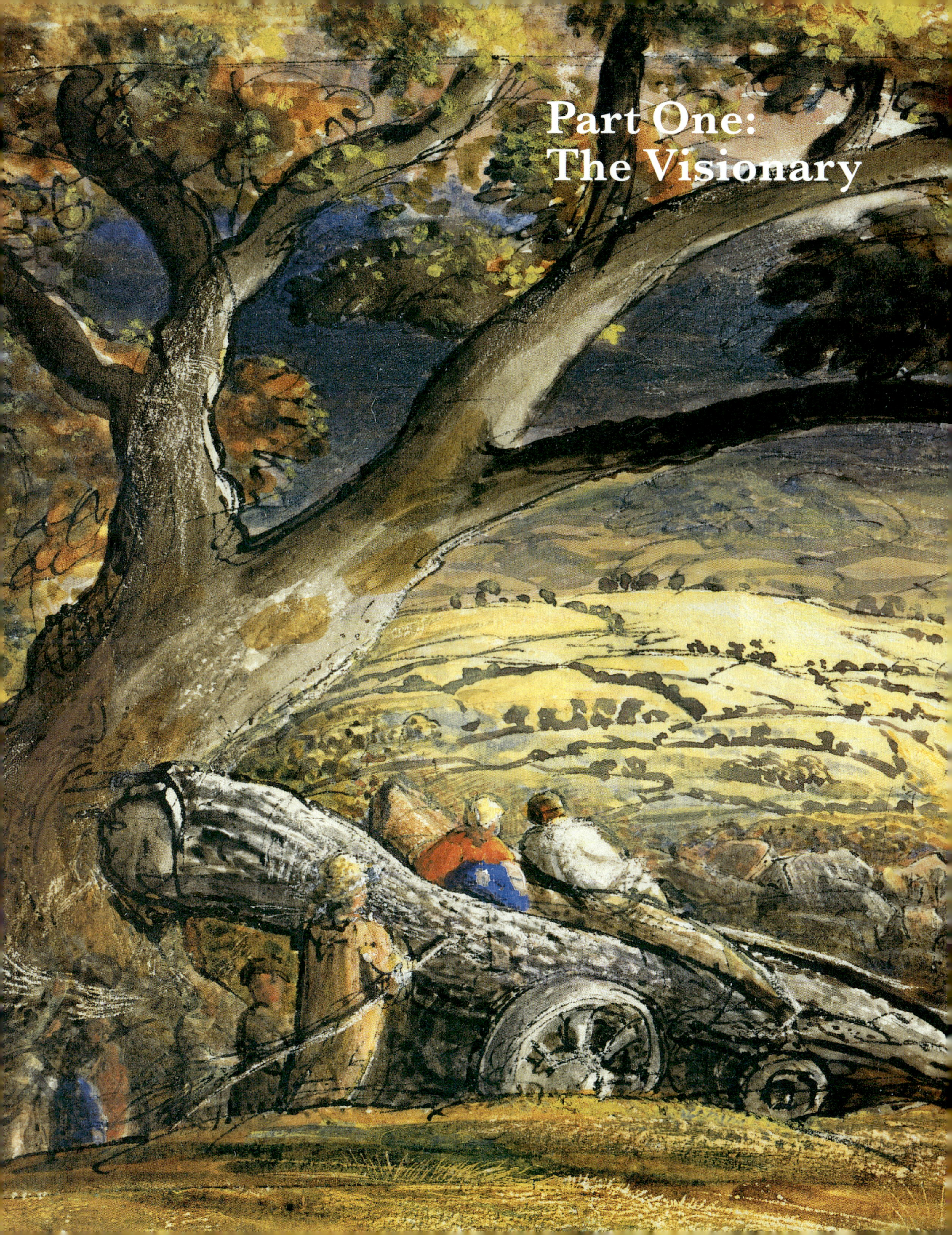

# 1. Early Years (1805–23)

*William Vaughan*

Palmer was born in 1805 into a middle-class family in Surrey Square, Newington, south London. His father, also called Samuel, was a bookseller and stationer in the City. His mother Martha (née Giles) came from a cultivated family, her father being a prosperous banker and an author. The Palmers were to have one other surviving child, William (born 1810), who also had ambitions to become an artist. These were never realized and he later became a warder at the British Museum.

Both parents implanted a love of literature in Palmer and his early ambition was to become a writer. This intention was strengthened by his nurse, Mary Ward, who particularly inspired him with an enthusiasm for John Milton. Palmer's parents, however, appear to have valued his artistic talents above his literary ones. His mother preserved an early drawing done by him at the age of seven, and encouraged him to copy prints of works of art. Already by the age of nine he was producing pictures for family and friends (*Letters*, p. 3). His father, meanwhile, encouraged his love of the spiritual and of natural scenery, taking him for walks around south London (then still largely rural), particularly the area between Greenwich and Dulwich (*Letters*, p. 823).

By 1818, when he was thirteen, Palmer had determined to become an artist. This decision may have been precipitated by two traumatic events that occurred about that time. A delicate child, he had been educated at home until the age of twelve. Then in May 1817, shortly after the family had moved to Houndsditch, he was sent to Merchant Taylors' School there. The experience was an unhappy one, and after six months he returned home. Two months later, while he was staying with his grandfather in Margate, he learned of the death of his mother. He later described how the news had 'pierced him like a sharp sword' (*L&L*, p. 6).

After it was decided that Palmer should become an artist, the painter William Wate was engaged to become his tutor. Wate was a landscape painter of moderate ability who encouraged Palmer to make studies from nature and introduced him to current instruction manuals, notably David Cox's *Treatise on Landscape Painting and Effect in Watercolour* (London, 1813). Under Wate's instruction Palmer rapidly developed a facility for landscape. A rare surviving early sketchbook (cat. 4) of 1819 shows that by the age of fourteen he had achieved a fair level of competence. He met with early success, too, having pictures exhibited at both the British Institution and the Royal Academy in 1819. One of the works exhibited at the British Institution, *Landscape: Composition* (BI no. 169), was sold (*L&L*, pp. 7, 407).

By 1820 Palmer's father had moved his shop and his family to 10 Broad Street, Bloomsbury. It was not a particularly salubrious location, being adjacent to Seven Dials, the notorious centre of the London underworld later described by Dickens in *Bleak House* (1853). However, the location had the advantage of being close to the British Museum where Palmer drew from the antique and also studied old master prints and drawings. It was also near the main artists' quarter in London around Charlotte Street, enabling him to make contact with fellow practitioners. The most important in these early years was John Linnell, who sought him out in 1822, having been impressed by some of his sepia paintings. This fateful meeting, which was to affect the whole of the rest of Palmer's life – he later married Linnell's daughter Hannah – encouraged Palmer to turn away from the naturalistic style evident in his early work to explore means of achieving archaic and 'visionary' effects. Unfortunately, no known works by Palmer survive from the crucial period 1821–3, so it is difficult to explore the stages by which this transformation took place. By mid-1824, however, as his sketchbook of that year shows (cat. 9), he was evolving a radically original, primitivist way of working.

**1**

## *Self-Portrait*, *c.*1824–5

Black and white chalks on buff paper, 29.1 × 22.9 cm (11½ × 9 in)

Lit: Brown 3; Lister 63

Oxford, Ashmolean Museum, 1932.211; purchased (Hope Collection) 1932

This remarkable image is rightly considered to be one of the most evocative and appealing self-portraits of the Romantic era. Its introspective mood has led it to be compared to the self-explorations of certain German Romantic painters, notably Caspar David Friedrich, and also to the later psychologically penetrating self-depictions by Vincent Van Gogh. Yet while it shares the sense of enquiry evident in such works, it is distinguished from these by its more ambiguous approach. It suggests that poignant mixture of adult and child that characterizes adolescence. It also seems to have affinities with the poet Keats's concept of 'negative capability': 'when man is capable of being in uncertainties, mysteries, doubts, without any irritable reaching after fact & reason' (*Keats Letters*, 21 December 1817, p. 43). It is the enticing mixture of certainty and uncer-

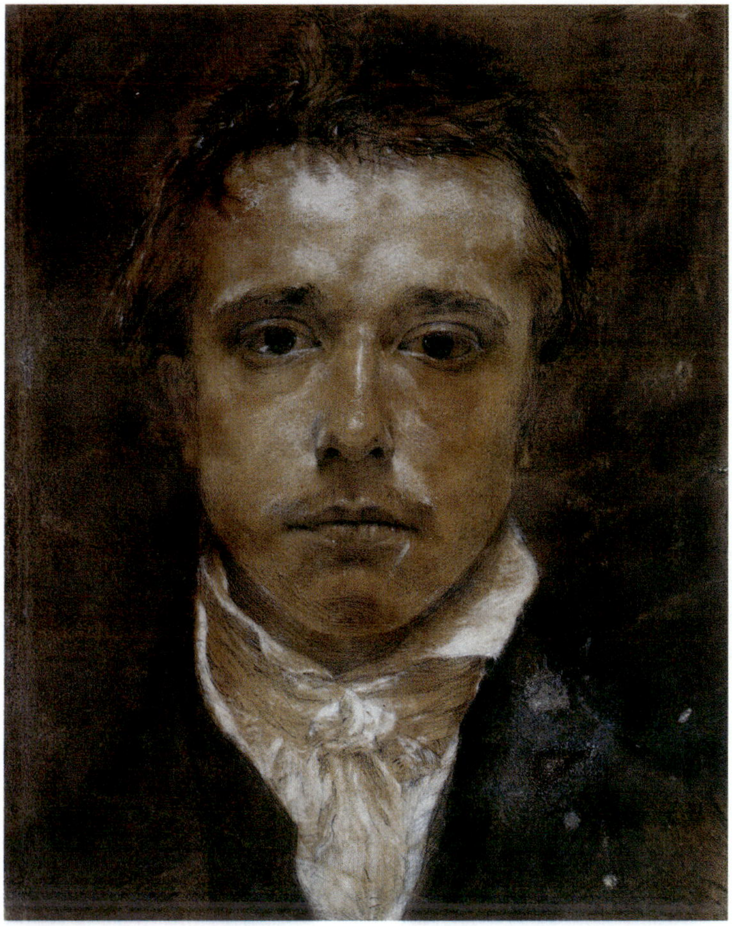

1

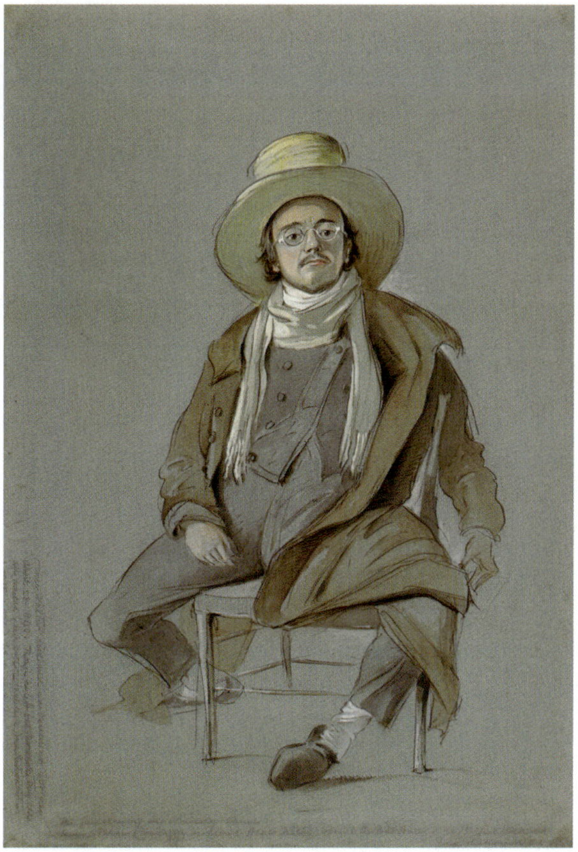

Fig. 24 Henry Walter, *Samuel Palmer*, *c.*1835, watercolour, British Museum.

tainty that make it such an expressive image, and one that also seems redolent of Palmer's own paradoxical character.

In this portrait Palmer studies his own head in close-up. He views himself slightly from below (presumably by tilting the mirror in which he was looking). The authoritative effect of such a pose is counterbalanced by the meditative expression. His eyes, nose and mouth are in sharp focus, which contrasts with the softer surround and produces a feeling of attentiveness and a flicker of determination. But it is perhaps the sense of varying light created by his subtle use of black and white chalk on a brown ground that enhances the work's reflective quality.

Various dates have been suggested for this work, ranging from 1824 to 1830. Grigson chose 1828, on the basis of similarities between it and pictures of Palmer by Richmond around that date (see cat. 54). More recently, however, Brown has observed that Palmer looks significantly younger than he does in the Richmond drawing, and proposed a date of *c.*1824–5, when he would have been nineteen or twenty. This seems highly convincing. Quite apart from the fact that Palmer looks here like a late adolescent, his hairstyle and dress seem to fit this date. In his early years Palmer was something of a dandy, with a fashionable coiffeur and cravat and white duck trousers. At the time of his 'conversion' to primitivism, however, he abandoned such stylishness, growing his hair and wearing a quaint coat made for him by his nurse Mary Ward. He is already shown in this attire in the cartoon that Richmond made of him in September 1825 (cat. 55), so it would seem most likely that this self-portrait dates from before that time.

Another support to the argument for 1824 is the relatively naturalistic style of drawing. The line that he uses to chalk out the contours of his features is more assured and confident than in earlier works and may well show the effects of his studies from the antique at the British Museum. On the other hand, the visionary intensity of the gaze suggests that he has already come into contact with Linnell and possibly Blake. He may already by this time have seen the 'visionary heads' of Blake. Brown suggests that for all these reasons the portrait most probably dates to the winter of 1824–5 and records the artist's moment of spiritual awakening, when the inspiration of Blake, ancient art and the scenery of Shoreham was stimulating a new sense of vision in him.

Palmer may have essayed this study in the hope of developing his skills as a portraitist. The genre was highly profitable and was proving to be a valuable resource for Linnell (as it was later to be for his close friend Richmond). The chalk drawing method used here was a common one for portraits at the time. It is known that Palmer was trying out portraiture in 1824. He exhibited a *Study of a Head* at the Royal Academy that year (RA no. 706), which could even be this work. Furthermore, he reported to Linnell in September 1824 that he had begun at Lullingstone, near Shoreham, 'a head on grey paper life size and tinted, also another sketch of the same person smaller'. As matters turned out, Palmer did not develop a portrait practice. Although there are a few further references to studies of heads made at Shoreham in the late 1820s, none of these survive. The present drawing is the only firmly established portrait drawing by Palmer now known.

The picture was kept by Palmer all his life and inherited by his son A.H. Palmer, who inscribed on the back of the old mount: 'Samuel Palmer by himself. His mouth was difficult to draw, sensitive and full of expression and feeling, not hard and defiant as in H. Walter's caricature in *The Followers of William Blake*. I gave this drawing to Mr. Richmond for his lifetime.' Henry Walter's 'caricature' is now in the British Museum (fig. 24). It was given by Richmond, who pronounced it to be a very good likeness. However, it does show Palmer at a later stage of his career and gives no sense of the inner world that is evoked in the present drawing.

The work is carefully drawn but there is also a sense of untidiness (highly characteristic of the artist), which is evident most strongly in the splashes of white wash that have fallen on his lapel. It is possible that this occurred at a later date, since there are signs that attempts have been made to clean them up.

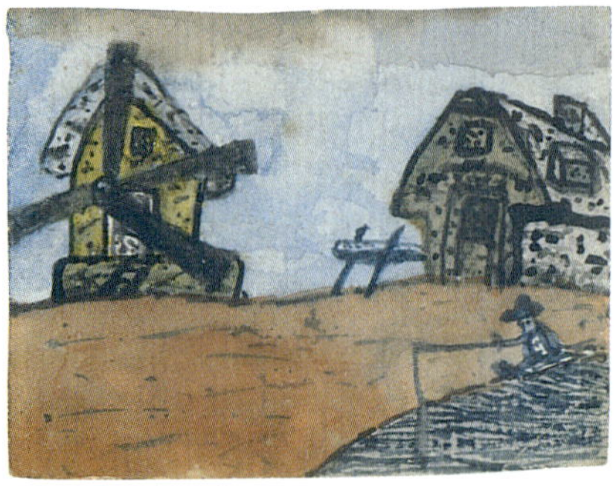

2

**2***

*Windmill and House*, 1812

Ink and watercolour, 4.1 × 5.4 cm (1⅝ × 2¹⁄₁₆ in)

Inscribed by the artist on verso in ink: *dec 19 1812*; in graphite: *The date is my dear Mother's writing. I gave this to dear Herbert Sept. 5 1862*

Lit: V&A 1926, 4; Lister 1

San Marino, The Huntington Library, Art Collections, and Botanical Gardens

As the inscription on the picture suggests, this childhood drawing, painted when the artist was seven, was preserved by his mother and was later passed by Palmer to his son. Its main interest is as a curio, although it does exhibit a sense of placement and organization. It is also a tiny work. This is not particularly strange for a child perhaps, but it is also interestingly predictive of Palmer's later habit of working on a small scale.

**3**

Henry Walter (1799–1849)

*Portrait of Samuel Palmer Aged Fourteen*, 1819

Graphite and grey wash, 29.5 × 22.5 cm (11⅝ × 8⅞ in)

Signed and dated: *July 20 1819*

Inscribed below in pencil (unknown hand): *Portrait of Samuel Palmer by Henry Walter Esq July 1819*

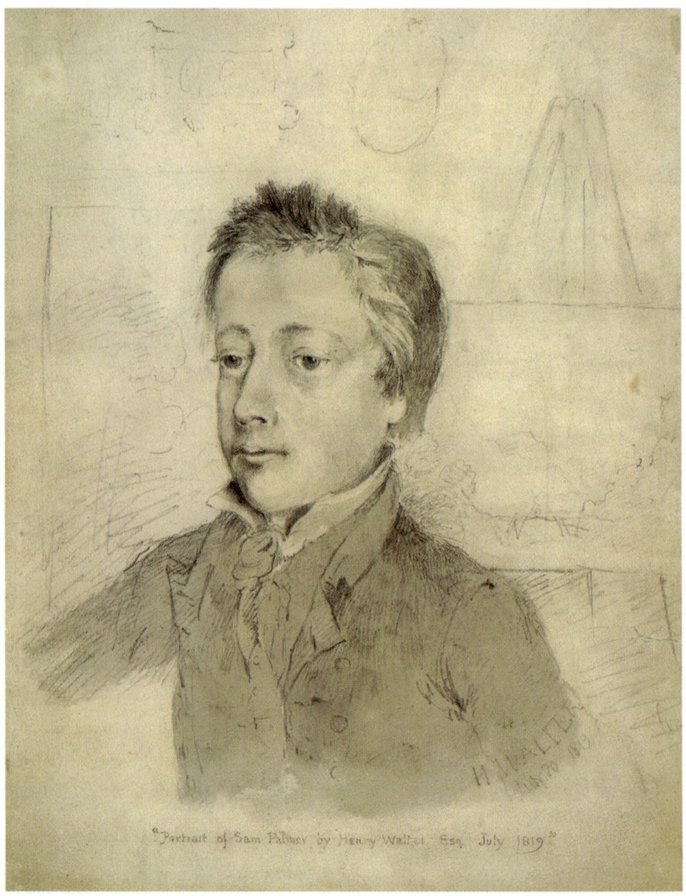


3

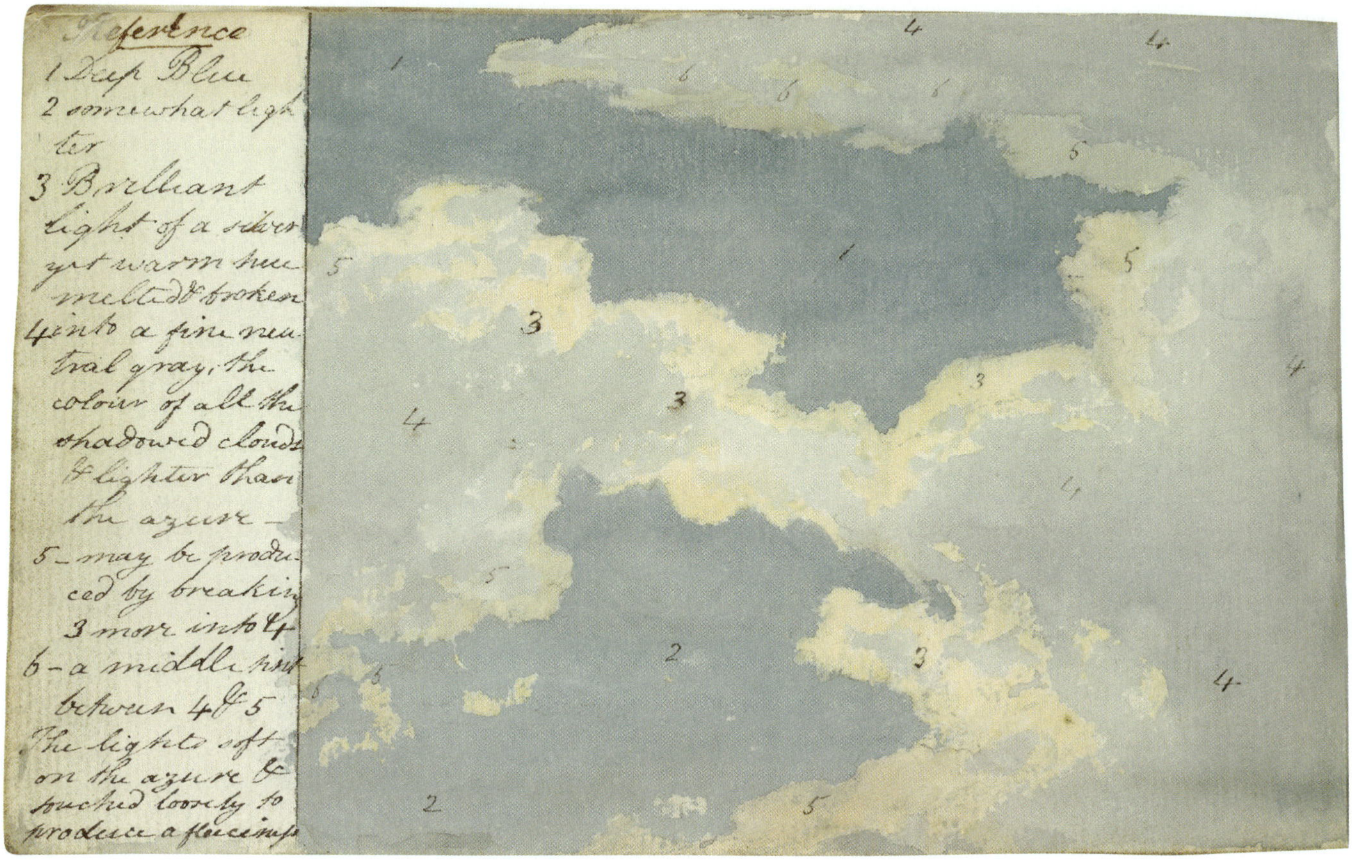


4a

Lit: Fitzwilliam 1984, 138; Brown 3
London, British Museum, 1936-4-9-56; H.L. Florence Fund

Henry Walter was a portrait and animal painter who became acquainted with Palmer at an early age and was later a minor member of the Ancients (see p. 17). This portrait was taken in the year following Palmer's decision to study to become an artist. Although still hardly more than a child, Palmer is shown with a serious and determined demeanour. Interestingly, he seems more assured here than in his own questioning self-portrait of some four to five years later (cat. 1). Perhaps this is because he was enjoying his first flush of professional success, having had three works accepted for exhibition at the Royal Academy and having sold a picture exhibited earlier in the year at the British Institution.

However, this sense of assurance may also have as much to do with the artist as with the sitter. As a professional portraitist, Walter tended to represent his sitters in a positive light, sometimes even with a degree of bravado, as is clear in the flamboyant portrait drawing he made of Palmer in *c.*1835 (fig. 24, p. 67). This is the one that A.H. Palmer dismissed as a 'caricature' (see cat. 1), though Richmond, who presented it to the British Museum, wrote a note on it vouching for its accuracy.

## 4

## Sketchbook (29 leaves), begun February 1819

Graphite, ink and watercolour; cover size: 11.7 × 19.4 cm (4⅝ × 7⅝ in)

Lit: Lister 12

London, British Museum, 1966.2.12.11

This volume, which once belonged to Palmer's brother William and was acquired by the British Museum from a member of the Palmer family, is one of two surviving sketchbooks from the artist's early years, the other being cat. 9. It was begun in the year that Palmer first had a work exhibited – at the British Gallery in February 1819 – and was used for several months, the last date recorded being 11 July 1819 (leaf 4 verso). The drawings and watercolours in it show him developing naturalistic and topographical skills in line with the instruction he had been receiving from William Wate.

The sketchbook contains views from a wide variety of locations both around London, particularly the southern regions between Greenwich and Battersea (his favourite haunts), and further afield, notably Margate (where his grandfather William Giles lived), Thanet and places in Buckinghamshire and Bedfordshire.

In contrast to Palmer's surviving sketchbook from 1824, this volume is almost entirely devoted to observed scenery. It does, however, share one

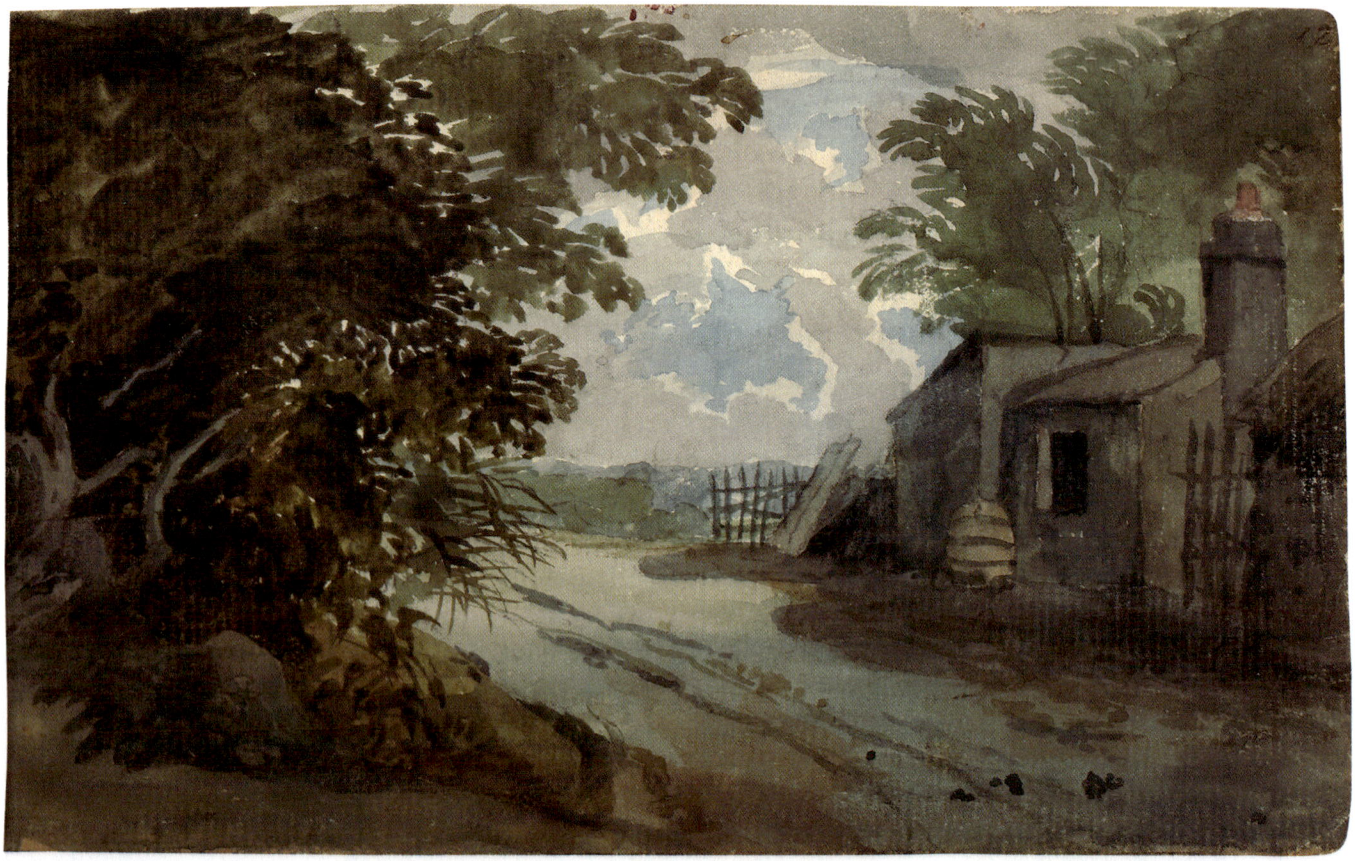

4b

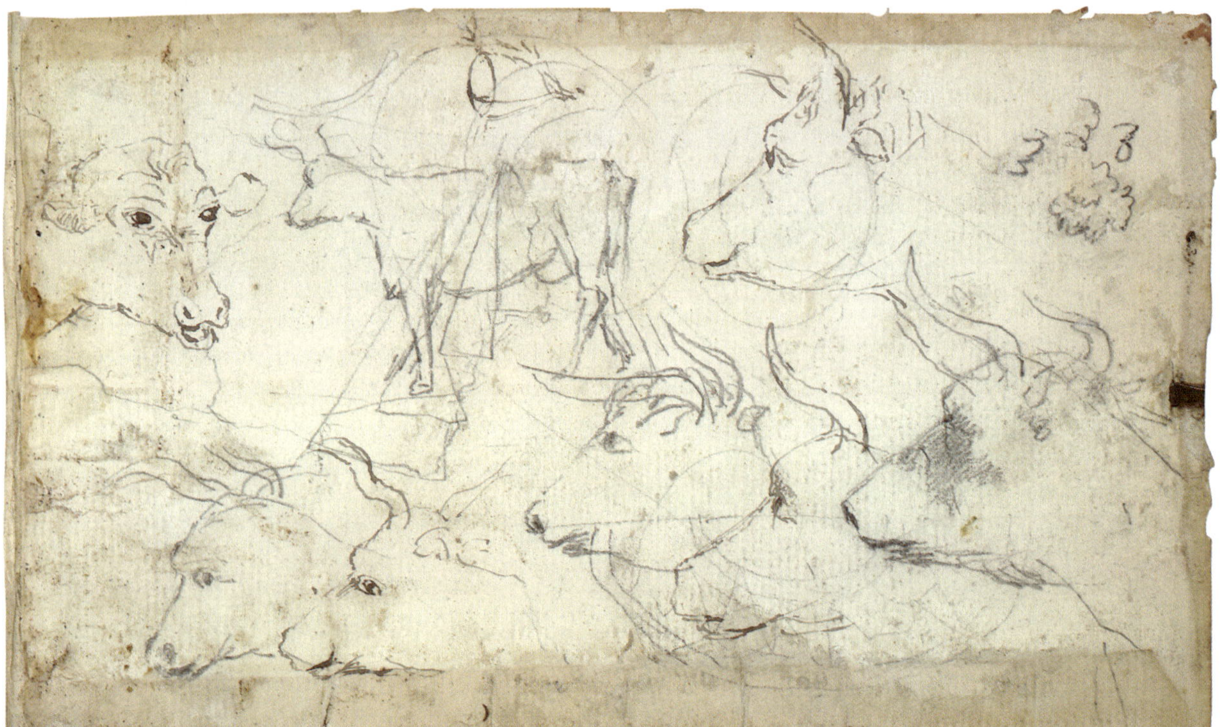

4c

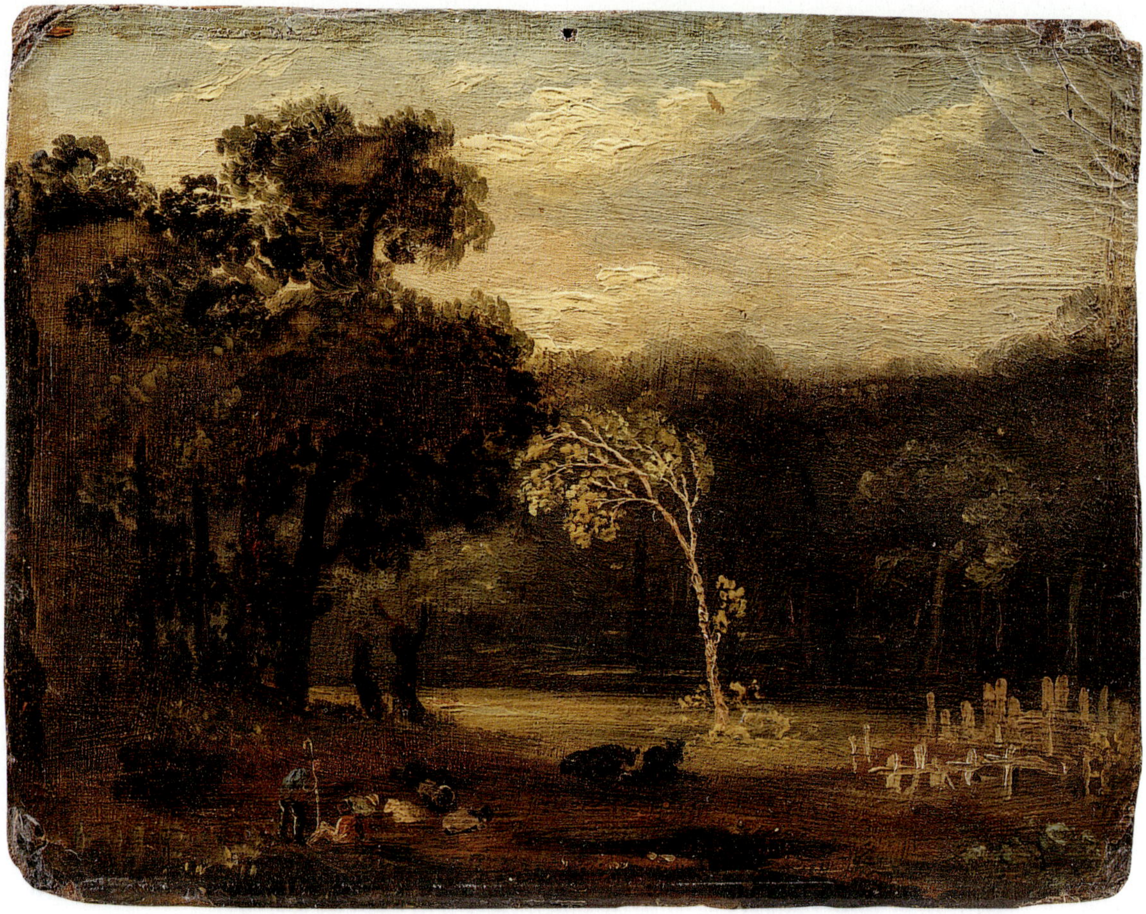

5

feature with the later sketchbook, namely the habit of making copious verbal notes to accompany his studies. Sometimes these supplement his sense of the inadequacy of his drawing skills as in leaf 4 verso, where he writes: 'This study though the sketch is uninteresting was very / good in nature – the left hand hedge was soft at the / edges & light & playful ...' He also wrote copious notes on colour effects.

## 4a

Leaf 2 verso: *Cloud Study*

Palmer was very much of his time in making detailed cloud studies. This study is more conventional that the experimental ones that Constable was to make soon afterwards. It fits more in the tradition of cloud compositions created by the eighteenth-century landscapist Alexander Cozens, whose work was much studied by artists, including Constable. Palmer's study is remarkable for the careful numbering and key given on the side, which show that he was trying to record the precise light effects and textures of sky and clouds.

## 4b

Leaf 4 recto: *Landscape*

This watercolour study of a country lane with cottages and trees is similar to studies of rural scenery that formed the basis of Palmer's first exhibited works. Like many small sepia compositions of the period, it seems to show the influence of David Cox's *Treatise on Landscape Painting.*

## 4c

Back cover: *Cow Heads*

These rapid studies of cows' heads give some hint of the expressive line that was later to play such an important part in Palmer's visionary work. In line with his predominantly pastoral subject matter, however, his most habitual animals in his mature work were not cows but sheep.

## 5

*Sketch from Nature in Syon Park*, 1819

Oil on linen laid onto millboard, 19.4 × 24.1 cm (7⅝ × 9½ in)

Inscribed on verso of original mount in black ink: *sketch from Nature – in Sion Park / the seat of his Grace the Duke of / Northumberland / S. Palmer Febr 6th 1819*

Lit: Lister 14

New Haven, Yale Center for British Art, Paul Mellon Collection, B1981.25.497

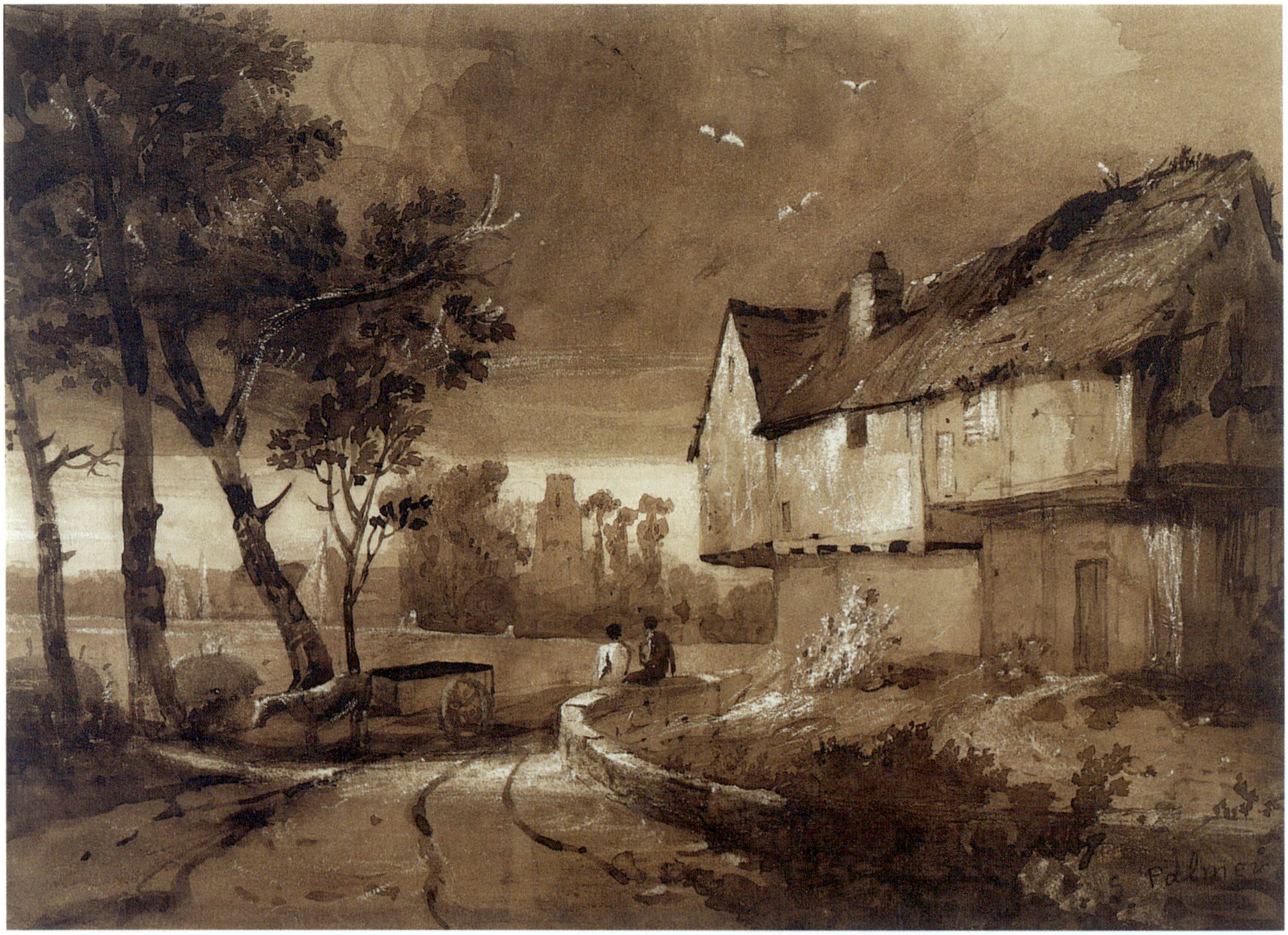

6

This is the earliest surviving example of the use of oil by Palmer. Oil sketching from nature had become a familiar method in Britain in the first decades of the nineteenth century and was being practised most extensively at this time by Constable. One of the earliest pioneers of direct landscape study was John Linnell (see cat. 21). At this stage, however, Palmer had not met Linnell and would probably not have been aware of such work.

Lister relates the handling of trees and foreground in this work to examples in David Cox's *Treatise*, particularly *Transient Effect – View in Battersea Marsh* (Aquatint 9, lower subject). A study of Syon house occurs in the sketchbook of 1819 (leaf 13 verso).

## 6*

### *Evening*, 1821

Brown ink and brown wash, 19 × 26.7 cm ($7\frac{1}{2} \times 10\frac{1}{2}$ in)

Signed at lower right: *S. Palmer*

Lit: Lister 27

London, Victoria and Albert Museum, 1579-1926

Palmer made several studies of buildings in brown wash or sepia at this period. This one, like cat. 7, is highly composed. It was possibly intended as an exhibition piece. An inscription on the back entitles it *Evening* and dates it to 1821. The stress on a time of day suggests Palmer developing skills in the representation of the times and moods of nature – something that can be seen as well in his watercolours of the period. It has been pointed out by Lister that the influence of Cox's *Treatise* is particularly evident in this work. He suggests that the modelling on the house can be related to *Hastings* and *Old Buildings, Lambeth* (Aquatint 4, right and left).

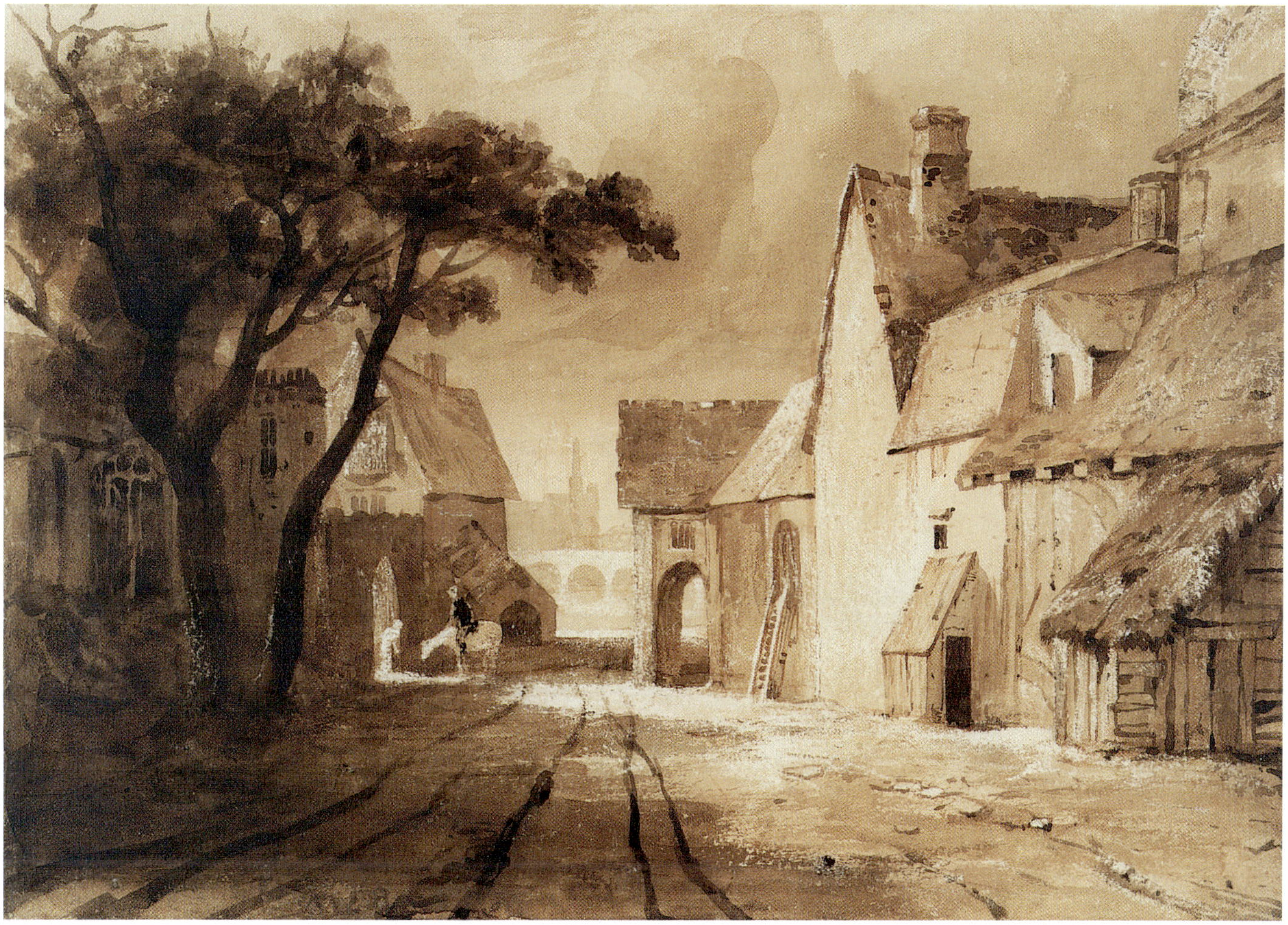

7

## 7*

*Study of Old Buildings*, 1821

Brown ink and brown wash, 19.2 × 26.7 cm (7½ × 10 in)

Signed at lower left, very faintly: *[PAL]MER*

Lit: Lister 28

New Haven, Yale Center for British Art, Paul Mellon Collection, B1975.4.1353

This study is similar in scale and design to *Evening* (cat. 6) and, like it, shows the impact of Cox's *Treatise*. There is a view of a bridge and river beyond, which is possibly the Thames, either at Battersea or Lambeth. He exhibited studies at Battersea at both the Royal Academy (49) and the British Institution (101) in 1821. There also seems to be an attempt at some subject: a man on a horse being admitted through a gate – possibly some ancient image of hospitality.

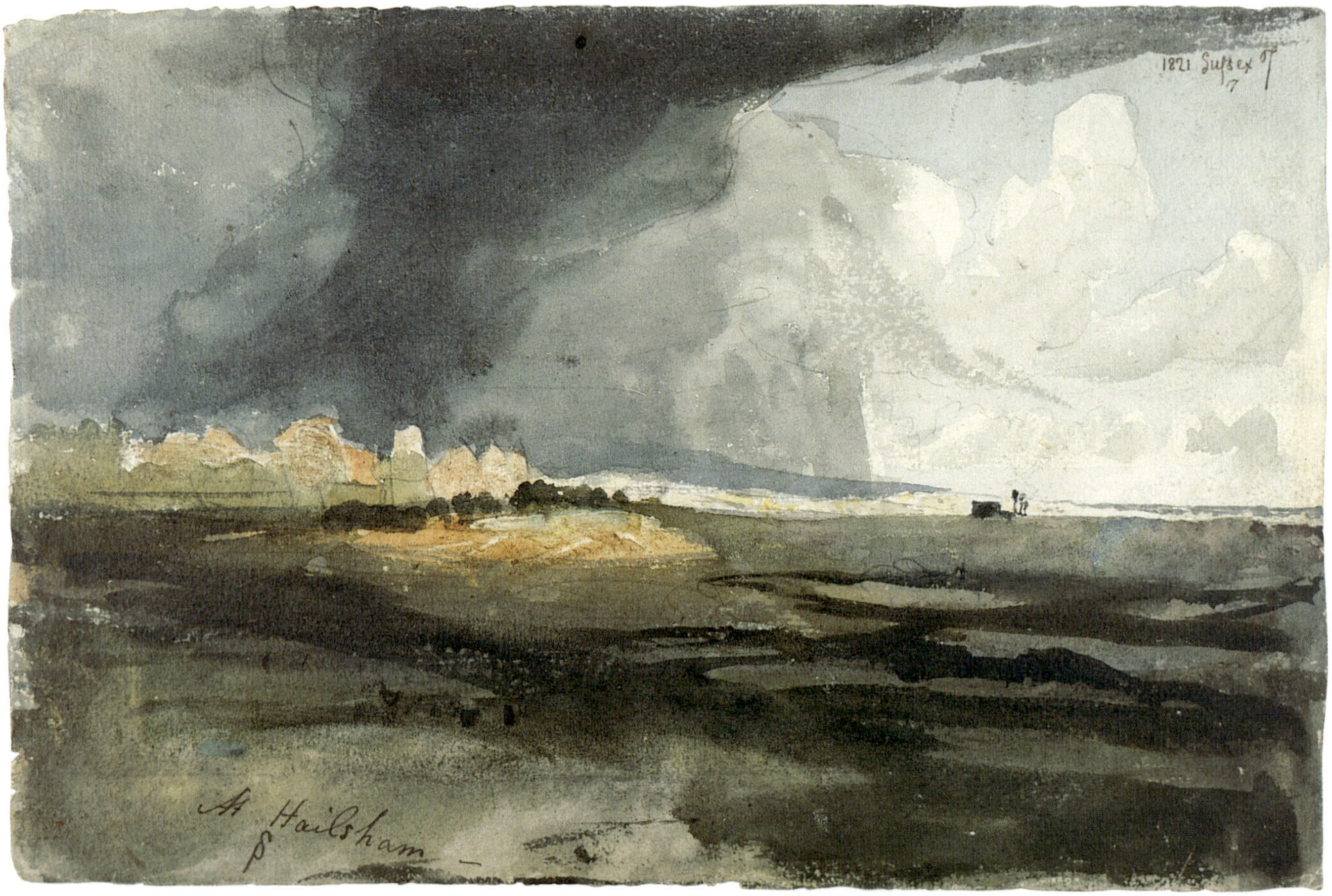


8

## 8

*At Hailsham, Sussex: Storm Approaching*, 1821

Watercolour, wash and gouache, 20.9 × 31.4 cm (8¼ × 12½ in)

Inscribed in the foreground, left: *At Hailsham SP* (monogram); at top right: *1821 Sussex 7/17*

Lit: *L&L*, p. 15; V&A 1926, 49; Lister 30

New Haven, Yale Center for British Art, Paul Mellon Collection, B1981.25.2656

Palmer exhibited a picture entitled *Hailsham, Sussex, Storm Coming on* (present location unknown) at the British Institution in 1822 (BI no. 106). It is possible that this sketch is a study for that work, as the inscription identifies it as Hailsham and it clearly shows the effects of a storm. An inscription on the back by A.H. Palmer claims that this work (which was in his possession) was a study for the Hailsham picture. There is a more finished version of the same subject in a private collection (Lister 31).

This picture shows how skilled the sixteen-year-old Palmer had already become in capturing atmospheric effects. He seems to have been aiming to master more dramatic forms of landscape at this time. Two years earlier, in 1819, he had been impressed by the blustery effects of Turner's *Entrance to the Meuse: Orange Merchant on the Bar, Going to Pieces*, which he saw exhibited at the Royal Academy (136). Later in life some of Palmer's most successful watercolours were stormy scenes – such as his views of Tintagel (cats 121 and 122) – and it is something of a surprise that he did not explore this genre further. The move towards more vigorous work at this point suggests that he was already dissatisfied with the picturesque scenery of Cox that he had been emulating. In *Life and Letters* A.H. Palmer records a criticism of Cox that Palmer made in 1824: 'Cox is pretty, is sweet, but not grand, not profound … Nature has properties which lie still deeper' (*L&L*, p. 15).

# 2. The Primitive Vision (1823–5)

*William Vaughan*

Around 1823, when Palmer was in his late teens, his art took a dramatic change of direction. He moved from being a promising but conventional painter of landscapes and topographical views to become the inventor of a highly original, primitivizing manner. Turning his back on the dominant naturalism of the day, he explored bold simplified shapes and rich effects of texture and design. These communicated an intense vision of nature of great spiritual force and psychological resonance. At the same time he brought his own revisions to the practice of painting, combining wash, watercolour, tempera and oil in an extremely individual manner as well as evolving a unique graphic style.

Palmer's conversion came after a period of growing dissatisfaction with his way of working. The catalyst for change was, by his own account, his meeting with John Linnell in September 1822. 'It pleased God', he later wrote, 'to send Mr. Linnell as a good angel from Heaven to pluck me from the pit of modern art.' (*L&L*, p. 8) Twelve years older than Palmer, Linnell was already a landscapist with an established reputation for sharply observed naturalistic painting. A deeply religious man, he was also a great promoter of the spiritual in art. A few years earlier he had befriended William Blake and was now helping the visionary artist by commissioning works from him. Linnell sought out Palmer because he had seen and admired some of the younger artist's sepias. He may well have thought of him as a prospective pupil. Certainly he gave Palmer advice from the start, encouraging him to extend his art studies by working from the antique and pursuing more intensive nature studies, while at the same time drawing his attention to the qualities of old master prints – telling him, among other things, to 'look at Albert Durer' (*L&L*, p. 15) and the work of Blake. It seems likely that Palmer rapidly outpaced Linnell in his direct emulation of the primitive, as soon Linnell was attempting to curb the younger artist's extremism in this by exhorting him to make detailed nature studies. This change of tack marked the beginning of a critical attitude towards Palmer that increased tragically in the years to come. During the first decade of their acquaintanceship, however, the differences between the two artists led to friendly and stimulating interchanges.

Since there are no known surviving works by Palmer for the years 1822 and 1823, it is hard to chart the stages by which his art changed at this critical moment. It is known from verbal accounts, however, that in 1823 he made his 'first attempt at figure design' in a now destroyed sketchbook. This was a St Christopher, hence signalling that he had by now determined to become a religious artist as part of his conversion to the primitive (*L&L*, p. 14). There are accounts of him, too, studying fifteenth- and sixteenth-century prints, and finally in autumn 1824 Linnell introduced him to William Blake. This proved to be the most influential encounter of his life. He was deeply impressed by Blake's character as an independent spiritual artist who held the world of the imagination to be more important than that of observation.

It would seem that Palmer was well prepared for the meeting with Blake. His one surviving sketchbook from the period, started in July 1824 (cat. 9) shows that he had already radically primitivized his manner of working and that he was at least acquainted with Blake's designs for Thornton's *Pastorals of Virgil* (cat. 19). Blake, on his side, seems to have recognized a special gift in Palmer and the two often met during the remaining three years of Blake's life. They would travel together to visit Linnell in Hampstead, where he had rented a farm. When Palmer settled in Shoreham in 1826 (a place he had visited on and off since 1824), Blake came to stay with him on at least one occasion.

Palmer emulated Blake most closely in the period between 1824 and 1826. Although there always remained differences between the two both in their art and in their politico-religious views, Palmer came nearest at this time to putting imagination before observation. This was the one point in his life when he seems to have seriously considered becoming a painter of religious figurative subjects.

While the personal contacts with Linnell and Blake were crucial for stimulating Palmer to develop his primitivizing manner, his transformation was part of a wider cultural movement at the time. It accorded with a widespread and increasing interest in the medieval in the post-Napoleonic period, which was characterized by a dislike for the growing detrimental social effects of industrialism and commercialism. Palmer's own medievalism and ultra-conservatism (so different from the radicalism that Blake and Linnell shared) fitted in with the growing reactionary backlash against the 'Liberal Toryism' of the governments in the later 1820s and early 1830s that gradually introduced social and political reforms, notably the Catholic Emancipation Act of 1829 and, most controversially of all, the Reform Bill of 1832. The taste for 'primitive' art – in reality that of Europe in the fifteenth century – fitted in with this mood by evoking the 'good old days' of a hierarchical, paternalistic society. It is a sign of the widespread nature of this feeling that Palmer was soon able to find other young artists, notably Edward Calvert and George Richmond (see cats 50–61), who shared his enthusiasm. Such conservative revivalism had been spearheaded on the continent in 1808 by the German artists, the Nazarenes. Palmer's decision to form, with his artistic friends, a breakaway group known as the 'Ancients' was almost certainly inspired by the example of the Nazarenes (see p. 17). While the activities of this group were at their height during Palmer's early years at Shoreham (see next section), the group had already come into existence by September 1824 when Palmer made an allusion to them in a letter to Linnell (*Letters*, p. 9).

Palmer encountered examples of 'primitive' art at the house of Charles Aders, a German merchant living in London who – following the lead of art collectors inspired by German Romanticism in his own country – had assembled a notable collection of early Flemish and German art. His knowledge of the prints of that period was based on works that he saw in the British Museum.

In 1826 Palmer's father gave up his bookshop and went to settle in Shoreham, where he was active as a Baptist lay preacher. This move seems to have precipitated Palmer into leaving London for Shoreham, which became his main area of activity for the next seven years.

## 9

## Sketchbook, 1824

Brown ink, graphite and watercolour, *c*.11.6 × 18.9 cm (4⁹⁄₁₆ × 7⁷⁄₁₆ in)

Lit: Butlin 1962; Lister 43

London, British Museum, 1964-11-4-1; single leaves in Victoria and Albert Museum (unless indicated otherwise, all illustrated leaves are from the British Museum)

The pages featured here are from an oblong Whatman notebook, bound in sheepskin and with a metal clasp originally containing ninety-two leaves. This sketchbook is the more remarkable of the two that survive from Palmer's early years. It records a combination of studies, compositions and writings from one of his most creative periods. It contains the first surviving record of his great 'visionary' years and includes some of the most original and striking drawings he ever made, as well as providing a unique insight into a mind in ferment.

Although Palmer had not met Blake at the time he began this sketchbook, he would already have known his work through Linnell. There seem to be echoes of Blake's wood engravings to *The Pastorals of Virgil* in some of the compositions and in the use of rich textural effects (see cat. 19). However, there is an equally strong impact from the graphic techniques of the sixteenth-century engravings that Linnell had exhorted him to study. Yet while 'Gothic' in overall appearance, these designs are very much his own and represent an extraordinary amalgam of observation and invention. All forms of preparatory design can be found here, from minute compositional sketches (see cat. 9b) to detailed studies of plants, animals and medieval buildings (see cat. 9d, i, o). As well as providing us with a vivid sense of how Palmer's landscape art was developing, it shows how he was also aiming to produce figurative (largely religious) designs. There is a particularly Blakean image of God (see cat. 9l), and there are some startling designs for the crucifixion, in which the bad thief seems to suggest the Gothic horror of Henry Fuseli, another hero of Palmer's at this time. Although Palmer was far less practised in designing figures than landscapes, he was making great strides in the former. This is the period when he was drawing from the antique in the British Museum.

As elsewhere Palmer frequently uses words to supplement his vision. Sometimes they describe anthropomorphic images of nature, as when he sees trees as men (cat. 9a); sometimes they are observations on art, as when he records a saying from Fuseli's *Lectures on Painting* (Fuseli), which remained a favourite text with him (*Letters*, p. 893). The book also contains many poems, a reminder that at this time Palmer had not altogether abandoned his literary ambitions. These tend to be highly descriptive of natural effects and support the view that the divine can be perceived in all forms of nature. As such, they are very much in harmony with the message conveyed by the images.

The drawings are produced largely in pen, although there are a few compositions in wash and watercolour is sometimes added. While the book is experimental throughout, it is clear that the primitivizing manner used in it is already well established. By all accounts Palmer had begun to work in this style about a year previously. Unfortunately no works from this earlier period appear to have survived.

The sketchbook is a unique record now, but it was not always so. Palmer is known to have kept a whole series of sketchbooks during this period, in which he recorded his thoughts, designs and observations. His son A.H. Palmer talks of 'more than twenty … large, clasped pocket-books' forming 'a kind of skeleton autobiography' (*L&L*, p. 12). Tragically, A.H. Palmer later burnt all but this volume because he felt that they showed 'unmanly' qualities and feared these would harm his father's reputation (*Letters*, p. xiii). Quite why this particular volume escaped the fire is not clear. It may always have been one with special connotations (Palmer had given it to Richmond, who in turn bequeathed it back to A.H. Palmer). However, the quotations that A.H. Palmer published in his 1892 life of his father (*L&L*) suggest that the thoughts at least in the other volumes were every bit as interesting.

A.H. Palmer extracted six leaves from this sketchbook for display in the 1926 exhibition of Palmer's work at the Victoria and Albert Museum (V&A 1926, 50). Two years later he presented two of these, along with three others that had not been displayed, to the museum. Some others were lost. Altogether sixteen of the ninety-two pages appear now to be missing (Butlin 1962, pp. 13, 45). After

A.H. Palmer's death the volume passed through the Palmer family to Miss Joan Ivimy Linnell and was acquired from her by the British Museum in 1964.

## 9a*

### Leaf 3 recto (5): *Tower with Crescent Moon and Profile of Old Man*

Inscribed at left: *These leaves were a gothic arch / done* [sketch of two Gothic cusps] *but sometimes trees are seen as / men I saw one a princess walking stately / with a majestic train. This wall should / be covered with Ivy*; at right: *The lower part of the foregoing continues /* [continued overleaf]

These two images are studies for a composition sketched out in full on the other side of the page (leaf 3 verso [6]). This shows the old man whose head is depicted here seated and reading a book. The image of the moon against the tower is in the background. The whole composition is vertical format with a pointed top. There is a note along the side indicating that it should have a gold frame.

The motif of the Gothic arch formed by leaves is a reminder that in the eighteenth century it was believed that the Gothic arch was first formed by the branches of two trees growing close to each other being tied together. The myth supported the notion that Gothic was a style derived from the forms of nature. Palmer frequently made use of this motif at this period, for example in *A Hilly Scene* (cat. 17). The moon presumably has a symbolic significance, perhaps indicating Christ. On the other hand, Palmer tends to associate the moon with the female (see cat. 9f).

## 9b*

### Leaf 4 recto (7): *Four Designs*

Inscribed in ink in lower right corner beside the lower right design: *Remember the / Dulwich sentiment / at very late twilight / time with the / rising dews (perhaps) / the tops of the hills / (quite clear) like a / delicious dream*

The four designs here, which focus, as the inscription suggests, on the effects of the setting sun with waxing sickle moon, contain elements that were to emerge a year or so later in two of the Oxford series, *Late Twilight* (cat. 13) and *The Skirts of a Wood* (cat. 14). The centralized tree and tranquil sheep in the top left-hand design suggest that he may already have known the first plate of Blake's *Job* (cat. 18) by the time he made these drawings.

The reference to 'Dulwich sentiment' in the inscription is a reminder that the experience of nature that he received viewing the hills around Dulwich was still uppermost in his mind at this time and had not as yet been replaced by the scenery in and around Shoreham. He seems to have begun visiting the Kent village in the summer of 1824 during the period when this sketchbook was being used.

## 9c*

### Leaf 14 recto (27): *Man Walking past Figures by a Tree*

This image of a traveller passing a pastoral scene has affinities with Blake's *Job* designs. The use of stippling and patterning to create textures seems also to reflect the engraving method used by Blake for that work. The subject may have been inspired by some journey into the countryside. On the other hand, the presence of a palm tree and the quasi-archaic costume of the figure with the pipe by the tree make it clear that this is no literal record.

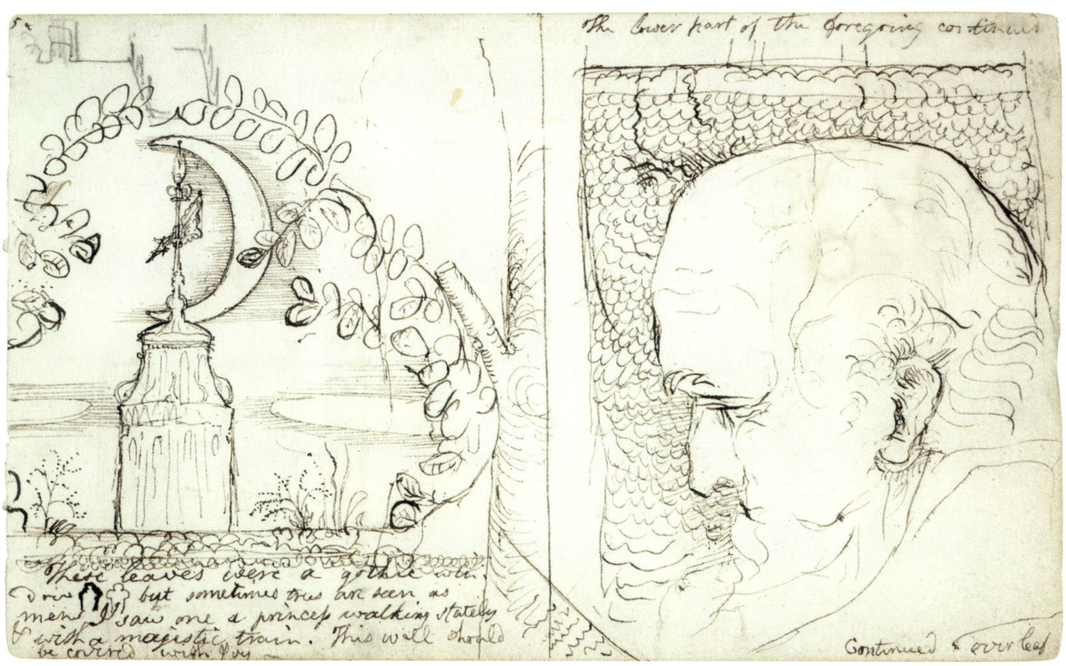

9a

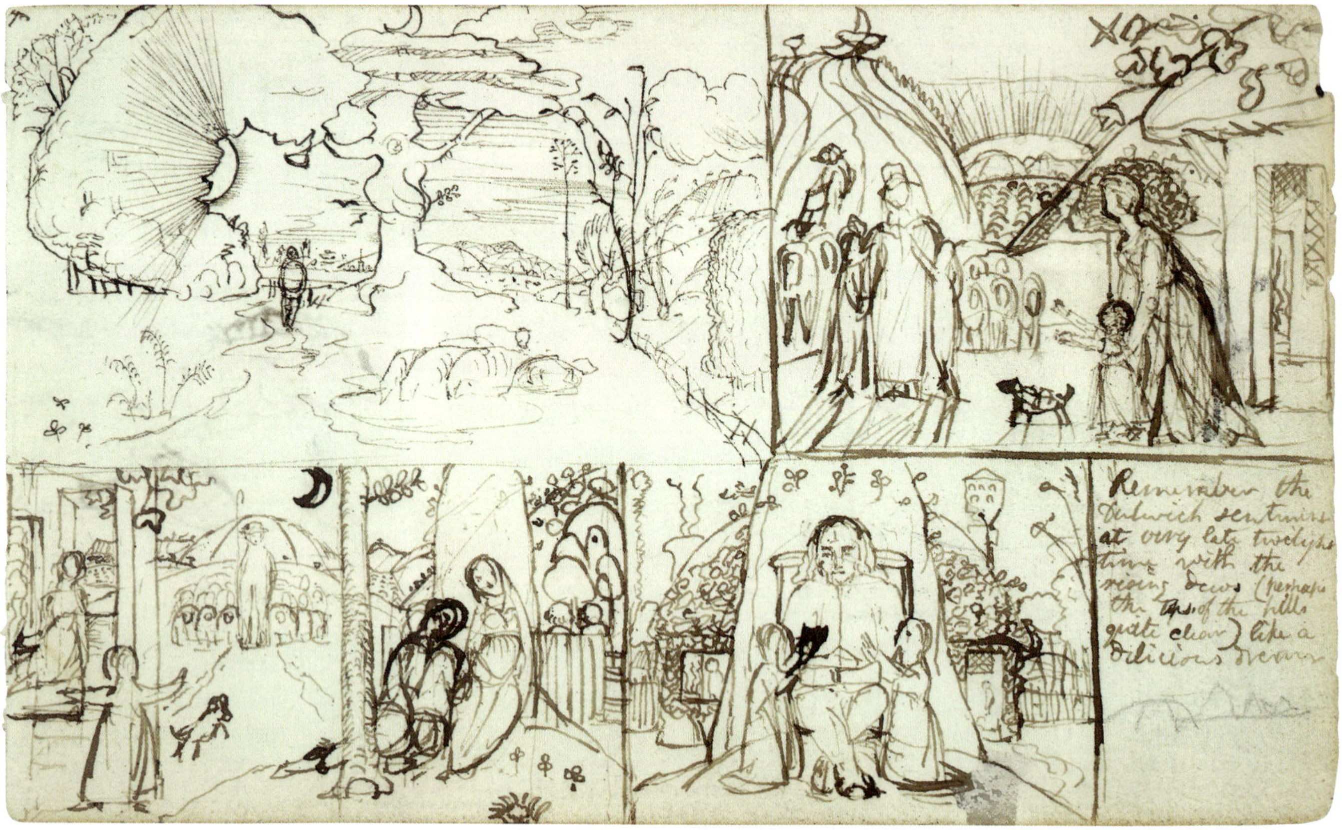
Remember the
Dulwich sentiment
at very late twilight
time with the
rising dews (perhaps
the tops of the hills
quite clear) like a
delicious dream

9b

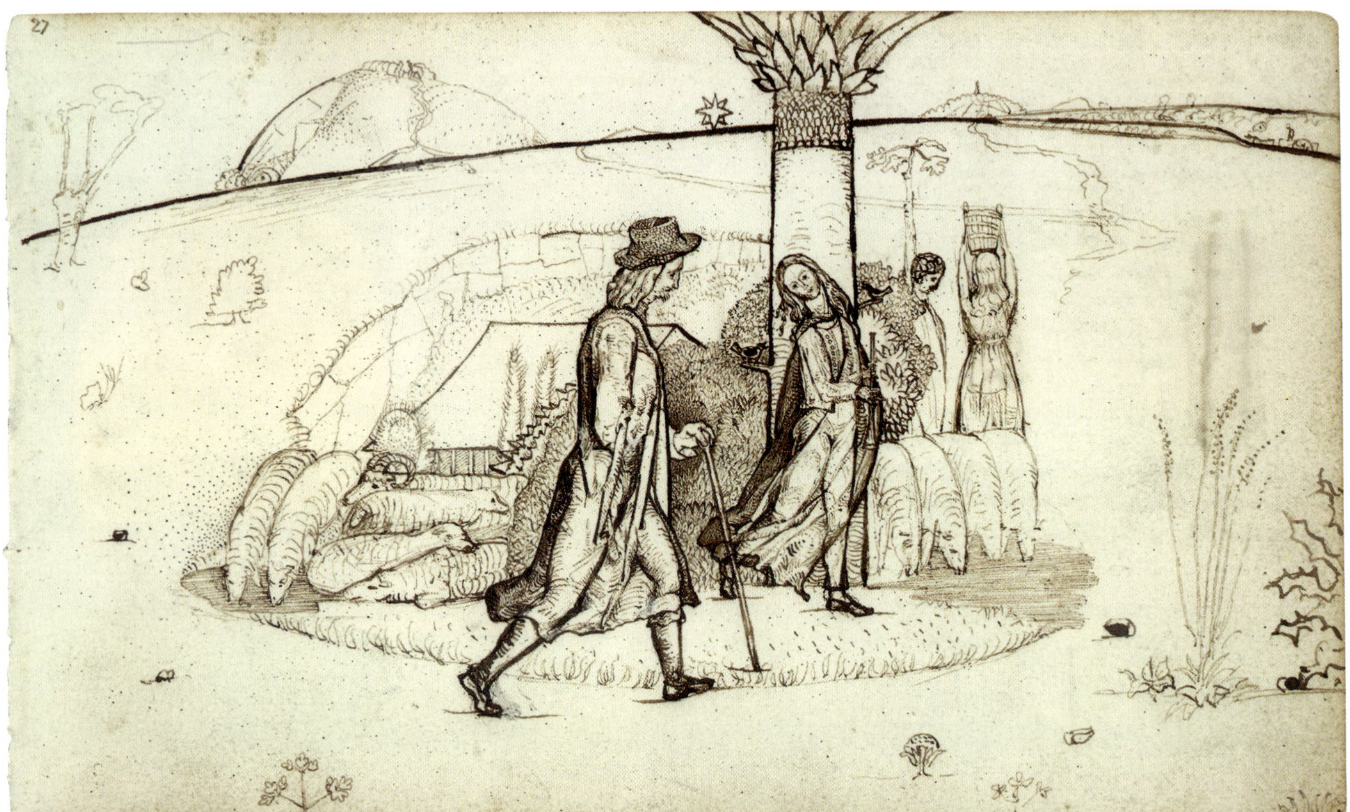

9c

## 9d*

### Leaf 17 verso (34): *Donkey-like Animal*

This splendid frontal view of an animal – reminiscent in technique of drawings of creatures by late Gothic artists such as Pisanello – seems to be more the product of imagination than observation. However, Palmer has emphasized features (such as the lengthy ears and flared nostrils) in a way that gives a strong sense of individuality. Like many of the visionary forms depicted by Blake, this invented being is drawn precisely. It is also viewed close-up – almost to the point of being threatening.

Palmer appears to have relished the emphatic and ungainly, as can be seen, for example, in his love for large-leafed chestnut trees (see cat. 70). This tendency is important for bringing a sense of instinctual earthiness into his visionary compositions.

## 9e

### Leaf 18 recto (35): *Three Animals*

These studies are close to those of the animal on the previous leaf (17 verso) and form part of the same spread of pages with it. While the bottom study might be of the same imaginary or real animal, the two smaller ones above are slightly different, with less exaggerated ears. These strengthen the possibility that Palmer was inspired to make these drawings after observing a donkey or mule.

## 9f

### Leaf 20 recto (39): *Harvest Celebration*

Inscribed top centre: *HARVEST MOON*; bottom left (beneath woman); *The / moon / also to / rule by night / for his mercy / endureth / for ever*; bottom right (beneath man); *Thou / [crown* deleted] */ crownest / the year / with thy / goodness*

Lit: Lister 43(20)

London, Victoria and Albert Museum, 2358-1928

This design for a picture focusing on the harvest moon apparently celebrates

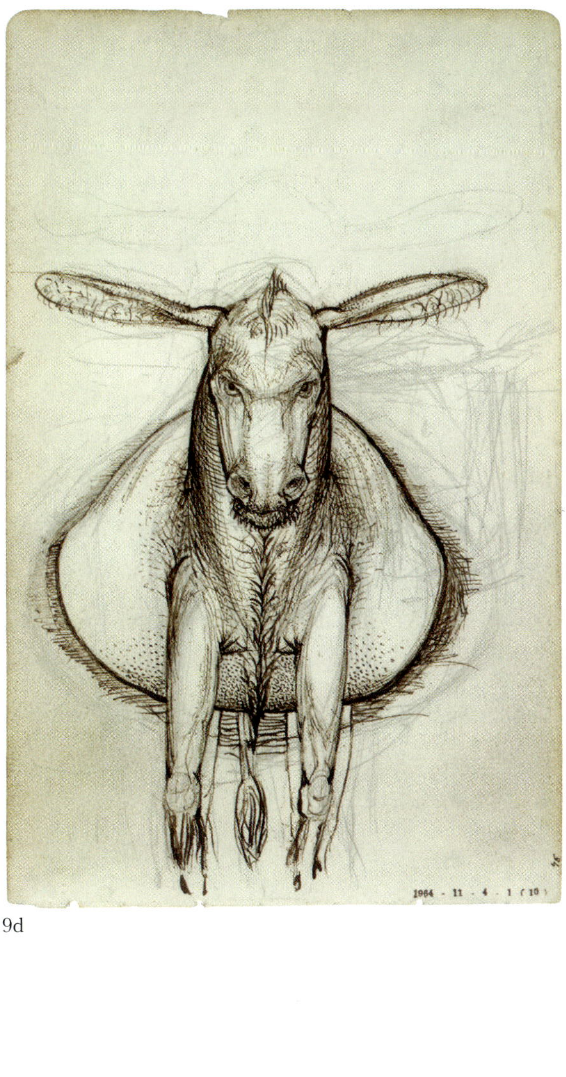

9d

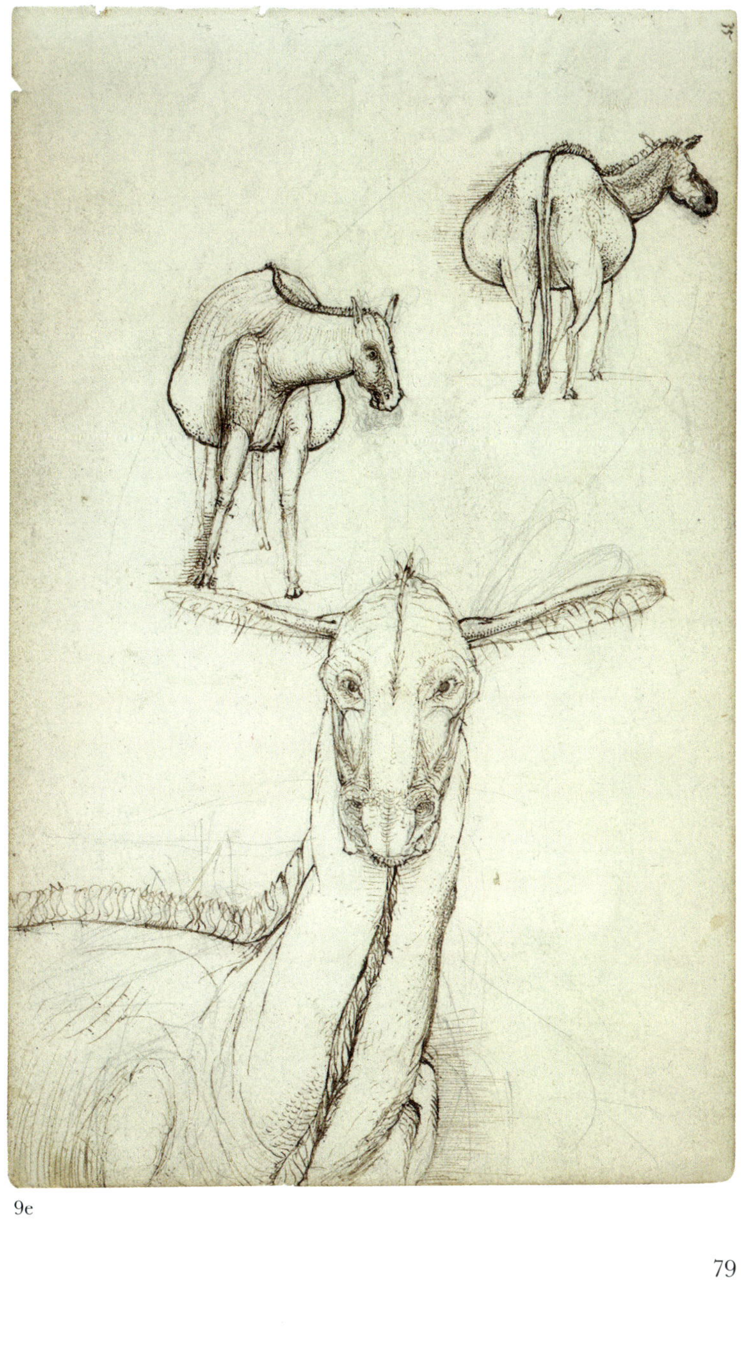

9e

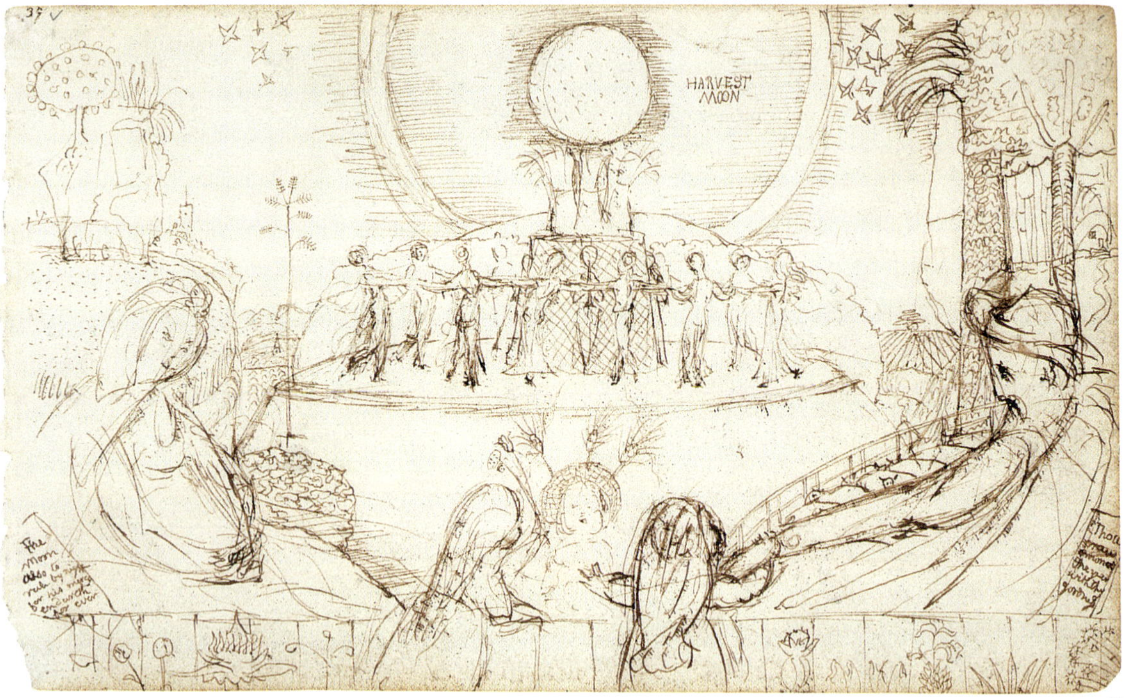


9f

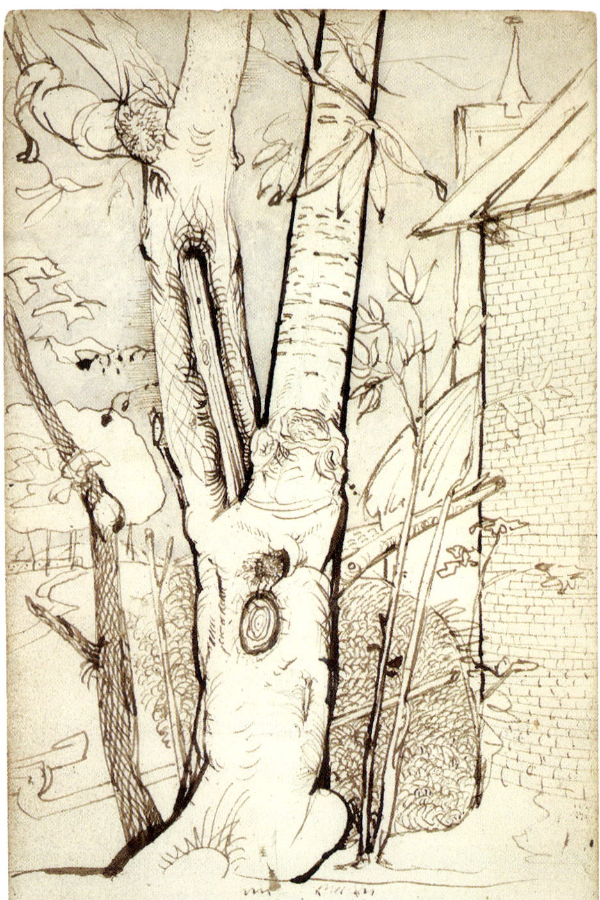

9g

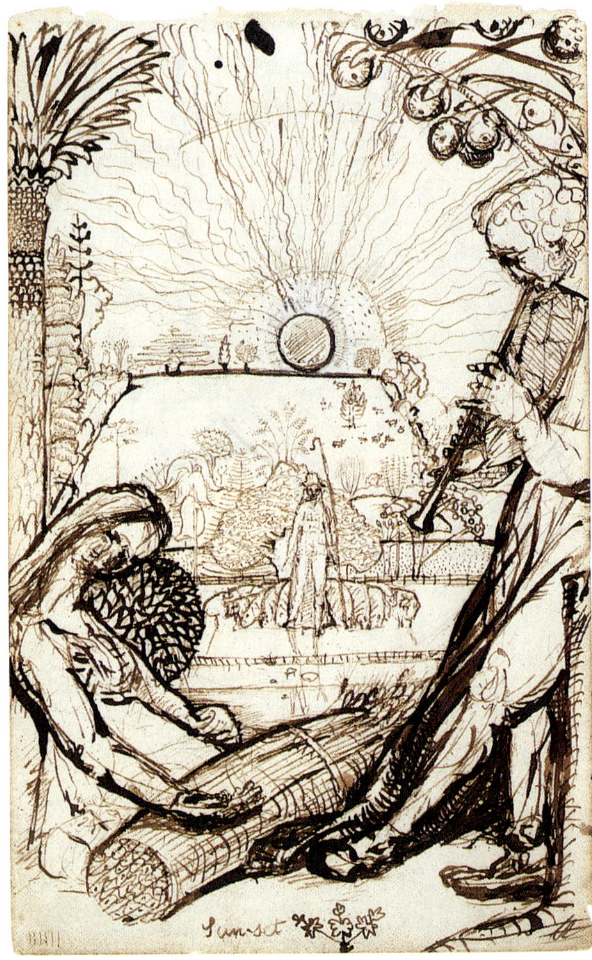


9h

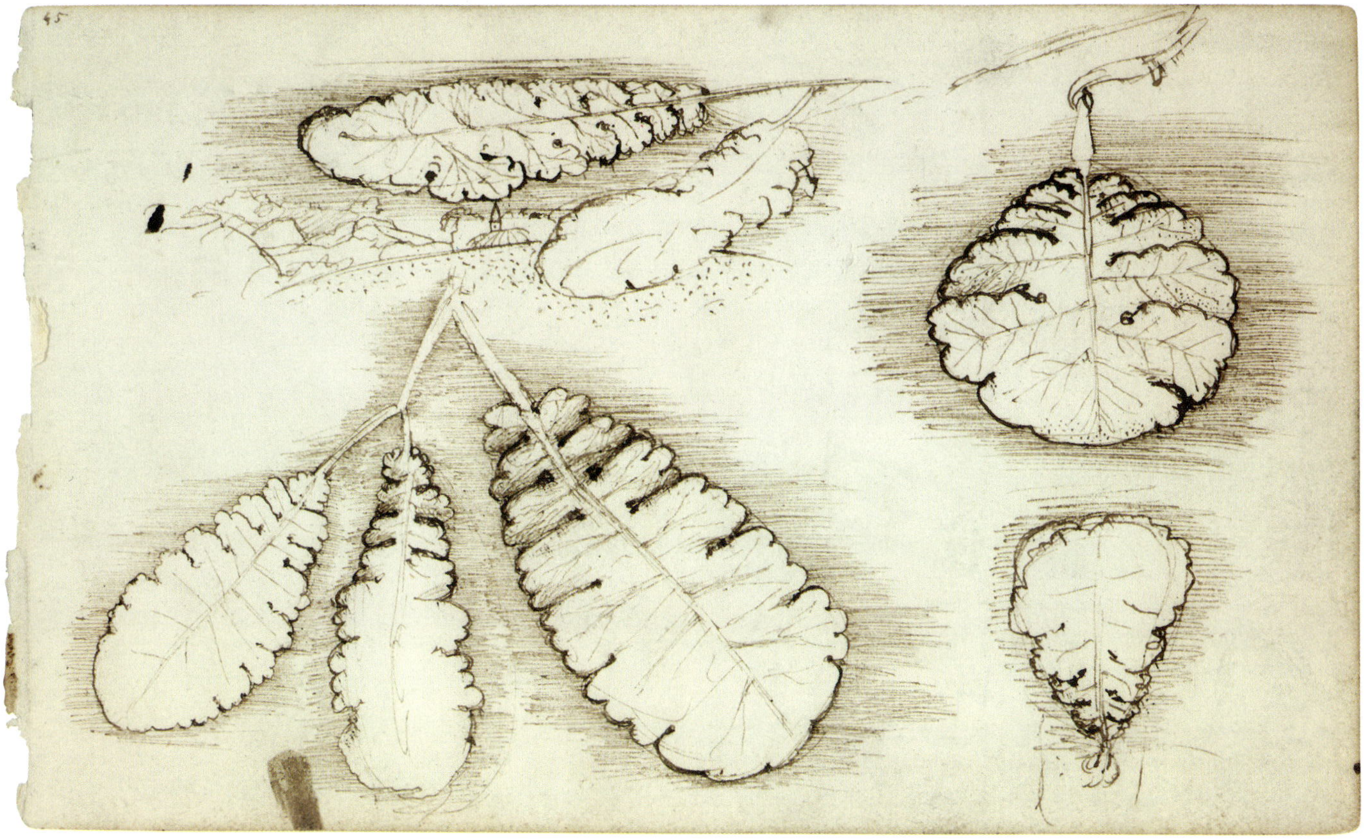

9i

fertility and divine benevolence. In the background a circle of figures dance on a round platform beneath the centrally placed and named harvest moon. In the foreground a man and woman recline facing each other, surrounded by children. The woman rests on an inscription (possibly in a book) adapted from Psalm 136: 9. The man rests on a matching inscription from Psalm 65: 11. This quotation is the same as that used for *The Valley Thick with Corn* (cat. 15), which suggests a connection between the two designs.

## 9g*

### Leaf 21 verso (42): *Forked Tree Trunk*

This richly textured study of a tree trunk prefigures some of the effects later produced in Palmer's drawings of oaks in Lullingstone Park (cats 46, 47). The detail on the trunk and the view past a brick building on the right to a church beyond suggest that this drawing might be based on direct observation.

## 9h

### Leaf 22 recto (43): *Sunset*

Inscribed at bottom of page: *Sunset*
Lit: Lister 43 (22);
London, Victoria and Albert Museum, 3514-1928

The inscription at the bottom of the page suggests that the scene is an evening pastoral idyll. A standing shepherd pipes on the right while a woman seated on the leaf rests the back of her hand on a sheaf of wheat. In the middle ground another shepherd stands with his crook surrounded by his flock, while a flaming sunset fills the horizon. The composition is framed by the branches of a palm and apple tree joined to form a Gothic arch (see cat. 9a). The subject, celebrating religion and fecundity with prominent male and female figures, has affinities with Palmer's composition showing the harvest moon (cat. 9f).

## 9i*

### Leaf 23 recto (45): *Study of Leaves*

This and other studies, including that of a tree trunk (cat. 9g), seem to be developed from observed natural forms. The stippling and textures show the influence of early engraving techniques. Magnified leaves were to be a prominent feature in Palmer's Shoreham designs.

## 9j*

### Leaf 26 verso (52): *Studies of a Kitten*

In all probability this kitten belonged to Palmer. Cats were Palmer's favourite pets and he kept them all his life. His first surviving letter – written to his father at the age of nine when staying at Margate in 1814 – says: 'Be so kind as to send me word how WATCH [his cat] does, give my love to him and tell him that I have written his name on the sands' (*Letters*, p. 4). In later life, when reminiscing about a recently deceased pet tabby, he writes to his friend Frances Redgrave of reading books with 'poor faithful "Tab" upon my knee, gently patting the leaves now and then, that I might take some notice of her' (*Letters*, p. 719). The inscription does not relate to this picture.

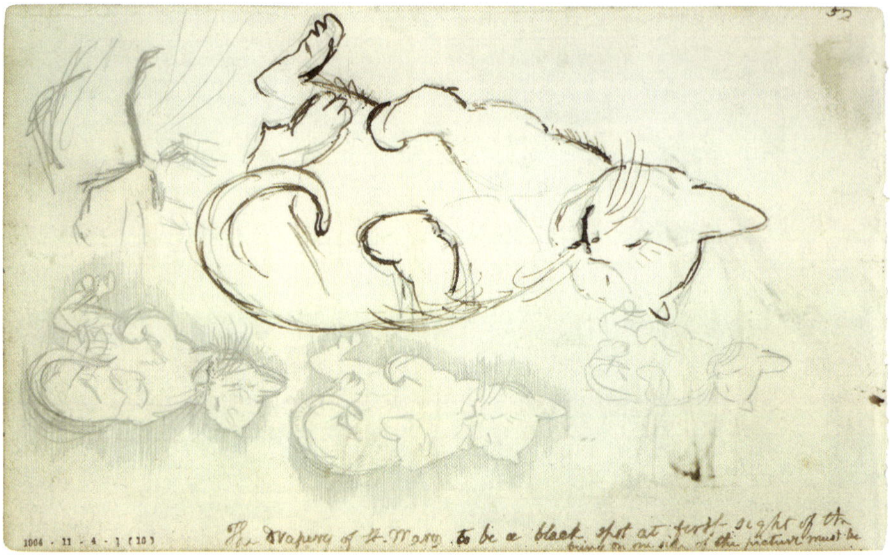

9j

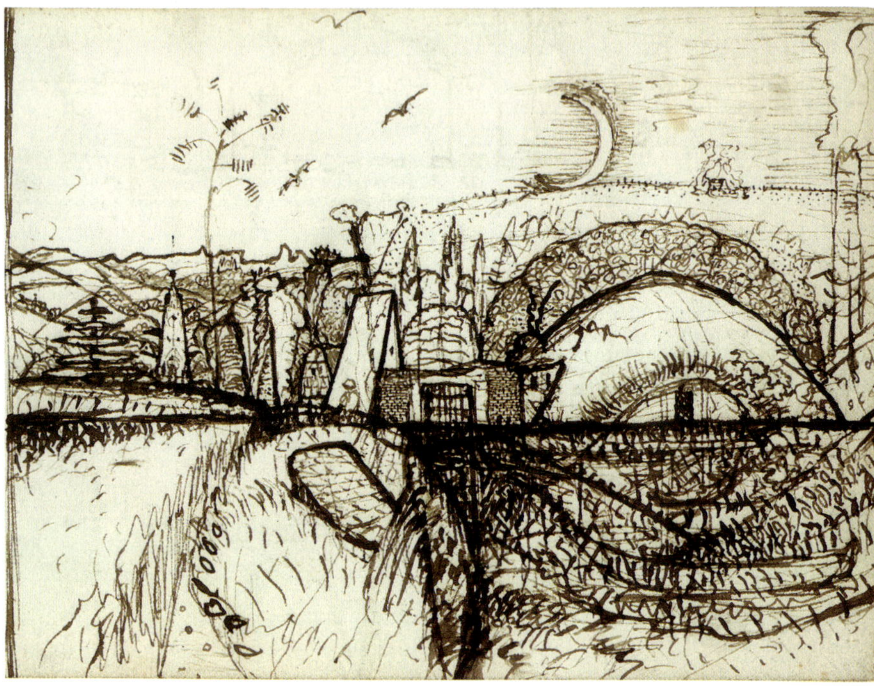

9k

## 9k*

### Leaf 29 recto (57): *Hilly Landscape*

This design relates to several others in the sketchbook that explore the effect of the waxing sickle moon resting on a hill in a landscape of folded hills, crops and dwellings. It is reminiscent of the phrase written in the first page of this sketchbook: 'Sometimes the rising moon / seems to stand tip toe on a / green hill top to see if the / day be going & if the time / of her vice-regency be come' (Lister 43[2]).

## 9l

### Leaf 31 recto (61): *God Creating the Sun and Moon*

This design appears to be part of a series of scenes telling the biblical story of creation, man's fall, and redemption by Christ. On another page in the sketchbook (leaf 29 verso) these scenes are shown as part of an architectural installation, perhaps a reredos in a chancel. Palmer may have been inspired to make these designs by Blake, who had similar dreams of creating great religious cycles in an architectural setting in the manner of Italian medieval and Renaissance artists. There is a Blakean vigour in Palmer's figure of God. Though very different in form, God's outstretched arms simultaneously creating the sun and the moon are reminiscent of Michelangelo's *God Creating the Stars* on the Sistine Ceiling. Palmer admired Michelangelo above all other artists at this time and referred to him as a mentor for his religious figurative compositions in particular.

## 9m*

### Leaf 33 recto (65): *Study of Trees*

Inscribed at lower left: *NB The chestnut ought to have / been in the middle*

The inscription suggests that these studies are based on observed trees. As in the study of the tree trunk (cat. 9g), there is strong emphasis on variety of texturing, though in this case it relates more to exploring the shapes and characters of different types of trees.

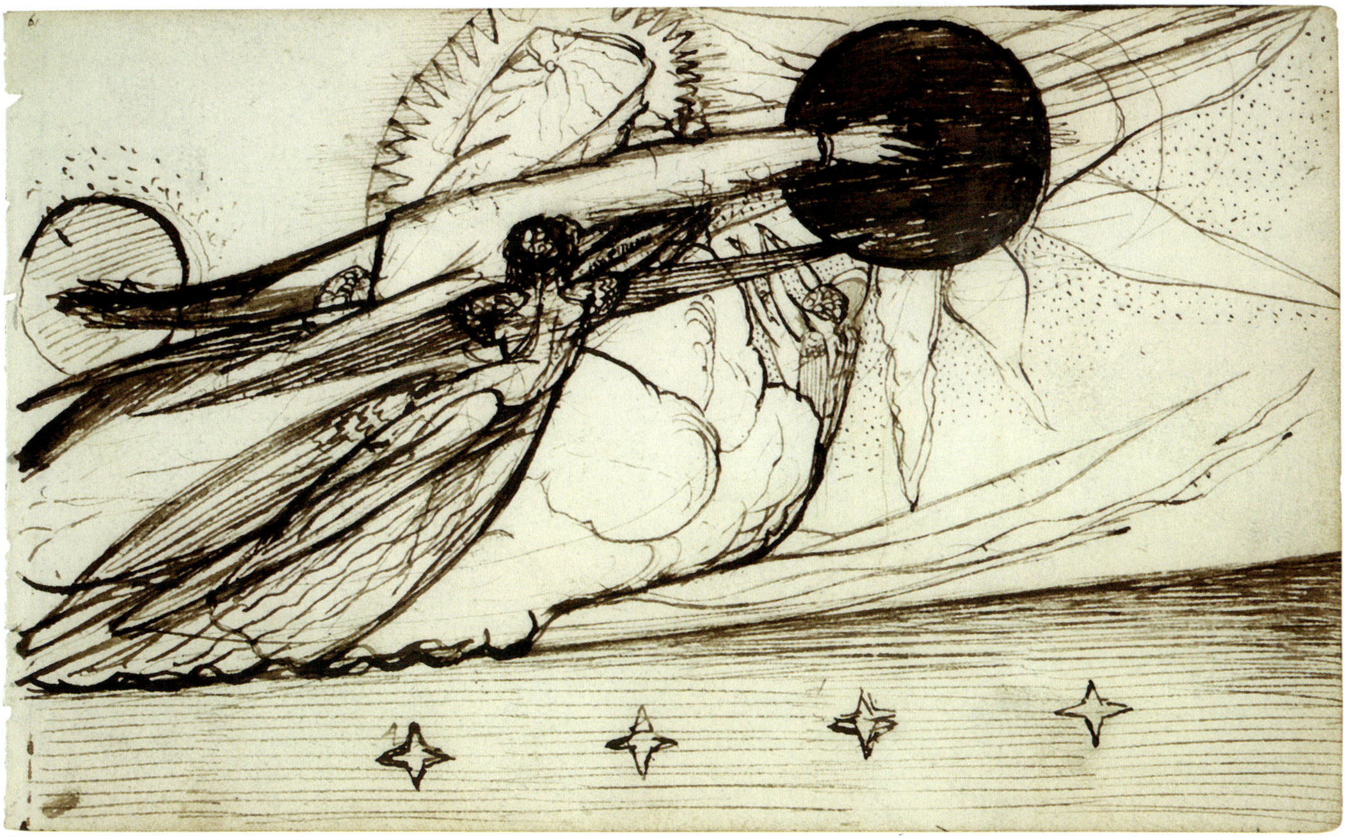

9l

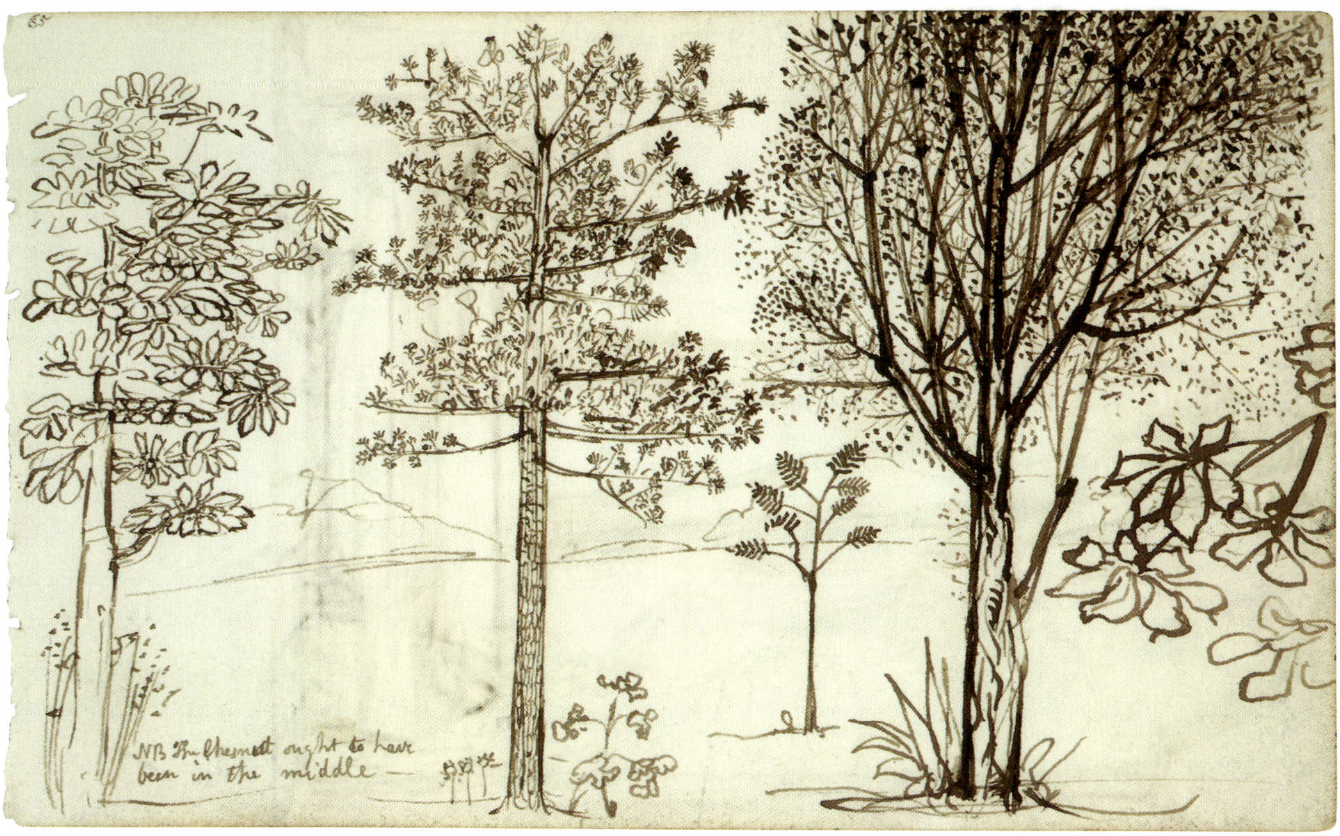


9m

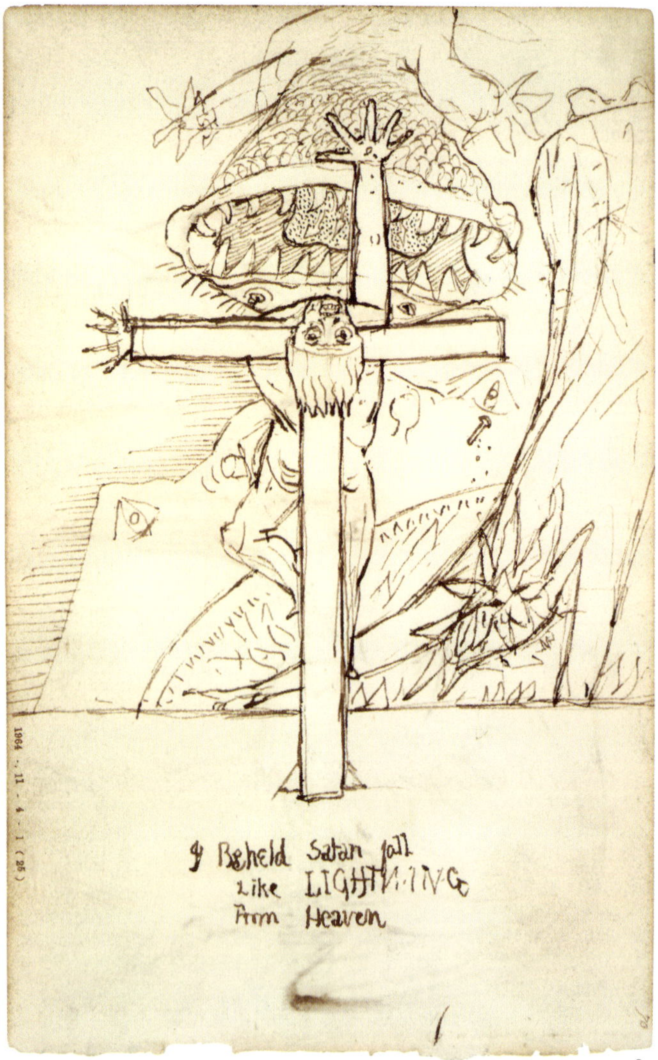


9n

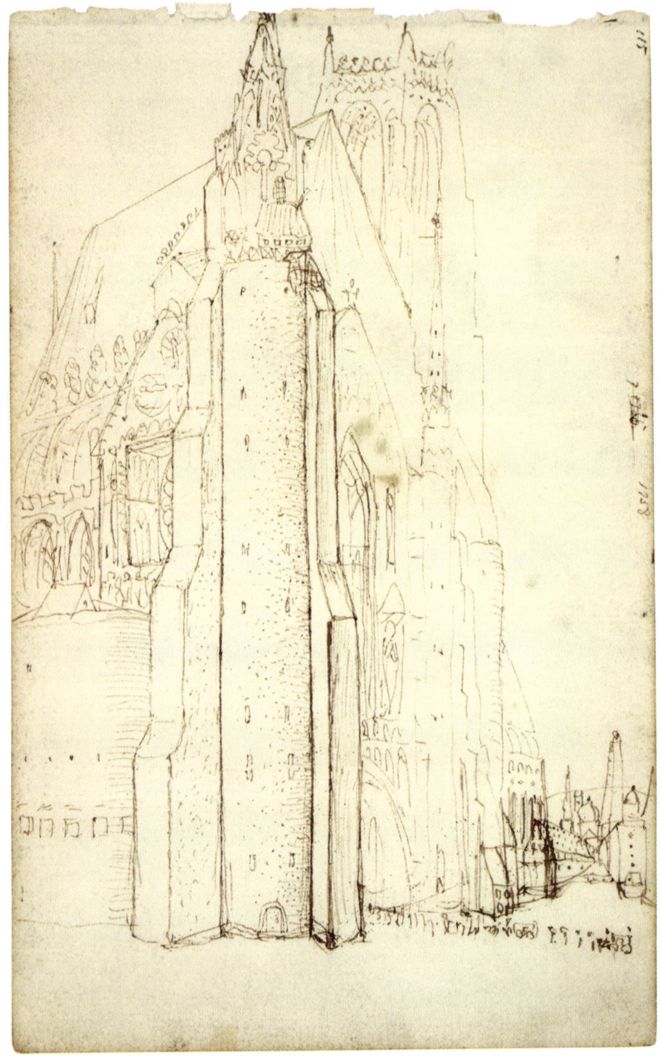

9o

### 9n*

## Leaf 35 verso (71): *The Bad Thief*

Inscribed in ink below image: *I beheld Satan fall / like LIGHTNING / from Heaven*

The quotation is from the Bible, Luke 10: 18. It describes an incident in Christ's ministry and is not connected to the Crucifixion. This is one of the most violent images in Palmer's work. The contorted form of the thief appears to reflect the influence of Henry Fuseli, an artist much admired by Palmer at this time. It is a study for a crucifixion scene in which the bad thief writhes in agony as he is attacked by a monstrous being, presumably a devil dragging him down to hell. This striking design is a reminder that Palmer had a gift for drama and expression that was only manifested in his art on infrequent occasions, as, for example, in some of his later stormy scenes (see cat. 120).

The subject may relate to the biblical cycles that Palmer was planning at this time (see cat. 9b). In one of the notebooks destroyed by A.H. Palmer – that used between November 1823 and July 1824 – he listed 'the repenting thief on the cross' among the 'delicious visions' of scenes from Christ's life that he hoped to turn into pictures (*L&L*, p. 13).

### 9o

## Leaf 58 recto (115): *Cathedral*

The sharp foreshortening in this view – leading the eye from a vast buttress across a Gothic façade to a street beyond – is an exaggerated version of an effect popular among topographers of the period.

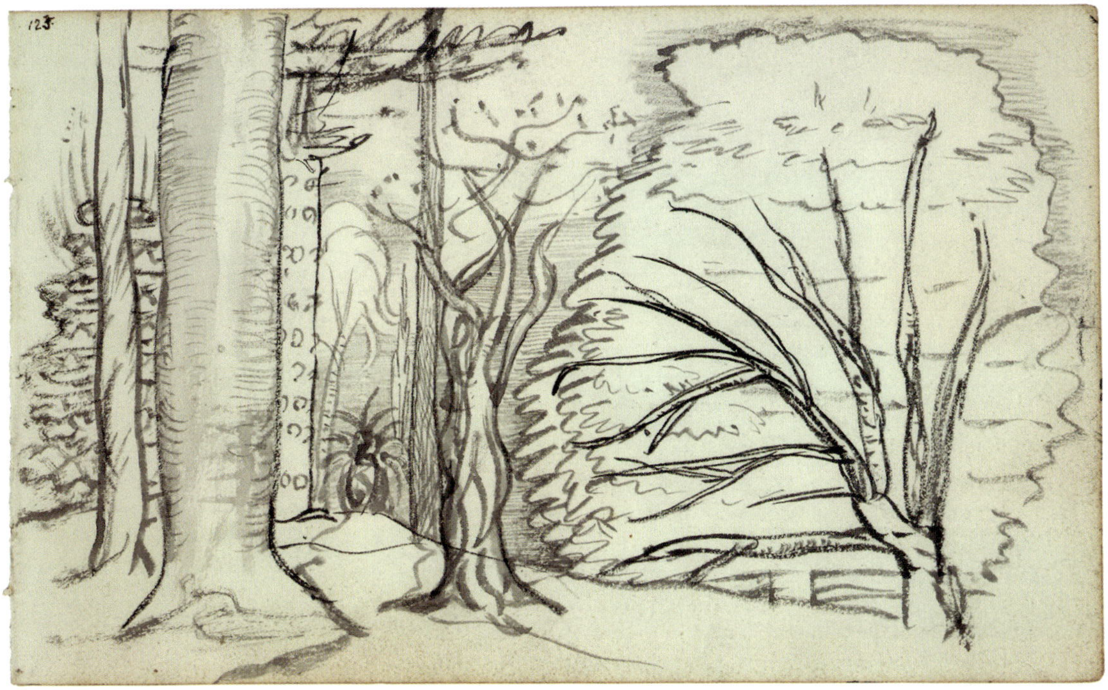

9p

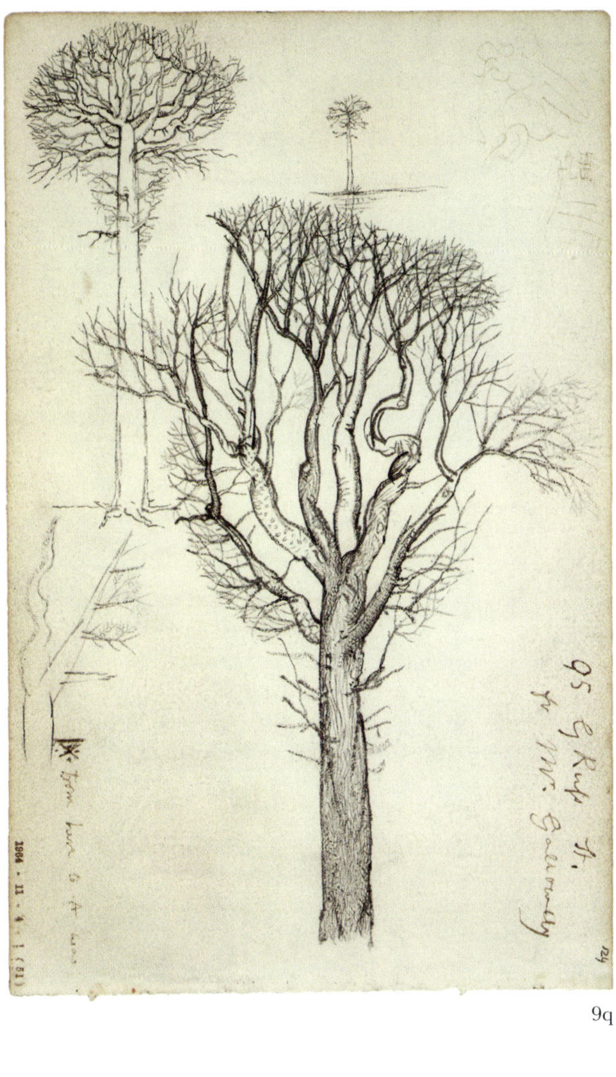

9q

## 9p†

Leaf 62 verso (123): *Tree Studies*

This woodland study focuses on the textures of tree trunks.

## 9q*

Leaf 62 verso (124): *Tree Studies*

Inscribed at lower left: *from here to A was;* and at lower right *95 G. Russ. St. / fr. Mr. Galloway*

This wintry study of trees was presumably made in the winter of 1824/5. The inscription at lower left, together with the sketch of a line of trees along a path, suggests that the picture was based on direct observation. As in other nature studies, however, there appears to have been a 'Gothic' emphasis on line, texture and emphatic profile.

## 9 r

### Leaf 68 recto (135): *Nude Male Torso*

This and no. 134 on the previous leaf form the most detailed figure studies in the sketchbook. The outstretched arms suggest that they may have been for a crucifixion subject, possibly that involving the bad thief (cat. 9n). As with the foliage and tree studies, details are emphasized by strong lines, in this case the sinews and muscles.

## 9 s*

### Leaf 86 verso (172): *Woodland by Moonlight*

This is the most elaborate tonal study of a landscape in the book. It is the earliest surviving example of Palmer's use of sepia or brown watercolour wash for the intense effects of his new form of primitivizing landscape that is shown fully developed in the Oxford series (cats 10–15).

## 9 t

### Leaf 89 verso (178): *Rocky Hill with Rabbit*

This sketchy composition is perhaps most remarkable for incorporating a rabbit, a motif to be found in the Oxford sepias (see cat. 12).

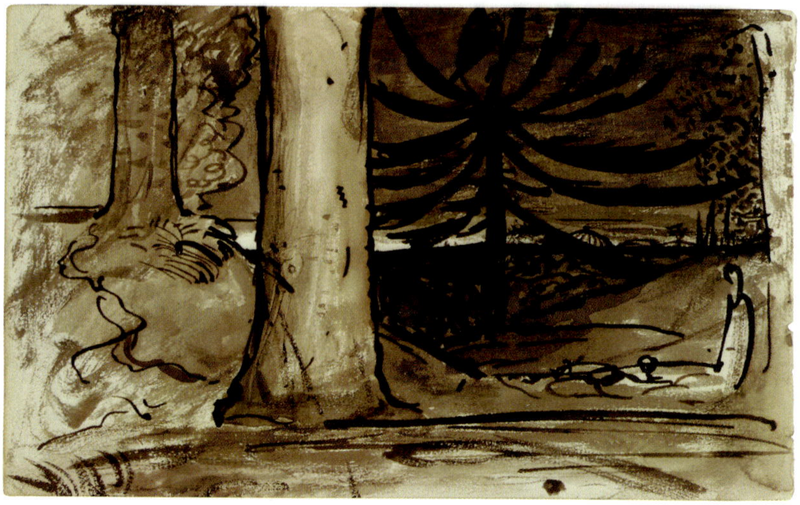

9s

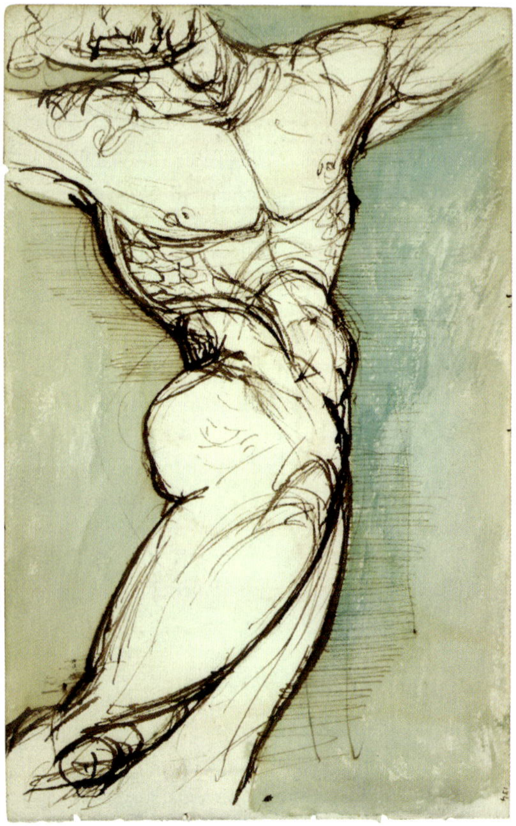

9r

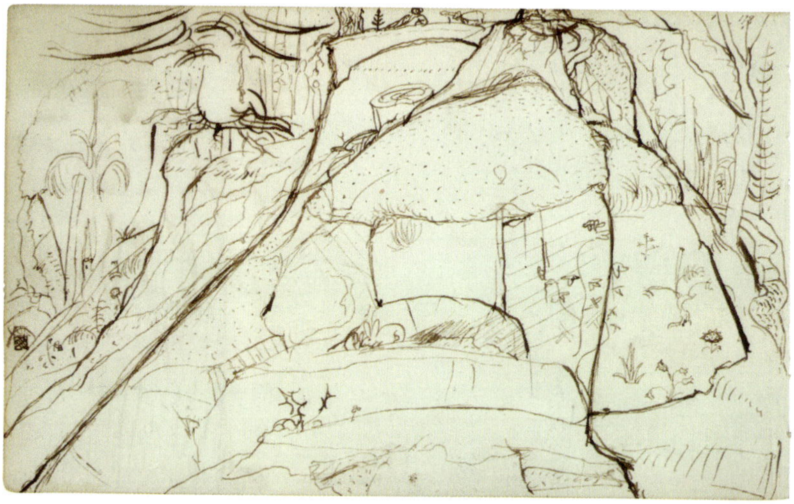

9t

## The Oxford sepia series of 1825 (cats 10–15)

This series of six ink, gum and sepia drawings (now preserved in the Ashmolean Museum, Oxford) are, like the 1824 sketchbook (cat. 9), a rare survival from Palmer's most 'primitive' period. Whereas the sketchbook reveals Palmer thinking and experimenting, these drawings are highly finished products, both in terms of composition and technique. It is a sign of this that all are boldly inscribed with the artist's name and all but one are dated.

The group seems to have been conceived as a series, although it is hard to ascertain if they share a communal theme. All depict fertile valley scenery enclosed by rounded hills reminiscent of the countryside around both Dulwich and Shoreham. The titles either evoke a time of day (for example *Twilight* or *Early Morning*) or draw attention to some natural phenomenon (for example *The Bright Cloud* or *The Edge of the Wood*). One is simply called *A Rustic Scene*. Taken together, they can be seen as a celebration of the mysterious wonder of the divinely created world and an image of man in his 'natural' rural state enjoying the God-given plenty. With the exception of *The Bright Cloud* they all show twilight, either late evening or early morning.

Each of the pictures had a text inscribed on the old frames that once enclosed them. These came from the Bible, Virgil or Bunyan. However, with the possible exception of *A Rustic Scene* the drawings do not seem to be literal illustrations of these texts. They differ in that respect from Palmer's later depictions of scenes from Virgil and Milton (see section 8, pp. 224–44). The texts cited here are used to draw attention to some phenomenon represented or to enhance the state of mind the picture aims to invoke. Their function is closer in that sense to that envisaged by Palmer's hero Turner when he used quotations from poems to accompany exhibited landscapes. The habit of exhibiting landscapes with excerpts from poems had in fact been common in Britain since the practice was allowed at the Royal Academy in 1798 (Butlin and Joll, p. 3) and expressed the close engagement between landscape and poetry at this time.

It is unclear, however, at what point the texts became attached to the pictures. The titles of three of them, *A Rustic Scene*, *Late Twilight* and *The Skirts of a Wood*, are the same as works exhibited at the Royal Academy in 1825 and 1826. None of these had texts attached to their catalogue entries. It may well be that the texts were added retrospectively by the artist later in life.

It cannot be established whether any of these works are the ones exhibited at the Royal Academy, although their extremely finished nature suggests that they were at least seen as works capable of exhibition. It is known, too, that some of Palmer's most extraordinary works did – despite their defiance of the conventions of naturalism – get accepted for exhibition at the Academy. A reviewer in the *European Magazine* was so startled by the appearance of one of Palmer's exhibits of 1825 (*A View in Kent* – untraced, Lister 47) that he recommended the artist exhibit himself as a curiosity (*European*, p. 85).

The imagery and its mode of representation are close to that explored in the sketchbook of 1824, though with greater attention to detail and richer handling of tonalities. The technique is based on the monochrome ink methods that Palmer had acquired from William Wate, but they take this practice in quite new directions. It has been observed by Sarah Herring that Palmer's dense working of ink and gum represents a change in the processes of ink painting that reflects similar developments in watercolour during the period (Herring). In the case of both ink drawing and watercolour painting a technique of applying layers of tone to an outline drawing – working from light to dark – was replaced by a denser way of working in which darks were put in and lights were recovered by means of scratching through to the paper or by adding white in gouache or some opaque medium. On the whole, however, this method was used for watercolour and Palmer was more unusual in revising Indian ink and sepia drawing along similar lines. Palmer further strengthened the density and richness of his tones by mixing gum with his ink (see p. 33). In this he may have been responding to Blake's method of strengthening watercolour by the addition of gum, something that he optimistically referred to as 'fresco'. It may be that Palmer, like Blake, believed that he was approximating the methods of the old masters they admired by adopting this method. In addition to mixing gum with the inks, Palmer seems to have applied an overall varnish to the finished work.

Though unknown outside the artist's immediate circle during his lifetime, this series attracted attention when exhibited at the winter show in Burlington House in 1893. It was here that the artist Charles Ricketts enthused about them to his friend Sturge Moore, who was later to make them well known through a celebrated publication in 1936 (Moore 1936).

The pictures remained with Palmer for most of his life. In his last years, however, he sold them to J.W. Overbury, a junior partner in the firm of his cousin John Giles. They were purchased from a member of the Overbury family by the Ashmolean in 1941.

**10**

### *A Rustic Scene*, 1825

Brown ink and sepia mixed with gum arabic, 17.9 × 23.5 cm (7 1/8 × 9 3/8 in)

Inscribed in lower right corner: *Samuel Palmer 1825*

Inscribed by the artist on former mount:
*Libra die somnique pures ubi fecerit horas,*
*Et medium luci atque umbris jam dividet orbem;*
*Exercite, viri, tauros, serite hordea campis,*
*Usque sub extremum brumae intractabilis imbrem.*
(Virgil, *Georgics*, I, 208–11)

Lit: Brown 5; Lister 53

Oxford, Ashmolean Museum, 1941.102; purchased 1941

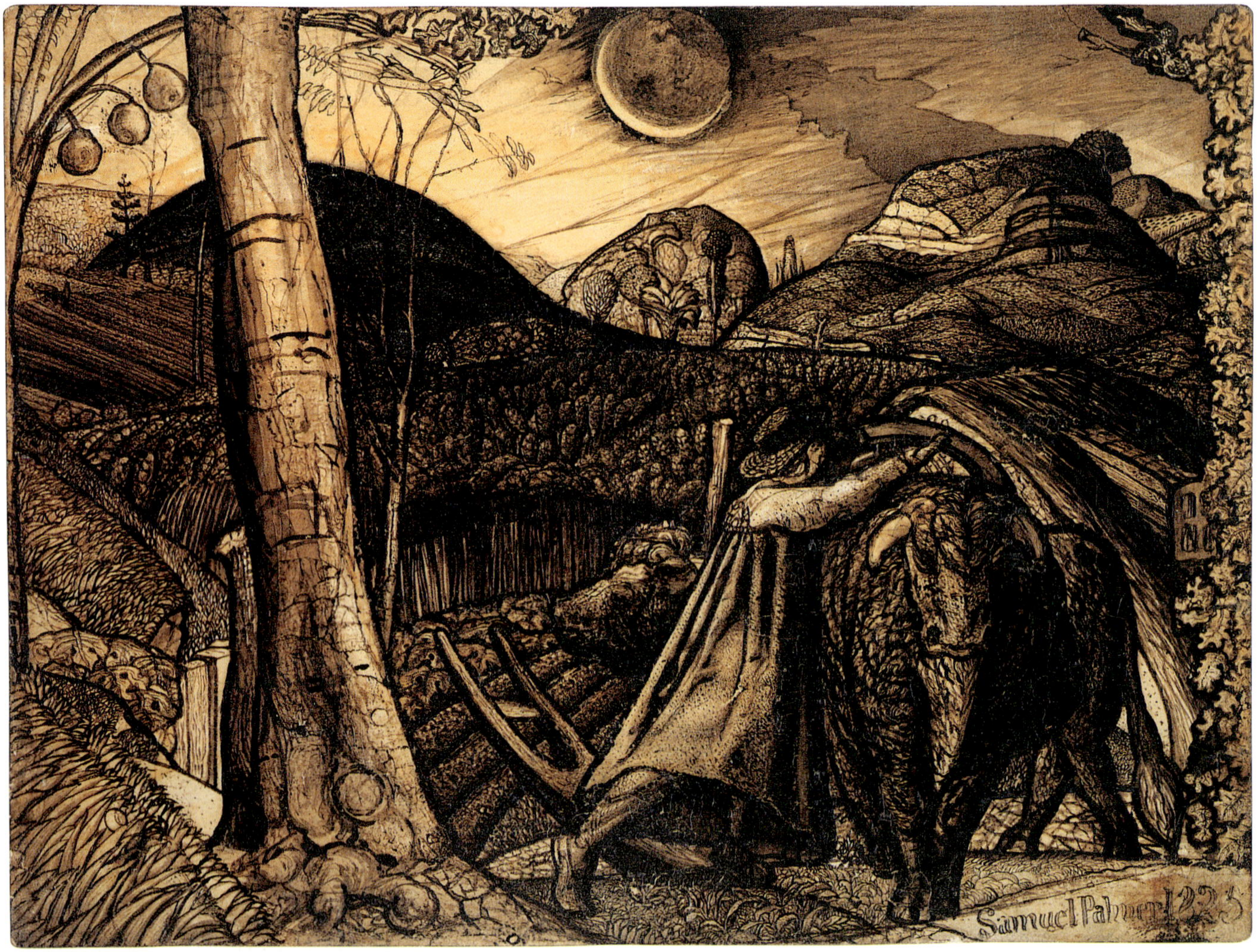

10

Palmer was a keen Latin scholar who had a particular admiration for the descriptions of rural life in the poetry of Virgil. The passage quoted has been translated more recently by Cecil Day Lewis as follows:

When the Scales make the hours for
  daytime and sleeptime balance,
Dividing the globe into equal
  hemispheres – light and darkness,
Then set your bulls to work, farmers, and
  sow your barley
Up to the last showers on the frost-bound
  limits of winter.

(Lewis, p. 21)

The text would imply that the ploughing represented was taking place at the time of the autumnal equinox. However ears of corn are still standing, which would suggest a slightly earlier season. It must in any case at least be late summer as there are some apples on the branch on the left-hand side of the composition. Perhaps Palmer was deliberately combining different seasons, as he is known to have done on other occasions (see cat. 17), to enhance an overall sense of abundance and fruitfulness. He has evoked early morning, correctly showing the waning sickle moon, which is only visible at dawn.

Ploughing scenes were common in British landscape painting in the early nineteenth century, particularly during the Napoleonic period when they were frequently used to emphasize the natural productivity of Britain and ability to withstand the onslaughts of the French. Virgil's *Georgics*, which provide detailed instructions for good husbandry, were frequently an inspiration behind such works (Payne 1993, p. 88). Although Palmer preferred pastoral scenes to agricultural ones, he did on occasion represent ploughmen throughout his life, most notably in his later etchings (cats 139, 140). In this work his image of the ploughman is particularly heroic, a view that accorded with his admiration for what he called in 1828 'our fine British peasantry' (*Letters*, p. 37).

*A Rustic Scene* was one of a group of pictures Palmer made for a Mr Bennett in 1825 (*Letters*, pp. 9–10). This may have been the work of that title exhibited at the Royal Academy in 1825 (RA no. 410).

**11**

## *The Valley with a Bright Cloud*, 1825

Brown ink and sepia mixed with gum arabic, 18.4 × 27.8 cm ($7^1/_4$ × 11 in)

Inscribed at lower centre: *Samuel Palmer / 1825*

Inscribed by the artist on former mount:
*This our life, exempt from public haunt,*
*Finds tongues in trees, books in ye running brooks,*
*Sermons in stones, and good in everything.*
(*As You Like it*, Act II, Scene i, lines 15–18: Duke Senior)

Lit: Brown 8; Lister 54

Oxford, Ashmolean Museum, 1941.105; purchased 1941

This woodland scene evokes the theme of rural retreat – alluded to by the quotation from the Duke's speech in Shakespeare's *As You Like It.* It is the most conventional representation of Arcadian scenery in the series and concentrates on the beauty of natural effects. However, although the picture does include stones and a stream (or river) in the middle ground, it is the soaring cloud that gains the picture its title and introduces a sense of the sublime. The 'Bright Cloud' was to become a favourite theme of Palmer's during his later years at Shoreham (see cats 75, 76, 87) and seems to suggest – as poetry referring to it then indicates – the image of a higher reality beyond the vale of comfortable rural peace, or 'Beulah' as it was referred to by Blake. Palmer had made sketches of clouds in his 1819 sketchbook, but nothing there compares to the voluminous power of this one. It is possible that he had been impressed by some of the vivid clouds in Constable's works. Later, in 1828, he was to write to Linnell expressing admiration for that artist's representations and saying that the 'glorious round clouds which you paint I do think inimitably, are alone an example how the elements of nature may be transmitted into the pure Gold of Art' (*Letters*, p. 50). Brown has commented that such massive cumulus clouds are common in the Darent valley where Shoreham is situated.

This idyllic world is unsullied by human presence (apart from that of the spectator), the mood being enhanced by the cooing birds in the foreground. Such amorous activity, as well as the fact that the trees seem to be newly in leaf, suggest the season of spring.

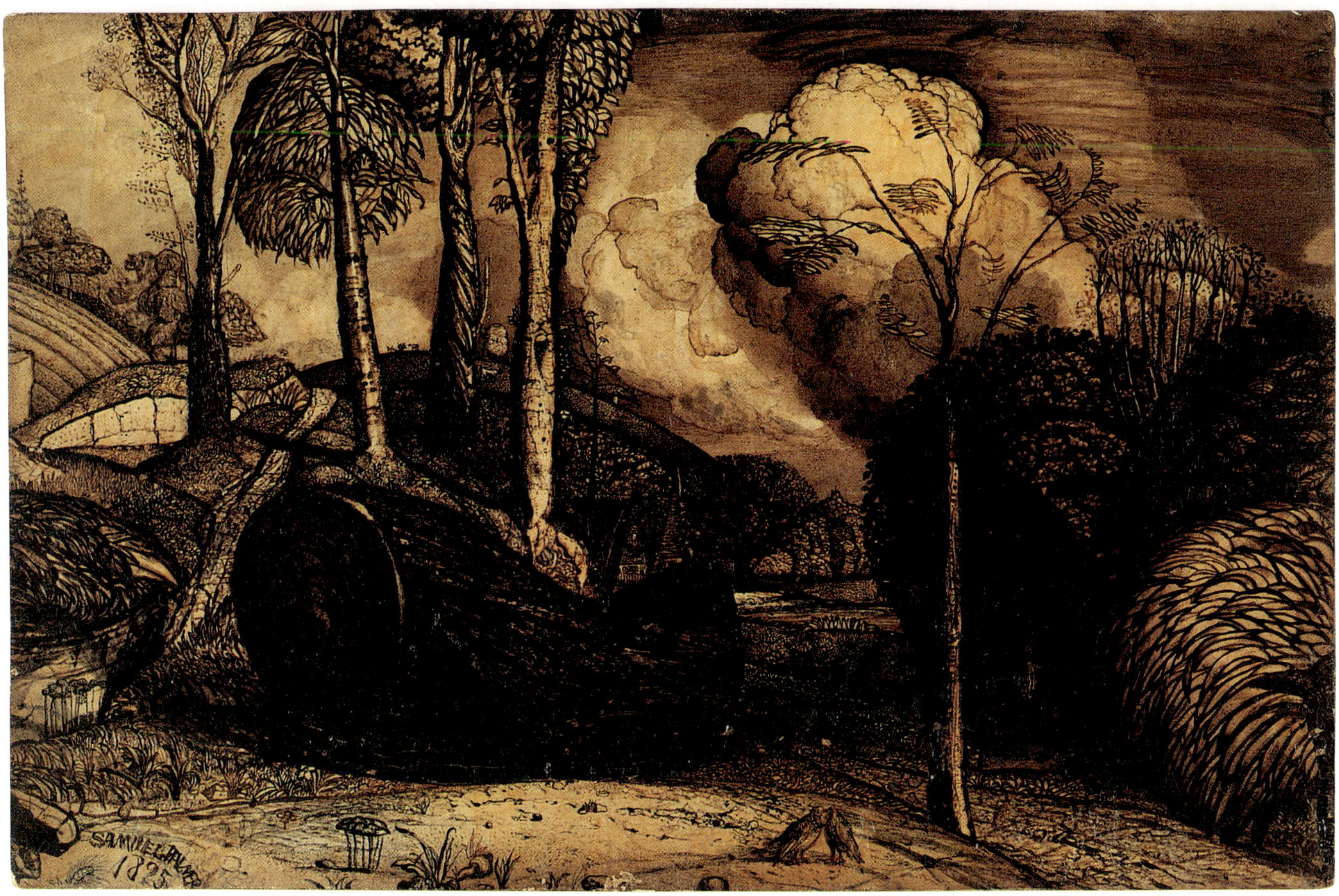


11

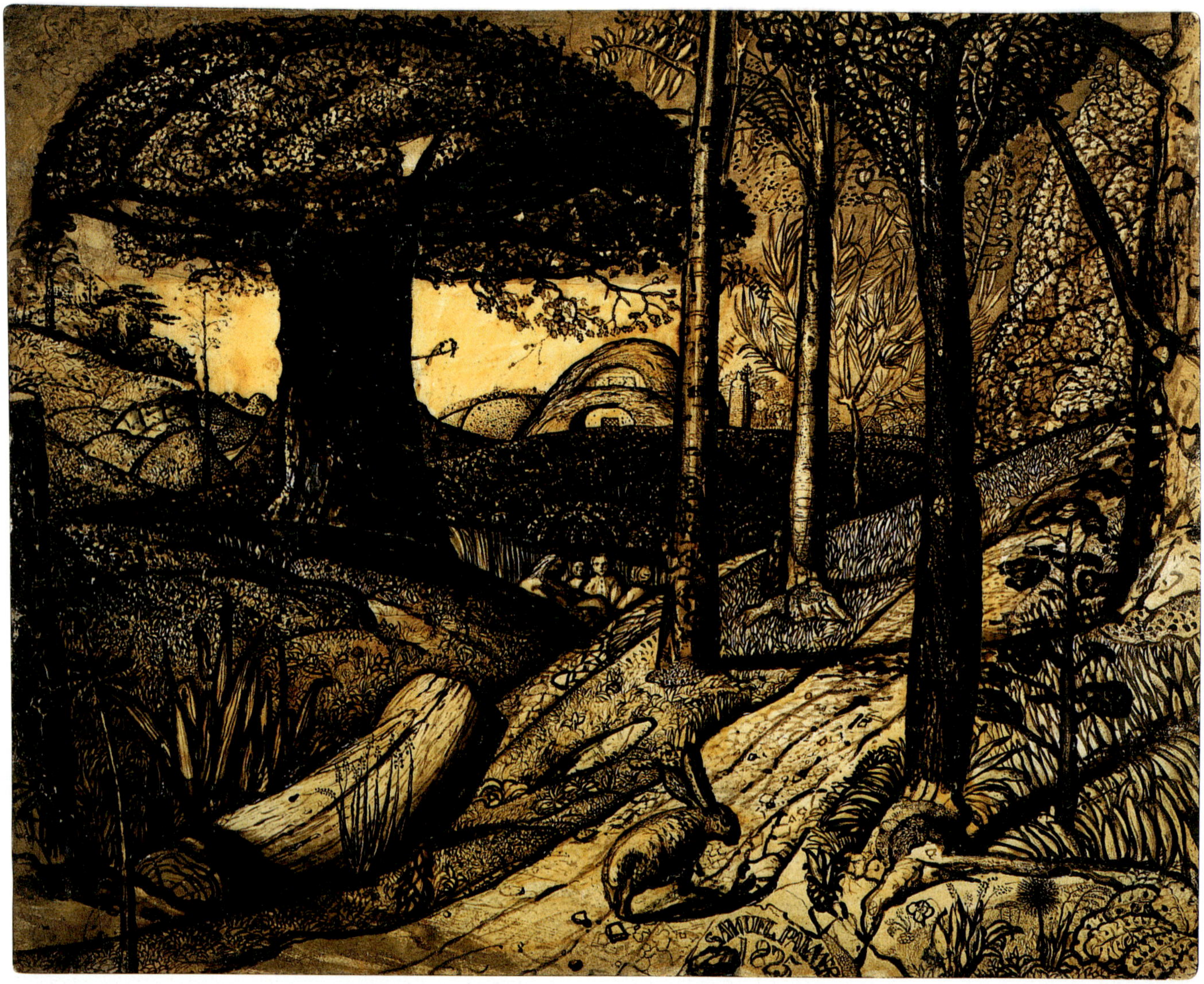

12

**12**

*Early Morning*, 1825

Brown ink and sepia mixed with gum arabic, 18.8 × 23.2 cm (7½ × 9³⁄₁₆ in)

Inscribed at bottom, right of centre: *Samuel Palmer / 1825*

Inscribed by the artist on former mount:
*I rose anone and thought I would be gone*
*Into the wode, to hear the birdes sing,*
*When that misty vapour was agone*
*And cleare and faire was the morning.*
*Chaucer*

Lit: Brown 10; Lister 55

Oxford, Ashmolean Museum, 1941.107; purchased 1941

In contrast to the *Rustic Scene*, with its heroic peasant, this representation of early morning is that perceived by a travelling knight. The quotation from the poem *The Complaint of the Black Knight* (lines 22–5) – thought by Palmer to be by Chaucer but now ascribed to John Lydgate – evokes a woodland idyll. It is closer in type from this point of view to the *Bright Cloud* (cat. 11), though it evokes most specially the quiet and clarity of the beginning of a fine day. The raking light – casting strong, long sideways shadows – makes clear both that the mists have indeed 'agone' and that the sun is still low in the sky. One prominent feature that suggests this and that is not alluded to in Lydgate's poem is the presence of the hare or rabbit in the foreground fearlessly treading a path. This introduction of animal consciousness heightens the sense of community with nature. Two birds sing or coo on a tiny branch on the curiously toadstool-like oak in the middle ground, which may itself be an echo of the tree in Blake's *Job* (see cat. 18).

There is more sign of human habitation here than in the *Bright Cloud*. Rounded cottages can be seen on the horizon echoing the shapes of hills. In a dell beyond the oak tree a group of people are seated, as though at a prayer meeting.

## 13

### *Late Twilight*, 1825

Brown ink and sepia mixed with gum arabic, 18 × 23.8 cm (7½ × 9[3]/16 in)

Inscribed by the artist on former mount: *LATE TWILIGHT / 'The west yet glimmers with some streaks of day' / Milton*

Lit: Brown, 7; Lister 56

Oxford, Ashmolean Museum, 1941.104; purchased 1941

The text inscribed on the mount is actually from Shakespeare's *Macbeth* (Act III, Scene iii, line 5: First Murderer). The misattribution to Milton of a quote from *Macbeth* is surprising, given the obsession with the 'Scottish Play' manifested by the Ancients in the 1820s. This suggests that the text may well have been applied later. The quotation draws attention to the glimmering light that Palmer has represented. He has captured a very particular effect when the sun has already sunk below the horizon, but the reflection of sunlight is still perceptible in the sky. He has accurately shown a waxing sickle moon here, which can be visible near the horizon around sunset. The halo around the moon is an indication of cold weather.

Palmer has concentrated on the darkening of the landscape towards the horizon, but close inspection shows that this has not obscured detail. A village can be discerned nestling in the trees. People can be seen returning home, passing stooks of corn (suggesting late summer). The stream to the left still catches some sunlight, as does the foreground in which a shepherd rests among his sheep.

Near the centre of the picture is a church steeple. This, combined with the symmetry of the composition and the presence of the moon (a common symbol for Christ) and the shepherd, suggests religious connotations for this pastoral. Brown quotes Grigson (1947) as arguing that the picture specifically represents Beulah, the earthly paradise described by Bunyan in *Pilgrim's Progress* and interpreted by Blake as a pleasurable state below the higher levels of vision.

The composition bears similarities to that of some pictures in the 1824 sketchbook (cat. 9) and perhaps even more closely to a page from a sketchbook now in the Yale Center for British Art (*c.*1825; Lister 44), which shows a very similar configuration of moon, hill and foreground tree.

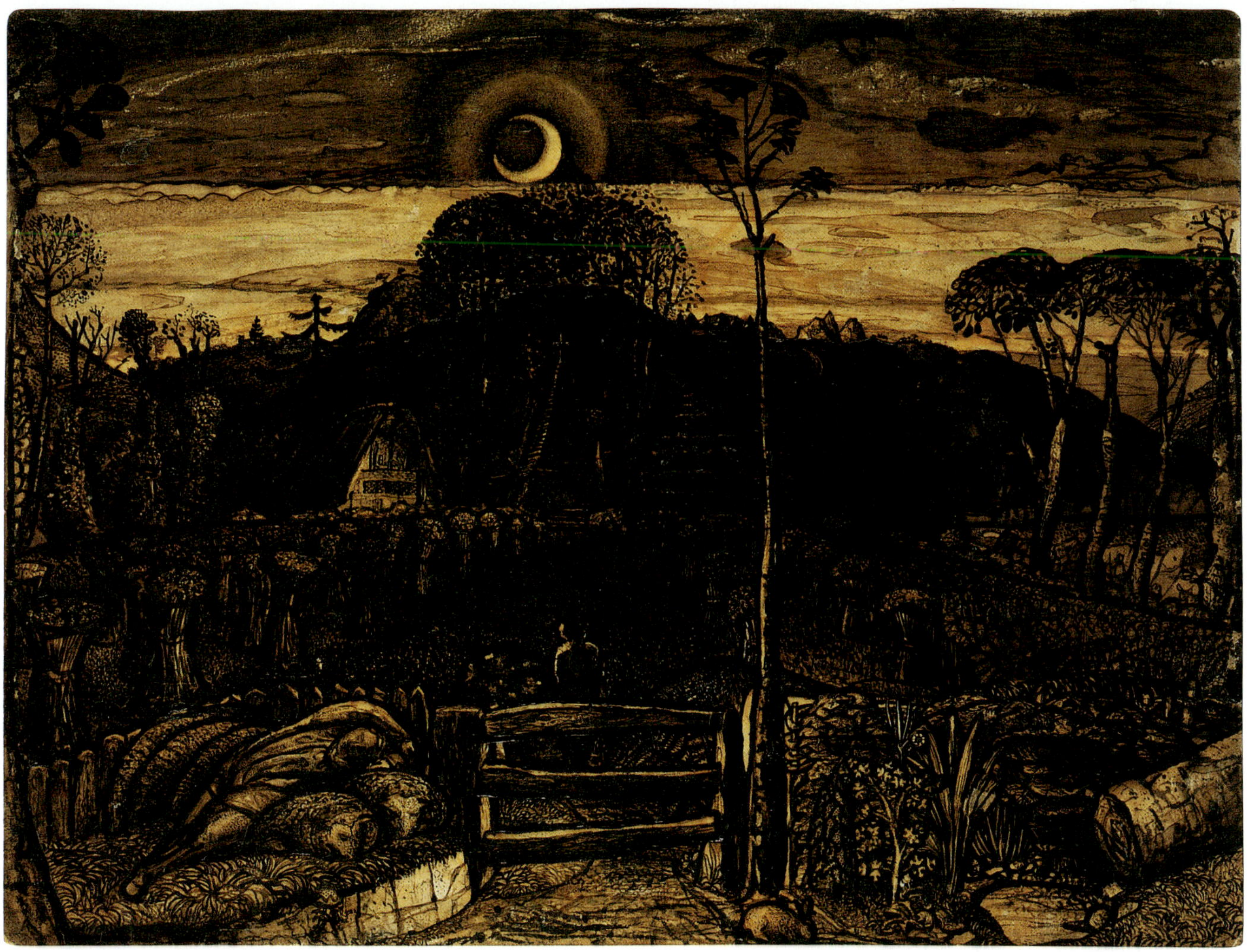

13

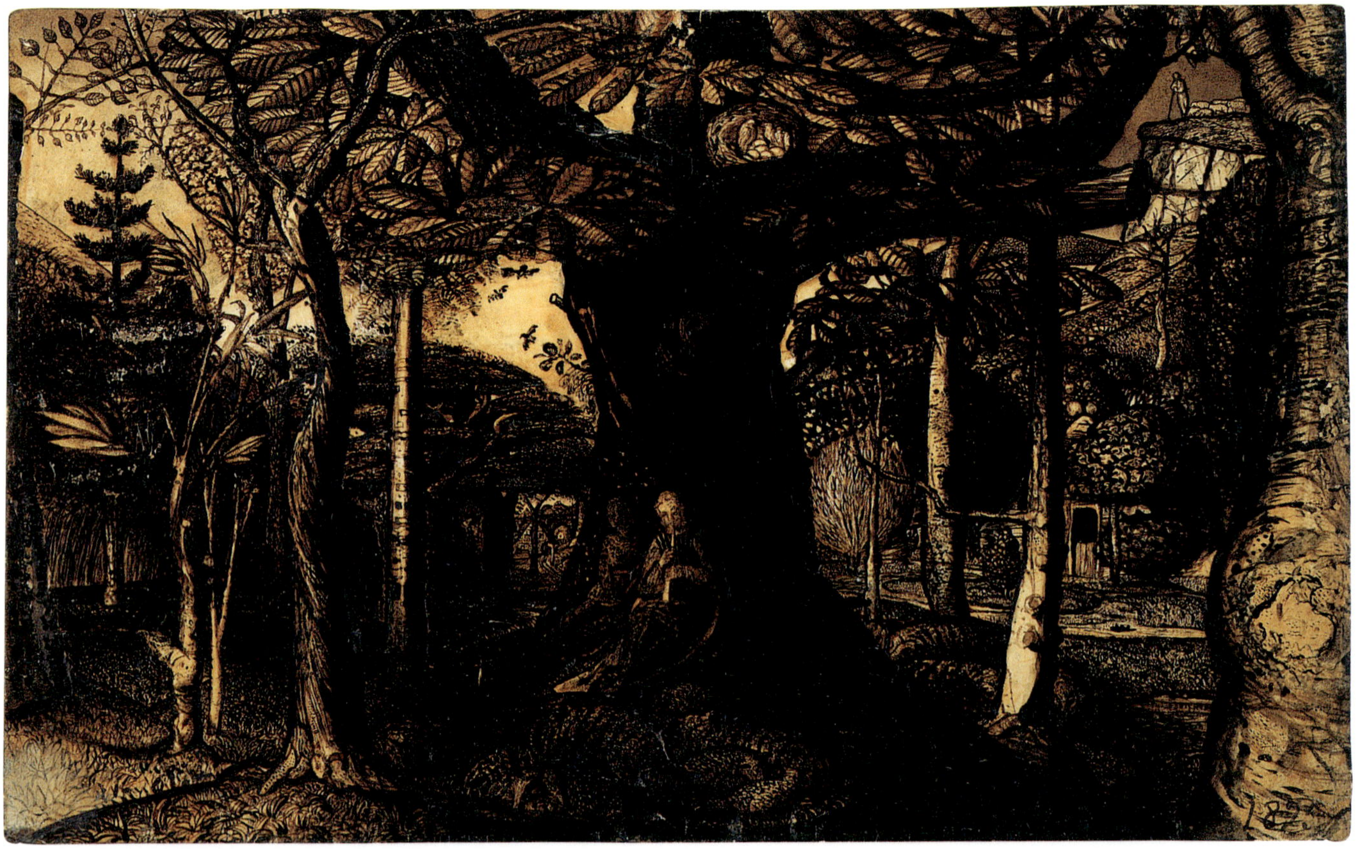

14

## 14

*The Skirts of a Wood*, 1825

Dark brown ink and sepia mixed with gum arabic, 17.4 × 27.7 cm (6 13/16 × 11 11/16 in)

Inscribed at lower right: *1825*

Lit: Brown 9; Lister 57

Oxford, Ashmolean Museum, 1941.104; purchased 1941

This is the only work in the series that is neither signed by Palmer nor given a quotation. There is, however, no doubt about its authenticity or rightful place in the series. To judge by the low level of light and the bats flying to the left of the central chestnut tree, this is an evening scene, representing a similar time to that in *Late Twilight* (cat. 13). The focus here is even more on the pastoral, with a shepherd piping beneath the tree and a further one with his crook and flock in the distance standing rather precariously close to the edge of a cliff. A village can be seen beyond the trees.

Brown has commented that this composition seems to show most strongly the influence of the first plate of Blake's *Job* (cat. 18), the work that Blake was engaged on when Palmer first visited him in autumn 1824. Despite a shared pastoral setting and crepuscular light, Palmer's emphasis is less on figures than on effects in nature, notably the haunting appearances of shadows and silhouettes. The scene is the most 'Gothic' of the series and is a reminder of the Ancients' penchant for nocturnal wanderings. As in his tree studies in the 1824 sketchbook, Palmer has enjoyed depicting rich textures and ungainly profiles in his trees. The predominance of the chestnut is particularly significant from this point of view. It shows Palmer's rejection of the conventional aesthetics of the picturesque movement in favour of more expressive and earthy forms. In his *Essay on the Picturesque* Gilpin had said that the chestnut could not be picturesque because of the ungainly size of its leaves. Palmer, however, who loved the chestnut, exaggerates the size of the leaves, as he does in later representations of the tree (see cat. 70).

## 15

*The Valley Thick with Corn*, 1825

Dark brown ink and sepia mixed with gum arabic, 18.4 × 27.5 cm (7 1/8 × 10 7/8 in)

Inscribed at lower centre: *Samuel Palmer / 1825*

Inscribed by the artist on former mount: *Thou crownest the year with Thy goodness: and Thy clouds drop fatness. They shall drop upon the dwellings of the wilderness; and the little hills shall rejoice on every side. Thy folds shall be full of sheep, the valleys also shall stand so thick with corn that they shall laugh and sing.* (Psalm 65: 11–13.)

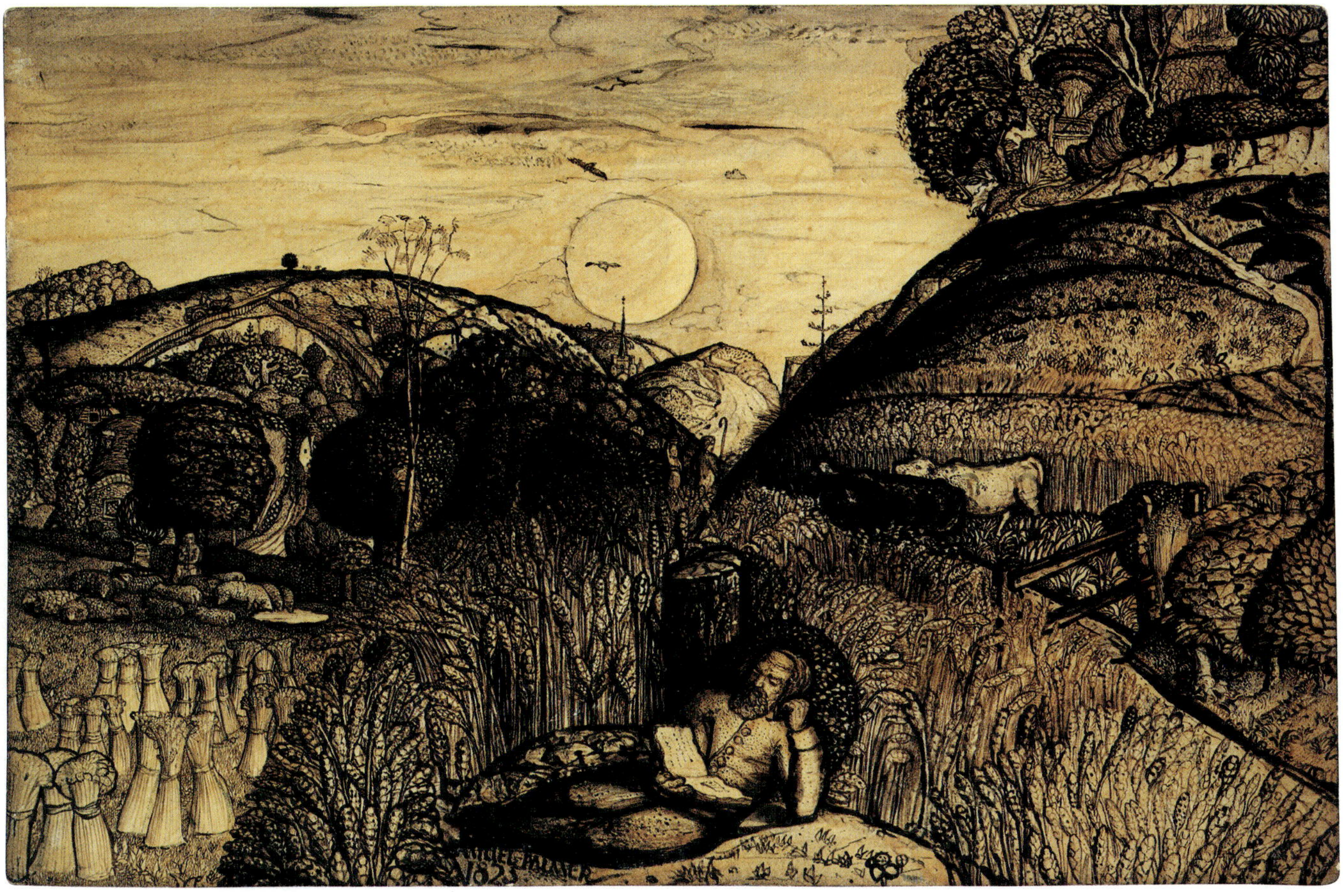

15

Lit: Malins, p. viii; Brown 6; Lister 58
Oxford, Ashmolean Museum, 1941.1043; purchased 1941

Brown has pointed out that a passage in the 1824 sketchbook envisaging a large field of corn 'with as it were islands peeping out of it – a clump of cottages completely inclosed [*sic*] and shaded by trees' seems to anticipate this composition.

The biblical evocation of plenty provided by divine benevolence is richly represented here, with flocks and crops emphatically portrayed by Palmer's thick lines and textural patterning. As elsewhere, the softening of distant forms (referred to by Palmer as 'aerial perspective') is banished so that the details of abundance can be traced up to the surrounding hills, where a cart makes its way home. Nestling between the hills, centrally placed, is a church steeple, doubtlessly stressing the religious aspect. The earthly abundance is matched by the amplitude of the full moon, with bats flitting across its surface. Given the brightness of the light and time of year, it is tempting to see it as a harvest moon. This association is strengthened by the fact that the quotation from Psalm 65 used here also occurs in Palmer's design celebrating the harvest moon in the sketchbook of 1824 (leaf 20 recto; cat. 9f).

The figure reading in the foreground has caused much speculation. It has been suggested, implausibly, that it might represent Edward Calvert, although why he should be in Elizabethan attire and sporting a beard (which he did not have at this time) is something of a mystery. More interestingly, Malins has associated the figure with Christian, the protagonist in Bunyan's *Pilgrim's Progress*, dressed in his new coat, resting and reading in the 'arbour' halfway up the hill called 'Difficulty'. Even though certain other features in the landscape (such as the gate and the two paths to the right) could be related to this interpretation, it seems difficult to match the details exactly. The general inspiration of landscape invested with religious meaning that Bunyan's book provided for Palmer is not in doubt, and he was later to illustrate scenes from *Pilgrim's Progress* (see cat. 120).

The reclining figure in a landscape, with head resting on arm, is a traditional image of melancholia. Palmer may be alluding to this tradition and perhaps revising it in Blakean manner as a means of returning imaginatively to the times of plenty in olden days through reading the Bible.

## 16*

### *Study of a Hand Holding a Knobbed Stick*, 1825

Brown ink, 11.1 × 8.2 cm (4 3/8 × 3 1/4 in)

Inscribed: *S. Palmer 1825*

Lit: Lister 52

London, Victoria and Albert Museum, 1303-1925

This study comes from a time when Palmer was working hard to develop his skills as a figurative artist in order to produce biblical paintings, such as the *Holy Family* (see cat. 28). The flatness of the form and the regularity of the hatching suggest that it may have been taken from an engraving. Copying engravings was standard practice for students of the period, as well as an activity much recommended by Blake.

## 17

### *A Hilly Scene*, *c.*1824–6

Watercolour and gum arabic on mahogany support, 20.6 × 13.7 cm (8 1/8 × 5 3/8 in)

Inscribed on verso: *No. 3 A Hilly Scene*

Lit: Lister 66

London, Tate, N5805; purchased 1948

This small panel is close in style to the Oxford series (see cats 10–15). Many of its features, such as the sickle moon, the chestnut with exaggerated leaves, magnified ears of corn, rounded hills and prominent church steeple, occur in the series. Although it is coloured, its form of drawing, with emphatic lines and texturing, is also highly similar. The symmetrical composition, moreover, has parallels with some designs in the 1824 sketchbook (see cat. 9). For these reasons it seems appropriate to suggest a date of *c.*1824–6 for the work. It is more primitive in style than works securely datable to the time after Palmer had settled fully in Shoreham in 1827. As with the Oxford series, the scenery seems to be inspired by an amalgam of features from Dulwich and Shoreham rather than representing any precise location.

The theme of this picture seems close to *Late Twilight* (cat. 13). Like that work, it shows a sickle moon and a centrally placed church. The symmetry of the picture emphasizes its religious mood. This is made even stronger by the bringing together of the branches of the two flanking trees in the foreground to resemble an arch, in a reference to the prevailing myth of the time explaining how the Gothic arch had been created. The significance of this myth was that it emphasized the notion of Gothic springing out of the forms of nature. Such an association would have been highly attractive to Palmer as a landscape artist with spiritual inclinations. The myth was used by German Romantic artists with similar inclinations, notably Caspar David Friedrich in his *Cross in the Mountains* (1808; Gemäldegalerie, Dresden).

The mystique of the work is heightened by its glimmering luminosity. The foreground light can hardly emanate from either the sickle moon or the sun, just beneath the horizon to the left: the glow suggests the supernatural. Palmer was particularly fond of making the familiar strange in this period by using exaggerated form and unusual low-light effects.

The mixing of watercolour and gum resembles Blake's 'fresco' technique and Palmer may have been influenced by the sight of some works in this manner when visiting his mentor. In style it is certainly the most primitive of all his extant paintings. As in a medieval miniature, the background is tilted forwards and packed with detail. Many suggestions have been made as to possible sources for individual features, but there are no clear connections with any of the works cited. It is possible that the primitivism of this work was inspired by some of the early Northern art that Palmer had recently seen in the collection of the

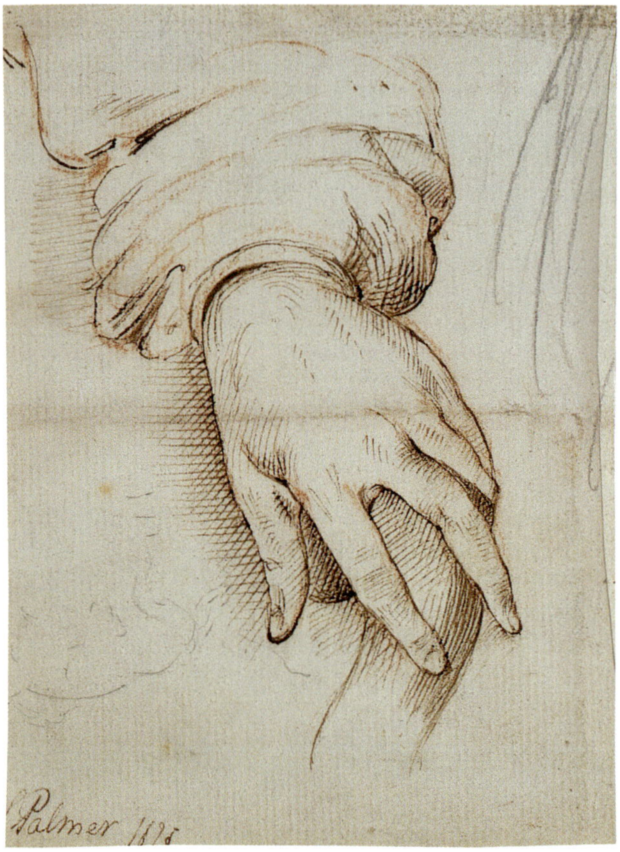


16

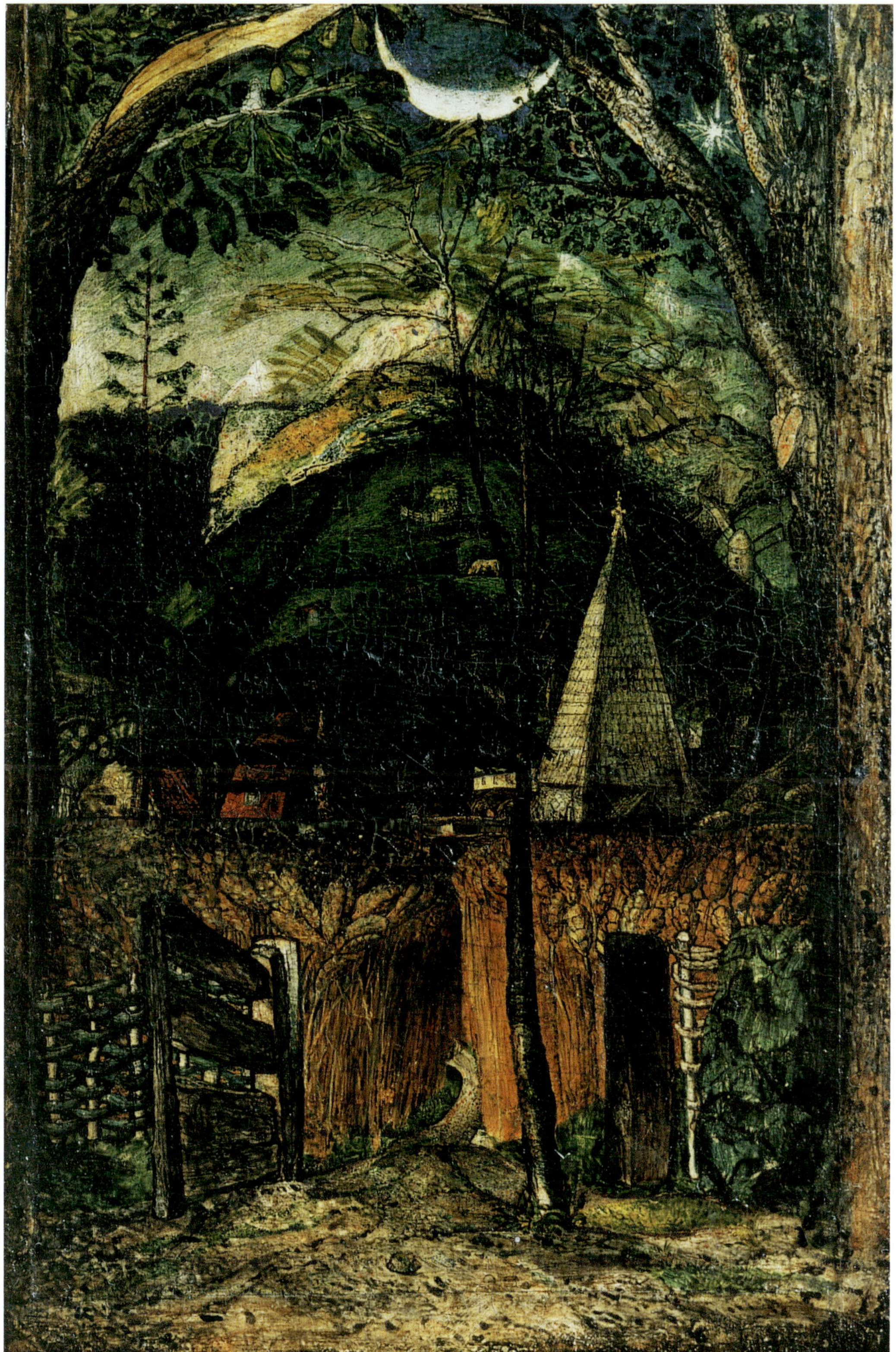

17

German merchant Charles Aders in London (see cat. 23).

The picture was acquired from Palmer by George Richmond in 1873. It was sold to the Tate by one of his descendants in 1948.

## 18*

### William Blake (1757–1827)
### *Illustrations of the Book of Job*, 1825–6

Engraving, 19.9 × 16.4 cm (7¾ × 6½ in)
Lit: Bindman 1978, 625, 639

#### 18a Plate 1 '*Thus did Job continually*'

London, British Museum, 1868-8-22-39-48

#### 18b Plate 14 '*When the morning Stars*', 1825–6

London, British Museum, 1868-8-22-39-61

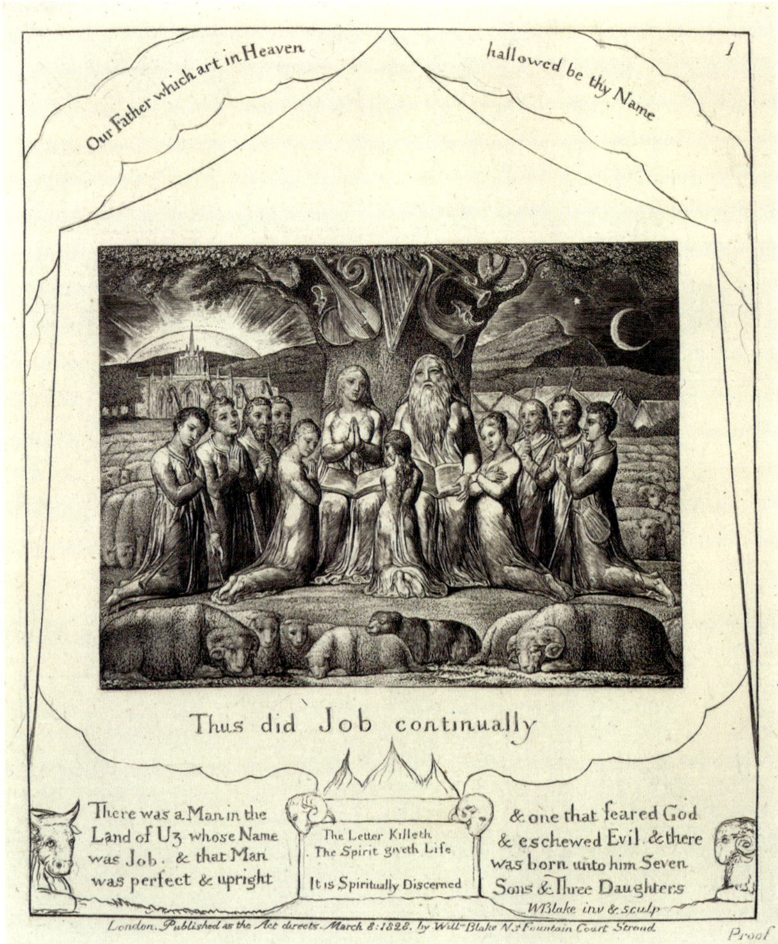


18a

Born in London, in humble circumstances, Blake now has a towering reputation as one of the greatest creative geniuses of the Romantic era, valued for the visionary power of both his poetry and his art. In his own time, however, he struggled to make ends meet as a jobbing engraver, mostly making copies of the works of others. Largely self-published, his writings attracted little attention beyond a small group of friends and enthusiasts and he was widely thought of – if thought of at all – as a harmless madman.

Samuel Palmer and his associates were part of the small group of people who admired Blake in his last years. The most important from a material point of view was the landscape painter John Linnell (see cat. 20), who befriended Blake around 1818 and was responsible for several of his last commissions, notably *The Pastorals of Virgil* (cat. 19), *Illustrations of the Book of Job* and a series of illustrations to Dante's *Divine Comedy*, which remained incomplete at Blake's death. Palmer, who was introduced to Blake by Linnell in September 1824, was perhaps the artist most affected by Blake in his own work. He and other members of the Ancients (see p. 17) venerated Blake and referred to his dwelling as the 'House of the Interpreter' in imitation of the character in Bunyan's *Pilgrim's Progress*. The other member of the Ancients perhaps to respond most directly to Blake's art was Edward Calvert (see cat. 59).

After his death Blake fell for a time into even deeper obscurity. However, interest in him revived during the Victorian period, spearheaded by Alexander Gilchrist's *Life of William Blake* in 1863 (Gilchrist 1863). Linnell and Palmer both gave Gilchrist (1828–61) first-hand accounts of Blake, which were key factors in shaping the Victorian view of Blake as a mystic visionary. The revival of Blake's reputation at this time also increased interest in the art of Palmer.

Blake's *Illustrations of the Book of Job* comprise a set of twenty-one plates. They were commissioned by John Linnell and jointly published by him and Blake in 1826. Though a critical success, they did little more than break even as a commercial venture.

The biblical story of Job – the righteous man who persisted in his faith in the Lord through all adversity and was rewarded in the end for his steadfastness – might seem to mirror that of Blake himself, who enjoyed a young circle of admirers in the last years of his life after decades of neglect and adversity. Typically, however, Blake gives his own interpretation of the story. For him Job had been at fault at the beginning of the story because he obeyed the form rather that the spirit of religion. At the end, after his adversities and mystical experience of the supernatural (cat. 18b), Job understood the world of the spirit and became enlightened. The first and last plates of the series show the opening

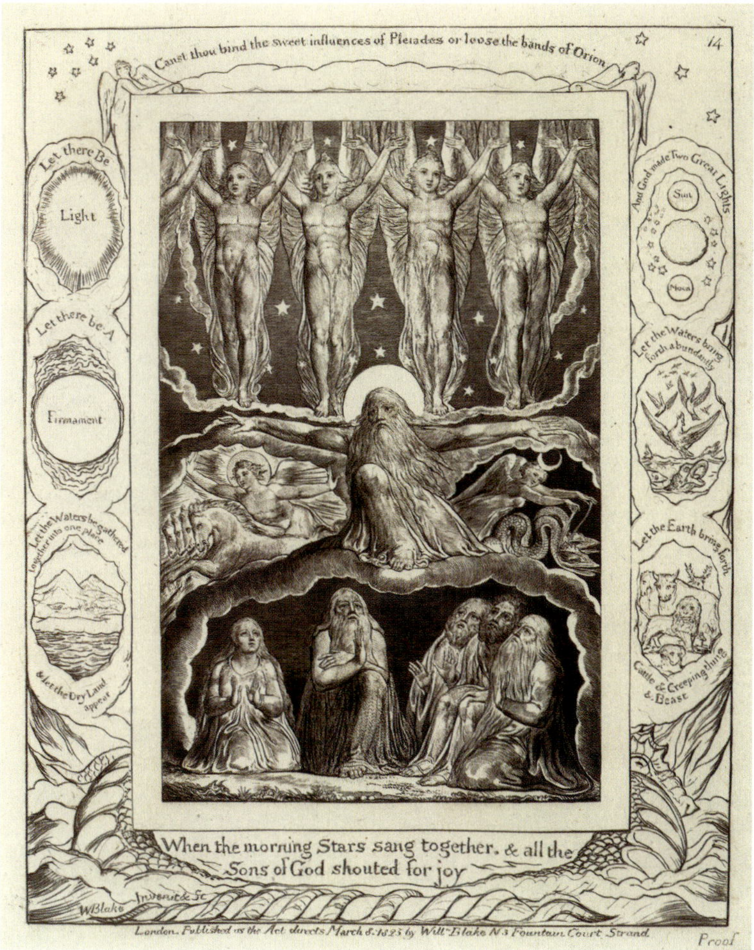


18b

and concluding moments of the story. In the first (see cat. 18a) Job and his family sit devoutly beneath a tree praying; in the last they rise up and sing and dance as though at a revivalist meeting.

It is unclear how far the complexities of Blake's interpretation of Job were understood by his young circle of admirers. Yet the imagery of the Job engravings had a profound impact. In a letter to Gilchrist Palmer describes how Blake was at work on the first of these plates when he first met him: 'the copper of the first plate – "Thus did Job continually" – was lying on the table where he had been working at it. How lovely it looked by the lamplight, strained through the tissue paper!' (Gilchrist 1863, vol. 1, p. 297). He cites these engravings and the wood engravings of *The Pastorals of Virgil* as having a particular relevance for him as a landscape painter. As well as the general importance of the pastoral imagery, the design of the first plate of *Job* seems to have had a direct impact on a number of Palmer's designs, such as *The Skirts of a Wood* (cat. 14).

Palmer may also have been inspired by Blake's method of engraving: in contrast to his earlier style, Blake here makes much use of stippling and patterning to heighten the sense of texture in his designs. While Blake had early been an admirer of Albrecht Dürer and other sixteenth-century engravers and printmakers, it seems that he was looking again at such work and discovering new qualities in them. This archaism in Blake accorded with the new fascination with the primitive felt by Linnell and Palmer at this time.

## 19*

### William Blake (1757–1827)

### Illustrations to Robert Thornton's *Pastorals of Virgil*, 1821

Wood engravings, proofs of blocks printed on two separate sheets, each approx. 16.4 × 10 cm (6½ × 4 in)

Lit: Bindman 1978, 602–18

London, British Museum, 1919-5-28-1 and 3; presented by Herbert Linnell

The wood engravings that William Blake made for Thornton's *Pastorals of Virgil* are among his most untypical works, in that they represent natural scenery and use an engraving method with which he was unfamiliar. Yet they became the most influential and talked about of his works in his lifetime.

Blake obtained the commission through an introduction to Robert Thornton by Linnell in 1818. Thornton, who wrote books mainly on medicine and botany, had produced a school edition of *The Pastorals of Virgil* in 1812. When Blake was introduced to him, he was preparing an illustrated version of the third edition. Thornton believed strongly in the power of imagery to fix information in the minds of the young, and for this reason he planned his edition to be lavishly illustrated with wood engravings. Blake was given one of the lesser sections to illustrate. His illustrations were not, in fact, to one of Virgil's *Eclogues* but to one of the imitations of Virgil by Ambrose Philips included at the end of the book, the pastoral poem 'Thenot and Colinet'.

Perhaps because he was unfamiliar with the methods currently used in wood engraving, Blake cut his blocks directly, so that the lines of the engraved block appeared white, rather than imitating the black lines of a drawing as was familiar in the use of wood engravings for reproduction work at that time. This unprecedented approach created an outrage at the publishers and Thornton was only persuaded to keep Blake's engravings in the book after representations on their behalf had been made to him by the President of the Royal

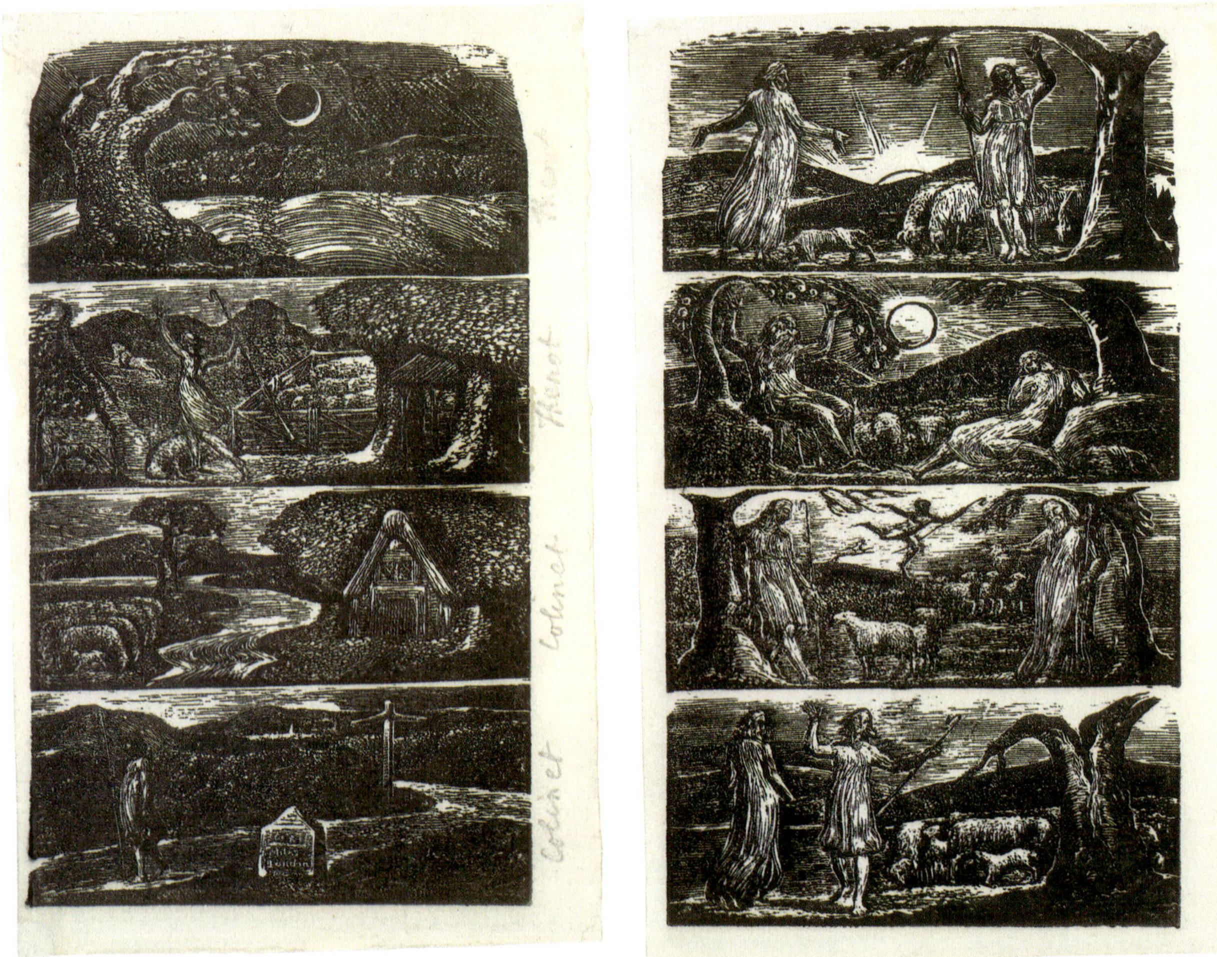

19

Academy, Sir Thomas Lawrence, and other leading figures in the art world. Even so, Thornton found it necessary to include a disclaimer about Blake's work in his book commenting that they 'display less art than genius, and are much admired by some eminent painters'.

Blake's wood engravings were greatly admired by Palmer, Linnell and their associates both for their bold use of pastoral imagery, which invested the features of the landscape with a primitive power, and also for their unusual cutting technique, which produced the effect of a low glimmering light. This may have been to some extent fortuitous, but it should be recalled that Blake admired the way that glimmering light effects produce a sense of the spiritual in landscape, praising Claude in particular for achieving this in his landscapes.

Palmer's high regard for these is recorded in one of his now lost sketchbooks, dated from November 1823 to July 1824 and quoted by A.H. Palmer in his life of his father:

> I sat down with Mr. Blake's Thornton's *Virgil* woodcuts before me, thinking to give their merit my feeble testimony. I happened first to think of their sentiment. They are visions of little dells, and nooks, and corners of Paradise; models of the exquisitest pitch of intense poetry. I thought of their light and shade, and looking upon them I found no word to describe it. Intense depth, solemnity, and vivid brilliancy only coldly and partially describes them. There is in all such a mystic and dreamy glimmer as penetrates and kindles the innermost soul, and gives complete and unreserved delight, unlike the gaudy daylight of this world. They are like all that wonderful artist's work the drawing aside of the fleshly curtain, and the glimpse which all the most holy, studious saints and sages have enjoyed, that rest which remaineth to the people of God. (*L&L*, pp. 15–16)

When he wrote this, Palmer had not yet met Blake, and after their meeting he obtained from the artist a signed page proof of prints from the blocks (Brown, p. 47). Superb though Palmer's evocation is, it does perhaps show more his preoccupations at the time than Blake's intentions in what was for Blake a relatively routine job creating designs for a type of subject for which he had limited approval. The earth was for Blake the place of limited vision. This accorded with his concept of 'Beulah', the earthly paradise mentioned in Isaiah and elaborated by Bunyan in *Pilgrim's Progress*. It would seem that Palmer's concept of Beulah was nearer the positive view of it that Bunyan had. Nevertheless the low glimmer in Blake's pastorals became a talisman for Palmer as he developed comparable effects in his own art.

**20***

## John Linnell (1792–1882)
## *William Blake at Hampstead*, *c.*1825

Graphite, 17.7 × 11.2 cm (7 × 4⅜ in)

Signed at lower right: *JL fecit*

Inscribed at lower left: *Wm Blake at Hampstead*; on mount, verso: *Mr Blake / on the hill before our cottage / at Hampstead c / 1825 I guess*

Lit: Keynes 1977, p. 139, pl. 33

University of Cambridge, Fitzwilliam Museum, PD.58-1950

In 1823 Linnell rented part of Collins's Farm on the west side of Hampstead Heath. In March 1824 he took over the whole of Collins's Farm, remaining there until 1828. During this period Linnell commissioned Blake first to do the illustrations to Job and then those to Dante. The two worked on the prints for Job, although this was largely done in London where Linnell maintained rooms at 6 Cirencester Place. However, Blake came to visit Linnell in Hampstead on a number of occasions, sometimes walking up from Bloomsbury in the company of Palmer. Despite his reservations about 'Beulah', Blake had a keen sense of natural beauty and enjoyed excursions to the Heath, though he worried about the effects of the air on his health. This sketch was presumably made on one such occasion. It shows Blake dressed as described by Palmer in a memory of visiting the Royal Academy with him: 'Blake in his plain black suit and *rather* broad-brimmed but not quakerish hat' (Gilchrist 1863, vol. 1, p. 278). Linnell was a shrewd and accurate – if not particularly flattering – portraitist, and this image of Blake is one of the most vivid we have.

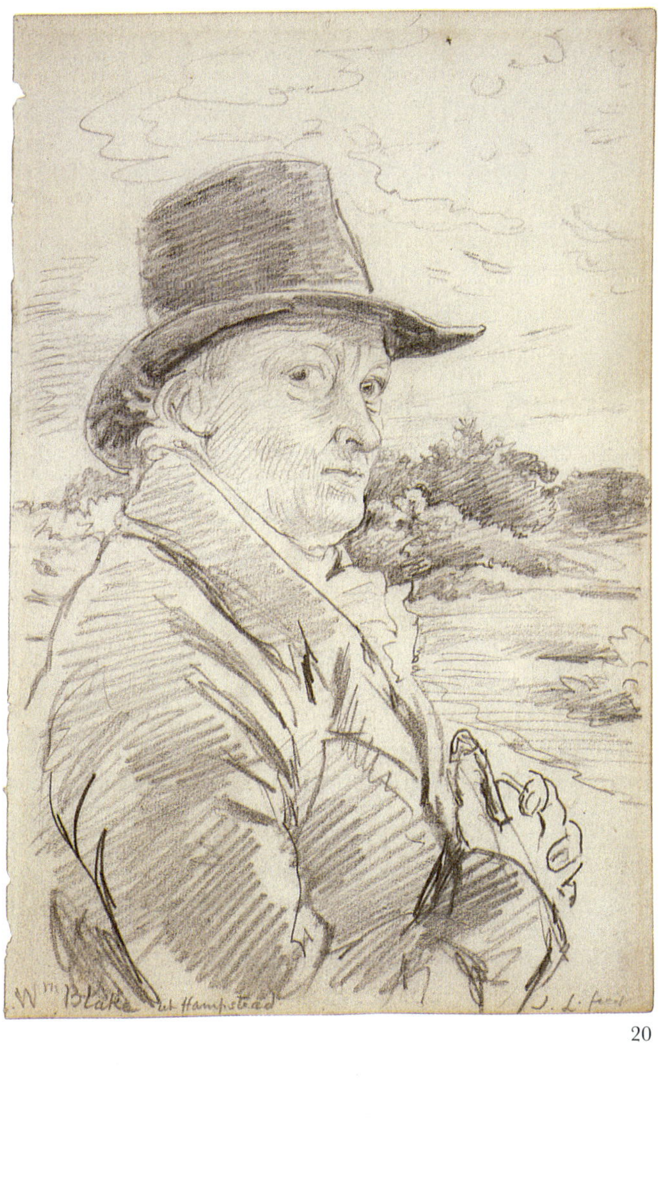


20

**21***

## John Linnell (1792–1882)
## *Study of a Tree*, 1811?

Watercolour, 14.9 × 10 cm (5⅞ × 4 in)

Lit: Crouan, p. xi; Payne 1982, p. 132

London, British Museum, 2002-10-26-6; presented by the National Art Collections Fund

The landscape painter John Linnell is now best remembered for the support that he gave Blake in that artist's last years (see cat. 46) and for the profound influence he had on Samuel Palmer, whom he met in 1822. Twelve years older than Palmer, he encouraged him to explore the primitive in art and introduced him to Blake. Both events were critical in Palmer's move to his own style of spiritualized primitivism during the Shoreham period. While admiring Palmer's art on some levels, Linnell was alarmed by his acolyte's departure from naturalistic conventions and attempted to discourage this. They also had differences in religion and politics, Linnell being a Nonconformist radical and Palmer a conservative member of the Church of England.

In 1837 Palmer married Linnell's eldest daughter Hannah, and from that time the relationship deteriorated, with Linnell attempting to play an increasingly controlling and negative role in Palmer's life. This has led to Linnell being treated somewhat unfairly in the Palmer literature. It should be remembered in his favour that he always felt excluded to some extent from the activities of Palmer's group, the Ancients. Furthermore his professional criticism of Palmer should be seen in the context of their respective careers. Palmer never succeeded in developing a successful, financially independent practice, while Linnell became in later years one of the most popular landscape painters of the Victorian era, deriving great wealth from his success.

In recent years Linnell's artistic reputation has to some extent revived. This has less to do with a reassessment of his Victorian landscapes than with the rediscovery of his innovative early pictures, which show an advanced realism in both technique and subject matter. Trained by John Varley, he was initiated by this artist into naturalistic sketching and took this practice so seriously that he even rivalled Constable as a naturalist. His earliest oil sketches date from his period of study with Varley, around 1806.

This study of a tree shows the sharpness of Linnell's vision in his early days. In 1811 Linnell underwent a strong religious conversion, becoming an ardent Baptist. It has been argued by both Crouan and Payne that this conversion increased his dedication to the study of nature, turning it into a form of spiritual exercise. It was the kind of work that Palmer would have encountered when he first met Linnell and would have inspired his admiration for the older artist. Like Constable, Linnell was an enthusiastic sketcher of trees. He later encouraged Palmer to make similar studies, provoking some of their most interesting artistic interchanges (see cat. 43).

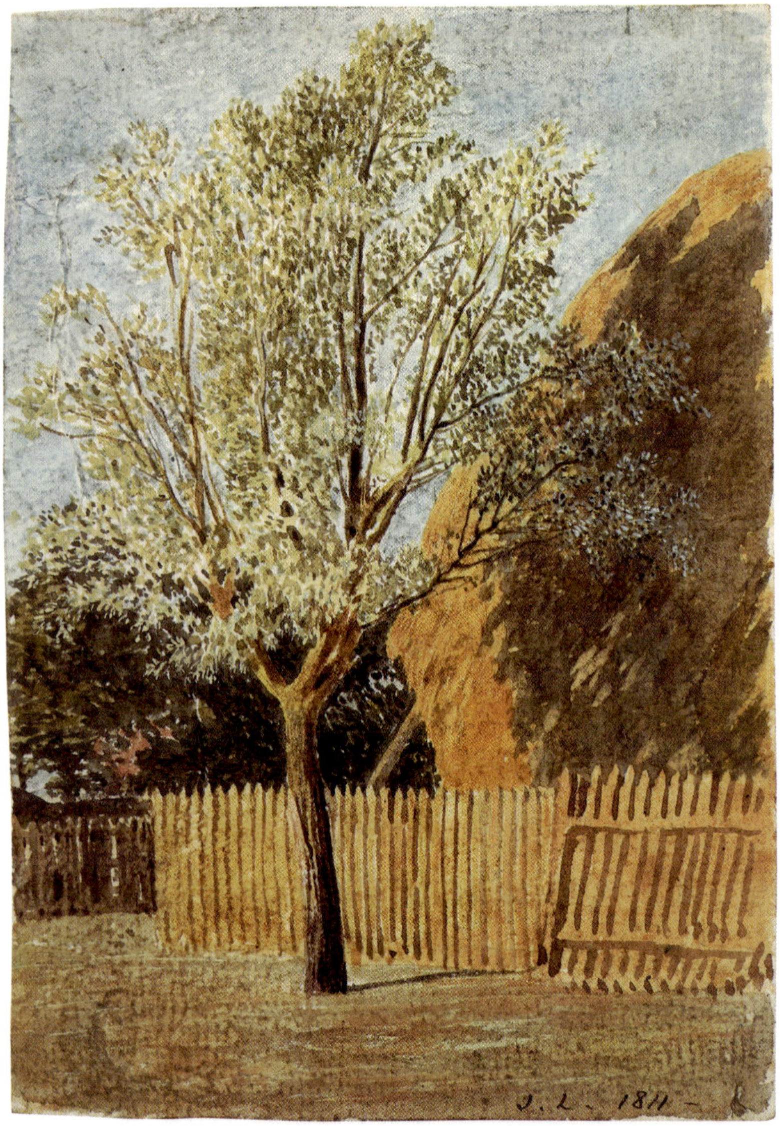


21

**22**

## John Linnell (1792–1882)

*The Favourite: A Group, with Portraits of the Artist's Children* (portrait of three of the artist's children: Hannah, Elizabeth and John), 1824

Watercolour miniature on ivory, 10.5 × 13.5 cm (4⅛ × 5⅜ in)

Lit: Linnell Autobiography; Story, vol. I, pp. 123–4, vol. II, p. 254; Graves 1906, vol. V, p. 65

Private collection, Linnell family

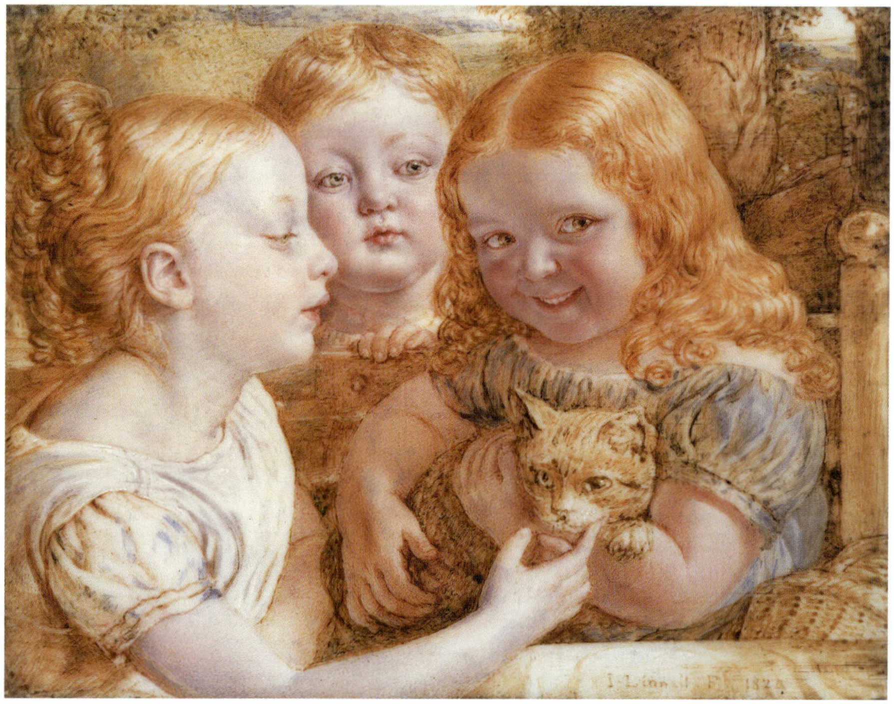

22

Linnell appears to have taken up miniature painting around 1816 at the suggestion of a neighbour. In his autobiography Linnell stresses that his portrait of his wife, Mary Ann Linnell, painted in 1818 was his first miniature, although he is now known to have been practising the art at least two years previously. Perhaps this slip underlines the importance to him of the miniatures of his family. The portrait of his three eldest children could certainly be claimed to be his finest work in the genre. It was exhibited at the Royal Academy in 1825 (RA no. 615). The title – which effectively turns the picture into a genre scene, with the children gathered around their pet cat – amply fulfils Linnell's desire to go 'beyond the locket and brooch style' then common among miniaturists (Linnell Autobiography). Together with Richmond, Linnell briefly restored miniature painting during the 1820s to the level of high artistic achievement that it had enjoyed in the sixteenth century. As such they could be seen as revivalists here as elsewhere in their art.

The picture is also of interest as the earliest portrayal of Palmer's future wife Hannah, seen on the left here stroking the cat under the chin. In the centre is John Linnell junior, destined like other male members of the family to become an artist. He was later to show great kindness to Palmer, softening to some extent the harshness of his father. Elizabeth, who remained unmarried, was to look after her parents in later life.

This is the period when the creative artistic interchange between Palmer and Linnell was at its height. Although never a full member of the Ancients, Palmer included Linnell at this time within the group, as he did indeed the children in this picture. In a letter to Linnell dated September 1824 Palmer concludes by sending 'love to the little ancients' (*Letters*, p. 9).

**23***

## John Linnell (1792–1882)

Copy of Van Eyck's *Righteous Judges*, 1826

Etching, 50.4 × 17.5 cm (20¾ × 7 in)

Lit: Story 1892, vol. I, p. 223

London, British Museum, 2002-7-28-92; presented by Frances Carey and David Bindman in honour of Neil MacGregor

This etching was produced by Linnell from a copy of one of the wings of Hubert and Jan Van Eyck's celebrated altarpiece, the *Adoration of the Lamb* (completed 1432), in St Bavon, Ghent. It was made from a copy of the altarpiece in the collection of Charles Aders, the German merchant whose collection of Northern primitives was much admired by Blake and the Ancients. According to Story, Linnell was commissioned to make the copy in 1826 by Aders's wife Eliza.

The etching is a meticulous work in which the influence of sixteenth-century engraving styles can be seen. It shows the extent to which Linnell, like Palmer, was engaged in the study of so-called 'primitive' art at this time. Linnell, however, may well have been drawn to Van Eyck because he represented the realist side of the fifteenth-century 'primitive' movement. For Linnell, unlike Palmer, there was no necessary conflict between the primitive and naturalism. Like Ruskin later, he saw the primitive in terms of direct and unprejudiced vision.

Linnell may have been influenced in his style of reproduction by the high quality lithographs after Flemish and German 'primitives' then being produced in Munich, notably those by Johann Nepomuk Strixner that were available in London booksellers at the time (Vaughan 1979, pp. 22–4).

Charles Aders's interest in collecting

Northern primitives very much reflected the tastes of his generation of Germans, largely inspired by the famous collection built up by the Boisserée brothers in Cologne and subsequently acquired by the Pinakothek in Munich. Like the Boisserées, Aders had profited from the expulsion of such works from religious institutions during the Napoleonic upheavals, buying early Flemish and German works at very low prices. The unusual feature about the Aders collection was that it was in London. Aders was well integrated into literary and artistic society in London, to a large extent through his wife, who was the daughter of John Raphael Smith and a talented artist in her own right. Their house in Euston Square became a focal point in the mid-1820s, a time when interest in German literature and Northern art was highly fashionable. Aders knew leading critics and artists in Germany and provided a crucial link between the two cultures on the visual side. Sadly his business failed in the 1830s and he was forced to sell his collection at knock-down prices. By then the vogue for the primitive that had flowered in the 1820s was on the wane, not to be revived until the age of the Pre-Raphaelites.

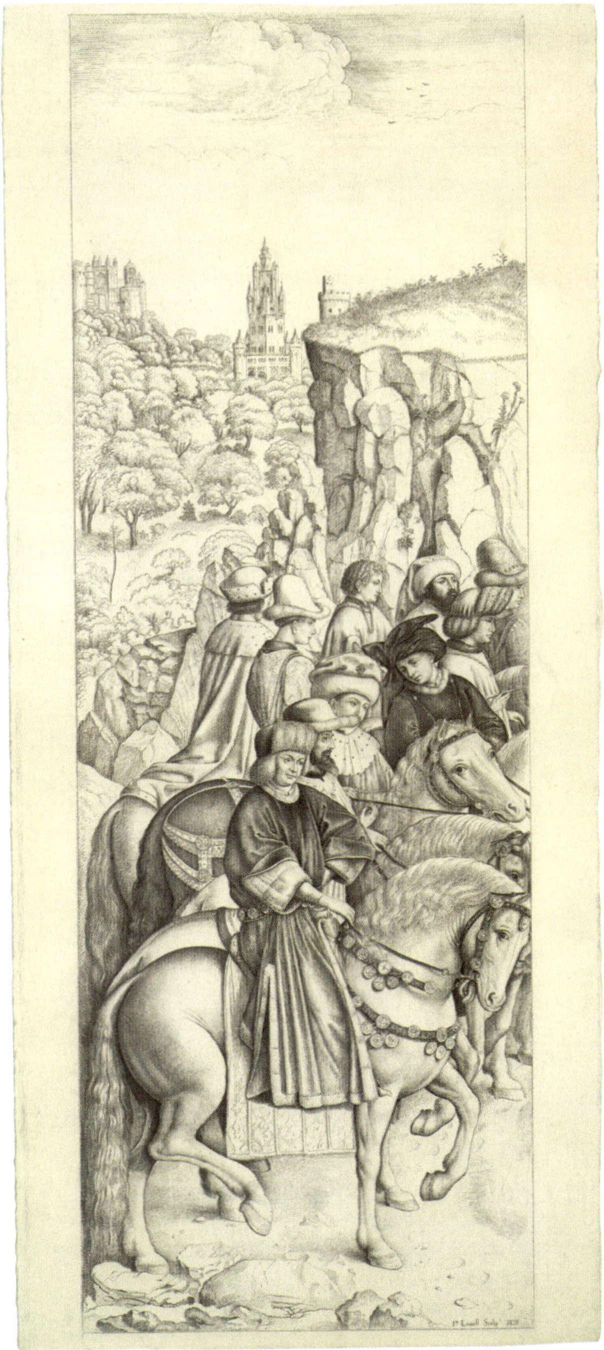

23

## 24

### Albrecht Dürer (1471–1528)

### *The Flight into Egypt*, *c.*1504 (from *The Life of the Virgin*, 1511 edition)

Woodcut, 29.7 × 20.9 cm (11 5/8 × 8 1/4 in)

Lit: *L&L*, pp. 15–16; Grigson 1947, pp. 15, 56

London, British Museum, 1895-1-22-634; donated by William Mitchell

The engravings and woodcuts of the great sixteenth-century German artist Albrecht Dürer were greatly admired by Palmer. In this he took his lead from his two early mentors, Linnell and Blake. Soon after meeting Linnell in 1822, Palmer recorded a conversation he had had with the older artist concerning art: 'Let me remember always, and may I not slumber in the possession of it, Mr. Linnell's injunction (delightful in the performance), "look at Albert Dürer"' (*L&L*, p. 15). Palmer seems to have been particularly fascinated by the bold manner in which Dürer used the simplifying methods of the woodcut to describe landscape features with vigorous linearity. Later in life he quoted with approval Blake's comment that 'his [Dürer's] most finished woodcuts, when closely examined, seemed to consist principally of outline; – that they were "everything yet nothing"' (*Letters*, p. 573). Palmer was deeply concerned with the expressive power of line and felt that Dürer's woodcuts provided this effect in its essence.

This image of the *Flight into Egypt*, published by Dürer as part of his series of the *Life of the Virgin*, was a particular

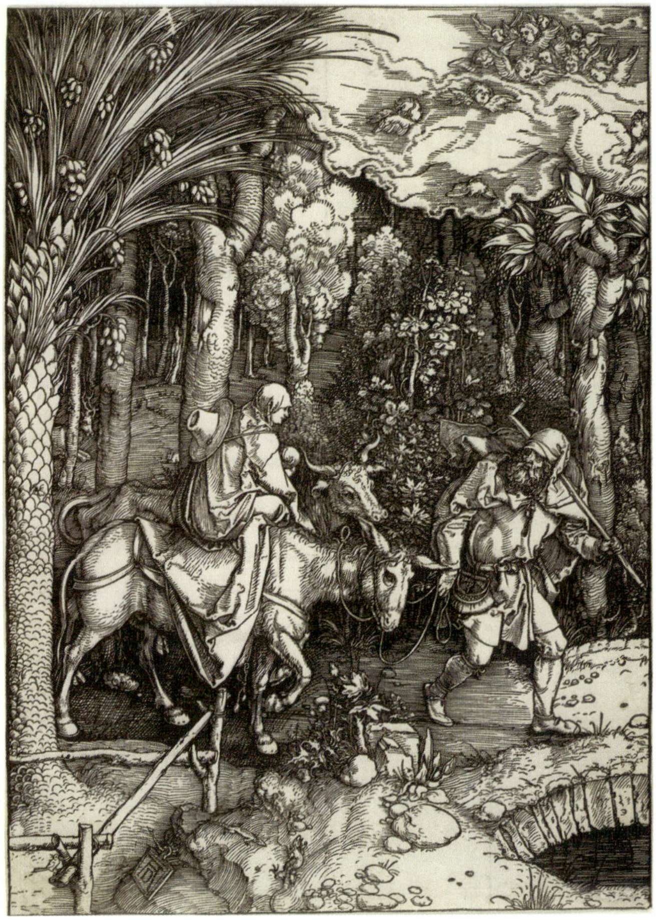

24

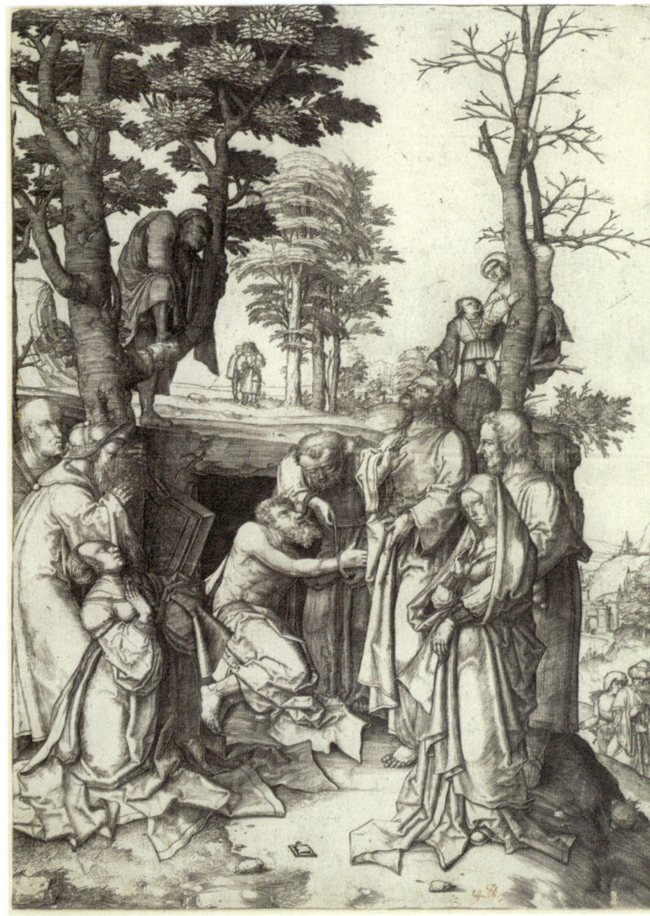

25

favourite of Palmer's. In a letter to P.G. Hamerton dated October 1871 he recommended it as an example to etchers for laying down the 'first lines' of a composition prior to filling this in with shading and further detail:

> Let any one look at a fine impression of Albert Dürer's Holy Family going through the wood, with the palm-tree on the left, and think what a comfort it would be to have such a preparation ready bitten on the copper, the ground removed, and a transparent one laid on for beginning the shadows. (*Letters*, p. 821.)

Palmer presumably already knew this work at the time when he was developing his 'primitive' vision. There appears to be a reference to the palm tree in it in the design on leaf 22 (recto) of his 1824 sketchbook (cat. 9h).

## 25*

## Lucas van Leyden (1494–1533)

### *The Raising of Lazarus*, 1505–7

Copper engraving, sheet 28.6 × 20.3 cm (11¼ in × 8 in)

Lit: *L&L*, pp. 12, 14, 16–17

London, British Museum, 1845-8-9-943

Lucas van Leyden was a Flemish painter whose engraving style was close to that of Dürer, whom he met in 1521. As with Dürer, Palmer was encouraged by Linnell (who owned a painting ascribed to van Leyden) to use van Leyden as a model for his landscapes. Palmer noted in his sketchbook of 1823–4 (now destroyed): 'look for Van Leydenish qualities in real landscape, and look hard, long and continually. Look for picturesque combinations of buildings, and elegant spires and turrets for backgrounds' (*L&L*, p. 14).

This quotation suggests that while Palmer turned to Dürer first for his powerful linearity, he seems to have been inspired by the more fanciful and decorative aspects of van Leyden's designs. He may also have been inspired by van Leyden's religious subject matter. In a list of subjects from the life of Christ in a lost notebook of 1822–4 he included the 'Raising of Lazarus' among the subjects he wished to paint. Speaking of these subjects he admonished himself to 'lay up, silently, and patiently, materials for them in your sketch-book, and copy the prints to learn such nicety in pen-sketching'.

**26*** (*illustrated as fig. 16, p. 48*)

## Giulio di Antonio Bonasone (1500/10–after 1574), after Michelangelo Buonarroti (1475–1564)

*The Holy Family*

Engraving, 40.3 × 26.8 cm (15⅞ × 10½ in)
Lit: Story 1892, vol. I, p. 225; *Letters*, p. 862
London, British Museum, 1866-7-14-66

The sixteenth-century Italian engraver Bonasone was admired by Palmer both for his consummate skills as an engraver and because much of his work was based on the designs of Michelangelo – venerated by all in the Blake circle as the most supreme of all artists. Many of Bonasone's engravings, including this Holy Family, are based on drawings by Michelangelo that are now lost. As with the Northern masters Dürer and van Leyden (see cats 24 and 25), Palmer appears to have been introduced to Bonasone first through Linnell, either from prints in his own collection or those that they viewed together in the Department of Prints and Drawings at the British Museum. Palmer seems to have been fascinated above all by the fine effects of shadow that Bonasone achieved. In a letter of 1872 to P.G. Hamerton he wrote:

> Bonasoni [*sic*] seems to me the greatest master of shadowing upon copper … let any one who can draw, copy exactly in pen and ink some boldly-shadowed limb of Bonasoni's, and afterwards turn it into a tree trunk by vigorous line work expressing the texture of the bark, and he will then see texture in its proper function, and shadow in its poetic sleep. (*Letters*, p. 862.)

The mysterious effects of shade achieved by Bonasone appear to have pleased Linnell himself less than what he felt were the clearer and more accurate engravings of Bonasone's famous contemporary Marcantonio Raimondi. In his life of Linnell Story notes that: 'Of all these old masters his favourite was Marc Antonio, whose style, though not perhaps so poetic as that of his pupil Bonasoni, was stronger, and showed more fidelity to the picture from which he worked.'

**27***

## Giulio di Antonio Bonasone (1500/10–after 1574)

*Tenere Medium Semper est Prudentiae*

Page CXXII of *Achillis Bocchi Bonum Symbolicarum*
Approx. 18 × 13 cm (7 × 5 in)
British Museum, PD 163* a 3; presented by G. Cumberland, 1820

As well as making high quality engravings, Bonasone also produced illustrations for emblem books, whose meanings appear to have fascinated Palmer. In 1825 he recorded Linnell's remarks about one of these: 'I was looking with Mr. L: [Linnell] at one of Bonasone's emblems, a rope-dancer balancing himself with the motto, *In medio est salus.* "Yes" said he emphatically, "for a rope-dancer; but the rope-dancer only keeps the middle that he may be not middling, but an excessive fine performer"' (*L&L*, p. 16).

This copy of the volume in which Bonasone's work appears (with a title that Palmer seems to have misremembered) was presented to the British Museum by George Cumberland, the patron of Blake, in 1820. Since Linnell and Palmer visited the Department of Prints and Drawings together in the 1820s, it is quite likely that this is the actual engraving they were looking at when Linnell made his remark.

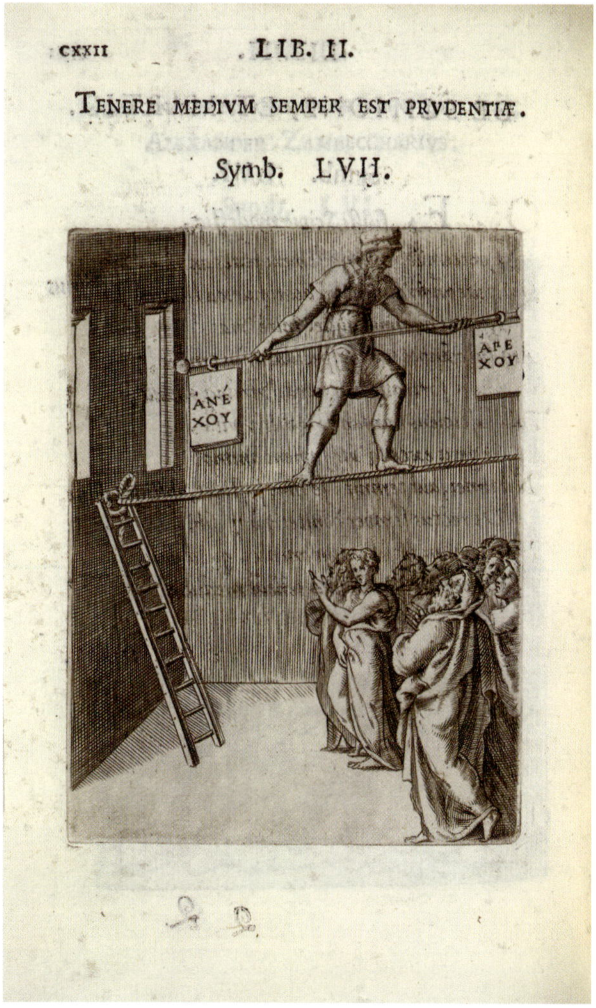


27

# 3. Shoreham and the Ancients (1825–30)

*William Vaughan*

The Kent village of Shoreham – some 30 miles south-east of central London – is the place now most strongly associated with Palmer's art. Although the main characteristics of his primitivizing style were formed in London, these reached their fullest and richest expression during his time in this village. Palmer himself later saw the seven years that he lived primarily in Shoreham as the happiest and most creatively fulfilling of his life. Afterwards, his style was to change dramatically. Yet much of the imagery that he developed at this time, the theme of the 'Sleeping Shepherd' for example (see cat. 89), remained a part of his repertoire. He preserved his Shoreham work in his studio, but, mindful of how strange it would seem to most contemporaries, he kept the boldest works, such as the *Magic Apple Tree* (cat. 69), in what he called the 'Curiosity Portfolio', shown only to a few trusted friends (V&A 1926, p. 36).

Palmer had been visiting Shoreham since at least September 1824 (*Letters*, p. 7). It seems that he was made aware of the village first by his father. A lay Baptist preacher, Samuel Palmer senior was attracted to Shoreham as a centre for Nonconformism. He only moved to Shoreham fully, however, after his brother Nathaniel offered him an allowance on the understanding that he would give up his bookshop in Bloomsbury and live as a retired 'gentleman' in the country. The contents of his shop were sold on 2 March 1827 (Grigson 1947, p. 50), and it is probable that he came to settle in Shoreham soon afterwards. Prior to that time Palmer junior had already been staying periodically in Shoreham with other members of the Ancients. Accommodation was often poor, Palmer taking a cottage that his friends referred to as 'rat alley'. In autumn 1828, however, his father rented Water House, a substantial property close to the bridge over the River Darent (see cat. 44). From that time onwards Palmer lived there with his father, brother William and nurse Mary Ward.

Palmer later said he was 'forced into the countryside by illness' (*Letters*, p. 824). He seems to have suffered much from bronchial trouble at this time. He was able to afford the move out of London because of a legacy from his grandfather William Giles, who had died in 1825. Relative freedom from financial worries in his early Shoreham years certainly provided Palmer with the opportunity to pursue his artistic inclination without hindrance. In his later Shoreham years, particularly after 1830, financial considerations played an increasingly important part in his life and were one of the reasons why he reluctantly decided to return to London in the mid-1830s. Yet, while enjoying life as an independent artist, Palmer always aimed at professional acceptance. During this period he sent work regularly to the Royal Academy for exhibition. Much was rejected, yet some of his most extreme work, *Ruth* for example (cat. 39), was shown. The critical reception was poor, and he does not seem to have sold work at this time except to relatives and close friends.

Since so few Shoreham works are firmly dated it is hard to be definite about how his art developed. What evidence there is suggests that the more severely primitive work, such as *A Shepherd and his Flock under the Moon and Stars* (cat. 30), dates from the early years. After 1827 – the year in which Blake died and Palmer seems to have settled permanently in Shoreham – his manner of painting becomes richer and more atmospheric, as in *Coming from Evening Church* (cat. 48), which is dated 1830. Palmer was at his most experimental technically at this time, practising a form of tempera painting inspired by Blake and creating monochromes in ink and mixed media. During the 1830s this tendency increased and Palmer moved away from visionary themes to more conventional though still intensely poetic evocations of the pastoral, as in *The Sleeping Shepherd* (cat. 89). It should be remembered, however, that this sequence remains largely conjectural, and that the changes may not have been exact or absolute. Furthermore, throughout his time at Shoreham he continued to produce naturalistically observed studies of nature alongside his imaginative work.

Palmer's early years at Shoreham were also the time when the Ancients were at their height as an artistic group. The group was set up around 1824 in London but continued to gather membership over the next three years. The principal figures were Edward Calvert (see cat. 58), George Richmond (see cat. 51), Francis Oliver Finch, Henry Walter (see cat. 3), Welby Sherman (see cat. 62) and Frederick Tatham. There were also some non-artist members, notably Palmer's cousin and constant supporter the stockbroker John Giles and Tatham's brother Arthur, an undergraduate at Magdalen College Oxford who later became a clergyman. John Giles's role appears to have been particularly significant, and he may indeed have been the initiator of the whole undertaking (see p. 18).

The details of how the group became established are not clear but it is assumed that Palmer had a leading hand in it. He was always the most enthusiastic 'Ancient' and may have been the only one to assume a special archaizing costume of the kind shown in

Richmond's miniature of him in 1829 (cat. 54). Others very close to him in these years were Calvert and Richmond. Yet while these both visited Shoreham, neither of them lived there. Calvert possessed independent means and could have afforded the move. However, he was already married and had a growing family. Richmond, younger than Palmer and his most enthusiastic follower, did not possess the means of living for an extended period in Shoreham. The son of a miniaturist, he was already building a career as a portraitist in London. Other members of the group were similarly sporadic in their visits, though Henry Walter, Frederick Tatham and Welby Sherman seem to have been resident for some time. In general, visits to Shoreham declined in the early 1830s and members of the group went their separate ways artistically while continuing, for the most part, to remain personal friends.

While short-lived as an artistic group, the Ancients did experience an intense sense of purpose and friendship (see p. 17). In many of their ideals and activities they foreshadowed the Pre-Raphaelites. As has already been said in the previous section, they were undoubtedly influenced in their decision to form a group and in their taste for medievalism by the German Nazarenes, the revivalist group based in Rome who enjoyed international celebrity in the 1820s. Perhaps because of their affinities with Nazarene art, their religious works achieved a degree of official support, if little commercial success. The President of the Royal Academy, Sir Thomas Lawrence, was a great admirer of the work of the Nazarenes (Vaughan 1979, p. 21). Some biblical pictures by Richmond and Palmer were accepted for exhibition at the Academy; Palmer himself was somewhat surprised that his works such as *Ruth* (cat. 39) were preferred over his landscapes (*Letters*, p. 54).

Despite the acceptance of *Ruth* and *The Deluge* (unknown – see p. 50), Palmer seems to have given up biblical figurative subjects soon after this. In 1830 and 1831 there were no pictures by Palmer in the Academy, presumably because all were rejected. From 1832 to 1836 he had works regularly in the exhibition. To judge by the titles of these, they all represented idyllic and pastoral themes that preoccupied him in his later years at Shoreham, when religious symbolism and eccentricity of effect were kept to a minimum.

Palmer's move away from extreme individualism in his art and lifestyle may have been partly due to growing adverse criticism in his own circle. A lost letter from him of *c.*1829 contains the following sentence that shows Linnell's disapproval of his secessionist tendency: 'I am startled by this sentence in a letter just received from my father, "Mr. Linnell … foretells that your voluntary secession from artists will end in the withering of your mind. He has known it to be so"' (*Letters*, p. 53).

## 28

## *Rest on the Flight into Egypt* or *Holy Family*, *c.*1824–8

Oil and tempera on panel, 31 × 39 cm (12¼ × 15⅜ in)

Lit: Pressly 1969, pp. 28–31; Brown 4; Lister 46

Oxford, Ashmolean Museum, 1932.2; presented by the National Art Collections Fund, 1932

This is a rare surviving example, along with *Ruth* (cat. 39), of a biblical subject painting by Palmer from this period. Other biblical subjects he is recorded as having depicted at the time include *Joseph's Dream* and *Naomi before Bethlehem*, as well as scenes projected from 'the books of Ruth, Daniel, and Jonah'. This is the only one of the group that represents Christ and could be said to have a devotional aspect. Perhaps this is because it was painted for his cousin and fellow Ancient, John Giles.

The subject – an apocryphal one of the Holy Family fleeing to Egypt and being fed miraculously on their journey through the desert by fruit from a palm under which they were resting – had been common in western art since the late Middle Ages. It would seem to be a highly appropriate one for a visionary landscape painter, stressing as it does divine benevolence in nature. Brown has pointed to treatments of the theme in an engraving by Martin Schongauer and a woodcut by Albrecht Dürer (cat. 24) as likely sources. Grigson 1947, p. 161, claimed that the picture illustrates the text 'the foxes have holes, and the birds of the air have nests; but the Son of man hath not where to lay his head' (Matthew 8: 20; Luke 9: 58). However, he gives no reason for this, and one must assume that this is no more than an ingenious speculation.

A sketch dated *c.*1824–5 now in the collection of the Yale Center for British Art (Lister 44) may be related to the composition of this picture.

A study in Princeton (cat. 29) has on the verso (apparently inscribed by the artist): 'The background of Mr Giles's Holy Family / Shoreham paddock'. Although not an exact match, there is a definite similarity of terrain. Shoreham paddock – a stretch of land to the south of the village – is mentioned by Palmer in his letters as a place that he liked to frequent. Pressly, who published the drawing, does not believe it is a study for the picture, but rather a later version of the same landscape, probably *c.*1828–30.

The date is problematic. It is normally assumed to be 1824, as on 2 January 1825 he wrote in his notebook that 'about the 15th of last July … I laid by the [Holy] *Family* in much distress, anxiety and fear'. The quote contains some difficulties. First, it is not clear that the *Family* referred to is this picture. The notebook in which the comment was made has not survived and it is known only in the form in which it was cited by A.H. Palmer (*L&L*, p. 13). A.H. Palmer puts 'Holy' in square brackets, thus indicating that it was an interpolation of his own. Second, Palmer says he laid the work by, but does not mention taking it up again. It is possible that, if this is the picture referred to, he nevertheless did not complete it until some time later.

Since Palmer was already visiting Shoreham by 1824 he could have been

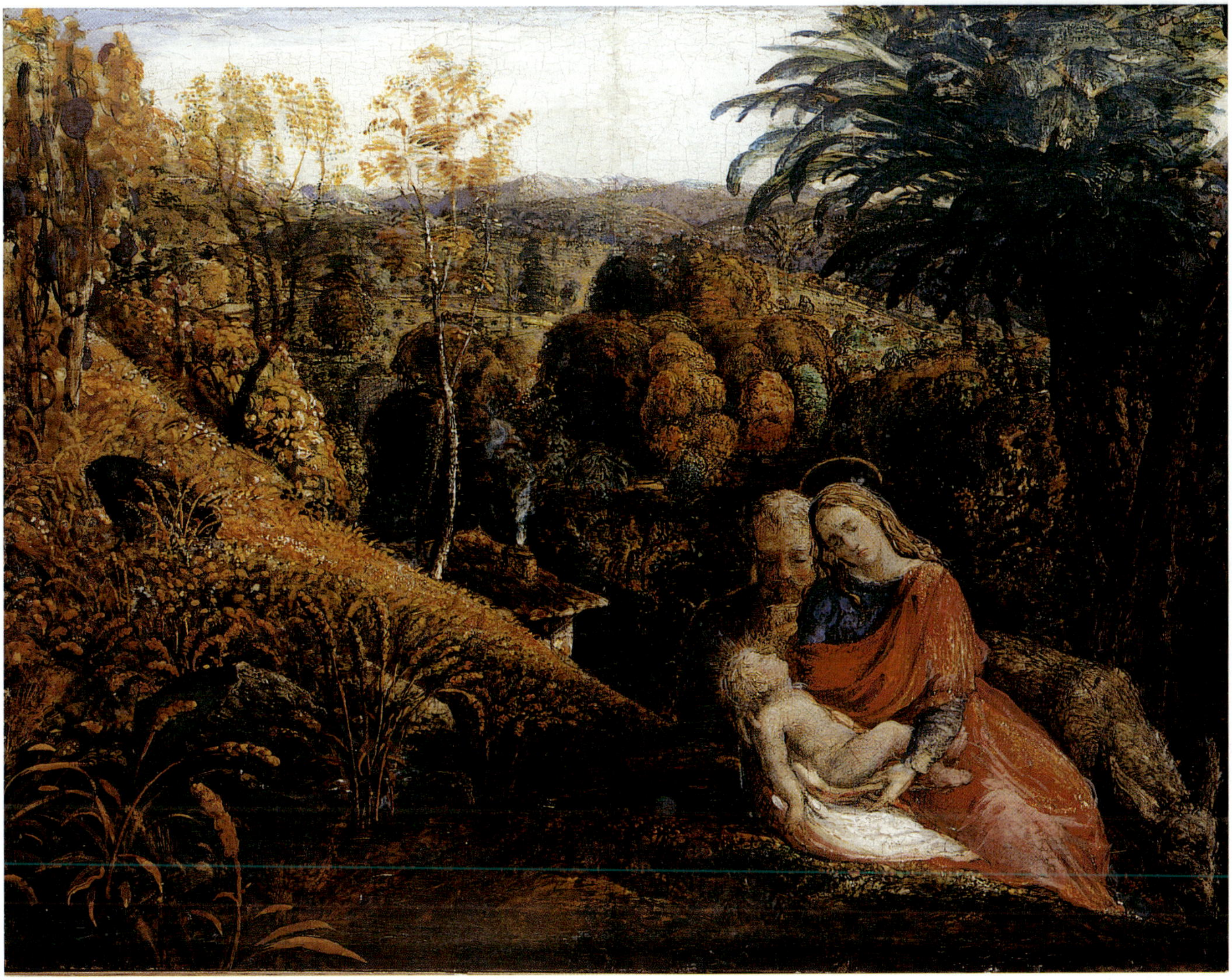

28

using sketches of the area in his religious works at that date. Brown feels that the autumnal look of the landscape suggests that it is based on his experience of Shoreham in the autumn of 1824. If this is the case, then the landscape would follow on after the time around July 1824 when, according to the comment in his notebook, he set aside his *Family*.

The technique used relates to Blake's manner of working in mixed media. Essentially, this involved painting in oil over tempera in imitation of fifteenth-century artists . Brown believes that 'it was probably his first essay in oils'. It is more conventional in treatment than the *Hilly Scene* (cat. 17), where tempera is used with watercolour, and seems closer to the more flowing style that developed after he settled in Shoreham. It is possible that, having set his Holy Family aside in July 1824, he only completed it when he had been in Shoreham for some time, perhaps even as late as 1828. He may only have added oil to the tempera base of the picture at the later date.

## 29

### *Shoreham Paddock / Hilly Landscape*, *c.*1826–8

Brown wash, 9.2 × 12 cm (3⅝ × 4¾ in)

Inscribed on verso in graphite: *The Background of Mr Giles's Holy Family / Shoreham Paddock*

Lit: Lister 116

Princeton, The Art Museum, Princeton University; gift of Frank Jewett Mather, Jr.

Although the designs are not identical, this view does bear a general relationship to that in the background of the *Holy Family* (cat. 28). Shoreham Paddock was a stretch of land to the south of the village that Palmer mentions in his letters and was fond of frequenting. Palmer is presumably looking down over this from the rising ground to the east of Shoreham. The hills on the west side of the Darent valley can be seen in the background. The loose and atmospheric manner evident here accords with the way Palmer tended to apply mono-

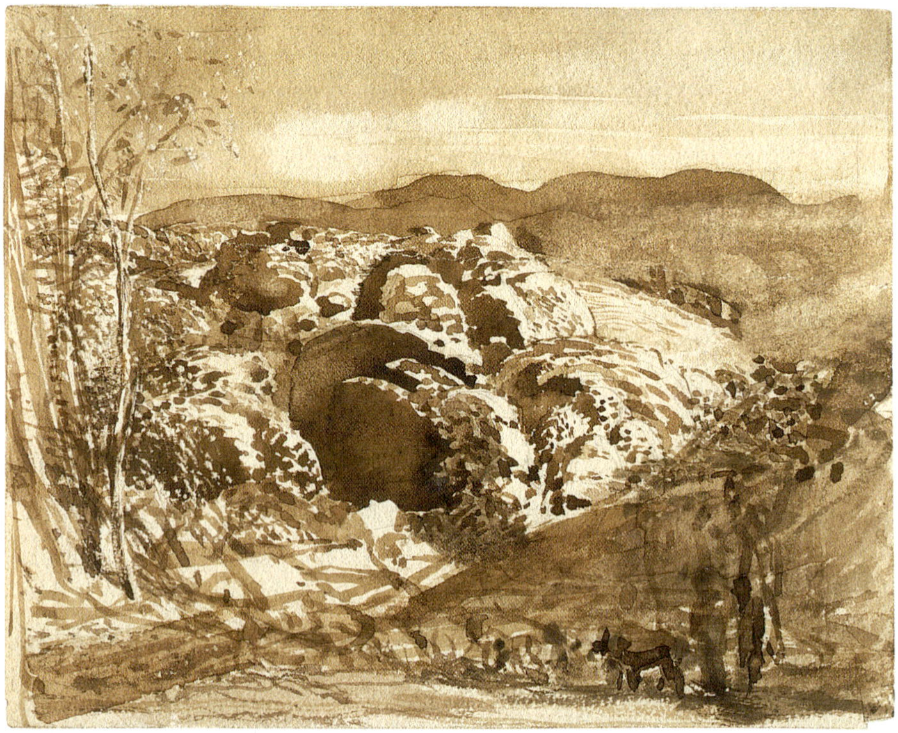

29

chrome washes after he had settled at Shoreham. It contrasts with the more hard-edged use of monochrome in the Oxford series of 1825.

## 30*

*A Shepherd and his Flock under the Moon and Stars*, c.1827

Black and brown ink, white gouache, some scratching out, 10.8 × 13 cm, (4¼ × 5⅛ in)

Lit: V&A 1926, 71; Fitzwilliam 1984, 14; Lister 72; Olson and Pasachoff 1998, pp. 163–4

New Haven, Yale Center for British Art, Paul Mellon Collection, B1977.14.2655

This is one of the freest of Palmer's 'blacks', the monochrome ink and wash paintings that became a speciality of his during the Shoreham years. The subject combines a pastoral scene – a shepherd and his flock – with startling nocturnal effects, in particular a vast waning moon and magnified stars. These are so prominent that they suggest some specific astronomical intention. In their book *Fire in the Sky* detailing the representation of comets in art, Olson and Pasachoff claim that this picture shows a comet with a double tail. This representation emphasizes, for them, the role of the comet as a portent of doom, something that accords with the 'Gothick' effects in the picture as a whole.

Palmer's treatment is so broad that it is hard to be certain whether the scratched lines by the star to the left are intended to be its tails or whether they are simply indications of light emanating from the moon, as the scratch beneath them presumably is. However, it is clear that Palmer was keen on astronomical phenomena and later made a painting showing Donati's comet over Dartmoor in 1858 (cat. 138). The picture certainly makes clear Palmer's fascination with celestial effects, communicated, for example, in one of his most ecstatic letters to Richmond in November 1827 (cat. 52).

Unusually for Palmer, the background also contains some decidedly Gothick elements, notably a castle to the right and a chapel or some other medieval building to the left. The strangeness of the whole scene is a reminder that the Ancients were fond of nocturnal wanderings, during which they would sometimes engage in readings from Macbeth and Mrs Ann Radcliffe's *Mysteries of Udolfo* (1794).

## 31

*Shepherds under a Full Moon*, c.1826–30

Pen and brown ink, brush and Indian ink mixed with gum, heightened with gouache on card, 11.8 × 13.4 cm (4¾ × 5⅜ in)

Lit: Lister 118

Oxford, Ashmolean Museum, 1934.287

The magnified forms and portentous use of the night sky resemble *A Shepherd and his Flock under the Moon and Stars* (cat. 30), which is similar in format and medium. There are echoes in the work of Blake's illustrations to Thornton's *Pastorals of Virgil* (cat. 19), both in the shape of the figures and in the general disposition of the composition. In the case of this picture, however, there is no clear indication of what kind of narrative, if any, was intended.

Like *A Shepherd and his Flock*, the work focuses on a spectacular nocturnal effect. In this case it is the full moon casting its light over an arc of fleecy small clouds. Mottled skies were a favourite of Palmer's in later life (see cat. 117). Here he is using it to suggest the tranformative effects of night. There are a number of other monochromes dated to the later 1820s that also explore the effect of full moon and mottled clouds, notably *A Kentish Idyll* (Lister 110), *Moonlight Landscape* (Lister 111) and *Shepherd Leading his Flock under a Full Moon* (Lister 112).

The experimental use of ink, gouache and gum is typical of Palmer's innovative primitivism in the mid-1820s. The forms are treated in a looser and more painterly manner than some works from this period, but this might be an aspect of the particular effect of moonlight on clouds being represented. Some commentators consider that this looseness makes the present work likely to date from the late 1820s or 1830, when other mottled moonlight scenes (see

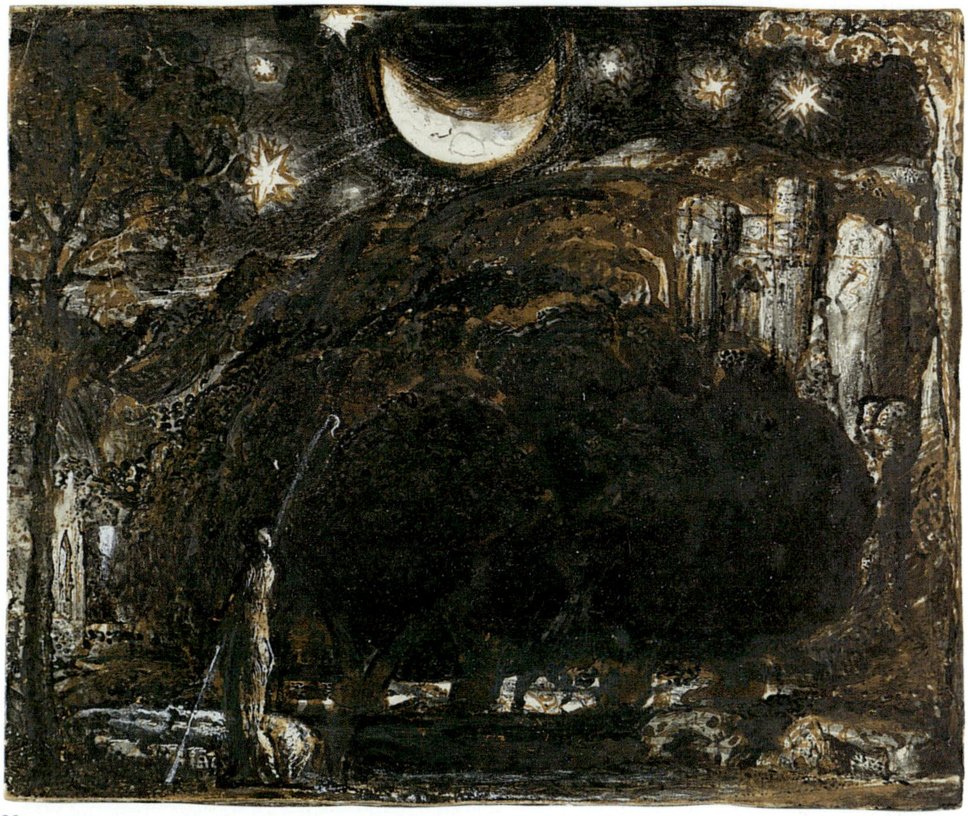

30

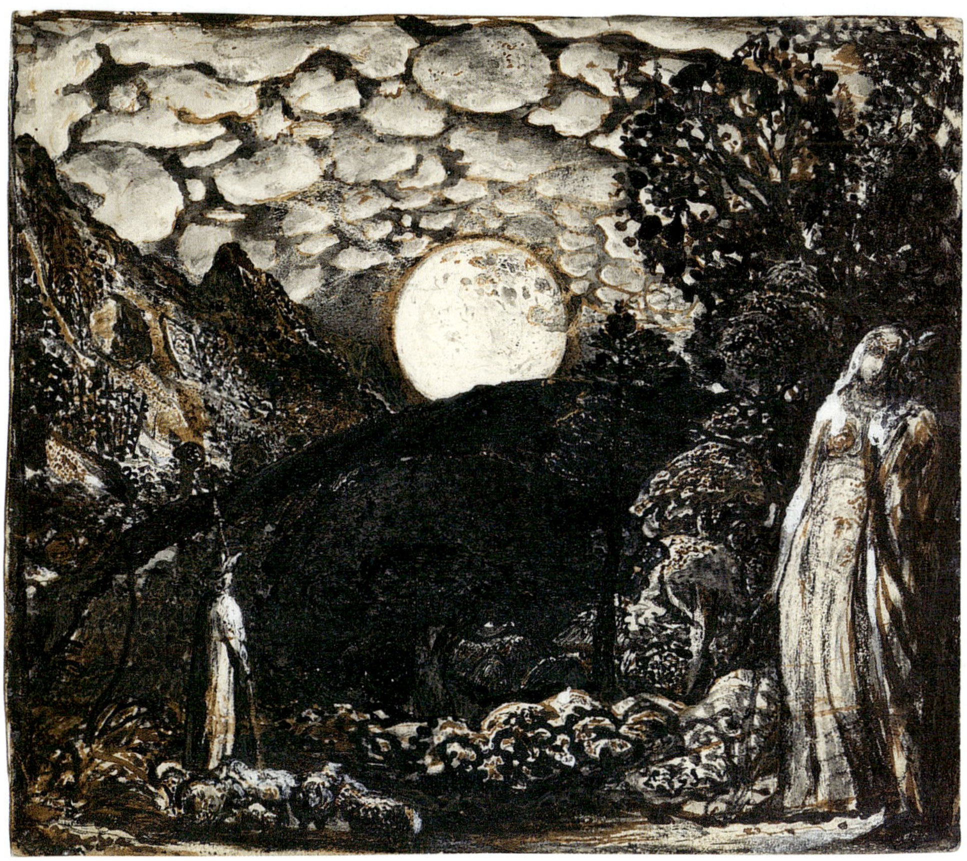

31

above) were apparently painted. Others (such as Grigson in 1960, p. 26) feel that the archaic motifs and experimental methods relate it more to the mid-1820s.

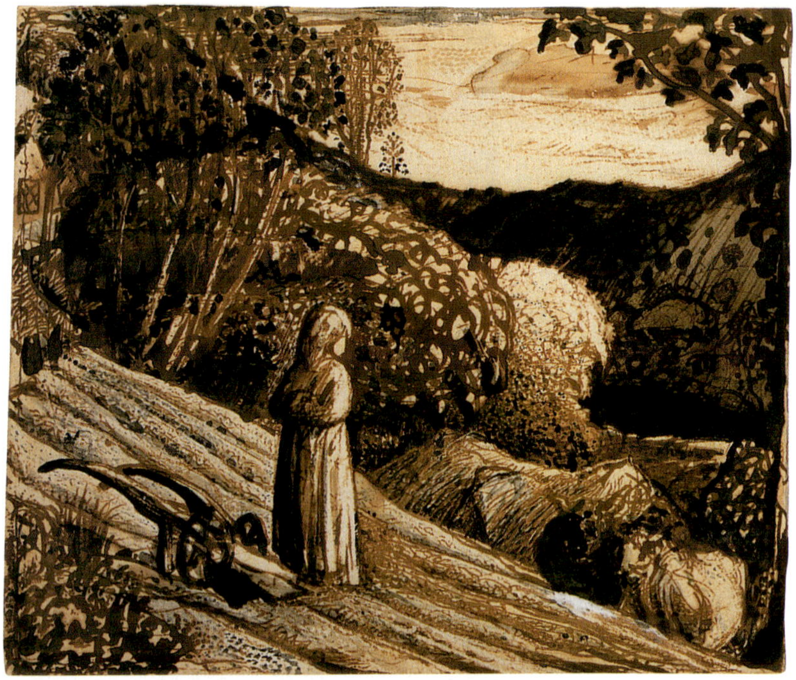

32

### 32*

*Landscape: Girl Standing, c.1826*

Ink and gouache on card, 11.4 × 13.3 cm ($4\frac{1}{2} \times 5\frac{1}{4}$ in)

Lit: Lister 64

London, Tate, N03701; purchased 1922

This scene – showing a girl standing by a plough in a sloping ploughed field – may be simply an evocation of rural life and have no symbolic or narrative meaning. Its design, particularly the strongly sloping field and rather compressed forms, suggest that it is close to Palmer's highly primitivizing phase and for this reason the work has usually been dated *c.*1826. The unconventional nature of the figure – so stiff as to almost resemble a sculpture – supports this early date.

This picture was particularly admired by Graham Sutherland for its bold composition (see p. 57) when he first saw it as a student in the 1920s.

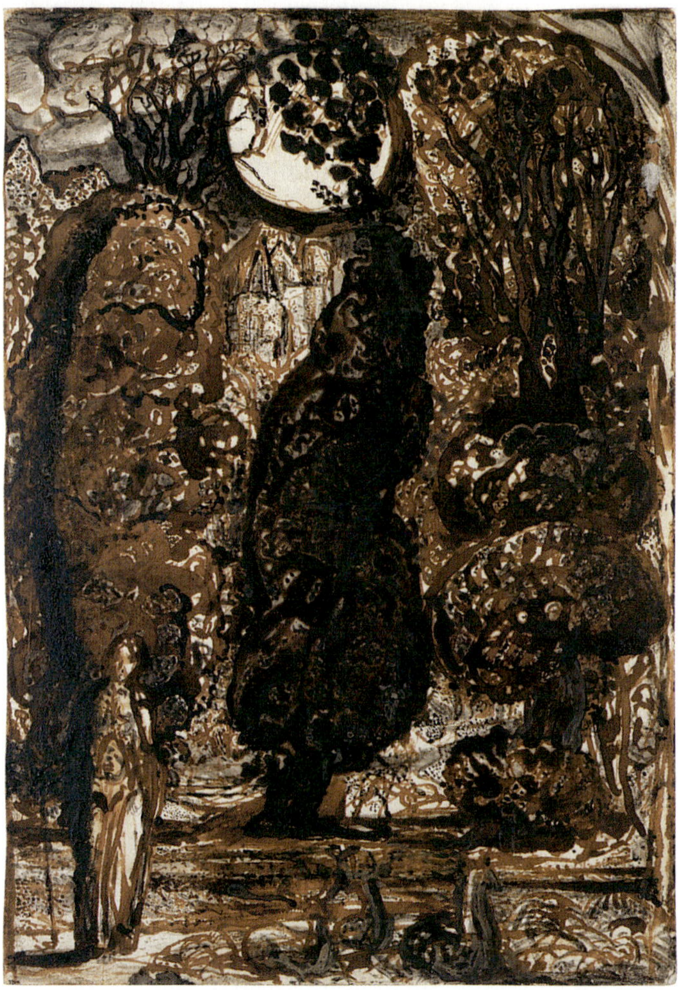

33

### 33*

*Landscape with Full Moon and Deer, c.1826–30*

Brown and black watercolour, 18.4 × 14.9 cm ($7\frac{1}{4} \times 5\frac{7}{8}$ in)

Lit: Lister 113

London, Victoria and Albert Museum, 644-1920

Like cat. 31, this loosely painted nocturnal scene represents the full moon, but this time the pastoral scene has the unusual addition of a deer.

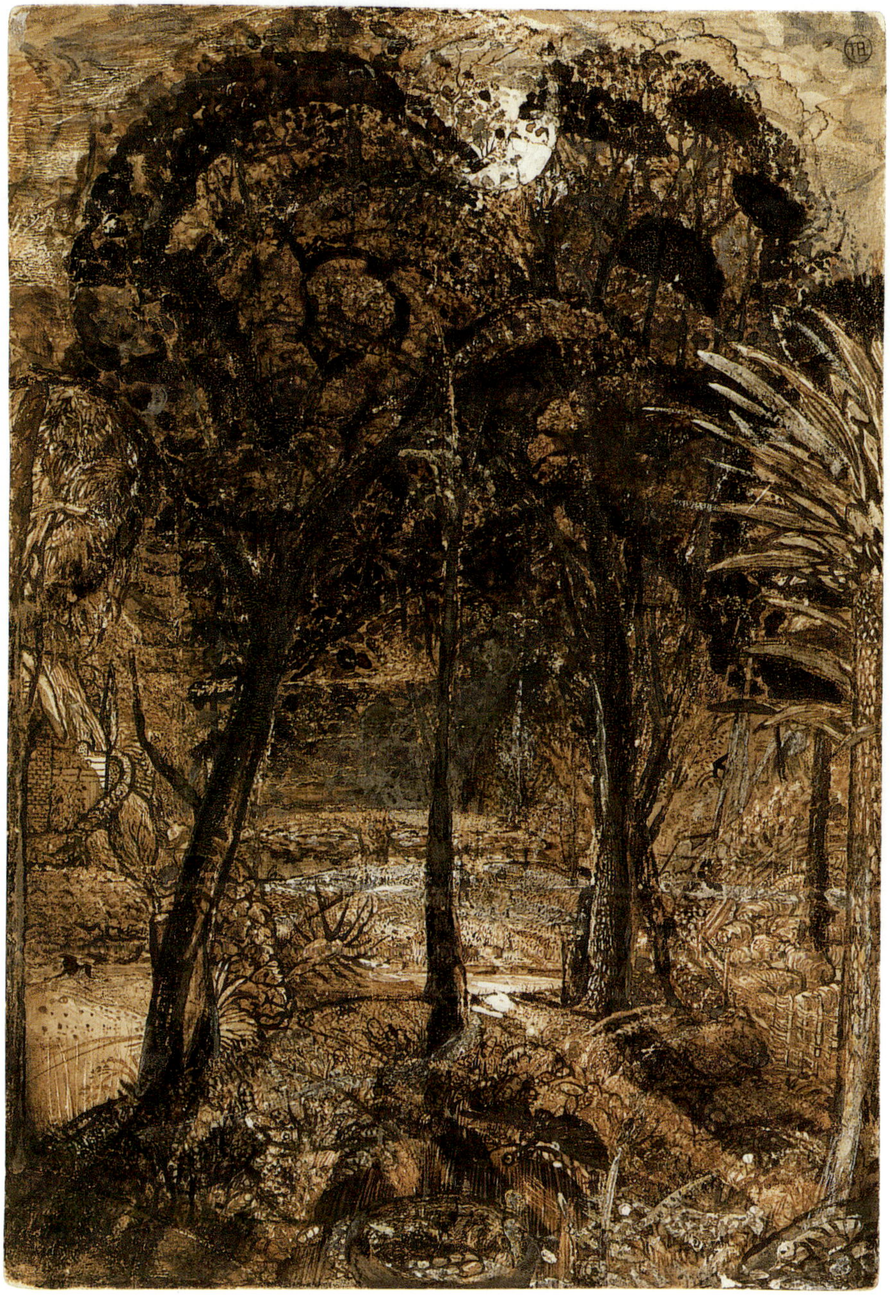

34

## 34*

*A Moonlight Scene with a Winding River*, *c.*1827

Black and brown wash and watercolour, 26.7 × 18.1 cm (10½ × 7 3/16 in)

Inscribed on verso: *From the collection of A.H. Palmer – 3863 24th Avenue West – Vancouver. BC. / Exhibited at Victoria and Albert Museum Oct. 1926 to Feb 1927 – at the Palmer exhibition / Number 60 in the official catalogue. / Sold at Christie March 4th 1929-*; plus miscellaneous scribbles in brown ink

Stamped on verso at upper right in black: *TEL* (Lugt 2420a: Thomas E. Lowinsky)

Lit.: V&A 1926, 60; Lister 73

New Haven, Yale Center for British Art, Paul Mellon Collection, B1977.14.4643

This exploration of the effect of moonlight glinting on a stream and viewed through trees combines elements from Shoreham with more exotic features, such as a palm tree on the right. It may aim to evoke the kind of ecstatic response to nocturnal effects that Palmer described in his letter to Richmond of 1827 (see cat. 52).

The technique is an unusual mixture of fluid and firm passages. While freer in treatment, the picture contains much detail and in that sense bears some resemblance to the Oxford sepias (cats 10–15). On the right, beyond a sheepfold, there appears to be a church. On the left there is a secular building that has been variously interpreted as a cottage (Grigson 1947, p. 168) and a 'water mill for grinding corn' (Lister). There are sheep in the fold to the right and in the foreground, a wreath-like form that has been read by Lister as a bird's nest with eggs. Whatever the precise content of the picture, it would seem to involve a celebration of natural bounty.

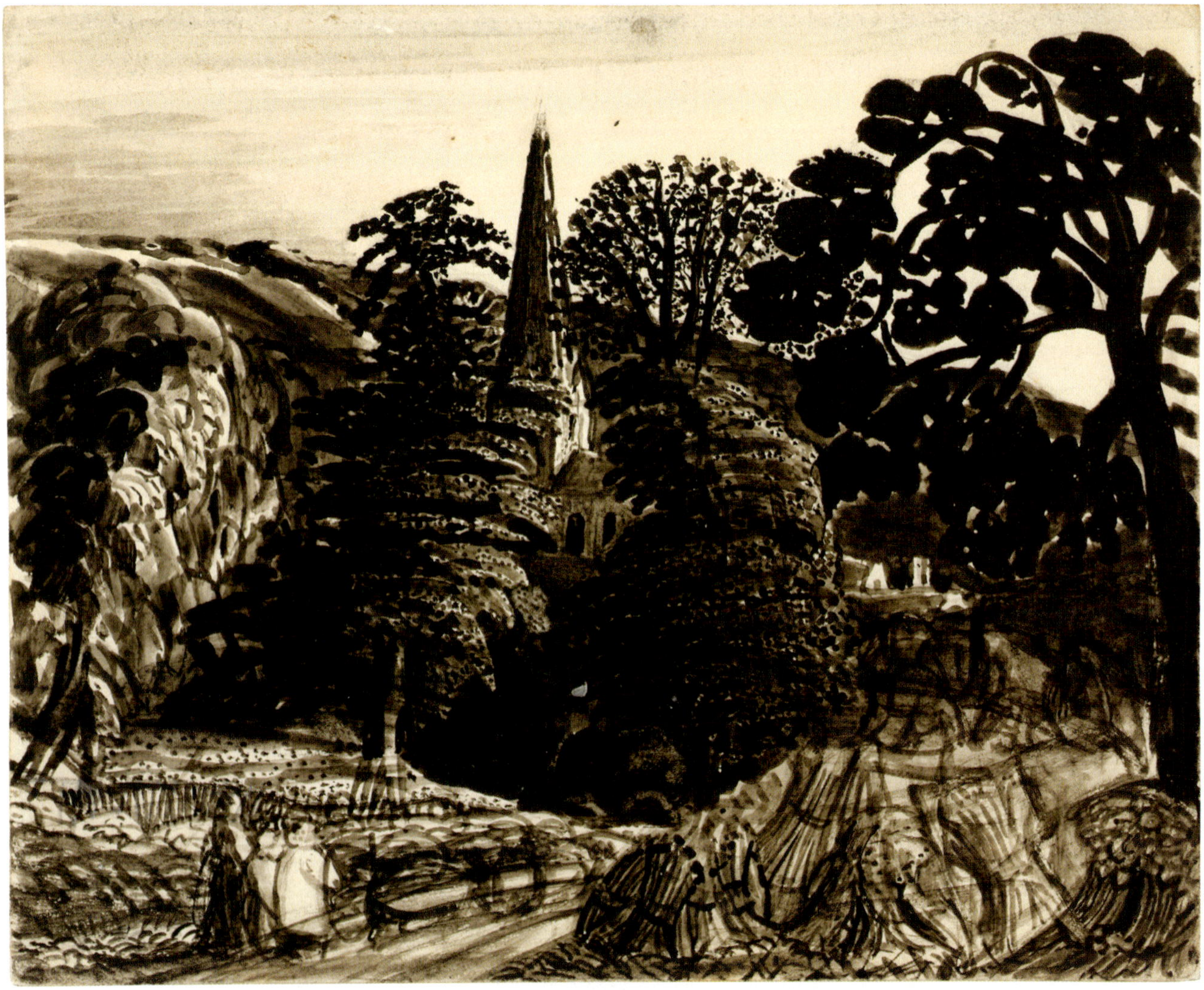

35

## 35*

*Evening: A Church among Trees*, *c.*1829–30

Ink on card, 15.2 × 18.4 cm (6 × 7¼ in)

Lit: Lister 115

London, Tate, N03698; purchased 1922

Figures walk towards a village past sheaves of corn in this evening harvest scene. The steeple of a church is prominent, as it is in many idyllic rural scenes prior to the rural unrest of 1832. Though no particular location can be identified, the terrain is highly reminiscent of the Darent valley in which Shoreham is situated.

In his representation of foliage Palmer still retains the magnified forms he evolved in the mid-1820s and makes highly effective use of textural variety and silhouettes, particularly with the large-leafed tree to the right of the composition. He shows, however, more concern for atmospheric effects than in his most primitivizing works, and it is for this reason that this work is usually dated towards the end of the 1820s, *c.*1829–30. The fine observation of evening light is a reminder of his great admiration of the tonal subtleties of the great French landscape painter Claude. It was perhaps the kind of effect he was describing when he claimed in a letter to Linnell in 1829 that two of his monochromes had more 'look of light' than he had achieved before (*Letters*, p. 54).

## 36*

*A Country Road, Leading towards a Church*, *c.*1828–30

Brown watercolour, 18.4 × 14.9 cm (7¼ × 5⅞ in)

Lit: Lister 126

London, Victoria and Albert Museum, 34-1953

This is a particularly bold treatment of the theme that so obsessed Palmer in the late 1820s: looking through foliage towards a church spire. According to an inscription on the mount by A.H. Palmer, it is 'one of numbers done at Shoreham showing the love of vivid contrasts of chiaroscuro'. It would seem that this work was probably executed as

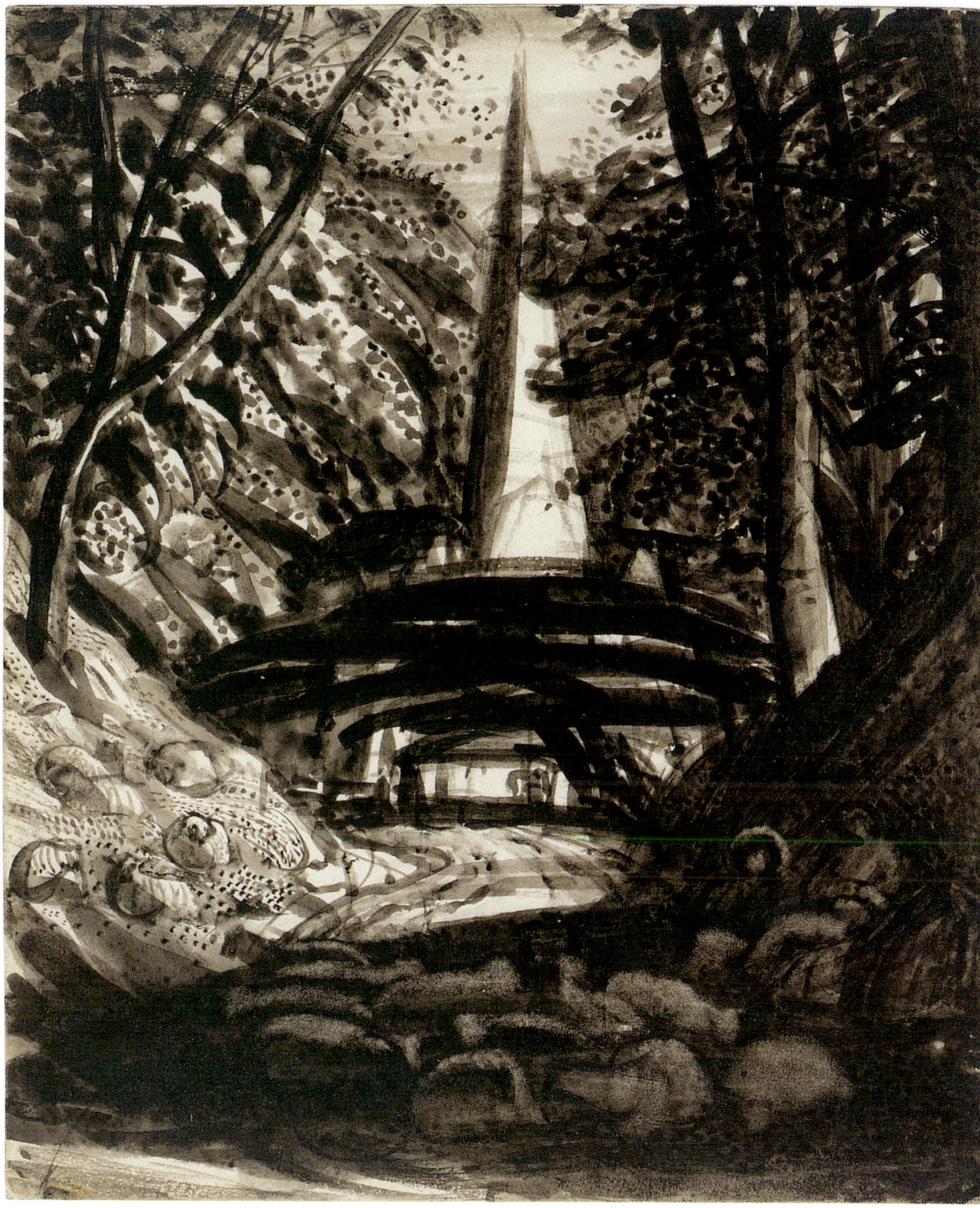

36

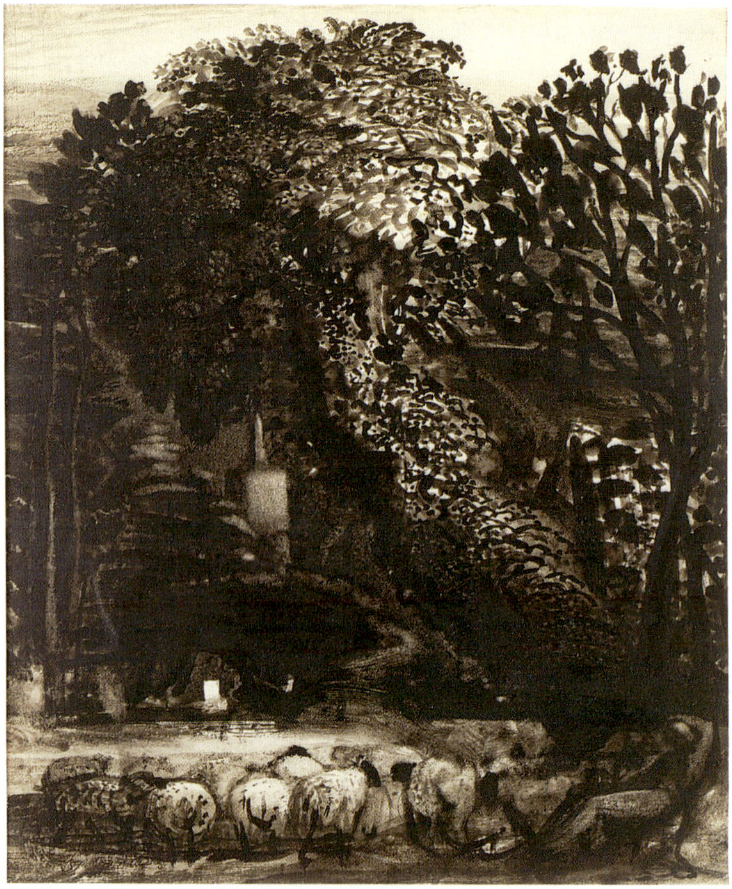

37

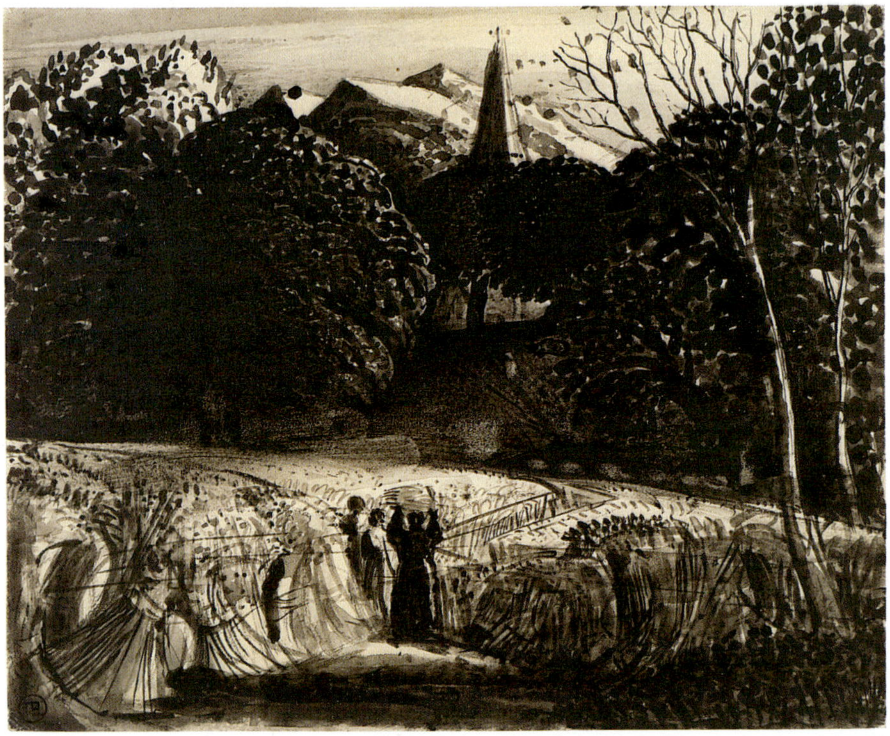

38

an experimental study. Its freedom of method can be contrasted with such elaborate and carefully finished 'blacks' as *A Church with a Boat and Sheep* (cat. 73), which are presumably similar to those sent for exhibition and intended for sale.

## 37*

*A Village Church among Trees*, *c.*1830

Black and grey wash on card, 18.3 × 15.2cm (7 3/16 × 6 in)

Lit: Lister 114

London, Victoria and Albert Museum, 33-1953

Another study in which broad wash effects are used, and stippling to create texture, this work is more conventional in its arrangement, with the foreground sheep distinctly separated from the dark middle ground and church beyond. The needle spire of the church has some similarities to that of Eynsford, the village immediately to the north of Shoreham in the Darent valley. This church, which can be viewed across a ford, was used as a motif by Palmer in many of his ink and wash paintings at this time, for example *A Church with a Boat and Sheep* (cat. 73).

## 38*

*Cornfield and Church by Moonlight*, *c.*1830

Black ink and wash, with point of brush, 15.2 × 18.4 cm (6 × 7 1/4 in)

Stamped at lower left in black ink: *TEL* (Thomas E. Lowinsky)

Lit: Lister, 119; Payne 1993, 67

New Haven, Yale Center for British Art, Paul Mellon Collection, B1977.14.4162

The motifs in this work are close to those in *Evening: A Church among Trees* (cat. 35). While identical in size and close in treatment, this picture has a more developed narrative. Female figures, one bearing a bundle, make their way through a cornfield towards a settlement in darkened trees with a silhouetted church spire rising above it. It could be assumed that they have been gleaning and are returning homeward in the evening. Such a theme would fit in with the idealized view of rural community that Shoreham inspired in Palmer before 1830. It is in effect the contemporary equivalent of the biblical subject *Ruth* that he was working on (cat. 39).

While frequently described as moonlight it would seem that this picture shows, like *Evening: A Church among Trees*, the raking light of the setting sun. Palmer tended to keep moonlight for scenes involving fantasy and transformation, whereas this picture evokes more a sense of the pastoral idyll. As with most ink and wash paintings of this period, there is little or no use of gouache to add in highlights. Lighter areas are all obtained by leaving the paper blank or, in one or two cases, scratching through the ink to the paper beneath.

## 39

## *Ruth Returned from the Gleaning, c.*1828

Ink, wash and gouache, over graphite, 29.4 × 39.4 cm (11⅝ × 15½ in)
Lit: V&A 1926, 58; Lister 81
London, Victoria and Albert Museum, 3449-1923

According to A.H. Palmer, this work is the one of this title exhibited at the Royal Academy in 1829 (641). It illustrates the moment in the biblical story of Ruth when she brought the barley she had gleaned in the field back to the city:

> So she gleaned in the field until even, and beat out that she had gleaned: and it was about an ephah of barley. And she took it up, and went into the city: and her mother in law saw what she had gleaned: and she brought forth, and gave to her that she had reserved after she was sufficed (Ruth 2: 17–18)

Ruth is shown striding towards the city with her ephah of barley under her massive arm. The exaggerated forms of this figure emphasizing power suggest Palmer's admiration for Fuseli, Michelangelo and the Italian Mannerists. It is an extraordinarily heroic concept of the female heroine of the biblical story. In the middle ground Ruth's mother-in-law Naomi can be seen before her cottage, reading a book by candlelight.

The theme of the Moabite woman who gradually gained acceptance among the Hebrews through the display of decency and modesty had a prominent place in Christian iconography because she was the great-grandmother of King David and hence an ancestress of Christ. The humane and sympathetic treatment of her story in Ruth was a further reason for her appeal.

Palmer may have been more attracted to the theme because of its resonances

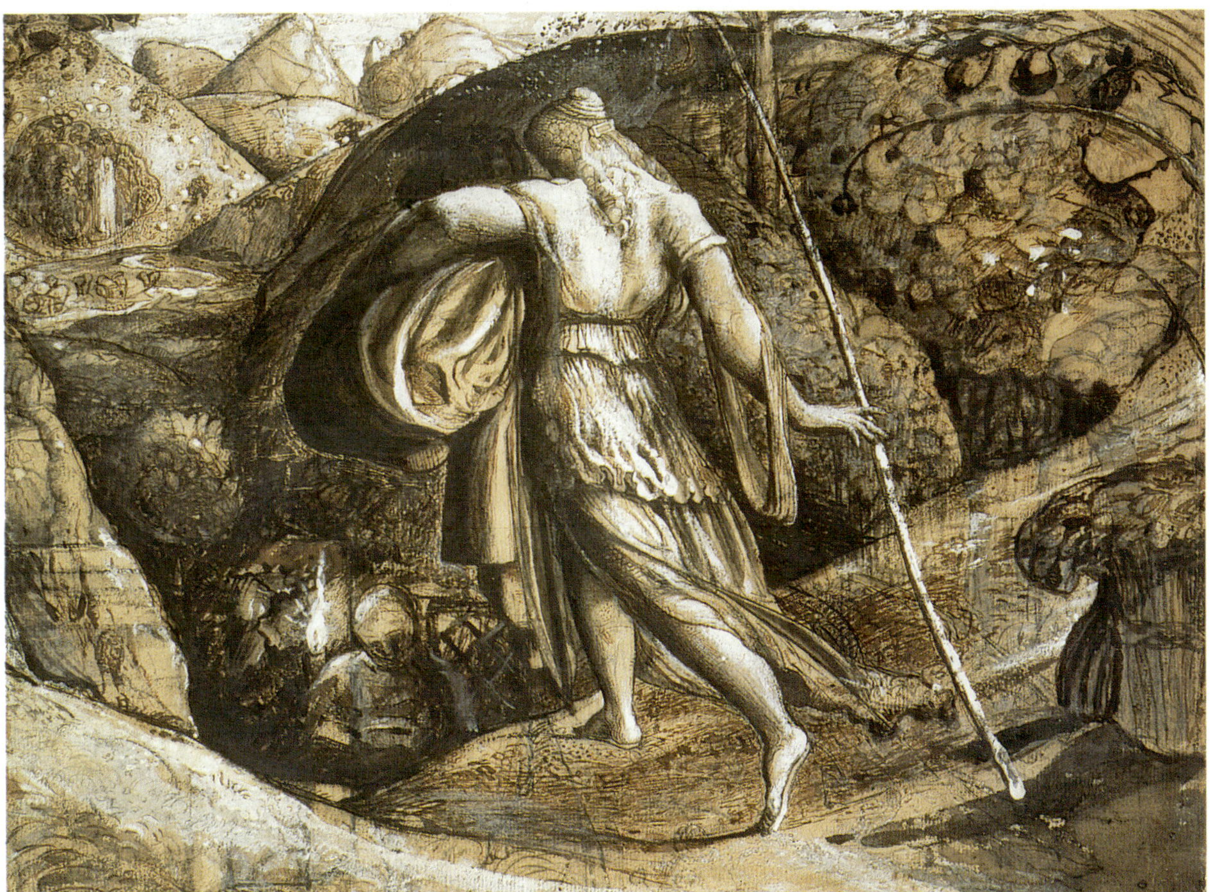

39

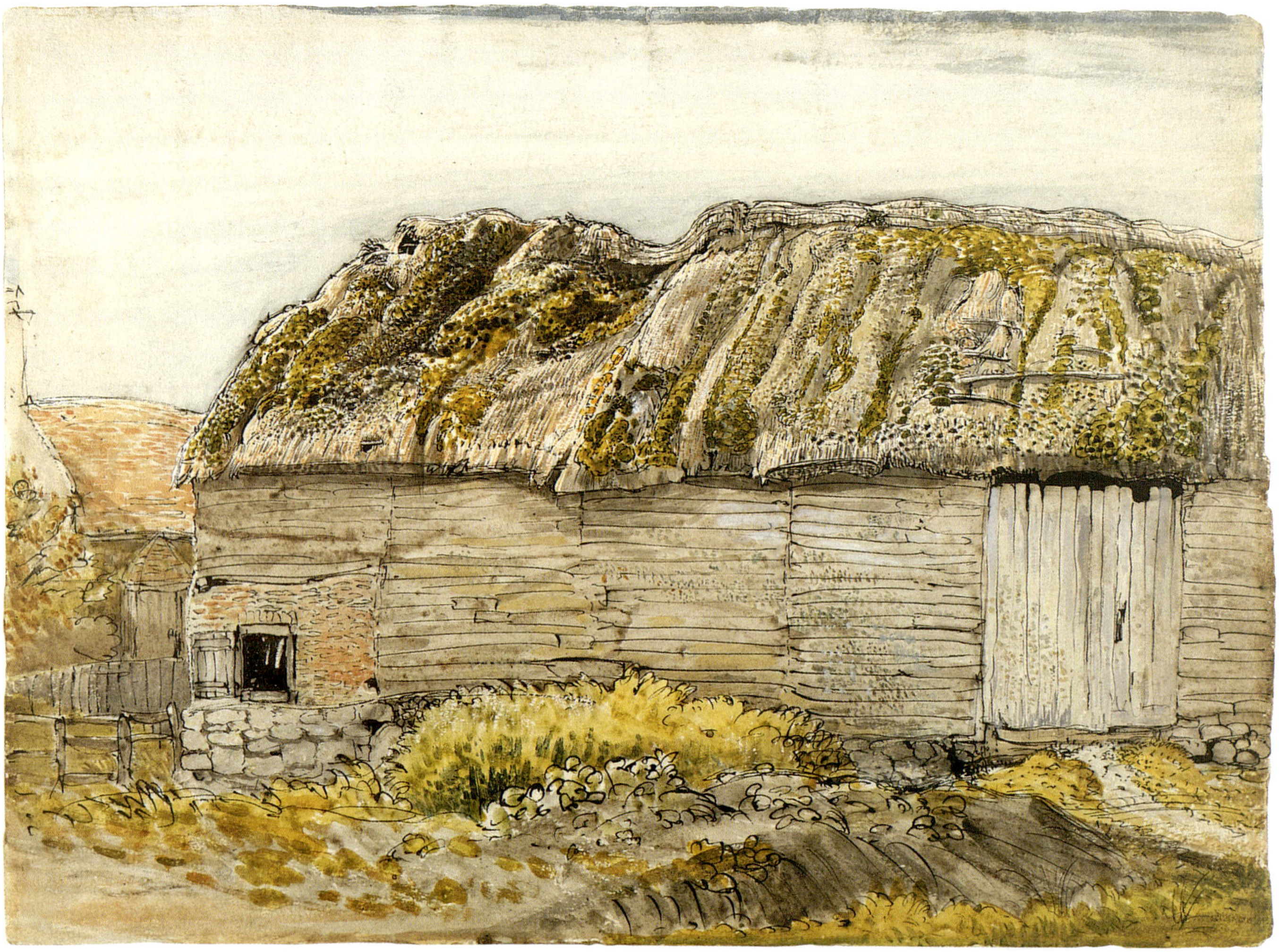

40

with the contemporary rural community (see cat. 48). This biblical scene of a gleaner returning home is the equivalent in that sense of his images of gleaners in Shoreham. Gleaning, furthermore, was a sensitive and much debated subject in rural economy of the time. Traditional farmers had always allowed the poor to glean from their fields after they had gathered the harvest in, while modern methods gathered more efficiently and thus denied the poor this bounty. Gleaning represented the humane 'old order' that the modern world was destroying.

## 40

### *A Barn with a Mossy Roof*, *c.*1828–9

Watercolour, gouache, tinted gum and pen and black ink, 27.8 × 37.7 cm (11 × 14⅞ in)

Inscribed on former mount in A.H. Palmer's hand: *One of a large series of outdoor studies which kept pace with the purely imaginative work*

Lit: V&A 1926, 85; Lister 96

New Haven, Yale Center for British Art, Paul Mellon Collection, B1977.14.5968

Palmer continued to make detailed observational studies throughout the Shoreham period, alongside his more imaginative compositions. This watercolour, together with the ones that follow (cats 41, 42), is usually dated *c.*1828 on the assumption that they all might be connected to Linnell's visit to Shoreham in the summer of that year. One, a view of *Ivy Cottage* (cat. 43), has a drawing by Linnell on the reverse. Linnell strongly encouraged Palmer to make large and detailed naturalistic studies, promising him, according to Palmer, that he could 'make a thousand pounds a year' through such work (*Letters*, p. 36).

Palmer's method in these pictures, however, is not simply naturalistic. Some, indeed, almost seem to have been created as a form of dialectic response to Linnell's artistic principles. As Palmer's letters of the time reveal, the two engaged in lively debate over artistic matters, as they did over religion and politics. While basing his technique on observation, Palmer characteristically focuses on certain details in this picture so intensely that they seem to move beyond representation to become a celebration of richly encrusted and textured patterning. In some ways the method prefigures that of the Pre-Raphaelites. Like these later artists, Palmer was inspired by the detailed realism in Northern fifteenth-century painting to work obsessively from nature. However, Palmer is unique in the sense of exuberance and excess that he brings to the process.

In this picture the mossy roof has captured Palmer's attention, causing him to work up its detail to a higher degree than the rest of the building and its surrounds. It is interesting to contrast this treatment with that of his earlier studies of rural buildings (cats 6, 7) made under the influence of the taste for the picturesque as communicated by such publications as David Cox's *Treatise on Landscape Painting* (see cat. 7). Like Cox, Palmer's attention is drawn to old, quaint and irregular buildings, but he now no longer arranges them in artistically 'balanced' compositions. Instead, he scrutinizes them head on, usually placing the main object of his interest flatly in the centre of the page. He has also abandoned in his later studies the nuanced tonalities that were regarded as so important for conveying a sense of the picturesque.

While some of the farm buildings that Palmer sketched (notably Sepham barn, which survived until the 1970s) have been identified, the one in this picture has not. There can be little doubt, however, that the study was based on an actual barn, which doubtless caught Palmer's eye because of the excessively decrepit nature of its roof.

## 41

### *A Cow-Lodge with a Mossy Roof*, *c.*1828–9

Watercolour, gouache, gum arabic and black ink, 26.7 × 36.5 cm (10½ × 14⅜ in)

Lit: Lister 97

New Haven, Yale Center for British Art, Paul Mellon Collection, B1975.4.1876

The watercolour is comparable in size and format to cat. 40 and was presumably made at much the same time. The composition mirrors that of the previous entry, which suggests, together with their similarity in size and handling, that they might have been conceived as a pendant pair. As in cat. 40, Palmer has focused in particular on the building's moss-encrusted roof, using watercolour and gouache with great power and

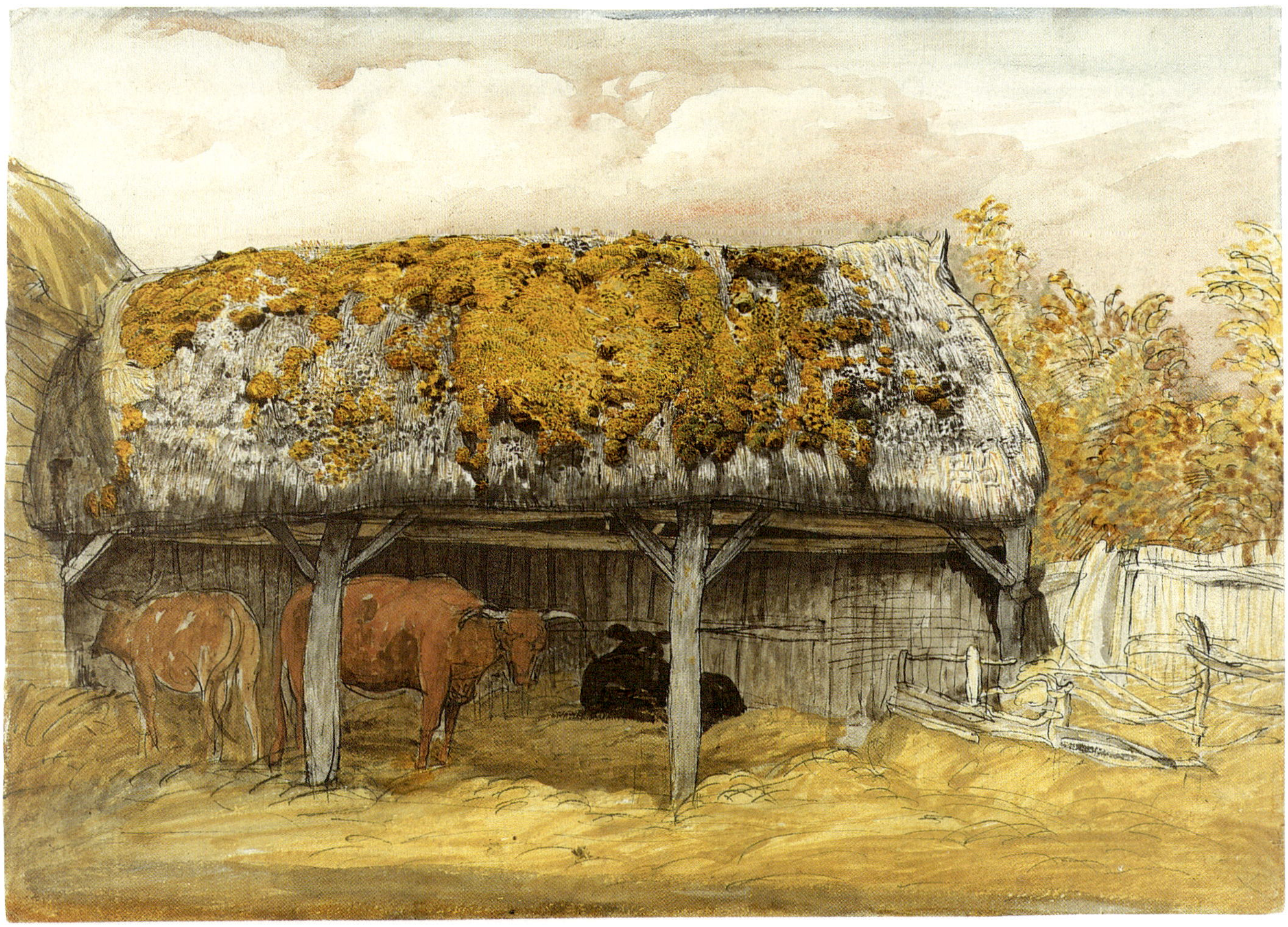

41

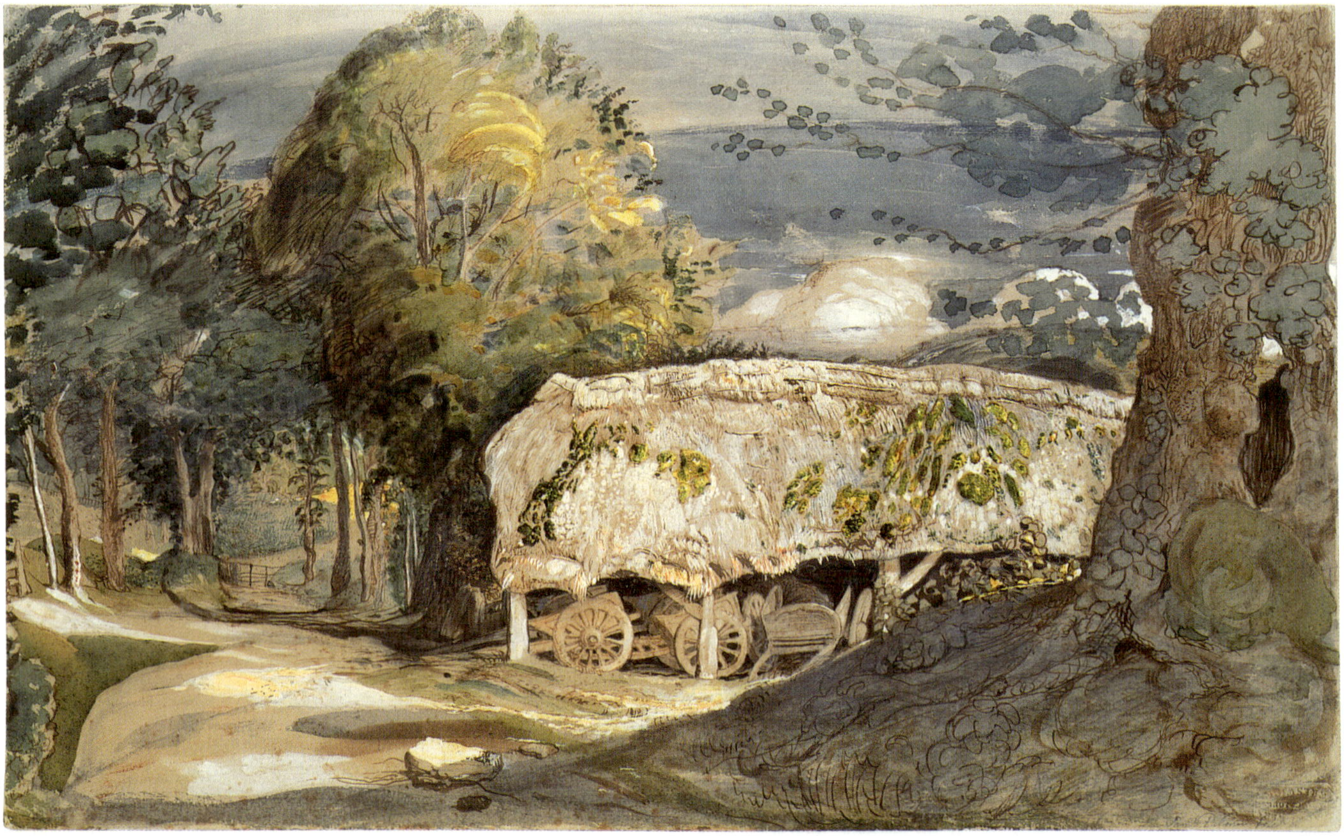

42

freedom to produce remarkable effects of texture and relief. Other parts of the cow-lodge and its surrounds remain loosely brushed in.

The colours in this work are strikingly vivid. They must always have been rich, with a strong emphasis on warm tones – yellows, reds and browns. However, the extraordinary pink of the sky seems to be the consequence of subsequent over-exposure. This caused the fading of a layer of blue wash that Palmer originally applied to the sky. There are signs of this blue surviving at the top of the picture, which was once covered by a mount. This study does show Palmer becoming bolder as a colourist, something that was soon to lead to such rich imaginative compositions as *The Magic Apple Tree* (cat. 69).

## 42

*Cart Shed and Lane*, 1828

Ink, watercolour and gouache, 27.8 × 45 cm (11 × 17¾ in)

Lit: Lister 89

London, Victoria and Albert Museum, 88-1937

Like cats 40 and 41, this is a large study of farm buildings, but more elaborately composed. In this case Palmer has stood further back from the building, viewing it across a lane. The picture shows a particularly vigorous handling of gouache.

Palmer's detailed studies of farm buildings at this time suggest that he might already have been thinking of developing more agriculturally based scenes of rural life. A few years later, in the early 1830s, he was to use such themes for his most ambitious and successful paintings, notably *The Shearers* (cat. 88) and *The Sleeping Shepherd* (cat. 89). Both these works are set at the entrances to barns.

The *Cart Shed*, like *Ivy Cottage* (cat. 43 recto), came from the collection of John Linnell. It is presumably one of the studies from nature that he made for Linnell at this time. This might explain why the design is, like that of *Ivy Cottage*, slightly more conventional than in the case of cats 40 and 41.

## 43

Recto: *Ivy Cottage, Shoreham*, 1828

Watercolour, gouache, and brown ink on blue wove laminated paper, 35.3 × 45.2 cm (14 × 17⅞ in)

Sheet blind stamped at upper right: *TURNBULLS CRAYON BOARD* (monogram with palette and brushes)

Signed at lower right in pencil: *S. Palmer*

John Linnell (1792–1882)

Verso: *Ploughing at Shoreham*, *c.*1828

Black wove and white chalk on blue laminated paper

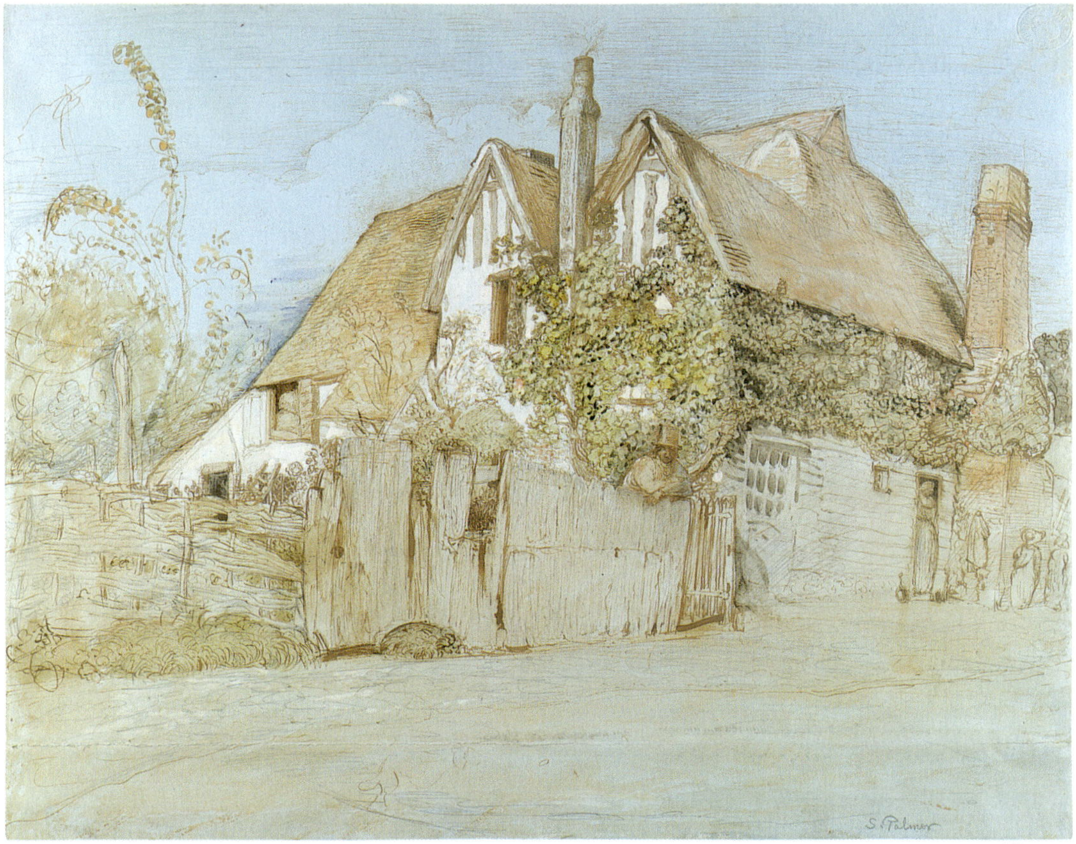

43 recto

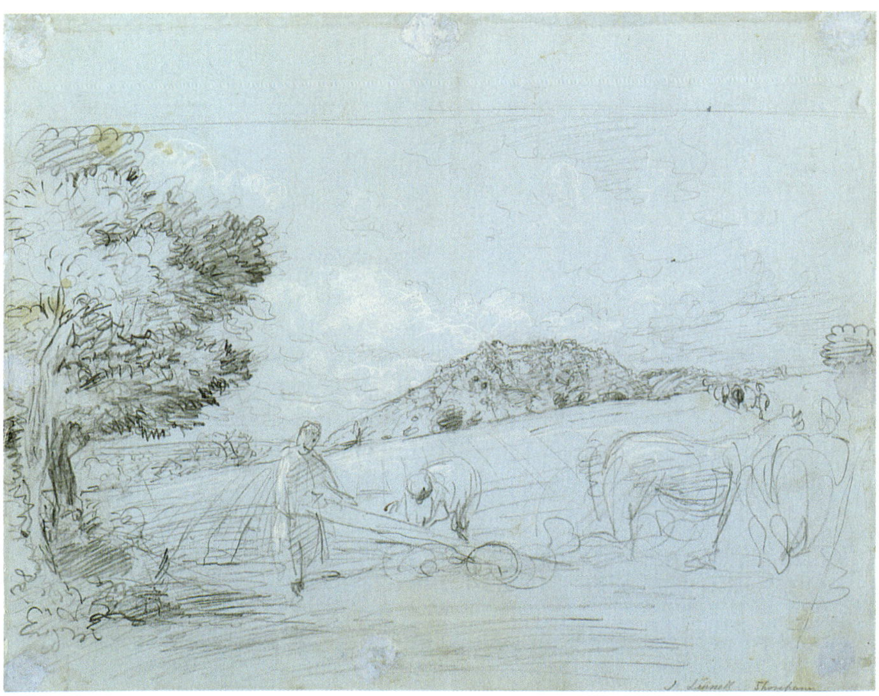

43 verso

Signed at lower right: *J. Linnell Shoreham*

Lit: Lister 90

New Haven, Yale Center for British Art, Paul Mellon Collection, B1977.14.307

This sheet comes from the collection of John Linnell and is almost certainly one of the studies that Palmer made for Linnell in 1828, a supposition strengthened by Linnell's drawing made in Shoreham on the reverse side.

Unusually for Palmer at this period, this is a balanced topographical drawing, using a conventional method of line drawing coloured in by watercolour wash. It was presumably Linnell's desire that Palmer should make factual studies to guide this highly traditional topographical approach. However, Palmer has characteristically expended a large amount of effort on capturing the detail and texture of the central part of the cottage.

Ivy Cottage still exists, on the road that leads out of Shoreham from the River Darent towards the church. It may

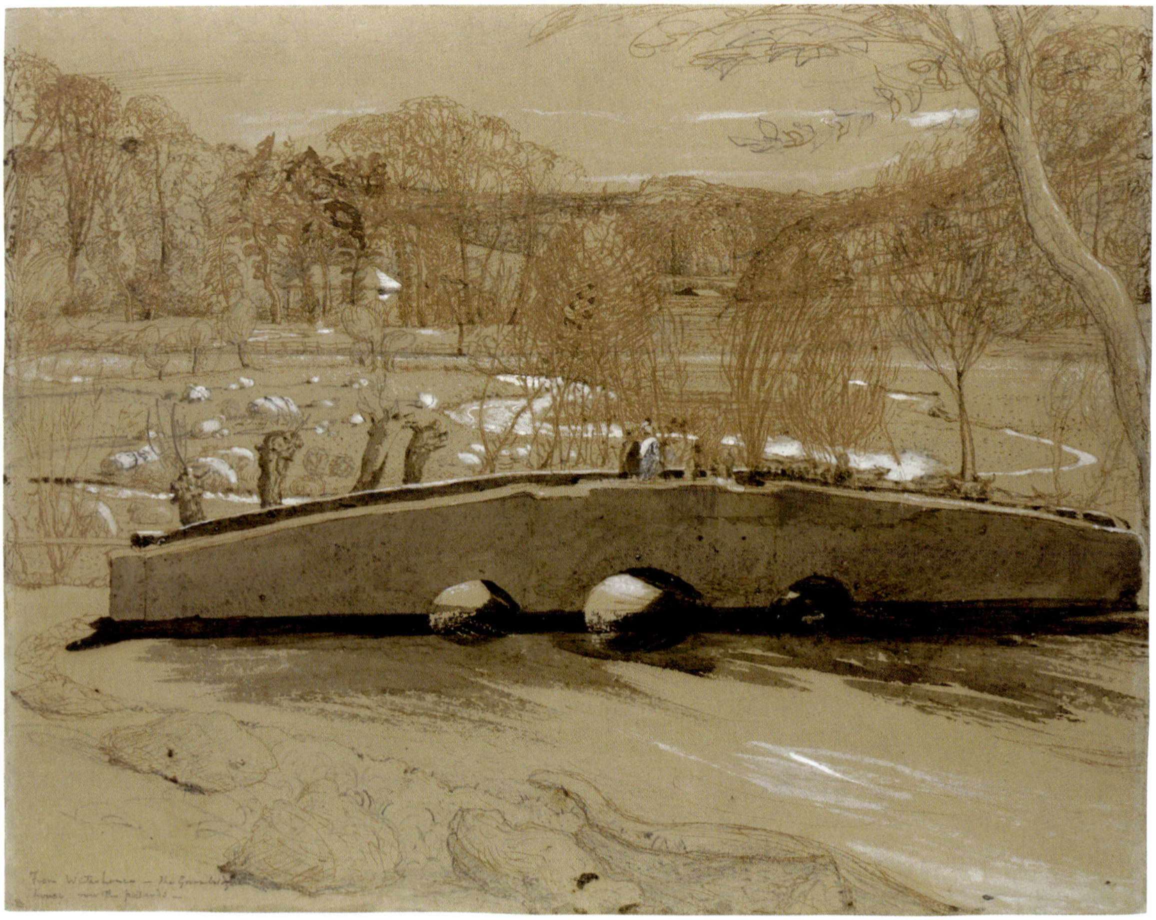

44

have had a particular resonance for the Ancients, since it probably contained the room used by them when they came to stay in Shoreham in *c.*1824–6 (*Letters*, p. 11). The cottage was occupied by the Tooth family, some of whose members are presumably the figures shown in the drawing.

The drawing also makes an attempt to depict rural life in accord with the conventions of the day. A 'rustic' – presumably the 'Mr. Tooth (the old gentleman)' referred to in a letter to Richmond (*Letters*, p. 12) – leans over the fence and regards us placidly, while at the back door of the cottage his wife appears to be bidding farewell to their daughters, who are heading up the road in the direction of the church.

Linnell's drawing of ploughing (presumably made prior to Palmer's painting) shows the artist characteristically exploring the working side of rural life. It is reminiscent of the bold realist compositions that he made a decade earlier. The drawing method is efficient and economical, showing none of Palmer's excess, which Linnell occasionally emulated around this time (see cat. 93).

## 44

*The Bridge at Shoreham, c.*1829

Pen and brown ink, brush and black and grey wash and white gouache, over graphite, on grey-brown paper, 22.1 × 27.8 cm ($8\frac{7}{8} \times 10\frac{7}{8}$ in)

Inscribed at lower left in graphite: *From Waterhouse – The Groombridge's / house over the pollards*

Lit: Lister 80; White and Saynor, p. 26

New York, The Metropolitan Museum of Art, 1972.118.292; bequest of Walter C. Baker, 1971

This study of the three arched medieval stone bridge over the River Darent at Shoreham was made from one of the windows in Water House, the large dwelling that was rented by Palmer's father from autumn 1828, when father and son moved in. Members of the Ancients frequently came to stay at Water House. Both house and bridge still exist, but there is considerably more foliage between the two now, rendering this view difficult to obtain.

Palmer may have been attracted to the bridge because of its antiquity. Known originally as 'Longebregge', it dated back to the thirteenth century (White and Saynor, p. 26). Though much repaired and remodelled since, it still retains the basic design of a medieval packhorse bridge. The house in the distance, further upstream above the bridge, is presumably that of Mr Groombridge mentioned in the inscription. Mr

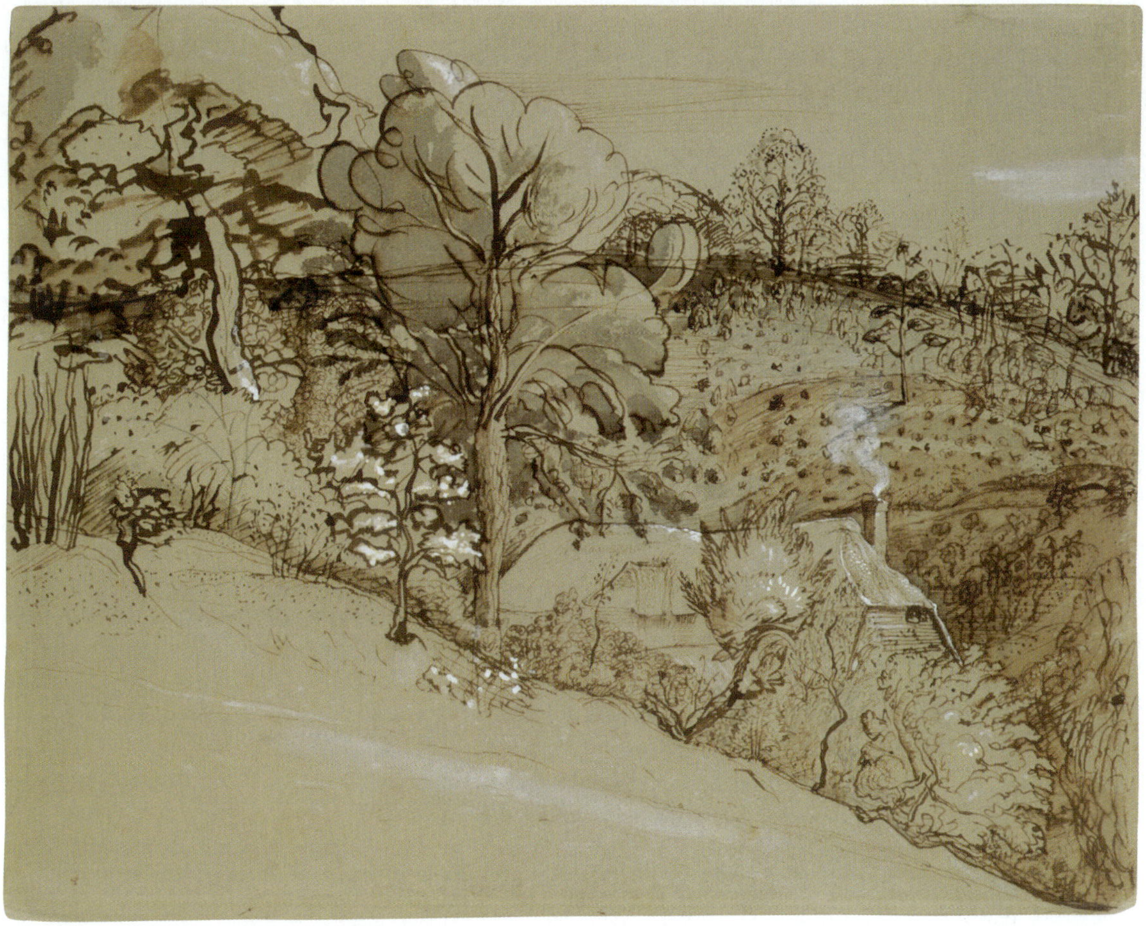

45

Groombridge was a farmer who owned an orchard mentioned in some of Palmer's letters.

Like the drawing of *Ivy Cottage*, this picture suggests a new interest in topographical work. It is freer in treatment, perhaps because it was intended for Palmer's own possession. Some of the sheep in the field beyond the bridge have lambs, which, together with the appearance of the trees, suggest early spring. A plausible date for the drawing, therefore, would be spring 1829.

## 45*

### *The Primitive Cottage*, *c.*1828–9

Brown ink, 22.4 × 30.2 cm (8 13/16 × 11 7/8 in)

Inscribed on verso in pencil in A.H. Palmer's hand: *qy use as illustration for proposed new life of SP / For Sir Frank Short 'The Primitive Cottage.' A subject dearly loved by SP throughout life.*

Lit: Lister 99

London, Victoria and Albert Museum, 452-1953

This nature study uses a drawing method similar to that in *The Bridge at Shoreham* (cat. 44), but with more ebullient handling. It seems, in fact, to combine some of the bold texturing effects found in Palmer's 'visionary' work with the more careful features of his nature studies. The drawing is presumably a study of a house on the slopes rising above Shoreham. It shows Palmer using the motif of view into a valley cut off by a foreground slope that recurs in several of his early Shoreham works, notably the *Holy Family* (cat. 28). Another view of a 'primitive cottage' – possibly the same building from another angle – is in the Yale Center for British Art (Lister 98).

## 46

### *Oak Trees, Lullingstone Park*, 1828

Ink and watercolour, 29.5 × 46.8 cm (11 5/8 × 18 1/2 in)

Lit: Lister 88; White and Saynor, p. 2

Ottawa, National Gallery of Canada, 4357; purchased 1937

Lullingstone Park – which contains Lullingstone Castle, seat of the Hart Dyke family since 1500 – lies immediately to the north of Shoreham along the Darent valley. The oaks there have considerable antiquity, being descended from the dense forestation that existed in pre-

Roman times. The name Darent derives from the Celtic word *derw* meaning the river surrounded by oaks (White and Saynor, p. 2).

This study is one of a series made for Linnell around 1828. The selection of trees as a subject may well have been suggested by Linnell, who himself made detailed paintings and drawings of trees in his early years (see cat. 21). Palmer never seemed totally happy with Linnell's commission or his encouragement to develop the observational side of his art. In October 1828 he wrote from Shoreham to George Richmond in London: 'Mr Linnell tells me that by making studies of the Shoreham scenery I could get a thousand a year directly. Tho' I am making studies for Mr. Linnell I will, God help me, never be a naturalist by profession' (*Letters*, p. 36). To Linnell himself Palmer wrote expressing his misgivings at the extent to which nature study could on its own achieve the higher reaches of art:

> I can't help seeing that the general characteristics of Nature's beauty not only differ from, but are in some respects, opposed to those of imaginative art …
>
> Universal nature wears a lovely gentleness of mild attraction; but the leafy lightness, the thousand repetitions of little forms … seem hard to be reconciled with the unwinning severity, the awfulness, the ponderous globosity of Art. Milton, by one epithet, draws an oak of the largest girth I ever saw; – 'Pine and *Monumental* Oak'; I have just been trying to draw a large one in Lullingstone; but the poet's tree is huger than any in the Park. (*Letters*, pp. 47–8)

As with his studies of farm buildings at this time, Palmer seemed to be trying to capture strong natural forms and find in them the grandeur that would lead to the 'ponderous globosity of Art', if not quite match Milton's epithet. In this picture he has reduced 'leafy lightness' to a minimum and tried instead to focus on the force and rotundity of the massive oak. Later in the letter to Linnell quoted above he talks of his attempt to avoid being distracted by 'the moss, and rifts, and barky furrows' and to catch the 'grasp and grapple of the roots; the muscular belly and shoulders; the twisted sinews'. The anthropomorphic language used by Palmer is significant, fitting in with a Blakean concept of the animate in nature being relatable to human form. There may even be, in these vast twisted shapes, a hint of the Wood of Self-Murderers depicted by Blake in his illustration to Canto XIII of Dante's *Inferno* (Butlin 1981, 812[24]).

This picture is the most elaborate of the surviving studies of oaks in Lullingstone Park. Palmer appears to have started with a careful chalk drawing and then used watercolour and gouache to emphasize the texture and rotundity of the foreground oak and contrast this with the woodland glade beyond.

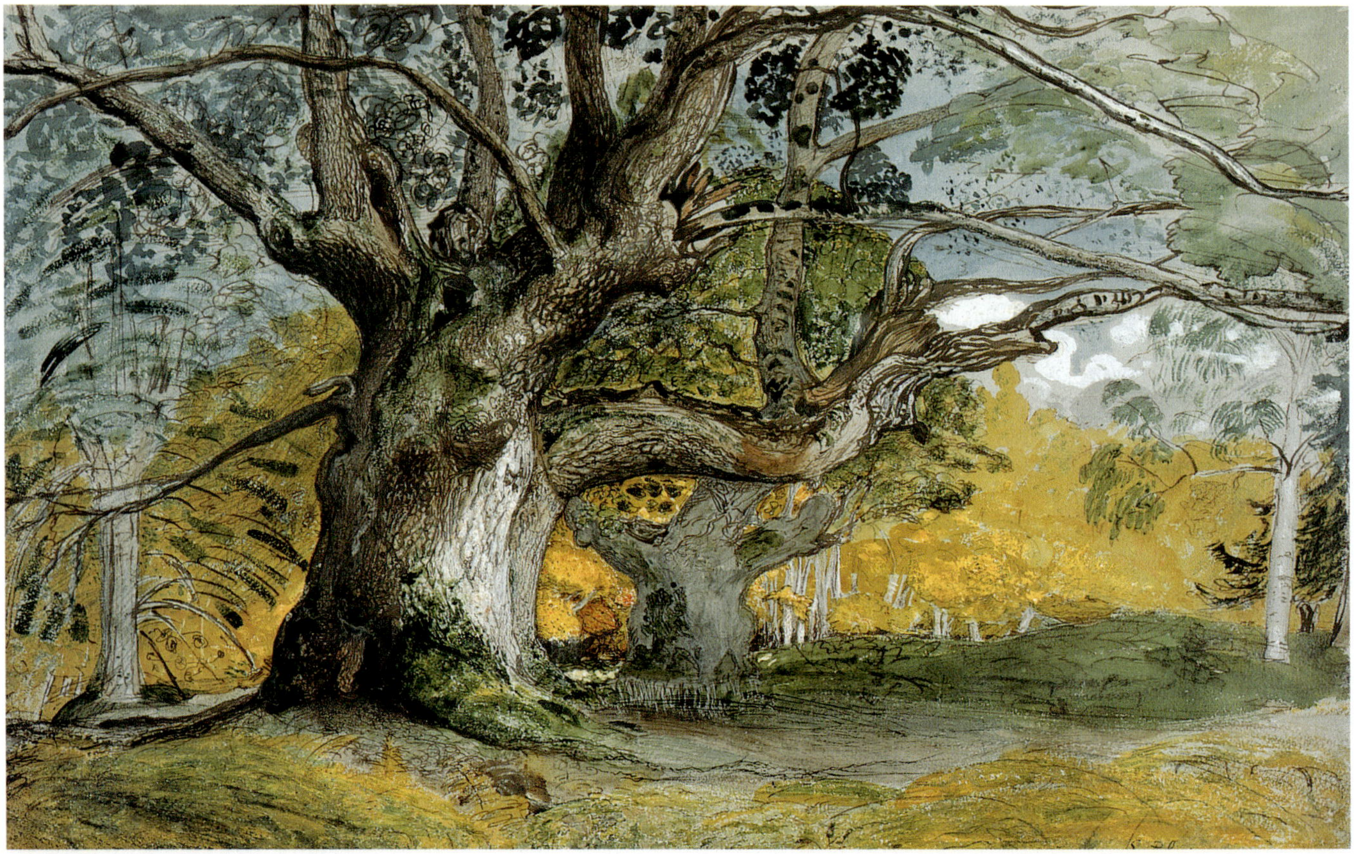

46

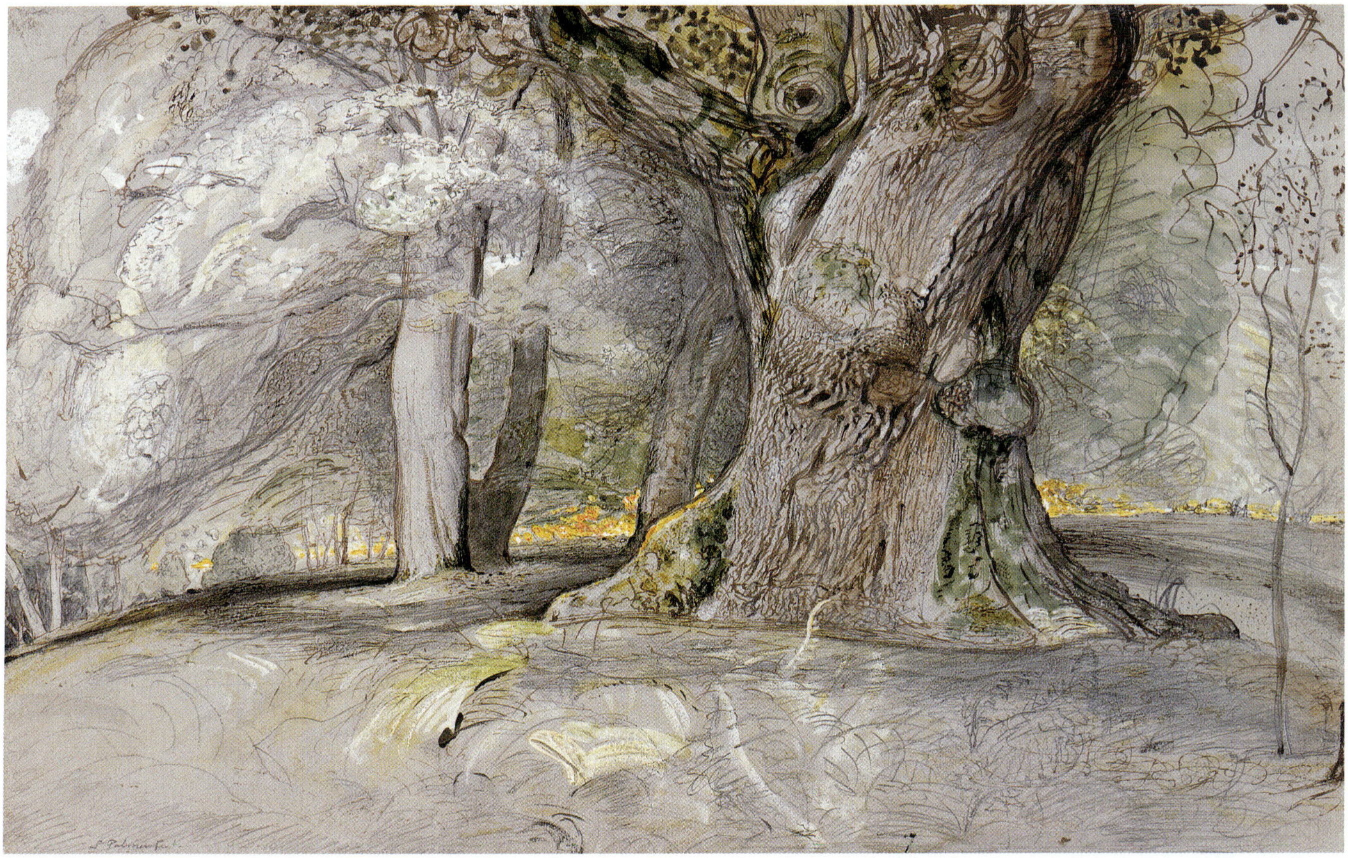

47

## 47†

*Oak Trees and Beech*, 1828

Brown ink, watercolour and gouache, over graphite, on grey paper, 29.2 × 46.6 cm (11½ × 18⅜ in)

Lit: Lister 86

New York, The Pierpont Morgan Library; collection of Eugene Victor and Claire Thaw

Like cat. 46, this study was made for John Linnell and remained in the Linnell family until the early twentieth century. It is similar in format to cat. 46 (though reversed in design) and concentrates in a similar manner on representing the volume and texture of the trunk of the oak in the foreground. There is, however, more emphasis on the use of the pen in this work and less colouring with watercolour and gouache.

## 48

*Coming from Evening Church*, 1830

Mixed media on gesso on paper laid down on panel, 30.5 × 19.7 cm (12 × 7¾ in)

Inscribed along lower edge: *Painted 1830 at Shoreham Kent S. Palmer*; on return edge of the relining canvas: *Painted at Shoreham Kent S. Palmer*; at lower right (added later): *and painted in tempera (no oil) by Samuel Palmer at Shoreham Kent, 1830*

Lit: Lister 123; Bindman 1985

London, Tate, N03697; purchased 1922

This painting is the most elaborate representation of the theme of the church and community to survive from Palmer's Shoreham period. It is also one of the very few works from this time that is clearly inscribed and dated. The repetition of this information in various forms suggests a particular significance. But although it firmly identifies the picture as being painted at Shoreham, it is not a literal representation of Shoreham itself. Shoreham church has no spire and it is set on the slopes of a hill removed from any immediate cottages.

The picture appears to show devout villagers coming from evening church service in an orderly procession and returning, presumably divinely inspired, to their cottages. The spiritual nature of the experience is emphasized by the framing trees, which form a Gothic arch, and by the full moon that shines on them behind the centrally placed church spire. Further links between nature and the rural community can be seen in the way the arched roofs of the cottages echo the Gothic arch of branches that frames the picture and the slopes of the hills behind. Many figures are also carrying flowers.

The figures wear generalized costumes and cannot be related to any particular historical period. They are selected, however, to represent all generations. A young couple with a family lead the procession, followed by a Blakean patriarchal figure. In the middle ground the parson can be seen surrounded by other members of his flock. The rhythmic movement of the people echoes that to be found in Blake's pastoral figures, such as his wood engravings for Thornton's *Pastorals of Virgil* (cat. 19) or the processing figure in 'Holy Thursday' from *Songs of Innocence* (1789).

There is no fuller presentation of Palmer's ideology at this time, and it recalls his intense debates with Linnell, where both expressed their unbounding admiration for the 'British peasantry', but where Palmer expressed the opinion that the old Tories had served them better than the modern Liberals: 'I ... as I love our fine British peasantry, think best of the old high tories, because I find they gave most liberty to the poor, and were not morose, sullen and blood-thirsty like the whigs, liberty jacks and dissenters' (*Letters*, p. 37).

The date of 1830, so firmly inscribed on this picture, may have been a significant one for Palmer, for this was when rural unrest began, preceding the 1832 Reform Bill that reduced the number of rural constituencies (see p. 29). Inspired partly by the revolution in France of that year and inflamed by increased rural poverty caused by bad harvests, rioting broke out in the countryside, and Palmer witnessed the burning of the haystacks of a local farmer from his house in September (see p. 32). It may be that Palmer saw 1830 as the year that brought to an end the rural harmony envisaged in this work and that he placed that date on it as a memorial. It was also the year in which Richmond's miniature of him in the garb of an 'Ancient' artist was exhibited at the Royal Academy (cat. 54).

This painting is the latest-known work by Palmer to adhere to a largely tempera technique. Like Blake and Richmond (cat. 57), he prepared his tempera by mixing pigment with various glues and gums, but he used a larger amount of gum than Richmond had done. This provides the picture with a glossier effect than such works by Richmond as *Abel the Shepherd* (cat. 53) or *Christ and the Woman of Samaria* (cat. 57). However, it has also led to the paint being more unstable. Like the *Holy Family* (cat. 28), the picture comes from the collection of John Giles.

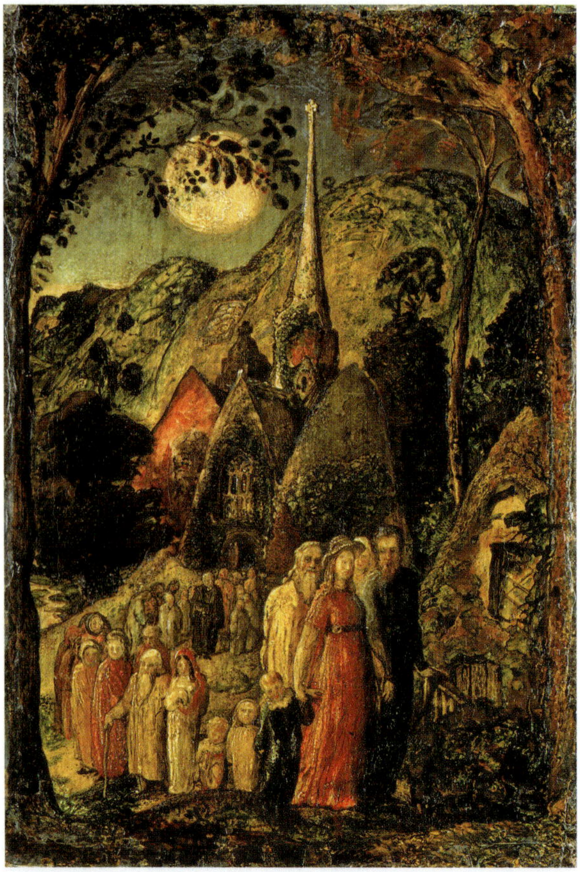

48

## 49

### *Cornfield by Moonlight, with the Evening Star, c.*1830

Watercolour and gouache, with brown ink, varnished, 19.7 × 29.8 cm (7¾ × 11¾ in)

Lit: Lister 117

London, British Museum, 1985-5-4-1; purchased with contributions from the National Heritage Memorial Fund, Henry Moore Foundation, British Museum Company, British Museum Friends and Sir Duncan Oppenheim

One of the largest and finest 'moonlights' from Palmer's early Shoreham period, this shows a man with smock, broad hat and staff walking with his dog through a cornfield that has already been cut and stacked in sheaves. The sky has a large waxing sickle moon and evening star. The ethereal nature of the work is heightened by the glimmering light, which is stronger than any that could have been cast by a sickle moon and has more of the character of full-moon light. No specific location has been indicated, but the rounded hills are highly reminiscent of the Shoreham area where this work was doubtless painted.

While the design of the picture is carefully composed, the handling is quite free, Palmer using vigorous strokes to depict the sheaves of corn. Its rich tonalities show how much Palmer developed as a colourist around 1830. Indeed, much of the allure of the work comes from the vivid way in which broadly applied tones interact with emphatic draughtsmanship. It was this kind of feature that so attracted the British Neo-Romantics in the mid-twentieth century to Palmer. This particular work was owned by Sir Kenneth Clark, a great admirer of Palmer and supporter of Neo-Romantics such as Graham Sutherland in his early years.

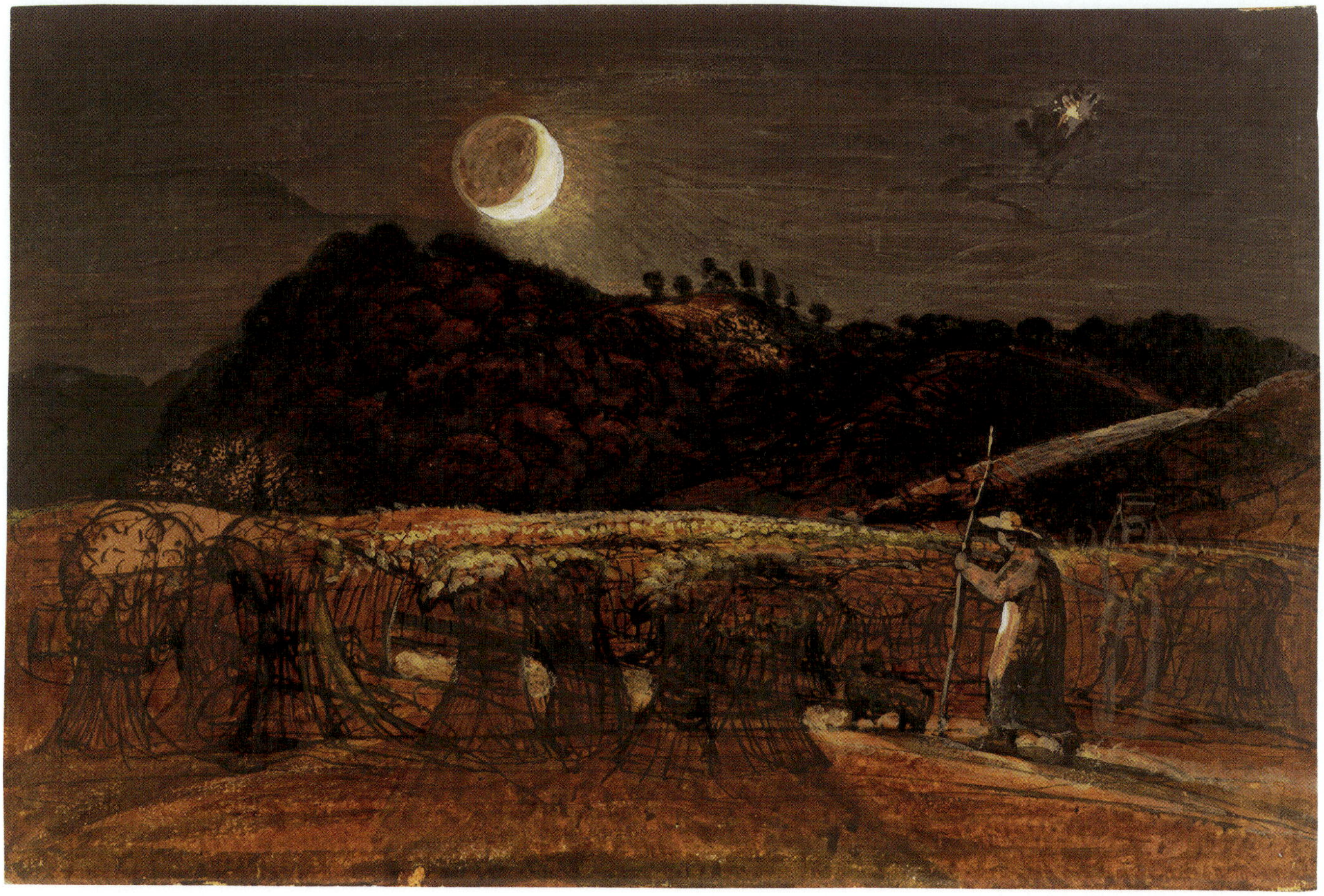

49

Lister suggests that this picture reflects the mood of the opening passage of Virgil's *Georgics*, quoting from the 1790 translation by Joseph Davidson: 'What makes the fields of corn joyous; under what sign, Maecenas, it is proper to turn the Earth and join the Vines to Elms … Ye brightest Luminaries of the World, that lead the Year sliding along the sky … your bounteous gifts I sing.' Virgil was one of Palmer's favourite poets. In later life he made a complete translation of the *Eclogues* (see cat. 163), and his ink painting of 1825, *A Rustic Scene* (cat. 10), had a passage from the *Georgics* attached to it. In this case, however, the inspiration appears to be general rather than specific. There is also perhaps a more religiously orientated contemplative awe in the picture than is suggested by Virgil's celebratory panegyric. Commentators in recent decades have been struck by the affinity of mood between works such as this and contemporaneous, religiously inspired scenes of figures contemplating the moon by the German Romantic painter, Caspar David Friedrich (Rosenblum, p. 59). Palmer never came closer to Friedrich than in this picture, although in technique their methods were utterly different.

## 50*

### *George Richmond Engraving the Shepherd*, 9 September 1827

Ink, 12.8 × 11.6 cm (5 × 4¾ in)

Dated at lower right in ink: *septr 9/1827*

Inscribed below date in ink in Welby Sherman's hand: *WS from GR*; along lower edge in pencil in George Richmond's hand: *Portrait of Geo Richmond engraving the Shepherd*

Lit: Lister 75; 'Shoreham notebook', Royal Academy, Richmond Archive, 397/GRI/1/2

San Marino, The Huntington Library, Art Collections, and Botanical Gardens, 68.25

This drawing was made of George Richmond when he was visiting Shoreham in 1827. In an account book covering the time of his visit to Shoreham Richmond subsequently (as an old man in the 1880s) wrote a recollection of his experiences there. He described it as 'amongst the very happiest weeks of my long life in which I engraved the Shepherd [cat. 51] and did much other work'. The visit was made possible by the sale of a portrait miniature.

Richmond walked out to Shoreham from London on 28 June 1827. As this was before the time that Palmer and his father had rented Water House (see cat. 44), lodgings had to be found for Richmond in the village. He stayed in the house of Mr Barham, 'a nice old labourer who had a bright and busy wife with two daughters. My rent was 2 shillings a week including service.' Richmond made a drawing of the room

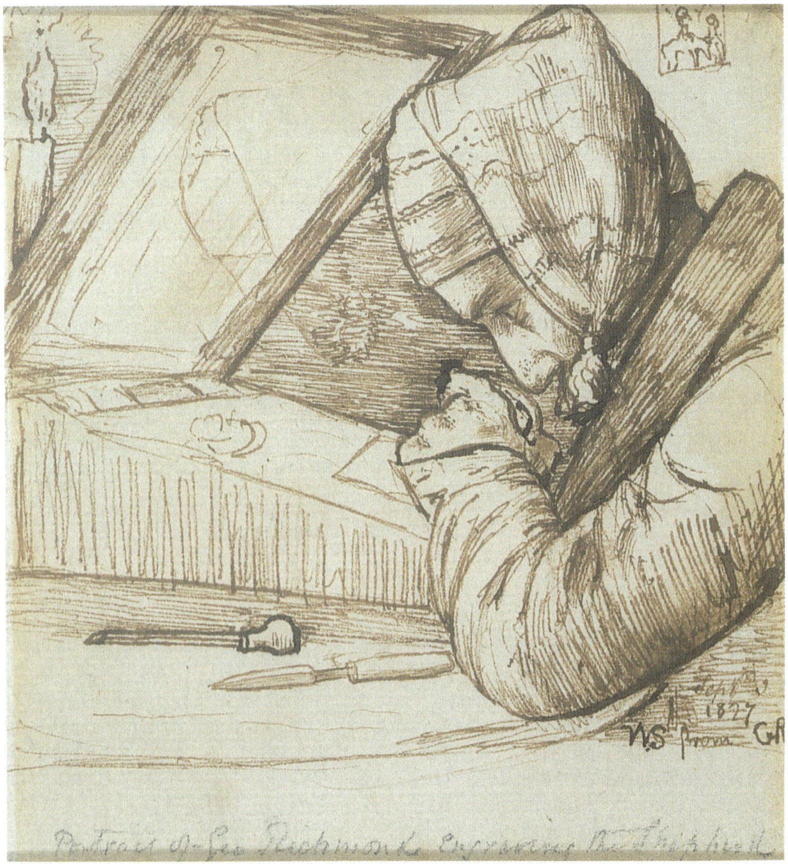


50

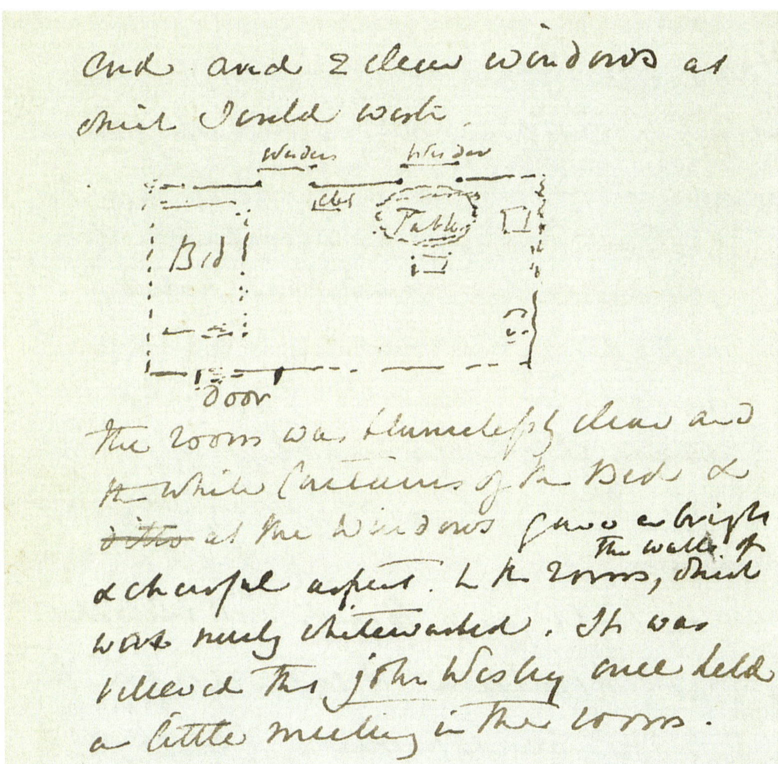
end and 2 clean windows at which I could work.



The room was blamelessly clean and the White Curtains of the Bed & ditto at the Windows gave a bright & cheerful aspect. The walls of the rooms, which was newly whitewashed. It was believed that John Wesley once held a little meeting in the room.

Fig. 25 George Richmond, *Page from notebook*, The Royal Academy

(fig. 25), which shows a table by a window, almost certainly the site at which Palmer sketched him engraving *The Shepherd*. He also noted: 'It was believed that John Wesley once held a little meeting in the room.' Shoreham's reputation as a centre for Non-conformism was probably the main reason that Palmer's father decided to settle there. Richmond also recorded in his memoir how he and his friends would read works by Shakespeare and Mrs Radcliffe in the room.

The drawing by Palmer shows Richmond at work at his engraving desk, with a mirror above, so that he can see the design reversed, and engraving tools beside him. He appears to have given this drawing at one time to Welby Sherman, who may have been advising him on engraving techniques at the time. It later returned to his possession and descended through the Richmond family. On the wall is a small drawing, possibly a design for a 'Flight into Egypt'.

## 51*

### George Richmond (1809–96)

### *The Shepherd*, 1827

Line engraving, 17.8 × 11.4 cm (7 × 4½ in)
Lit: Fitzwilliam 1984, 96
London, British Museum, 1932-5-13-1; presented by Henry Robinson

George Richmond was four years younger than Palmer and not more than fourteen or fifteen when the Ancients were set up. The son of a miniaturist, he was a student at the Royal Academy Schools at the time when Palmer was settling in Shoreham. Always more at home with figurative work than Palmer, he produced the most remarkable biblical paintings of the Ancients group and ones that show that he embraced primitivism as fully as Palmer did himself. He also painted pictures that most resembled those of the German Nazarenes, although his paintings are more idiosyncratic in their archaisms.

Richmond was soon to have a thriving career and went on to become one of the most successful portrait painters of the Victorian era. He remained Palmer's closest personal friend. He and his wife accompanied Palmer and Hannah on their trip to Italy in 1837 (see pp. 179–80). He continued to attend the monthly meetings that the former Ancients held in later life and was present at Palmer's deathbed.

This pastoral scene is heavily dependent on figures in Blake's wood engravings for Thornton's *Pastorals of Virgil* (cat. 19). The shepherd is based on Thenot and the sheep on those in the frontispiece. The anatomy of the shepherd, however, shows Richmond's study of Italian Mannerist prints, in particular those of Bonasone (see cats 26, 27). Richmond said that he began this engraving in April 1827 and worked on it substantially while in Shoreham during the summer of that year. Samuel Palmer made a drawing of him at work on it (cat. 50). However, the engraving was never completed: the arms and areas in the background are unfinished.

## 52
## Letter to George Richmond dated 14 November 1827

Lit: *Letters*, pp. 15–17

New York, The Pierpont Morgan Library, MA3455

Palmer was a prodigious letter writer. Unfortunately not many letters from the early years survive. Those that do – particularly those to his close friend George Richmond – reveal the depth of his artistic and spiritual enthusiasm as well as the complexity and interest of his personality.

This letter was written by Palmer to Richmond soon after the latter's sojourn in Shoreham during the summer and early autumn of 1827 had ended. It is an intensely emotional letter (as many of his to Richmond are) and gives a sense both of his visionary intensity and of his humour. Palmer was clearly feeling lonely and isolated after his friends had left.

In the early part of this long letter Palmer expresses his enthusiasm for the effects of nature observed during his wanderings around Shoreham in some of his headiest visionary language:

> I have beheld as in the spirit, such nooks, caught such glimpses of the perfumed and enchanted twilight – of natural midsummer, as well as, at some other times of day, other scenes, as passed thro' the intense purifying separating transmuting heat of the soul's infabulous alchymy, would

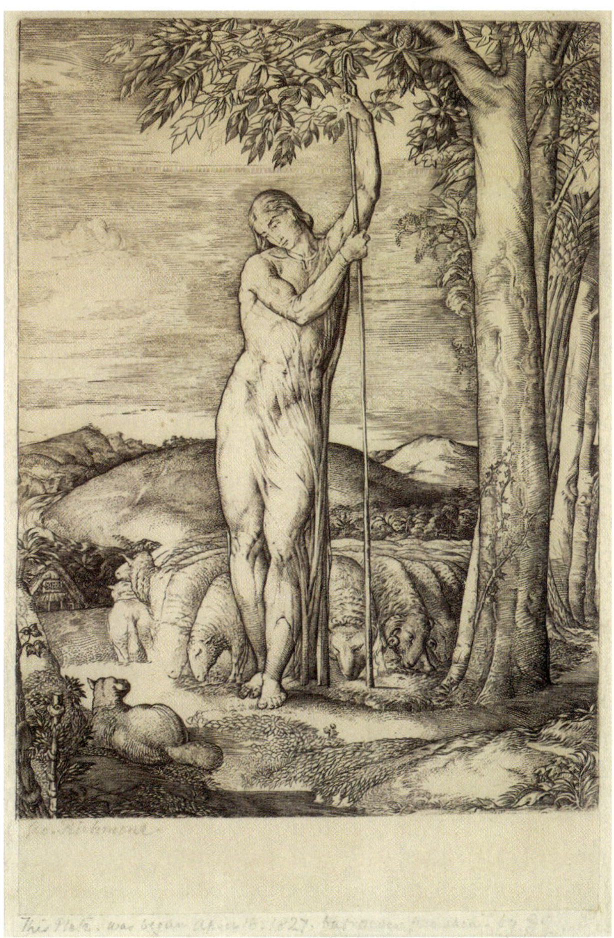

51

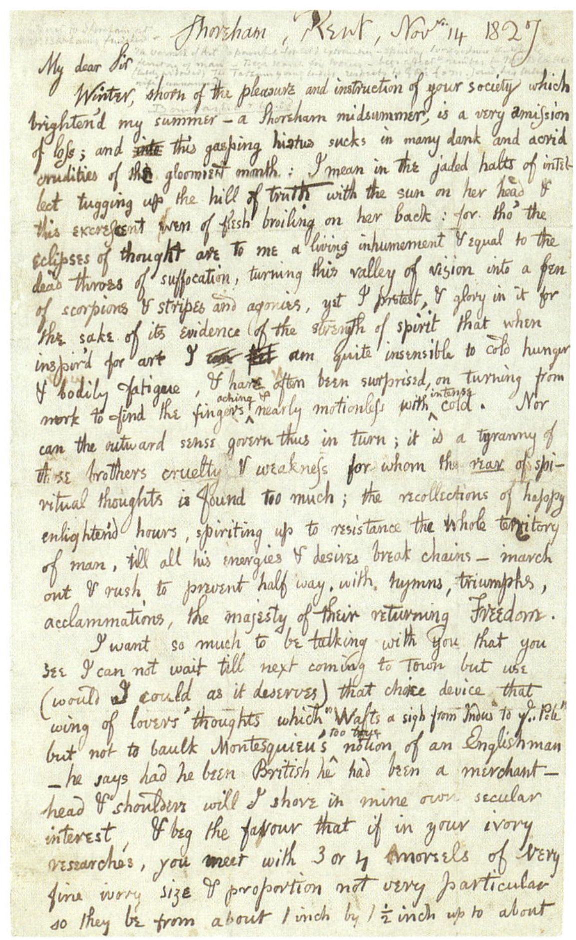

Shoreham, Kent, Novr. 14 1827

My dear Sir

Winter, shorn of the pleasure and instruction of your society which brighten'd my summer – a Shoreham midsummer, is a very amission of loss; and this gasping hiatus sucks in many dank and acrid crudities of the gloomiest month: I mean in the jaded halts of intellect tugging up the hill of truth with the sun on her head & this excrescent oven of flesh broiling on her back: for tho' the eclipses of thought are to me a living inhumement & equal to the dead throes of suffocation, turning this valley of vision into a fen of scorpions & stripes and agonies, yet I protest, & glory in it for the sake of its evidence of the strength of spirit that when inspir'd for art I am quite insensible to cold hunger & bodily fatigue, & have often been surprised, on turning from work to find the fingers aching & nearly motionless with intense cold. Nor can the outward sense govern thus in turn; it is a tyranny of these brothers cruelty & weakness for whom the emiss of spiritual thoughts is found too much; the recollections of happy enlighten'd hours, spiriting up to resistance the whole territory of man, till all his energies & desires break chains – march out & rush to prevent half way, with hymns, triumphs, acclammations, the majesty of their returning Freedom.

I want so much to be talking with you that you see I can not wait till next coming to Town but use (would I could as it deserves) that choice device that wing of lovers' thoughts which "Wafts a sigh from Indus to ye Pole" but not to baulk Montesquieu's too true notion of an Englishman – he says had he been British he had been a merchant – head & shoulders will I shove in mine own secular interest, & beg the favour that if in your ivory researches, you meet with 3 or 4 morsels of very fine ivory size & proportion not very particular so they be from about 1 inch by 1½ inch up to about

52

divinely consist with the severe and stately port of the human, as with the moon thron'd among constellations, and varieties of lesser glories, the regal pomp and glistening brilliance and solemn attendance of her starry train.

Later in the letter, however, Palmer turned to amorous matters, sending greetings to the beautiful sisters of his fellow Ancient, Frederick Tatham, one of whom was later to elope with Richmond. Remembering the occasion of some earlier meeting with the Tatham sisters, Palmer blames the state of his 'goggles' for his failure to communicate his ardent passion to the young ladies:

Tell them that herein is my disadvantage – whereas mine eyes are dim save when I look at lady fair – and whereas I can only see their lustre thro' my goggles, those said goggles so scratch'd and spoil'd that all the fire of the love darting artillery of my eyes is lost upon *them* and redounds not to my advantage, the ladies seeing only two huge misty spheres of light scratchd and scribbled over like the sun in a fog or dirty dish in a dark pantry.

Palmer concludes the letter with the comment: 'I am looking for a wife.'

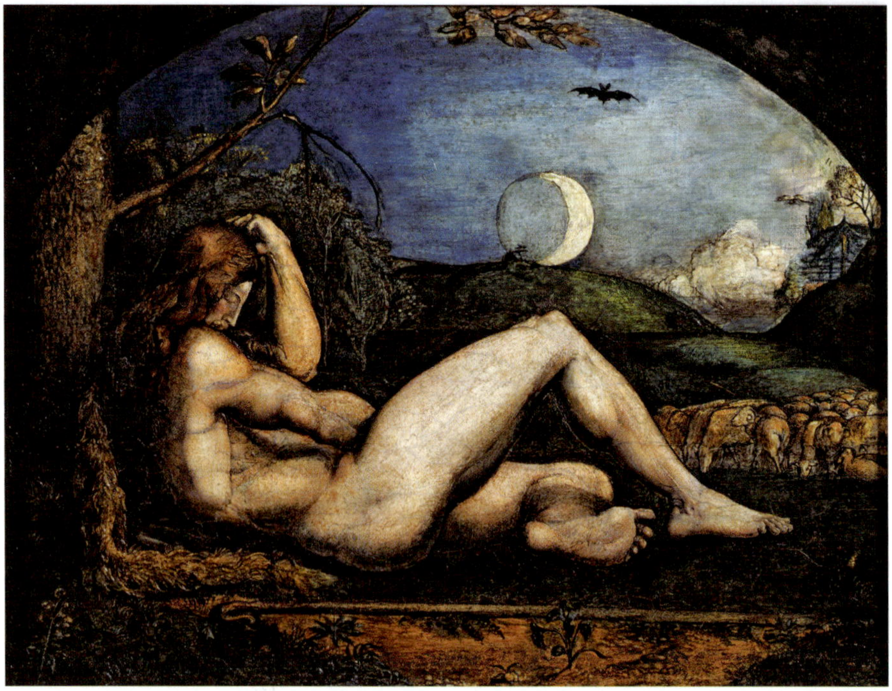

53

## 53

George Richmond (1809–1896)

*Abel the Shepherd*, 1825

Tempera on oak, 23 × 30.8 cm (9⅛ × 12⅛ in)

Inscribed at top left: *Abel the Shepherd. 1825*; at top right: *G.R. Pinx*; at bottom right: *1825*

Lit: Gilchrist 1887, p. 261; Fitzwilliam 1984, 94

London, Tate, N05858; purchased 1948

*Abel the Shepherd* was the first picture exhibited by Richmond at the Royal Academy, when he was sixteen. It shows Abel as a 'keeper of sheep', as described in Genesis 4: 2, and its pastoral subject accorded with the interests of both Palmer and Blake, who was then coming to the end of his engraving of *Job*. Blake had earlier treated the theme in the *Body of Abel Discovered by Adam and Eve*, and Linnell possessed a drawn version of this, which could also have been seen by Richmond. Richmond had recently met Linnell, who had introduced him to both Palmer and Blake around this time. H.H. Gilchrist records that this 'was Richmond's first picture; one that was submitted to Blake, who made a careful correction drawing of the shepherd's arm in his pupil's sketchbook'. This drawing, formerly in the collection of Sir Geoffrey Keynes, is published in Butlin (Butlin 1981, 802.1).

The body of Abel shows a debt to Michelangelo's statue of *Night* from the Medici tomb, which Richmond would have known through engravings. The tempera method that he used was presumably inspired by Blake, who had applied this in his own *Body of Abel Discovered by Adam and Eve* (Butlin 1981, cat. 664). In the Fitzwilliam catalogue Lister pointed out that there seem to be strong affinities between the drawing style used here and Palmer's Oxford sepia series (cats 10–15). There are also some shared motifs, for example the flying bats, which resemble those in *The Valley Thick with Corn* (cat. 15).

Presumably the decision to treat this theme as a nocturnal one relates to the interests of the Ancients in night and the occult. The picture is, in a sense, a prototype for one of Palmer's most successful and enduring motifs, that of the *Sleeping Shepherd* (cat. 89).

The picture is painted in tempera, a medium that Richmond was then using, like Palmer, under the influence of Blake. When Richmond consulted Blake about the process, the latter copied out a passage from a modern edition of the fourteenth-century treatise by Cennino Cennini describing it. Richmond appears to have used tempera in a more conventional manner than Palmer did (see cat. 89).

## 54

### George Richmond (1809–96)

*Portrait of an Artist (Miniature of Samuel Palmer)*, 1829

Inscribed in ink on card mount, probably in the artist's hand: *Saml. Palmer Esq. (Painter) / Painted by Geo Richmond in Half Moon St in Novr / 1829 / Exhibited at Rl. AcY., 1830*

Watercolour and gouache on ivory, 8.3 × 7 cm (3¼ × 2¾ in)

Lit: Ormond, p. 356; Fitzwilliam 1984, 100

London, National Portrait Gallery, 2223

This remarkable image was exhibited at the Royal Academy in 1830 (no. 668). It demonstrates Richmond's supreme skills as a miniaturist and the genial approach to his sitters that made him such a successful portraitist in the Victorian era. To judge by other images of Palmer (including those by Richmond himself), the representation of Palmer is somewhat idealized. His Christ-like appearance and apparently medievalizing dress recall portraits of the Nazarenes, for example that of Franz Pforr by Friedrich Overbeck (fig. 3, p. 19), and would seem to have a similar function as a manifesto of the artist's beliefs. Exhibited as *Portrait of an Artist*, Palmer's portrait seems to have been used to exemplify a type. As well as associations with Christ, Richmond might well have had one of Dürer's spiritualized self-portraits in mind when creating this work.

Richmond had already recorded Palmer's eccentricities of dress in 1825 (see cat. 55), but it would seem that the present garb was one worn for the occasion of this portrait rather than his normal attire. However, Palmer had adopted the beard and hairstyle by this time. Earlier in the year, on 17 May 1829, Palmer had written to Linnell concerning the wearing of beards: 'The artists have at last an opportunity of wearing the beard unmolested; I understand from the papers it has become the height of fashion! I hope they will avail of this.' (*Letters*, p. 54.) Presumably he followed his own advice soon after this, if he had not done so already. A chalk study of Palmer in the National Portrait Gallery shows the artist in a similar pose and is presumed to be the study for this work; although the physiognomy is alike, Palmer is looking down and his face does not bear the same degree of reflective passion. Altogether Ormond lists eight drawings of Palmer by Richmond, all of which are in more informal situations and are less idealized.

## 55*

### George Richmond (1809–96)

*Caricature of Samuel Palmer*, 1825

Pen, touched with white, 15.2 × 14.3 cm (4¾ × 4 in)

Inscribed: *sambo Palmer*; *22 September 1825*

Lit: V&A 1926, 6

London, Victoria and Albert Museum, 1298-1925

This caricature was made in the year that Richmond and Palmer first met. It shows Palmer after he had abandoned his early stylishness (still evident in his self-portrait, see cat. 1), grown his hair long and adopted the broad-brimmed

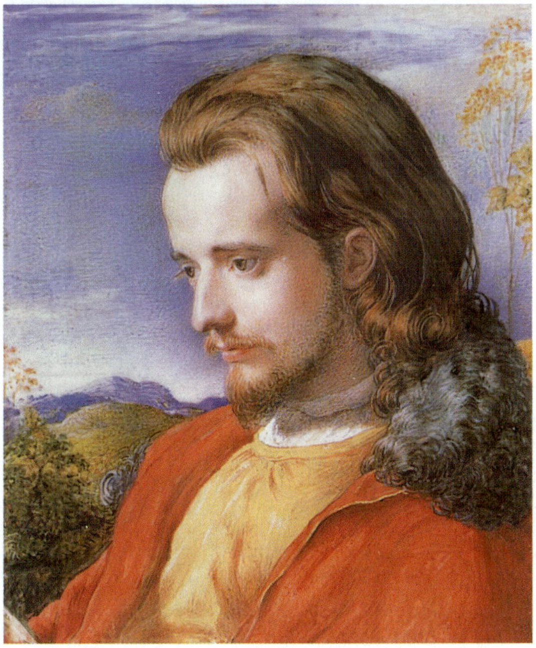

54

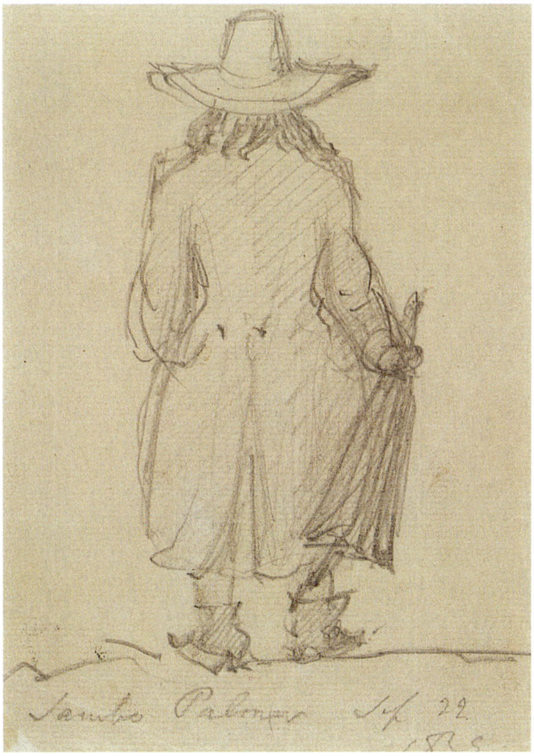

55

hat and long coat that became his trademarks. There is a hint of Palmer's absent-mindedness as the caricature shows him holding his umbrella upside down. The picture forms an interesting contrast to the glamorized miniature of Palmer as a Christ-like artist in full Ancients' garb made some five years later (cat. 54). It is a reminder of the strong vein of humour that ran through the Ancients' activities. Palmer himself combined visionary fervour with self-mockery, as can be seen in his letters to Richmond (see cat. 52).

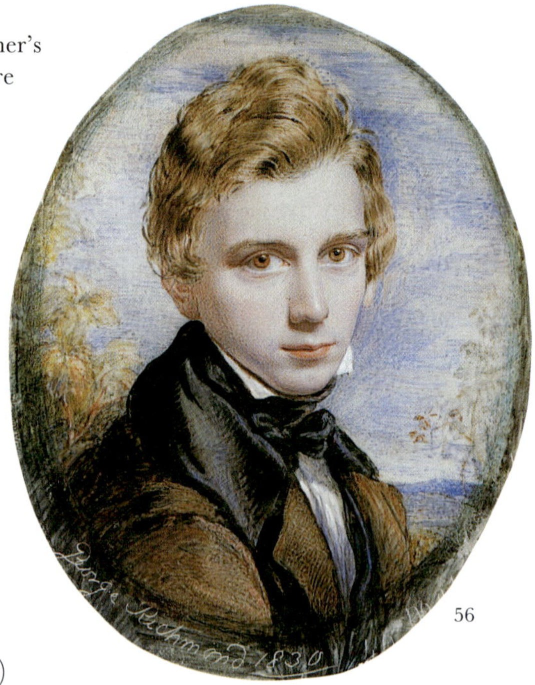


56

## 56

### George Richmond (1809–96)

### *Self-Portrait*, 1830

Gouache on ivory, oval, 8.9 × 6.8 cm (3½ × 2⅝ in)

Inscribed on verso: *George Richmond, painted by himself for our marriage*

Lit: *Richmond Papers*, pp. xiii, 34; Lister 1981, p. 160

London, National Portrait Gallery, 6586

Like cat. 55, this work shows Richmond's great skills as a miniaturist. It also makes clear, however, that Richmond did not follow Palmer in his dress or appearance. Richmond was by this time building a successful career as a portraitist and would not have risked this by adopting the eccentricities of his fellow Ancients. Instead he shows himself as a clean-shaven and fashionable young man, albeit one with a distinctly soulful expression. The latter is possibly related to the fact that the miniature was a marriage gift to his bride. The only concession to the Ancients in this self-portrait appears to be the landscape background, which recalls similar ones in fifteenth-century paintings.

## 57

### George Richmond (1809–96)

### *Christ and the Woman of Samaria*, 1828

Tempera on wood, 41 × 49.8 cm (16⅛ × 19⅝ in)

Lit: Fitzwilliam 1986, 97

London, Tate, N01492; presented by the artist's family, 1897

The scene is taken from the story of Christ and the Woman of Samaria, as related in John 4: 1–30. On a journey to Galilea Christ paused to rest at Jacob's Well, outside the town of Sychar in Samaria. There he astonished a Samaritan woman who was drawing water by a request for a drink. The traditional antipathy between Jews and Samaritans was such that they would not drink from the same vessel. Christ's gesture was taken by Christians as an indication that his message was for all people and not just for Jews, hence its significance for Christians in general. As the woman was an adulteress, Christ talking to her was also a sign of his refusal to condemn people who had transgressed conventional mores.

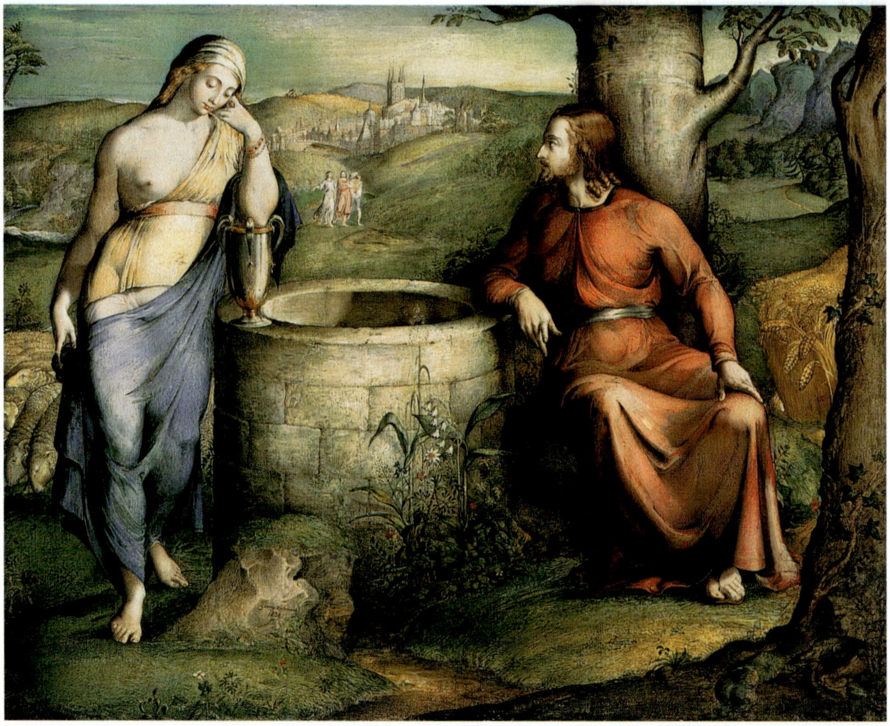

57

Richmond has followed the traditional pattern, familiar from such examples as the version by Michelangelo, then owned by the Liverpool merchant William Roscoe but probably known to Richmond through the engraving after it by Nicholas Beatrizet. Certainly a print after Michelangelo's drawing was of particular interest to Palmer, since he wrote to Linnell in May 1826: 'If, happening at any time to lay your hand on the prints from M. Angelo of Christ and the woman at the well or the Conversion of St. Paul, you would lay them by, I should be delighted by a sight of them' (*Letters*, pp. 10–11).

Christ sits beneath a shady tree. Richmond has shown the woman with one breast exposed and braided hair – conventional signs for a courtesan. In the background is the city of Sychar. The figures approaching are Christ's disciples, who in the story express surprise to find him talking to a Samaritan woman. Although Richmond had depicted biblical subjects before, this was his first representation of Christ. The figure of Christ bears a passing resemblance to Palmer as he was depicted by Richmond a year later (see cat. 54).

Like *Abel the Shepherd* (cat. 53), this work is in tempera and shows a similar interest in both Blake and early Italian art. Its pastoral imagery, particularly the sheep, have echoes of Blake's *Job* engravings (see cat. 18). A squared-up study for this painting is in the Tate collection (T02103).

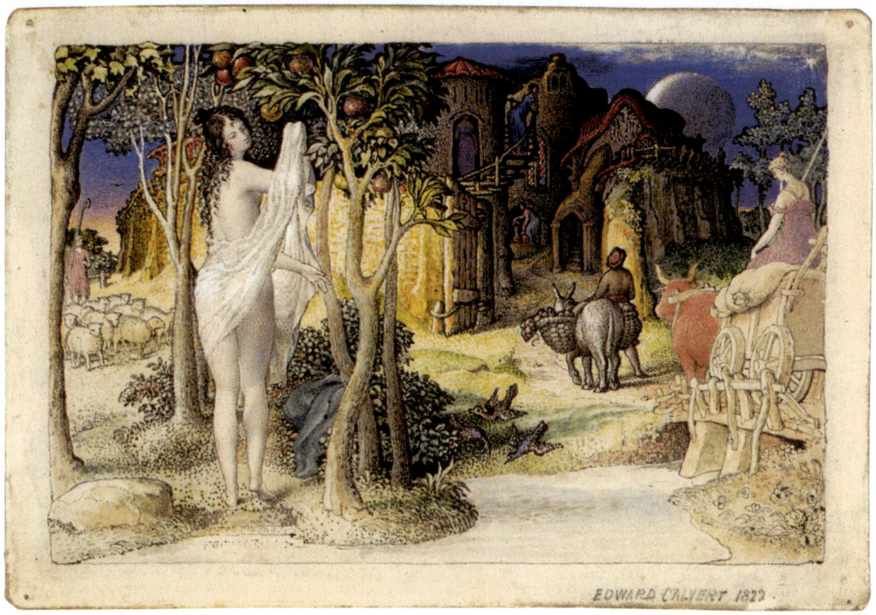


58

## 58

### Edward Calvert (1799–1883)

### *A Primitive City*, 1822

Watercolour, 7.7 × 10.2 cm (3 × 4⅛ in)

Signed and dated at lower right of sheet in pencil: *EDWARD CALVERT 1822*

Lit: Calvert, pp. 11–12; Fitzwilliam 1984, 110

London, British Museum, presented by the National Art Collections Fund, 1947, 1947-2-17-1

Calvert is best remembered for the brilliant and highly original wood engravings that he produced between 1827 and 1831, when the Ancients were at their most creative as an artistic group. Born in the West Country, the son of a military officer, he first had a career in the Navy, leaving the service after witnessing the death in action of his closest friend. A man of independent means, he determined at this time to devote his life to art. After studying drawing in Plymouth with Ambrose Bowden Johns, he moved to London in 1824, where he enrolled as a student at the Royal Academy. Soon after this he was introduced to Palmer by the latter's cousin, John Giles, who happened to be the stockbroker involved in selling some shares for Calvert. He also met Blake at much the same time and became a member of the Ancients. Calvert was by this time already married with children, and for this reason he only made visits to Shoreham, remaining resident with his family in Brixton.

Together with Richmond and Palmer, Calvert was one of the most innovative members of the Ancients in the late 1820s. He was inspired, like Richmond and Palmer, by Blake's illustrations to Thornton's *Pastorals of Virgil* (cat. 19). In his case, however, he focused on the actual medium Blake used: wood engraving. The outcome was a series of fine prints of rustic subjects, which developed Blake's practice of using the marks made by the engraver to produce positive white lines and marks in the print. Little known in his own day, his work was to prove inspirational to wood engravers in the twentieth century.

Unlike the other Shoreham artists, Calvert did not base his vision on Christian poetry such as that of Milton or Bunyan. A pantheist, he favoured the world of pagan antiquity, even erecting an altar to Pan in his garden in London. His rustic scenes are inspired by Theocritus and other pagan idylls, and represent the sensual in a more overt and even sexually explicit way than do the other Ancients. Like Palmer, Calvert's vision of the primitive began to wane after 1830. In his case, however, he never successfully managed to develop a new mode of working and produced little of interest in his later years. He remained one of Palmer's closest friends, staunchly supporting him through personal crises.

This exquisite miniature depicts a pagan golden age. Sheep are being driven home and a wagon laden with grain and grapes is making its way towards the city. While these images could be either Christian or pagan, the naked figure in the foreground unequivocally suggests the latter. In its gem-like use of miniaturist techniques, and detailed and emphatic depiction of forms, this work seems to bear all the hallmarks of the work of the Ancients. Surprisingly, however, it was produced before Calvert had moved to London and before the Ancients had even been formed. It may well be, however, that Calvert already had some knowledge of Blake. A year later, in 1823, when he was still living in Plymouth, he paid for a copy of Blake's *Job*. This appears to have been via his teacher, A.B. Johns, who had links with the London art world and was a friend of Turner's. It is not impossible that Johns had by that time introduced Calvert to other published works by Blake, since there appear to be traces of both the *Songs of Innocence* and *The Pastorals of Virgil* in the *Primitive City*.

## 59

## Edward Calvert (1799–1883)
## *The Cyder Feast*, 1828

Wood engraving, state 3, 7.6 × 12.7 cm (3 × 5 in)

Lit: Fitzwilliam 1984, 114

London, British Museum, 1887-5-2-113; presented by Samuel Calvert in 1887

This impression includes the lettering 'BY THE GIFT OF GOD IN CHRIST', which the artist later cut from the block. The image, however, has no obvious Christian message but seems rather to exude the paganism that was the central theme in Calvert's life. As Lister says, it 'owes more to Virgil and Theocritus than to Christ', the cavorting couple in the foreground seeming about to join some bacchanalian revel already being enacted by further couples in the background against a harvest moon.

The technique used for cutting the wood block shows the strong influence of Blake. The rich textures achieved also suggest a debt to Palmer's drawing style in its most primitivizing phase, as, for example, in *Early Morning* (cat. 12). The figures dancing before a huge harvest moon in the background is reminiscent of a similar motif in the admittedly more devout and regulated harvest festival that occurs in Palmer's 1824 sketchbook (cat. 9).

## 60

## Edward Calvert (1799–1883)
## *The Bride*, 1828

Engraving, state 2, 7.6 × 12.9 cm (3 × $5\frac{1}{8}$ in)

Lit: Lister 1962, pp. 77–81

London, British Museum, 1932-3-12-86

Like *The Cyder Feast* (cat. 59), this impression contains a religious inscription that was removed for later impressions: 'THE WATERS OF THIS BROOK SHALL NEVER FAIL TO THE MARRIED WIFE OF THE LORD GOD'. As with *The Cyder Feast*, this inscription seems to problematize the Christian message of eternal salvation through Christ by investing it with sexual overtones. It is possible that Calvert was aiming to find a secular meaning for such messages in the notion of life continuing eternally via procreation rather than through the salvation of the individual soul.

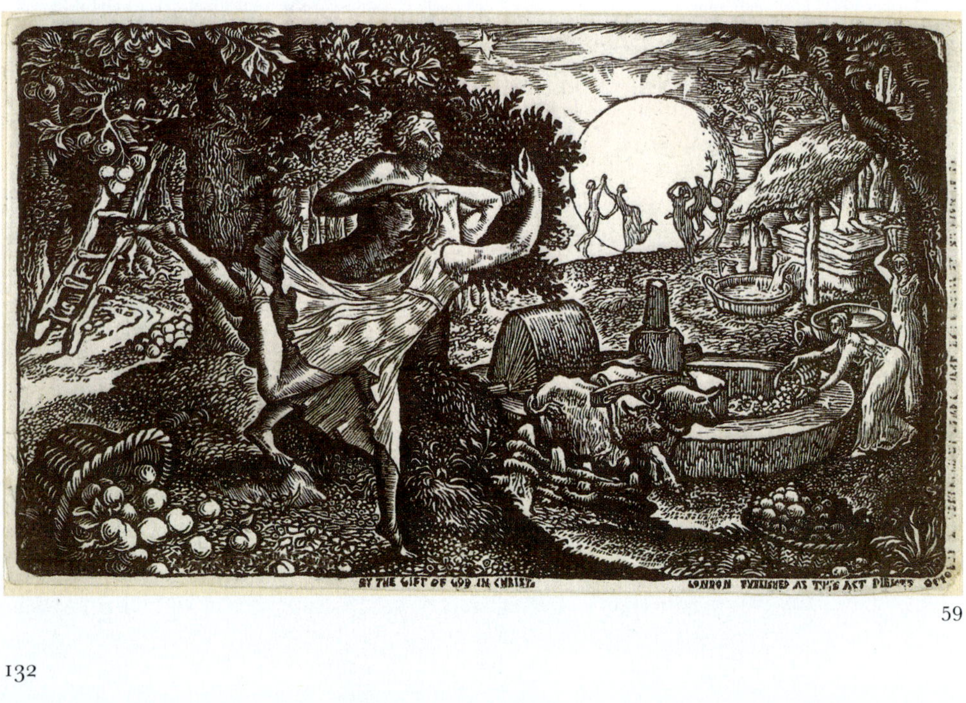


59

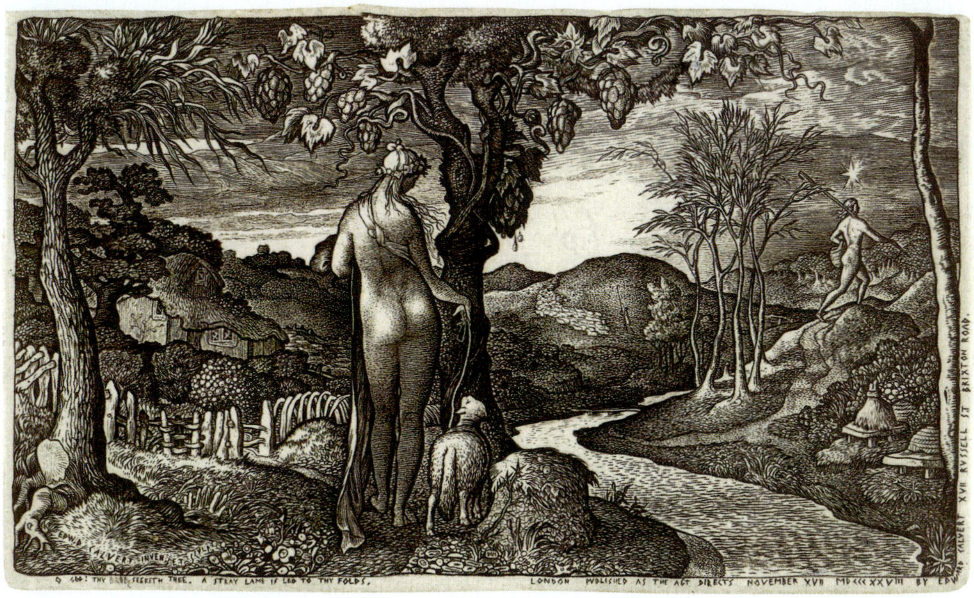

60

The landscape emphasizes fruitfulness, the vine around the central tree containing huge bunches of grapes, one of which is oozing drops of juice. Further pastoral richness is suggested by a hive surrounded by bees in the left-hand tree from which honey gushes forth in streams. The bride in the foreground, viewed naked from behind, recalls similar figures on antique gems that Calvert collected.

Like Blake's *Job* illustrations (see cat. 18), this work is a conventional line engraving. The richness of textures achieved here, however, seem to show the effects of Calvert's experiments in wood engraving.

## 61

### Edward Calvert (1799–1883)

### *The Chamber Idyll*, 1831

Wood engraving, 4.1 × 7.6 cm (1⅝ × 3 in)

Lit: Fitzwilliam 1984, 121

New York, The Metropolitan Museum of Art, 31.87.41; Harris Brisbane Dick Fund, 1931

This erotically charged scene of rural nuptials is widely regarded as Calvert's finest work. It was also his swan song as an engraver, as he made no more prints afterwards. Unlike his earlier engravings, which show continual debts to Blake's *Pastorals of Virgil* illustrations and provide, thematically, a pagan counterpart to Palmer's pastoral themes, this subject is very much Calvert's own. It brings to a head the earthy sense of fertility and sexuality that underlies all Calvert's best work.

We are provided with a view into the chamber of a young couple. It is a warm night and the cottage door lies open, providing us with a view of a fruitful land. There is a plough on the horizon, emphasizing the end of a day's labour (and possibly symbolic of the forthcoming night's activities). Inside a basket of apples – a sign of fruitfulness – stands beside the young woman as she undresses before her expectant lover. Interestingly, the woman – based on images in Calvert's collection of antique gems – is shown taking a dominant role. As well as being an erotic masterpiece, this wood engraving is a technical tour de force. The fine lines, textures and light effects show that Calvert had become a consummate master of the craft he had only taken up four years previously.

Since he had achieved so much, one wonders why Calvert went no further. As a man of independent means, he did not have to fear the financial consequences of taking risks with his art, as Richmond and Linnell did and as Palmer increasingly had to do when his legacy began to

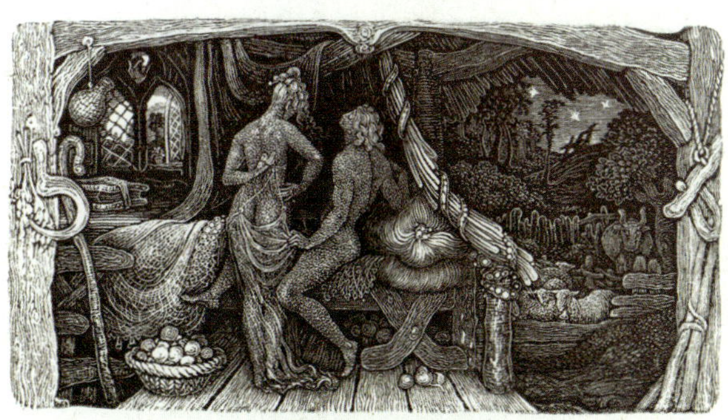

61

run out in the mid-1830s. Perhaps it was simply the pressure of the growing prudery that was emerging in the 1830s and that we now see as the dominating public mores of Victorian society. While financially secure and a free thinker in religious matters, Calvert was acutely aware of his social position as a gentleman and as the father of a family. Whatever the reason, his later work became tamer and more decorative, though containing wistful echoes of his great period of creativity.

## 62

### Samuel Palmer, with engraving by Welby Sherman (active 1827–34))

### *Harvest under a Crescent Moon*, *c.*1828

Wood engraving on Japanese vellum, 2.65 × 7.7 cm (1 1/8 × 3 1/8 in)

Lit: Lister P1

London, British Museum, 1944-12-11-1; donated by Arthur K. Sabin

This impression is from a woodblock that belonged to A.H. Palmer, who gave it to Martin Hardie in 1920, and is one of a group of fifty prints taken from the original block by A.K. Sabin at the Temple Sheen Press in January 1932. The block was destroyed by enemy action in 1940.

While the design is generally accepted as being by Palmer, there has been much dispute about the level of his involvement with the cutting of the block. Palmer had no experience of printmaking at this time, although he was familiar with Blake's wood engravings and his close friend Edward Calvert was also producing wood engravings of high quality (see cat. 59). Calvert's method of cutting is quite distinct, however, from that employed in this block. Both in its shape and its use of white lines cut into the block this engraving suggests a debt to Blake's engravings for Thornton's *Pastorals of Virgil* (see cat. 19).

Whether or not Palmer was actually involved at any stage in the cutting of the block, it is clear that Welby Sherman was responsible for finishing it. This can be seen by a letter written by Palmer to Richmond on 3 January 1828, in which he states: 'Would you do me the favour to give my best respects to Mr. Sherman and tell him I rather wish that my block should not be proved and retouch'd … Therefore I should be obliged to Mr. Sherman if he would complete the cutting without obliterating the drawings.' (*Letters*, p. 18.) Sherman was trying to establish a career as an engraver at this time, and Palmer occasionally engaged him to make prints after his work (see cat. 94). Those favouring the authorship of Palmer for the block have pointed out that the method used – that of engraving white lines on the block – suggests that the engraver was developing the design as he cut rather than making a facsimile copy of a drawing.

The possibility that Palmer may have been directly involved in wood engraving at this time has also been raised in connection with impressions from wood blocks in the recently discovered Ionides album (see cat. 63). The cutting of the wood in the problematic prints in that album is cruder than in this block and it seems unlikely that they are by the same hand as the engraver of this work.

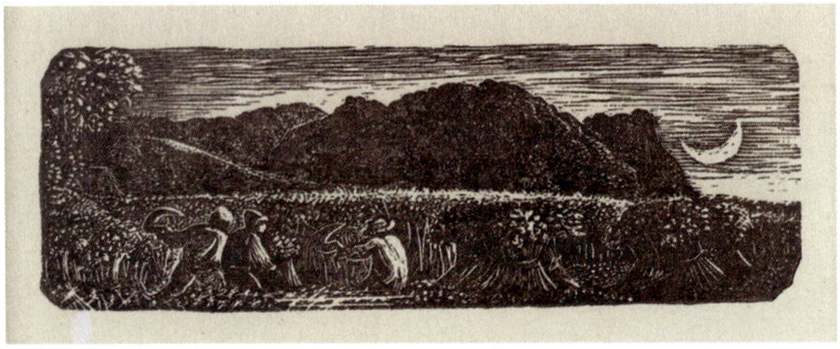

62

## 63

### Album formerly owned by Alexander Constantine Ionides

Paintings, drawings, prints and photographs mounted on pages, 23.5 × 18 cm (9 1/4 × 7 1/8 in)

Page 2 recto (ten wood engravings: eight illustrations to 'Thornton's Virgil' by William Blake, *The Baccante* by Welby Sherman after Edward Calvert and *Peace* attributed to Samuel Palmer) illustrated

Lit: Evans 2002

London, Victoria and Albert Museum

This album contains drawings, prints and photographs of works of art collected by the Greek Maecenas Alexander Constantine Ionides and members of his family. Its main interest in this context is the presence in it of a number of wood engravings by Blake, Calvert and other artists connected with the Ancients, including possibly Palmer. In his article on the album Evans draws attention to Ionides's relationship with Calvert, which seems to have been particularly close in 1826–7 when Ionides was a pupil at the school in Brixton run by Calvert's old friend Joseph Hine. Calvert himself was living in Brixton at that time and may even have offered drawing lessons at Hine's school.

The contact between Calvert and Ionides occurred at a time when Calvert was at the height of his creative powers as a wood engraver and the album contains impressions of both some of his finest work and the wood engravings by Blake for Thornton's *Pastorals of Virgil* (see cat. 19) that inspired him and other Ancients. Most intriguing of all is the presence of a number of crudely cut wood engravings that combine pastoral motifs, similar to those in the 'blacks' that Palmer was then painting (see cats 30, 31), with the erotic themes to be found in Calvert's engravings. There are no other records of these extraordinary images. Their position in the album confirms both that they were highly prized by Ionides and that they are related (as their appearance would suggest) to Calvert and his circle.

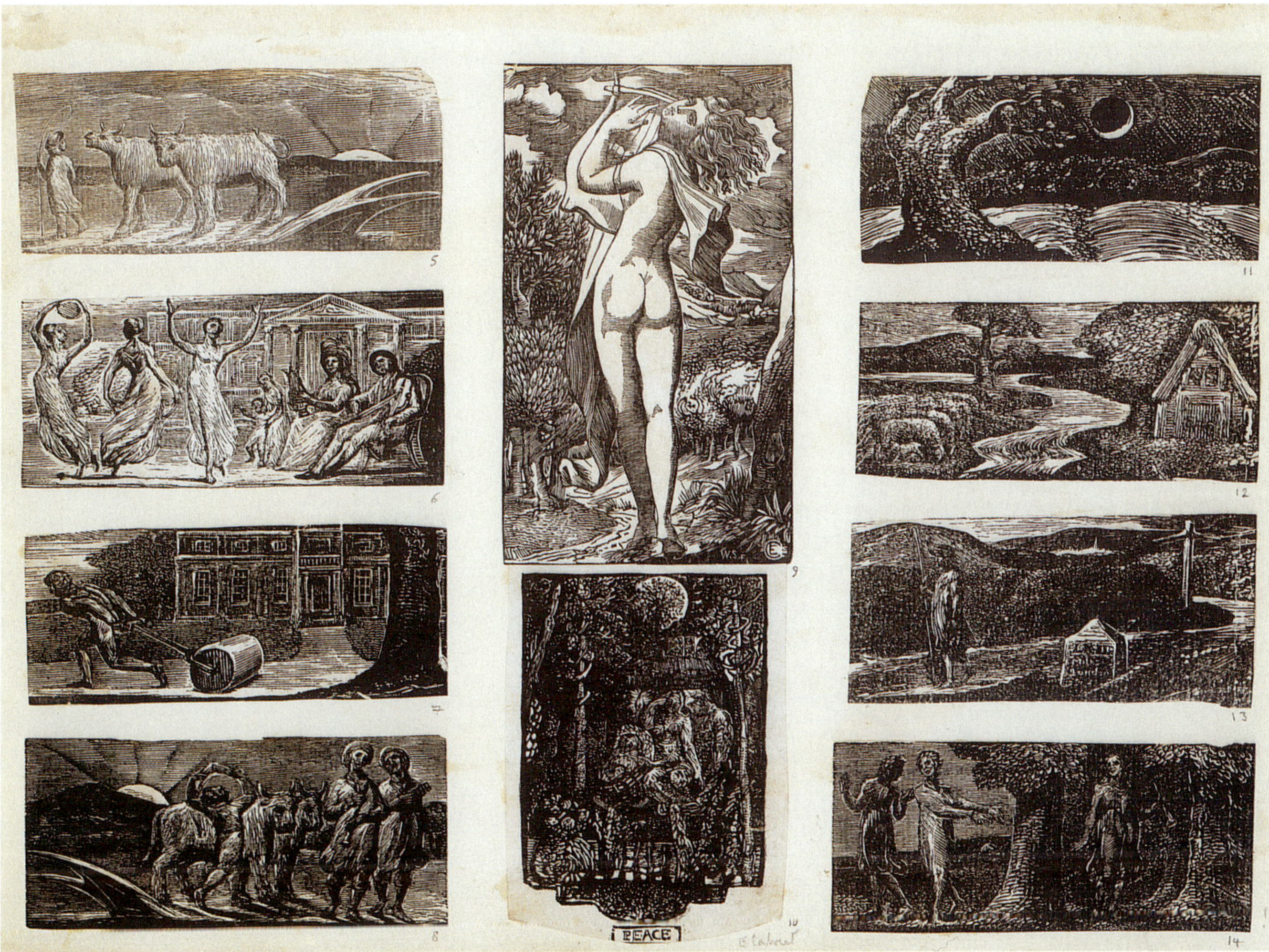


63

In his article Evans speculates that these wood engravings might be by Palmer. There are certainly strong arguments in support of this claim. Palmer is known to have been interested in wood engraving at this time, collaborating with Sherman on one block (see cat. 62). The roughness of the cutting could be explained by Palmer's inexperience in the practice of wood engraving. Palmer is not known to have produced other sexually explicit scenes, yet letters by him from the period certainly reveal a strong erotic obsession. Since so much of his early work was destroyed by his son, it is quite possible that risqué pictures might have been undertaken and not have survived.

Another possibility is that the wood blocks may have been engraved by Ionides himself. A drawing of a classical figure by Ionides occurs in the album, and while this is of a totally different nature to these wood engravings, it does at least confirm that he had artistic aspirations at this time. Evans himself dismisses the notion that Ionides could have made the engravings. His main argument is that, if Ionides had produced such works, they would have been more likely to reflect the work of Calvert than of Palmer. Yet the figures do have affinities with Calvert's, and Ionides would surely have had access to Palmer's images if he was close to Calvert at this time. On the other hand, it might be argued that the wood engravings, while crude, show a boldness of conception unlikely to be found in an inexperienced amateur.

Another intriguing possibility, raised by Elizabeth E. Barker in an essay in this volume (p. 48), is that these designs could have been made by Calvert in *c.*1824–6, prior to the time when he had fully mastered the engraving process.

The identity of the cutter of these wood engravings must remain unclear at this point. What is certain is that the artist was intimately acquainted with the work of Blake and the Ancients. It is hoped that the present book and exhibition will assist in determining whether they are in fact by Palmer.

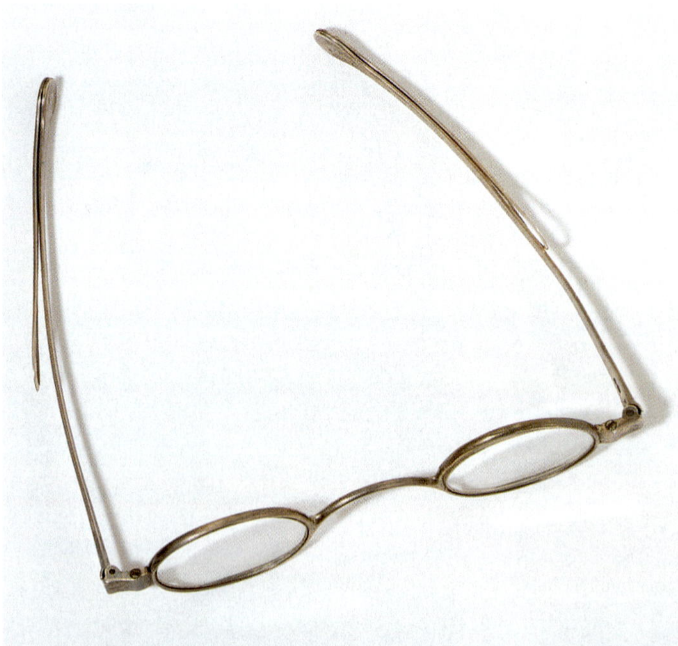

64

## 64

### Samuel Palmer's silver spectacles, 1819-20

Lit: V&A 1926, 18

London, Victoria and Albert Museum, E. 3979-1923; presented to the V&A by A.H. Palmer

According to A.H. Palmer in the 1926 exhibition catalogue, his father 'used these spectacles for nearly seventy years' and wore them for all his work. Possibly they are the pair he had on in the portrait of him by Henry Walter of *c.*1835 (fig. 24, p. 67), though the resemblance does not appear to be exact.

A.H. Palmer's claim that these spectacles were used by Palmer for all his work differs somewhat from the earlier account of them in *Life and Letters*: 'A Pair of old-fashioned silver spectacles with very broad rims was used for distant objects; but on state occasions aforesaid, these were exchanged for spectacles of the ordinary pattern' (*L&L*, p. 132). As Palmer was short-sighted, it would naturally be the case that he would wear glasses particularly to study distances. He also appears to have entertained a dialogue with his glasses, which seemed at times to offer him an alternative vision. In his lost sketchbook of 1823–4 he wrote: 'The least bit of natural scenery reflected from one of my spectacle-glasses laughs me to scorn and hisses at me' (*L&L*, p. 13). On another occasion he blames his glasses for undermining his amorous aspirations, by disguising the 'darting artillery of my eyes' (see cat. 52).

It was perhaps because of his obsession with glasses that Blake's widow gave him Blake's after the latter's death. A.H. Palmer states that 'Blake's great, round, steel-rimmed glasses, bleared by many years of use, were among my father's very few personal treasures' (*L&L*, p. 132).

# 4. Later Shoreham (1830–35)

*Colin Harrison*

*Coming from Evening Church* (cat. 48), inscribed so carefully 'PAINTED 1830 AT SHOREHAM KENT S. PALMER', marked the end of Palmer's overtly archaic style, but he remained at Shoreham for a further five years, during which time he produced some of his most extraordinary works. They marked the high point of his individuality, when the model of Blake had receded, and the domineering influence of Linnell had not yet induced the self-doubt that was to afflict Palmer's work in Italy. The last works Palmer produced at Shoreham were exhibited in 1835, by which time he had already begun looking for new horizons, new subjects and a new style.

Apart from a handful of long letters to Richmond and Linnell, and a few notes to other friends and relations, Palmer's correspondence from this period is scarce. They are mostly addressed from Shoreham, where Palmer spent much of the year. However, he was becoming increasingly isolated, as his fellow Ancients left the Darent Valley to pursue their careers in London. In January 1830 George Richmond ran away with Julia Tatham to be married at Gretna Green; the couple rarely visited Shoreham after their wedding. Calvert and Finch remained faithful friends, but spent most of their time in London. Only the least interesting Ancients, Welby Sherman and Henry Walter, still lived at Shoreham. Palmer was often lonely, and frequently complained that he needed a wife. He remained on good terms with Linnell and in 1832 began to show an interest in one of Linnell's daughters, Hannah, then aged fifteen, whom he would marry in 1837. Linnell even visited Shoreham again, in 1833, when he emulated Palmer's bold, swirling pen in a few landscapes at Underriver (cat. 93).

During this period Palmer's life was changing materially. In the *Literary Blue Book* of 1830 he was listed as living at both Water House, Shoreham, and 2 Temple Street, Fleet Street, London, and specializing in 'design'. In the following year he began negotiations to purchase two cottages at Shoreham, and by 1832 he had also bought a small house in London, at 4 Lisson Grove, Marylebone. It was from the latter address that he sent in works to the Royal Academy between 1832 and 1837. His London house also provided him with a base for teaching, a source of income mentioned by his son but otherwise undocumented at this period. However, his frequent protestations of poverty must be taken literally: a memorandum records that, in his later years at Shoreham, he managed to reduce his weekly expenditure to 5*s.* 2*d.*

The rapidly changing political climate caused Palmer to burst into print in 1832 with *An Address to the Electors of West Kent* (cat. 95). This was written in response to the threats to both the constitution and the countryside from a series of laws, culminating in the Reform Act of 1832. The supremacy of the Established Church was abolished, the right of its rural clergy to tithes questioned and Palmer's High Tory principles under attack. For much of 1830 the countryside around Shoreham was in turmoil, with the 'Captain Swing' riots and widespread rick-burning. Palmer feared that the pastoral landscape with which he identified so closely would be destroyed by the political changes and, as a last resort, wrote in defence of the status quo that prevailed during his first years at Shoreham. The pamphlet is hysterical and unreasonable, but reflects the very real mental and emotional disturbance Palmer suffered.

The political changes profoundly affected Palmer's art, as religious subjects gave way to the pastoral. He continued to submit work to the Royal Academy, where it was rejected in 1830 and 1831, but accepted in the following years: seven works in 1832, five in 1833, six in 1834, but only two in 1835. A passing reference in one of his letters to 'my blacks' in 1832 has led scholars to deduce that some or all of his submissions in that year were monochrome drawings. Unfortunately, the titles of exhibited works are too vague and repetitive to make identification certain. The drawings in Indian ink are among Palmer's most accomplished works, the technique highly sophisticated and the feeling remarkably intense. The oil paintings of this period, most of which were presumably made for exhibition, were on prepared wooden panels or commercially made board, and continued to be experimental, though without the thick layers of gum used until 1830. The subject matter of both drawings and paintings was the flock and the harvest, often by moonlight, serene and balanced but charged with emotion. Sometimes Palmer reworked in oil a subject that he had already treated in ink a year or more previously; such are the origins of the paintings known as *The White Cloud* (cat. 86) and *The Bright Cloud* (cat. 87). Only in a few finished works did Palmer reveal his development as a colourist, notably in *The Golden Valley* (cat. 85) and *The Shearers* (cat. 88), both more controlled and subtle than the private pastorals such as *Ivy Cottage* (cat. 71). At the same time Palmer continued making nature studies: those done for Linnell in 1828–9 were succeeded by several of the most original drawings of Palmer's career, notably *In a Shoreham Garden* (cat. 66). In his later years at Shoreham Palmer preferred to make tiny studies in sepia, notations of composition as well as effects of light. Only a few studies of

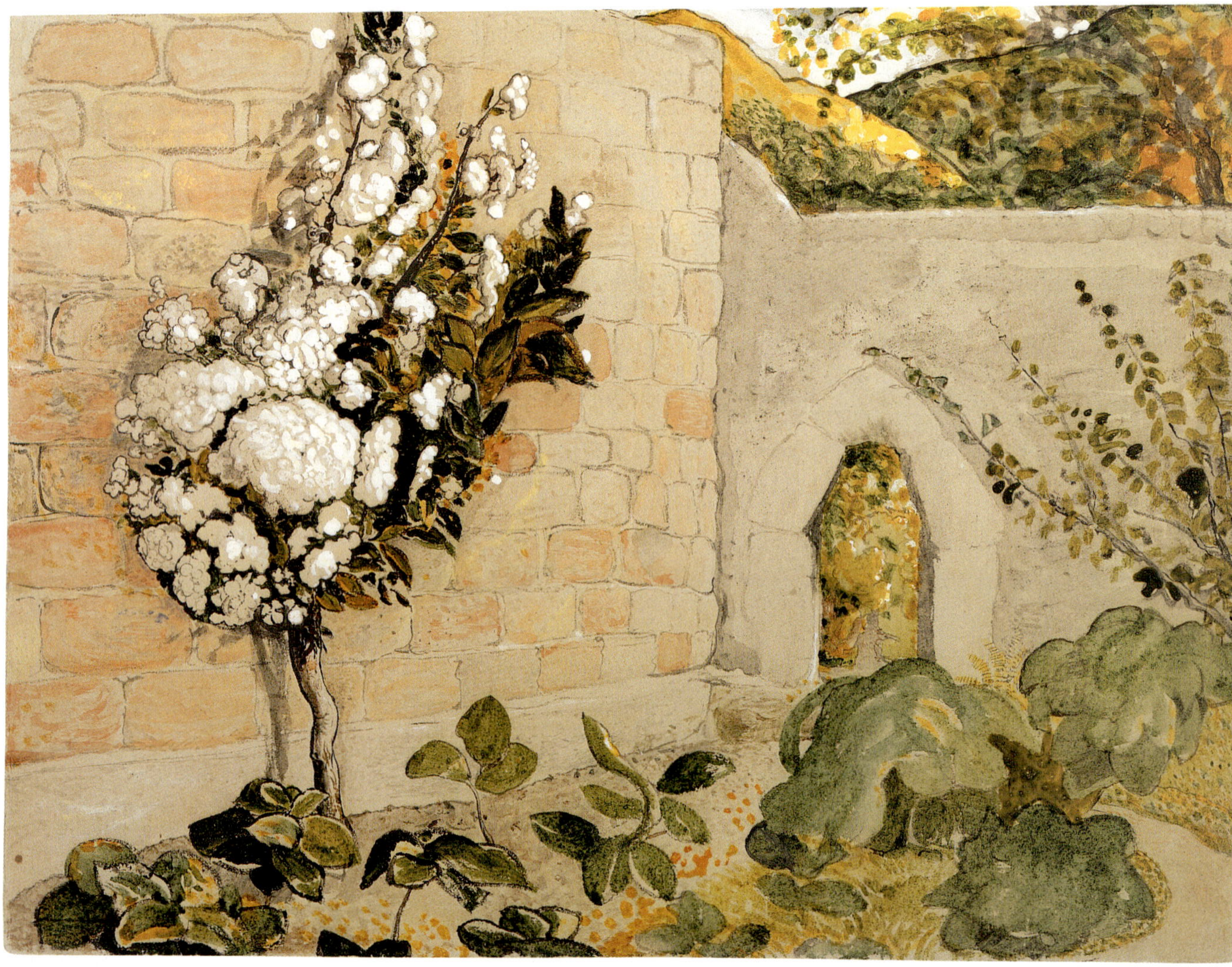

65

details survive, which were probably all from *c.*1834–5 and are the most conventional of all Palmer's drawings.

In spite of the numerous setbacks in his life and his career, Palmer wrote in 1834 that 'I feel more energetic and ambitious for excellence in art than ever, but yet I hope with a more innocent and less selfish enthusiasm' (*Letters*, p. 64). He also longed to see 'some first rate distances' (16 October 1834: *Letters*, p. 66). In the summer of 1834 he made a journey to Devon, apparently inspired by a cheap print in a shop window. This was the first time he had travelled far from Shoreham, and it gave him a taste for new landscapes that eventually took him to Italy on his honeymoon.

## 65†

### *Pear Tree in a Walled Garden, c.*1829

Watercolour and gouache with gum arabic, over preliminary indications in brush and grey wash, with traces of graphite, on grey paper, 22.2 × 28.2 cm (8¾ × 11⅛ in)

Lit: V&A 1926, 56; Grigson 77; Lister 102

New York, The Pierpont Morgan Library, Collection of Eugene Victor and Claire Thaw, 1980.37

Together with the following work, to which it is closely related, this is one of the most exuberant of Palmer's Shoreham drawings, combining close observation of detail with an almost abstract delight in the irregularities of nature. The limited palette and subtlety of colouring are natural developments from his studies of the oak trees in Lullingstone Park (cats 46, 47). The egg-yolk yellow is the same, but the drawings are conceived in a more pictorial spirit, carefully composed and boldly executed. The pear tree in blossom is integrated into a portrait of a real garden, complete with a tall stone wall and a path leading under a Gothic arch into an even more riotous display of abundance beyond. Behind are the hills of the Darent Valley, with the brilliant white clouds balancing the blossom.

A.H. Palmer (V&A 1926) proposed that the garden was Palmer's own at Water House, while later commentators have made the less convincing suggestion that it belonged to a Mr Groombridge, whose house is indicated in a note by A.H. Palmer on the drawing *The Bridge at Shoreham* (cat. 44). A passage in Palmer's celebrated letter to John Linnell in December 1828 has been associated with this drawing and its companion:

> Terrestrial Spring showers blossoms and odours in profusion, which at some moments 'Breathe on earth the air of Paradise': indeed sometimes, when the spirits are in Heav'n, earth itself, as in emulation blooms again into Eden; rivalling those holden fruits which the poet of Eden sheds upon his landscape, having stolen from that country where they grow without peril of frost or drought or blight – 'But not in this soil'. (*Letters*, p. 49.)

## 66

### *In a Shoreham Garden*, *c.*1829

Indian ink with watercolour and gouache on prepared board, 27.9 × 22.2 cm (11 × 8¾ in)

Lit: V&A 1926, 62; Grigson 78; Lister 103

London, Victoria and Albert Museum, 32-1926

A.H. Palmer was the first to describe this as a 'companion to *The Magic Apple Tree*' (V&A 1926), and the two have come to be regarded as the summit of Palmer's achievement, his most individual contributions to the history of English art. Like its companion, *In a Shoreham Garden* was 'shown to scarcely anyone' (A.H. Palmer to F.L. Griggs, 27 June 1926, Ashmolean Museum) and presumably kept in Palmer's special Shoreham portfolio. The two drawings are, however, very different in style, technique and effect, although the aim in both was to celebrate the 'excess [that] is the essential vivifying spirit, vital spark, embalming spice … of the finest art'.

The drawing is dominated by an apple tree in full bloom, growing at the edge of a garden path. Framed by its branches, at the end of the path stands a graceful female figure in profile, wearing a flowing red dress, and gazing away to the right. Apart from the edge of a wooden building in the foreground, everywhere else is a profusion of blossoms and leaves, both within and beyond the garden. Tall trees reach into the sky at the right and left, and even the sky is punctuated by pink and white apple blossoms exploding like fireworks on the ends of their branches.

The idea for the drawing may have come to Palmer in his own garden at Water House, from which he painted the bridge across the Darent (cat. 44) and possibly the *Pastoral with a Horse Chestnut Tree* (cat. 70). Alternatively, it may have been another garden at Shoreham, attached to one of his own properties or elsewhere. It is unlikely, however, to have been that of Mr Groombridge, who seems to have grown fruit commercially in an orchard. The technique of the drawing is similar to that of the *Pear Tree in a Walled Garden*, though on a slightly different support. The outlines of the leaves and blossom are drawn in thick black Indian ink, both under and over the body colours – green, white, pink and egg-yolk yellow – applied with varying touches, from tiny dots to broad shading. The white body colour is so thickly applied that at one point a large blob has come away, almost as though the blossom has exploded.

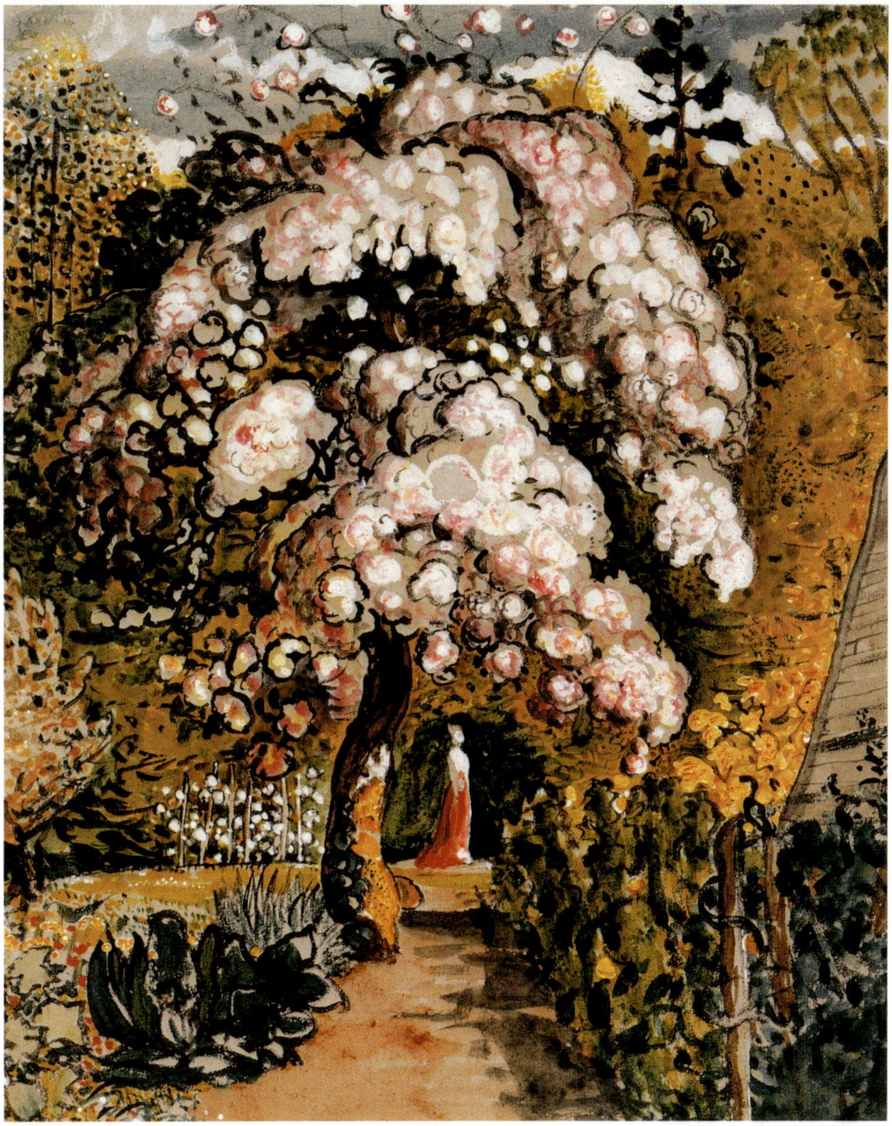

66

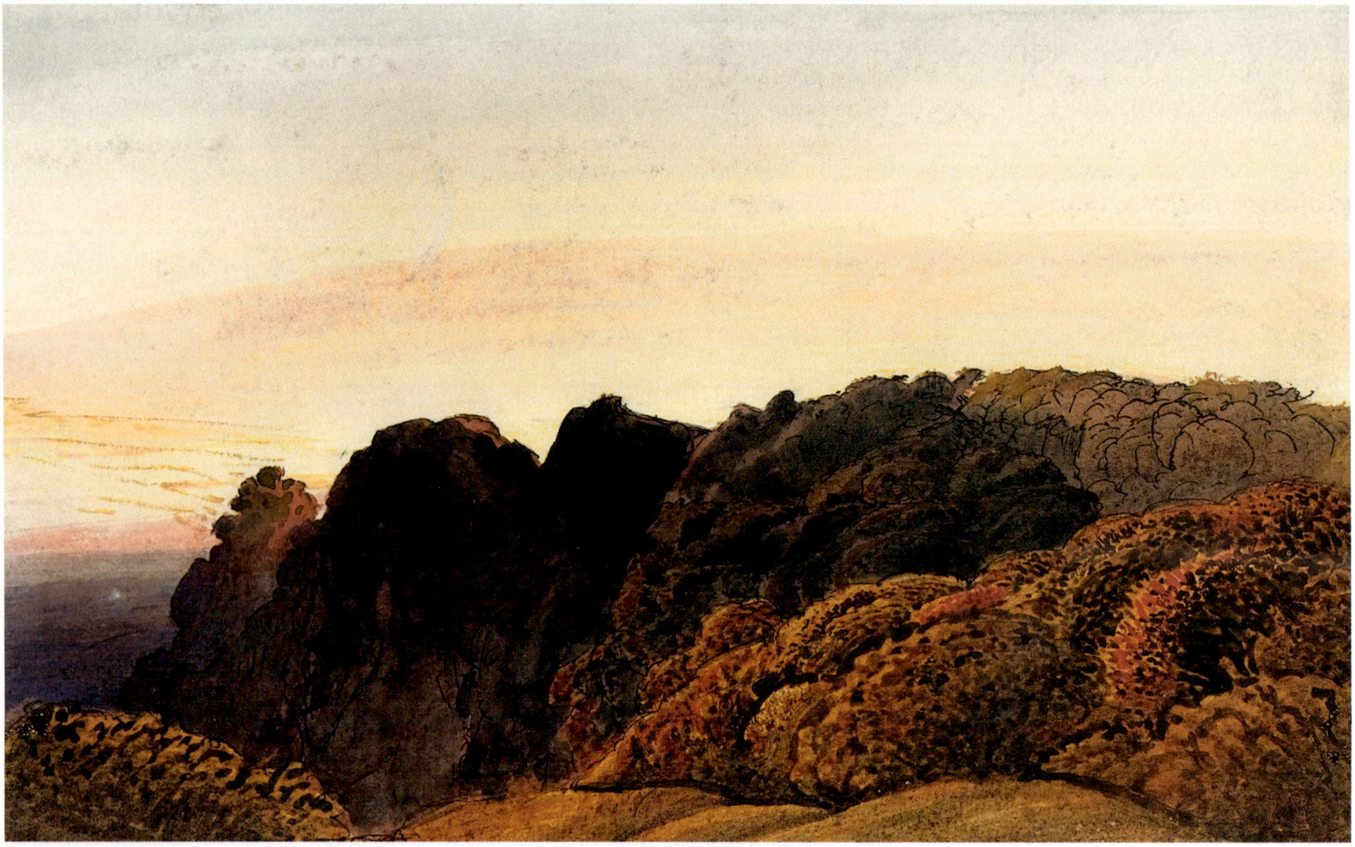

67

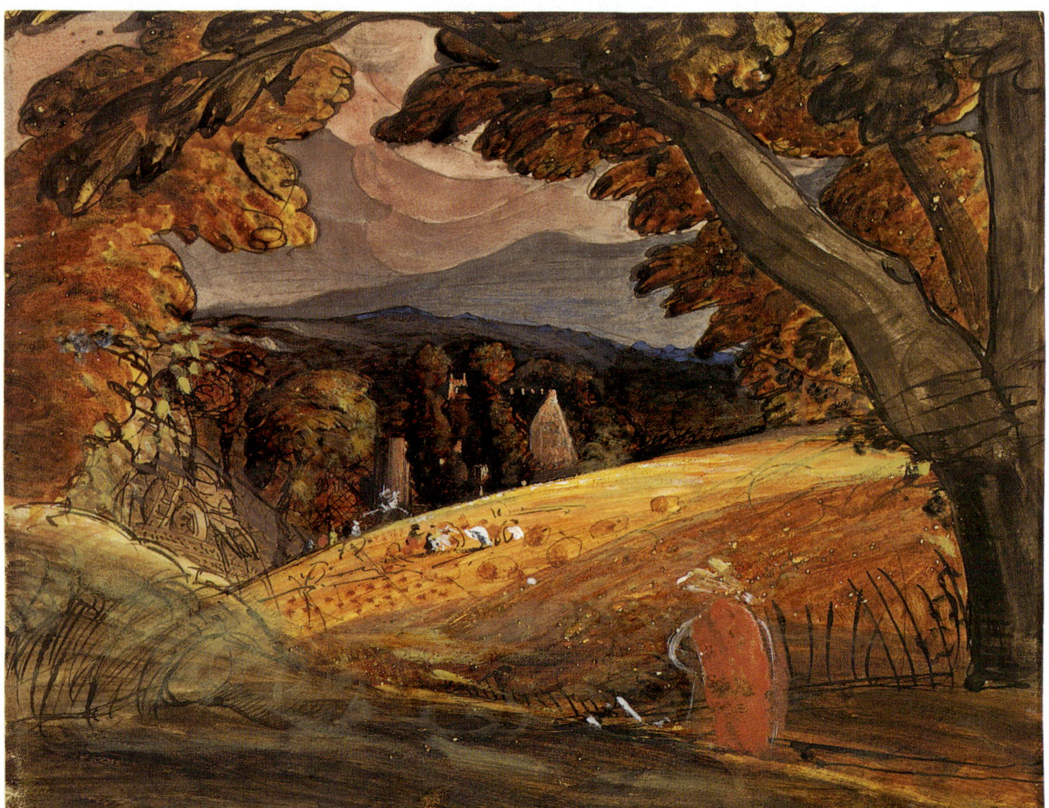

68

## 67

### *Yellow Twilight*, *c.*1830

Watercolour and gouache with pen and black ink and gum arabic, 16.5 × 27.5 cm (6½ × 10¾ in)

Lit: V&A 1926, 65; Grigson 89; Lister 120

Private collection, UK

One of the first treatments of a motif that became a favourite with Palmer when he was working around Underriver in the 1840s, this watercolour is also remarkable for being among the earliest nature studies without the presence of human beings or habitation. The wooded ridge may be in the Darent Valley near Shoreham or further afield, perhaps near Underriver, where Palmer had worked in *c.*1828–9 (Lister 100). It might be an illustration of one of Palmer's most elliptical notes: 'RIDGES OF MOUNTAIN ALONG OPEN COUNTRY' (*L&L*, pp. 54–5).

Grigson (1947, p. 95) coupled this work with *The Magic Apple Tree* as 'two exceedingly, supremely exquisite works of vision'. He evidently knew the work well, writing that 'in a half-lit room, the drawing seems luminescent; both startling and tender', and reserved some of his most poetic appreciation for it: 'It is a tender, imaginative truth, a sunset sky which is, precisely, a visible image of an invisible, hardly attainable blessedness. In few things painted by an English artist is vision held so securely and with such simplicity and such delicate, grave concentration.' (Grigson 1947, p. 96.)

The colours have faded slightly over the last fifty years, but the *Yellow Twilight* remains Palmer's most intensely coloured panoramic landscape, in which no single element of the composition destroys the equilibrium of sentiment. The economy and harmony of the colours, the sureness and variety of touch, and the calligraphic fluency of the penwork articulating each different area of vegetation, all demonstrate Palmer's mastery in his mid-twenties. A.H. Palmer (V&A 1926) recalled that he was so fond of this work that his father gave it to him in *c.*1870. He subsequently gave it to Sir Eric Maclagan, Director of the V&A.

## 68†

### *Harvesters by Firelight*, *c.*1830

Black ink with watercolour and gouache on wove paper, 28.7 × 36.7 cm (11¼ × 14 7/16 in)

Lit: Lister 125

Washington, DC, National Gallery of Art, 1986.72.12, Paul Mellon Collection

The title of this work has been suggested by an inscription on the back of the picture apparently signed by A.H. Palmer with his initials: 'The reflection of one of the incendiary fires / fires [*sic*] in Kent; I think about 1830 done I think / the next day – The building is, I think / Ightham Mote / A.H.P. / Subject the harvesters hurrying away the / last of the harvest'. The writer of the inscription is alluding to the incendiary fires caused during the 'Captain Swing' uprisings in Kent in 1830. Palmer was well aware of these, since some occurred in Shoreham (see p. 31). It is certainly possible to read the clouds in the sky as coloured by the reflection of a fire. However, as Lister points out, the incendiary fires were aimed at stacks and barns, so there would be no reason for the harvesters to be hurrying the crops out of the field. Lister further observes correctly that there is no sign of haste in the harvesters. Ightham Mote is a medieval house close to Shoreham that Palmer sketched (Lister 83), but the building in this picture does not resemble it.

It would seem therefore that any relationship between this picture and the incendiary uprisings in Kent around 1830 is highly tenuous. Lister is uncertain whether the inscription is by A.H. Palmer, and others have even questioned whether the work is by Palmer. Close study of the inscription, however, suggests that the writing is A.H. Palmer's. His inaccuracy about the subject is not untypical. He was also well aware of the Kentish uprisings, and appears to have had more sympathy with the insurgents than his father had (*L&L*, p. 51). Stylistically, the picture is compatible with the highly experimental use of colour and vigorously simplified forms to be found in many works of around 1830 (see, for example, cats 42 and 82). It is hoped that comparisons made possible by the present book and exhibition will help in resolving any uncertainties about the identity of this picture. WV

## 69

### *The Magic Apple Tree*, *c.*1830

Brown ink, watercolour and gouache with gum arabic, 34.9 × 26 cm (13¾ × 10¼ in)

Lit: V&A 1926, 61; Grigson 92; Fitzwilliam 1984, 21; Lister 127

University of Cambridge, Fitzwilliam Museum, 1490

Palmer's son remembered that 'This design dwelt apart from some of its Shoreham fellows in "The Curiosity Portfolio," so labelled by Palmer' (V&A 1926), which was shown only to intimate friends. He coupled it with *In a Shoreham Garden* (cat. 66) as comprising the supreme expressions of Palmer's belief in the abundance of God's gifts in nature, as expressed in Psalm 65: 'Thou crownest the year with thy goodness; and thy paths drop fatness. They drop upon the pastures of the wilderness: and the little hills rejoice on every side. The pastures are clothed with flocks; the valleys also are covered over with corn; they shout for joy, they also sing.' While these lines, especially the final phrase, are highly appropriate, A.H. Palmer also believed that the two drawings expressed his father's 'passionate love for Ceres and Pomona [which] has led him from the land of plain fact into fairy-land' (*L&L*, p. 48). He sustained his interpretation of the present drawing by giving it the present title, *The Magic Apple Tree*, justifying it by claiming that the tree is 'apparently leafless and it supports by magic a tremendous and utterly abnormal crop of large ripe apples' in 'a conflagration of colour' (V&A 1926).

However, as Grigson remarked, A.H. Palmer's title and interpretation are wholly misleading, for there was nothing

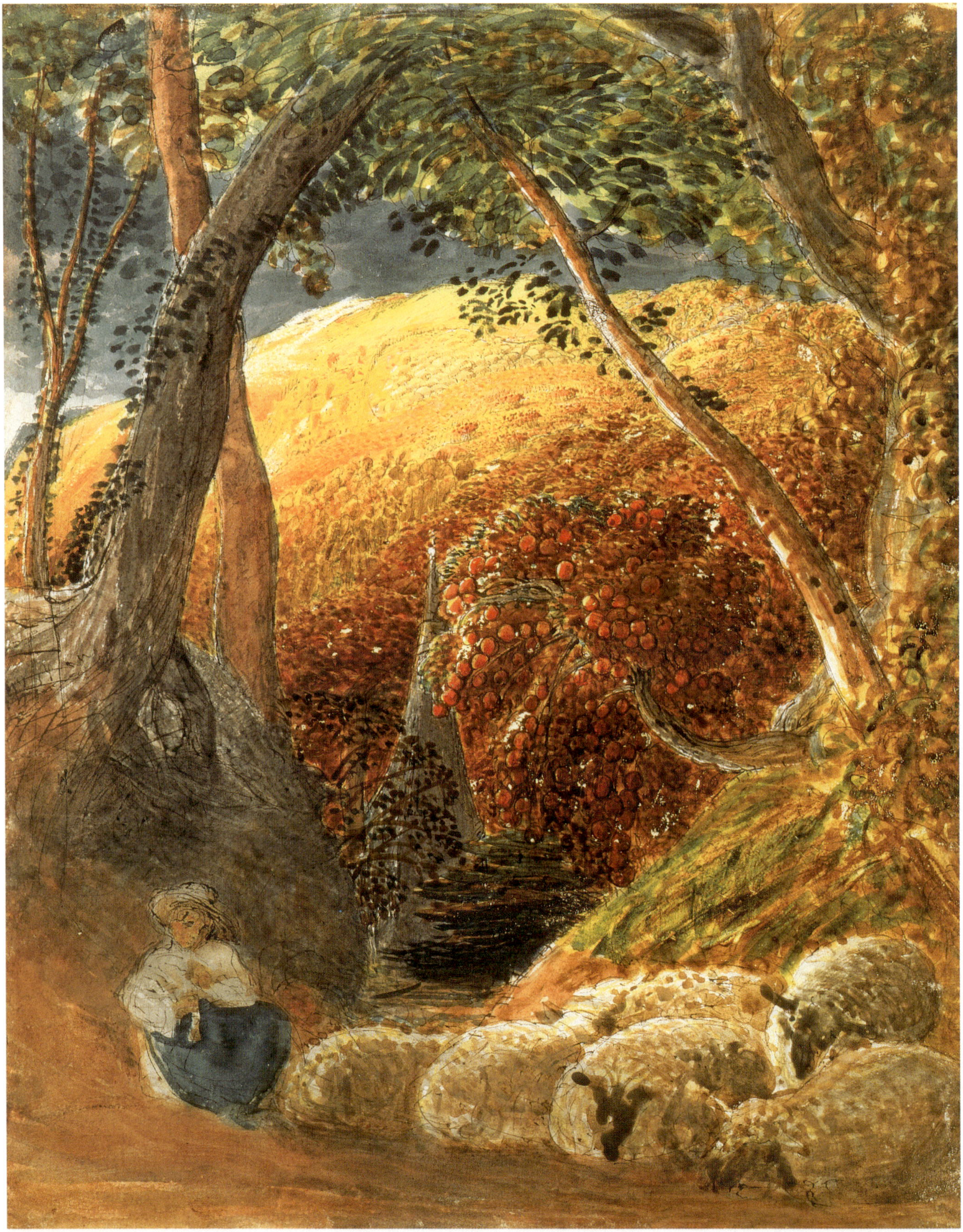

69

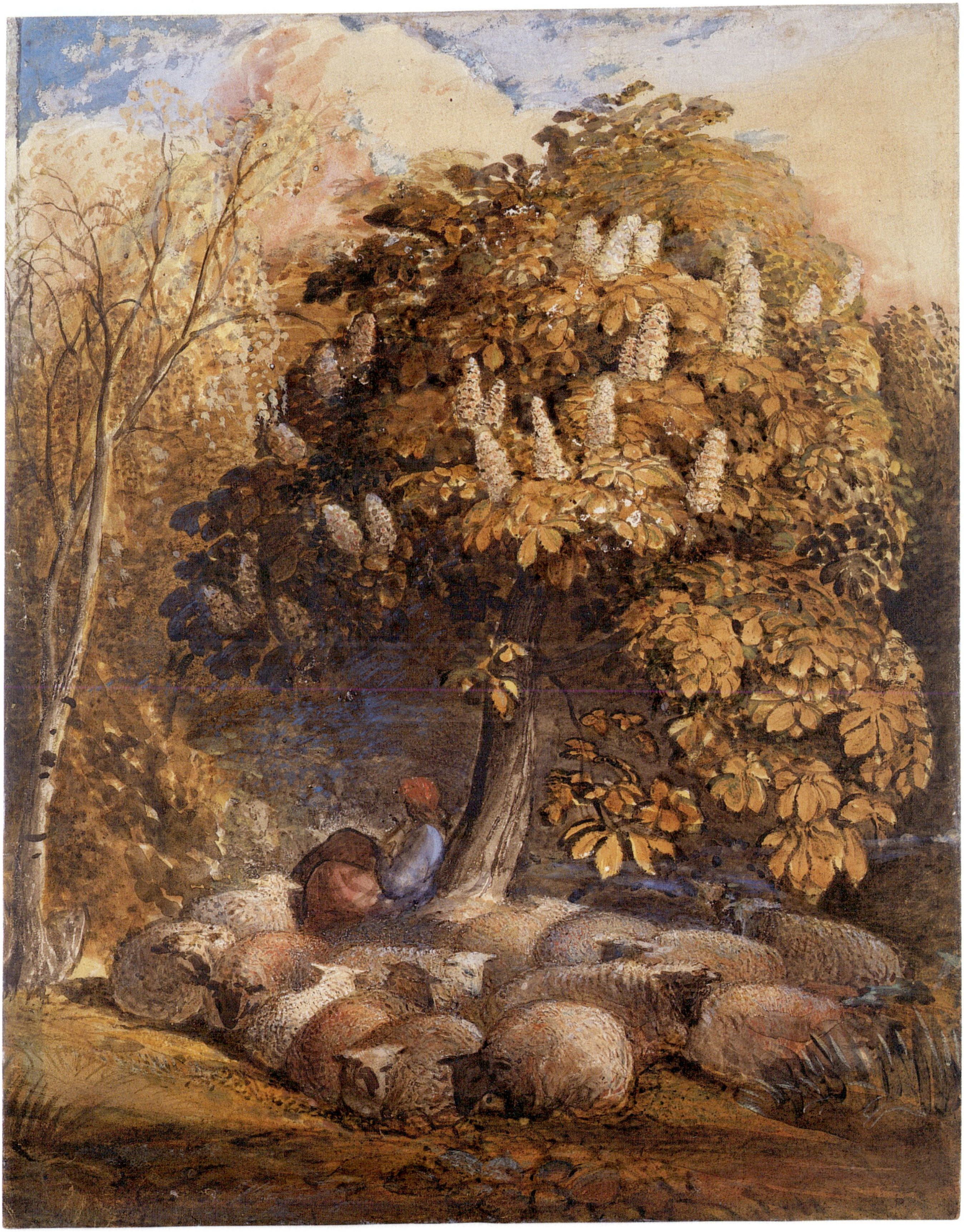

70

magical in Palmer's Neoplatonic vision of fecundity, which depended rather on the munificence of a bountiful God. Indeed, in this drawing the apple tree is only one manifestation of this bounty, which can be seen in the densely wooded hillsides, the golden fields of ripe corn and the large woolly sheep in the foreground. At the centre of the composition, as in several other works of this period, is the church, its spire echoed in the arch of trees framing the composition, emphasizing the religious significance of the scene. It is, indeed, a peculiarly Christian pastoral vision.

## 70

### *Pastoral with a Horse Chestnut Tree, c.*1831–2

Watercolour and gouache with gum arabic over preliminary indications in pencil, on buff paper, 33.4 × 26.8 cm (13¼ × 10⅝ in)

Lit: Grigson 96; Brown 14; Fitzwilliam 1984, 22; Lister 131

Oxford, Ashmolean Museum, 1929.37; bequeathed by the Revd William Fothergill Robinson through the National Art Collections Fund, 1929

Palmer has transformed what might have been a conventional representation of the pastoral – a shepherd piping while his flock of sheep rest – by placing the whole scene beneath the flowers and foliage of an almost supernatural horse chestnut tree. Unlike *The Magic Apple Tree* (cat. 69), the scene is entirely pagan, with no religious reference, and Palmer may have been following his friend Calvert in this path.

Earlier commentators have noted the scarcity of iconographical precedents for the chestnut tree. Although it was introduced from Asia in the seventeenth century, and recommended as suitable for creating avenues in gentlemen's parks by John Evelyn and others, it was denounced by William Gilpin in his *Remarks on Forest Scenery* (1791) as 'a glaring object' and seldom depicted. It was, however, symptomatic of Palmer's individuality that he should have made studies of it from his youth: a drawing of the whole tree appears on the left of a sheet of studies of trees in the sketchbook of 1824, with the comment 'The chestnut ought to have been in the middle' (cat. 9m), and there is a drawing of the foliage on another sheet from the same sketchbook. The chestnut is also prominent in the *Skirts of a Wood* of 1825 (cat. 14). By the early 1830s, the probable date of the *Pastoral*, he would have been familiar with its structure and growing habits. Indeed, the specimen growing today on the banks of the Darent in front of Palmer's house, Water House, at Shoreham may have been planted in Palmer's lifetime.

While the *Pastoral with a Horse Chestnut* has been grouped with the other drawings of trees from Shoreham (cats 65, 66, 69), it is less experimental and less extravagant. The exaggerated size of the leaves, each one carefully outlined in black, and the giant candles of flowers are balanced by a much more restrained use of colour, no longer applied in thick unmodulated blobs, but carefully mixed and integrated with, for example, the pink, white and brown of the fleeces. Palmer has also achieved a much more subtle harmony of colour, the pink of the sheep echoed in the red of the shepherd's costume and the rosy cloud above. The dating of *c.*1831–2 is

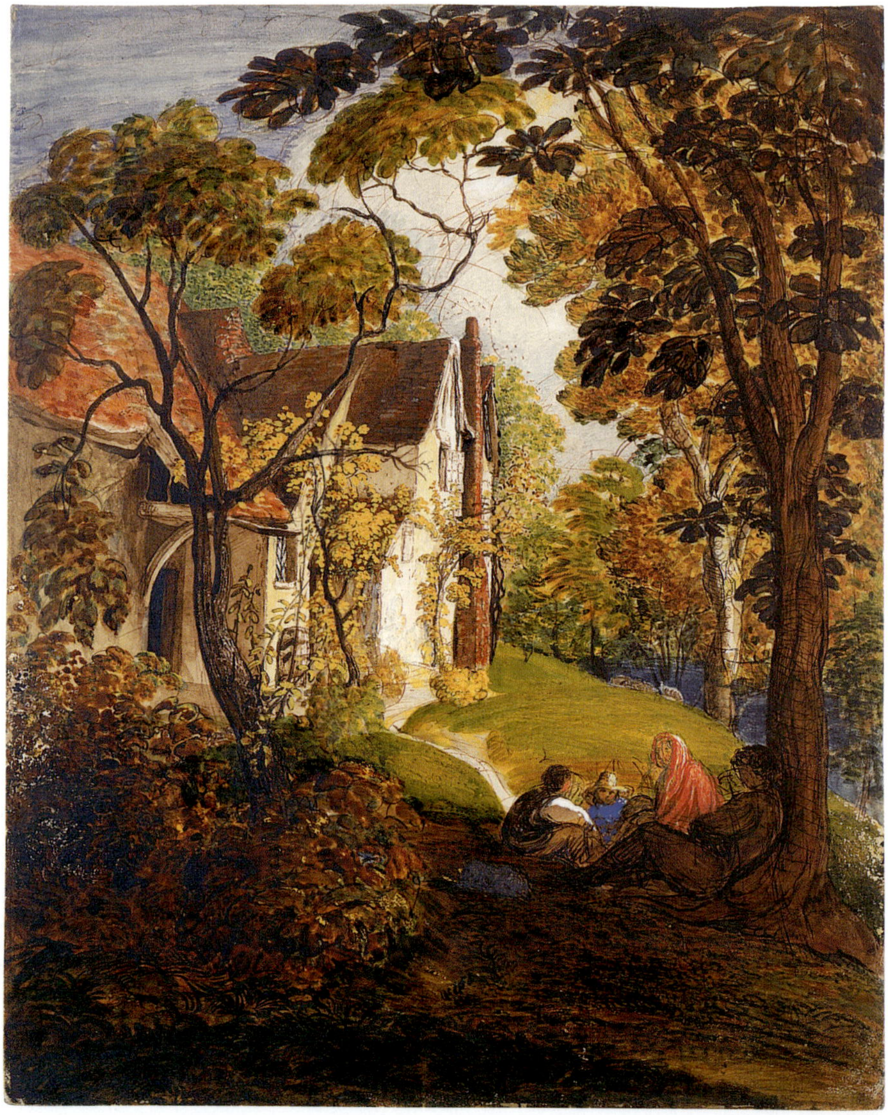

71

supported by the lack of penwork, and the similarity of brushwork with some of the 'blacks', though without the extensive scratching out that they usually show. Unlike *The Magic Apple Tree* and *In a Shoreham Garden* (cat. 66), this work was not exhibited at the V&A in 1926, having passed out of the Palmer family's possession into that of John Giles and later that of George Richmond's son-in-law, William Fothergill Robinson.

## 71

### *Ivy Cottage, Shoreham, c.*1831–2

Watercolour and gouache with gum arabic over pen and brown ink and graphite, 40.3 × 32.2 cm (15⅞ × 12¾ in)

Lit: V&A 1926, 69; Grigson 97; Brown 15; Lister 132

Oxford, Ashmolean Museum, 1942.113; purchased 1942

When it was shown at the V&A in 1926, this drawing was simply entitled *Old House on the Bank of the Darent*; it was not until the 1950s that the house was identified as Ivy Cottage. It was therefore Palmer's second study of the cottage – the first dates from 1828 (cat. 43 recto). The earlier drawing was made during John Linnell's visit to Shoreham, and conforms to his precepts of nauralism. In the second the cottage is subsumed into a richly coloured and intensely unrealistic vision of pastoral contentment.

The drawing is notable for the range of techniques Palmer has used, from the vigorous underdrawing in pencil, pen and ink to the broad washes of green, brown and blue and the minute stippling in gouache of the tree nearest the house. The figures are rustic but generalized: one wears a broad-brimmed straw hat, his back to the sheep he is tending, talking to another, while a third, female and in a shocking pink-red shawl, listens in the characteristic pose of thoughtfulness, her head resting on her hand. A fourth, reminiscent of the sleeping shepherd (see cat. 78), rests his back against tree, while a dog sleeps at his feet.

## 72

### *The Flock and the Star, c.*1831–2

Indian ink and wash over graphite and brown ink, on white card, 14.9 × 17.7 cm (5⅞ × 6$^{15}/_{16}$ in)

Lit: Grigson 98; Brown 17; Lister 133

Oxford, Ashmolean Museum, WA 1940.64; purchased 1940

In a letter of 21 September 1832 Palmer referred to the return of 'my blacks which were in the exhibition'. At the Royal Academy that year, he showed seven works, all of which have generally been assumed to have been 'blacks', that is monochrome drawings rather than oil paintings. Three of the blacks shown in 1832 were twilight subjects, their titles so vague as to make them unidentifiable with surviving works: *A Pastoral Scene:*

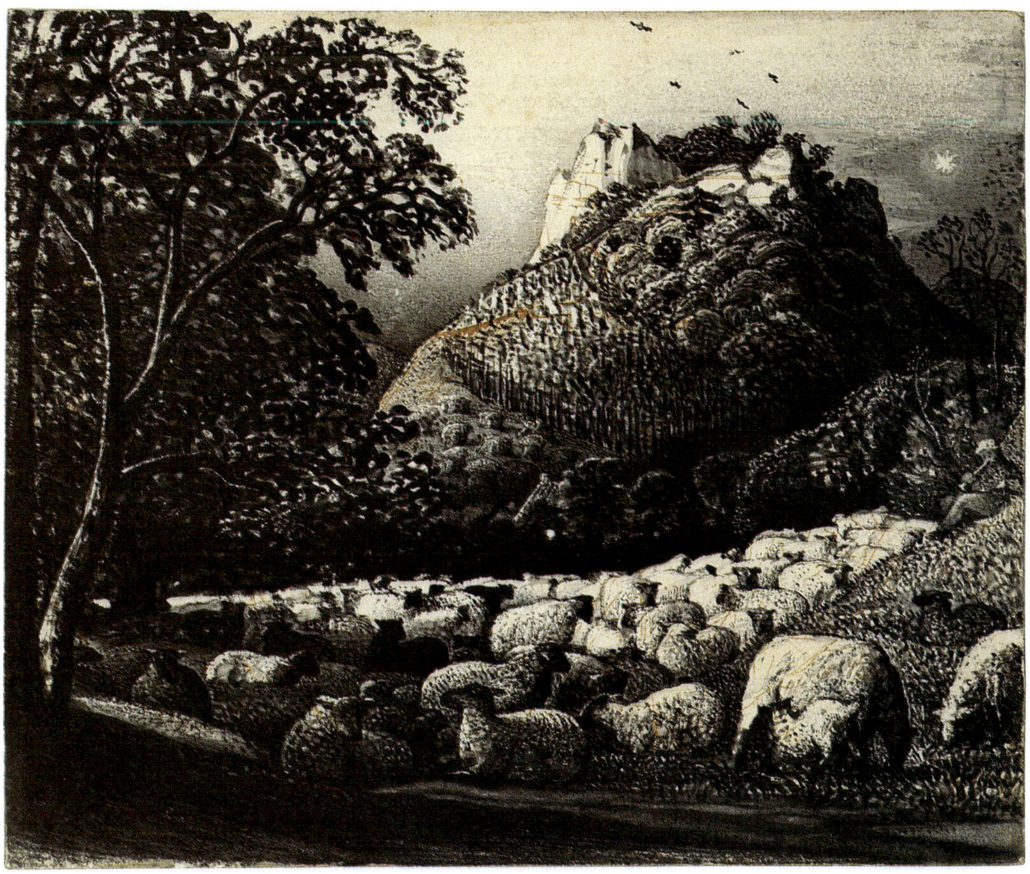

72

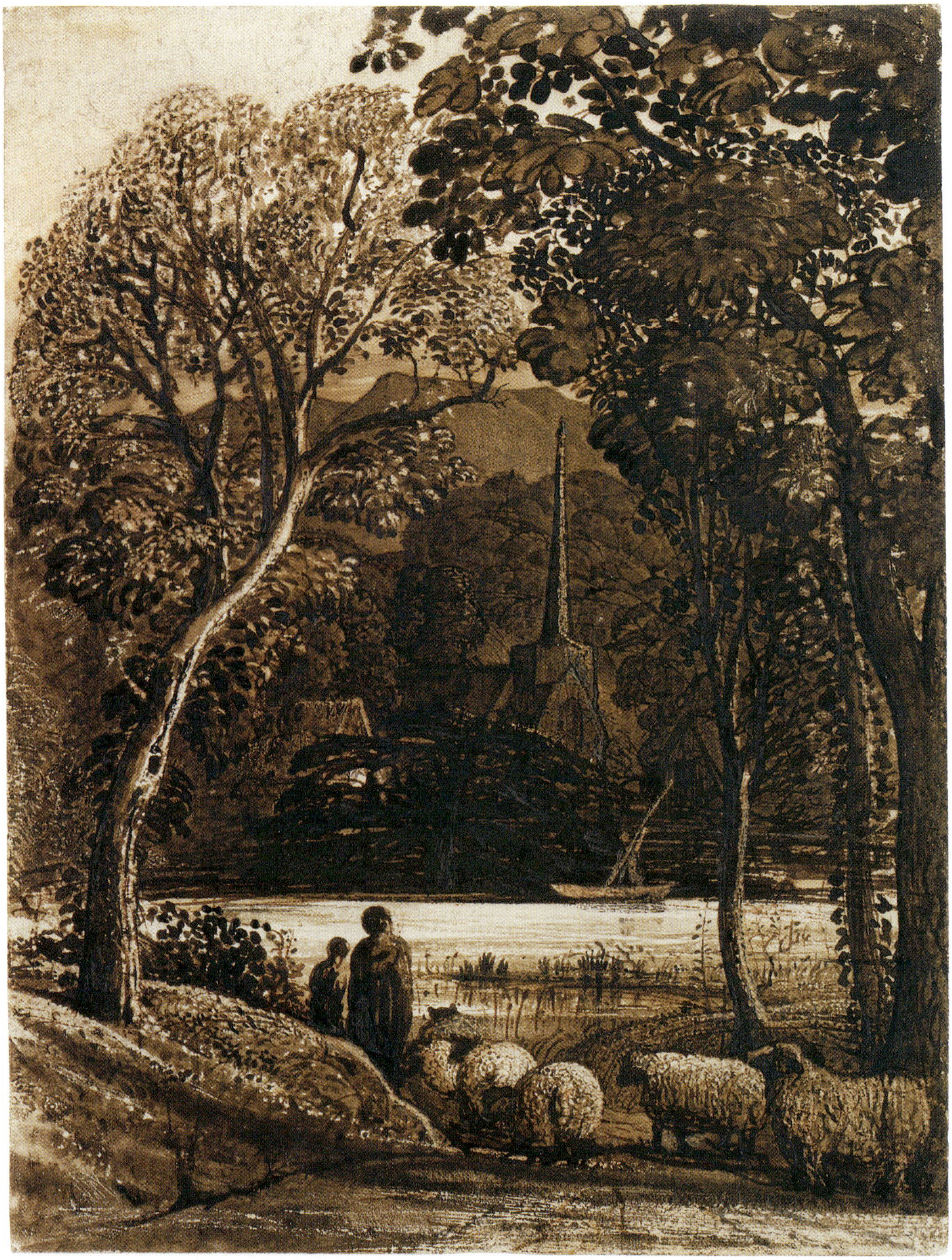

73

*Twilight*; *Landscape: Twilight*; and *Late Twilight*. *The Flock and the Star* may have been one of the exhibited twilight scenes, and is similar in technique, and presumably in date, to *The Folded Flock* (Lister 135) and *A Cornfield, Shoreham, at Twilight* (Lister 134). In all three much of the composition is defined by robust scratching out with a knife or pen nib over extensive underdrawing in brown ink.

Here, the landscape is still, save for a lamb enthusiastically feeding in the foreground, while a shepherd pipes on the slope on the right. At the centre of the composition is a brightly lit cottage window at the foot of a hill with a curiously craggy summit. The lower slopes of the hillside are carefully cultivated with corn, while above them are a field of hops and forestry over much of the summit. The pole star shines brightly in the sky, but the landscape is illuminated by a full moon, out of sight on the left.

**73**

*A Church with a Boat and Sheep*, *c.*1831–2

Sepia, 18 × 13.5 cm (7¹⁄₁₆ × 5⁵⁄₁₆ in)

Lit: Lister 130

Private collection, USA

This is an extremely fine and carefully worked example of one of the monochromes that Palmer referred to as 'blacks' but were often dark brown in tone. It appears to be the kind of twilight scene that Palmer was sending for exhibition around 1830 and that he felt had 'more look of light than I have got before' (*Letters*, p. 54). Like most of the monochrome ink paintings of this period, this work seems to have been executed almost entirely with the brush, with no addition of gouache and only the minimum of scratching out to strengthen highlights. It demonstrates the mastery of his technique for painting 'blacks' by this time.

The view across the river to a village dominated by a church with a needle spire strongly resembles Eynsford, the village to the north of Shoreham where there is a ford and church with a needle spire. Palmer would doubtless have experienced it under light conditions similar to this during one of the nocturnal ramblings that he undertook with fellow Ancients during the late 1820s. The image of figures waiting with sheep for the ferry to cross the river may well be rooted, too, in direct experience, as well as symbolizing the idea of moving from this life to the next.

WV

**74**

*Young Man Yoking an Ox*, *c.*1831–2

Brush in Indian ink with scratching out on off-white paper, 14.9 × 18.6 cm (5⁷⁄₈ × 7³⁄₈ in)

Lit: Grigson 36; Brown 16; Lister 136

Oxford, Ashmolean Museum, 1940.63; purchased 1940

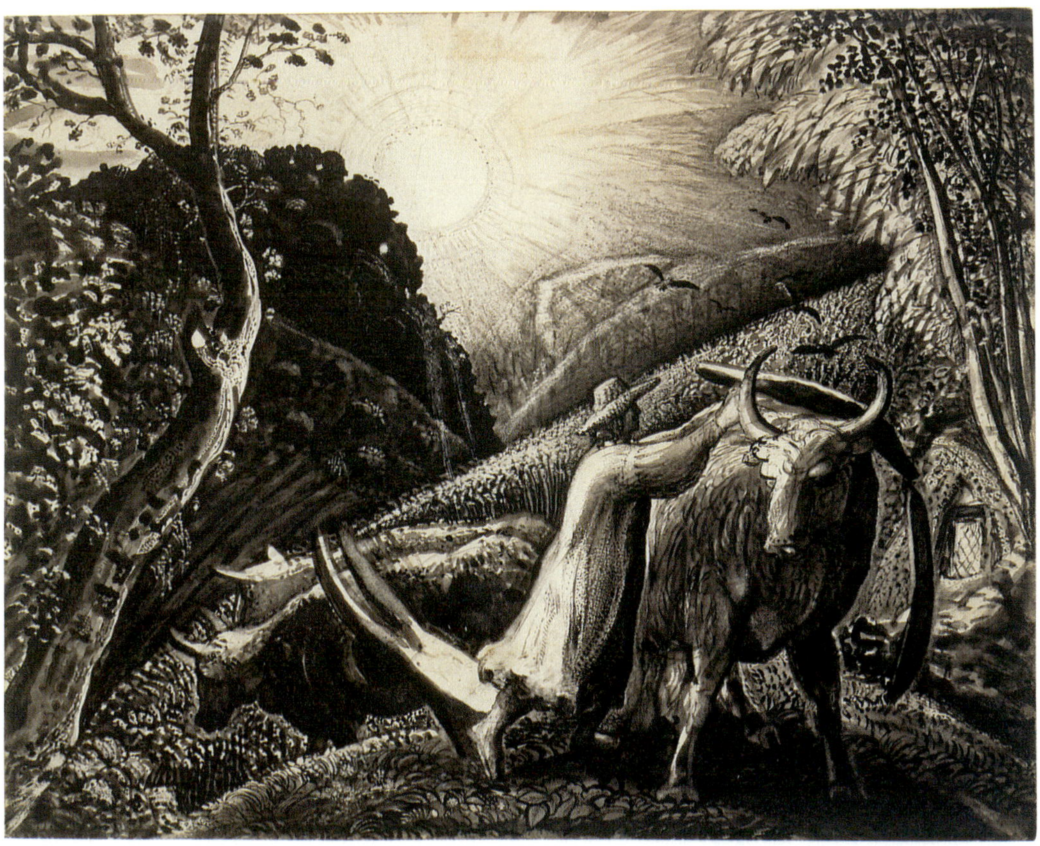

74

Although Palmer made many variations on similar themes, he rarely repeated himself, especially in the Shoreham period. This drawing is therefore unusual in being a reworking of *A Rustic Scene* of 1825 (cat. 10). Most of the elements of the composition are similar, but the effect is quite different: the scene is now illuminated not by a crescent moon but by a brilliant sun, one of Palmer's boldest, and the whole mood is much less static. The young man wears a smock and Palmer's favourite straw hat, and is probably unyoking the ox before going home to the cottage with the light in the lattice window. (This interpretation seems to be confirmed by the studies of the yoke on the verso.) The great variety of textures is common to many drawings of the period, as are the framing trees and the diagonals of the hillsides.

## 75

### Drawing for *The Bright Cloud*, *c.*1831–2

Indian ink and wash on card, 22.7 × 30.3 cm (10 × 10¾ in)

Lit: Grigson 118; Lister 138

London, Tate, N03312; presented by Hugh Blaker through the National Art Collections Fund

Binyon described this drawing and the following simply as versions of *The Bright Cloud* (cat. 87; Binyon 1925, p. 22), and Grigson mistakenly identified them as studies for the eponymous oil painting. In fact, the compositions are quite different, for, while they share the diagonal ridge sloping from right to left in the middle distance, the foreground of both drawings is occupied by a shepherd and shepherdess tending a flock of sheep, whereas in the painting a procession of villagers wends its way home.

All three compositions are dominated by the billowing cumulus that Palmer had earlier incorporated into *The Valley with a Bright Cloud* (cat. 11). Unlike the clouds of his contemporary, Constable, who made a scientific study of them, they were for Palmer further manifestations of the divine in nature, as expounded in such writings as William Paley's *Natural*

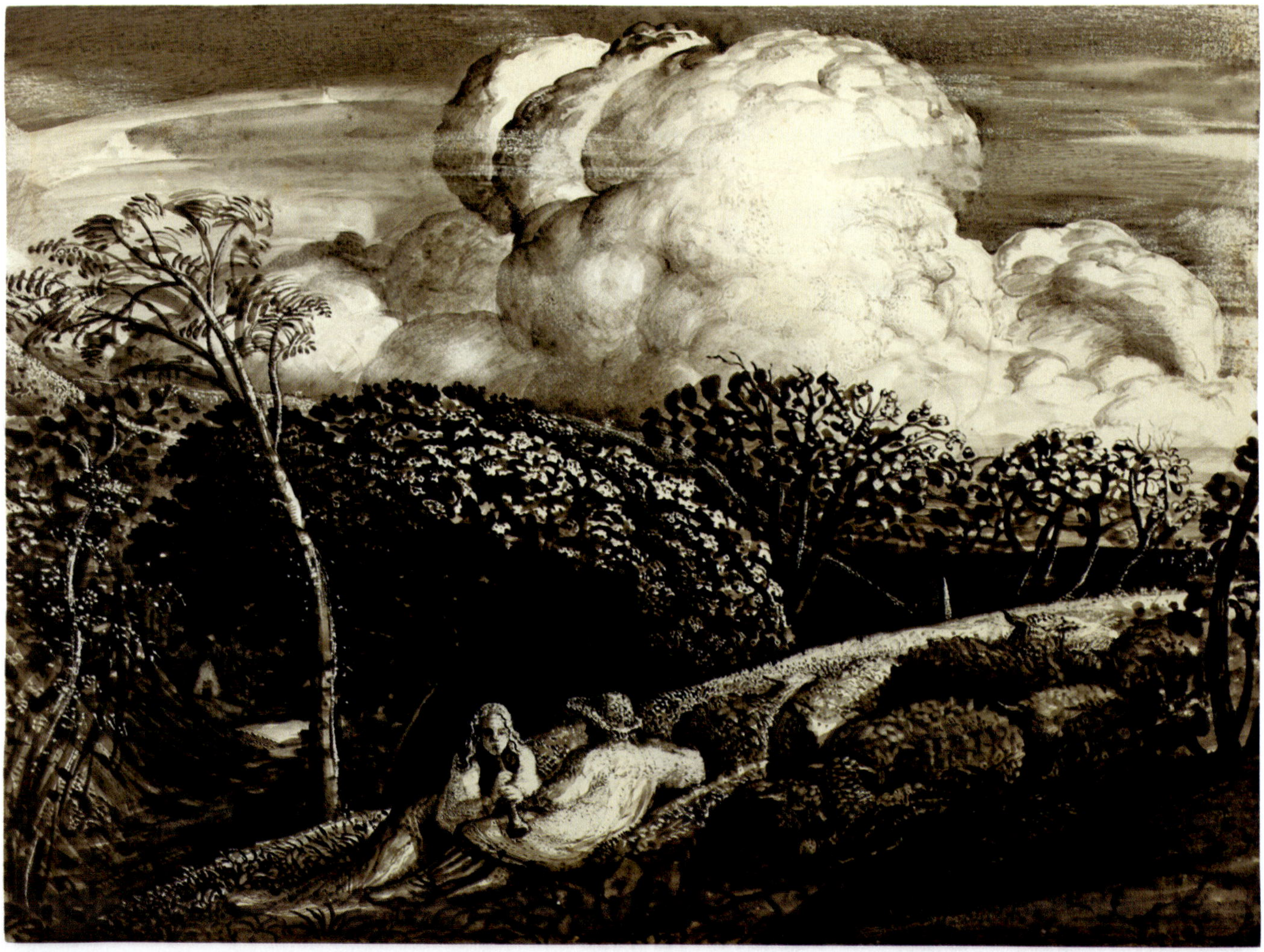

75

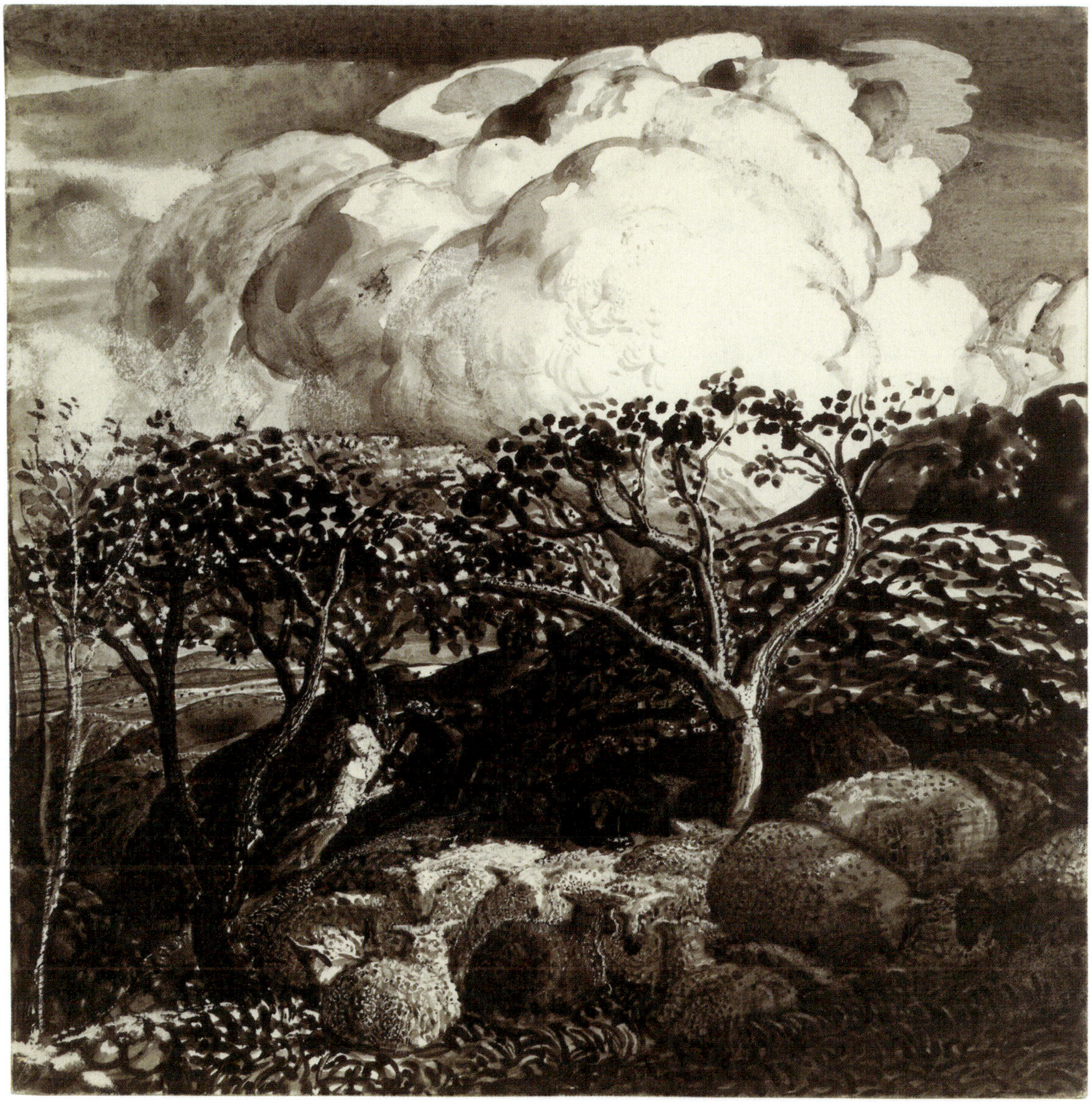

76

*Theology, or Evidences of the Existence and Attributes of the Deity, collected from the Appearances of Nature* (1802), which Palmer would probably have read.

## 76

### Drawing for *The Bright Cloud*, *c.*1831–2

Indian ink with scratching out, 15.2 × 15 cm ($5^{15}/_{16}$ × $5^{7}/_{8}$ in)

Lit: Grigson 119; Fitzwilliam 1984, 25; Lister 137

London, British Museum, 1927-5-18-10

The fluid technique suggests that this drawing was adapted from that in the Tate (cat. 75). It demonstrates Palmer's mastery of working in monochrome, creating the white of the clouds and highlights mostly by leaving the paper blank, with only a little scratching out to finish.

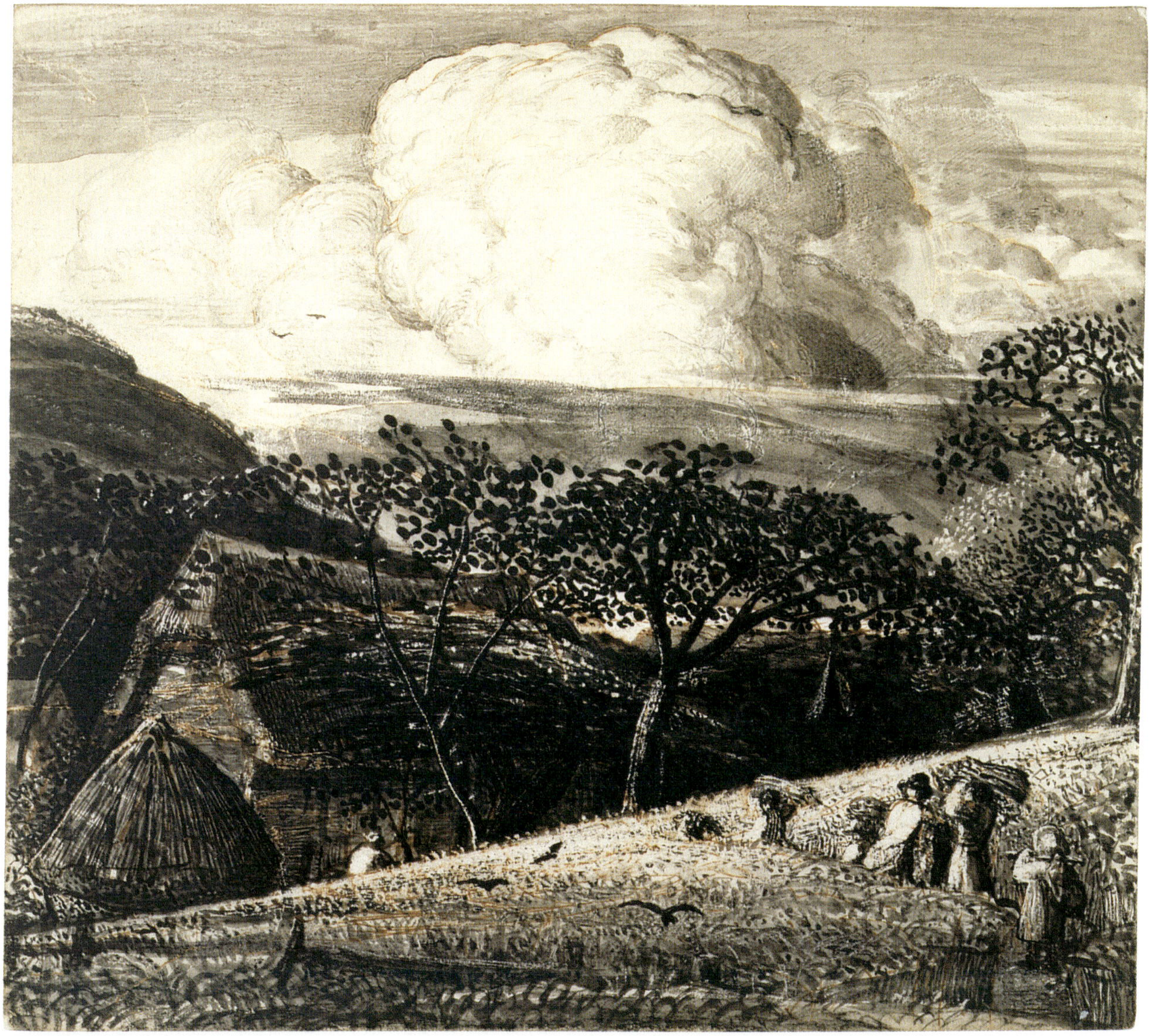

77

**77**

## Drawing for *The White Cloud*, *c.*1831–2

Indian ink, over pencil and pen and brown ink, 14.5 × 16.1 cm (5¾ × 6⅜ in)

Lit: Grigson 120; Brown 19; Lister 144

Oxford, Ashmolean Museum, 1934.288; purchased 1934

Unlike the two *Bright Cloud* drawings (cats 11, 12), this is indeed related to the oil painting (cat. 87) and corresponds to it closely, down to the birds flying over the corn in the foreground. Since the oil was two or three years later, it must be assumed that Palmer did not sell the drawing and decided to rework it as an exhibition piece.

John Commander (Arts Council 1956, no. 47) was the first to notice a similarity in the composition between this work and Pieter Brueghel's *Corn Harvest* (1565; New York, Metropolitan Museum). However, the points of comparison are few, and probably irrelevant, since the painting was inaccessible to Palmer and not engraved. Nevertheless, Palmer may have known engravings after other paintings by Brueghel of the harvest.

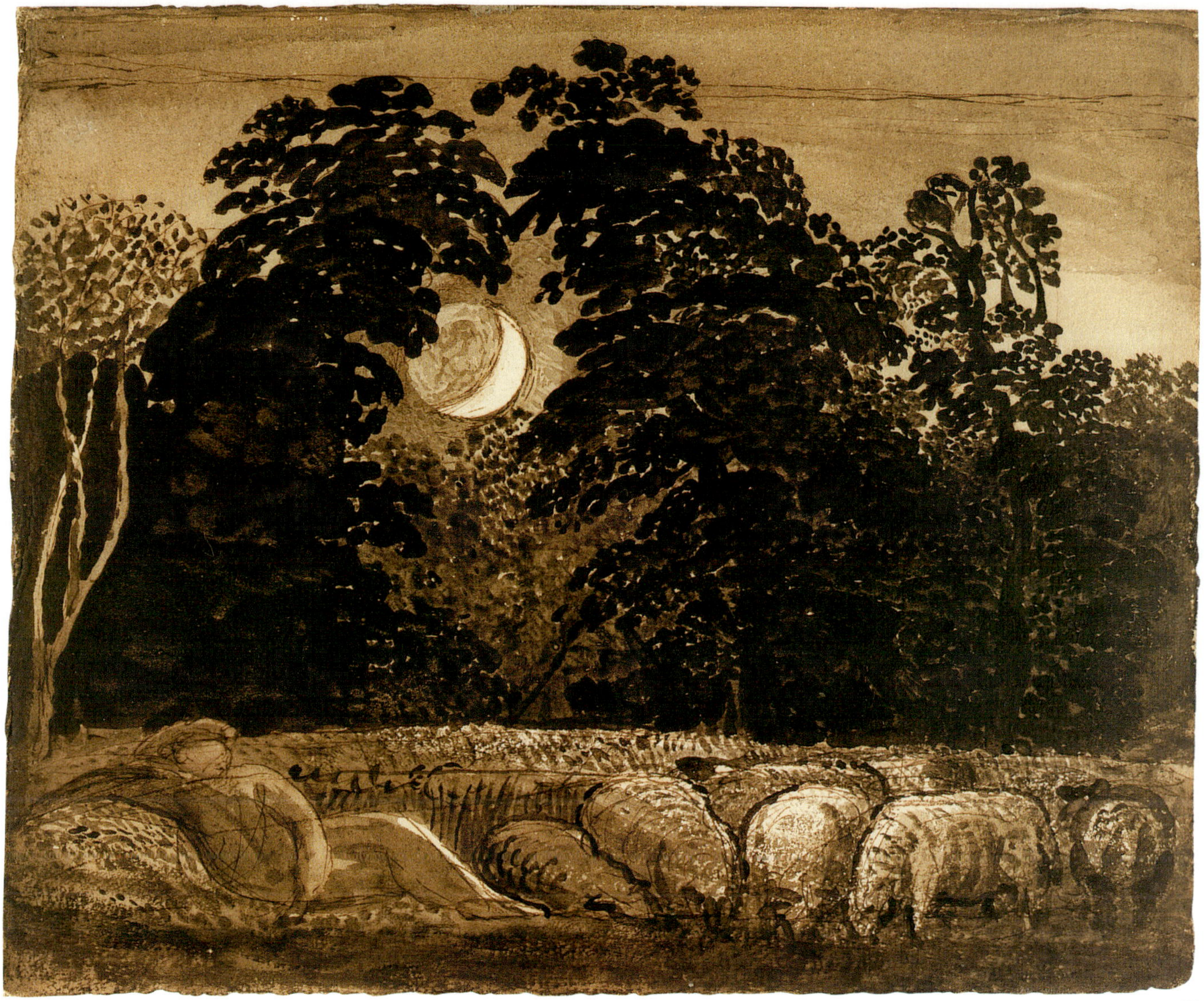

78

## 78

*The Sleeping Shepherd*, *c.*1831–2

Brown ink and brown watercolour, 15.7 × 18.8 cm (6¼ × 7½ in)

Lit: Grigson 113; Fitzwilliam 1984, 24; Lister 142; Nugent 2000, p. 210

University of Manchester, Whitworth Art Gallery, D/2/1954

In Palmer's pastoral landscapes the shepherd is to be found conversing with a companion, piping to his flocks or sleeping. He first treated the theme of the sleeping shepherd in a number of sheets in the sketchbook of 1824 and incorporated the figure at its most ungainly in the *Late Twilight* of 1825 (cat. 13), where he is uncomfortably draped on the backs of his sheep. In this monochrome drawing of the early 1830s the shepherd occupies the foreground, loosely drawn, leaning against a mound of earth. His sheep feed in front of a field of corn, while the crescent moon shines through a gap in the trees and casts an almost supernatural light over the landscape. The composition is all the more effective for its simplicity.

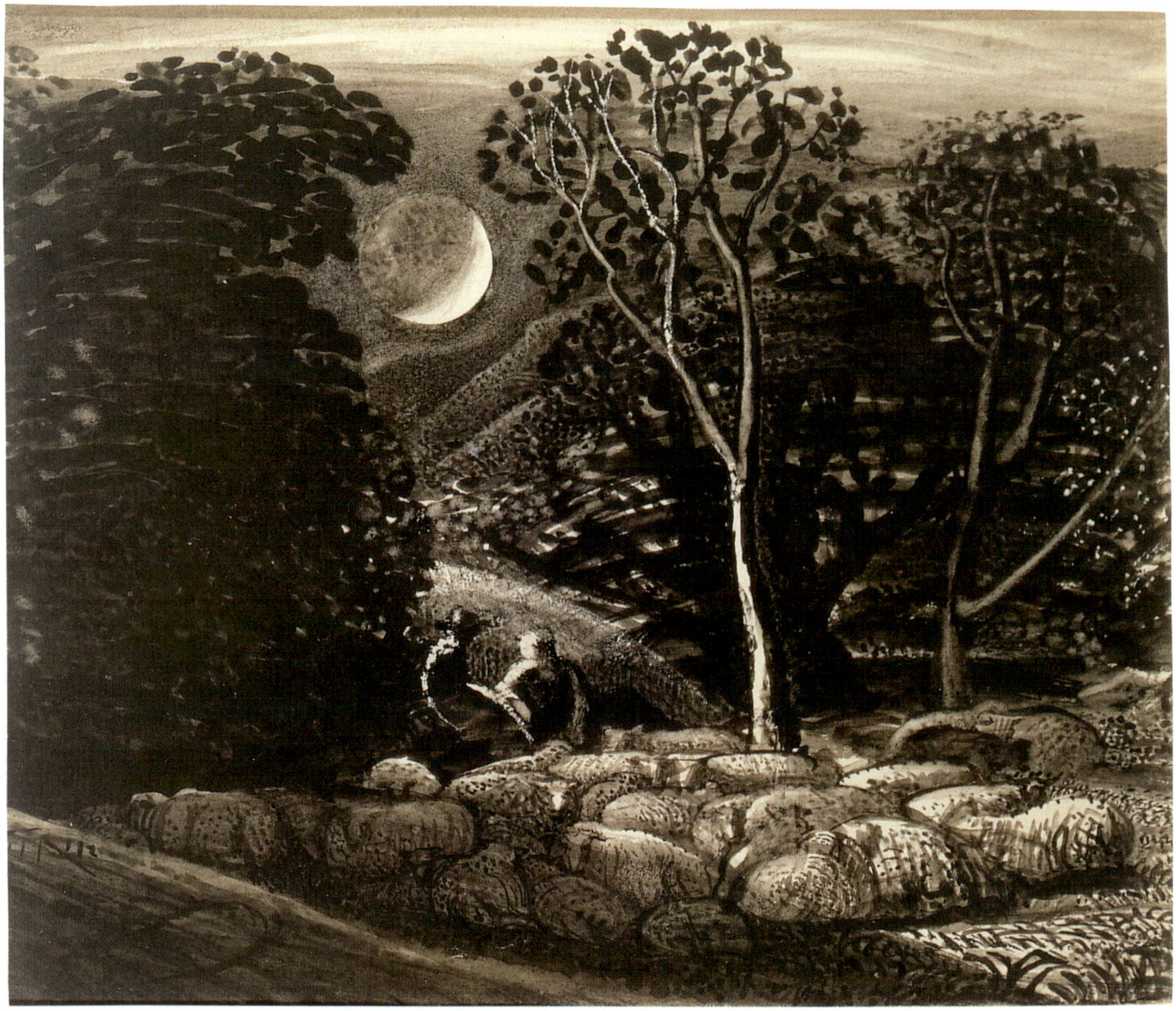

79

**79***

*Moonlight: A Landscape with Sheep*, *c.*1831–2

Indian ink and wash on card, 15.2 × 18.3 cm (6 × 7¼ in)

Lit: Grigson 114; Lister 143

London, Tate, N03700; purchased 1922

This may have been one of the 'blacks' exhibited in 1832 (see cat. 72), three of which were moonlit scenes. Under the strong moonlight a shepherd and shepherdess sit conversing, while their flocks sleep peacefully. The technique is more complicated than in some others of this series, and the drawing notable for the sophistication of the scratching out to create highlights in, for example, the edge of the grassy knoll in the centre; the outline of the figures, the trunk and branches of the tree and the backs of the sheep in the foreground; and the burst of tiny lights on the right. Lister compares the composition with that of Sherman's mezzotint, *Evening*, of 1834 (cat. 94), though in the print there is a cottage and the solitary shepherd is dozing or sleeping.

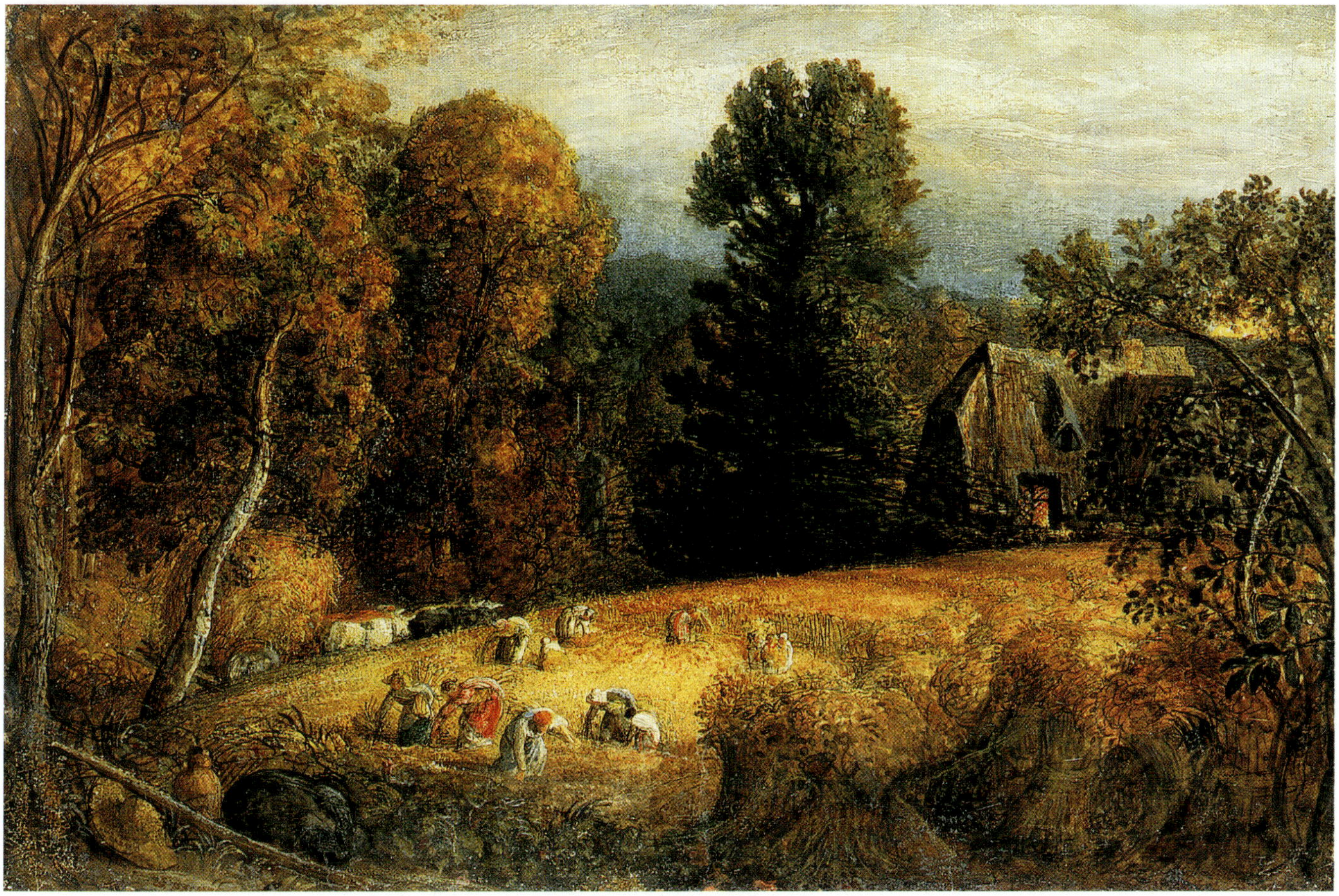

80

## 80

*The Gleaning Field, c.*1833

Oil and tempera with pen and ink on panel, 30.5 × 43.8 cm (12 × 17¼ in)

Signed: *S. PALMER*

Lit: Grigson 130; Fitzwilliam 1984, 26; Lister 164

London, Tate Gallery, C04842; bequeathed by Mrs Louisa Mary Garrett, 1936

The large signature suggests that, like *The Harvest Moon* (cat. 81), this was one of Palmer's submissions to the Royal Academy. While it has been identified as the work of this title shown in 1833, this is not certain, since another *Gleaning Field* had been exhibited the previous year. Certainly, the insistent reworking of the whole composition in pen and ink suggests a more experimental approach than the varied but consistent technique of *The Harvest Moon.* Moreover, the foreground and middle ground are all on the same plain, suggesting that Palmer had not yet settled on the sloping ridge that he used for his later harvest scenes. In this work he has packed in his favourite motifs: a wagon laden with hay drawn by a team of oxen moving towards the glowing window of the farm on the right; the stooks of corn and the gleaners at work in the field; and the golden sun setting on the far right.

## 81

*The Harvest Moon*, 1833

Oil and tempera with graphite on paper laid down on panel, 22.1 × 27.7 cm (8¾ × 11 in)

Signed: *S. PALMER*

Lit: Grigson 129; Lister 168

New Haven, Yale Center for British Art, Paul Mellon Collection, B1977.14.65

A label in Palmer's hand stuck to the back of the panel suggests that this painting was a submission to the Royal Academy. It is generally identified as the *Harvest Moon* shown in 1833, which failed to attract a buyer. It was inherited by A.H. Palmer, who described it as a typical example of the oil paintings of this period, 'full of the Shoreham sentiment, and … not without some of the accompanying peculiarities' (Palmer 1892, pp. 46–7).

In contrast to many of the other Shoreham oils, Palmer has included an open view into the distance, suggesting that he was already experiencing the restlessness that took him to Devon in the following year. There he found the sea; in Kent he had only a winding river, reminiscent of 'Sabrina's silvery flood' in Virgil's *Eclogues*. The high relief of the moon and stars provides almost dazzling light to the field of harvesters, who are unusually numerous, some wearing brightly coloured smocks. A loaded wagon drawn by three pairs of oxen – almost ghostly in the moonlight, so faintly are they outlined – moves towards the farmhouse with the lighted window, the symbolic sanctuary at the end of a day's work.

One technical peculiarity of this work is the unusual use of paper as a support for an oil painting. While there is no visible sign of underdrawing, certain elements in the foreground, especially the figures, have been characteristically articulated in graphite.

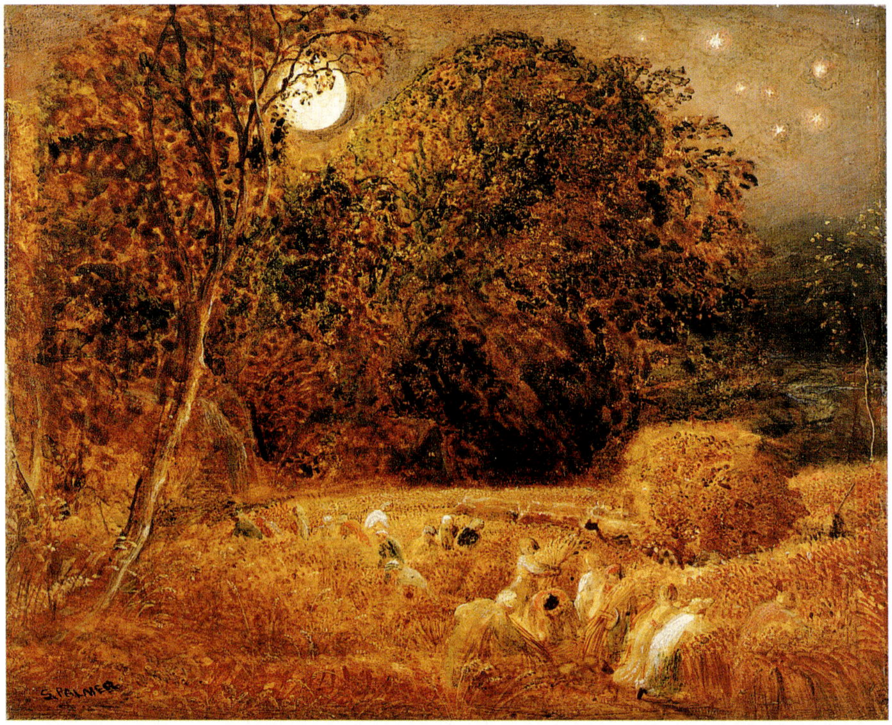


81

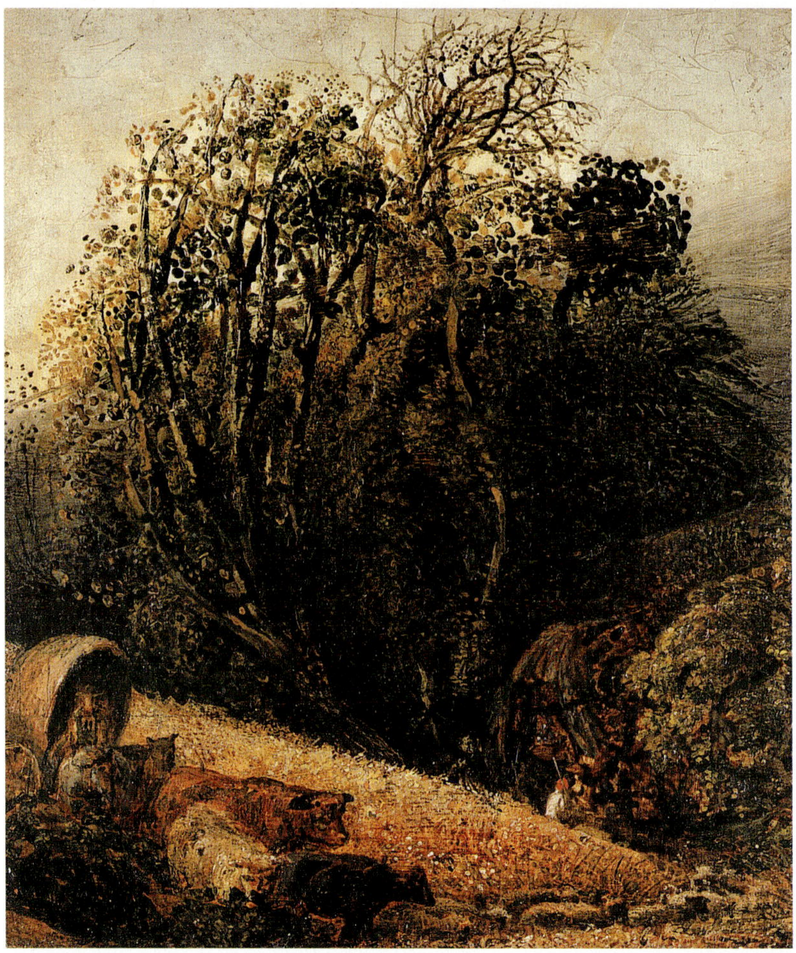

82

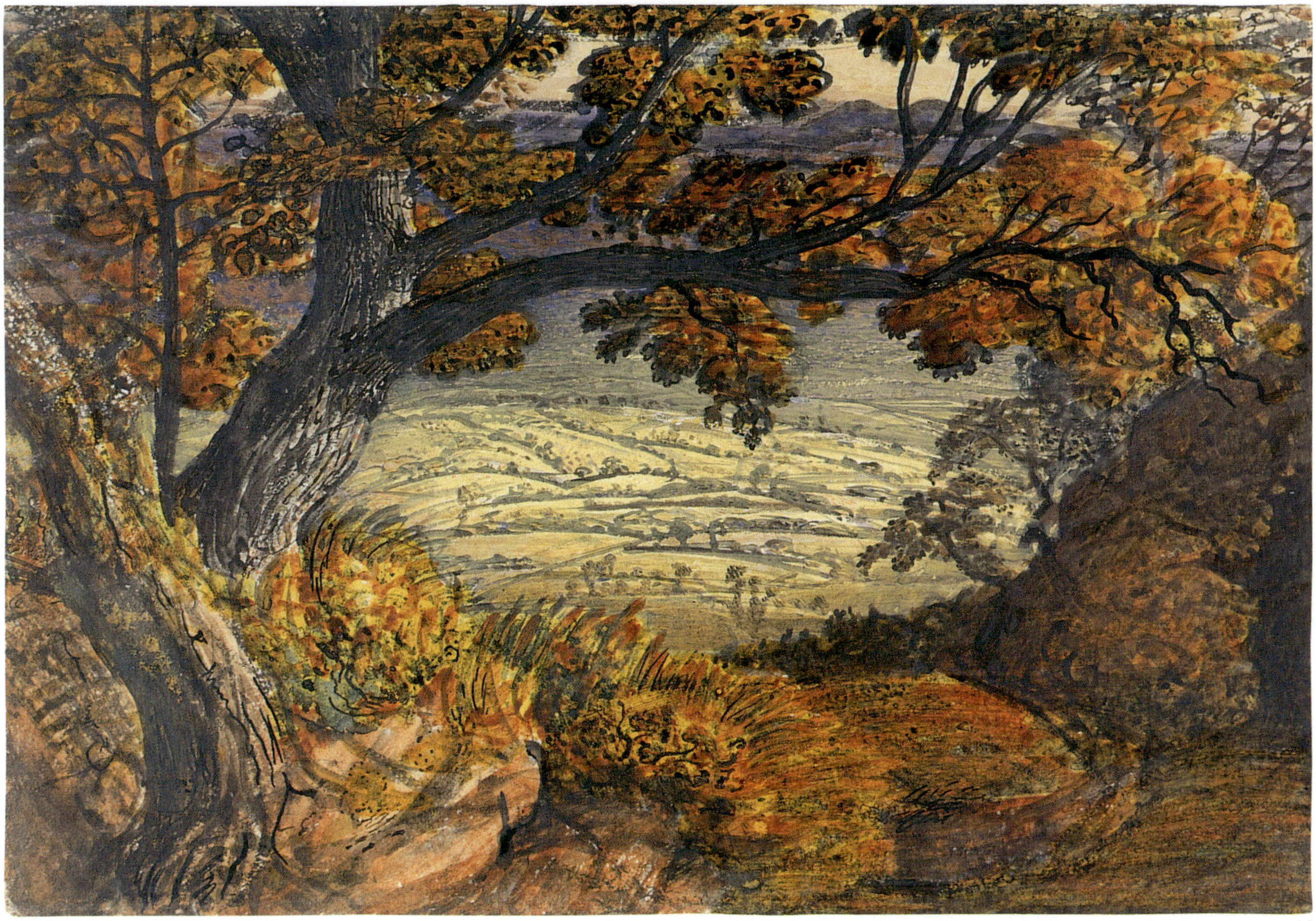

83

## 82*

*A Cornfield Bordered by Trees, c.*1833–4

Oil and tempera on panel, 17.1 × 14.5 cm (6 11/16 × 5 11/16 in)

Lit: Brown 21; Lister 171

Oxford, Ashmolean Museum, 1947.168; purchased 1947

Brown may be correct in proposing that this freely painted panel is 'a very rare example of an oil sketch by Palmer', though the elements of the composition are familiar from many works of the later Shoreham period. It is Palmer's smallest surviving oil.

## 83

*The Weald of Kent, c.*1833–4

Indian ink, watercolour and gouache, with pen, Indian ink and gum arabic on heavy paper, 18.7 × 27.1 cm (7 3/8 × 10 3/4 in)

Lit: Lister 172; Barton and Tong 1995, p. 8

New Haven, Yale Center for British Art, Paul Mellon Collection, B1981.25.2654

This drawing and the following have been linked since 1926, and are similar in technique and conception. In a return to the enclosed compositions of the late 1820s Palmer has depicted a panoramic view of the Weald of Kent seen beneath the heavy boughs of a massive oak tree. The drawing was probably made from nature, perhaps in the summer of 1833 or 1834. It has generally been considered a study of the Darent Valley, but more recently Barton and Tong have identified the view as Underriver (near Sevenoaks, Kent) from Carter's Hill. The watercolour has been applied with an unusually thick brush, the outlines of the trees made more pronounced with gum arabic and the foreground reworked with characteristically wiry penwork.

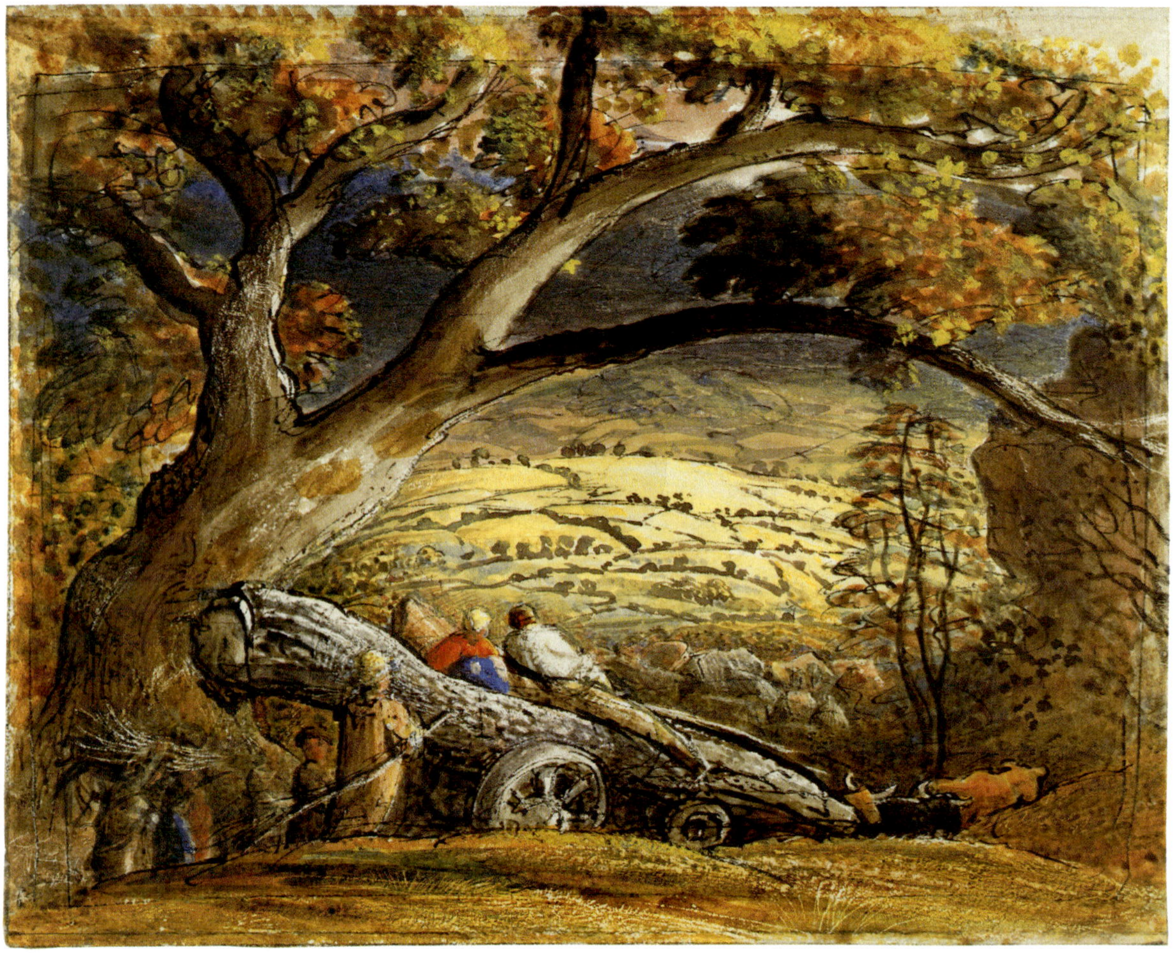

84

## 84

*The Timber Wain*, c.1833–4

Watercolour and gouache, 12.7 × 15.5 cm (5 × 6⅛ in),

Lit: V&A 1926, 53; Grigson 133; Lister, 173

New Haven, Yale Center for British Art, Paul Mellon Collection, B.2001.2.1087

This seems to have been developed from the previous drawing, and shows a similar view of the Weald of Kent. Here, however, Palmer has returned to his favourite compositional device of figures descending diagonally into the valley: a great tree trunk is dragged by a team of oxen, while other peasants carry stooks of corn beside it.

The old mount was inscribed with lines 488–91 from Milton's *Paradise Lost*, Book II:

> As when from mountain tops the dusky clouds
> Ascending, while the north wind sleeps, o'er spread
> Heaven's cheerful face, the lowring element
> Scowls o'er the darken'd landskip snow or shower.

The mount no longer survives, and the relevance of the inscription is not obvious. It may have been made by A.H. Palmer, to whom the drawing was given in the 1860s. He described it in 1926 as 'without the full vehemence of the true Shoreham mood; or any of the "Prudential"' qualms of later years'.

## 85

*The Golden Valley*, c.1833–4

Watercolour and gouache with graphite, pen and ink, and scratching out, 12.7 × 16.5 cm (5 × 6½ in)

Lit: V&A 1926, 54; Grigson 134; Fitzwilliam 1984, 27; Lister 174

Michael and Judy Steinhardt Collection, New York

When first exhibited, at the V&A in 1926, this watercolour had the title *Harvesting with Distant Prospect*, emphasizing its close relationship with many other works of Palmer's mature years at Shoreham. The present title, first used by Binyon in 1925 but not sanctioned by A.H. Palmer, is less specific but more poetic. The artist himself gave no title, but his son, perhaps with his father's authority, inscribed on the mount lines 492–5 from Milton's *Paradise Lost*, Book II:

> If chance the radiant sun with farewell sweet
> Extend his evening beam, the fields revive,
> The birds their notes renew, and bleating herds
> Attest their joy, that hill and valley rings.

*The Golden Valley* is Palmer's broadest and most brilliant panorama, a prospect from a ridge down into a lush agricultural landscape, with gently rolling hills dissolving into mist and cloud on the horizon. The complex mesh of interlocking fields is described in pen and ink with tiny dabs of jewel-like colour, and the foreground in Palmer's spiky style of penwork with extensive scratching out. Once again, a procession of figures moves rhythmically down the hillside, a heavily laden wagon drawn by a sprawling team of oxen at its head, and three timeless female figures carrying burdens on their heads bring up the rear. As always, their goal is the cottage below. The balance of the composition seems to acknowledge the aims of Claude, whose models Palmer was to seek in Italy a few years later, and of Turner, Claude's most assiduous modern disciple. The picture is probably based on a view of Underriver. There are strong similarities between the scene and a drawing of Underriver by Linnell (cat. 93).

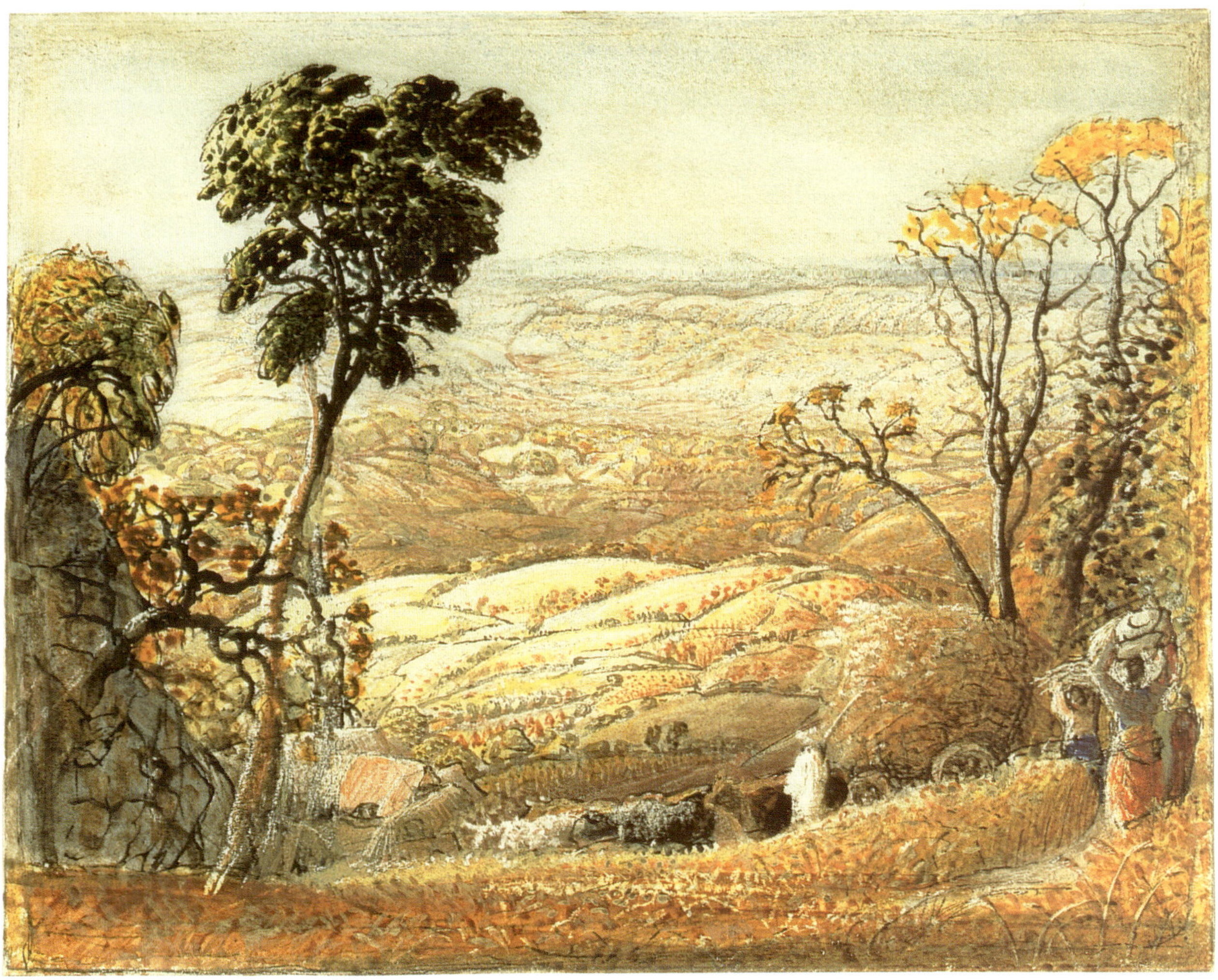

85

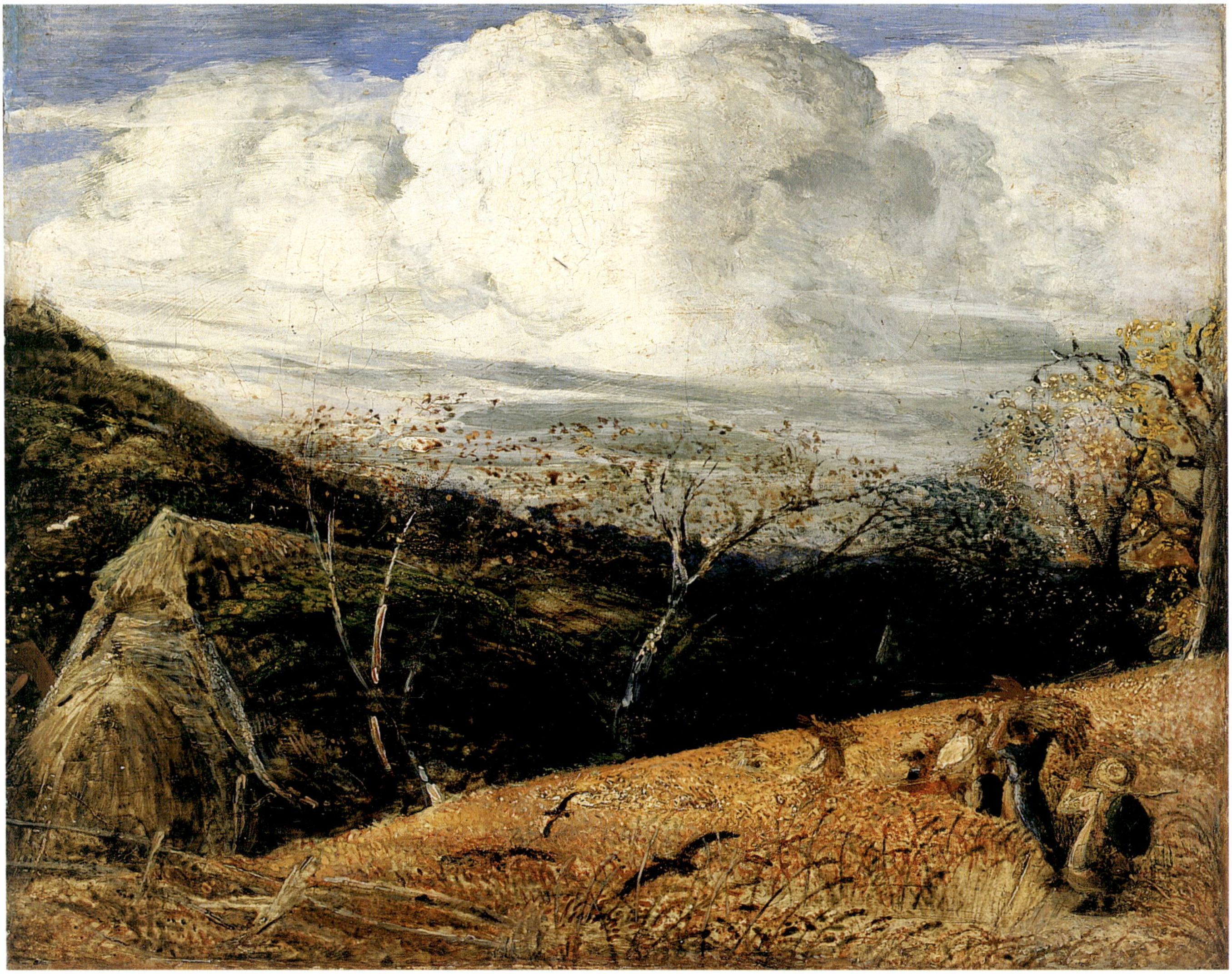

86

## 86

*The White Cloud, c.*1833–4

Oil and tempera, transferred from millboard to canvas, 22.2 × 26.7 cm ($8^3/_4$ × $10^1/_2$ in)

Lit: Grigson 135; Lister 175

Oxford, Ashmolean Museum, 1987.68; bequeathed by I.L. Phillips, 1986

The two paintings now known as *The Bright Cloud* (cat. 87) and *The White Cloud* are closely related – the composition of one is approximately a mirror image of the other – and mark the culmination of Palmer's fascination with clouds. This had begun as early as 1819, when he made careful studies of the colouring and shape of clouds in his sketchbook, and can later be seen in such works as *The Valley with a Bright Cloud* of 1825 (cat. 11). The only significant difference between the painting and its related drawing (cat. 77) is the removal of a figure in front of the cottage, as if his presence might disturb the narrative of the returning peasants.

*The White Cloud* was yet another work owned by George Richmond, whose daughter married William Fothergill Robinson, later a Queen's Counsel and Vice-Chancellor of the Duchy of Lancaster, in 1869. Richmond gave the painting to them on their twenty-fifth wedding anniversary in 1894.

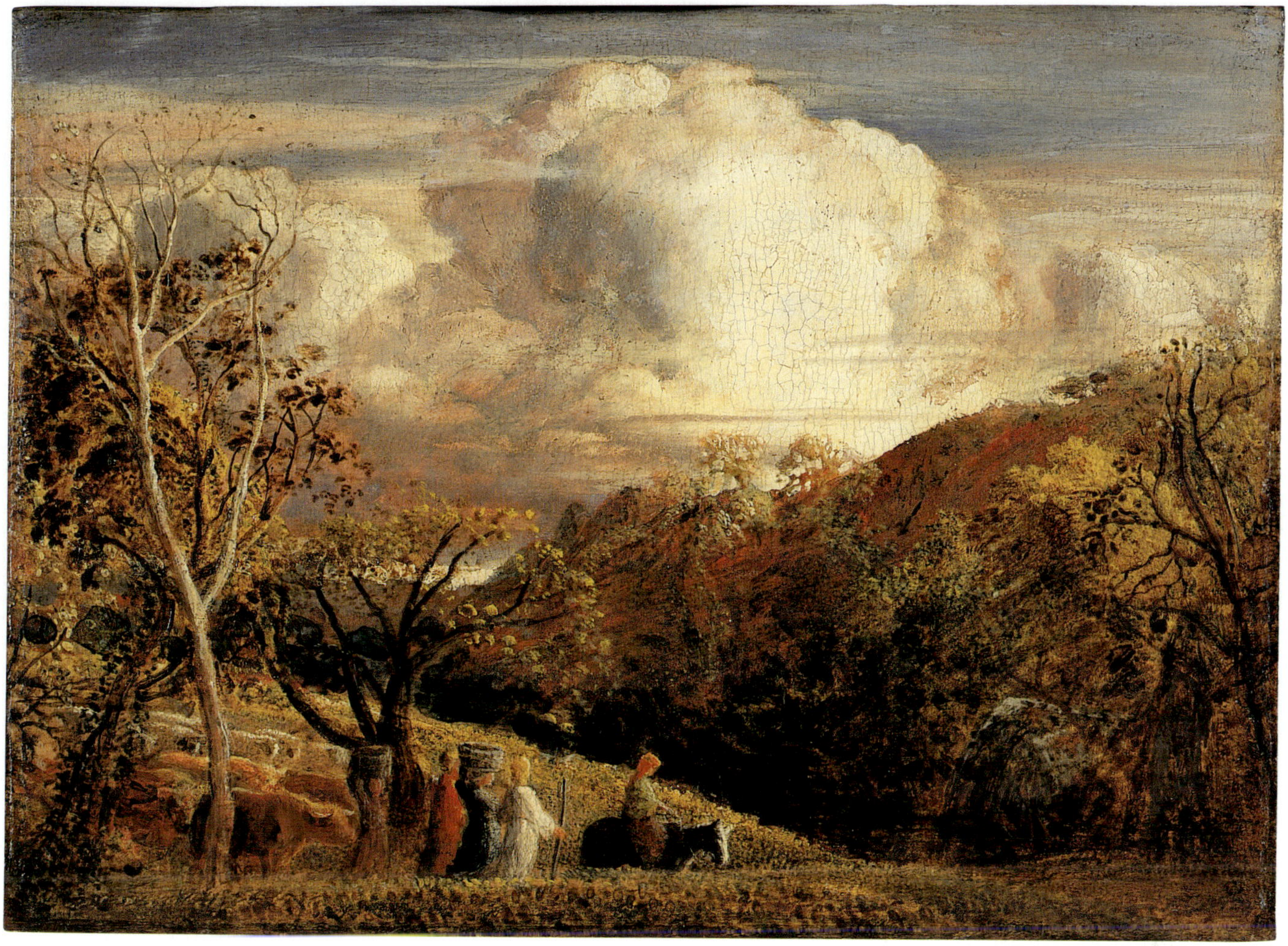

87

## 87

*The Bright Cloud*, *c.*1833–4

Oil and tempera on mahogany panel, 23.2 × 31.7 cm (9⅛ × 12½ in)

Lit: Grigson 136; Fitzwilliam 1984, 28; Lister 169

Manchester City Galleries, 176-82

An old label indicates that this painting was previously entitled *A Rustic Scene* and exhibited at the Royal Academy in either 1833 or 1834. It had acquired its new title by 1881, when it was shown in the retrospective at the Fine Art Society and F.G. Stephens wrote a long and warmly enthusiastic appreciation of it in the catalogue. Palmer's own title is preferable, for the painting is another variation on the theme of peasants returning home, rather than a study of clouds or weather. Unlike many of the contemporary panels, the landscape is painted in daylight, with billowing piles of cumulus clouds in the sky and the procession of peasants watched but not followed by herds of cattle and sheep. The four figures have strong biblical associations: one rides a donkey, two carry baskets on their heads, and a third holds a staff.

Like many of the Shoreham works, it first belonged to John Giles and then, after his sale in 1881, went to George Richmond's son-in-law, William Fothergill Robinson.

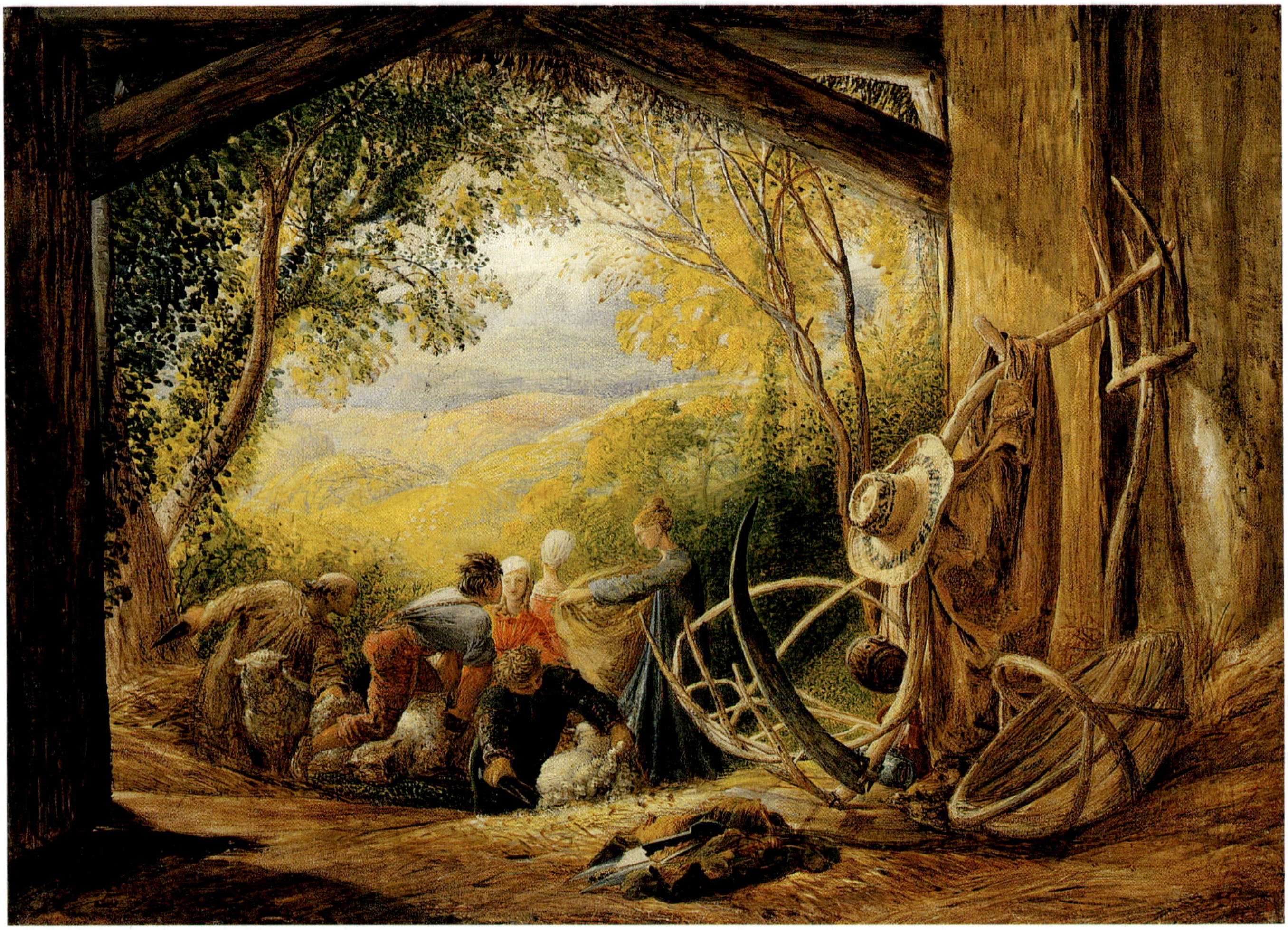

88

## 88

*The Shearers*, *c*.1833–4

Oil and tempera over black chalk on heavy oak panel, 51.4 × 71.1 cm (20¼ × 28 in)

Lit: Grigson 139; Fitzwilliam 1984, 29; Lister 177

Lent courtesy Richard Nathanson, London

Palmer's most ambitious work before his journey to Italy, *The Shearers* is also one of his most enigmatic. The importance and poses of the figures give the picture the pretensions of a history painting, yet there is nothing conventionally noble about their work. It is tempting to link contemporary political and social developments in the countryside with this brutal explosion of work into Palmer's pastoral world, and in some sense to see *The Shearers* as a farewell to the ideals of Shoreham. Unfortunately, there is no mention of the work in Palmer's correspondence, and although it has all the hallmarks of an exhibition piece, it was never exhibited, at least under its present title, and not mentioned in print until A.H. Palmer gave a brief description of it in his biography. Any attempt to interpret the painting must therefore remain a matter of conjecture.

From the interior of a large barn, its great double doors open, the viewer looks out onto a rolling downland landscape, brilliantly lit in the manner of *The Golden Valley* (cat. 85). Against one of the doors is an elaborate still life of farming implements, including a wooden fork, a scythe with its blade aggressively pointed towards the viewer, threshing implements and a basket. Prominent in the arrangement is 'the large patterned straw hat, [which] became one of his father's most cherished symbols of his Shoreham days' (*L&L*, pp. 47–8), together with a barrel and bottle for refreshment, and a spare pair of shears and discarded clothing. Just outside the barn are the shearers, three men and three women. They are tightly grouped in a frieze-like arrangement of consciously varied poses, the men on the left struggling to control the sheep they are shearing, two women behind gathering the wool, and the third looking out into the landscape.

The figures seem to be quotations from works by other artists: Lister has suggested sources in Blake's prints and in antique gems, but they were probably more wide-ranging. The old man on the left, for example, might be Abraham from a Sacrifice of Isaac, his folded shears resembling a dagger, while the figure in the centre is slightly reminiscent of an antique wrestler. The third shearer, and the three women, all have affinities with Henry Fuseli's figures. The general composition may also incorporate memories of other artists' work. At the British Institution exhibition in 1819, when Palmer showed his first works and when he was at his most impressionable, he would have seen Rubens's *Barn in Winter* (*c.*1630) from the Royal Collection, a work that almost immediately inspired the *Village Snow Scene* (1819; version at Yale Center for British Art) by Palmer's friend and fellow 'extollager' (see p. 19), Robert Hills. Rubens offered a precedent for showing the interior of a barn looking out, the reverse of the usual viewpoint in biblical subjects such as the Adoration of the Shepherds. More recently, Palmer's friend William Mulready, whose dappled style he adopted in his oil paintings, had exhibited an *Interior of an English Cottage* (1828; Royal Collection), which shows an extensive landscape through a large open window. While it is not difficult to suggest pictorial sources, it is probable that Palmer may also have found inspiration in the Bible or among his favourite poets, Milton, Virgil and Bunyan. Unfortunately, none of the passages describing shearing in the Bible or Virgil's *Eclogues* corresponds closely, so any literary source also remains unidentified.

However, no source, literary or pictorial, can fully elucidate the radical nature of Palmer's figure painting. For, as Christiana Payne has shown, the depiction of rural labour was rare in English art, most artists contenting themselves with portraying the picturesque, rather than the physical, side of farming. Only a few eccentrics, such as James Ward and the provincial Thomas Barker of Bath, were prepared to show the brutal reality of life in the countryside. Palmer may therefore have been commenting not only on contemporary politics but on contemporary painting too, and the refusal of his fellow artists to engage with rural life. The fact that Palmer never returned to either the subject or the spirit of this painting might confirm that he himself realized that it was unique and that it symbolized his final departure from Shoreham.

Just as Linnell had set Palmer to make landscape studies in 1828, so he apparently encouraged him to study still life in 1834. The most substantial result was an oil painting sent by A.H. Palmer to F.L. Griggs in 1924, 'a little Shoreham oil picture ... a careful study of still life' (Grigson 122). This may have been the *Study from Nature* exhibited at the Royal Academy in 1834. Regrettably, neither work has been identified. However, Palmer made use of these studies in two of his later Shoreham oils, *The Sleeping Shepherd* (cat. 89) and *The Shearers*.

Two similar studies of the farming implements in *The Shearers* are known: fig. 26 and another one, now untraced but reproduced as the frontispiece in A.H. Palmer's *Memoir*. They may be referred to in a letter apparently dated 18 September 1835 and written from London: 'I had just succeeded in setting a model in my room – scythe etc.' (*Letters*, p. 73). Fig. 26 depicts a scythe, sheep shears, harvest barrel and the personal possessions of a farmer: coat, straw hat, umbrella and stick. The other drawing omits the umbrella and stick, but includes an indication of the edge of the open doorway and straw on the floor, making a more complete composition.

It is interesting that, as late as 1861, Palmer should recommend to his son Thomas More the study of 'picturesque farm implements in a like juxtaposition', that is 'the near against the distant' (*Letters*, p. 600).

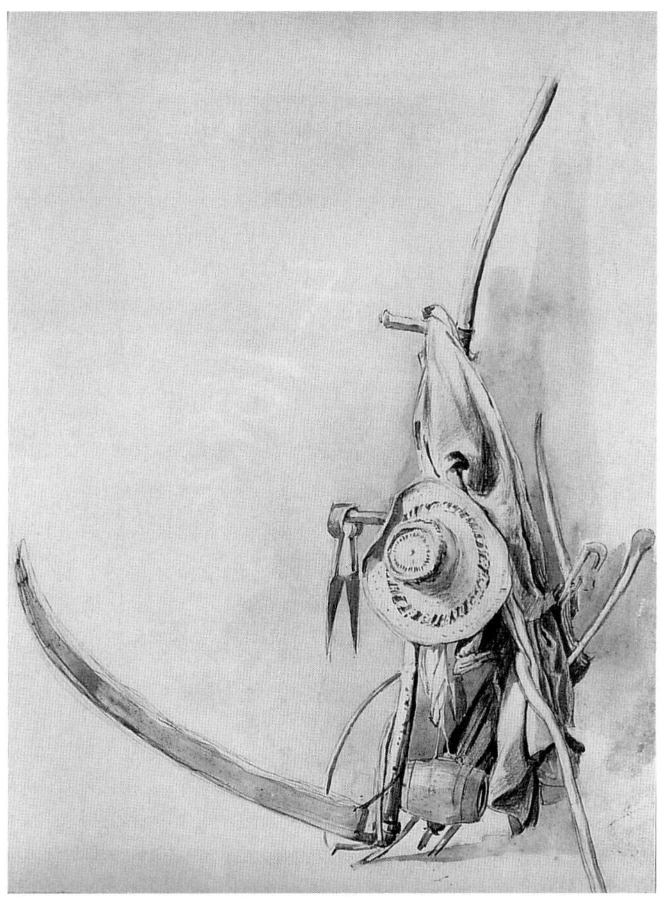

Fig. 26 Study for *The Shearers*, *c.*1834–5, brown and grey wash and graphite, collection of Mr and Mrs Paul Mellon.

## 89

### *The Sleeping Shepherd*, *c.*1834–5

Tempera and oil over chalk with scratching out on board, laid down on panel, 38.1 × 51.4 cm (15 × 20¼ in)

Lit: Grigson 140; Lister 179

James Fairfax, AO

Following his treatment of the theme of the sleeping shepherd in the sketchbook of 1824, a sepia drawing of 1825 and a 'black' of the early 1830s (cat. 78), Palmer returned to it in this oil, which has been variously dated 1833–5. A passage in a letter to George Richmond of October 1834 has been linked to the painting:

> One of the very deepest sayings I have met with in Lord Bacon seems to me to be 'There is no excellent beauty without some strangeness in the proportion'. The sleeping Mercury in the B. Museum has this hard-to-be-defined but most delicious quality to perfection so have the best antique gems and bas reliefs and statues. (*Letters*, p. 67.)

He described the British Museum sculpture more poetically in later life:

> More than two thousand years ago the sculptor bade that marble live. It lived, but slept, and it is living still. Bend over it. Look at those delicate eyelids; that mouth a little open. He is dreaming. Dream on, marble shepherd; few will disturb your slumber. (*Letters*, p. 706.)

The sculpture is now known to represent the shepherd boy, Endymion, whose beauty captivated Diana, the goddess of hunting (fig. 29, p. 211). The pose of Palmer's shepherd, however, is not very similar to that of the antique marble, and the inspiration was general, rather than specific. Lister suggested that a possible literary source was a passage from one of Palmer's favourite works, *The Faithful Shepherdess*, a play by John Fletcher (1579–1625). But the sleeping shepherd was a stock figure in pastoral literature, from Virgil on, and it may be vain to seek a specific source of inspiration. Lister's further suggestion that Palmer was thinking of the shepherds who came to Bethlehem to adore the new-born Christ is also improbable.

The composition of the painting is similar to that of *The Shearers* (cat. 88): a landscape seen from inside a barn, with

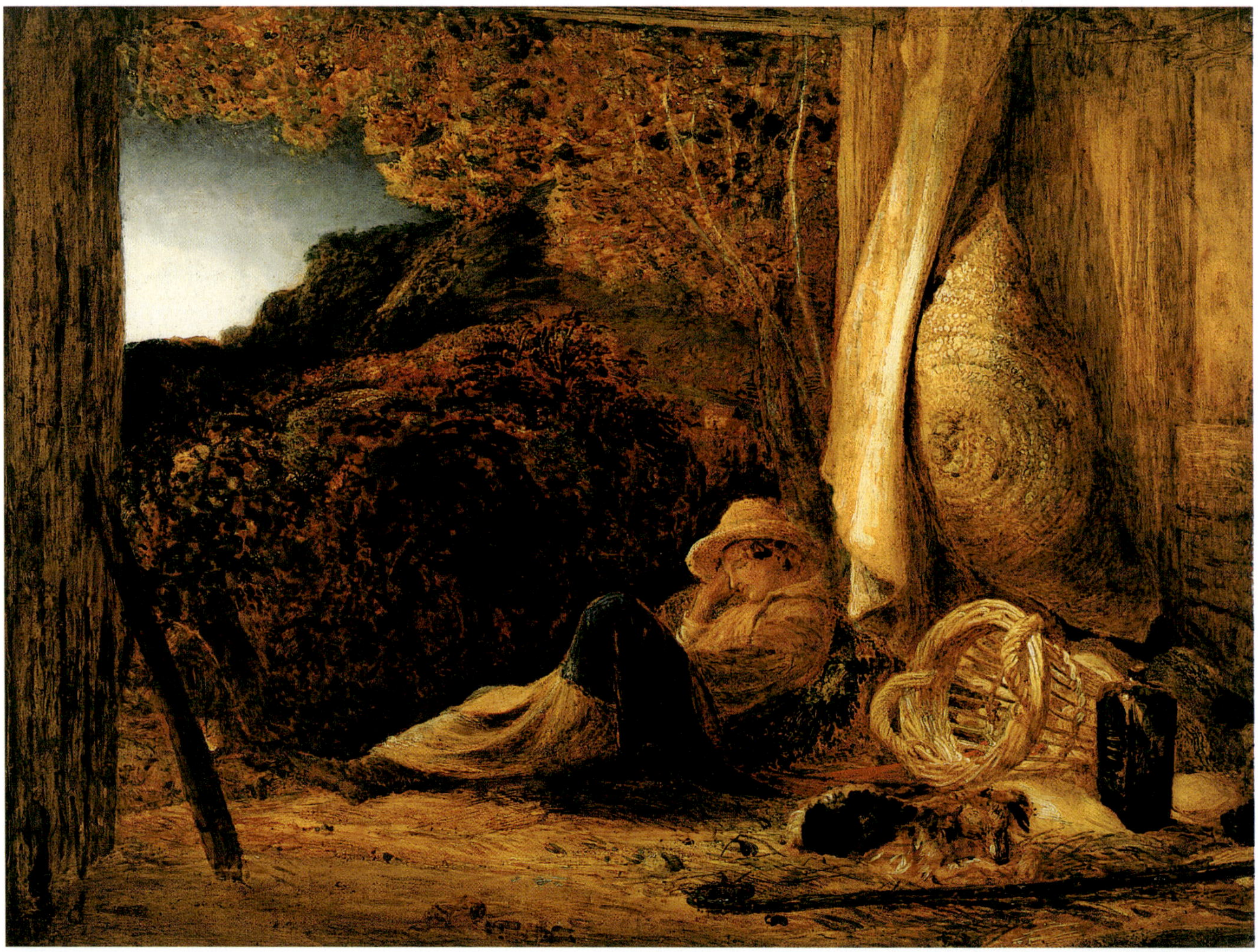

89

an elaborate array of farming utensils at the right. Here, a huge rush basket hangs on the wall, while on the ground, which is strewn with straw, are an outsize bottle, an elongated wicker basket, the shepherd's crook and a sleeping dog. The shepherd himself sleeps with his head resting on one hand and one knee raised, propped up against the door post. Behind him, a curtain has been pushed back, as though the whole scene might be shut out when he awakes. Beyond, in the valley, the night sky shows bright behind the hills on the horizon. A cottage with a light in the window, the shepherd's home, can be seen in the valley. *The Sleeping Shepherd* is painted largely in tempera, with the highlights in white body colour applied with great delicacy in places (such as the rim of the hat). The bold perspective of the barn receding slightly to the right is confidently handled, and might confirm the dating of 1834–5. The support is, unusually, a commercially prepared board, rather than the heavy panel that Palmer normally used for his oil paintings.

In the inventory of the collection of J.W. Overbury (private collection) this painting is recorded as having been 'bought of the artist by Mr [John] Giles who gave it to me in 1874 as a wedding present'. It remained with Overbury's descendants until 1984.

## 90

*Landscape – Twilight, c.*1834

Oil and tempera with pen and ink on panel, 23 × 28 cm (9 1/8 × 11 1/8 in)

Lit: Grigson 141; Lister 182

Richard L. Feigen

A label attached to the panel gives the title and 'No. 6', indicating that this work was submitted to the Royal Academy. It was probably the *Landscape – Twilight* shown in 1834, rather than one of the works with this title shown in 1832 or 1833. However, the identification is made less certain by A.H. Palmer, who in a letter to F.L. Griggs of 9 August 1926

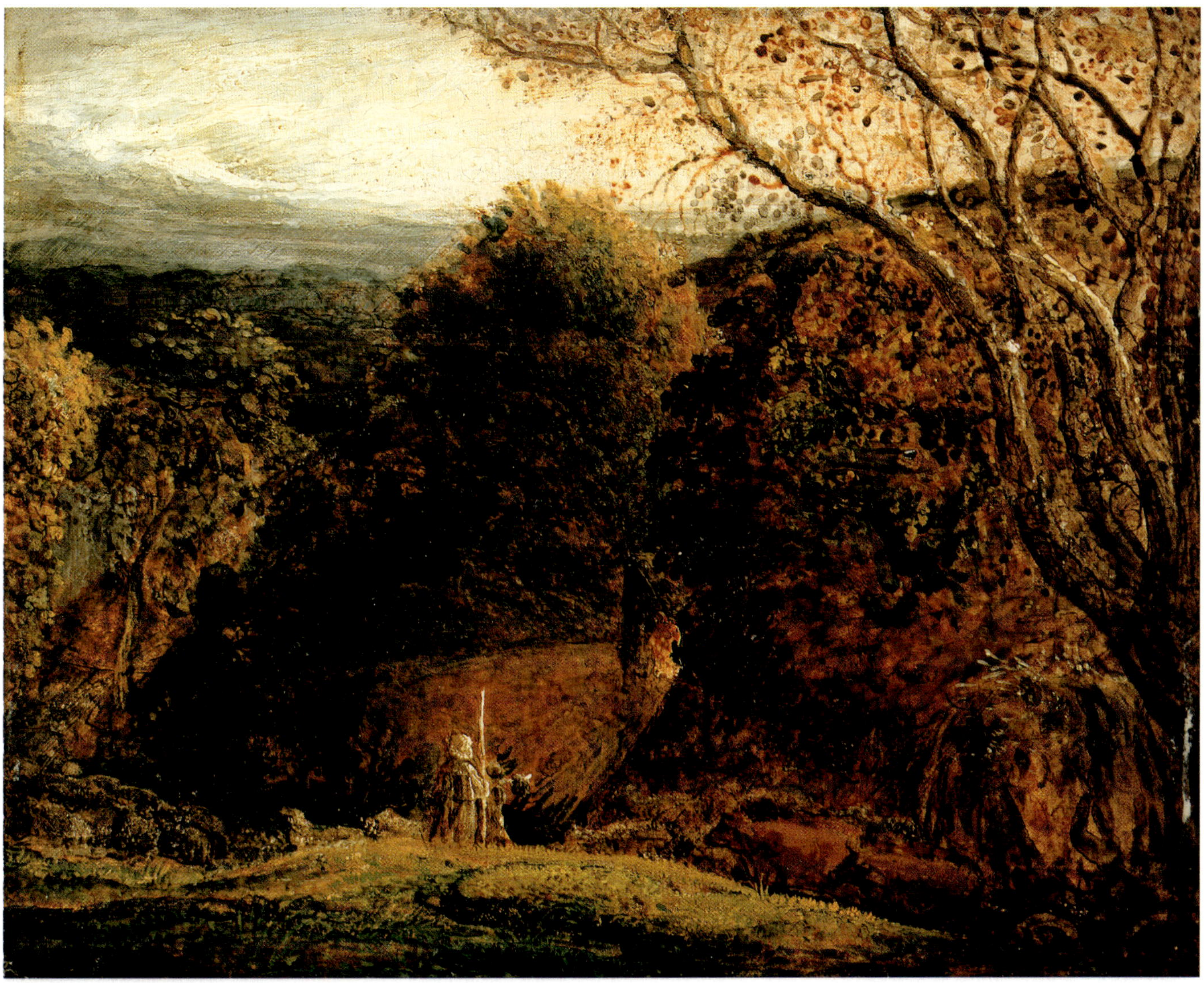

90

(Ashmolean Museum) reported that he was sending for the V&A exhibition the last of the Shoreham panels in his possession, *Landscape – Twilight*, and that he was 'particularly anxious to have your opinion of what *I* have called "Twilight – The Cottage Window"'. Lister 182 is certainly the work that he sent in 1926, but his alternative title was also one used by his father for another work exhibited in 1834. The uncertainty emphasizes how similar many of Palmer's compositions were and how deliberately unspecific his titles.

The drawing identified by Grigson as a study for *Landscape – Twilight* (V&A, Lister 163) is not identical in composition, but the focus in both drawing and painting is on the light streaming from the cottage window into the landscape. In the painting, however, it catches the figure of the peasant and integrates him more fully than any other variant of this composition into the hearth at his journey's end.

A.H. Palmer was especially fond of this painting, retaining it in preference to *The Shearers* and others, which he sold in 1909. In 1892 he attempted to explain the extraordinary power that the Shoreham panels hold: they are 'remarkable for their suggestiveness, calling forth our more timid imagination, and leading it away to explore the recesses of a romantic country without allowing us to realize the fact that our explorations are really bound by a little paint upon a wooden panel'. In the letter to Griggs mentioned above, he felt it had 'a spell about it. The imagination enters that cottage & what it sees there and thinks it sees all round about in the quiet mysterious woods and valleys far surpasses to my mind the same kind of thing in *Christmas*.' He also explained why the panel showed signs of neglect – his father kept it unframed in a cupboard all his life.

## 91*

### *A Pastoral Scene*, 1835

Oil and tempera on panel, 30 × 40 cm (11 13/16 × 15 3/4 in)

Lit: Grigson 156; Brown 22; Lister 215

Oxford, Ashmolean Museum, 1940.21; purchased 1940

Palmer's first extended journey away from London and Kent was a trip to Devon in the summer of 1834, the importance of which he recorded in a letter to George Richmond in October 1834: 'I would not have been without the Devonshire reminiscences on any

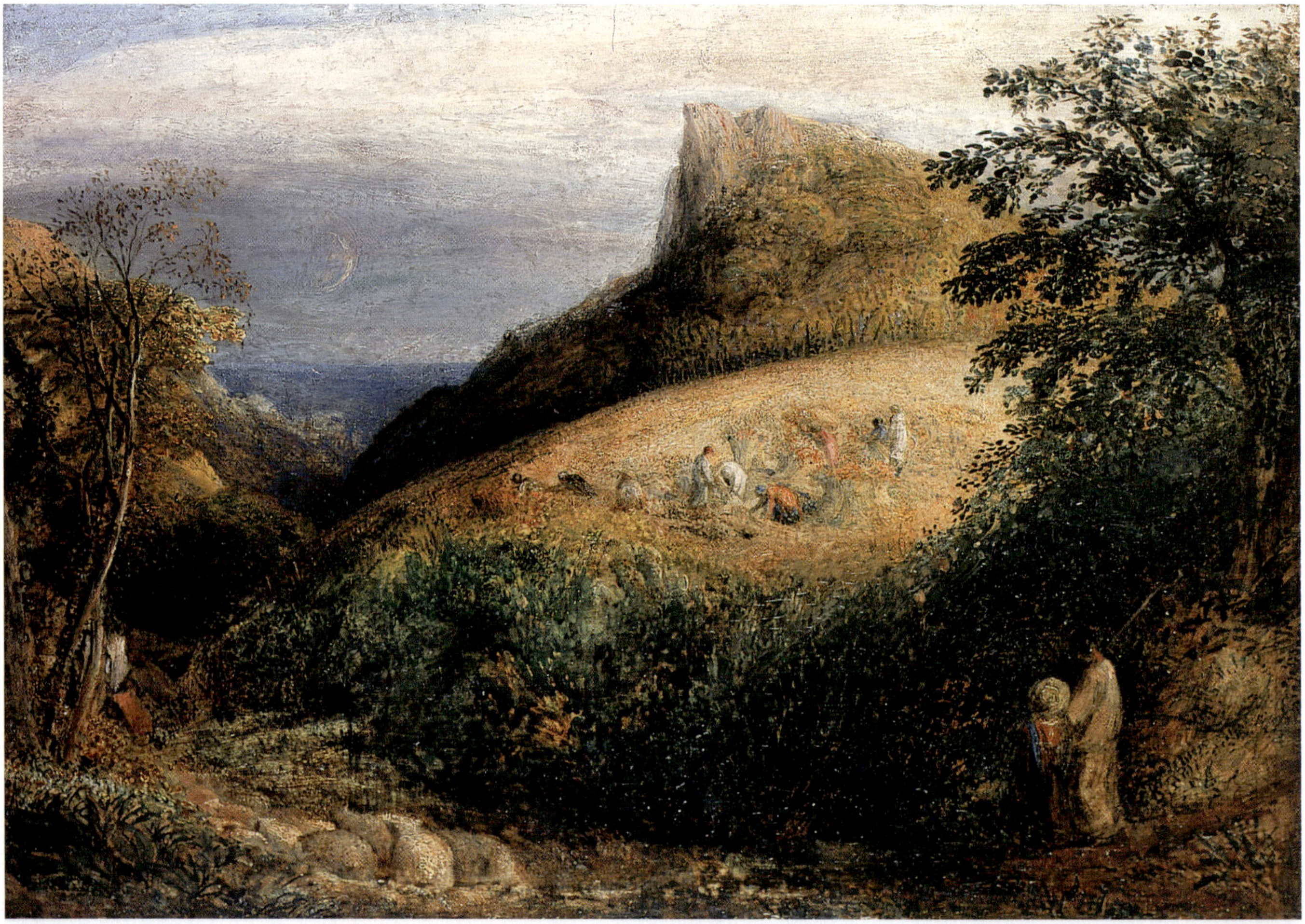

91

account – I hardly ever try to invent landscape without thinking of them' (*Letters*, p. 66).

It is probable that among the landscapes he was inventing in the winter of 1834 were the two shown at the Royal Academy in the following spring, the *Scene from Lee, North Devon* (cat. 97) and *The Cornfield* (Lister 208). Although Lister gives confusing provenances, there is little doubt that the painting now known as *A Pastoral Scene* was, in fact, the second of Palmer's exhibits at the Academy. More than *Scene from Lee*, it combines the pastoral sentiment of Shoreham with the topography of 'dear, spongy Devon' and is one of the artist's most impressive and carefully resolved oil paintings. It was based on two studies (Lister 213/cat. 92 and Lister 214): the first probably a topographical notation; the second taming the jagged shapes of the rocks on the right, placing them at the summit of Kentish hills and rearranging the composition to make it more balanced and to give the harvesters greater prominence. Brown has speculated that the painting might have begun as a straightforward Shoreham landscape, which would account for the extensive pentimenti. If this is the case, Palmer has been remarkably successful in assimilating the topography of Devon into his pastoral vision.

Palmer kept the work for nearly forty years, eventually sending it as a wedding present to George Richmond's daughter Julia, who married William Fothergill Robinson in 1874: 'The "Harvest-field" sent herewith I have kept by me until now for occasional revision, and I do not see what more could be done without mixing styles or manners of working incident to different periods of one's life' (*Letters*, pp. 901–2).

## 92*

### Drawing for *A Pastoral Scene*, 1834

Brush and brown ink with scratching out, 9.5 × 11.4 cm (3¾ × 4½ in)

Lit: Grigson 154; Lister 213

New Haven, Yale Center for British Art, Paul Mellon Collection, B1977.14.5824

First reproduced in 1892 by A.H. Palmer, who simply called it a 'Design at Shoreham', this tiny drawing was later identified by Grigson as a study for the painting *A Pastoral Scene* in the Ashmolean (cat. 91). It was probably drawn from nature on Palmer's first visit to Devon in the summer of 1834, and preceded the more finished and stylized drawing formerly owned by John Giles and now in the Tate (Lister 214). The view has not been conclusively identified, but the topography is reminiscent of the area around Ilfracombe. Grigson proposed Lee Abbey near Lynmouth, while Commander (Arts Council 1956, no. 156) preferred the rocks between Ilfracombe and Watermouth. More recently, it has been suggested that the distinctive rock formation on the right might be in the Valley of the Rocks, near Lynton. The crescent moon provides unnaturally strong illumination for the landscape, which is alive with activity: the harvesters in the field, heavily laden wagons going up and down the hill and a woman carrying faggots in the foreground.

When A.H. Palmer sent the drawing as a gift to Martin Hardie, he wrote that it 'used to hang among some special favourites in my room when I was a boy'.

## 93

### John Linnell (1792–1882)

### *Underriver – The Golden Valley*, *c.*1833

Pen and brown ink and wash over graphite on white wove paper, 28 × 27.5 cm (11⅛ × 10⅞ in)

Signed: *JL*

Lit: Crouan 64

Private collection; promised gift of Jeffrey Berenson to the Metropolitan Museum of Art, PG63

Linnell's nature studies are for the most part carefully executed, in pencil or ink, and reminiscent of those of his master, John Varley. However, in a handful of

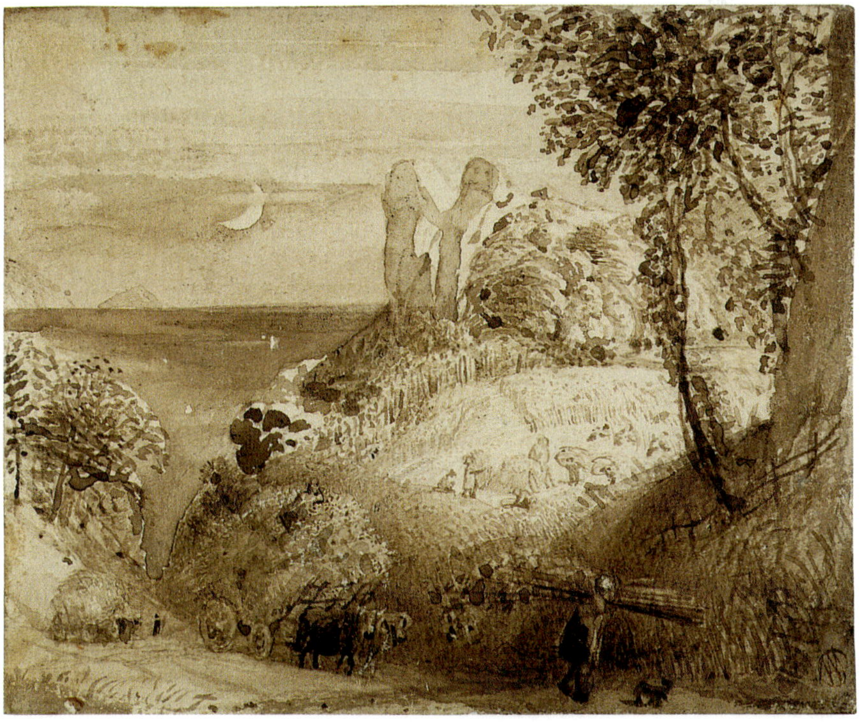

92

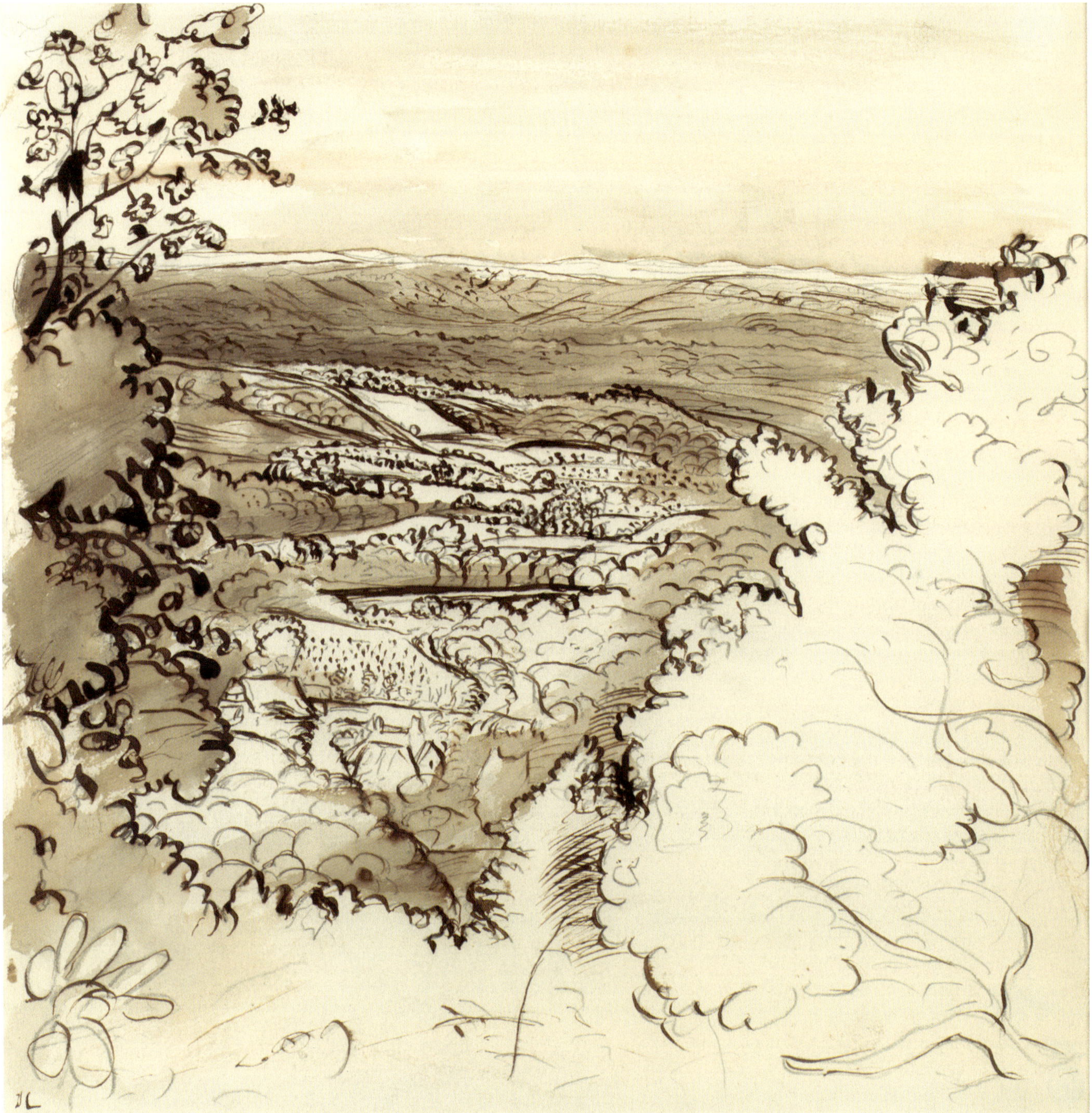

93

drawings, he adopted Palmer's flamboyant and cursive style in pen and ink. This sheet is comparable with *The Weald of Kent*, signed and dated 1833 (Fitzwilliam Museum; Crouan 63), which shows a similar view down a valley from a high vantage point. Both must have been made on an otherwise unrecorded visit to Kent in the summer of 1833, presumably on a visit to Palmer at Shoreham. The view has been variously identified as being taken from Poll Hill, south-west of Shoreham, and more convincingly as looking down onto Underriver from the ridge west of Carter's Hill (Barton and Tong 1995, p. 8). Palmer used the same view in *The Golden Valley* (cat. 85), and he and Linnell may very well have worked side by side. However, Linnell's drawing is stylistically closest to Palmer's sketches of the late 1820s, such as *The Primitive Cottage* (Lister 99), though his penwork is more regular and controlled than Palmer's abandoned exuberance.

## 94

### Welby Sherman (active 1827–34), after Samuel Palmer

### *Evening*, 1834

Mezzotint,
image 14.8 × 17.8 cm (5 13/16 × 7 in),
sheet 22 × 24.3 cm (8 11/16 × 9 9/16 in)

Lit: Campbell Dodgson, 'The Engravings of George Richmond and Welby Sherman', *Print Collectors' Quarterly*, XVII (1930), pp. 352–62 (361–2); V&A 1926, 66; Grigson 142; Fitzwilliam 1984, 133; Lister P3

London, Tate, N03869; presented by Herbert Linnell, 1924

In addition to his etchings after Palmer, Calvert and Richmond, and his possible participation in Palmer's own woodcut (see cat. 62), Welby Sherman made a single mezzotint, *Evening*. The technical sophistication of this print, especially when compared with his earlier work, has led some commentators to speculate that he was trained in this technique rather than straightforward intaglio methods. While it is impossible to be certain who Sherman's teacher might have been, it is worth noting that John Linnell began making mezzotints in 1830–31, both portraits and subject pictures after popular artists such as William Collins, and may have taught Sherman or been a fellow pupil elsewhere.

Only three impressions of the print are known, of which two are before letters (one touched in chalk). The published state includes the inscription:

> 'EVENING LATE, BY THEN THE CHEWING FLOCKS / HAD TA'EN THEIR SUPPERS OF THE SAVOURY HERB / OF KNOT-GRASS DEW-BESPRENT' / PAINTED BY SAMUEL PALMER / ENGRAVED BY WELBY SHERMAN / Published by Samuel Palmer, 4 Grove Street, St. Marylebone 1834. Price 2/6.

On the basis of the inscription 'Painted by Samuel Palmer', all commentators agree that the original composition

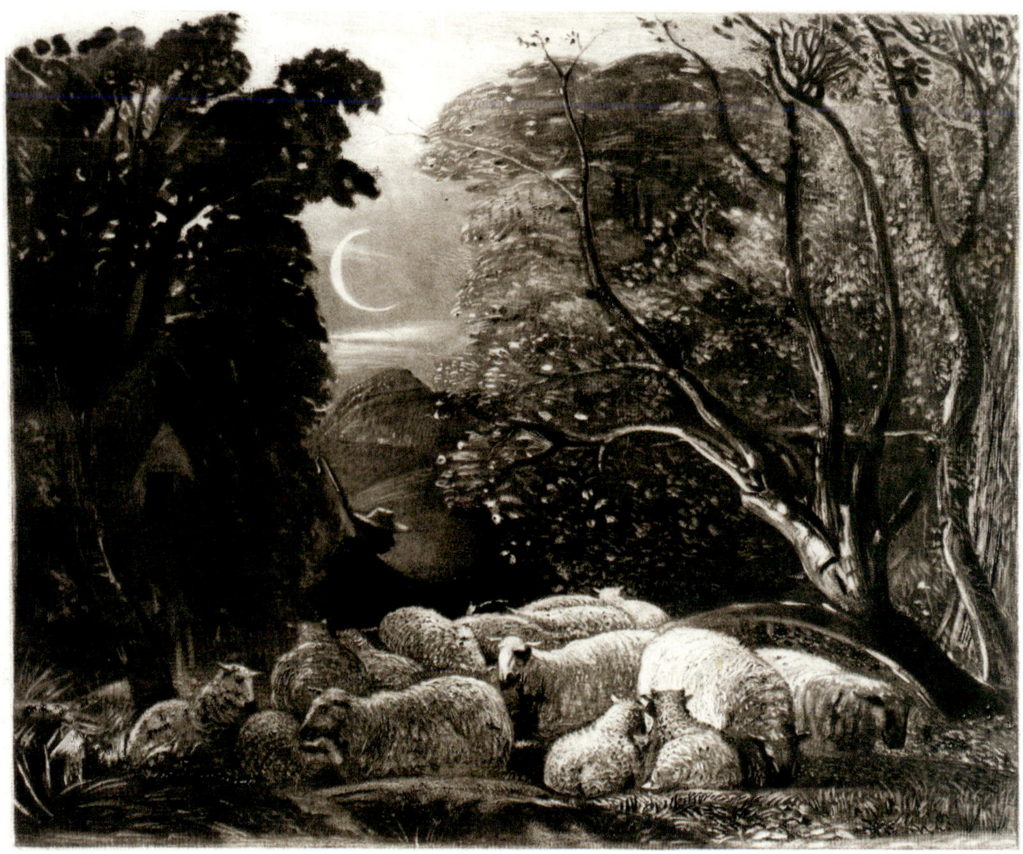

94

was an oil painting once in the possession of A.H. Palmer, which he referred to in later life: 'In the little panel picture (once in my possession) which was engraved by Sherman the young moon was an absolutely essential feature. But Linnell painted it out and ruined the picture.' Lister confused this panel with another Linnell retouched in 1875, a 'small woody landscape' now known as *The Farm* (perhaps the painting *At Filston Farm* Palmer exhibited at the British Institution in 1835). The model for Sherman's mezzotint remains untraced, and there must remain the possibility, in spite of A.H. Palmer's memory, that it was a watercolour, perhaps one of the 'blacks' of the early 1830s. Certainly, the technique would have been highly appropriate for translating Palmer's twilight monochromes.

Just as Linnell had taken up mezzotint for commercial reasons, so, it seems, had Sherman. In a letter to George Richmond of 14 October 1834 Palmer asked him 'if as you kindly promised you would let the little mezzotint flock hang up somewhere where it can be seen as it might be of some service to Sherman or myself who are both at present pinched by a most unpoetical and unpastoral kind of poverty' (*Letters*, p. 62). The touched proof in the V&A is dated in pencil by Palmer 'March 21 1834', and Sherman must have completed the published state that spring or summer. The lines after the title are from Milton's *Comus* (1637), lines 540–42.

Although the print was published by Palmer, with his address, he had no means of selling it and did not have a regular dealer to handle it. In fact, all three surviving impressions remained within Palmer's close circle: those in the British Museum and the V&A belonged to Palmer himself, and the present impression to Linnell. Linnell's mezzotints were published by leading print dealers such as Colnaghi, Thomas Boys and Francis Graves. He would presumably have interceded on behalf of the Ancients to publish their prints, but to no avail.

Two years after this collaboration, Sherman won a great deal of money from Palmer's brother William in a game of billiards and fled to France in ignominy (*Letters*, p. 20 n. 2).

## 95*

*Address to the Electors of West Kent*, 1832

Pamphlet, 21.7 × 13.9 cm (8⅝ × 5½ in)
Lit: Bindman 1985; Lister 1987, pp. 241–54
Maidstone, Centre for Kentish Studies

The existence of Palmer's only writing published in his lifetime was known solely from references in his son's *Memoir* to 'a fiery squib' until a copy of the pamphlet came to light in 1985, when it was published by David Bindman. Its rarity (this is still the only known copy) is not surprising, as it was by nature ephemeral. Palmer wrote it in support of the Tory candidate, Sir William Geary, Bt., in the General Election of December 1832 following the passing of the Reform Act.

Although the title page bears the imprint of the London printer Joseph Shackell, the pamphlet was probably published at Palmer's expense. The contents are intemperate in tone and profoundly reactionary in sentiment, a last-ditch attempt to defend the Church of England against the reforms that Palmer believed would bring about the end of the way of life in the countryside that he loved. He sent copies of the pamphlet to the *Kentish Observer* (supporting the Tory stance) and the *Kentish Gazette* (for the reformers). Only the latter deigned to review it, calling it 'The ravings of this maniac'. Palmer's candidate was bottom of the poll.

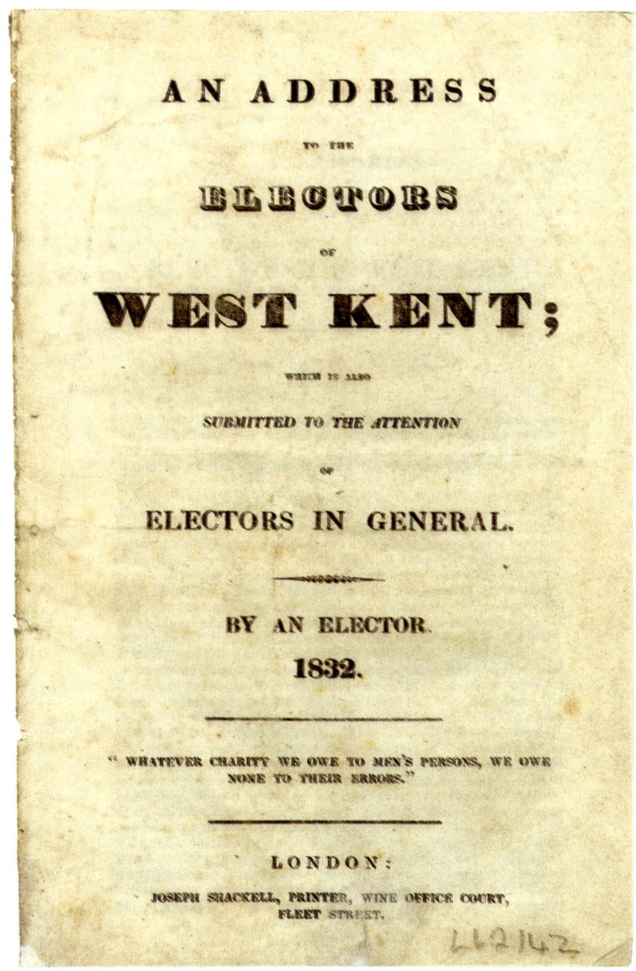

AN ADDRESS
TO THE
ELECTORS
OF
WEST KENT;
WHICH IS ALSO
SUBMITTED TO THE ATTENTION
OF
ELECTORS IN GENERAL.

BY AN ELECTOR.
1832.

"WHATEVER CHARITY WE OWE TO MEN'S PERSONS, WE OWE NONE TO THEIR ERRORS."

LONDON:
JOSEPH SHACKELL, PRINTER, WINE OFFICE COURT, FLEET STREET.

95

OPPOSITE
*Christian Descending into the Valley of Humiliation*, 1848 (detail, cat. 120)

# Part Two: The Victorian

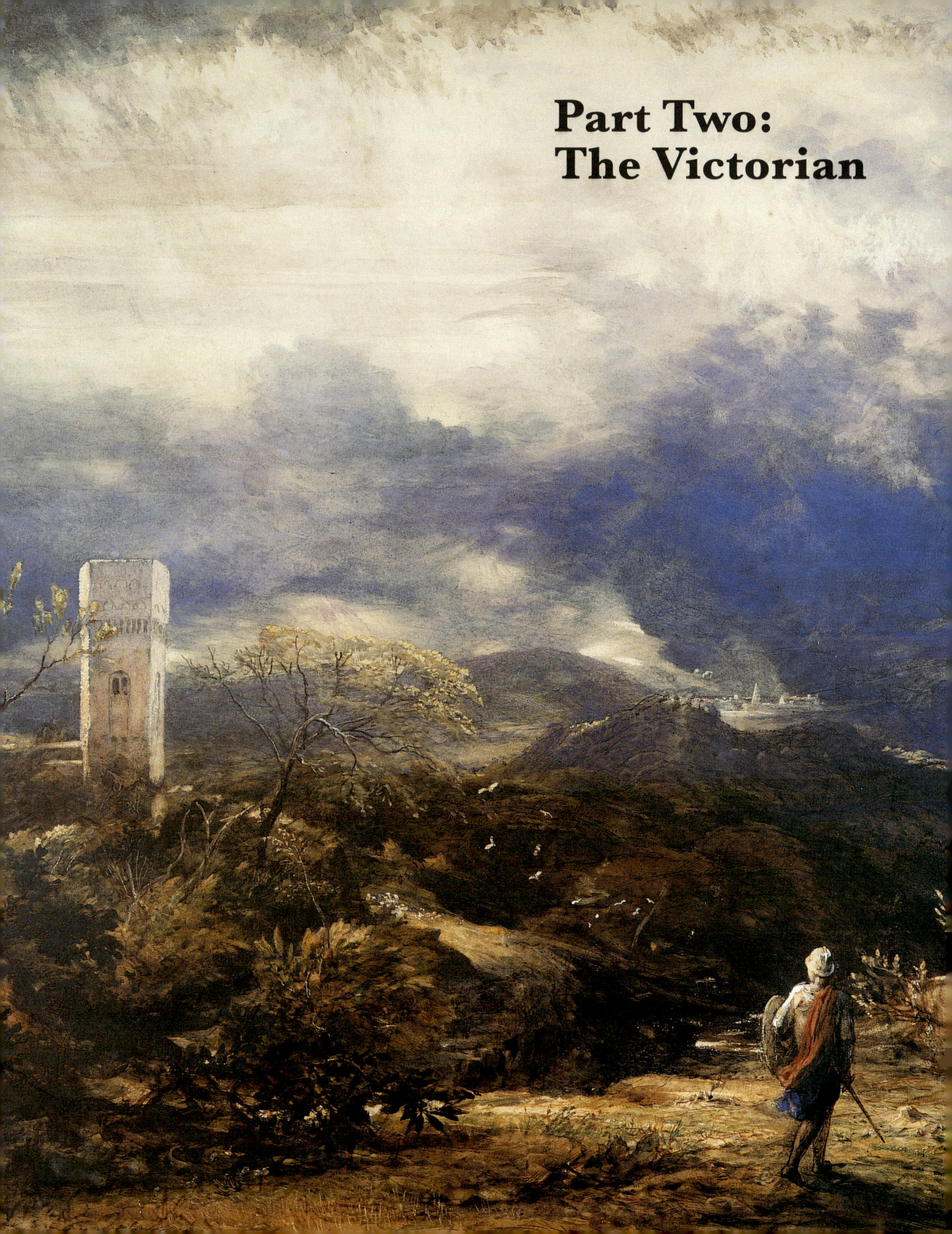

# 5. The Traveller (1835–7)

*Elizabeth E. Barker*

The year 1835 proved a watershed for Palmer. In January the artist marked his thirtieth birthday, and at some time before mid-September he moved from Shoreham to London. Palmer had purchased a ten-room house in Marylebone (4 Grove Street, Lisson Grove) in 1832, calling it his 'teaching headquarters' in the city (Grigson 1947, p. 150 n. 11). Moving there placed him within easy reach of friends: around the corner from Frederick Tatham (20 Lisson Grove North), a brief walk to Edward Calvert (Park Place, Paddington) and George Richmond (16 Beaumont Street, New Road, St Marylebone), and half-an-hour's stroll to John Linnell (38 Porchester Terrace, Bayswater).

More than a change of scene or re-engagement with an artistic community, Palmer's departure from the 'Valley of Vision' signalled a new course for his art. In leaving Kent and moving to London, Palmer withdrew from his youthful ideal of 'Imaginative Art' (*Letters*, p. 47), which had been an 'eternal abstraction from cloggy corporeal existence' (*Letters*, p. 43). During a series of tours of the British countryside Palmer would seek the very 'Universal nature', whose 'leafy lightness' and 'thousand repetitions of little forms' he had once derided (*Letters*, p. 47). As a result, the artist's landscape studies from this period reveal a free, exploratory manner that bears little immediate resemblance to the drawings of the Shoreham period.

Palmer began his travels in the south-west of England, in Dorset and Devon, inspired to visit the latter by a print of Watermouth Bay glimpsed 'in a shop window in Gt Russell St' (*Letters*, p. 721). The region provided the subjects for paintings exhibited in 1835 (RA nos 90 and 153; cats 97, 98) and fostered in Palmer a lifelong admiration for the area's 'infinite richness' (*L&L*, pp. 55, 405, 407; *Letters*, p. 474).

In the summer of that year Palmer made his first journey to Wales in the company of Henry Walter (see cat. 3; *Letters*, pp. 71, 73, 83–4). They explored the exotic land from north to south, visiting Conway, Snowdon, Betwys-y-Coed, Dolgellau and Tintern. The following summer, Palmer returned to Wales, this time with Calvert, and sketched the area near Betwys-y-Coed at greater length (*Letters*, p. 75). At a lodging house in the Coed-y-Brenin forest Palmer met the former Blake associate, Henry Crabb Robinson, who – taken by Palmer's 'eye of deep feeling and very capacious forehead' – invited the young artist to visit the nearby waterfalls with him (Robinson 1869, vol. 2, p. 221). Robinson recorded the excursion in his diary:

> We ... entangled ourselves in a forest, but the mountain torrent afforded us great pleasure. In less than two hours we came to the waterfall Rhaiadyr y Mawwdach [Rhaeadr Mawddach] which is a double and very fine one especially on the South side on which we were – Above the fall is a bridge – We crossed it and after looking at the fall on this side we came to the spout of the Cayne [Pistyll Cain], a single lofty and most elegant fall which I left Mr. P: to take a sketch of, which I mean hereafter to buy. (Robinson 1869, vol. 2, p. 221).

True to his word, Robinson purchased 'A waterfall with a distant view of Snowdon' (untraced) from Palmer for 10 Guineas in November of that year (Grigson 1947, p. 131).

The mountains, waterfalls and castles of Wales offered dramatic subjects for Palmer's new naturalistic study of the world. He approached his subjects with an almost scientific curiosity, seeking to capture specific places in precise moments. He made many of the Welsh sketches on tinted or light-brown paper, securing the essential forms with a pencil before elaborating the primary subject (typically located in the middle distance) in watercolour and black chalk. These are unquestionably working drawings: large portions of the sheets are left unfinished, and the margins and images are heavily inscribed with notes. If the light probing lines of the Welsh sketches depart from the bold certain strokes of Palmer's youthful 'blacks', the artist's continued preoccupation with texture and the calligraphic quality of his marks recall his earlier manner.

In making a tour of Wales, Palmer followed a trail blazed by many others, including Wilson, Sandby, 'Warwick' Smith, Ibbetson, de Loutherbourg, Turner, Cotman, Girtin, Müller, Prout, Jackson, Cox, John Varley and Linnell (Moir 1964; Wilton 1984; Andrews 1989, pp. 84–107, 108–51; Woof and Hebron 1998, pp. 102–80; Lord 1998, p. 37; Lord 2000, pp. 129–66, 279–310; Story 1892, vol. 1, pp. 80–85; Linnell 1994, pp. 28–9.) As this roster suggests, from the mid-eighteenth century, a tour of Wales had become almost routine for British artists, who traipsed the southern Wye Valley in search of the picturesque scenery and ruins praised by William Gilpin (Gilpin 1783), and hiked the northern area near Betws-y-Coed to admire the Romantic vistas and waterfalls later celebrated by Thomas Roscoe (Roscoe 1836, 1844).

For Palmer, then, the journey to Wales must have seemed a rite of passage. It was also an opportunity to broaden his experience, enlarge his reputation and secure the means of establishing an independent household. For artists of

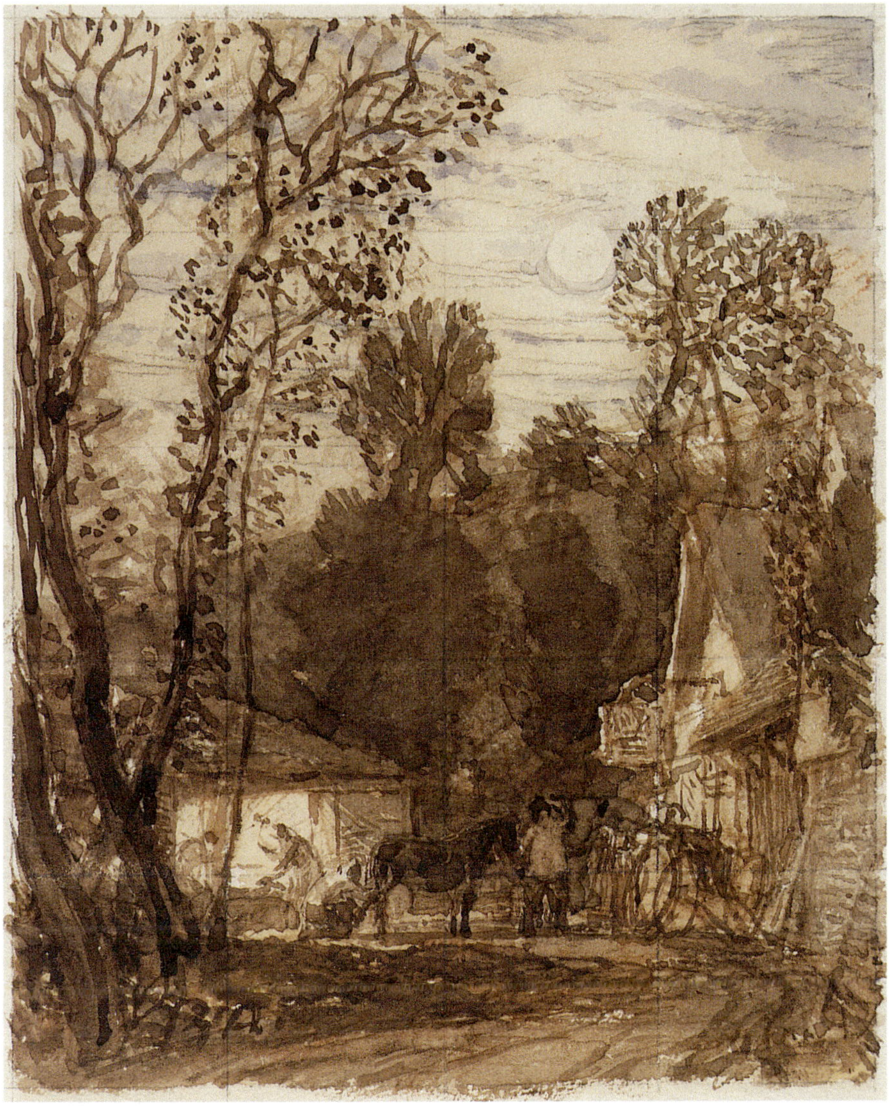

96

Palmer's generation, views of Wales comprised a distinct, commercially viable sub-genre of British landscape painting, and Palmer hoped that his Welsh studies would be 'the foundation ... of solid attainments' (Smith 2002, table IV, p. 10; *Letters*, pp. 83–4). Disappointingly, however, Palmer would have difficulty selling his Welsh watercolours and would ultimately come to regard his drawings from this period as 'unworkable' (*Letters*, p. 256).

## 96

### *The Wayside Smithy*, *c.*1835

Brown ink, blue wash and graphite on off-white Whatman paper (watermarked), image 12.7 × 10.2 cm (5 × 4 in), sheet 25.1 × 18.7 cm ($9\frac{7}{8} \times 7\frac{3}{8}$ in)

Inscribed in graphite at bottom in A.H. Palmer's hand: *Contrast of Moonlight & Fire or candle light – which SP loved*; at lower left: *See back–*; at lower right: *For Capt Martin Hardie*; on upper verso: *Design Illustrating one of S. Palmer's Favorite themes – Moonlight & artificial light – See Christmas etching*

Lit: V&A 1926, 113; Lister 203

New Haven, Yale Center for British Art, Paul Mellon Collection, B.2001.2.1087

Deft marks of graphite and ink capture the essential forms; select strokes of wash establish the composition in light and shade. Beneath a blue-and-brown-streaked sky illuminated by a full moon (a circle of clean white paper) a tree-lined lane leads towards an inn. Opposite it a blacksmith's shop shines against the night, its artificial light, by contrast with the moon, tempered by a thin application of wash. Within the bright structure, a smith raises his hammer, observed by a second figure. Others stand in the darkened road, grooming the horse whose broken shoe has prompted the nocturnal repair.

The sheet's restricted palette of brown and blue relates to a method that Palmer later recommended to his pupil, Louisa Twining (cat. 131): by using only the brown pigment Cologne earth, the blue pigment cobalt and the carbon-based brown ink bistre, an artist could 'save *much* time' when sketching from nature (*Letters*, p. 717). The light, searching draughtsmanship, broken lines and extensive use of graphite link this drawing to similar works such as *The Young Traveller* and *Man Carrying Faggots*, which must also date to this time (Lister 184, 160). Perhaps, during a period when Palmer ranged farther than ever before, images of journeys and travellers held a special appeal.

At some time, possibly years after its completion, Palmer squared the sheet in graphite, as if preparing to transfer the design onto another working surface. He may have intended to develop it into a finished painting or – considering its intimate size and luminous composition – an etching. No further versions of the design, however, are known.

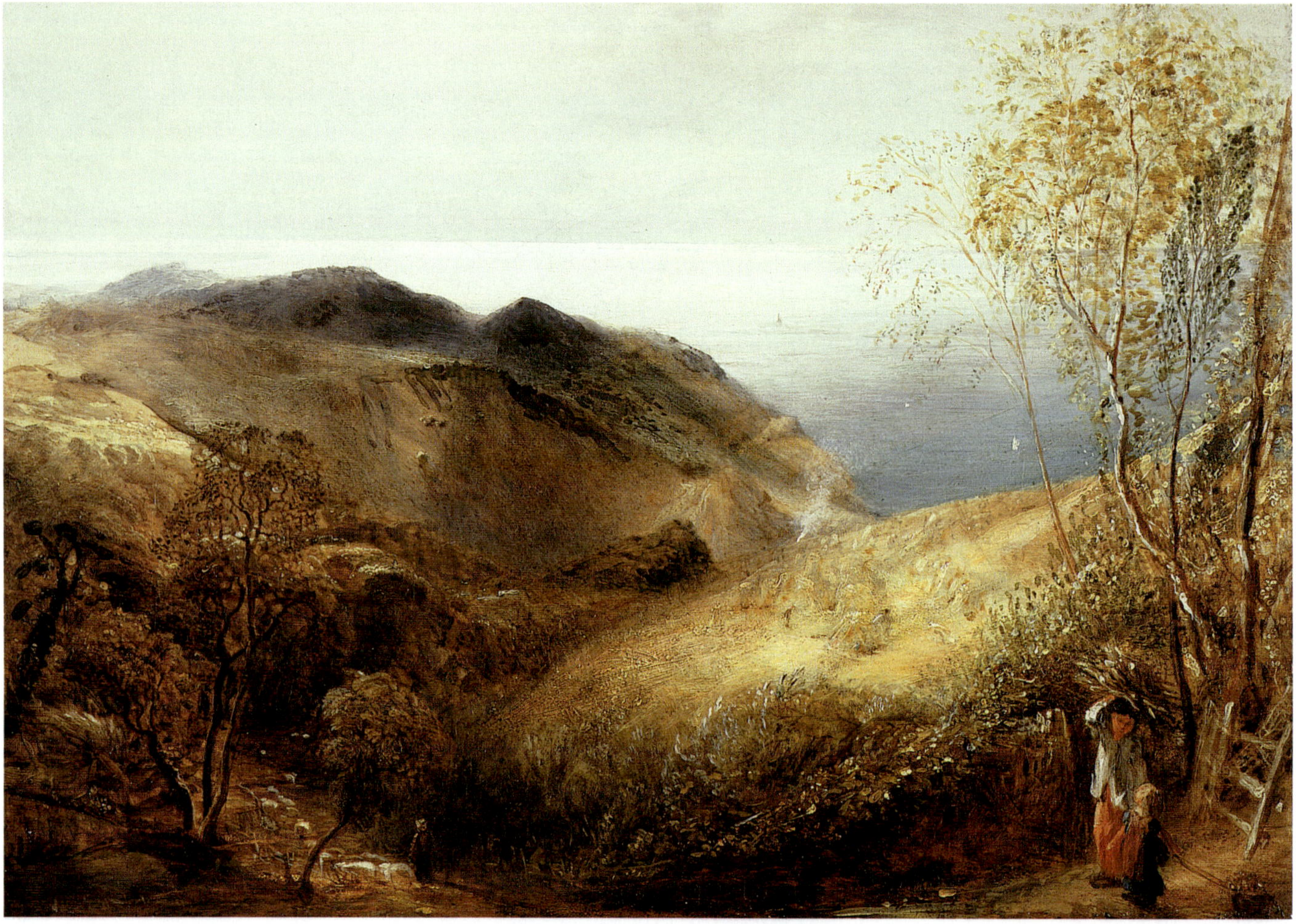

97

## 97

*Scene from Lee, North Devon*, 1835

Oil on canvas, 26.7 × 38.1 cm (10½ × 15 in)

Lit: Lister 219

University of Cambridge, Fitzwilliam Museum; bought from the Fairhaven Fund with contributions from the National Art Collections Fund and the National Lottery through the Heritage Lottery Fund, 2003

Although an old label identifies this painting's subject as 'On Chaldon Down, Dorset', it actually depicts a site in Devon that remains largely unchanged: the view of Lee from the coastal path to Ilfracombe. The exact date of Palmer's visit to the region is unrecorded, but it must have preceded his exhibition of this painting at the Royal Academy in May 1835 (RA no. 90), and may well have occurred the previous autumn. Not surprisingly, this post-Shoreham painting seems to summarize the artist's previous accomplishments and predict the work to come: the globular forms of the foreground leaves, and the distant sheep and wisp of chimney-smoke recall the earlier works; the accomplished aerial perspective and rustic children relate to other works of the mid-1830s; the naturalistic profile of the hills, subdued sky and cool-toned palette forecast the later landscapes.

In painting the sunlight glinting on the water, Palmer may have taken inspiration from Claude, the artist he later described as 'the greatest landscape-painter who ever lived' (*Letters*, p. 671). Palmer never forgot Blake's delighted description of a painting by Claude in which he had discerned 'upon the focal lights of the foliage, small specks of pure white which made them appear to be glittering with dew which the morning sun had not yet dried up'. Decades later, Palmer recalled that, as Blake spoke, 'He warmed with his subject, and it continued through an evening walk. The sun was set; but Blake's Claudes made sunshine in that shady place' (*Letters*, p. 573).

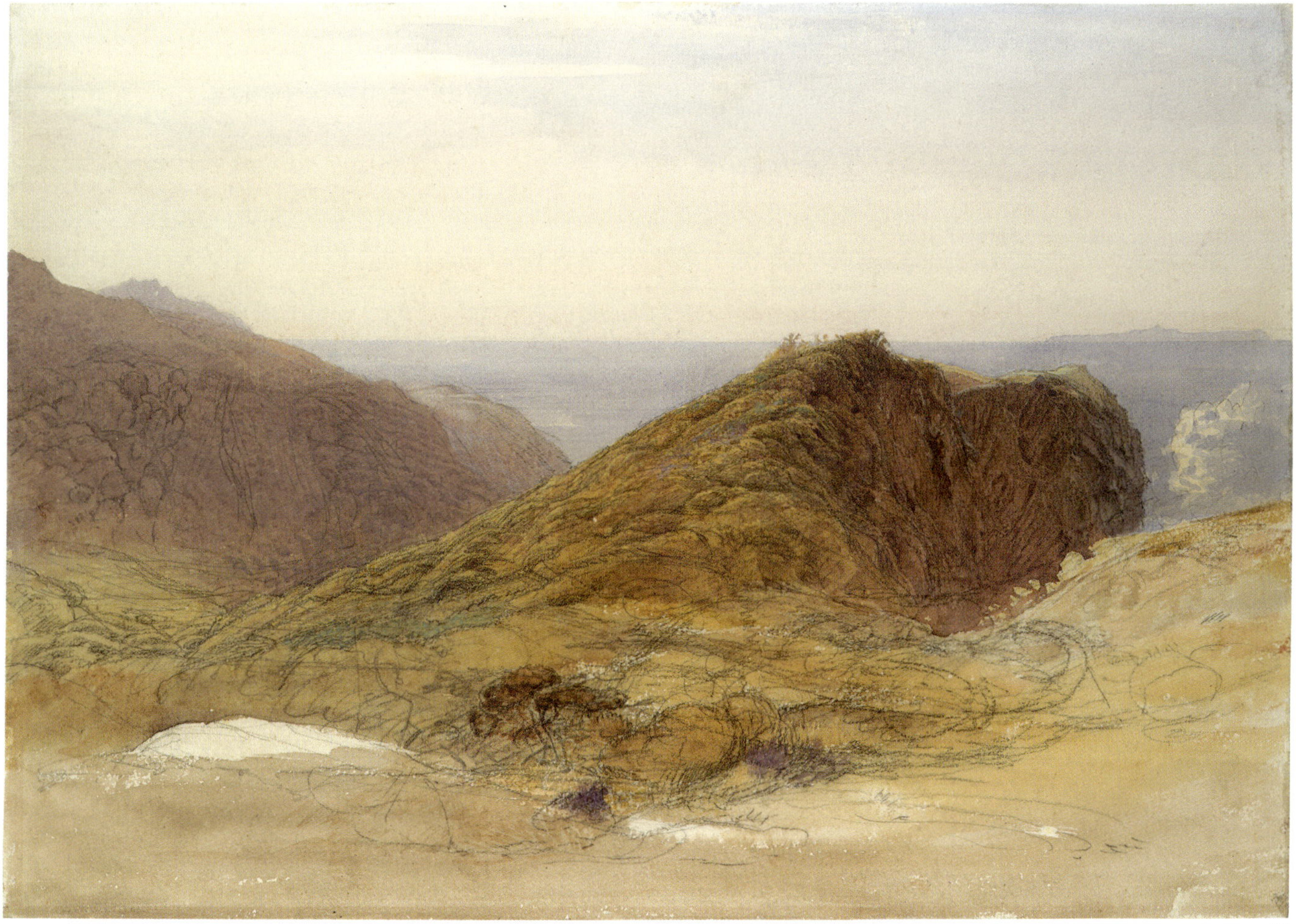

98

## 98

*On the North Coast of Devon, Lundy Island in the Distance*, 1835

Watercolour, gouache, black chalk and graphite on off-white wove paper, 27.1 × 38 cm (10¾ × 15 in)

Lit: Lister 217

New York, The Metropolitan Museum of Art, 1970.178; Rogers Fund, 1970

Fresh and energetic, abbreviated and extravagant by turns, this expressive watercolour proclaims the process of its creation. Light notations in graphite and black chalk establish the profiles of the hills and surface of the sea; watercolour washes of yellow, brown, blue, green and purple (a distinctive shade that Palmer may have mixed himself) refine the forms. In the central areas, such as the golden promontory in the middle of the scene, layers of watercolour combine with passages of black chalk to yield rich textural effects. In the distance, looser notations form the cool-toned hill, and smoothly blended washes of pale colour describe a luminous sky. In the foreground, areas of clean white paper contrast with strokes of watercolour dragged with a dry brush, and animated passages of black chalk re-inscribe the spontaneous quality of the initial sketch onto the finished work.

Palmer took this view from Clovelly, looking north-west across Barnstaple or Bideford Bay: Lundy Island's long profile marks the right edge of the horizon. He presumably made it, perhaps in more than one sitting, during a visit to 'dear, spongy Devon' in 1834 or early 1835 (*Letters*, p. 712). The style reflects the transitional date: the vibrant palette and near-obsessive attention to selected details associated with his earlier work here serve a naturalistic vision. Palmer's 'intense love of Devonshire' – his mature ideal of British landscape – inspired numerous subsequent visits (*Letters*, p. 14). Indeed, the artist defined his 'habitable latitudes' as those found 'south of the railings of Hyde Park' with 'their kernel in Devonshire' (*L&L*, p. 56).

## 99

### *A Study at Tintern – Drawn on the Spot*, 1835

Brown ink, watercolour, gouache, graphite and black chalk on off-white paper toned pinkish-brown (originally grey), 37.2 × 47.5 cm (14¾ × 18¾ in)

Lit: Brown 23; Fitzwilliam 1984, 32; Lister 232; Harrison 22; Woof and Hebron 1998, no. 114

Inscribed in brown ink at lower left side: *Weir End*; at lower left: *A / In one part of the wall the interstices had been fill'd with mortar so that the breadth of stones / and of mortar between were of the same colour – there was a gradation from the marked divisions / to a mingling together in which the distinctions of stones were almost lost* –; at lower right in graphite: *45*

Oxford, Ashmolean Museum, 1939.75; purchased 1939

On 19 August 1835 Palmer wrote to Richmond from Tintern Abbey, Monmouthshire, near the English border with Wales, 'a nook', he described, for which he 'would give all the Welch mountains, grand as they are' (*Letters*, p. 71). The opinion was not unusual: artists and tourists had long admired the Wye Valley and visited its celebrated picturesque ruins – Tintern Abbey, Goodrich Castle and Chepstow Castle (Woof and Hebron 1998, pp. 103–7). Yet if Palmer's destination was conventional, his response to Tintern was strikingly original.

The artist selected for his subject not the typical distant ruin framed by trees but a close-up view of an overgrown garden beside a modest house. Palmer evidently searched for the forms, discovering them as he drew. He initially sketched the roofline higher and wider across the sheet, then changed his mind, and covered the discarded marks with pale blue wash. He elaborated his initial sketch selectively, developing the central areas – the fig tree growing against the wall, the pink blossom of the hollyhocks, the dark interiors glimpsed through windows and doors – with touches of yellow, green, pink, white and brown. The design becomes freer at the edges, where large, looping squiggles trace the lower right and upper left corners of the scene. In the foreground wall expressive lines of brown ink describe each stone, and a diluted application of white gouache completes the cell-like structure.

Palmer may well have referred to this garden in his letter to Richmond: 'Hard by, I saw a man this evening literally "sitting under his own fig tree" whose broad leaves mixed with holyoaks and other rustic garden flowers embower'd his porch' (*Letters*, p. 71). Palmer's biblical quotation (Micah 4: 4) refers to the peace of the kingdom of God. But the artist's own experiences in Wales would end on a discordant note. Palmer's letter to Richmond concludes with a plea for the loan of 3 pounds to convey him home:

> Poetic vapours have subsided and the sad realities of life blot the field of vision – the burthen of the theme is a

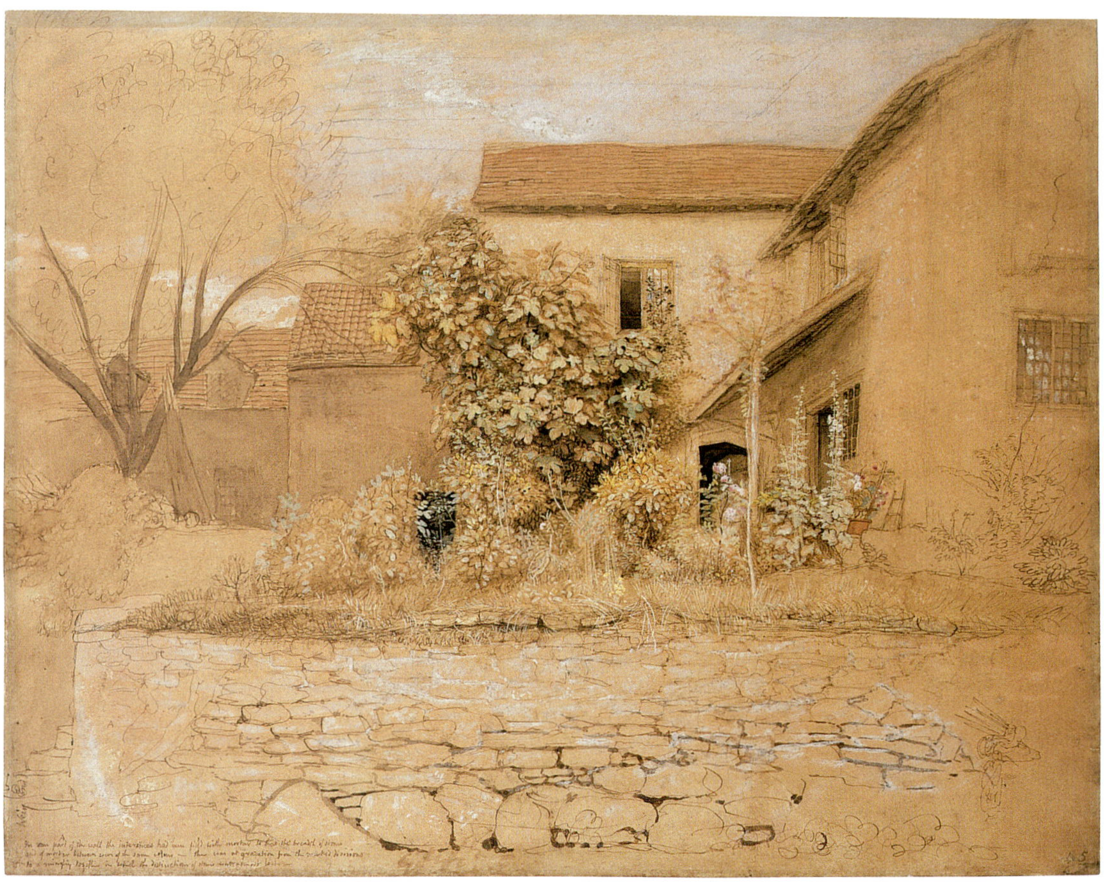

99

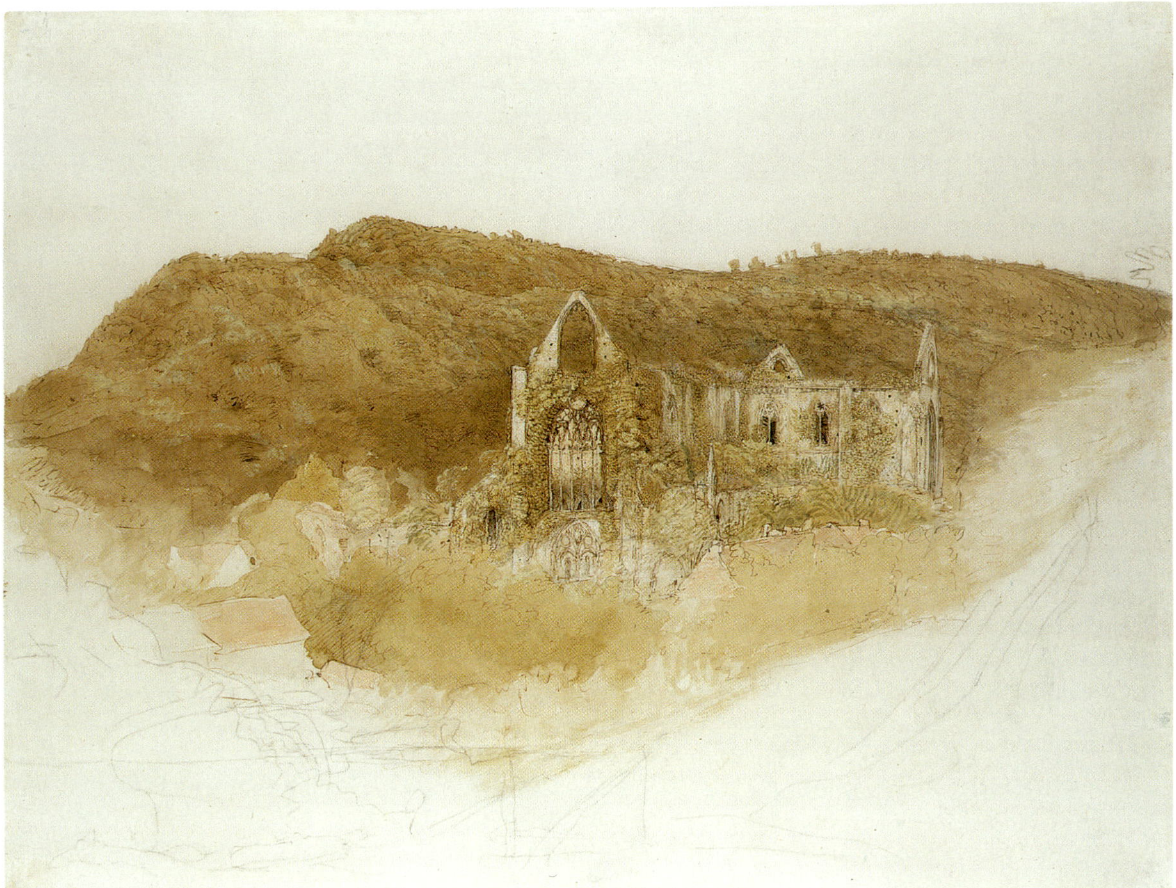

100

heavy one I have not cash enough to carry me to London – O miserable poverty! how it wipes the bloom from everything around me. Had I conceived how much it would cost I would as soon have started for the United States as Wales (*Letters*, p. 72).

Fortunately, Richmond, who had received a loan of 40 pounds from Palmer when he needed it most (to elope with Julia Tatham in 1831), did not hesitate to help (*Richmond Papers*, p. 32).

**100**

*Tintern Abbey*, 1835

Watercolour, gouache, brown ink and black chalk on white laid paper, 36.8 × 48.6 cm (14½ × 19⅛ in)

Lit: Lister 233; Woof and Hebron 1998, no. 112

London, Victoria and Albert Museum, 1902-1919

Palmer's 1835 letter from Tintern (*Letters*, pp. 71–3) includes a rapturous description of the local landmark: 'such an Abbey! the highest Gothic; trellised with ivy, and rising from a wilderness of orchards, and set like a gem amongst the folding of woody hills' (*Letters*, p. 71). Palmer made four studies of the late thirteenth-century Cistercian ruin (Lister 233–6), three of which are known. The present drawing shows the south-west view, the tracery of the west front's central window framed by ivy, and the Wye river (out of sight) behind. As with other studies from about this time, Palmer enriched central areas of the sheet while leaving outer portions unembellished. The sketch at the base remains undeveloped, but the middle and upper portions of the design have been progressively worked: washes of pink and green distinguish roofs and foliage, lines of brown ink elaborate architectural details, and a pale grey tone designates the sky.

In 1783 William Gilpin had teasingly proposed the 'judicious' use of a mallet to remove the 'disagreeable' gable-ends that 'confound the perspective' in the abbey's cross aisles (Gilpin 1783, pp. 32–3.) But Palmer took a nostalgic view, more in the spirit of Wordsworth's 'Lines composed a few miles above Tintern Abbey' (Woof and Hebron 1998, pp. 103–7). Palmer revelled in the unclassical architecture, lingering over the slight asymmetry of the tracery as if to emphasize its Gothic craftsmanship and the passage of time. He expressed his fondness for such qualities in his letter: 'I feel here a most grateful relaxation and am become once more a pure quaint crinkle-crankle goth – If you are a Goth come hither, if you're a pure Greek take a cab and make a sketch of St. Paul's Covent Garden before Breakfast' (*Letters*, p. 71).

## 101

### *Conwy Castle, North Wales*, 1835?

Black chalk, watercolour, wash and gouache on light brown paper laid down onto a buff board support, 32.7 × 45.5 cm ($12\frac{7}{8}$ × 18 in), irregular

Inscribed at lower right in brown ink: *Conway Castle from near the Old Llanrwst Road – North Wales.*; at lower left in black chalk: *N.B. central mass with ye same gradg – relatively a little dark –*; on the tree at centre left: *Ivy no line to repeat [those of ye towers?]*; to left of tree: *thick wall*

Lit: Lister 271

New Haven, Yale Center for British Art, Paul Mellon Collection, B1977.14.5969

The design is focused like a lens or a view glimpsed in a Claude glass, or diminishing mirror (p. 37), with its richly coloured, comparatively detailed central object encircled by looser sketches. Nestled by trees and houses, Conwy Castle in North Wales rises from a broad landscape before a blue river and purple hills. In the foreground on the left descriptive texts inscribed on the relevant areas of the design record effects that Palmer did not have the time or inclination to draw: ivy climbing a tree trunk and a thick stone wall. A faint sketch on the right indicates a stand of trees; a brief line indicated by an arrow marks a point at which to crop the design.

Few of Palmer's extant Welsh landscapes can be dated with certainty: four are signed and dated 1835; none are dated 1836 (from north to south, Lister 225, 226, 230, 231; Lister 276 is inexplicably inscribed '5 July 1837', although the artist is not known to have visited Wales in that year). Given its somewhat tentative handling, the present sheet may well date to the earlier tour of 1835.

## 102

### *Moel Siabod from Tyn-y-Coed*, 1835 or 1836

Watercolour, gouache, brown ink and graphite on brown paper, 37.8 × 47.6 cm ($14\frac{7}{8}$ × $18\frac{3}{4}$ in)

Inscribed at lower right in brown ink over graphite in Palmer's hand: *Mount Siabod from Tyn-y-Coed near Capel Curig. on the Road to Bettws-y-Coed.*; in graphite at lower right of verso: *97*

Lit: Lister 254

New Haven, Yale Center for British Art, Paul Mellon Collection, B1977.14.5967

In his 1835 letter from Wales (*Letters*, pp. 71–3) Palmer lamented the fine, unromantic weather of his mountain tour:

> Our Ossian Sublimities are ended – and with a little more of McPhersons

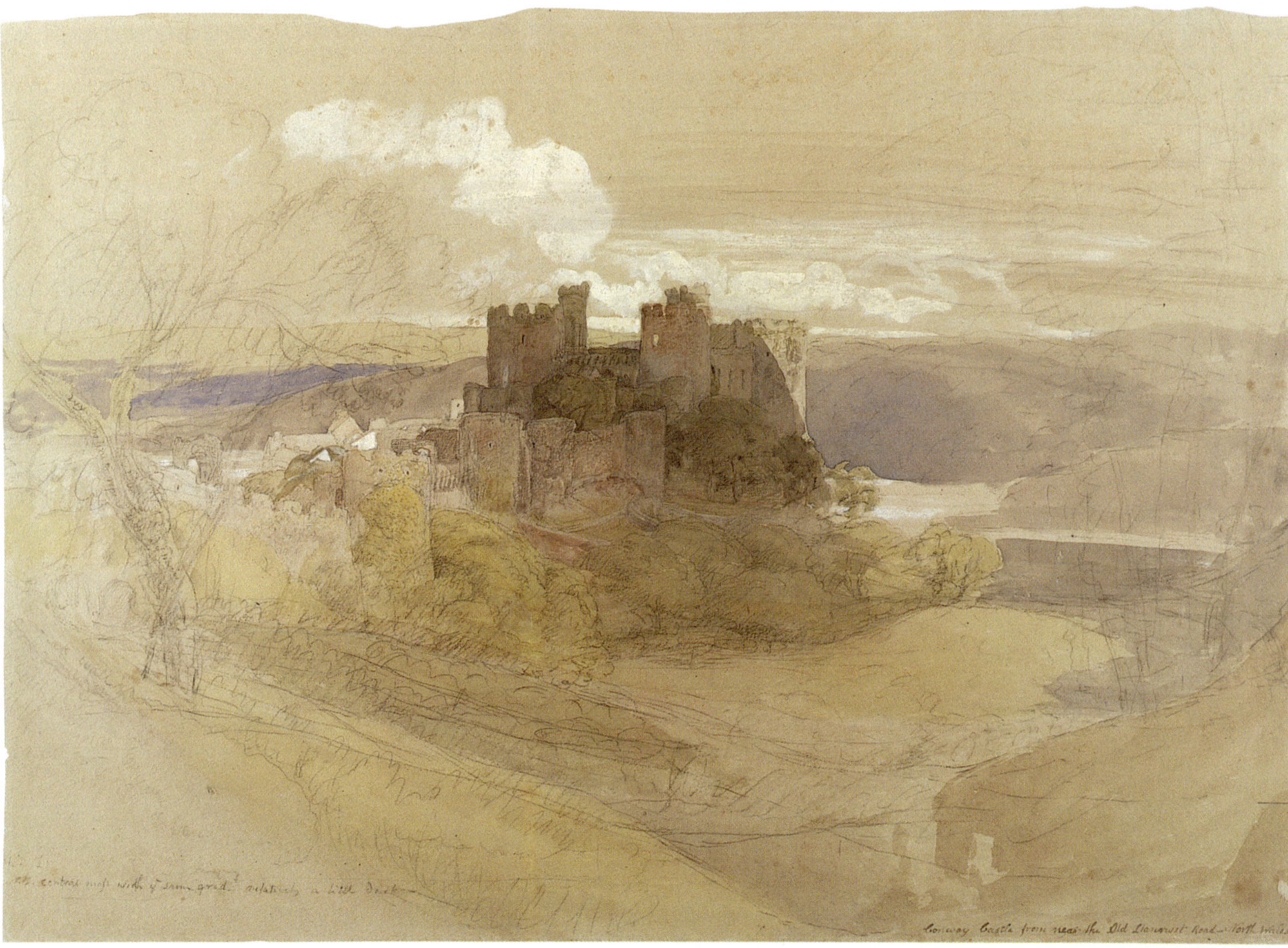

101

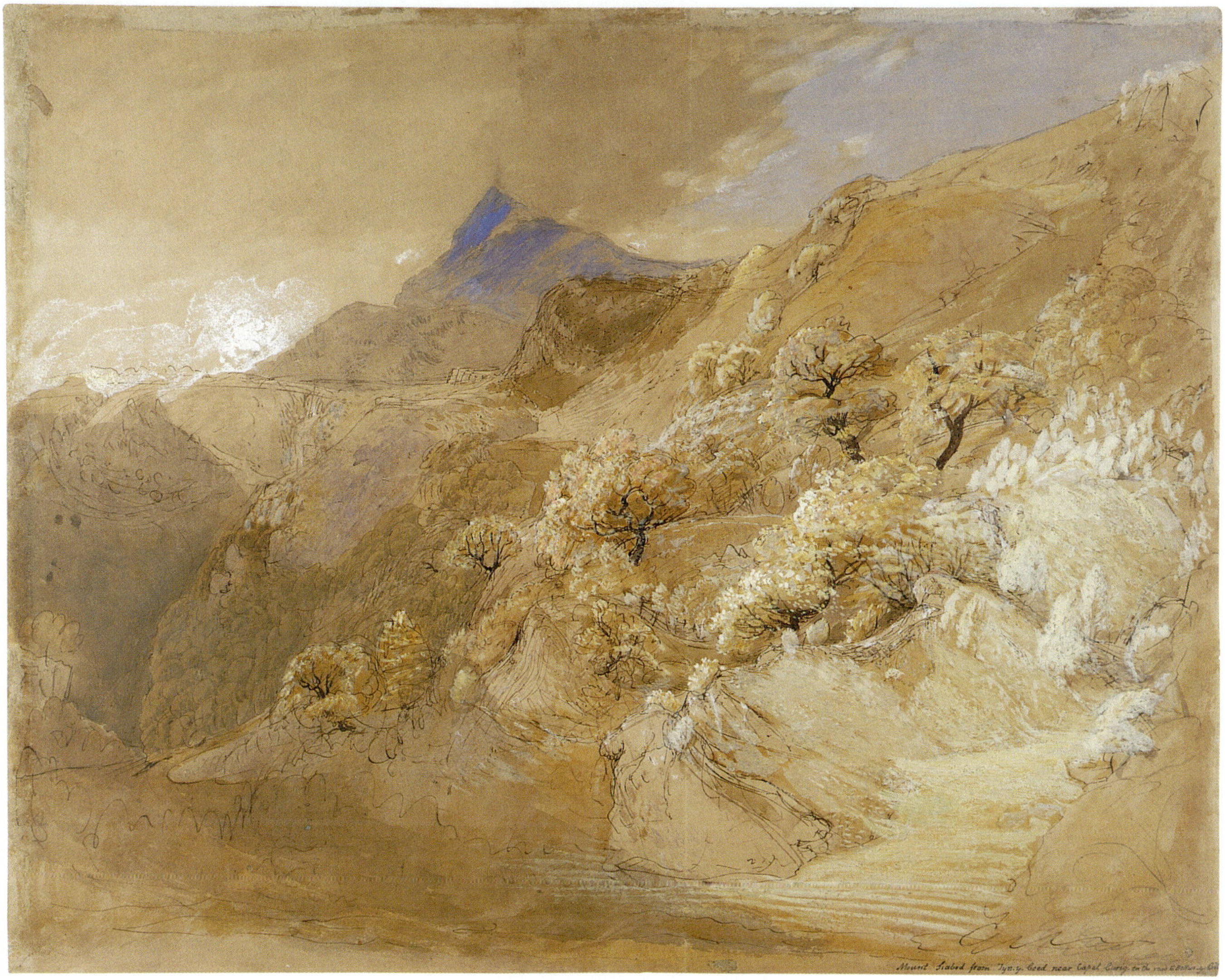

102

> mist and vapour, we should have had much more successful sketching – but unfortunately when we were near Snowdon we had white light days on which we could count the stubbs and stones some miles off – we had just a glimpse or two one day thro' the chasms of stormy cloud which was sublime. (*Letters*, p. 71.)

Here, Palmer captured the clear view of another mountain in northern Snowdonia: Moel Siabod. It looms above the viewer, who seems to stand at its base, assessing the climb towards the bright blue peak. Palmer sketched the view in graphite, then elaborated the forms with animated dashes, dots and squiggles of ink, watercolour and relatively dry gouache. Swooping lines and tiny points of brown ink shape the contours of the hill; purple-grey washes convey passages of shadow. The manner of describing the trees recalls the Shoreham period: curving pen strokes form the trunks and branches, and dabs of white, yellow, pink and grey complete the foliage.

Palmer's astute critic, Geoffrey Grigson, found such studies deeply personal, 'struck out in a quick, masterly way, but embodying, as Constable's pictures so often do, a sense of uneasiness and disturbance'. Grigson continued: 'These [Welsh] watercolours show a direct, untainted grasp of nature, but they are a nature without paradise, and they are what Palmer called "a batch of imitation," material to be worked up' (Grigson 1947, p. 132). No highly finished versions of the present subject, however, are known, perhaps because the artist found such outdoor sketches difficult to translate. Indeed, by 1838 Palmer had come to regard his Welsh studies as 'unworkable'; to correct the unmediated quality that he regarded as their flaw, Palmer in his later (Italian) sketches often added to nature 'on the spot' (*Letters*, p. 256).

## 103

### *A Cascade in Shadow, Drawn on the Spot, near the Junction of the Machno and Conway, North Wales*, 1836?

Watercolour, gouache, graphite and brown ink, 46.4 × 37.5 cm (18¼ × 14¾ in)

Inscribed at lower left with point of brush: *No 7 / Samuel Palmer*; at lower centre, partly obscured: *Cascade … at the junction of the rivers … Machno, Wales*

Lit: Lister 241; Libson 1990, p. 29; Leger Galleries 1992, no. 5; Lyles and Wilton 1993, no. 226

Malcolm Wiener Collection

A.H. Palmer described his father's Welsh waterfall studies as 'elaborate and true to nature', and recalled: 'His soul was in this work; he rejoiced in the rugged beauty of wild, impetuous currents, no less than in the still translucent depths; and held that a landscape, however lovely, was never perfect without at least some glint of water' (*Memoir*, p. 9). In the present work Palmer enlivened a *plein air* pen sketch with watercolour, ink and gouache to capture the changing effects of a cascade and pool, still and rushing water in sunlight and shadow. The site can be identified as the Fairy (or Fairies') Glen (also called Ffos Noddum or Foss Nevin), a celebrated beauty spot on the Conwy River, about two miles south of the village of Betws-y-Coed.

By the time of Palmer's visits to Wales in 1835 and 1836 the area around Betws-y-Coed, which offered ready access to the Conwy, Lledr and Llugwy river valleys and to Snowdonia, was known to artists (Lord 2000, p. 281). During the Victorian era it would become one of the most popular destinations in all of Wales (Roscoe 1844; Lord 1998, p. 37). By 1860, when James Bridge Davidson published Roger Fenton's stereograph of the site, the Fairy Glen had become a favourite spot of visiting artists: 'in summer … a troop of artists … take up various positions on the rocks, and enliven their labours with occasional chants, and other vocal efforts more or less amusing' (Daniel 2004, pp. 44–5, figs 27–8). Greater numbers arrived following the extension of the railway to Betws-y-Coed in 1868, prompting the Voelas Estate (which owned the property) to install a turnstile and charge admission to the Fairy Glen (Lord 1998, pp. 69, 71). By the time *The Gossiping Guide to Wales* (1872) described it as a 'spot that might well be transferred to canvas', the practice had become commonplace (Lord 1998, p. 171 n. 197).

Palmer, however, arrived before the hoards. He probably visited the area in 1835 and certainly did so in 1836, when in late May or early June he drafted a letter listing his return address as 'at Mrs. Elinor Roberts's not Roberts', Betwys-y-Coed, Near Llanwrst – By Corwen, North Wales' (*Letters*, p. 1093). Palmer's known interest in sketching waterfalls during this second tour and the technical proficiency of the present work suggest a date of 1836.

Significantly, this watercolour cannot be identified with any of the finished views of waterfalls in North Wales that Linnell assisted Palmer in selling in 1838 (*Letters*, pp. 98–9, 115, 135, 145–6, 205). Instead, the artist kept it in his own collection 'for reference' until at least 1871, when he appears to have sold it to his important patron, Leonard Rowe Valpy, for 80 guineas (*Letters*, p. 829; *Memoir*, no.77, p. 102).

The 'No 7' inscribed at the bottom of the sheet links *A Cascade in Shadow* to a series of large-scale views of North Wales, of which six others (bearing numbers between twelve and twenty-nine) are known (Lister 230, 270, 272, 256, 252 and 223).

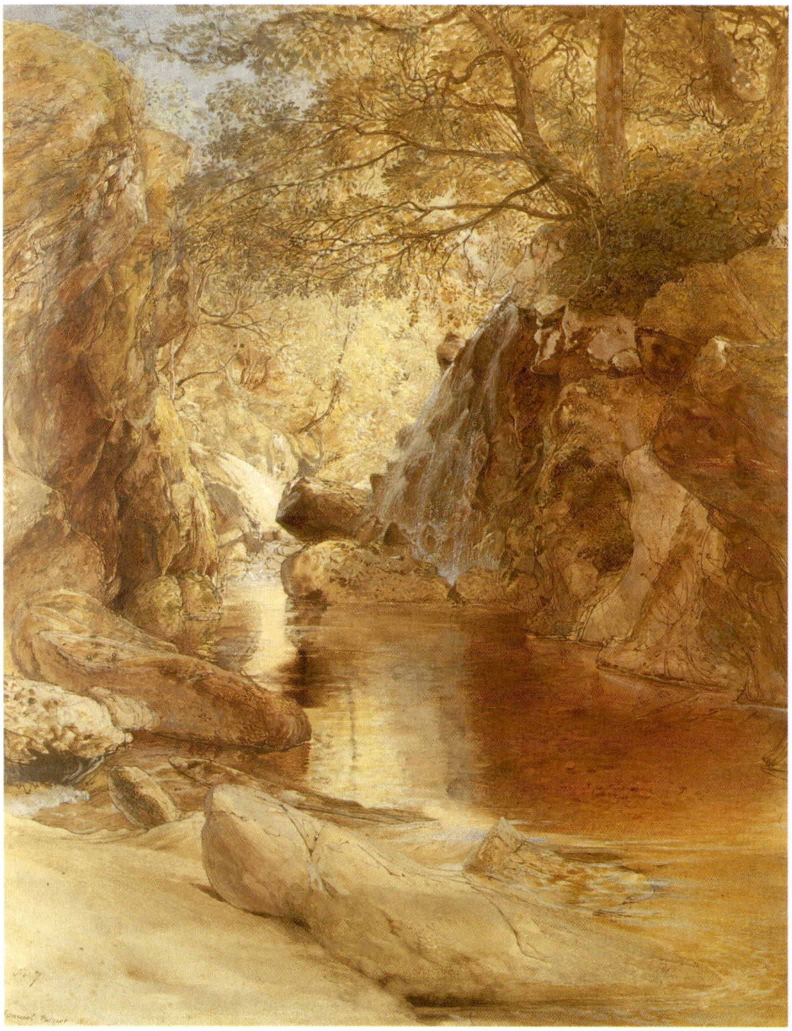

103

# 6. Italy (1837–40)

*Elizabeth E. Barker*

Every landscape painter should see Italy. It enlarges his idea of creation ... he sees the sun and air as fresh as from the hand of their maker.
Samuel Palmer to Elizabeth Linnell, July 14, 1838 (*Letters*, p. 155)

The year 1837 began on a sad note: on 18 January, the nineteenth anniversary of Palmer's mother's death, the artist's beloved childhood nurse, Mary Ward, died (*Letters*, p. 82). Yet the year would also bring happiness. On 30 September Palmer married Hannah Linnell, the eldest of John Linnell's nine children, in a civil marriage ceremony (upon which Linnell insisted) at the Marylebone Registrar's Office. Despite the difference in their ages – Samuel was thirty-two, Hannah just nineteen – the couple were well matched. As a child, Hannah listened to Blake's stories and learned the fundamentals of art from her father. As an adult, 'Anny' – whom Palmer teasingly called 'Bantam' for her small size, or the 'Head of the House' to his own 'Tail' (*Letters*, pp. 567, 857) – expressed a wide-ranging curiosity and passionate enthusiasm similar to her husband's (*Letters*, p. 74 n. 3, actually from 1836). Their long marriage, although marked by the tragic loss of two children and the burden of Palmer's debilitating asthma, would be characterized by mutual kindness and affection (*Letters*, p. 462; *Memoir*, p. 37).

On 4 October the newlyweds departed for Italy in the company of George and Julia Richmond, and their four-year old son Tommy (Thomas Knyvett Richmond, later Canon of Carlisle). Palmer had long dreamed of seeing Italy; he was fortunate to have the opportunity to travel when he did. After the defeat of Napoleon in 1815 the journey had become less expensive, less arduous and (following recent French excavations) more revealing than ever before. Palmer was also fortunate to have Richmond as his friend; the younger artist generously loaned Palmer £300 to undertake the trip.

The Palmers departed with a sense of excitement. But the bride's parents feared the dangers – unsanitary food, unheated lodgings, cholera, Roman Catholicism, *banditi*, volcanic eruptions – and begged the young couple to write to them every fortnight. In the resulting correspondence (cited frequently in the following pages) the young artists documented the trip in their own refreshingly direct language.

The Palmers travelled from London to Calais and spent a week in Paris (where they admired Veronese's *Marriage at Cana*, 1562–3, and paintings by Titian and Giorgione in the Louvre), before passing through Lausanne and over the Simplon Pass to Lake Maggiore. After three days in Milan (where they saw Leonardo's *Last Supper*, *c.*1495–7) they headed south, through Parma and Bologna, over the Apennines to Florence, where they rested for four days (visiting the Duomo, Santa Croce, Santissima Annunziata, the Baptistry and the Uffizi Gallery), before continuing to Rome, which they reached in mid-November. They spent the following winter there – painting, reading Bulwer-Lytton's *The Last Days of Pompeii* (1834) and meeting other expatriot artists, including Joseph Severn, John Gibson, Penry Williams, Thomas Dessoulavy and William Collins (*Letters*, p. 143).

In May (when the Richmonds returned to Florence) the Palmers, loaded with painting gear, travelled to Naples, where they encountered the painters Edward Lear and Thomas Uwins. They spent July in Pompeii, where they witnessed a minor eruption of Vesuvius – and where they resisted the temptation to pocket a few antique 'souvenirs' (*Letters*, p. 151). They passed the hot months of August and September sketching in Torre Annunziata, Salerno and Corpo di Cava – where they met the

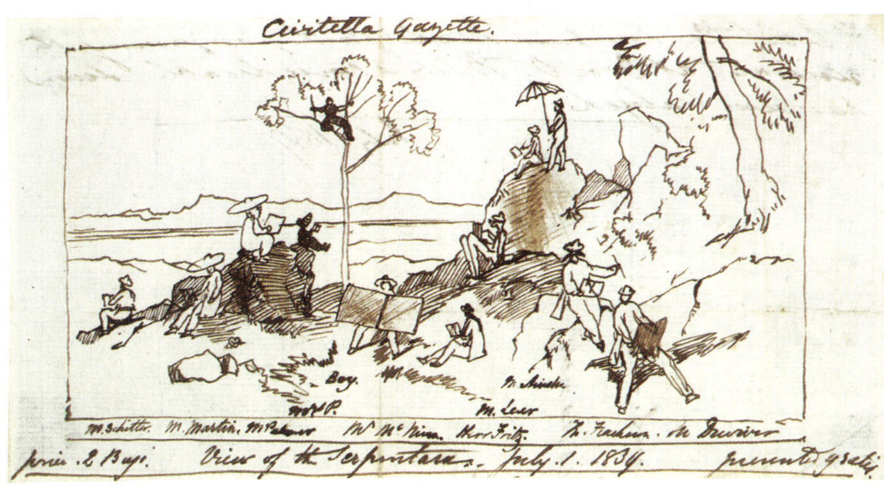


Fig. 27 Penry Williams (1798–1885), *Civitella Gazette: View of the Serpentara, July 1, 1839*, pen and brown ink, British Museum.

artist John Frederick Lewis – before returning to Naples, visiting Pausillippo and reaching Rome in late October. Following a brief excursion to Pozzuoli, they spent most of November and December working in Tivoli, then passed January to May 1839, as they had the previous winter, in Rome. There they prepared paintings for the Roman exhibition, read Lady Morgan's *Life of Salvator Rosa* (1824), saw – but did not enjoy – Donizetti's *Roberto Devereux o il Conte di Essex* (1837), learned of the invention of the daguerreotype and met up with Albin Martin, a pupil of Linnell who would become their frequent companion (*Letters*, pp. 284, 333, 291 n. 1, 304).

In the summer they finally turned towards the north and home, visiting Subiaco and Civitella in June and July. There Palmer suffered in an attempt to give up snuff, and Penry Williams captured them at work amid other artists: Samuel in a hat and spectacles on the crest of a rock, Hannah in her bonnet perched nearby, and Albin Martin seated below (fig. 27; *Letters*, p. 356). They visited Papignia and Terni in August, and spent September and October in Florence. By late November 1839 they had returned to England, stopping on the way to sketch the Château de Polignac, near Le Puy, France.

Throughout this period of almost daily practice and her husband's tutelage, Hannah Palmer's skills as a draughtswoman and watercolour painter grew by leaps and bounds. Samuel Palmer's art, likewise, was transformed by his experiences abroad. Brilliant southern sunlight inspired a more vibrant – initially somewhat garish – palette. Broad Italian views prompted larger designs, rendered in more complex perspective. Various sites and motifs – from the Colosseum to cypress trees – provided the staffage of Palmer's later idyllic landscapes.

## 104

### *The Colosseum and the Arch of Constantine from the Palatine, Rome, c.*1837–9

Watercolour and graphite, 13.7 × 27.9 cm (5 3/8 × 11 in)

Lit: Fitzwilliam 1984, 37; Lister 321

Tate, T01008; presented by the National Art Collections Fund (Herbert Powell Bequest), 1967

In October 1838 Palmer wrote of the Eternal City:

> Rome is a thing by itself which, once seen, leaves the memory no more – a city of Art which one has dreamed of before, and can scarce believe one has really seen with these ocular jellies – to which London seems a warehouse, Paris a trinket-shop. What must it have been in its antique glory? (*Letters*, p. 233.)

Among the ancient sites that vied for a visitor's attention, the massive, august Colosseum offered a striking mix of ancient violence and modern Christianity. (At the time of the Palmers' visit the Colosseum had been consecrated by Pope Benedict XIV and displayed the Stations of the Cross.) The Palmers must have sought it out early in their Italian sojourn and seen much of it during their prolonged stays in Rome. In keeping with a favourite practice of the period, they planned to visit it by moonlight, which they had been told 'is a fine sight with the torches. It is a splendid thing by daylight and quite strikes you with awe when you approach it' (*Letters*, p. 120; Powell 1998, p. 33).

In this fresh study, evidently sketched on the spot, Palmer captured the view of the Colosseum from the south in early afternoon. The panoramic proportions of this sheet – approximately twice as long as it is high – distinguish it from Palmer's earlier drawings, and herald what would become a standard format for the artist's mature work. (For Palmer's 'little long', 'middle long' and 'large long' sizes, see p. 192.)

## 105a*

### *A View of Modern Rome*, 1838

Watercolour, gouache and graphite on buff paper laid down on board, 40.9 × 57.8 cm (16 × 22 3/4 in)

Signed and dated at lower right (in gold): *Samuel Palmer Rome / 1838*

Lit: Fitzwilliam 1984, 36; Powell 1987, pp. 182–5; Lister 285; Liversidge and Edwards 1996, no. 29; Powell 1998, pp. 13–14

Birmingham City Museums and Art Galleries, P16'46; purchased (Feeny Charitable Trust), 1946

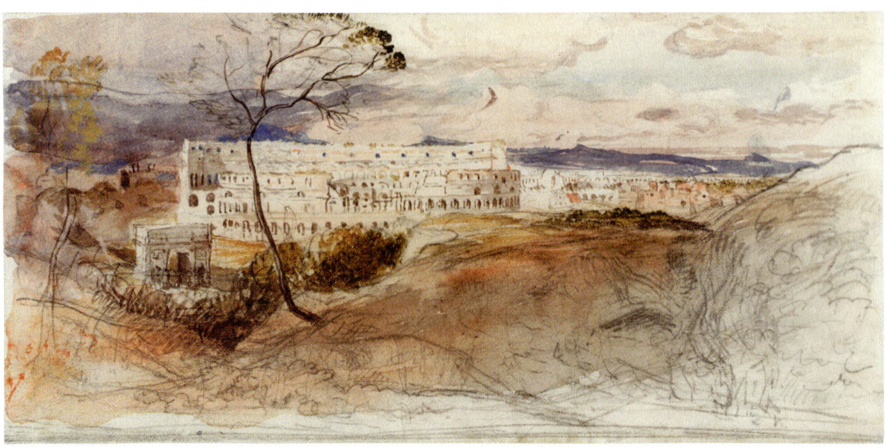

104

## 105b

### *A View of Ancient Rome*, 1838

Watercolour, gouache and graphite on buff paper laid down on board, 41.1 × 57.8 cm (16¼ × 22¾ in)

Lit: Fitzwilliam 1984, 35; Powell 1987, pp. 182–5; Lister 288; Wildman 1991, no. 83; Liversidge and Edwards 1996, no. 30; Powell 1998, p. 26

Birmingham City Museums and Art Galleries, P15'46; purchased (Feeny Charitable Trust), 1946

On 25 March 1838 Palmer wrote to Linnell from Rome with news of an ambitious project:

> I have spent much time on a finished drawing rather more than two feet long of Modern Rome during the carnival with Bacchic Masquers and a car covered with garlands for the foreground. What I thought necessary to be introduced or composed I did on the spot while the impression of the whole was fresh – and spent on it the last degree of pains and study of which I was capable. (*Letters*, p. 124.)

George Richmond kindly brought this drawing to the attention of a potential patron: John Baring, a British visitor to Italy seeking views of ancient and modern Rome to give his father, the banker and amateur artist, Sir Thomas Baring, 2nd Baronet. Carrying the watercolour to the site from which Palmer had taken his view – the fashionable terraced gardens of the Pincian Hill (completed in 1834) – Richmond and Baring were surprised to find that Palmer had introduced into his drawing 'more matter than could be seen from any one station', although all could be discerned by 'moving a few yards to the right or left' (*Letters*, p. 124).

This strategy allowed Palmer to include virtually every notable sight. At the left the twin churches of S. Maria di Montesanto and S. Maria dei Miracoli flank the Via del Corso, where riderless horses race on a track erected for carnival. Behind them the Castel Sant' Angelo and St Peter's Cathedral rise in the south-west. Before them the Obelisk of Ramses II marks the centre of the oval Piazza del Popolo; modern hemicycles (erected during Giuseppe Valadier's 1816–24 redesign of the piazza) and the Porta del Popolo complete its boundaries. Baring and Richmond, familiar with the distinguished tradition of *veduti ideali*, approved of the composite view – indeed, Richmond pronounced that no one 'but Turner could have treated the subject so well' (*Letters*, p. 124).

*Modern Rome* bears little resemblance to Palmer's previous work. Its scale, complexity and high-keyed palette suggest a response to the light and monuments of Italy, and to Veronese's *Marriage at Cana*, which had overwhelmed Palmer in the Louvre with its 'highest key of light' and 'purest brilliancy of colour' (*Letters*, p. 213). *Modern Rome*'s uniform attention to detail, moreover, marks a clear departure from Palmer's 'unworkable' Welsh sketches (*Letters*, p. 256). By contrast to those unsaleable works, this watercolour attracted a buyer: Baring commissioned a duplicate of *Modern Rome* (private collection, Lister 286) for 40 guineas – a sizeable amount for Palmer, but one that Linnell thought undervalued by half (*Letters*, p.129 n. 5) Palmer immediately began to prepare a pendant, a process that proved a 'hard grapple' (*Letters*, pp. 127, 146).

To compose *Ancient Rome*, the artist integrated a series of south-eastern views from the Capitoline Hill, taken from the tower roof, window and adjoining alley of the Palazzo Senatorio (*Letters*, p. 257). After two or three days of 'intense suffering' – Palmer reported becoming 'so yellow and thin that I could pull out my waistcoat three inches from my body' (*Letters*, p. 146) – the painter emerged victorious. Whereas *Modern Rome* displays an uncertain relationship of foreground to background, and a central open space that inadvertently deflects attention to the margins, *Ancient Rome* presents a masterfully integrated composition that leads the eye along a deliberate path: past the Arch of Septimus Severus and dome of SS. Martina e Lucca (on the left) and the Temples of Saturn and Vespasian (on the right); across the Forum, marked by the Column of Phocas, Temple of Castor and Pollux, Arch of Titus and Arch of Constantine; towards the Colosseum and S. Giovanni in Laterano; as far as the aqueducts of the Campagna and snow-capped Alban Hills. Palmer described this watercolour, with its comparatively sober, predominately green palette (possibly inspired by Titian: *Letters*, p. 340), loose handling and simple foreground, as 'the most striking thing I have done' (*Letters*, p. 257).

Interestingly, in 1838 Turner exhibited in London *Modern Italy – the Pifferari* (Glasgow Art Gallery and Museum) and *Ancient Italy – Ovid Banished from Rome* (private collection, USA), followed in 1839 by *Ancient Rome; Agrippina Landing with the Ashes of Germanicus* (Tate) and *Modern Rome – Campo Vaccino* (Earl of Rosebery) (Butlin and Joll, nos 374, 375, 378, 379). Palmer learned of the Turners from the Linnells, and asked them how Turner had differentiated his subjects, but no reply is recorded (*Letters*, pp. 152, 372 n. 15). In fact, Turner's 'ancient' and 'modern' pendants are quite different from Palmer's, since they treat specific historical events, while Palmer's views show general incidents in contemporaneous settings. Palmer seems to have used 'ancient' and 'modern' in the manner of nineteenth-century travel-books: to refer to eras typically associated with specific sites, rather than to indicate the representation of particular historical moments (Powell 1987, pp.182–5).

Palmer's foreground figure groups, rather than his titles, seem to provide clearer indications of his meanings. In *Ancient Rome* figures descend solemnly by torchlight beneath the gaze of a single dove; in *Modern Rome* carnival revellers dance with sensual abandon. Palmer, a devout Anglican both attracted and repelled by the Roman Catholicism that he encountered in Italy (*Letters*, pp. 228–35), may have used the different groups to contrast the heroic struggle of the early Christian church with the debased pageantry of contemporary Catholicism.

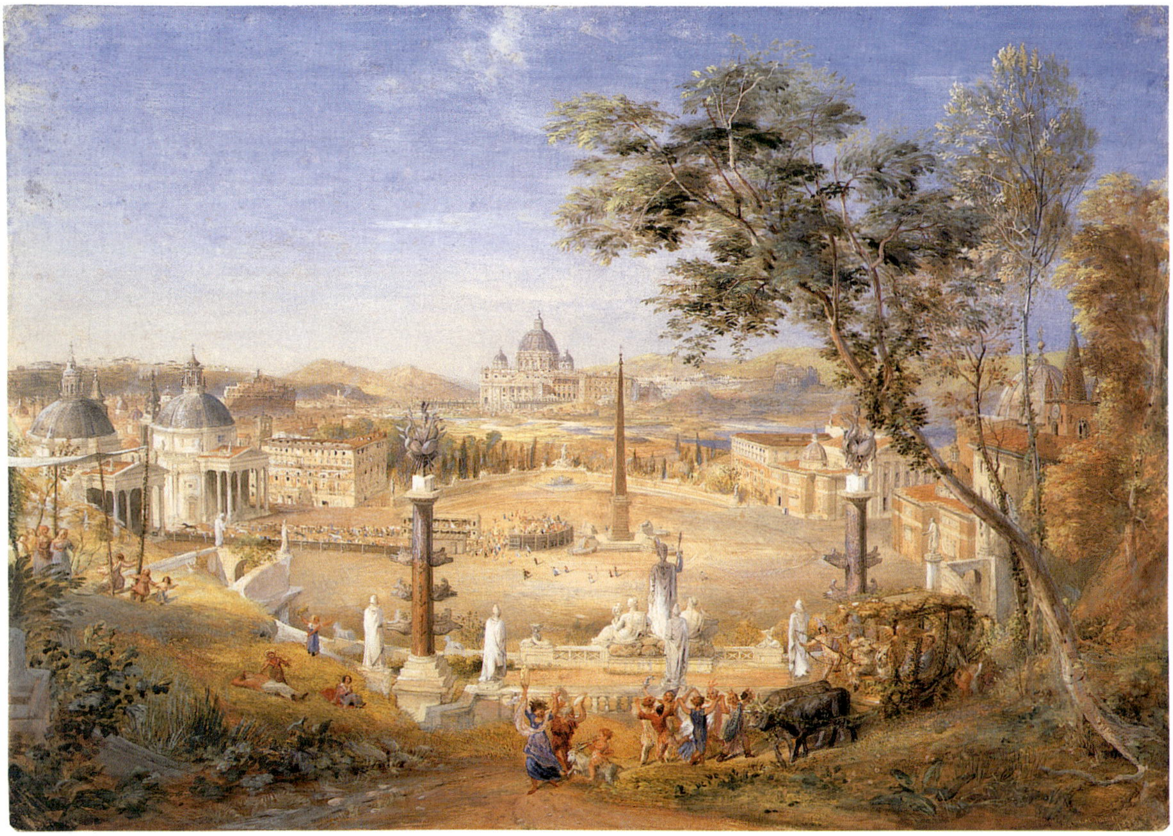

105a

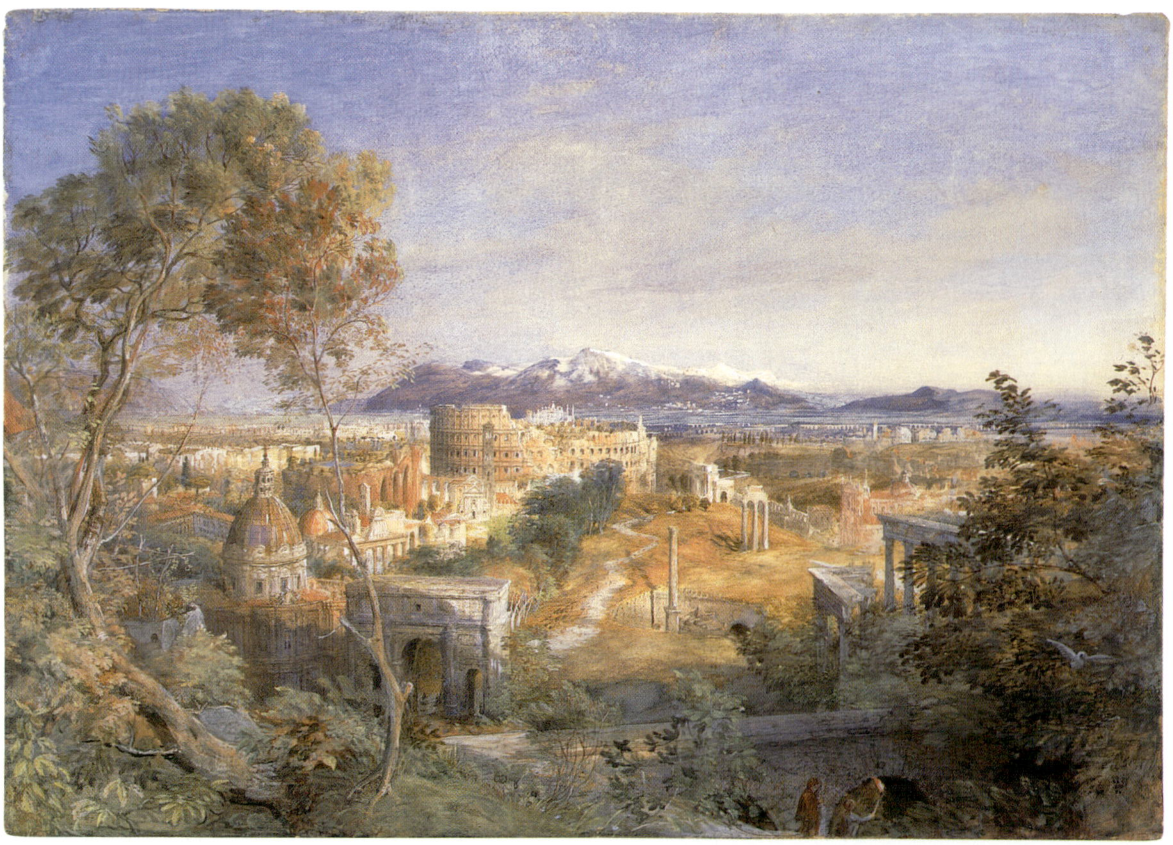

105b

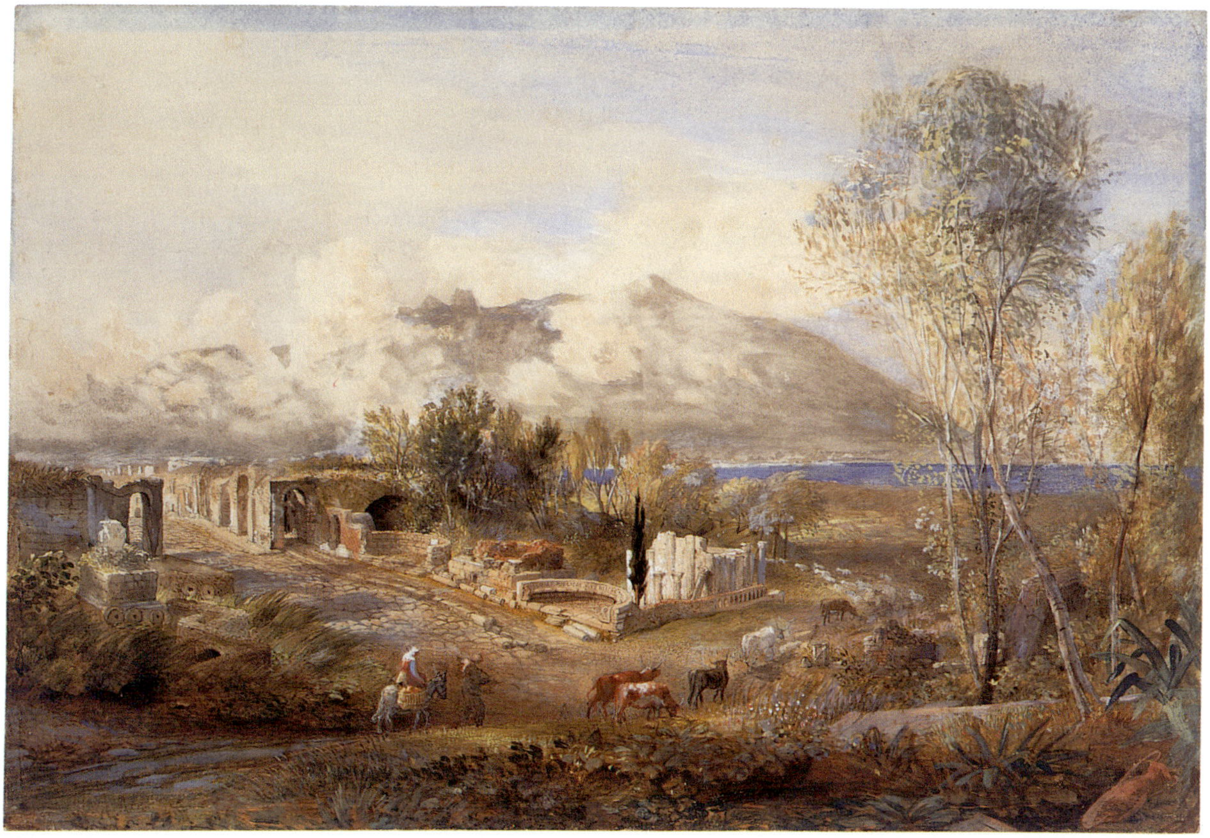

106

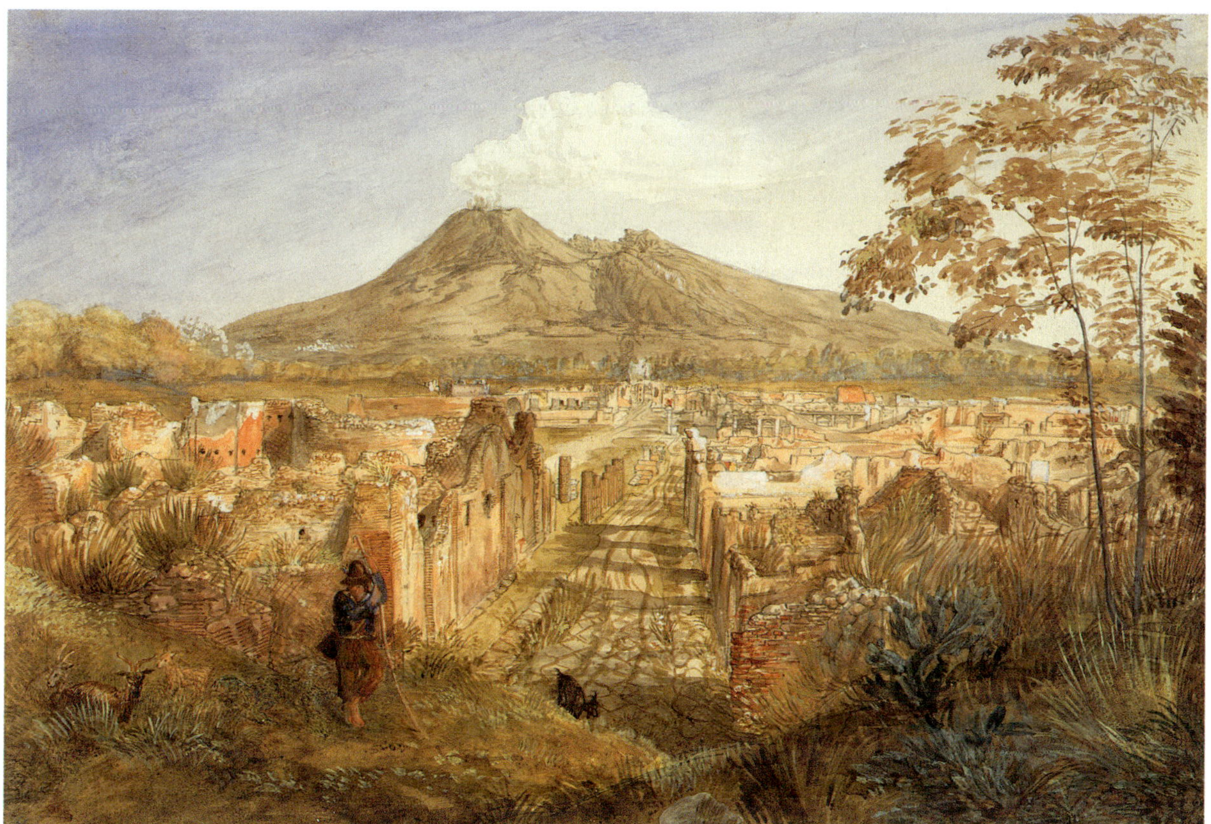

107

Palmer exhibited both views in the 1839 spring exhibition of the Accademia di San Luca in Rome. Yet despite their prominent location, side-by-side opposite the entrance, neither attracted a buyer (*Letters*, p. 270). (Baring purchased a pendant view of *Ancient Rome* from another, unidentified, artist.) More disappointing still, Baring's replica of *Modern Rome* would be the only commission that Palmer received during his entire Italian sojourn. Hannah Palmer's plan to etch these views, as part of a series of ten prints after her husband's Italian landscapes (also to include *Street of Tombs, Pompeii*, cat. 6.3), was never realized (*Letters*, p. 179).

## 106

### *Street of Tombs, Pompeii*, 1838

Watercolour, gouache, graphite and brown ink on card, 28.9 × 41.9 cm (11$^{3}/_{8}$ × 16$^{1}/_{2}$ in)

Inscribed in brown ink on the exedra: *MAMIAE PUBLICAE: V. VS BLICAE[?]*

Lit: V&A 1926, 126; Lister 305

London, Victoria and Albert Museum, P28-1919

In May 1838 the Palmers travelled to Naples. From their hotel – where Edward Lear and Thomas Uwins were also staying – they sketched the bay that 'filled up' their window, sparkling by moonlight 'like diamonds on ebony' (*Letters*, p. 217). In July the Palmers moved to Pompeii, where both Hannah and Samuel prepared five drawings of the city and the volcano that had simultaneously destroyed and preserved it in AD 79 (*Letters*, pp. 173, 190). At the end of their month-long stay a minor eruption of Vesuvius reminded them of Bulwer-Lytton's *The Last Days of Pompeii* (1834; *Letters*, p. 143). As Hannah recounted it, 'fearful rumblings' and 'dreadful noises like the discharge of cannon' had followed a nocturnal spectacle of 'vivid flame showering red hot stones which at that distance seemed like a fountain of sparks, and spreading out in fiery clouds' (*Letters*, p. 192).

Most of their Pompeian sojourn, however, was characterized by the 'deathly quiet and silence' of the ruins, where every structure carried morbidly romantic associations (*Letters*, p. 150). The Palmers particularly admired the Street of Tombs, and both made drawings of it (Hannah's: cat. 107). Samuel's large watercolour presents a crossroads near the Porta Ercolano. On the left the paved, empty Street of Tombs appears lined with ruins and barred with shadows. On the right rustic figures and cattle traverse a track leading to a grassy plain. At the intersection a single cypress grows between the exedra and colonnade of the tomb of the priestess Mamia. In the distance, beyond the blue strip of Castellamare, Vesuvius appears surrounded by clouds. The view recalls Bulwer-Lytton's description of the site:

> From the gate stretched the long street of tombs, various in size and architecture, by which, on that side, the city is as yet approached. Above all, rode the cloud-capped summit of the Dread Mountain, with the shadows, now dark, now light, betraying the mossy caverns and ashy rocks, which testified the past conflagrations, and might have prophesied – but man is blind – that which was to come! (Bulwer-Lytton, p. 135.)

Palmer exhibited a work entitled *Pompeii: The Street of the Tombs* in 1840 (RA no. 1005), possibly the present work (although Lister tentatively identified it as his 304). Palmer later adapted the central left portion of this design for the vignette illustration on the title page of Dickens's *Pictures from Italy* (cat. 110).

## 107

### Hannah Palmer (1818–93)

### *Street of Tombs, Pompeii*, 1838

Watercolour, gouache and graphite, 18.4 × 26.7 cm (7$^{1}/_{4}$ × 10$^{1}/_{2}$ in)

Signed in graphite at lower left: *Hannah Palmer*

Inscribed on the old mount in a twentieth-century hand: *By Hannah Palmer (then about 20 years old) Drawn on the spot; when she and her husband were living in Pompeii. See her signature / 121 / 0680*

Lit: V&A 1926, 43; Powell 1998, p. 29, fig. 12, no. 12; Agnew's 2004, no. 78

University of Wisconsin-Madison, Chazen Museum of Art; Edward Blake Blair Endowment Fund and Walter A. and Dorothy Jones Frautsch: Purchase Fund purchase, 200430

Hannah Palmer, like her husband, made five studies at Pompeii (*Letters*, p. 173). She ranked one of them among her best works (*Letters*, p. 275):

> It is twilight over Pompeii, looking up from one of the solemn streets with the moon just rising over the fine mountains of Cava and a bat wheeling his drowsy flight over the foreground – a few goats and a shepherd winding up a path finish this sketch, which much delighted me in nature. (*Letters*, p. 293.)

The present sheet, which shows the Street of Tombs approached by a goatherd with Vesuvius in the distance and was presumably made on the spot, gives some indication of that drawing's appearance. The cautious, unbroken graphite lines that describe the mountain's contours, the meticulously rendered foreground plants with their precise touches of colour, and the light, feathery trees in the right foreground all resemble other identified works by Hannah Palmer, such as *Below Papigno* (private collection) and *Bridge at Corpo di Cava* (Yale Center for British Art).

Hannah Palmer aspired to become, in her husband's words 'a fine original Artist', an achievement that he valued more highly 'than a whole Hogshead of other accomplishments' (*Letters*, p. 209). Admiring her ability 'to make really consistent, beautiful, and I think saleable drawings from nature', Samuel hoped that her supplementary income as a painter would provide her with 'many comforts and enjoyments' during their life together (*Letters*, pp. 209, 203). During their honeymoon the couple worked side-by-side in the field, hired a model for their shared use and took turns 'grinding colour and replenishing our [paint-]boxes' (*Letters*, pp. 283, 242); their letters mention plans for the arrangement of 'our' studio and public showroom upon their return to London (*Letters*, p. 159).

Although few of Hannah Palmer's post-Italian drawings have been identified, scattered references suggest that she continued to work following their return to England. She exhibited Italian landscapes at the British Institution in 1840, 1841 and 1842 – the last was only months after the birth of their first child, Thomas More (Graves 1908, p. 413). Later that same year Samuel refused his father's request to lodge with them, noting that it 'would bring more domestic labour upon my wife – whereas at present she already has as much as possibly can be united with drawing' (*Letters*, p. 416). A letter from 1846 mentions an art dealer's request that Hannah prepare a copy after Titian, but no reply is recorded (*Letters*, pp. 441–2). A letter from 1849 evokes the image of seven year-old Thomas More 'sitting out in Kensington Gardens with your Mamma, reading to her while she is sketching and trying with the pencil yourself' (*Letters*, p. 468). And a letter from 1859 refers intriguingly to 'Annie … doing those drawings for the queen' – possibly in reference to Queen Victoria – but nothing else of the project is known (*Letters*, p. 551).

## 108

### *The Cypresses at the Villa d'Este,* 1838

Brown ink, watercolour, gouache, graphite and black chalk on blue paper, 31.5 × 22.9 cm (12½ × 9 in)

Inscribed in graphite at lower right in A.H. Palmer's hand: *The Cypresses at the Villa d'Este Tivoli – drawn on the spot.*; and at lower left in Martin Hardie's hand: *Samuel Palmer / given to me by A.H. Palmer See his note on back / M.H.*; in graphite at lower left of verso in a modern hand: *SAMUEL PALMER CYPRESSES AT VILLA D'ESTE / TIVOLI / B1977.14.4645*

Lit: V&A 1926, 92; Fitzwilliam 1984, 39; Lister 328

New Haven, Yale Center for British Art, Paul Mellon Collection, B1977.14.4645

In November 1838 the Palmers travelled to Tivoli. The Villa d'Este's celebrated hillside gardens, with their splendid fountains, grottoes and water organ, inspired them to remain until late December, when bitter cold forced their return to Rome. On 16 December Palmer lamented:

> I wish we had known of the Villa d'Este before we went southward though it might have stopped farther movements – it is surer game for me than all the rest – and I have seen nothing like or second to it. There are several views of the old cypresses which would be sure money and surer improvement. (*Letters*, p. 255.)

Palmer probably secured the present study around 2 December, when he informed Hannah's sister Lizzy (Elizabeth Anne Linnell): 'I have got a finished study of pines and cypresses – the latter 300 years old and wonderfully fine' (*Letters*, p. 249 and n. 22; Brown, under no. 26).

Palmer's satisfaction is understandable. This assured *plein air* study ranks among his finest of any period, and remained in his possession 'all his life as a source of inspiration' (V&A 1926, 92). Palmer approached the trees as a discrete subject, isolated from their surroundings, with only the faintest sketch of a human figure to suggest the massive scale. He began the drawing in graphite and black chalk, initially positioning the highest tree further to the left, then added colour: green watercolour for the middle tones, precise touches of pink and light green gouache for the lights, and brown wash for the shadows. Finally, he elaborated selected details in black chalk, graphite and brown ink. He worked from left to right, and stopped at an attractive stage of incompletion, before the right side of the sheet appeared as finished as the left.

Ruskin seems to have just such a study in mind when he ranked Palmer as an artist 'deserving of the very highest place among faithful followers of nature': 'His studies of foreign foliage especially are beyond all praise for care and fullness. I have never seen a stone-pine or a cypress drawn except by him; and his feeling is as pure and grand as his fidelity is exemplary.' (Ruskin 1846, p. 402.)

In 1839 Palmer used this drawing while designing two exhibition water-colours of the Villa d'Este at Tivoli (Ashmolean, and Victoria and Albert Museum; Lister 314, 333; *Letters*, p. 252); in 1845 he returned to it when composing *Tivoli and the Campagna of Rome* (private collection, UK; Lister 397). Palmer's affection for the subject never waned. In 1858, two decades after his Italy journey, the artist mused: 'One might draw the cypresses in the Villa D'Este for a year and not exhaust them' (*Letters*, p. 540).

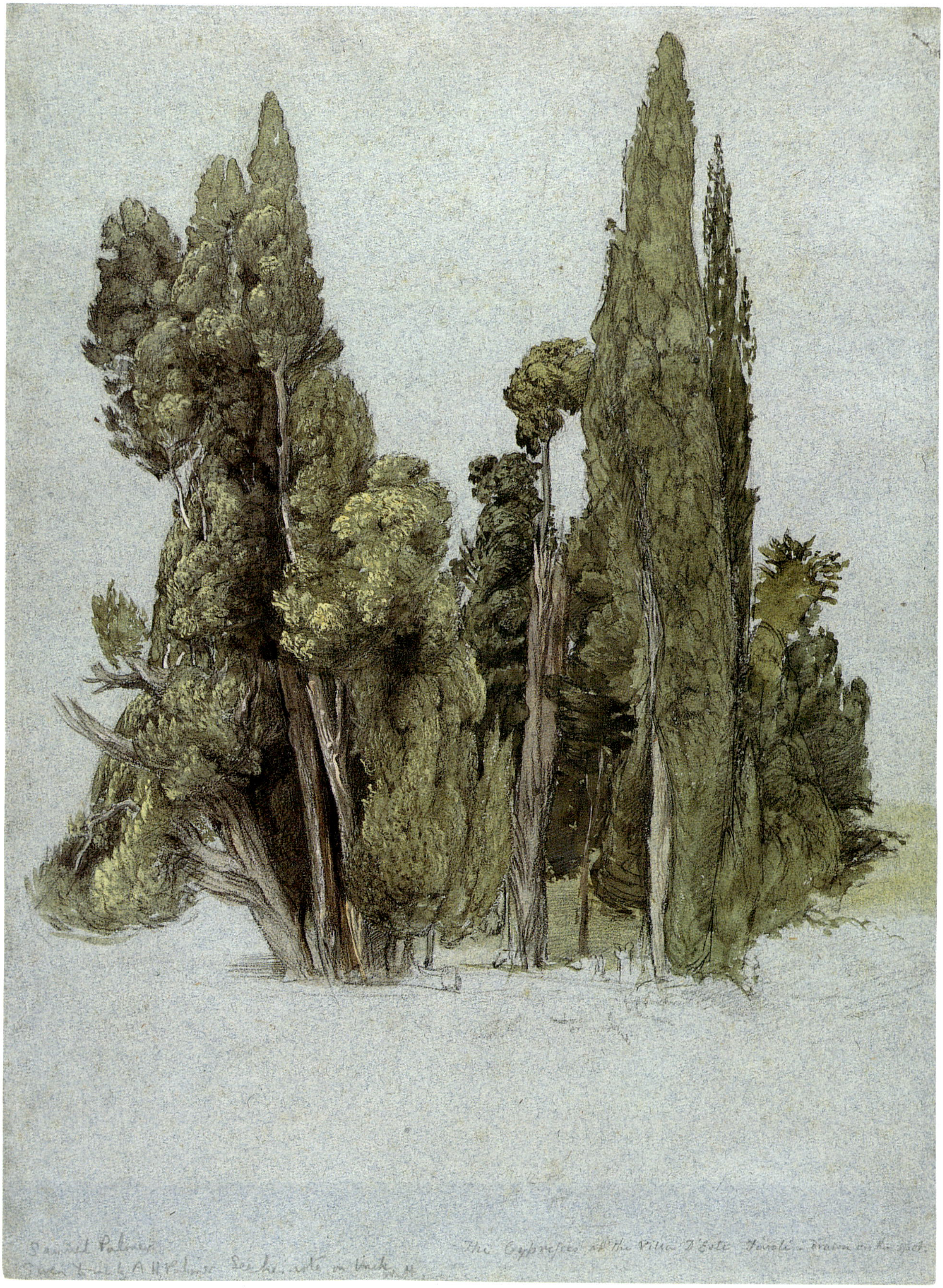
Samuel Palmer
The Cypresses at the Villa D'Este Tivoli – drawn on the spot.

108

## 109†

### *The Villa d'Este from the Cypress Avenue*, 1838

Black chalk, watercolour and gouache on blue-grey paper, 45.7 × 31.9 cm (18 × $12\frac{5}{8}$ in)

Inscribed in graphite at lower left: *Villa d'Este Tivoli – drawn on the spot*; and at left: *Terminations of clusters in / shadow were soft and fluffy like / these.*

Lit: Fitzwilliam 1984, 40; Lister 315

New York, The Pierpont Morgan Library, purchased as Gift of the Fellows, 1962.18

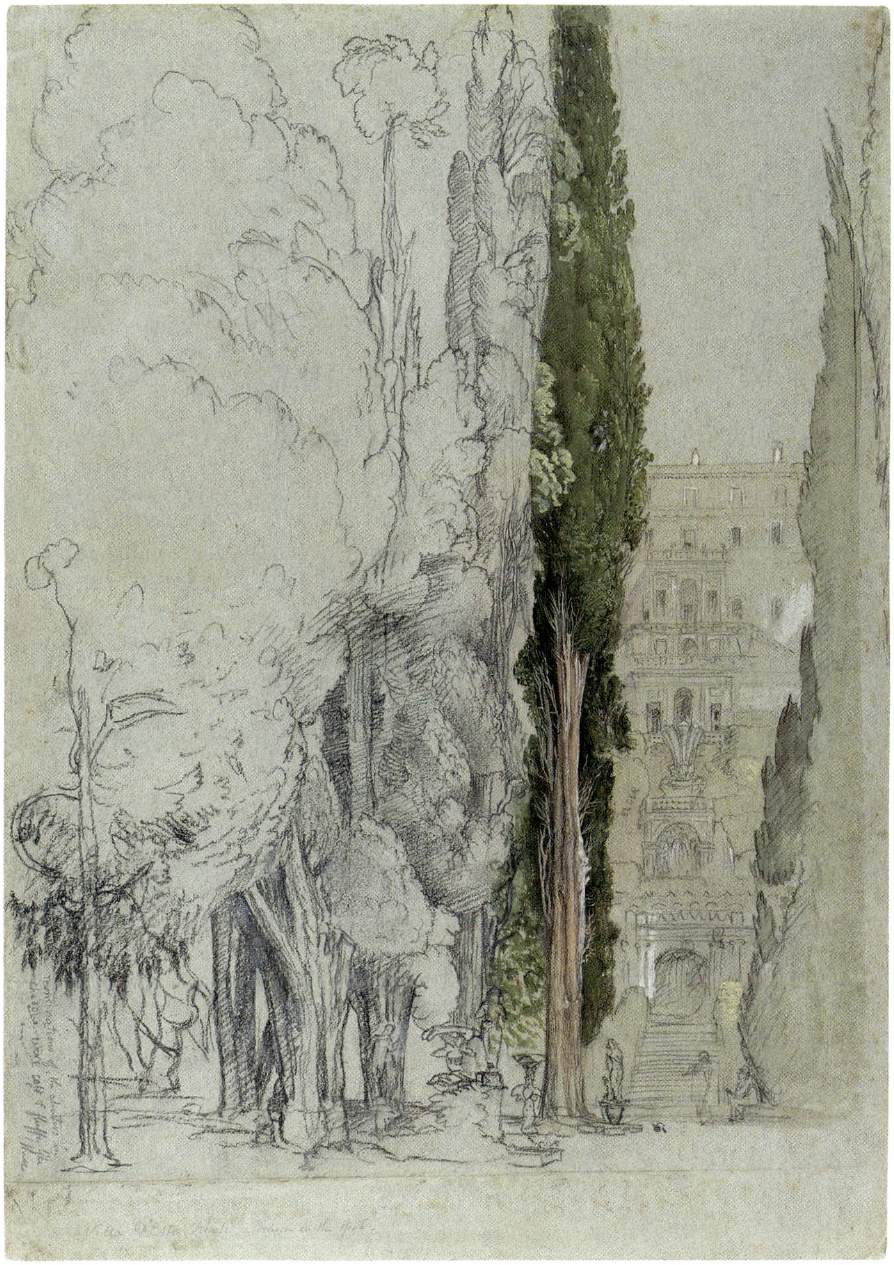

109

In this dramatic view of the Villa d'Este from the Cypress Avenue Palmer adopts an unusual vertical, tightly framed composition. Efficient strokes of black chalk capture the basic forms; touches of wash and gouache describe the steep façade; and a single cypress stands in colour, fully painted. While Palmer might well have devised this compelling arrangement on his own, he seems likely in this instance to have taken inspiration from a colleague.

In the spring of 1837 William Collins, a Linnell family friend then touring Italy with his wife and sons (including Wilkie, the future novelist), prepared a closely similar watercolour study (fig. 28; private collection, UK; Agnew's 2003, no. 59), later used for the oil painting, *The Villa d'Este* (Victoria and Albert Museum; RA 1842; Collins 1848, vol. 2, p. 205). The following winter the Collinses travelled to Rome. On 21 February 1838 the Palmers wrote to the Linnells that the recently arrived Collinses were 'very friendly' and had recommended various picturesque sites (*Letters*, pp. 109, 113). Samuel went on to relate that he had just seen 'a study of some most noble cypress trees planted in Ariosto's time at Tivoli – which with a figure or two would make a very grand subject' (*Letters*, p. 115). Although Palmer does not name the artist of that study, Collins seems the most likely candidate, considering the context of the remark, the two artists' acquaintance and the close similarity of their respective sketches.

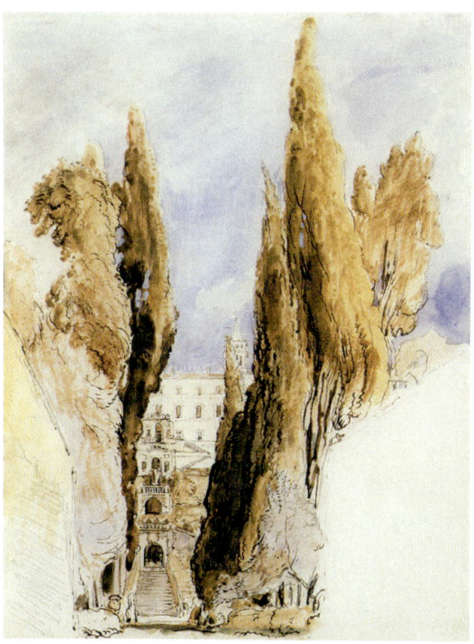

Fig. 28 William Collins, RA (1788–1847), *Villa d'Este, Tivoli*, 1837, brown ink and watercolour over graphite, private collection, UK.

**110**

## After Samuel Palmer

### *The Villa d'Este*

Plate 2 of Charles Dickens, *Pictures from Italy*, Bradbury and Evans, London, 1846

Wood engraving, page 17.5 × 11.1 cm ($6^{7}/_{8} \times 4^{3}/_{8}$ in)

Lit: Lister B1(ii); Bowen 2000, p. 203

New York, The Metropolitan Museum of Art; A. Hyatt Mayor Purchase Fund, Marjorie Phelps Starr Bequest, 2004.482

In March 1846, six-and-a-half years after Palmer's return from Italy, Charles Dickens approached him with the request to provide illustrations for a forthcoming book: *Pictures from Italy*, a collection of literary sketches inspired by the author's recent experiences in Italy (*Letters*, pp. 439–440).

Palmer does not appear to have been the first choice of illustrator: Dickens seems initially to have considered his friend Clarkson Stanfield for the project, but the Roman Catholic artist appears to have withdrawn his participation when he learned (from the serial publication of its chapters) of the book's marked anti-Catholicism (Paroissien 1973, pp. 247–9; Tillotson 1977, p. 517 note). Dickens then asked the art dealer Colnaghi to recommend 'any clever young artist or Student who had been in Italy, and had brought home a portfolio of such Sketches as I want' (Tillotson 1977, p. 521). Palmer appears to have been the choice; Dickens visited Palmer's studio to see his drawings, and within days offered him a welcome commission of 20 guineas for four vignette illustrations of the type used in Samuel Rogers's enormously successful *Italy* (a copy of which Dickens lent to Palmer; Tillotson 1977, p. 546).

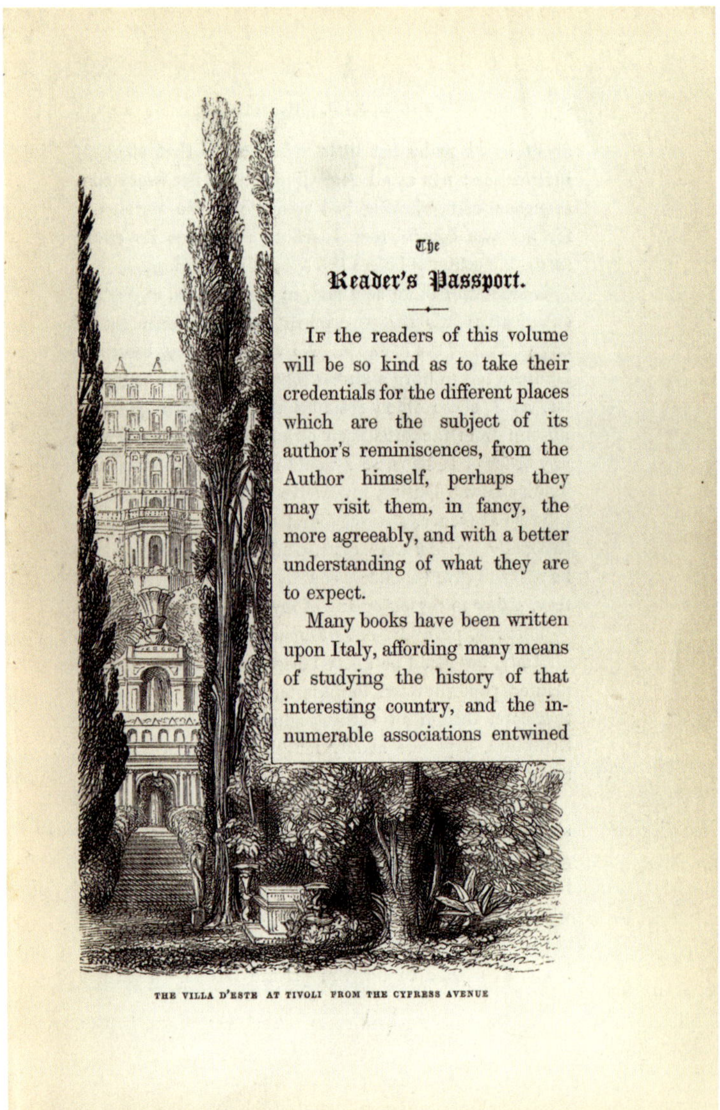

The Reader's Passport.

If the readers of this volume will be so kind as to take their credentials for the different places which are the subject of its author's reminiscences, from the Author himself, perhaps they may visit them, in fancy, the more agreeably, and with a better understanding of what they are to expect.

Many books have been written upon Italy, affording many means of studying the history of that interesting country, and the innumerable associations entwined

THE VILLA D'ESTE AT TIVOLI FROM THE CYPRESS AVENUE

110

In this, as in the other vignettes in *Pictures from Italy*, Palmer did not illustrate a specific passage in the text, but rather evoked a general memory of the country. In the present instance Palmer adapted his existing study of *The Villa d'Este from the Cypress Avenue* (cat. 109), shifting the palace to the left edge, moving the central cypress tree to the right and extending the landscape at the lower right, creating a frame that would surround the text. He developed the new design in an intermediary drawing (Morgan Library; Lister 412ii) rendered exclusively in black and white and scaled to the size of the print. He then transferred that design (in reverse, so that the print would appear in the same direction as the original) onto a block of wood and oversaw the professional engravers who removed the negative areas of the design from the block, yielding a network of raised lines that formed the printing surface. Trial proofs covered with corrections for the wood engravers attest to Palmer's frustrations with the process (Lister B1).

Bowen characterized Palmer's collaboration with Dickens on *Pictures from Italy* as 'one of those great non-encounters of literary history' (Bowen 2000, pp. 206–7). It is indeed regrettable that Palmer's commission was so hurried and so limited. A paucity of illustrations – a mere four in total – distinguishes this volume from Dickens's other published works, creating the paradoxical achievement of a *Pictures* book with very few pictures. To amend this conspicuous omission, the book's 1862 republication included extra illustrations by Marcus Stone.

## 111

### Hannah Palmer (1818–93), after Titian (Tiziano Vecellio, ?1485/90–1576)

### *Sacred and Profane Love*, 1839

Graphite and brown wash on an off-white lightweight wove paper page of George Richmond's memoranda book, 1837–9, tab T, bound in leather, with alphabetical tabs and the gold-tooled title 'G R / MEMORANDA', 12.8 × 9.6 × 1.6 cm (5 1/16 × 3 3/4 × 5/8 in)

Inscribed in graphite in George Richmond's hand beneath the image: *drawn by Mrs. Palmer*

London, Royal Academy of Arts, The George Richmond Archive 397/GRI/1/4

In February 1839 Hannah Palmer wrote to her parents with news of her latest accomplishment:

> We went the other day to the Palazzo Borghese and we saw the most splendid Titian. (Sacred and Profane love). We inquired for permission to copy, found only one person was allowed to copy at once and that my turn would not come for eight months. I then made friends with the Russian lady who is now painting it and succeeded in obtaining 6 days – from 9 until 3 o'clock; yesterday was my last, and by working as hard as a horse I have finished my best copy of the finest picture I ever saw. Such landscape!! My copy is more than a foot long … Mr. Palmer thinks you will jump for joy at this. (*Letters*, p. 292.)

Hannah Palmer's large copy of *Sacred and Profane Love* (*c*.1514; Borghese Gallery, Rome) is untraced, but the present sketch – drawn in the memoranda book of George Richmond, opposite that artist's quick outline of the same – suggests her attention to Titian's landscape background and his broad massing of light and shade.

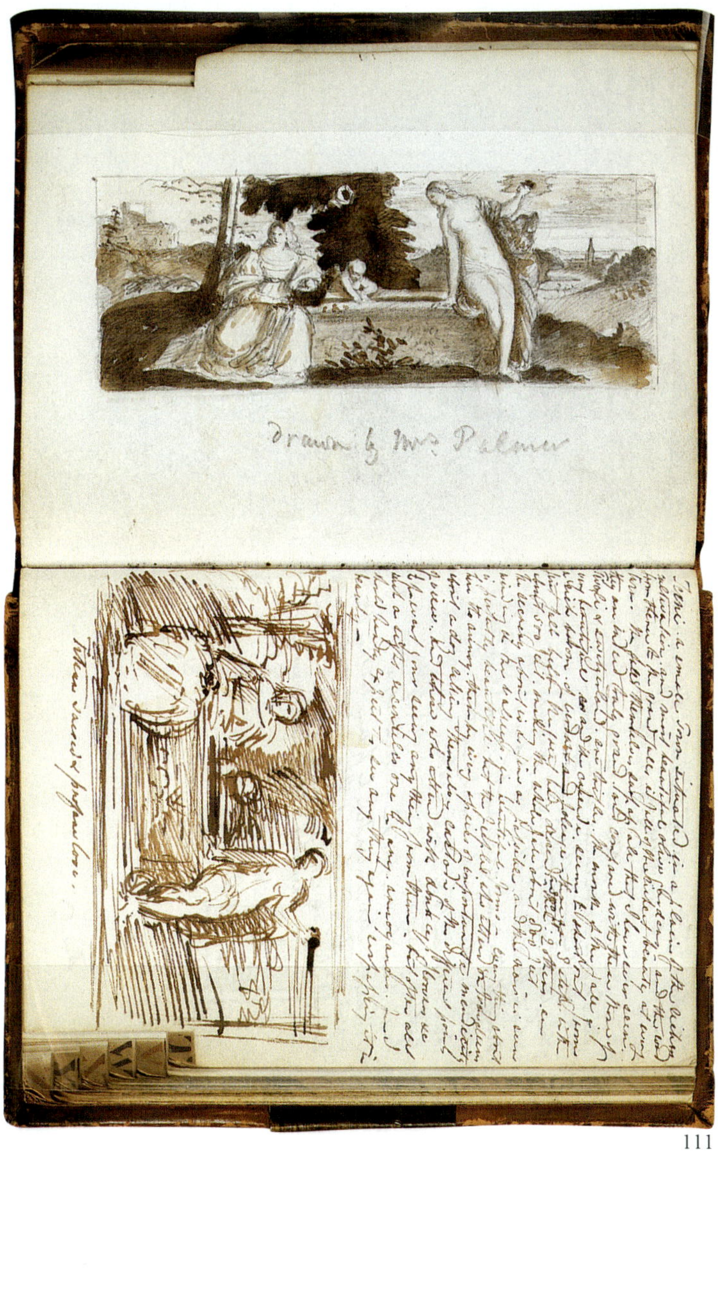


111

## 112a

### John Linnell (1792–1882), after Michelangelo Buonarroti (1475–1564)

### *The Fall of Man and Expulsion from the Garden of Eden*, 1834

Mezzotint with etching printed in light brown ink on chine collé laid on a buff-coloured paper support, sheet size 30.5 × 36 cm (12 × 14 1/4 in)

Private collection, Linnell family

## 112b

### John Linnell (1792–1882), after Michelangelo Buonarroti (1475–1564)

### *The Fall of Man and Expulsion from the Garden of Eden*, published 1834, coloured in watercolour and gouache by Samuel Palmer, 1839

Mezzotint with etching printed in light brown ink on chine collé laid on a buff-coloured paper support, sheet size 30.5 × 36 cm (12 × 14 1/4 in)

Lit: Lister 330

Private collection, Linnell family

Hannah Palmer travelled to Italy with two commissions from her father: to paint small-scale copies after Raphael's frescoes in the Vatican loggia and to colour a set of prints after Michelangelo's frescoes in the Sistine Chapel. The loggia designs would not be realized as planned, and are now unknown (*Letters*, pp. 259, 325–6). *The Fall of Man and Expulsion from the Garden of Eden* relates to the latter

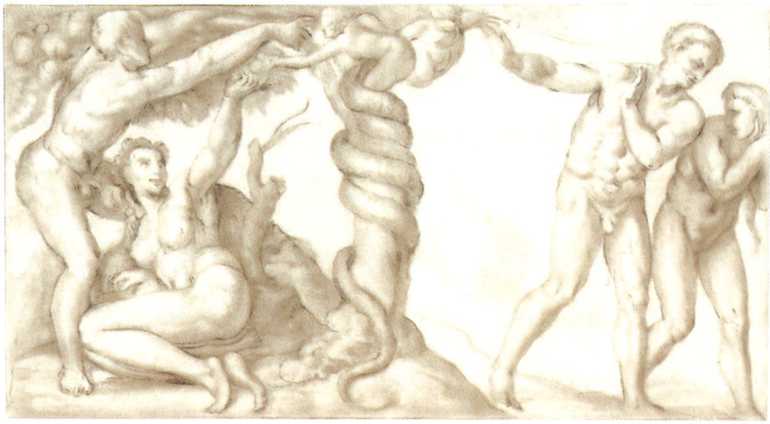

112a

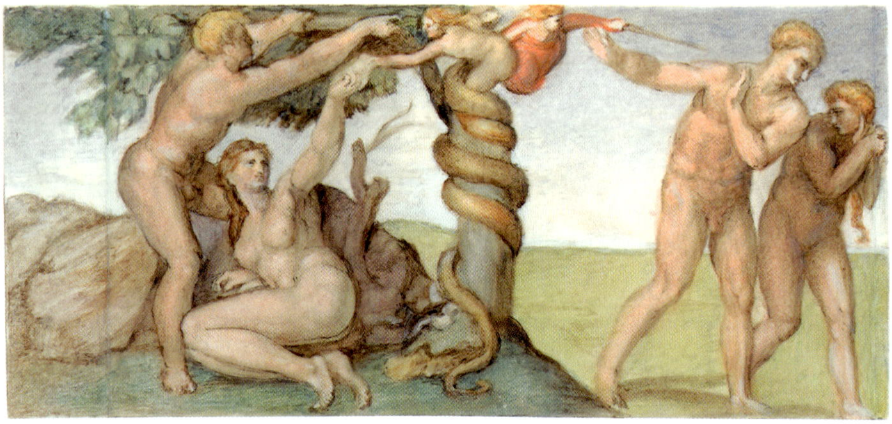

112b

project. Linnell had engraved it as part of a set of forty-one prints whose subtle combination of etching and mezzotint drew the praise of Ruskin and Constable (Constable's letter of 30 July 1835, John Linnell Archive, Fitzwilliam Museum, Cambridge, Ms. 497-2000; Story 1892, vol. 1, p. 221; Malins 1968, p. 48). (Linnell, who never travelled to Italy, based the prints on studies that he regarded as Michelangelo's preparatory designs for the Sistine Chapel; sold, Christie's, London, 15 March 1918, lot 130.)

In commissioning his daughter to colour a set of prints after the original frescoes, Linnell sought to assist her with an immediate source of income and to provide all his children with potential future employment in colouring additional sets based on Hannah's models (*Letters*, p. 279 n. 6). In fact, the project proved difficult to realize, hampered by bad weather, Hannah's persistent illness, restricted access to the chapel, the poor lighting conditions within it and the sheer magnitude of the task (*Letters*, p. 259). But Hannah persevered. She obtained the official permission to draw with help from her Italian teacher's brother (*Letters*, p. 295). She bought an opera glass and a small mirror to scan details and to reflect light onto specific areas of the frescoes – already brightened by lengthening days and a fortuitously timed cleaning. Most importantly, as her health became strained, she accepted her husband's assistance (*Letters*, p. 259).

With Samuel Palmer involved, the project took on new life. In little more than a fortnight (between 18 February and 15 March 1839) every sheet had received some attention, as Samuel worked to correct the chiaroscuro, and Hannah applied the colours (*Letters*, pp. 299, 291, 295). Palmer wrote to Linnell relating their progress and explaining their admittedly diminished aims: no longer to replicate the original frescoes, but only to capture the effect of 'successful original little *sketches*' or 'vigorous sketches from nature done before breakfast' (*Letters*, pp. 295, 320).

Nevertheless, Samuel's engagement in the project steadily increased, until he had devoted nearly three months, often working alone, to its completion (announced in a letter to the Linnells on 23 May 1839; *Letters*, p. 336). Palmer extensively reworked the printed scenes, revising 'nearly all the whole of the Sistine Chapel' with particular attention to the Prophets and Sibyls. He corrected virtually every composition against the original frescoes – in the present instance, by notably extending the left side of the sheet – until 'held up and against the originals they seemed to have the same breadth and grandeur in the general proportions of form colour and effect' (*Letters*, p. 324).

Surprisingly, only one complete set of coloured impressions ever appears to have been commissioned (from a 'Mr. Boddington' in 1840, *Letters*, p. 279 n. 6). Given its unrivalled quality, and apparent Linnell family provenance (the backs of several mounts bear scraps of paper inscribed with John Linnell's address), the set of thirty-eight hand-coloured prints to which the present work belongs (formerly in the collection of Joan Linnell Ivimy Burton) may reasonably be identified as the original, coloured in Rome (sold, Christie's, London, 15 March 1918, lot 88). Significantly, *The Fall of Man and Expulsion from the Garden of Eden* is presented in a manner similar to that which Palmer had proposed: 'cut out and mounted on something like cream color'd Bristol Board' (*Letters*, p. 321).

## 113

### *The Village of Papigno on the Nar, between Terni and the Falls*, 1839

Brown ink, watercolour, gouache and black chalk on grey-brown wove paper, 31.6 × 42.1 cm (12½ × 16⅝ in)

Lit: Fitzwilliam 1984, 42; Lister 345

London, Victoria and Albert Museum

In August 1839 the Palmers and their friend Albin Martin visited Papigno, a picturesque village in the Umbrian hills near the dramatic Cascata delle Marmore, the waterfall that Joseph Addison identified as the site visited by the fury Allecto in the *Aeneid* (Malins 1968, pp. 111–12):

> ... There is a spot
> In central Italy where the mountains are,
> A noted place, heard of in many lands,
> The Valley of Amsanctus. Flanks of forest,
> Dark with leaves, close in on either side,
> And in the midst a torrent rumbles down
> A twisted channel, swirling through the rocks.
>
> (Fitzgerald, *Aeneid*, VII, p. 216.)

To cover the region's steep terrain, the artists hired a man to carry the sketching gear and a donkey for Hannah to ride. After quipping that the 'donkestrian exercise' had done her good, Hannah reported to her parents: 'I have made a drawing of the falls – and Mr. P. is making a large striking view' (*Letters*, p. 365).

The present watercolour may be that view. It shows the hilltop town, its buildings traced in brown ink, its streets populated with minuscule figures, high above the white River Nar that flows through a valley lined with olive trees. Blue and purple mountains rise in the distance, their deep colours balanced by the strong green of the tangled plants that frame the scene. That proficient foreground passage reveals a preoccupation of the moment. Palmer wrote to Linnell from Papigno:

> I would not have returned to England on any account without seeing what I have lately seen – since I have turned my attention particularly to foregrounds I have been happy enough to light on some very beautiful and *poetic* specimens and have found some which with the least touch of distance would make most poetic pictures. (*Letters*, p. 366.)

Palmer exhibited the drawing with the Old Water-Colour Society in 1844, accompanied by a quotation from Wordsworth's 'Upon Westminster Bridge': 'The river glideth at his own sweet will.'

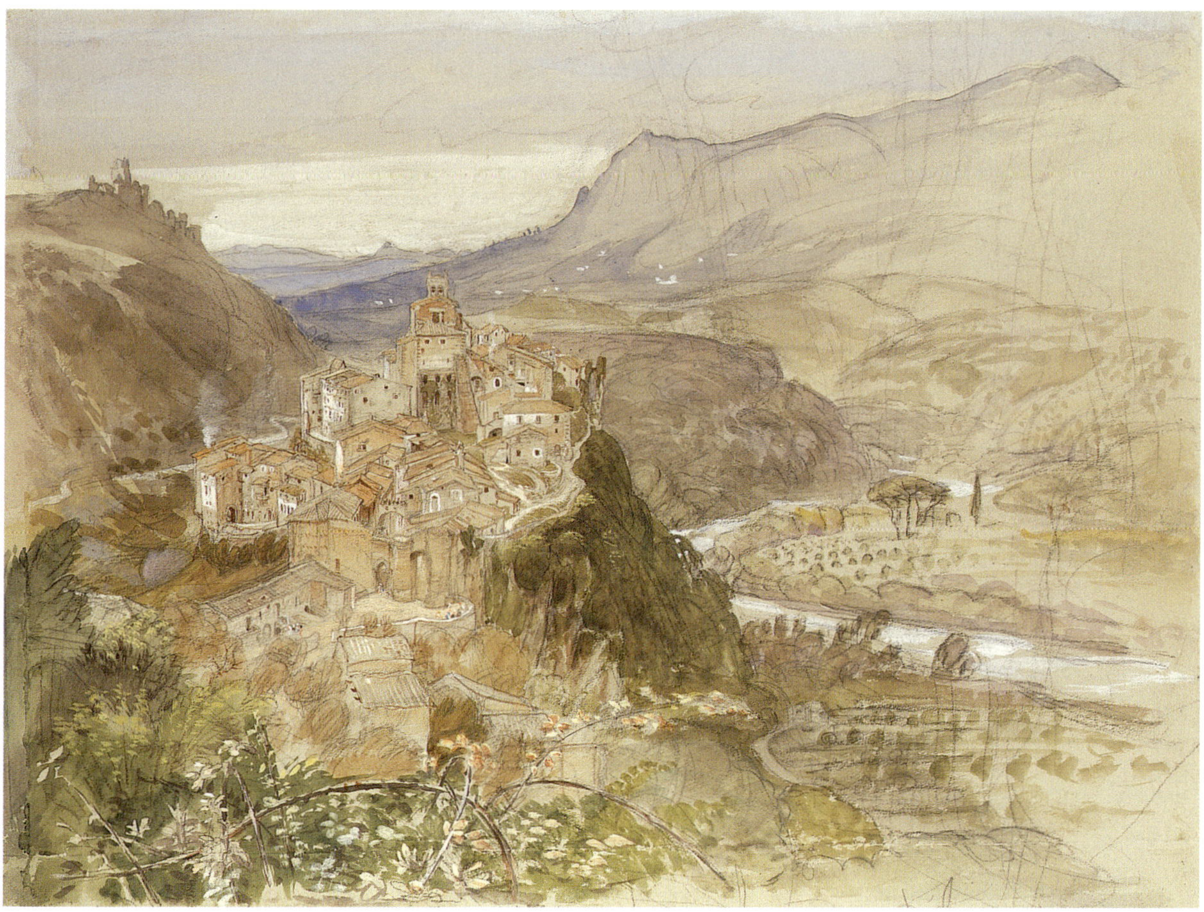

113

# 7. Sketches and Idylls (1840–*c.*1865)

*Elizabeth E. Barker*

The Palmers returned from Italy in November 1839 and settled in Samuel's Marylebone house. They would spend the next two decades in London, during a period of marked personal and professional change.

In 1842 Hannah Palmer gave birth to their first child, Thomas More Walter George Palmer (called 'Thomas More' or 'More'), followed in 1844 by a daughter, Mary Elizabeth Palmer. Mary died suddenly during the winter before her fourth birthday, and the following spring of 1849 the distraught family moved to an 'ancient' thatched cottage at 1A Victoria Road, Kensington (*Letters*, p. 462 n. 1). But death pursued them: Samuel Palmer, Sr., passed away that autumn, and Henry Walter died the following spring. In 1851 the Palmers moved again, to another house in Kensington: 6 Douro Place. There, in 1853, a second son, Albert Herbert Palmer (called 'Herbert' or 'Hub') was born; the only child of Hannah and Samuel to reach adulthood, A.H. Palmer would become his father's etching-printer and first biographer.

Faced with the responsibility of a growing family, Palmer sought to establish his reputation with large-scale, strongly coloured, richly textured exhibition watercolours of subjects drawn from his travels or from literature. In 1843 Palmer had been elected an associate of the Society of Painters in Water-Colours (the Old Water-Colour Society), a group established in 1804 that offered practitioners of the medium a professional imprimatur and exhibition venue other than the Royal Academy where oil paintings claimed the spotlight (*Letters*, p. 420); he became a full member in 1854.

Palmer's landscapes could be readily discerned in exhibitions by the distinctive panoramic format – approximately twice as long as high – that the artist adopted some time before 1852 (*Letters*, p. 489). (By 1844 Palmer had already noted the convenience of 'Newman's Un-hot-pressed Royal London Board' for cutting into '6 Long Shapes' of dimensions identical to *The Colosseum*, cat. 104; Correspondence.) Palmer offered this trademark format in three standard sizes, whose dimensions seem to represent fractions of commercially available paper and artists' boards: 'little long' (about 7½ × 16½ in / 19 × 42 cm), 'middle long' (perhaps 10 × 20 in / 25 × 51 cm) and 'large long' (about 12¼ × 27½ in / 31 × 70 cm). (The exact dimensions are uncertain; Lister confusingly cites his cat. 401 as 'little long', omits 'middle long' and refers to his cat. 598 as 'large long', although it is close in size to 401; Lister 1988, pp. 6–7.)

Critics generally – and increasingly – admired Palmer's powerful depictions of sunsets, sunrises and twilight, and applauded the poetic or 'idyllic' character of his landscapes (see p. 45). Expanding on this view, the Pre-Raphaelite artist, critic and collector, F.G. Stephens, characterized Palmer as 'the painter of the Dorian mood', a reference to an ancient Greek tribe of Doris or Doria that had lent its name to one of the ancient Greek modes of music (the authentic mode on the note of 'D'). (Stephens 1872, p. 162; Powers; Vergo.) As Poussin used the term – in a celebrated analogy between the modes of music and the styles of painting – the Dorian mode was 'stable, grave, and severe' and therefore suited to 'subjects which are grave and severe and full of wisdom' (letter dated 24 November 1647 to Paul de Fréart, Sieur de Chantelou, translated and reprinted in Holt 1982, p. 155). For Palmer's contemporaries, then, his mature landscapes presented a learned (but unaffected) synthesis of the stern, the classical, the simple, the natural, the harmonious and the refined.

The works usually found buyers, but despite this apparent success, Palmer continued to struggle. The prices of his watercolours simply did not compensate for the time lavished on their preparation. As Palmer wrote to Linnell in 1854,

> [my watercolours] are like some apples which will not ripen till they have been kept a long while in the cupboard … [I] sometimes work on 4 or 5 in one morning – lay them aside when tired of them and take them out a month afterwards with a fresh eye but still they will not come *ripe* till a great deal of time first and last has been spent on them. (*Letters*, pp. 494–5.)

For this reason, by 1843 Palmer had returned to teaching as a means to supplement his income (*Letters*, p. 421; Grigson 1947, p. 150 n. 11). Most of his pupils were women: many from the upper classes, several introduced by Richmond (whose daughters studied with Palmer) and Linnell. For lessons given at his students' homes Palmer charged one guinea for two (or two-and-a-half) hours or 10*s.* 6*d.* for one hour; for instruction at his own house he charged only 7*s.* per hour (*Letters*, pp. 428, 447, 449). While the pricing was piecemeal, the practice was comprehensive, requiring Palmer to provide complete terms of regular instruction before receiving payment for the entire 'season' at its conclusion (*Letters*, p. 536).

In a typical lesson Palmer would prepare a drawing while describing his methods and principles as his pupils watched, listened and took notes. Students then kept Palmer's model to copy in preparation for their next meeting. To ensure a ready supply of suitable teaching material, Palmer 'would suffer the "weeds" and grasses of the small suburban garden [in Kensington] to reach their unshorn maturity, and would then use them as a lesson from the windows' (*Memoir*, p. 13). A generous and attentive teacher, Palmer maintained long friendships with former students such as Louisa Twining and Julia Robinson (née Richmond), offering them advice, encouragement and the loan of his own works to copy (*Letters*, pp. 715–16). During the years 1857 to 1859 Miss Mary L. Meakin, a miniature painter and figure-drawing instructor, resided with the Palmers, and the two artists may possibly have arranged to teach students together or in coordinated succession (*Letters*, p. 542 n. 2).

The obligations of teaching kept Palmer in London long into the summers, when he would have preferred to be travelling. But he usually managed to make at least one brief sketching tour each year, often in August. During the period considered here Palmer visited Shoreham (in the summer of 1840), Reigate (in August 1843), Wales (in October 1843), Guildford, Surrey (in October 1844), Princes Risborough, Buckinghamshire (in August and September 1845), Margate, Kent (in August 1846 and 1856), Cornwall (in July 1848 and again in 1857, together with his elder son), Devon (in July and August 1848, June and July 1849, July and October 1858, August 1859 and probably 1860), probably Red Hill (in 1849), and Hastings (in May and June 1859).

His sketching apparatus on such tours – almost always made on foot – was 'simplicity itself':

> There were no costly umbrellas, elaborate boxes, or well-filled portmanteaus. A narrow deal case, or, at other times, a capacious sketching portfolio, slung round the shoulders with a strap, held a good supply of paper, with two large but very light wooden palettes, set with clots of colour a quarter of an inch thick, upon a coat of enamel formed of flake-white and copal. A light hand-basket held the remainder of the more bulky materials, with the lunch or dinner, and a veteran camp-stool which had survived the Italian campaign. A quantity of capacious pockets were filled with sharp knives, chalks, charcoal, crayons, and sketch-books; and a pair of ancient neutral-tint spectacles carried, with a little diminishing mirror, specially for sunsets, completed the equipment.
>
> (A.H. Palmer 1884, pp. 148–9.)

Indeed, when the artists Richard Redgrave and Charles West Cope first met Palmer, at a Welsh inn during the artist's 1843 tour, he appeared similarly encumbered, causing the others to mistake him for a pedlar, since he bore 'his whole painting apparatus, clothes, and necessaries of travel upon his own person' (Redgrave 1891, p. 51).

That meeting would be fortuitous, inspiring Palmer's lifelong friendships with the Redgrave and Cope families. And it may well have prompted Palmer's first foray into etching, the medium in which he would create some of his finest work. Palmer took up the etching needle in 1850, the year in which he completed four prints and was elected to membership in the Etching Club. He continued to make etchings for the rest of his life, working for intense periods squeezed between the demands of watercolour painting and teaching (see p. 47).

On 11 July 1861 Palmer experienced the traumatic event he described as 'the catastrophe of my life' (*Letters*, p. 1071): the death, apparently from a ruptured blood vessel, of his eldest son, Thomas More Palmer, following a long illness at the untimely age of nineteen (*Letters*, pp. 604–5). Palmer's grief at the loss of his beloved child, a promising young scholar and musician who shared his father's interest in the church, cannot be exaggerated. Within hours of Thomas More's death Palmer fled the site – a rented farmhouse at High Ashes, near Dorking, Surrey – never to return; later, he could not bring himself to attend his son's funeral or visit his grave (*Letters*, pp. 605–8). Thomas More's death seems to have caused an emotional estrangement between Hannah and Samuel: although they would draw close again in later years, during the period immediately following their loss he seems to have sought solace in solitary work, while she took comfort from her family (*A Vision Recaptured*, p. 21). Palmer's relationship with his father-in-law, increasingly distant since Hannah and Samuel's marriage, remained cool.

In May 1862 the Palmers moved to Furze Hill House, Mead Vale, Redhill, a suburban villa near the Linnells' home, where Palmer would spend the rest of his life (*Letters*, p. 649).

## 114†

### *Near Underriver, Sevenoaks, Kent, c.*1840

Watercolour and brown ink on off-white paper, 27.2 × 38.4 cm (10¾ × 15⅛ in)

Lit: V&A 1926, 95; Lister 371

Providence, Museum of Art, Rhode Island School of Design, 69.154.13; anonymous gift

Within a violet-streaked sky a luminous sliver of reserved white paper describes a waxing crescent moon. Beneath it rapidly sketched trees and plants washed with colour frame richly textured slopes and meadows before distant purple hills. The lessons of Italy have been fully learned: from the earthy foreground to the ethereal background each element relates harmoniously to every other, all within the artist's firm control.

This study shows the hilly landscape around Underriver, Sevenoaks, Kent, near Palmer's youthful 'Valley of Vision'. Lister identified the drawing as one mentioned in a letter of January 1843 as 'sketches of rock' and a 'pen and ink sketch of the Underriver distance – seen in a slice between the banks of rooks hill lane' (*Letters*, p. 419). (The description recalls another view entitled *Rooks Hill* – Lister 374 – but Lister identifies that as Rooks Hill, Sussex, not Rooks Hill, Kent.) Although neither description

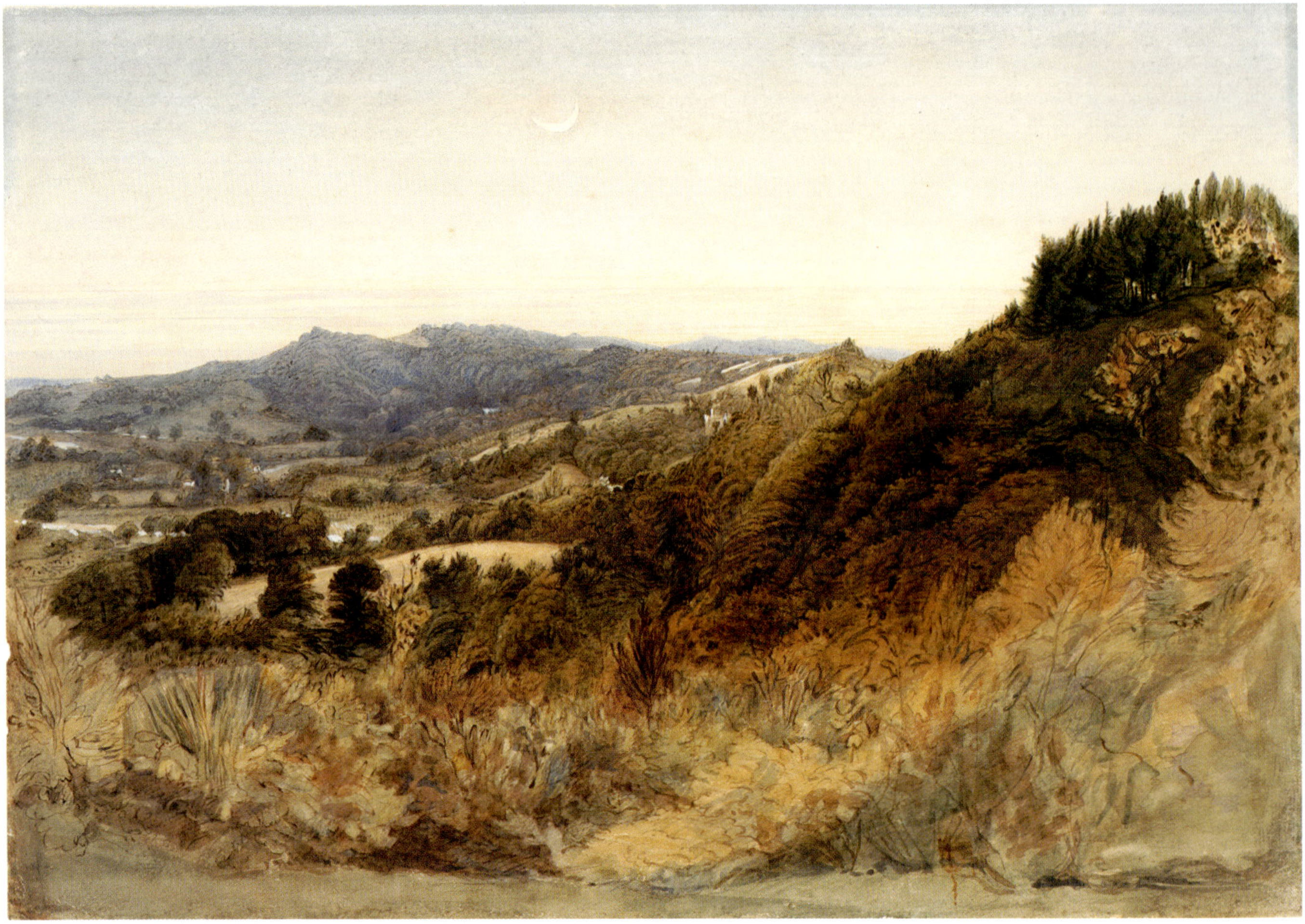

114

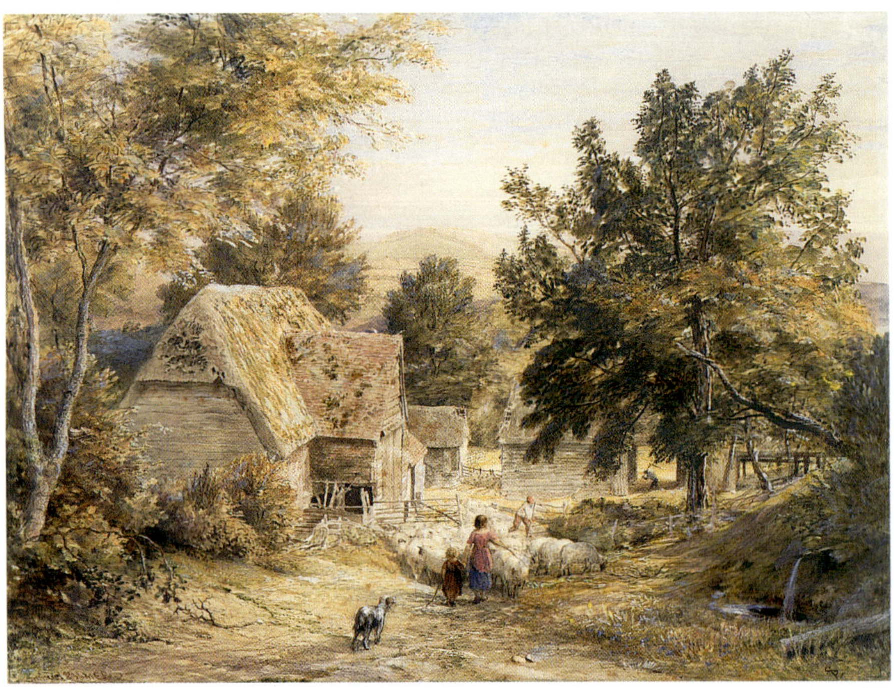

115

mentioned in the letter seems to suit the present work, a date in the early 1840s does seem reasonable. Palmer's certain visit to Kent in 1840 (when he and Hannah summered in Shoreham) and this drawing's stylistic similarities to his late Italian drawings, such as *Papigno* (cat. 113), support a date soon after his return to England.

## 115*

### *A Farmyard near Princes Risborough, Bucks*, 1846

Watercolour, 39.2 × 54 cm (15 7/16 × 21 1/4 in)

Signed at lower left: *Samuel PALMER.*

Monogram at lower right: *SP*

Inscribed on a label formerly attached to backboard of the frame in ink: *A Farm-yard / near Prince's Risborough, / Bucks. / N.B. No picture either in oil or / water colours should be so*

*/ hung as to receive direct / sunlight during any part of / the day. S.P.*; on a card behind the drawing and now apparently lost: *Entering the Farm Yard. Size of mount to be ordered 27¾ × 21½*

Lit: *L&L*, pp.80–82; V&A 1926, 121; Lister 416

London, Victoria and Albert Museum, 23-1919

In the autumn of 1845 Palmer spent a month at Princes Risborough in Buckinghamshire and made several sketches of farm buildings in the neighbourhood. This watercolour – which is probably the one entitled *A Farm Yard Near Risborough, Bucks* that was exhibited at the Old Water-Colour Society in 1846 (201) – is the most finished composition to have been worked up from these studies. Palmer made a replica of it, a practice that he sometimes engaged in when he did not want to lose a composition on sale. A.H. Palmer records that the work 'used to hang on the wall, Furze Hill House, in a picked position' (V&A 1926).

The picture is one of the elaborately composed English rural scenes that Palmer continued to produce in the 1840s alongside his continental subjects. Unlike his later idylls, these focus more on daytime activities rather than evening or nocturnal effects. This scene shows a young girl driving a herd of sheep towards a farmyard where a man is opening the gate. The title, 'Entering the Farm Yard', given on the card that was once attached to the drawing before the picture was mounted, would suggest that Palmer originally intended this event to be the picture's main theme. He was probably aiming to rival such popular painters of rustic genre scenes in the 1840s as William Collins and William Mulready. WV

## 116*

## *The Watermill*, c.1848

Water and body colour, mixed in parts with gum arabic, 51.3 × 71.2 cm (20³⁄₁₆ × 27¹⁵⁄₁₆ in)

Inscribed in pencil on verso, probably by A.H. Palmer: *The Water Mill*

Lit: *L&L*, pp. 85, 88; Brown 34; Lister 443

Oxford, Ashmolean Museum, 1925.12; presented by the Revd William Fothergill Robinson in memory of Alfred and Mary Eleanor Robinson, 1925

The title for this picture comes from a pencil inscription on the verso, apparently in A.H. Palmer's hand. A meditative picture of a building by water, which is viewed in the shadow of a copse of trees silhouetted against the setting sun, it represents a new direction for Palmer, one that was to lead to the deeply toned idylls for which he was most famous in his later years. Although no one reason can be given for the change, it may be that the traumatic event of the death of his three-year-old daughter in December 1847 after a long and painful illness affected this change of mood.

Prior to this event, however, it would seem that Palmer had been determining to develop a new and bolder direction in his art. In *Life and Letters* A.H. Palmer quotes from a memorandum of 1847 that expresses this resolve: 'I must, D.V., strike out at once into a new style, SIMPLE SUBJECT; BOLD EFFECT; BROAD RAPID EXECUTION.' Like his *Pilgrim's Progress* (cat. 120) and *Tintagel* pictures (cats 121, 122) of this period, *The Watermill* seems to be a product of this resolve. The handling of the picture is particularly free and confident. Brown notes that there is no indication of preparatory pencil work in the composition. While the other pictures explore the new boldness in terms of storm-tossed scenes, this one is quiet and reflective. It was, moreover, to presage the direction that he would follow most assiduously in his later career. While utterly different in technique from his Shoreham pictures, the motif of viewing silhouetted forms against the setting sun re-introduced the world of shadows that had been so prevalent in that earlier period.

The picture shows the earliest manifestation of a striking sky effect that typified the artist's late style. This is what he referred to as 'Margate-Mottle', a mackerel sky with the rows of fleecy white clouds thrown into highly coloured relief by the rays of the setting sun. The effect was given its name by Palmer because he first captured it when on one of the frequent visits to Margate that he made in the 1840s. A.H. Palmer records Palmer as saying: 'This year [1848] I made a great advance in the estimation of artists by my mottled-sky drawing begun at Margate.' A.H. Palmer explains that, while appreciated by fellow artists, the work did not sell:

> The drawing alluded to was not sold … The execution is somewhat slight, but the composition and light and shade are pleasing. The sun sets in the midst of that beautiful dappled glory sometimes described as a 'mackerel sky' … the sky (though it is luminous), judged by the standard of my father's later works is somewhat faint and vapid in colour, giving the impression of the fading of some pigment such as Indian yellow, which he certainly used about this time.

A small copy of this work was made in oils by John Reed, a deaf-mute artist whom Palmer had befriended and who was godfather to A.H. Palmer. That copy is now lost. WV

## 117*

## Study for *The Watermill*, 1848?

Watercolour, 12.7 × 17.8 cm (5 × 6⁸⁄₁₀ in)

Lit: Leger Galleries 1992, 13

Private collection (c/o Lowell Libson Ltd)

This freely painted watercolour appears to be an early compositional study for *The Watermill* (cat. 116). It focuses on the central visual effect of that work – a view of trees silhouetted against a sunset sky. The sky itself is marked by a particular 'mackerel' effect, its rows of fleecy clouds differentiated by the rays of the setting

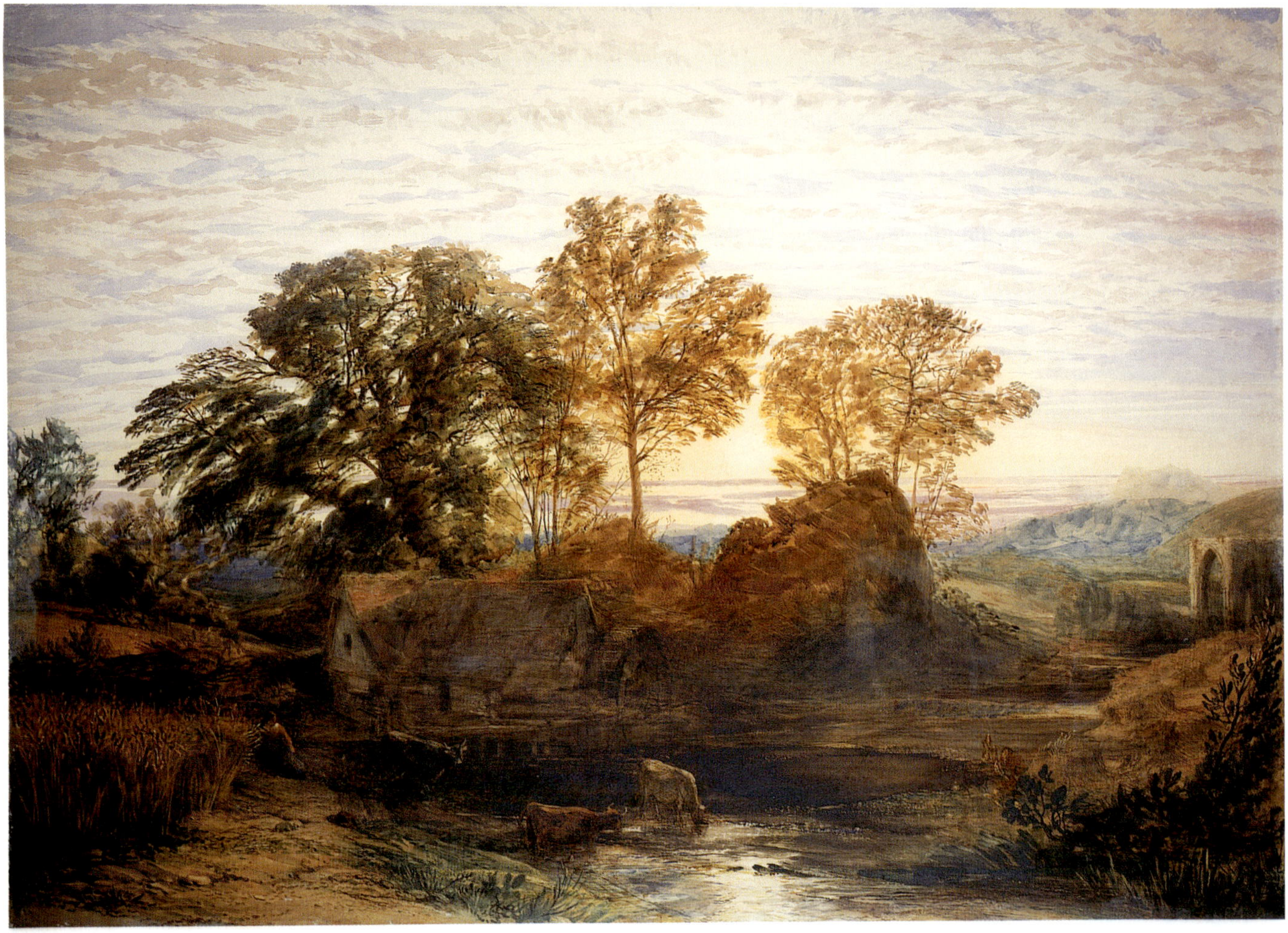

116

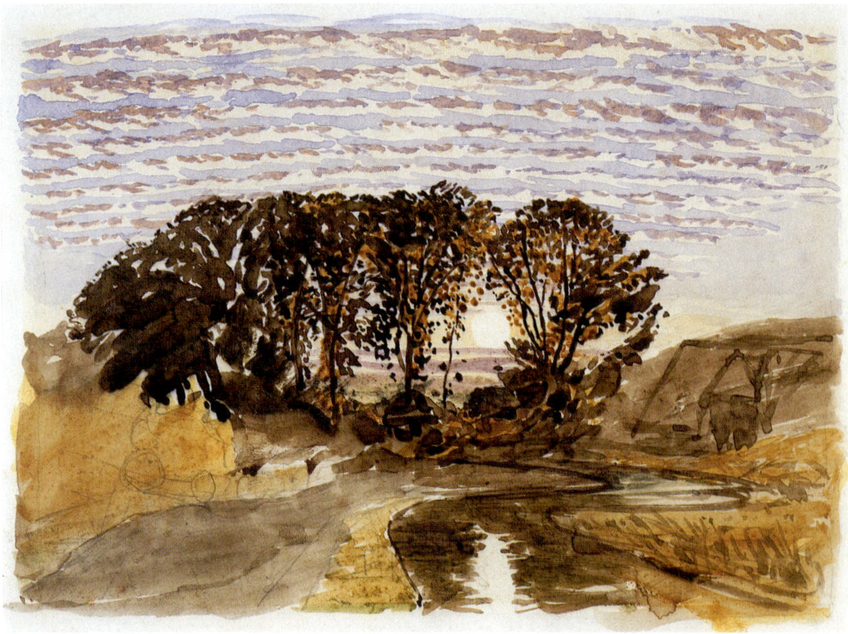

117

sun. According to A.H. Palmer, Palmer was particularly proud of this effect, which he first captured successfully when at Margate, and which he subsequently called 'Margate-Mottle'.

The configuration of trees against a sunset is similar to the central part of a watercolour, *Near Margate, Twilight*, owned by Eton College (Lister 356) and dated by Lister to *c.*1840. It seems more likely that this is a studio design than an outdoor study, so it is unlikely to be the actual work that won the 'estimation of artists' for Palmer (see cat. 116). WV

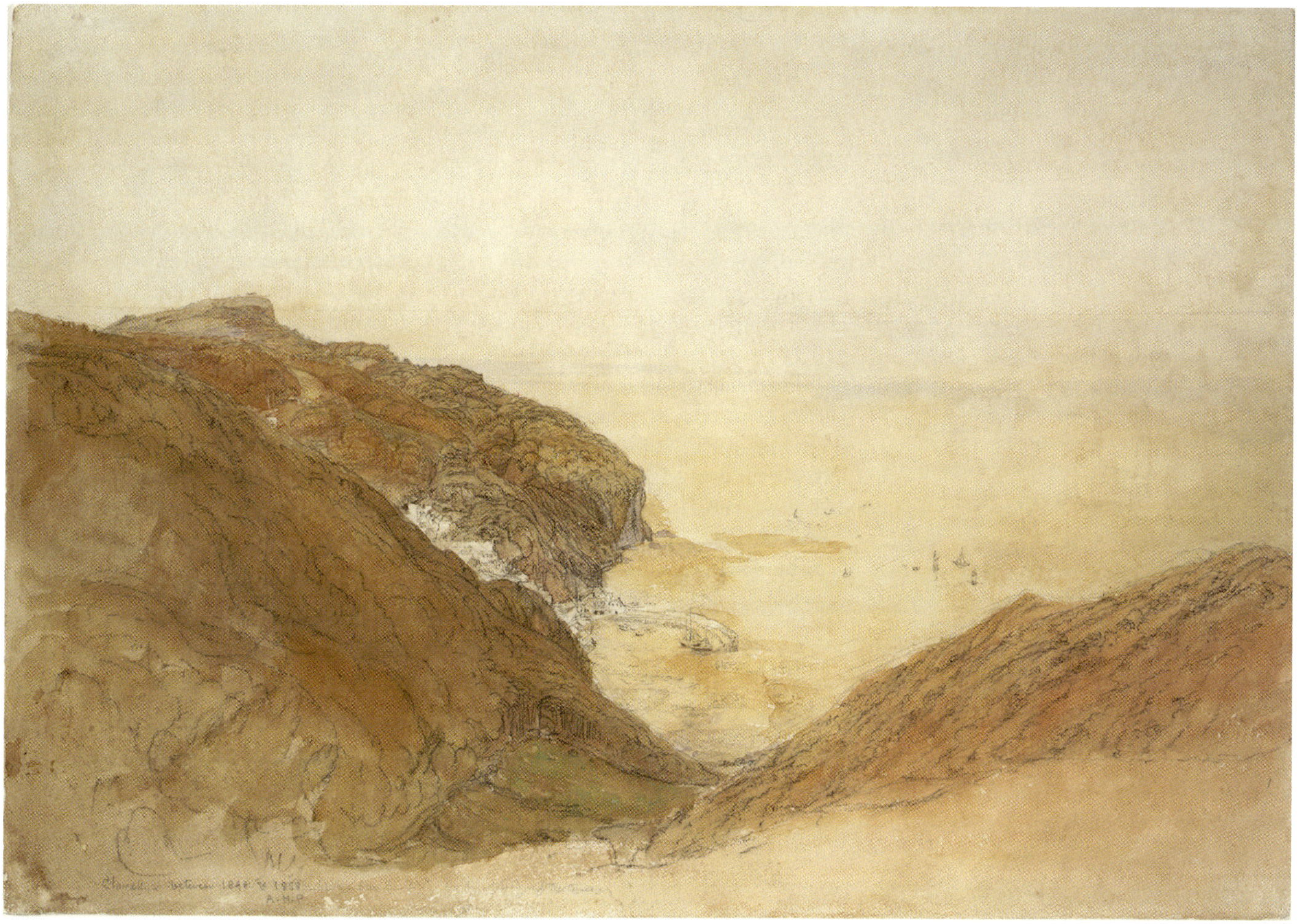

118

## 118

*View of Clovelly, Devon*, *c.*1848–9

Watercolour, gouache, black chalk and graphite on Bristol board, 27 × 38 cm (10⅝ × 15 in)

Inscribed in graphite at lower left in A.H. Palmer's hand: ... *'See The Message from the Sea'* ... *Lundy Island in Distance*; and in graphite in A.H. Palmer's hand on top of (and partially obscuring) the earlier inscription: *Clovelly – between 1848 & 1858 / A.H.P.*

Lit: Lister 476

New York, The Metropolitan Museum of Art, 1979.135.5; bequest of Mary Cushing Fosburgh, 1978

As is indicated by A.H. Palmer's inscription on this sheet, this view depicts Clovelly, a north Devon town overlooked by hills and distinguished by a large harbour with a curving quay. Clovelly, like other towns along this coast, offers views of Lundy Island, whose familiar profile appears here, lightly sketched in graphite at the upper right.

As in an earlier study that included the island (cat. 98), in the present drawing Palmer elaborated his initial graphite sketch with washes of watercolour and gouache, and passages of black chalk. Confident that he had already captured the essential elements, Palmer left large portions of the design unfinished, allowing quick notations of sailboats to float beneath a pencil stroke marking the horizon and dashes of blue suggesting the sky. The vertiginous angle and powerfully massed lines of black chalk correspond closely to studies of the late 1840s, such as *View at Tintagel* (cat. 121) of 1848, indicating a similar date for the present work. Palmer visited Devon in July and August of 1848 and June and July of 1849 and presumably made this drawing during one of those tours.

## 119

## *Memoranda of Sunsets on the Devon Coast*, 1849?

Watercolour on buff wove paper laid down on card, 27.3 × 26.5 cm (10¾ × 10⅜ in)

Inscribed in graphite (beneath upper sketch): *Hay cut – intensely bright but narrow threads of glossy light on hay – The mirror like brightness of all such / lights on foregrounds must always be remembered in facing the light – about 7 p.m. – 10 July.*; and (beneath lower sketch): *past 8 p.m. – 10 July / It was a disagreeable sunset – too much vapour over sky & sea – The sun being in vapour had not power / to light edges in distance – which therefore resembled twilight – The intensely bright glossy lights on / foregrounds become of course more sparing as the sun gets low – because the shadowed sides of the [illegible] becomes more numerous as the angle of illumination is diminished.*; and on verso in A.H. Palmer's hand: *Sunset memoranda in Devon with Lundy Island / Kensington Period. / A.H.P. Never Exhibited / Included in the list mailed Oct 5 1928.*

Lit: Lister 484

New Jersey, Princeton, Princeton University Art Museum, 47-187; gift of Frank Jewett Mather, Jr.

As Palmer grew older, his art addressed increasingly personal concerns. His landscape subjects evoked a pastoral idyll in sharp contrast to the realities of life in an industrialized age. He presented such subjects in suitably elusive conditions at sunset or twilight during the warm 'Italian' days of harvest, 'that dazzling weather when all the air seems trembling with little motes' (*Letters*, p. 544). Since 'very transitory effects, e.g. sunsets … are generally quite lost through trying to do too much', Palmer focused his attention at such moments on capturing 'the characteristics of the effect' with a minimum of lines or washes, and supplementing the resulting sketch with extensive written memoranda (*Letters*, p. 426).

In this rapid sky study made on the coast of Devon on '10 July' – probably of 1849, given the artist's long sojourn in Clovelly during that year – fluid strokes of yellow, orange, brown and violet capture the changing colours of twilight progressing into sunset. Palmer must have made many such invaluable studies. The present sheet may belong to a project that the artist would later recall as his 'most valuable piece of past study': 'The doing each sunset for three weeks over the *same* piece of rock and sea –

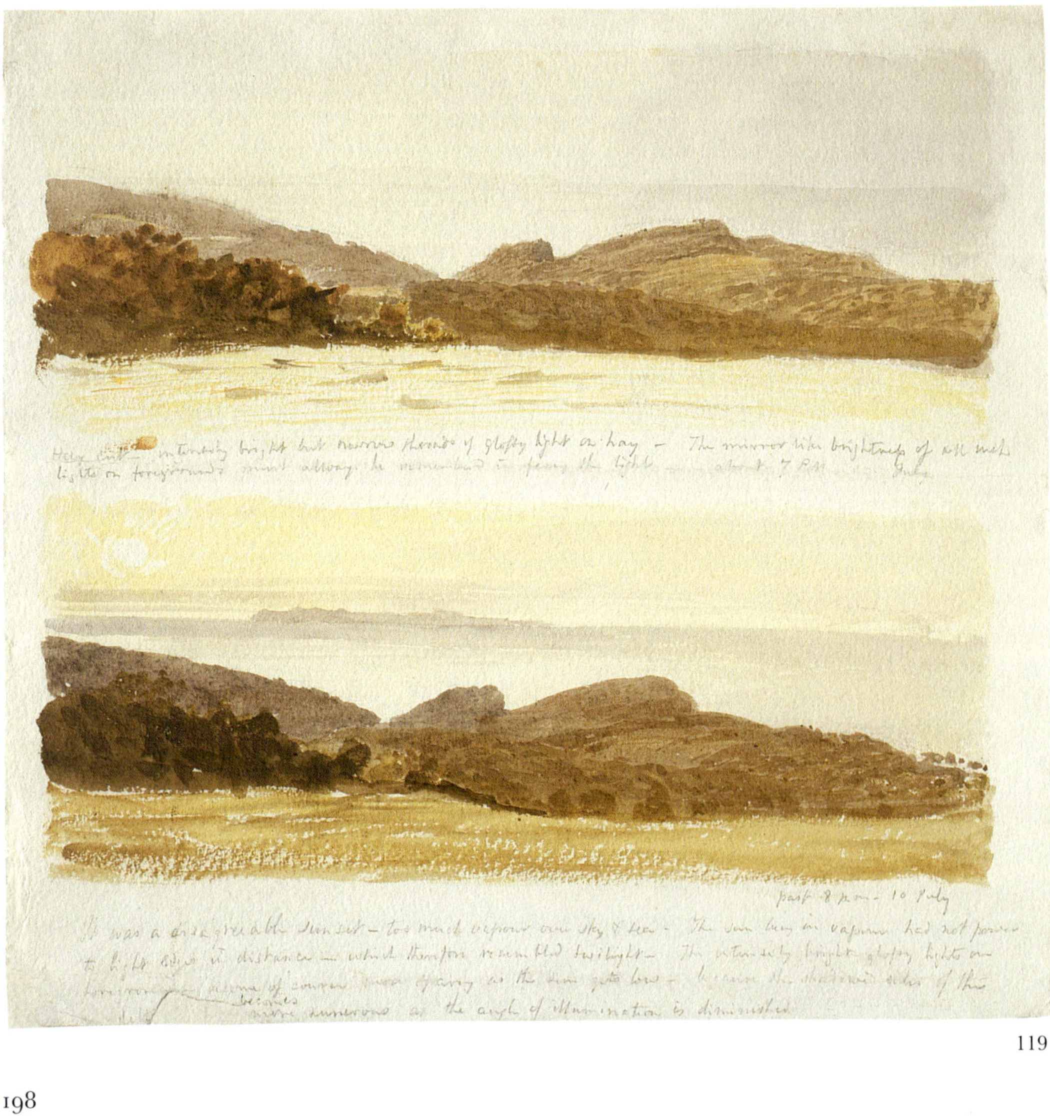

119

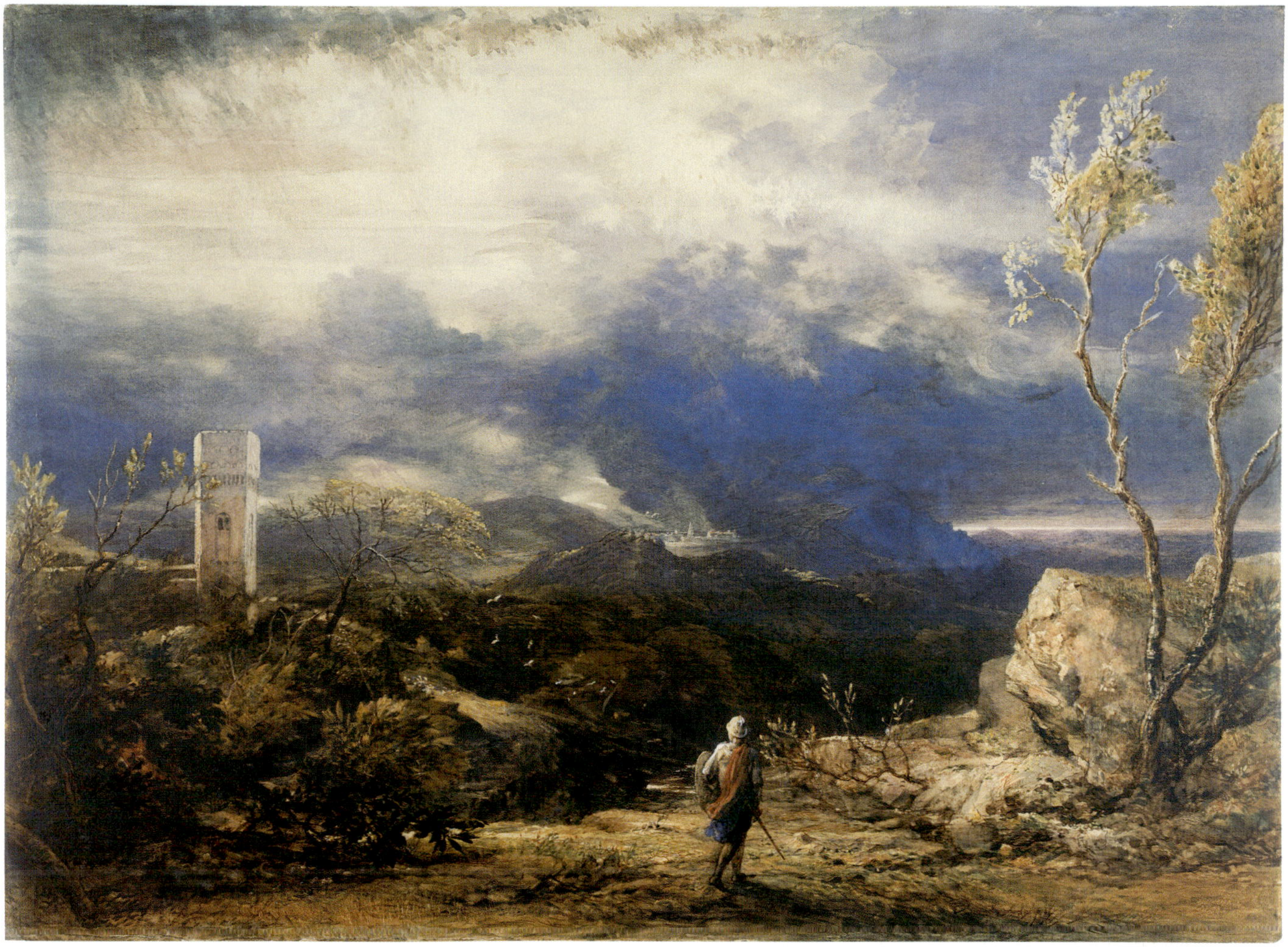

120

and such an opportunity from the unshadow'd bed room window – of watching sky and distance would I think, from my increased experience be still more useful.' (*Letters*, p. 602.)

**120**

## *Christian Descending into the Valley of Humiliation: Vide 'Pilgrim's Progress'*, 1848

Watercolour, gouache, black ink, black chalk and gold over faint squaring notations in graphite on off-white lightweight artist's board, 51.9 × 71.4 cm (20³/₈ × 28¹/₈ in)

Inscribed in graphite on verso, probably in A.H. Palmer's hand: *Christian Descending into the Valley of Humiliation / Exhib in 1848*

Lit: Brown 35; Lister 444; Harrison 31

Oxford, Ashmolean Museum, 1929.35; bequeathed by the Revd William Fothergill Robinson through the National Art Collections Fund, 1929

Bands, speckles and starbursts of violet, blue and grey form the broad, transitional sky. The bright area above the tower on the left, balanced by the narrow, luminous strip of reserved paper at the horizon on the right, suggests a receding (or approaching?) storm. Every detail of this dramatic prospect has been deliberately rendered, from the birds in the lower centre – some painted, others scratched out – to the trees in the right foreground, where areas of reserved white paper gleam beside painted and scratched-out passages and touches of gold.

Palmer took his subject from John Bunyan's *The Pilgrim's Progress from This World to That Which is to Come* (1678), an allegory of the progress of the Christian soul that ranked among Palmer's favourite books (*Letters*, pp. 438, 771). Palmer shows the protagonist, Christian, embarked on his journey through the ominous Valley of Humiliation, pausing in a moment of reflection not narrated by Bunyan. Wearing the armour that Discretion, Prudence, Piety and Charity had given him – 'sword, shield, helmet, breastplate, all-prayer, and shoes that would not wear out' – Christian turns towards the House Beautiful where he had slept in 'a large upper chamber' named Peace, presumably one of the prominent arched windows visible in the tower (Bunyan, p. 52). The red cloak that falls from Christian's shoulder hints at the approaching scene: because he had no armour for his back (and could not

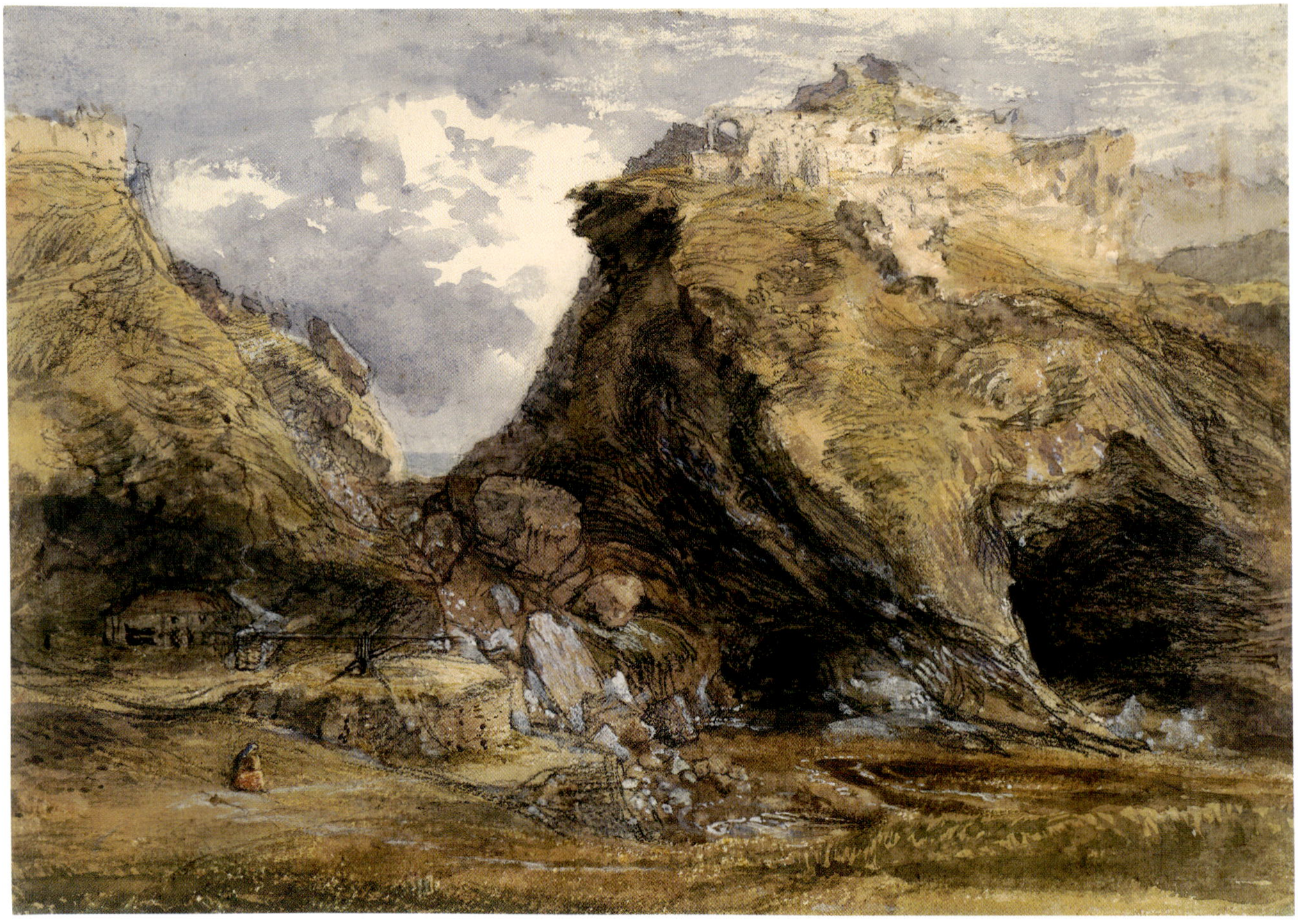

121

safely flee) the hero would resolve to stand and fight the poem's greatest battle against the foul fiend Apollyon, 'clothed with scales, like a fish ... wings like a dragon, feet like a bear ... fire and smoke [out of his belly], and ... the mouth of a lion' (Bunyan, pp. 54–5).

Many artists before Palmer had illustrated the *Pilgrim's Progress*, including William Blake (Norvig 1993, Appendices A and B, pp. 214–29; Butlin 1981, no. 829 [1–29]). Palmer knew Blake's late watercolour designs and must have considered them when he came to paint the present work. Yet *Christian Descending* bears little resemblance to Blake's designs, nor indeed to those of any other predecessor, none of whom treated the exact subject in which the protagonist stands alone and prepares for action.

Palmer's ambitious painting claimed many sources of inspiration: the heroic landscapes of Salvator Rosa (as Lister noted); the classical heroes of Claude (as Harrison proposed); the sublime settings of early Turner; and the vibrant palette of Linnell (as Brown observed). Frustratingly, however, Palmer's watercolour would remain unsold.

**121**

*View at Tintagel*, 1848

Black chalk, watercolour and gouache on off-white wove paper, 26.2 × 37 cm (10¼ × 14⅝ in)

Lit: Fitzwilliam 1984, 48; Lister 452; Stainton 1991, no. 83

British Museum, London, 1910-7-16-17

For commentary see cat. 122.

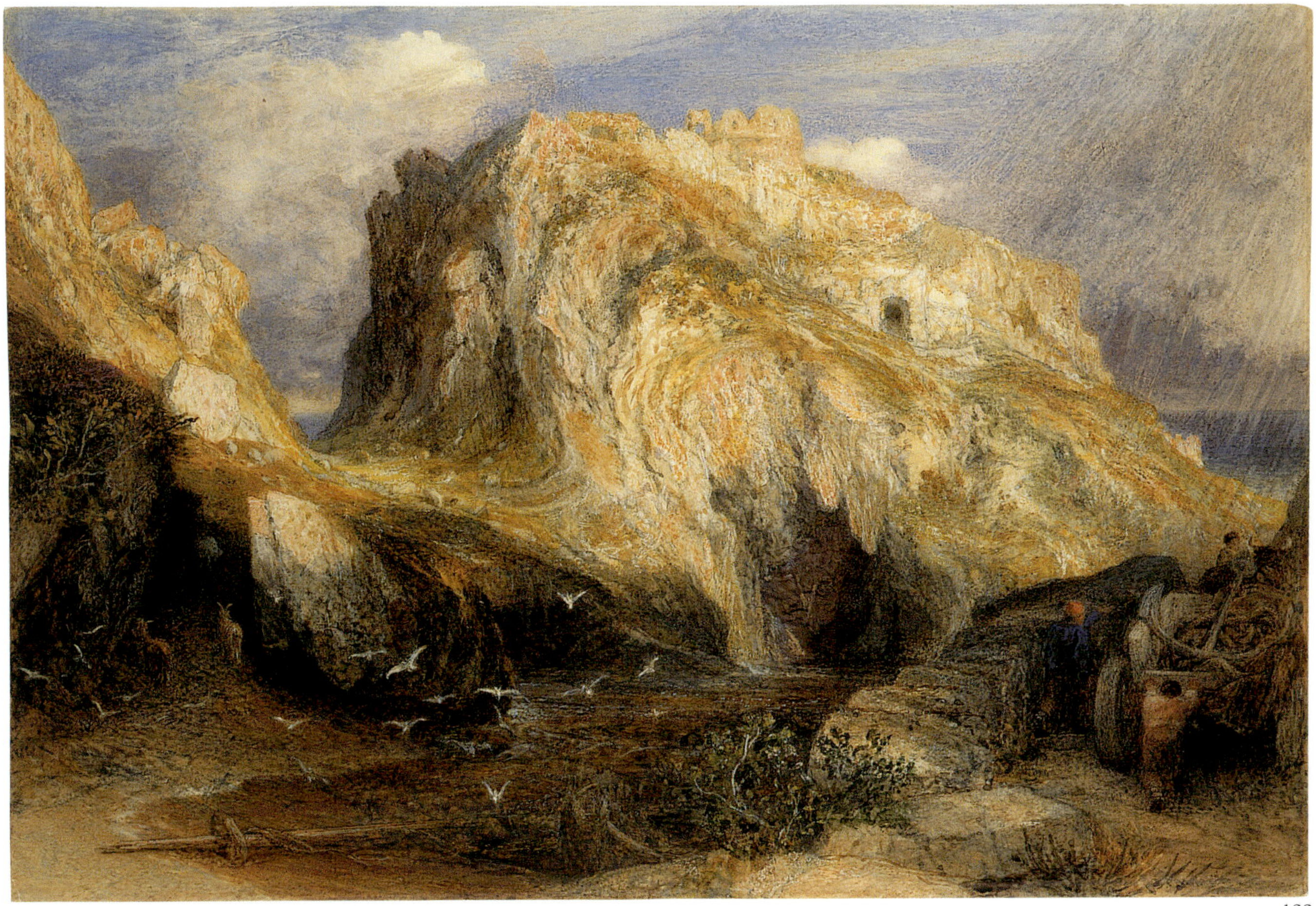

122

**122**

*King Arthur's Castle, Tintagel, Cornwall*, 1848–9

Watercolour, gouache, graphite, black chalk and brown ink on buff wove paper, 30.2 × 44.2 cm (11 7/8 × 17 3/8 in)

Signed at lower right with point of brush: *S. PALMER*

Lit: Brown 31; Fitzwilliam 1984, 49; Lister 453; Harrison 33; Harrison 1997, fig. 5

Oxford, Ashmolean Museum, 1942.27; presented by Percy Moore Turner, 1942

In the summer of 1848, during a sketching tour of Cornwall and Devon, Palmer wrote to Calvert:

> The north Cornish coast is very wild, but the country above treeless and desolate. There is one most curious place on the peaks of two cliffs, which are gradually tumbling by huge fragments into the sea, viz. Tintagel Castle, the birth-place and palace of King Arthur. It was a mouldered ruin in the days of Henry the Eighth. Some turreted fragments remain which are very quaint and strange. (*Letters*, p. 460.)

In the British Museum's bold sketch of Tintagel (cat. 121) powerful strokes of black chalk shape two massive rock formations lapped by waves and separated by a deep cleft. On the right a rugged peak pierced by a cave bears the ruins of the twelfth-century castle. On the left a crane stands upon a circular platform.

Palmer developed the subject in the Ashmolean Museum's exhibition watercolour, a work described by Lister as the 'zenith' of the artist's post-Italian work (Lister 1985, no. 57). The vantage point is slightly shifted, so that the promontory with the castle occupies the middle distance, and a road bordered by a stone wall fills the right foreground. There, figures steer an ox-drawn cart transporting an enormous anchor and chain. Gulls, delineated in rapid strokes of gouache, hover above the waves, and goats seek shelter in a passage beneath the rocks.

## 123

### *Farewell to Calypso!*, 1848–9

Watercolour, gouache and gold on London board, 52.8 × 74.4 cm (20¾ × 29¼ in)

Signed at lower right with point of brush: *S. PALMER*

Lit: Fitzwilliam 1984, 50; Lister 461; Nugent 2002, p. 209

The University of Manchester, The Whitworth Art Gallery, D.1937.17; Jesse Haworth Bequest, 1937

The scene is inspired by (but not narrated in) Book V of the *Odyssey*. Odysseus, freed from long captivity by the beautiful sea-nymph Calypso (daughter of Atlas), sails from the island of Ogygia for Ithaca, the distant home where his beloved wife Penelope awaits him. Raising his arm in farewell, the hero stands on the stern of the raft he had built for the journey, outfitted with a sail and steering oar and supplied with wine, water and food. Calypso, a red cape billowing around her 'silvery gown of subtle tissue, drawn about her waist with a golden belt' (Fitzgerald, *The Odyssey*, p. 89), extends her arms towards her departing lover in a gesture of release (and longing), the palm of one hand shining with reflected light. Near the shore seabirds skim the shimmering waters, beneath. At the horizon an unpainted circle, outlined in white and ringed in dotted brown, forms a glorious setting sun, its razor-sharp rays of purple, yellow and glittering gold extending across the sheet.

While the glittering light and expansive composition suggest a debt to Claude, the dramatic sun is entirely Palmer's own. The artist admitted to a certain 'sun-and-moonism' and justified the apparent mannerism by asserting: 'the earth is never so fair without its luminaries – *they are its eyes*; and if it border on mannerism often to introduce them, it is the same often to omit them' (*Memoir*, p. 52). Palmer created his celestial orbs using a common technique of the day – affixing 'a small covering of paper, cut to the shape required, and slightly attached by gum' to the luminous paper or board before painting (*Memoir*, p. 53).

In the present work the glittering light and expansive composition suggest a debt to Claude. Yet some time before the autumn of 1850 Palmer would jot himself a note to 'forswear HOLLOW compositions like Calypso … and forswear great spaces of sky' (*L&L*, p. 103). Fortunately, he seems to have taken little heed of his own advice. Palmer re-exhibited the present work in 1853 at L'Exposition Universelle,

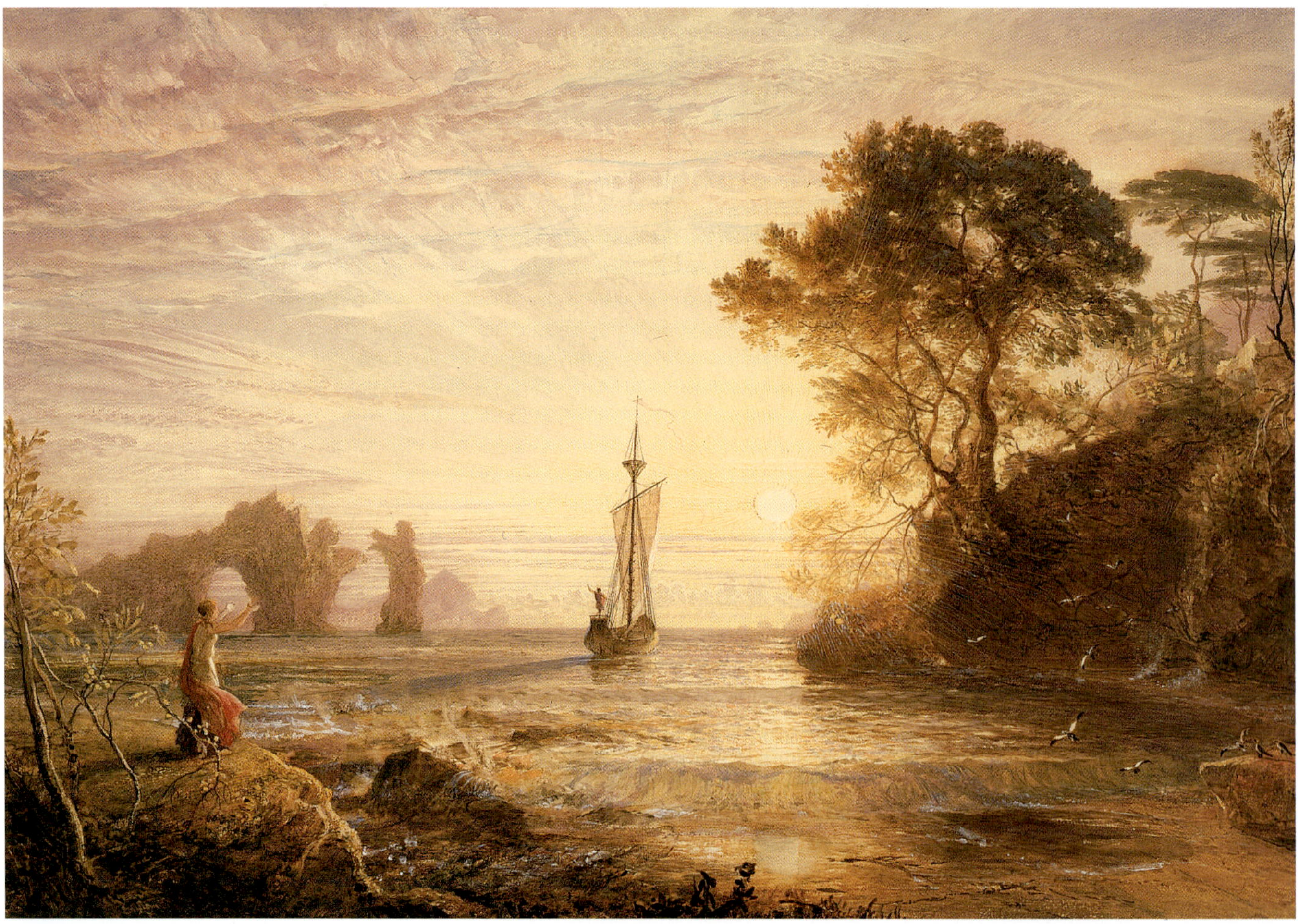

123

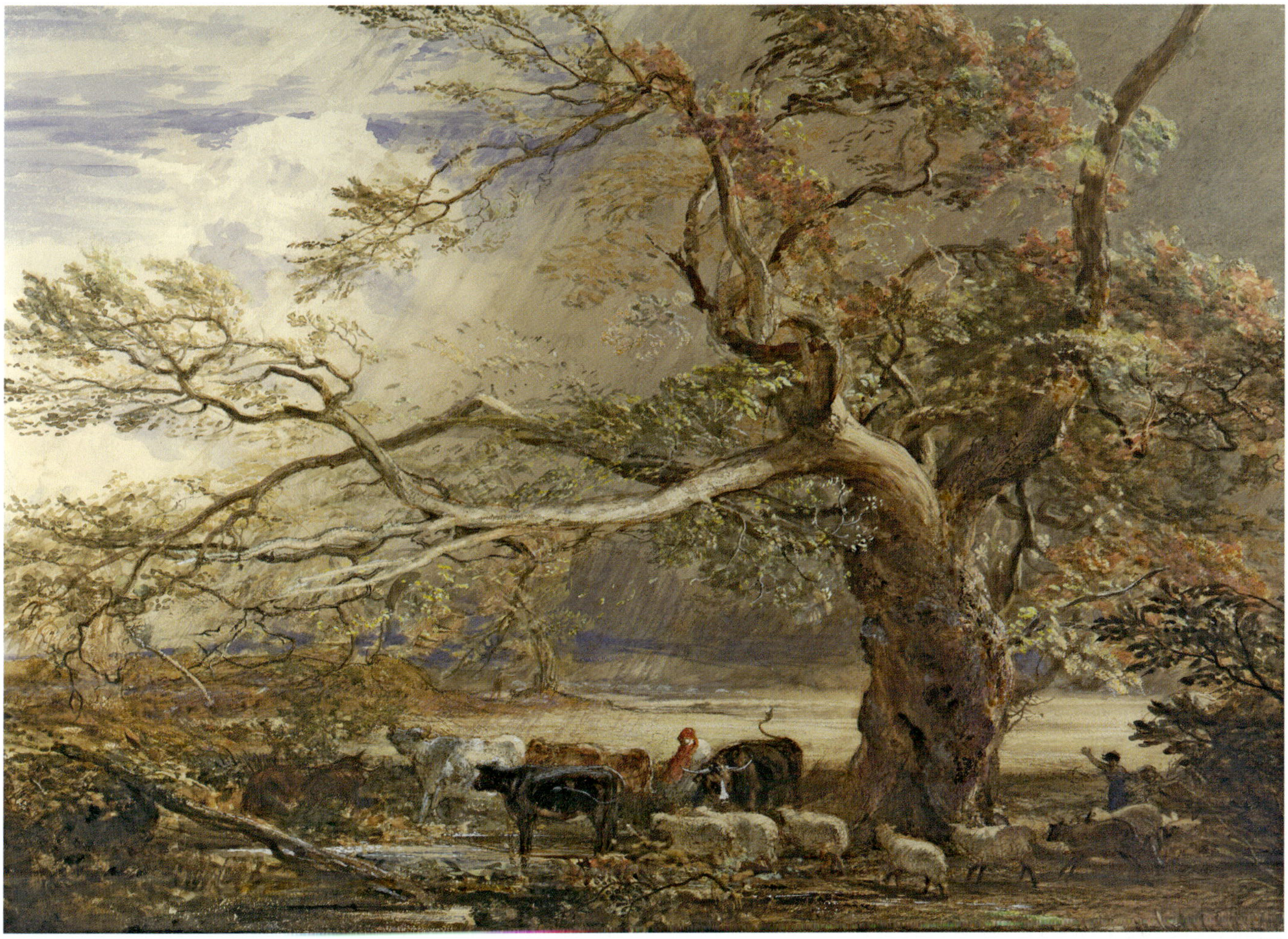

124

Paris (no. 1063), and repeated its composition in various works (Lister 549, 568, B5, 609, 616). Ultimately, the particular combination of forms seems to have proved irresistible. In 1862 Palmer mused:

> Why, from childhood onwards, are we ever dreaming of capes and caves, and islets and headlands, and the marriage of the land and sea? Yet what attracts us like Acrasia's bower, and Armida's gardens, and that *Isle of Isles* where Calypso sang, and Ulysses built his ship? (*Letters*, p. 680.)

**124**

*Sheltering from the Storm*, 1849

Watercolour and gouache on buff paper, 50.2 × 69.2 cm (19¾ × 27¼ in)

Lit: Lister 467

New York, Collection of Gilbert and Ildiko Butler, Promised Gift to The Metropolitan Museum of Art

Surprised by a sudden shower, a woman huddles beneath a massive oak, and a boy herds his cattle to safety as another child raises his arms in alarm. Behind them, beyond the nearby stream or pool, a shepherd drives his flock across the light-struck middle distance. Masterful touches of mauve, brown, orange, green and black describe the tree trunk; pale green, orange, yellow and red form the leaves. At the upper right streaks of blue watercolour painted over a layer of grey describe the falling rain; at the upper left strokes of blue applied directly to the clean paper indicate a patch of bright sky.

Palmer exhibited the present work – along with seven others, including *Farewell to Calypso!* (cat. 123) and *King Arthur's Castle, Tintagel, Cornwall* (cat. 122) – at the Old Water-Colour Society in 1849. There it would have been subjected to the scrutiny of other artists, visitors, critics and potential purchasers. Not surprisingly, Palmer appears to have developed the bold composition and striking textures with such viewers in mind. By demonstrating the medium's capacity for large size, brilliant colour, rich impasto and ambitious subject matter, Palmer and his fellow water-colour painters challenged the perceived superiority of oil painting.

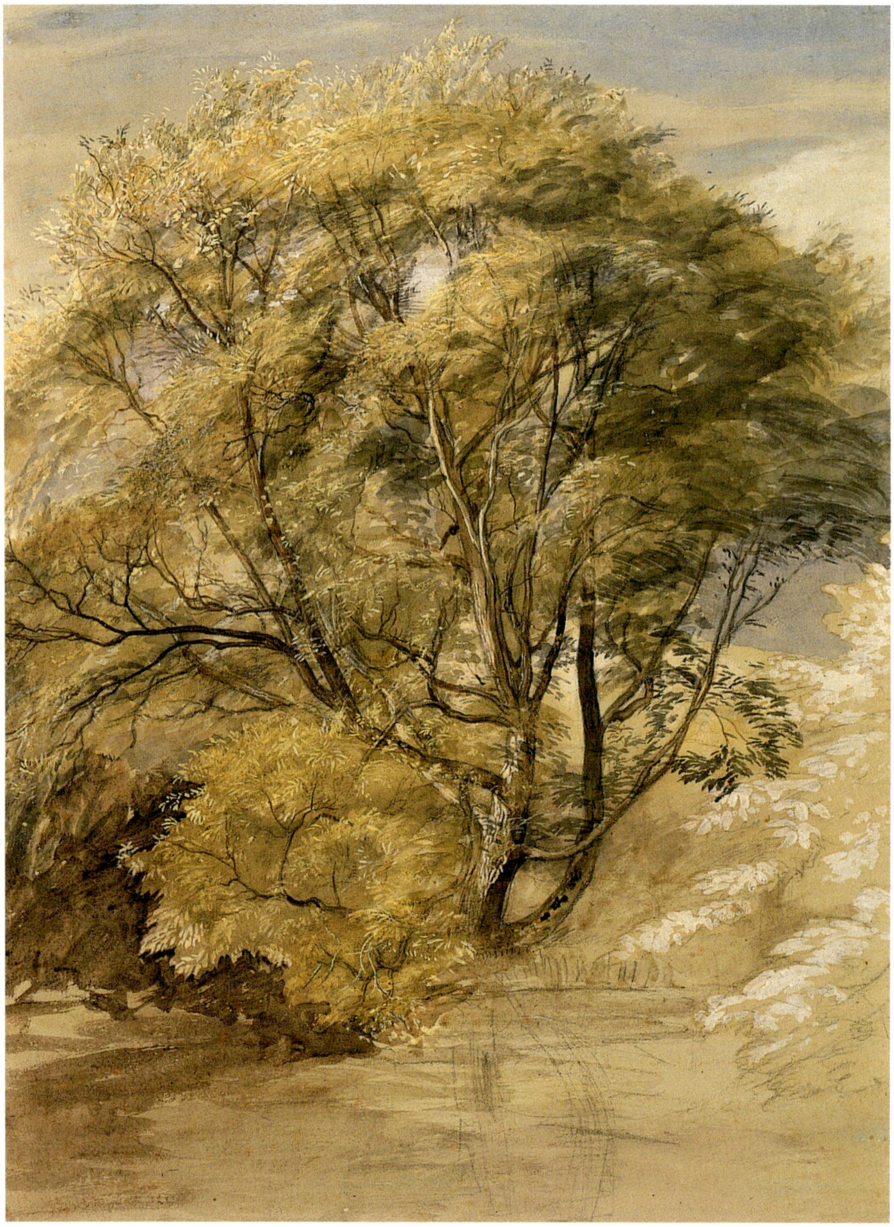

125

## 125*

*The Willow*, *c.*1850

Watercolour, 37 × 26.5 cm (14 9/16 × 10 7/16 in)

Lit: Lister 487

Manchester City Galleries, 1936-196

Throughout his career Palmer produced vivid tree studies, a habit perhaps encouraged in the first place by Linnell, who had commissioned him to make studies of the oaks in Lullingstone Park (cats 46, 47). Taken as a group, these tree studies provide one of the most revealing commentaries on the ways in which Palmer's observational methods developed and changed. The Lullingstone Park oaks are emphatically drawn, with all the encrustation and magnification so typical of Palmer's 'visionary' years. His fine studies of cypresses at Tivoli (cat. 105) – the only work by him ever to be praised in public by Ruskin – show the botanical exactitude that developed around the time of his journey to Italy. They are detailed, careful and precise – almost forensic in their investigative probing. The present study of a willow – made in all probability a year or so before the etching that was based on it – shows the new breadth and vigour that emerged in his art in the late 1840s and that is celebrated in his *Watermill* (cat. 116).

Typically for Palmer, the study, while elaborate, conceals none of its stages. It shows the bold 'first lines' that mapped out the whole and that enabled the sketch to retain a sinuous vigour so appropriate for the pliable wood of the willow. Over this framework Palmer built up washes of paint and topped these with layers of directly applied dryer brushstrokes, giving the impression of the leaves in movement. While retaining the basic form of the tree and its situation on the bank of a river, Palmer elaborated the design in the etching (cat. 126) by adding a swan, cows and some background scenery. WV

## 126

*The Willow*, 1850

Etching, sheet 18.8 × 14.6 cm (7 3/4 × 5 3/4 in), plate 12 × 8.2 cm (4 7/8 × 3 1/8 in), image 9 × 6.6 cm (3 1/2 × 2 5/8 in), state 2 of 3

Signed on plate at lower left: *S. PALMER 1850*

Inscribed in graphite at lower left in Martin Hardie's hand: *Ar[ii] – Proof by A.H.P. on his private press*; at lower centre: *Martin Hardie Colln. / A.H. Palmer.*; at lower right: *M.H.*

Lit: Alexander, 1(ii); Lister E1(2)

New Haven, Yale Center for British Art, B.1977.14.10940

*The Willow* was Palmer's first etching. (For more on Palmer's work as an etcher, see essay, pp. 47–54.) On 19 February 1850 the artist submitted it to the Etching Club of London, an association of professional artist-printmakers formed in 1838 to promote the medium by sharing expertise and opinions at regular meetings, as well as the expenses and profits of group publications (Fredericksen 2002, Chambers 1999). After studying Palmer's probationary plate, the assembled members elected him unanimously to their ranks. Their opinion of *The Willow* may have been similar to F.G. Stephens's, who regarded Palmer's 'tentative effort' as 'remarkable for its delicacy and some timidity, the latter being, of course, due to a newly tried and difficult process'. (Stephens 1872, p. 166.)

To compose the scene, Palmer adapted the tree study in Manchester Art Gallery (cat. 125) and added cows, a distant building and a swan. A dense network of cross-hatched lines conveys the shaded areas, darkest beneath the tree, along its lowest branch and at the lower right. The artist's son, A.H. Palmer, printed this fine, evenly inked proof before the etching's publication in *The Life and Letters of Samuel Palmer* (1892): he gave it to Martin Hardie, the art historian and artist who did much to revive interest in Palmer's work in the third decade of the twentieth century (*L&L*, p. 2).

The whereabouts of the original copper plate reprinted by Hardie, Griggs and Short in 1926 and then cancelled is unknown.

## 127a

### Etching needle used by Samuel Palmer

Wood, metal alloy and steel

Lit: V&A 1926, 19

London, Victoria and Albert Museum, E.459-1953; presented by Dorothea Short

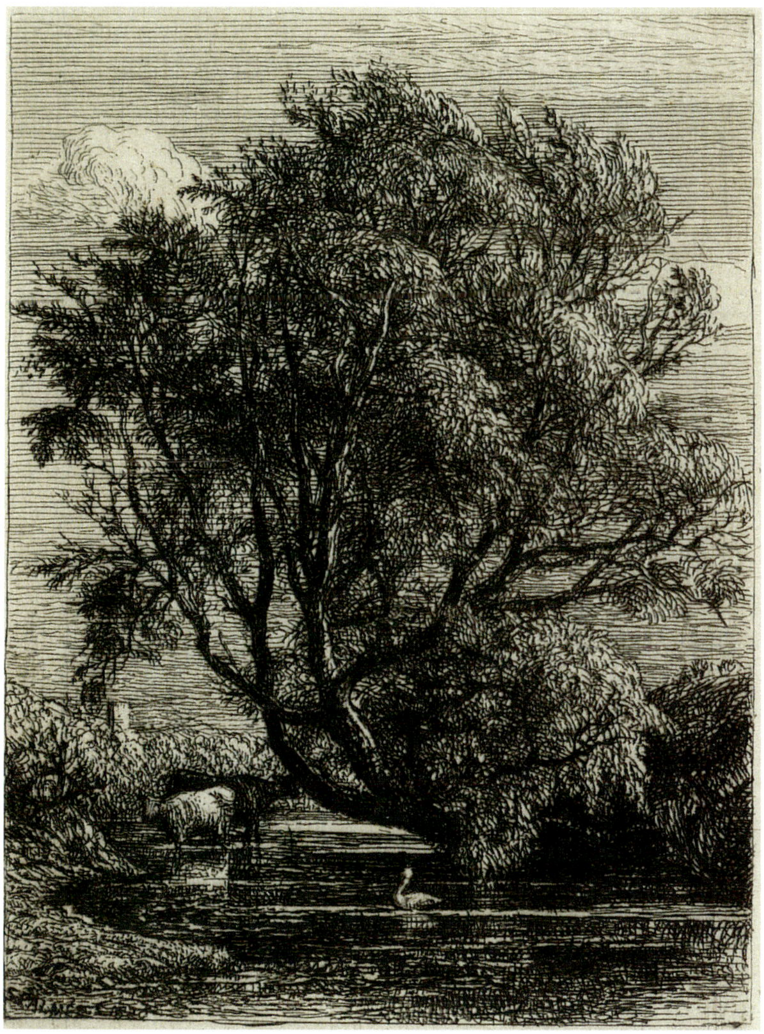

126

## 127b

### Short burin used by Samuel Palmer

Wood, metal alloy and steel

London, Victoria and Albert Museum, E.460-1953; presented by Dorothea Short

## 127c

### Long burin used by Samuel Palmer

Wood, metal alloy and steel

Inscribed (in etching) on ferrule (possibly in Palmer's own hand): *Samuel / Palmer*; on steel point (in another hand): *Samuel Palmer's burin / Given to me by Martin Hardie – 1937 / ROBERT AUSTIN*

London, Victoria and Albert Museum, E.3980-1923; presented by Martin Hardie

## 127d

### Scraper used by Samuel Palmer

Wood, metal alloy and steel

Lit: V&A 1926, 20

London, Victoria and Albert Museum, E.4530-1923; presented by Martin Hardie

In 1850, at the age of forty-five, Palmer took up etching, an intaglio printmaking method whose autographic qualities appealed to many nineteenth-century painters. (For Palmer's work as an etcher, and the etching process in general, see essay, pp. 47–54.) These were his etching tools: an etching needle (a sharp point used to draw on the prepared ground of a printing plate); short and long burins, or gravers (straight-shanked, four-sided blades with lozenge-shaped cutting points used to make broader lines on the plate), and a scraper (a tapered blade with three concave sides used to remove burr or smooth out areas of the plate).

The artist's son, A.H. Palmer, who printed many of his father's plates, gave the tools to the 'Trio' of printers who had collaborated in a sensitive reprinting of Palmer's five surviving etching plates, published in 1926: Sir Frank Short, the great master printer, Royal

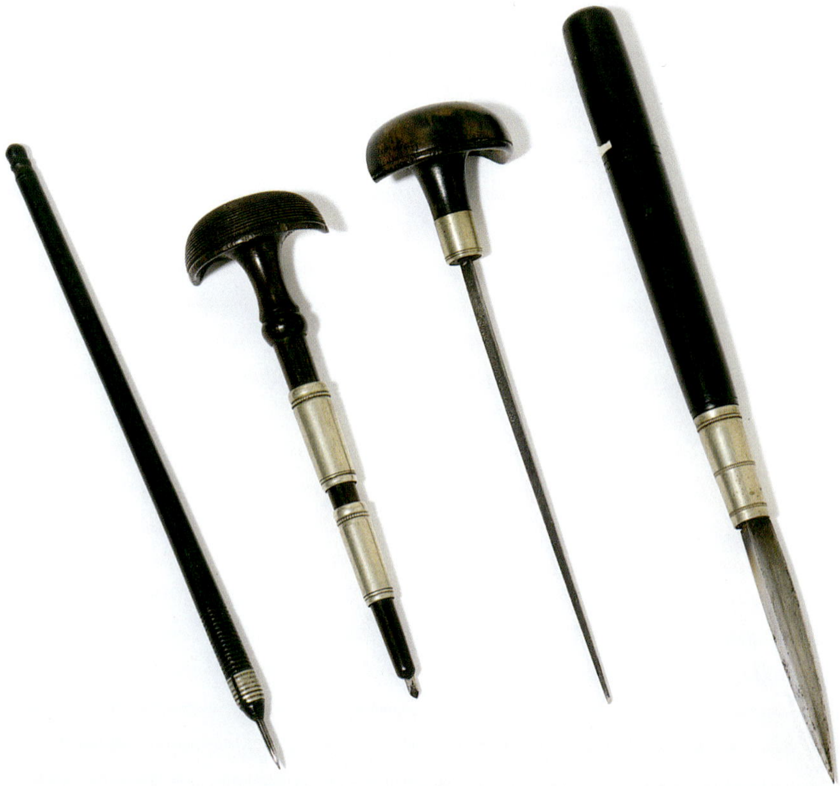

127 a b c d

Academician, 2nd President of the Royal Society of Painter-Etchers and Professor of Engraving at South Kensington; Martin Hardie, the artist, art historian and curator, who wrote extensively about Palmer's work and organized the important 1926 retrospective at the Victoria and Albert Museum; and F.L. Griggs, the etcher, watercolour painter and printer, on whose Dover House Press at Chipping Campden the 'final edition' of Palmer's etchings were printed. (Hardie and Short each donated two of Palmer's etching tools to the Victoria and Albert Museum; Griggs's tools – assuming that he also received some – are unknown.)

In a note sent to Martin Hardie in 1923 A.H. Palmer recalled that the tools with 'German silver fittings were made by one Donaldson, in industrious, between bibulous, intervals – a noted man at his craft.'

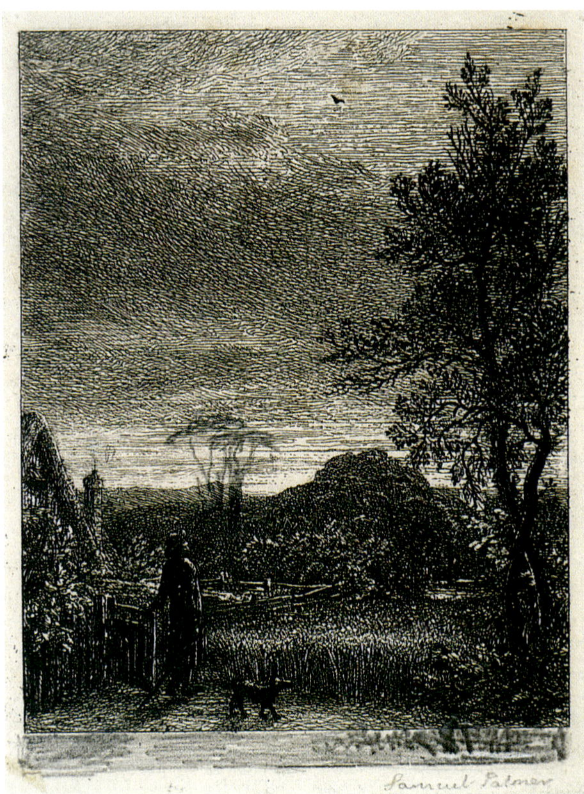


128a

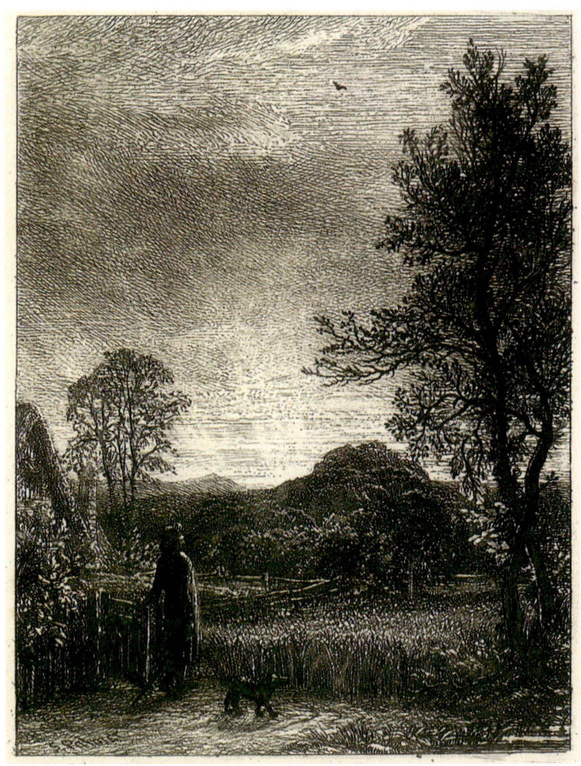

128b

## 128a

### *The Skylark*, 1850

Etching, touched in graphite, printed on buff paper laid down onto card, sheet 12.3 × 10.1 cm (4⅞ × 4 in), plate 12.4 × 11.6 cm (4⅞ × 4⅝ in), image 9.5 × 7.4 cm (3¾ × 2⅞ in), working proof 2 of 2, before state 1 of 8

Signed in graphite at lower right of image: *Samuel Palmer*; at lower right of sheet: *M.H.*; at upper left of verso: *3*; at bottom: *Martin Hardie / Request for Exhibition.*

Lit: V&A 1926, 163; Alexander 2(i); Lister E2(1)

New Haven, Yale Center for British Art, B1977.14.10932

## 128b

### *The Skylark*, 1850

Etching on chine collé, sheet approx. 25 × 35 cm (9⅞ × 13¾ in), plate 11.9 × 9.8 cm (4⅝ × 3⅞ in), image 9.7 × 7.6 cm (3¾ × 2⅞ in), state 7 of 8, before lettering

Lit: Alexander 2(vii); Lister E2(7); Goldman 1991, no. 2

London, British Museum, 1872-5-11-983; presented by Samuel Palmer, 1872

In *The Skylark*, Palmer's second etching (completed in the same year as the first), his astonishing skill as a printmaker fully appears. The subject comes from Milton's 'L'Allegro' (II, lines 41–4):

> To hear the Lark begin his flight,
> And singing startle the dull night,
> From his watch-towre in the skies,
> Till the dappled dawn doth rise …

As Pressly observed, Palmer's mood of religious reverie also recalls the passage in Samuel Taylor Coleridge's 'Fears in Solitude' (1798), in which a humble man listens to a skylark's song at dusk and 'dreams of better worlds' (Pressly 1970, p. 14, no. 2).

Palmer developed the design from a brown wash drawing of the early 1830s (untraced, Lister 140), which also served as the basis for a small oil painting (National Museum of Wales, Cardiff, Lister 375) that A.H. Palmer dated to the Shoreham period and described as 'strong and rich in colour' (V&A 1926, 166). To prepare the etching, Palmer made an ink drawing (Cleveland Museum of Art, Lister 497) the same size as the plate with the design reversed, so that the printed image would repeat the original orientation.

The working proof preserved at Yale reveals Palmer's early arrangement of the composition, before the first state. Dissatisfied with the effect, Palmer marked the sheet extensively in pencil, lengthening the image at the base with rough indications of plants and a path, inserting a tree in the middle distance and adding a branch to the tree on the right.

The subtle tonalities and luminous sky were hard won. Palmer recalled spending 'a whole day in nearly burnishing out' the sky, which had been over-bitten by a 'perverse acid' that '*would* bite skies and nothing else' (*L&L*, p. 99). Undeterred by technical glitches, however, Palmer pursued the effect he sought until he achieved what A.H. Palmer described as 'the delicate upward flush of early dawn over thin vaporous cloud' (*L&L*, p. 99).

Palmer referred to this etching as 'Dawn' until November of 1856, when he selected the title *The Skylark* for use in *Etchings for the Art Union of London by the Etching Club* (1857), where it appeared as plate 17. The original steel plate was destroyed (*Letters*, p. 1028).

## 129

### *Christmas* or *Folding the Last Sheep*, 1850

Etching on Japanese paper, sheet 15.8 × 12.2 cm (6¼ × 4¼ in), plate 12.4 × 10.2 cm (4⅞ × 4 in), image 9.8 × 8.1 cm (3⅞ × 3⅛ in), state 3 of 5

Signed in etching at lower right: *S. Palmer*; inscribed in graphite in Samuel Palmer's hand beneath image: *Folding the last sheep: from Bamfylde's Sonnet*; in brown ink (the first word over traces of graphite): *Samuel Palmer*; in graphite at lower right: *Christmas / Artist's Proof / Japanese Paper*; in graphite at lower centre: *A 4 III of 5 / C26905*; in graphite on a slip of paper attached to the mount in Sir Frank Short's hand: *Printed by me F.S.*; and on another slip: *Pattern / but no darker / Return to Sir F. Short*

Lit: Alexander 4(v); Lister E4(5)

Oxford, Ashmolean Museum, 1954.112; purchased 1954

Three small children greet a man who opens a sheepfold gate for the last of his entering flock. Beside them, within a bright cottage, a fourth child hands plates to a woman setting a table. The homely subject and masterful juxtaposition of silvery moonlight and glowing lamplight make *Christmas* 'one of Samuel Palmer's most successful plates' (*Memoir*, p. 17 note).

Palmer took the subject from John Bampfylde's 'Sonnet on Christmas' (1778):

> Old Christmas comes, to close the
>   waned year;
> And ay the Shepherd's heart to make
>   right glad;
> Who, when his teeming flocks are
>   homeward had,
> To blazing hearth repairs, and nut-
>   brown beer,
> And views, well-pleas'd, the ruddy
>   prattlers dear
> Hug the grey mongrel; meanwhile
>   maid and lad
> Squabble for roasted crab[apple]s.

Palmer prepared the plate in 1850, but the dating of the present impression remains uncertain. Confusingly, inscriptions on the work itself conflict with others on the mount. Two slips of paper attached to the mount state that Sir Frank Short printed this impression as a model for the posthumous edition of Palmer's etchings published in 1926 (see essay, pp. 47–54). But this impression does not resemble others from the 'final edition', which show the plate in its fifth state after the removal of the lettering (introduced by 1877 and still present in 1882; *Memoir*, frontispiece) and following the addition of a triangle etched in the lower left margin. Moreover, this impression bears various annotations (excluding the apparent signature) in Palmer's own hand.

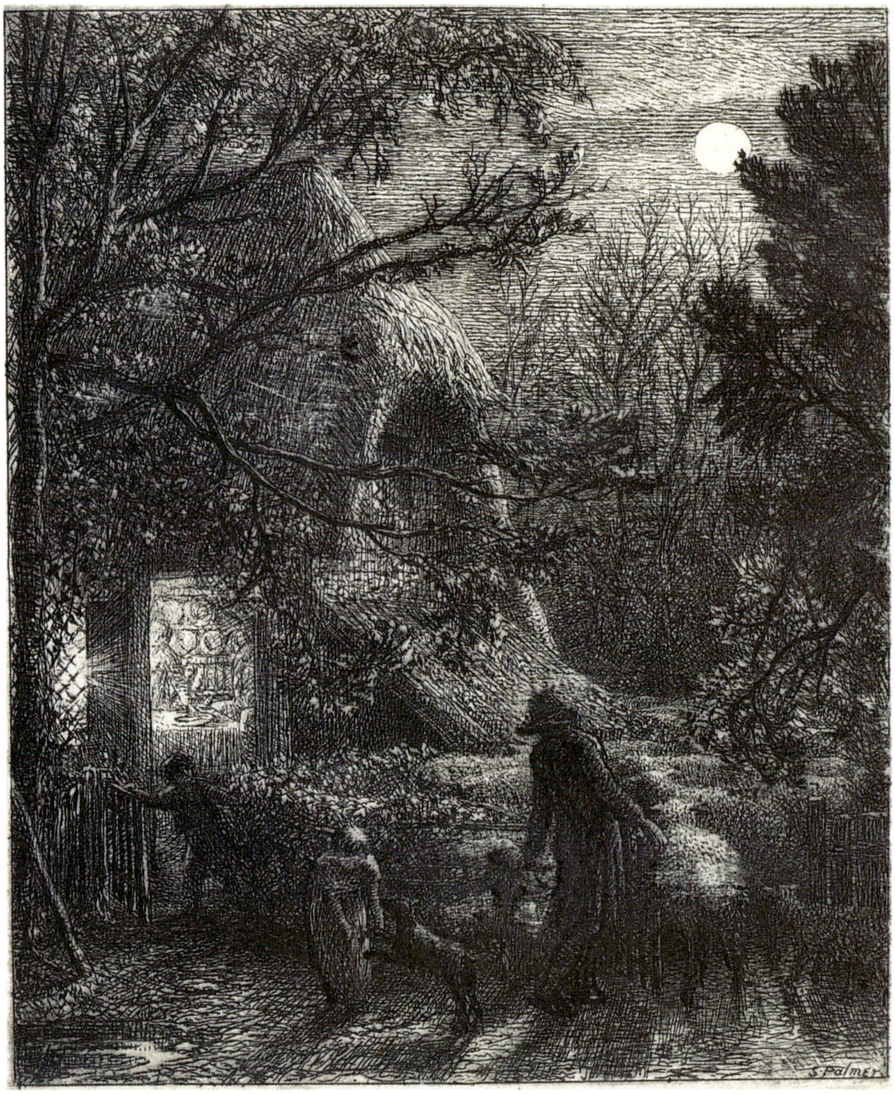


129

Given its penultimate state and inscriptions by Palmer, this impression would appear to have been printed during the artist's lifetime, and later to have become inadvertently linked to Short's comments (presumably made in reference to a different impression). It seems likely that Frederick Goulding, or possibly A.H. Palmer, printed this impression between 1873 and 1877, when the master printer instructed the etcher's son in 'artificial printing' techniques using this plate, and pulled at least one (other) proof on old Japanese paper (V&A 1926, 173–4). The cancelled steel plate for *Christmas* is now in the Victoria and Albert Museum.

## 130

### *Old Cedar in the Botanic Garden, Chelsea*, 1854

Black chalk on off-white paper, 26.5 × 36.6 cm (10½ × 14½ in)

Inscribed in graphite at upper left of verso, possibly in the artist's hand: *An old cedar in Botanic Garden Chelsea / drawn as a lesson to Mr. Aston afterds member of Institute 1854.*; in graphite in Martin Hardie's hand: *C.R. Aston, 1832–1908 / M.H.*; in red chalk: *256*; in blue ink in Martin Hardie's hand: *S. Palmer / Cedar in Botanic / Gdns Chelsea / 1854*; and in graphite in Martin Hardie's hand: *Martin Hardie*

Lit: Fitzwilliam 1984, 53; Lister 522

New Haven, Yale Center for British Art, Paul Mellon Collection, B1977.14.5932

A web of fine black chalk describes the natural specimen, a sinewy cedar tree. Palmer found his subject in south-west London, in the Chelsea Physic Garden, established in 1673 by the Society of Apothecaries, and saved from closure in 1722 by Sir Hans Sloane, founder of the British Museum.

Palmer prepared this study as part of a drawing lesson given to Charles Reginald Aston, a great-nephew of Sir Thomas Lawrence and subsequent member of the Royal Institute of Painters in Water Colours. The circumstances of its creation – Palmer at work with his chalk, explaining his methods and principles as he demonstrated them to his rapt pupil – are conveyed in the reminiscences of another student:

> It was not only a rich treat to watch him painting the beautiful pictures which were developed out of his imagination from day to day, and formed the lesson (afterwards possessed by me), but also to listen to his original and striking conversation, combined with the profoundest rules and directions concerning art. (Twining 1893, p. 20.)

## 131

### 'Egg Classification' from 'Notes taken during the Lessons in Watercolor Painting from Samuel Palmer to Louisa Twining', 1856

Bound manuscript notes in graphite and watercolour, page 20.5 × 16.4 cm (8⅛ × 6½ in)

Inscribed in graphite: *Egg Classification / The half tints or delicate half / shadows which seem to / grow out of the shadow / into the light seem / to take definite shapes / or to suggest them / The high light, or lights / also have a shape / Look for shapes in lights shades & half / tints /* [drawing of a seven-sided figure, labelled A at top, B at base] *A If exposed to sky cool / B affected by colour, or colours of the ground /* [drawing of a tree] *a cool light from sky / warm light from Sun /* [drawing of three connected planes labelled A in centre, B at base] *a mixture of A & B / it being exposed to reflex from both sky & earth. / Practically if you prepare your*

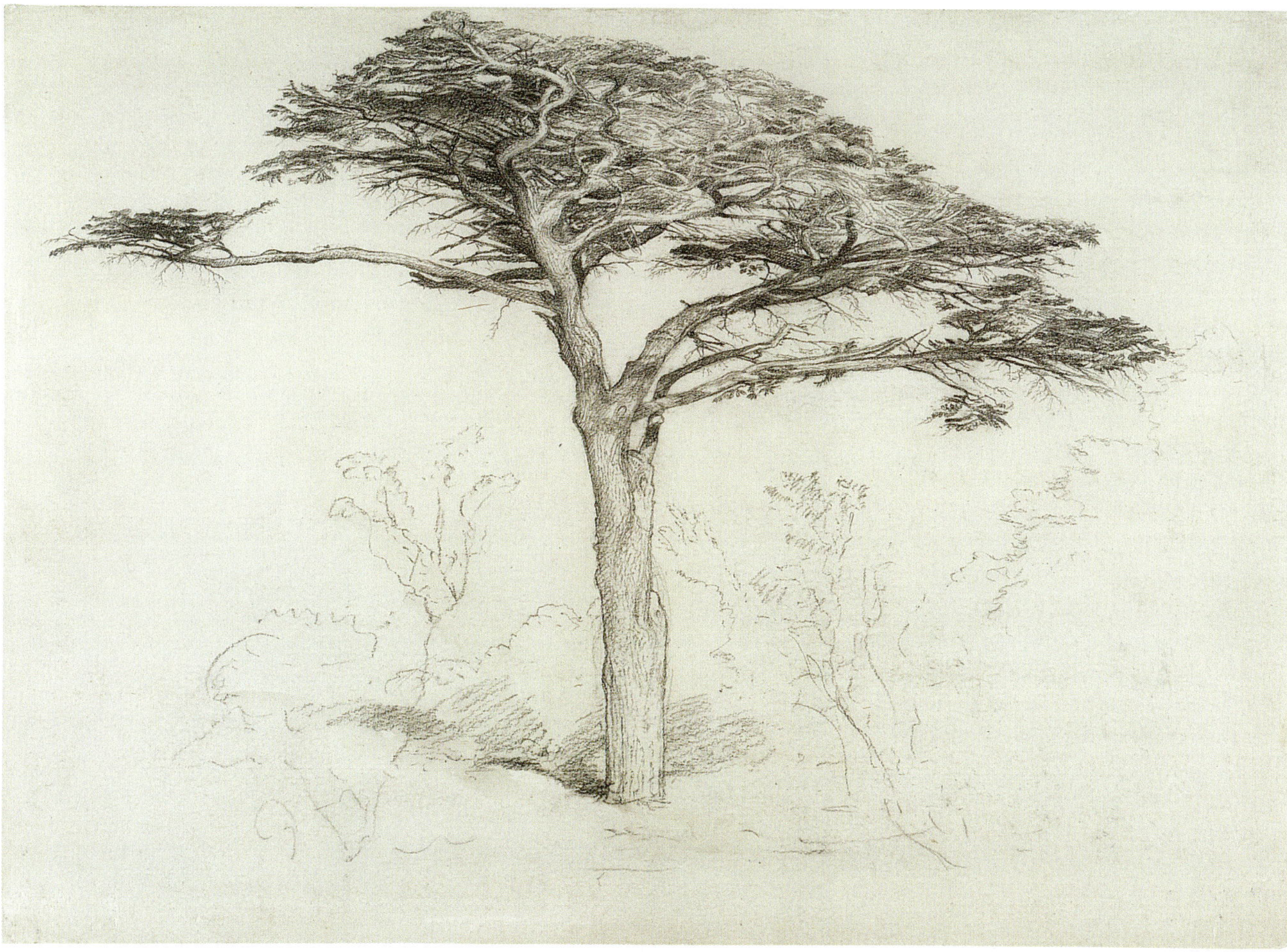

130

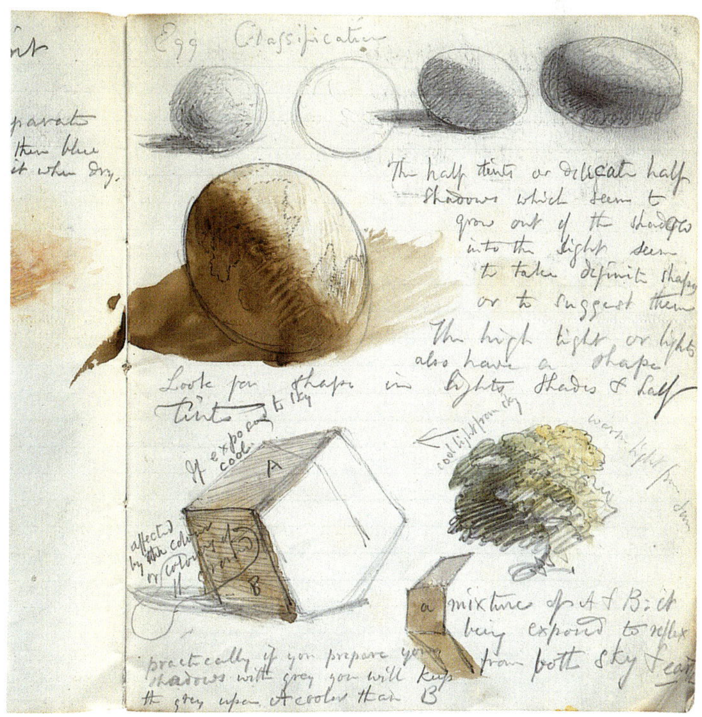
Egg Classification
The half tints or delicate half shadows which seem to grow out of the shadows into the light seem to take definite shapes or to suggest them
The high light or lights also have a shape
Look for shapes in lights shades & half tints
A
B
a mixture of A & B it being exposed to reflex from both sky
practically if you prepare your shadows with grey you will keep the grey upon A cooler than B

131

*shadows with grey / you will keep the grey upon A cooler than B.*

Oxford, Ashmolean Museum, 1954.131.2

Palmer made these notes on light and shade as part of a series of lessons in watercolour painting given to the tea and coffee heiress, author and philanthropist, Louisa Twining, in 1856. The serious subject and methodical explanation typify Palmer's manner of instruction, which sought to ground all pupils in the fundamentals, regardless of their level of interest or expertise. The eggs shown at the top of this page often served as models. A.H. Palmer recorded that his father would set his pupils 'to draw an egg in black and white chalk' as a training exercise, and would himself sometimes 'go to school to a potato' for the same reason (*L&L*, pp. 105–6).

Other pages contain additional notes on light and shade, and on outline and form; lists of recommended colours; methods for combining colours to make tints, and for layering tints upon the paper; on colour wheels; and on capturing distances, sunsets and the 'EXPRESSION' of nature.

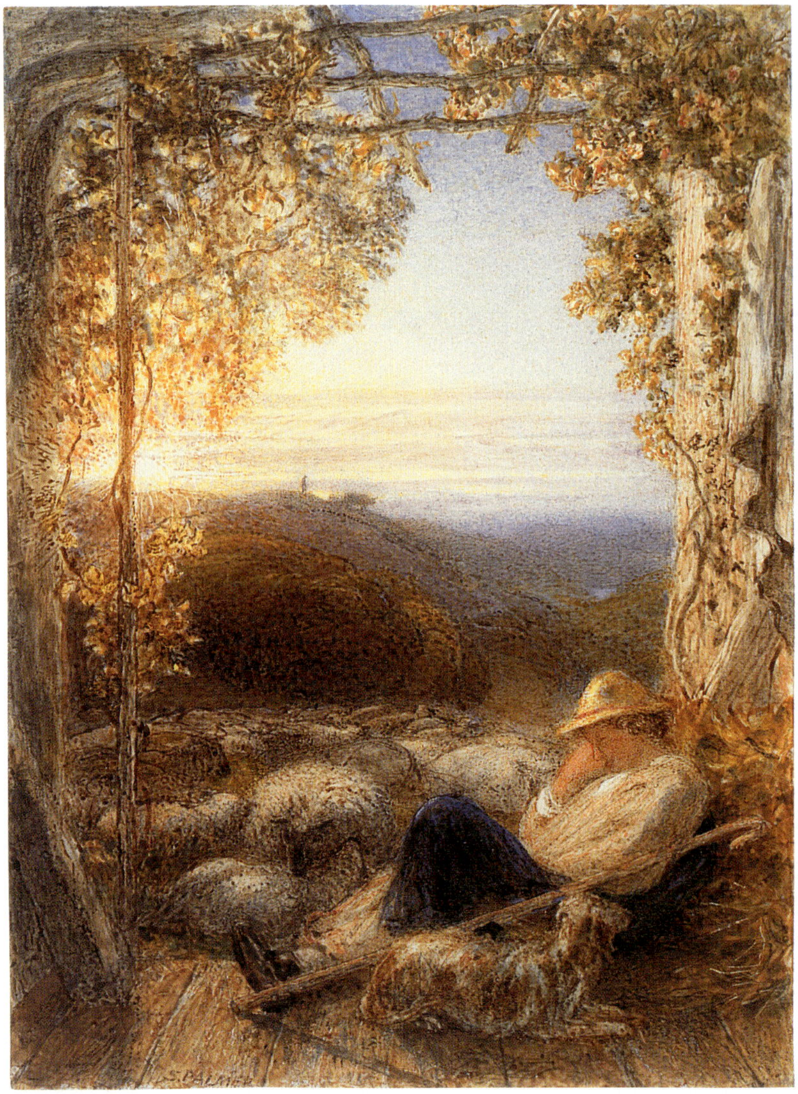

132

## 132

### *The Sleeping Shepherd, c.*1854

Watercolour, gouache, gum arabic, brown ink and traces of graphite on off-white wove paper laid down onto secondary support, 24.5 × 17.8 cm (9⅝ × 7 in)

Signed at lower left with point of brush: *S. PALMER*

Lit: Fitzwilliam 1984, 54; Lister 539

University of Cambridge, Fitzwilliam Museum, PD34-1980; bequest of Miss E.M. Williamson, 1980

The composition reprises Palmer's earlier *Sleeping Shepherd* of the late Shoreham period (cat. 89), but transforms that picture's rustic barn into an arbour teeming with blossoms and shifts the viewpoint to encompass a broad landscape illuminated by the setting sun. The contrast between the toiling ploughman and the slumbering shepherd evokes traditional representations of the active and the contemplative life. Palmer probably completed this accomplished watercolour (previously dated *c.*1857) by 1854, when he began to prepare the etching adapted from its design (cat. 133).

The shepherd's reclining pose has many precedents, but (as Lister noted) Palmer may well have considered his favourite sculpture in the British Museum when he came to design his own peaceful sleeper (fig. 29, see also cat. 89; *Letters*, p. 67). For Palmer 'that peerless shepherd of the Townley gallery' evoked 'the tenderest pastoral' and offered a 'sure test of our imaginative faculty' (*Letters*, pp. 880, 706).

## 133

### *The Sleeping Shepherd – Early Morning, c.*1854–7

Etching on chine collé, sheet 29.7 × 21.7 cm (11¾ × 8½ in), plate 12.4 × 10.3 cm (4⅞ × 4 in), image 9.5 × 7.8 cm (3¾ × 3⅛ in), state 3 of 4

Inscribed in graphite at lower left: *B. Museum*; on verso at upper left: *laid aside for B. Museum*; at centre: *5*

Lit: Alexander 6(iii); Lister E6(3); Goldman 1991, no. 6

London, British Museum, 1872-5-11-984; presented by Samuel Palmer, Esq., 1872

At the meeting of the Etching Club on 4 November 1854 Palmer reported that

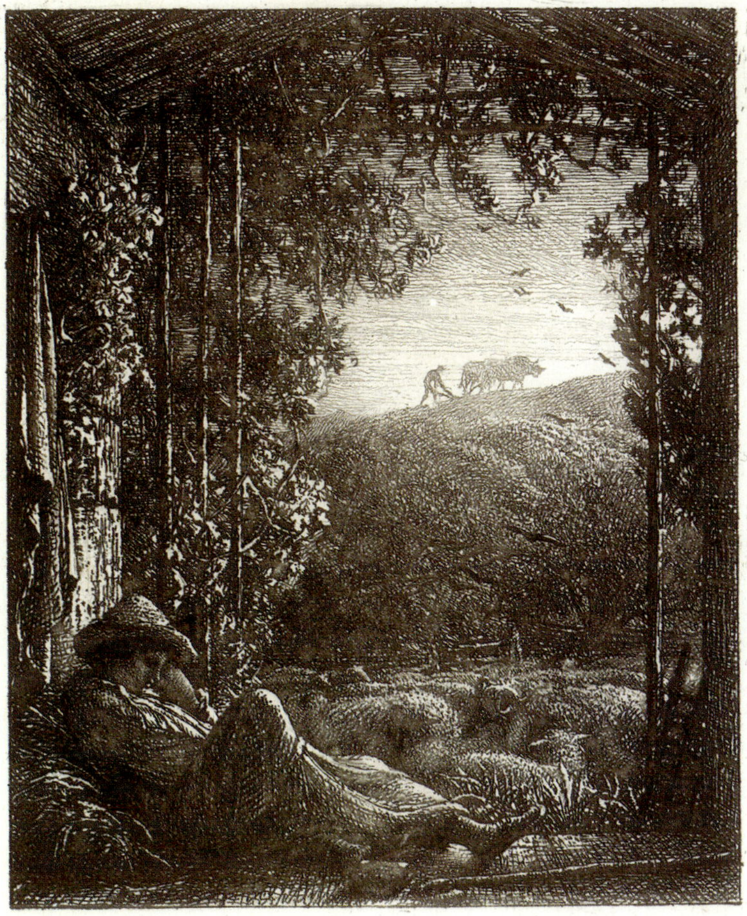

133

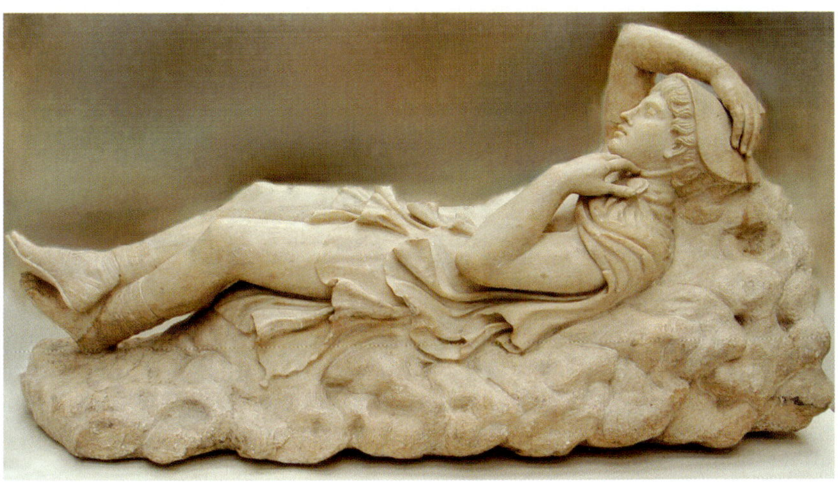

Fig. 29 *Endymion the Shepherd Boy Asleep on Mt Latmos*, marble, late second century AD (figure restored and upper surface reworked in the eighteenth century), found by Gavin Hamilton at Roma Vecchia, Rome, in 1774 or 1776, British Museum.

he had new works in progress: this plate appears to have been one of them. It may be the 'Shepherd from Sonnets' named on 12 February 1855, is probably the 'Shepherd Boy – Morning' mentioned on 12 March 1855 and is certainly the 'Early Ploughman' listed on 17 and 23 May 1856. Palmer would inscribe the words 'Peace and Quiet' on an impression exhibited in 1857 (Pressly 1970, no. 6). But the print is best known by the title (determined by the 4 November 1856 club meeting) under which the final state would be published (as plate 5 of *Etchings for the Art Union of London by the Etching Club*, 1857): 'The Sleeping Shepherd'.

To accommodate the small vertical plate favoured for his early etchings, Palmer altered the design of the Fitzwilliam Museum's picture (cat. 132) in various details – widening the arbour, repositioning the crook, replacing the dog with a book, raising the shepherd's knee, moving the hill and ploughman nearer, and adding a fence and rooks. The intermediary design, presumably a black ink line drawing the size of the etched image (like Lister 497), is lost.

In February 1872 Palmer sent the present impression to his friend F.G. Stephens with the note:

> The 'Sleeping Shepherd' is I think the best impression that has been taken – and probably I threw it aside because the rooks were so large that a single one would have made a good family pie – but I have clipped their wings with the point of a penknife. (*Letters*, p. 838.)

Palmer's judicious removal of small portions of the print's surface remains visible in the sky. Stephens had requested *The Sleeping Shepherd* (and other etchings) to complete the set of Palmer's prints that he deposited in the British Museum later that spring (*Letters*, p. 843). When Stephens described this print in an article (Stephens 1872, p. 167), he quoted the following lines, evocative of Milton and Thomas Gray, but possibly composed by Palmer: 'The ploughman seeks the upland lawn; / O'er-watched, the shepherd nods at dawn.' Lister, though,

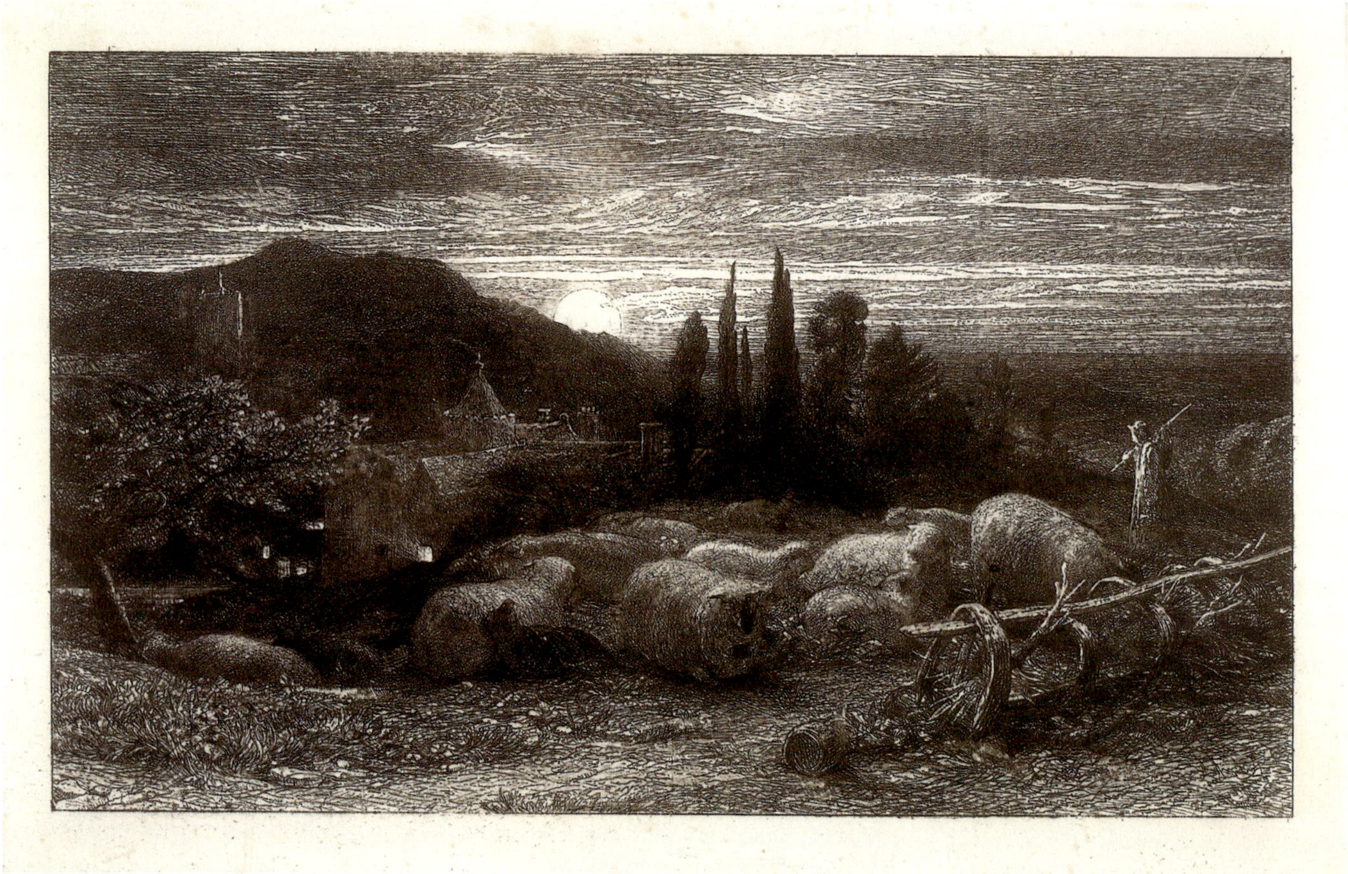

134

related different lines to the scene: Milton's 'L'Allegro', II, 63–8 (Fitzwilliam 1984, 85.)

An impression of the first state coloured by hand, apparently by Palmer himself, is in the National Gallery of Art, Washington, DC (Lessing J. Rosenwald Collection). The original plate, one of a set of four made of steel, was destroyed (*Letters*, p.1028).

## 134

### *The Rising Moon* or *An English Pastoral* or *Evening Pastures*, *c.*1855–7

Etching on off-white wove paper trimmed to the plate margins 14.5 × 22.4 cm ($5^3/_4 \times 8^7/_8$ in), image 11.7 × 19.1 cm ($4^5/_8 \times 7^1/_2$ in), proof of state 2 of 9, touched with graphite

Lit: Alexander 7(ii); Lister E7(2); Goldman 1991, no. 7

London, British Museum, 1872-5-11-977; presented by Samuel Palmer, 1872

On 29 October 1855 Palmer presented 'a new etching' to the Etching Club. That plate was almost certainly *The Rising Moon* or *An English Pastoral*, later published as plate 10 of *Etchings for the Art Union of London by the Etching Club* (1857). In addition, Palmer would refer to this print variously as 'The Flock – Evening', 'Evening Pastures' and 'my moonlight-flock-etching' (Minutes, 17 May 1856; RA 1865, no. 872; *Letters*, p. 792).

Horizontally orientated and substantially larger than Palmer's previous etchings, *The Rising Moon* initiates a new format for the artist's prints. A shepherd, his belongings suspended in a bundle from a stick, pauses beside his flock, as the full moon illuminates the mottled sky and roofs of a nearby village. Palmer composed the scene from numerous motifs, imagined and observed, from different periods in his career. The solitary figure, woolly animals and moonlit sky recall the Shoreham period; the hills evoke Devon and Wales; the cypresses elicit memories of Italy; the 'bars of moonlight' relate to studies made at Margate (*Memoir*, p. 18); and the provender trough reappears in many later works.

One element, however, is unique: the 'exaggerated perspective' described by P.G. Hamerton in 1880, which makes the 'monstrously big' sheep dwarf the 'pigmy'-sized man (Hamerton 1880, p. 260; comparison with Palmer's later treatment of a similar subject, *Opening the Fold*, cat. 162, reveals the difference). Hamerton – who admired Palmer's work and praised *The Rising Moon* for its serene subject and abstractly rendered sky – only hinted at the possible reason for the distortion, demurring that 'it would be out of place to enter fully into the subject here'. Hamerton's reluctance to elaborate, combined with his admission that such perspective might well be 'scientifically true', suggests that he was referring (with polite obliqueness) to an effect associated with photography (Hamerton 1880, p. 260).

The notion is not outrageous: Victorian artists may have been averse to acknowledging the use of photographs as models of design, but many employed them nevertheless. (For the examples of William Frith and William Dyce, see Sutton 1863, Cowling 1989, Willsdon 1988, Neve 1970.) While there is no documentary evidence to suggest that Palmer used photographs in this manner, his letters of the 1860s do attest to a growing familiarity with photography (*Letters*, pp. 291 n. 1, 702, 761, 768, 782, 869), and he almost certainly knew of the camera obscura (used by Linnell) and camera lucida (a variant of which, the Graphic Telescope, had been invented and patented by Cornelius Varley, brother of Palmer's friend John Varley). Yet Hamerton's attribution of the anti-intuitive proportions of *The Rising Moon* to an effect first seen with lenses seems misplaced. In fact the problem appears to lie entirely in the outsize figure, which was more likely to have resulted from Palmer's practice of combining elements from various sketches in his final designs.

Palmer extensively reworked the plate over many years (*Letters*, p. 1066). This proof of the second state provides a glimpse into his working processes: at the base of the left-most cypress (where it meets the backs of the sheep) Palmer darkened the shadows with touches of graphite. A.H. Palmer recorded that several counter-proofs of the plate were taken 'in brownish ink, and on drawing paper, with a view of colouring them', but no such impressions are known (V&A 1926, 188). The copper plate was destroyed (*Letters*, p. 1028).

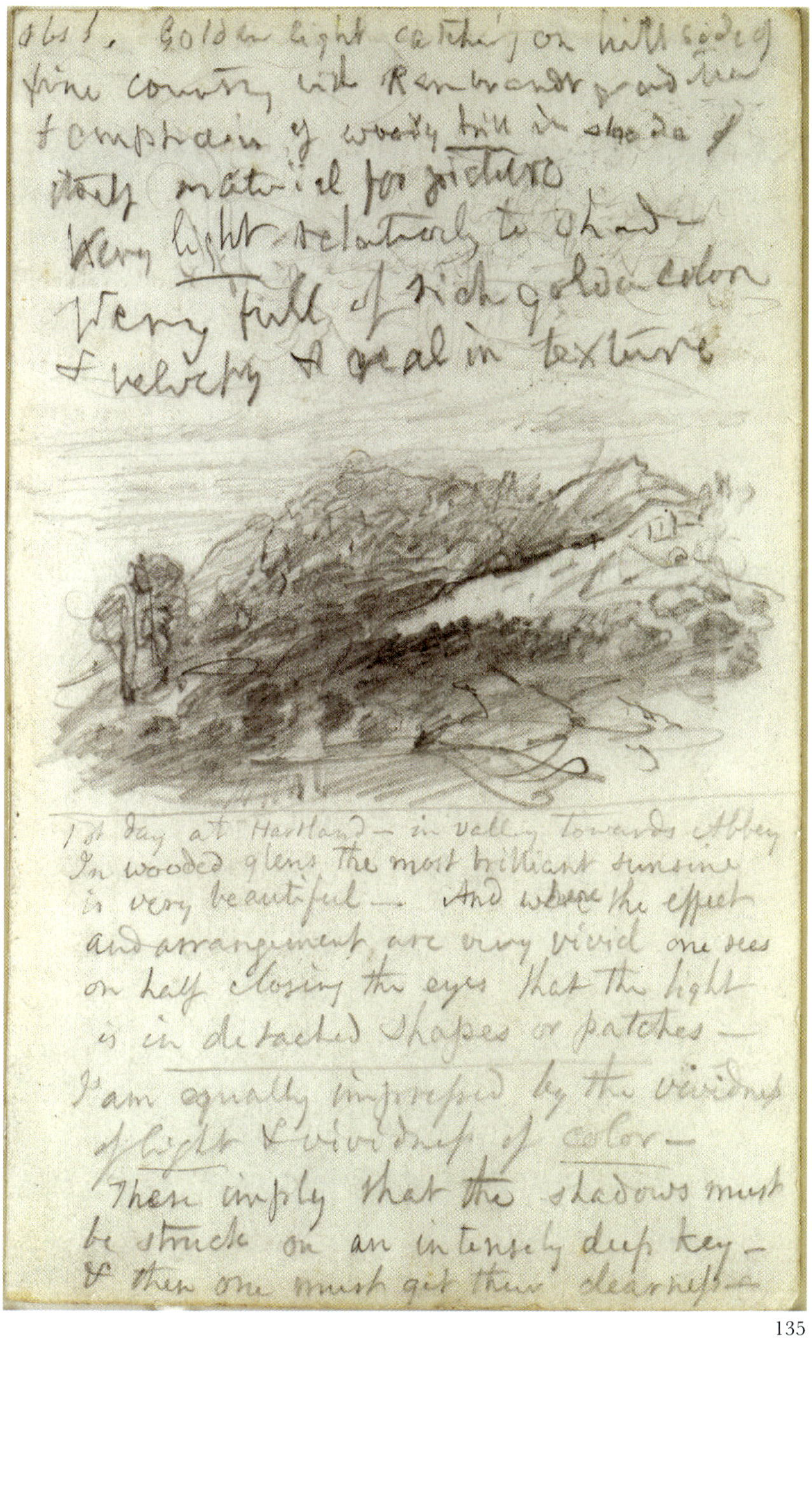

135

## 135

### Page from Sketchbook, *c.*1858

Graphite on off-white wove paper, 18.3 × 11.2 cm (7¼ × 4½ in)

Inscribed in graphite in the artist's hand on recto: *Obs 1. Golden light catching on hill side of / fine country with Rembrandt gradation / & emphasis of woody hill in shade of / itself material for picture / Very* light *relatively to shade / Very full of rich golden colour / & velvety & real in texture /* [landscape sketch] */ 1st day at Hartland – in valley towards Abbey / In wooded glens the most brilliant sunsine* [sic] */ is very beautiful – And where the effect / and arrangement are very vivid one sees / on half closing the eyes that the light / is in detached shapes or patches – / —— / I am equally impressed by the vividness / of* light *& vividness of* colour *– / These imply that the shadows must / be struck on an intensely deep key – / & then one must get their clearness –*; on verso: *Sky grey lights & reflected lights as one / can – / Sir James Hamlyn William 21 Upper Grosvenor / St /* [sketch]; in another hand at lower left: *2/4*

Lit: Lister 556, 680

New York, The Metropolitan Museum of Art; bequest of Mary Cushing Fosburgh, 1978

The dating of this sketchbook page has been inconsistent. In 1892 A.H. Palmer published a selection of notes from this sketchbook and assigned them to 1858 (*L&L*, pp. 111–12). In 1988 Raymond Lister catalogued the notes transcribed by A.H. Palmer (which he described as lost) among the works of 1858 (Lister 556) but re-catalogued (as a different work) the Metropolitan Museum of Art's sheet and dated it tentatively to 1878 (Lister 680).

Lister presumably based the second, later dating on the sheet's shaky calligraphy; yet the handwriting's considerable variation – orderly beneath the sketch but slovenly at the top – makes it an unreliable indicator of date. Since the continuous content suggests that the various inscriptions date to the same moment, the differences in calligraphic style would seem to indicate some change in the writer's circumstances, rather than his age at the time of writing. Palmer may have begun to write at the bottom of the page, but run out of space, and so continued at the top (across the sky of his sketch), presumably working hurriedly in fading twilight.

The text itself provides further clues. The inscription, '1st day at Hartland – in valley towards Abbey', indicates that Palmer prepared this sheet in Devon. The village of Hartland (about four miles from Clovelly) is distinguished by Hartland Abbey, an eighteenth-century estate whose name derives from its medieval use as a monastery. A second (hitherto overlooked) inscription on the verso reads 'Sir James Hamlyn Williams 21 Upper Grosvenor St.', presumably a reference to Sir James Hamlyn-Williams, 3rd Baronet of Clovelly and Edwinsford, whose seat at Clovelly Court contained a fine picture collection and whose estate harboured some of the area's best views. Palmer may well have jotted the London address of Sir James during a visit to Devon with the intention of contacting him upon his return to the city. Although no further connection between the two men is known, the death of Sir James in 1866 establishes a last possible date for the present work.

The dates of Palmer's post-Italian tours narrow the scope further: the artist certainly visited Devon in July and August of 1848, June and July of 1849, July and October of 1858 and August of 1859, and he may also have travelled there in 1860. Of these possibilities, A.H. Palmer's 'original' dating of 1858 seems the most likely, given the close correspondence of the present work to two other detached sketchbook pages. One, dated 18 July 1858 (Lister 555), contains notes on twilight observed in Cornwall and Margate that A.H. Palmer transcribed immediately before that of the present study, indicating their nearness in date (*L&L*, p. 111). The other (Lister 460) has nearly identical dimensions to the present work, contains pencil sketches drawn in a similarly brisk manner, bears extensive annotations concerning the 'velvet depth' and 'vibrating gradations' of twilight, and was exhibited in 1926 amid the works of the 1850s (V&A 1926, 114).

## 136

### *Study of Bough Laden with Apples, c.1855?*

Black chalk, 29.2 × 45.1 cm (11½ × 17¾ in)

Inscribed: *Principle of size / Medium or large Apples universal bright / Exceptions / Some still a little larger & / some very much smaller – often / in graduated clusters / Gen. Effect in bright sun the whole / tree apples & leaves very golden / in the same tree will be some / boughs of darker apples / dim in relief but exquisite / in finish / boughs next in size to smallest / twigs – are I think of a crusty / texture and a pale dead gold. / Apple boughs fall in long shapes / like the branches – or the / same foreshorten'd which / is fine, the boughs are / pull'd down by the / weight. N.B some / trail along on the / green ground*; in a different hand: *1830*

Lit: V&A 1926, 63; Grigson 90; Fitzwilliam 1984, 20; Lister 124

University of Cambridge, Fitzwilliam Museum, 1491

Given the emphasis Palmer placed on foreground material in many of his early works, and Linnell's insistence that he should make extensive studies from nature, it is surprising how few drawings of the individual elements of his landscapes survive. This drawing of the bough of an apple tree has been associated with the watercolour in the Fitzwilliam, *The Magic Apple Tree* (cat. 69), since A.H. Palmer lent it to the V&A in 1926. In the catalogue he described it as 'Shoreham period, but analytical', in contrast to the 'ultra Shoreham sentiment' of the watercolour. However, the link is tenuous, and the date of 1830, inscribed by an unknown hand, is almost certainly incorrect. The style of the work suggests a later period, possibly the 1850s. Palmer's own

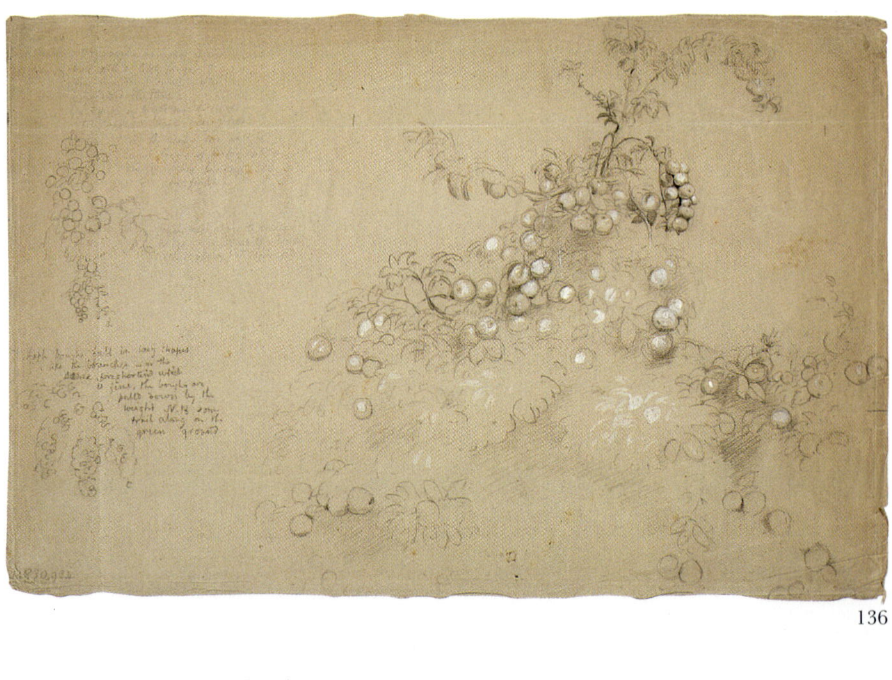

136

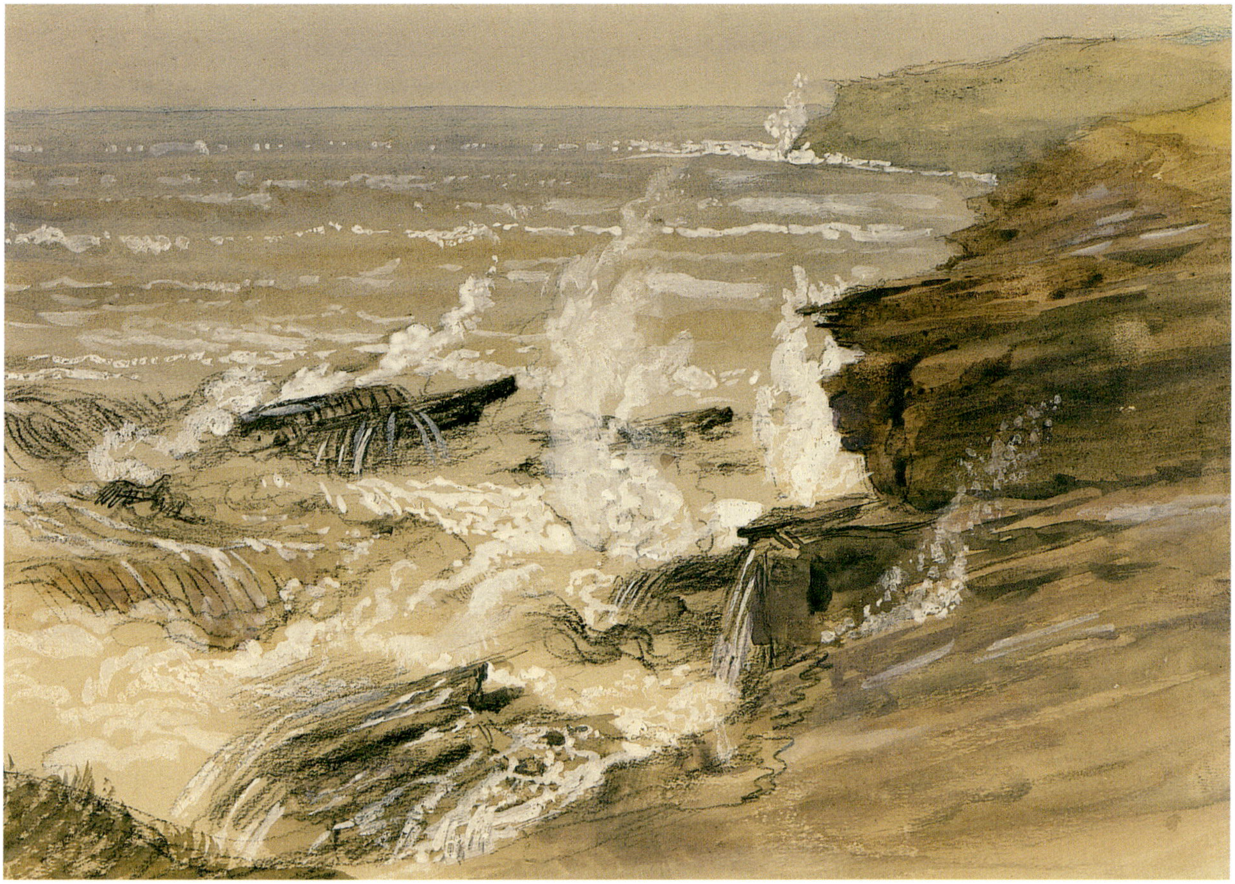

137

annotations are characteristically concerned with the depiction of bright sunshine through the leaves and fruit of the tree. CH

## 137

*Storm and Wreck on the Cornish Coast*, *c.*1858

Watercolour, gouache, brown wash and black chalk on grey paper, 18.8 × 27.4 cm ($7^3/_8 \times 10^3/_4$ in)

Inscribed in graphite on verso: *35*

Lit: Lister 563

Manchester City Galleries, 1936.192; bequeathed by Mrs Louisa Mary Garrett, 1936

Waves crash against a rocky shore marked by fragments of a shattered vessel. Deft marks of black chalk, swift strokes of brown wash and staccato touches of white describe the windswept view. A bold stroke of fluid blue wash forms the high horizon line and positions the viewer in direct confrontation with the surf. Fingerprints visible amid the sea-spray at the centre, and the beach edge at lower right, record Palmer's physical grapple to capture the stormy view.

A.H. Palmer described a smaller variant of this study as 'one of the best of S.P.'s sketches from nature' and recorded that it formed the basis of a watercolour exhibited with the Old Water-Colour Society in 1862 (no. 291): *Wrecked at Home – A Husband and a Brother Saved* (untraced; V&A 1926, 103; Lister 598). The Manchester Art Gallery's drawing belongs to a group of coast studies made during a visit to Cornwall in 1858; its closest counterpart is a graphite-and-black-chalk wave study of comparable dimensions executed on a similar grey sheet in the National Gallery of Canada (Lister 562).

## 138

*The Comet of 1858, as Seen from the Heights of Dartmoor*, 1858–9

Watercolour and gouache, 31.1 × 69.9 cm ($12^1/_4 \times 27^1/_2$ in)

Lit: Lister 574; Olson 1990, pp. 795–6; Olson and Pasachoff 1998, 234–6, fig. 130

Private collection, England

A stream of light – Donati's Comet of 1858 – illuminates the sky above a panoramic landscape, executed in Palmer's 'large long' size (see p. 192). (The comet, discussed below, was named for the Florentine astronomer credited with first sighting it.) To the left of the winding river a shepherd stands transfixed beside his flock. To the right a woman extends her hand, indicating the brilliant spectacle to the small child in her arm and the others seated before her. Behind them a hooded figure sits within an arched cave-like space, its warm

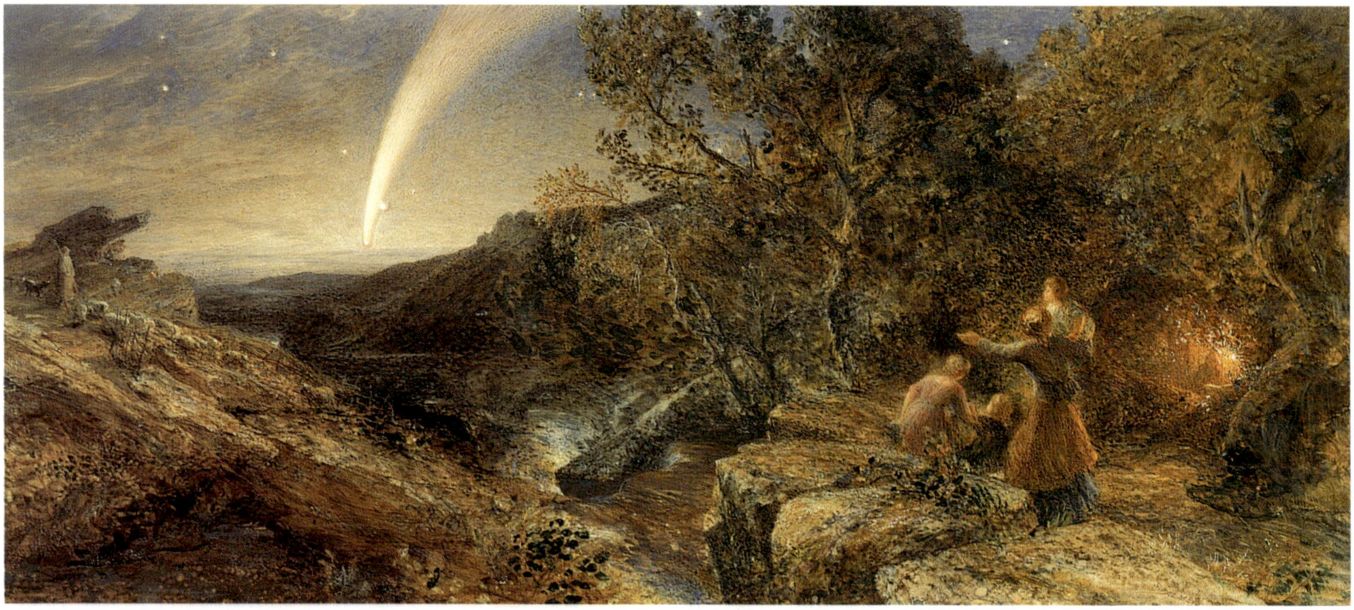

138

lamplight contrasting with the cool-toned celestial object.

Palmer described the unusual subject of this work in a letter to his friend (the Blake biographer) Alexander Gilchrist, who apparently possessed the watercolour in the period following its exhibition at the Old Water-Colour Society in 1859:

> I have never had a proper title to my Comet drawing – for want of knowing on what day of the month I saw the thing represented – viz.: the passing of Arcturus *through* the comet … if you have not the dates by you never mind – only *then*, have the goodness to alter the label – merely putting 'The Comet of 1858 as seen from the heights of Dartmoor'. (*Letters*, p. 603.)

The correct date was 5 October 1858, the night Donati's Comet passed before the bright star Arcturus, shown here to the right of the comet's tail (Olson 1990; Olson and Pasachoff 1998, pp. 234–6). As Olson observed, Palmer's placement of the visible stars of the Boötes and Corona Borealis constellations, and his depiction of the comet's white centre of condensation and orange-and-red coma are astronomically accurate, but his portrayal of the tail – in fact, a 'large, curving, scimitar-like dust tail and two thin plasma tails' – appears simplified, presumably because England's humid atmosphere obscured the view.

Donati's Comet remained visible from Earth by telescope for nine months (2 June 1858–4 March 1859), for more than three of which (19 August–4 December 1858) it could be seen with the naked eye (Olson 1985, pp. 93–7; Olson and Pasachoff 1998, pp. 227–44). Given its long duration and unrivalled beauty – 'certainly more beautiful than the famous comet of 1811' (*The Times*, 1858) – Donati's Comet claimed international attention. Not surprisingly, various artists, including William Turner of Oxford (White 1977, no. 194; Wilcox and Titterington 1984, no. 87; Olson and Pasachoff 1998, pp. 232–3, figs 126, 127) and William Dyce (Pointon 1978; Pointon 1979, pp. 169–74, 193; Willsdon 1990; Olson and Pasachoff 1998, pp. 237–40, fig. 133), attempted the timely subject.

Like those artists, Palmer seems to have explored the celebrated celestial body as a display of heavenly light, rather than as a scientific phenomenon. (Significantly, the artist's extensive correspondence contains only one other reference to a specific astronomical event: being called outdoors to witness a lunar eclipse in October 1856; *Letters*, p. 524.) Indeed, the correspondence of certain elements to traditional Christian motifs – the Announcement to the Shepherds, the hermit saint at prayer within a cave – suggests a moral meaning (*Letters*, p. 935). For Palmer, Donati's Comet may have served primarily as a luminous reminder of the divine Creator: 'Can we wonder that Kant never thought without awe of the starry heavens, or of our moral responsibility?' (*Letters*, pp. 985–6.)

## 139a

### *The Weary Ploughman* or *The Herdsman* or *Tardus Bubulcus*, begun 1858

Etching, sheet 21.8 × 29.3 cm ($8\frac{5}{8} \times 11\frac{1}{2}$ in) irregular, plate 19 × 26.2 cm ($7\frac{1}{2} \times 10\frac{3}{8}$ in), image 13.2 × 20 cm ($5\frac{1}{8} \times 7\frac{7}{8}$ in), state 1 of 8

Inscribed in graphite at lower left in Samuel Palmer's hand: *1st impression*; at lower right: *No 1*; in graphite at lower centre in another hand: *A8 I? of 8 The Weary Ploughman (From the F.L. Griggs & Thomas Pergam Collections)*; at upper right: *11*; on verso in graphite at top: *Duplicate not required for Exhibition*

Lit: Alexander 8(i); Brown 44; Lister E8(1)

Oxford, Ashmolean Museum, 1966.75.1313; presented by Mr Arthur Mitchell, 1964

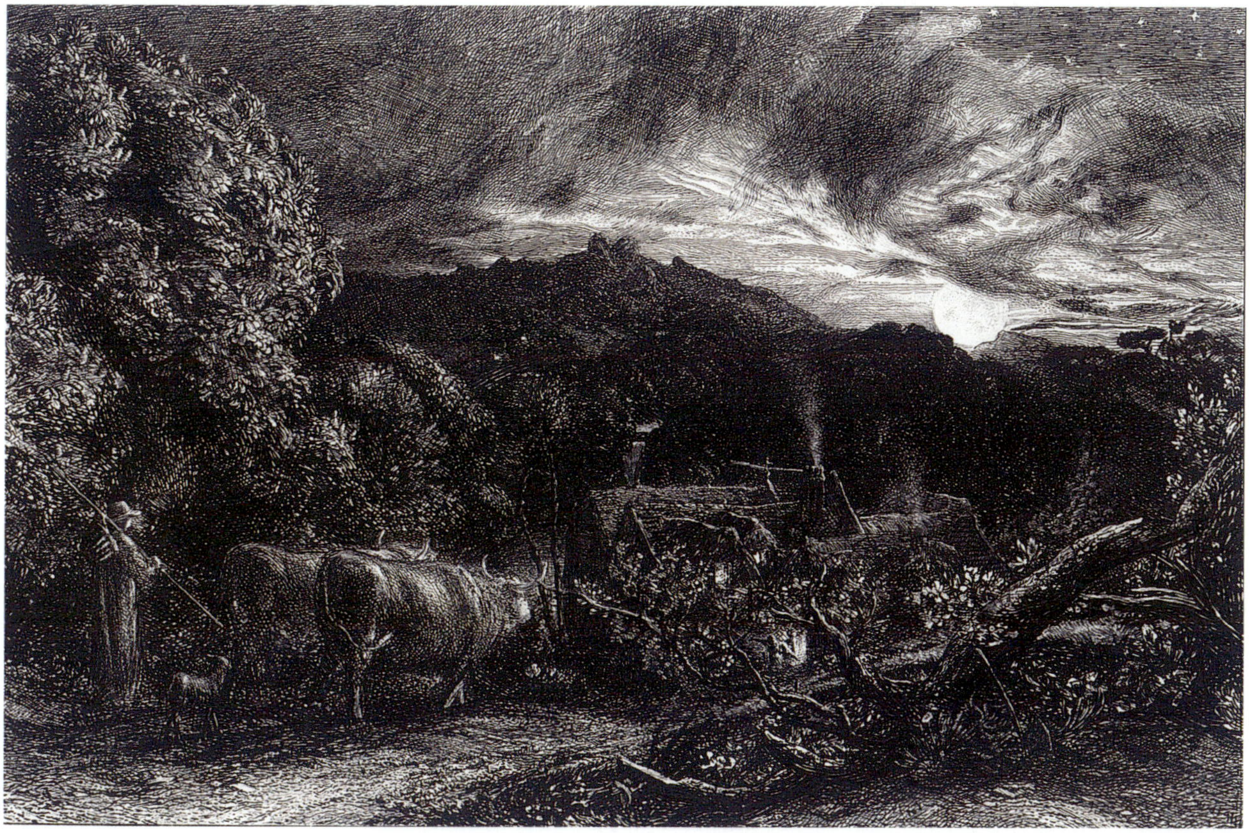

139a

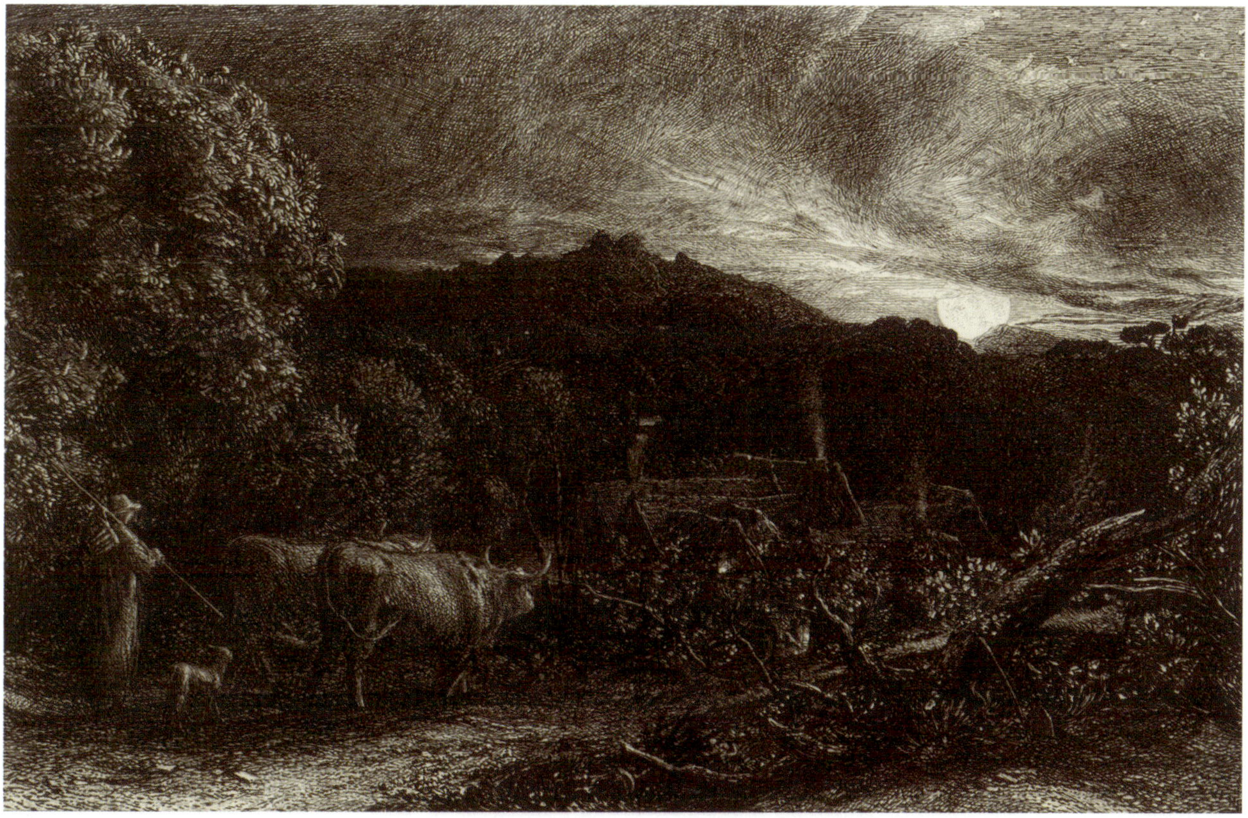

139b

## 139b†

### *The Weary Ploughman* or *The Herdsman* or *Tardus Bubulcus*, begun 1858, printed 1864

Etching, plate 19 × 26.2 cm (7½ × 10⅜ in), image 13.1 × 20.1 cm (5⅛ × 7⅞ in), extensively annotated proof of state 7 of 8

Inscribed on recto in graphite at top: *Should Mr. Martin wish to take some sample proofs Mr. Palmer sends this as [a sample] / while printing / Sample for printing from / when the proofs are drawn they should look something like this / the hill behind the farm dark – and the farm not blotty but / about this colour – ; at left: Please take care / [of] this & let me / [h]ave it when done with / Keep as much ink as you / can behind the oxen just / over the dog / The man's stick, however, / should not be blotted out / but be as it is here –*; at right: *Furze Hill House / Red Hill Surrey /* [sketch] */ Under the moon close to the / right of the dark Hill B / is a more distant hill A / just where A touches the / moon it should be a little / lighter – therefore, when / the plate is wiped & / ready for the press / please to take piece / of rag quite clean / and wipe that line very carefully – it is / only a little strip of the hill 1/16th of an inch / broad that wants it / as much as I have below enclosed in a faint dotted / line* [sketch] */ do not wipe more than that / dotted line includes*; at bottom: *I don't want it darker than than* [sic] *this / but when the print is drawn wet from the / press this would be about the mark* – ; on verso in graphite at upper right: *24 Herdsman, working proof 3. / Palmer's sample for / printing by Aug 1864*

Lit: V&A 1926, 194; Alexander 8(vii); Lister E8(7)

Washington, DC, National Gallery of Art, 1943.3.9132; Lessing J. Rosenwald Collection

## 139c

### *The Weary Ploughman* or *The Herdsman* or *Tardus Bubulcus*, begun 1858

Etching on Japanese paper, sheet 15.8 × 20.2 cm (6¼ × 7 15/16 in), plate 19 × 26.2 cm (7½ × 10⅜ in), image 13.1 × 20.1 cm (5⅛ × 7⅞ in), state 8 of 8

Numbered in lower margin of plate: *4*

Lit: Alexander 8(viii); Lister E8(8)

New York, The Metropolitan Museum of Art, Harris Brisbane Dick Fund, 1917

Palmer developed this plate during six intense weeks between late May and early July 1858, noting in his 'common-place-book' each detail of its progress – from the concentrations of the mordants and the timing of the acid baths to the areas of stopping-out and the passages reworked with a graver (V&A 1926, 189, pp. 76–8; *Letters*, p. 546). Those records, combined with the annotations preserved on subsequent impressions of the print, make *The Weary Ploughman* one of Palmer's best-documented etchings.

The three impressions exhibited here trace the development of the plate, as Palmer elaborated the design and balanced the distant sunset with the highlights in the fore- and middle grounds. In the impression of the first state in the Ashmolean Museum (cat. 139a) many of these dark tones remain undefined, especially in the sky, where a simple circle serves to indicate the moon. Gad, the professional printer used by the Etching Club until 1863 (see essay, pp. 47–54), presumably pulled this print: Palmer names him in his memoranda of 1858 (cited above), and his name is inscribed on an impression of the second state in the Princeton University Art Gallery (Pressly 1970, no. 9).

Following its printing by Gad, the *Weary Ploughman* plate passed to

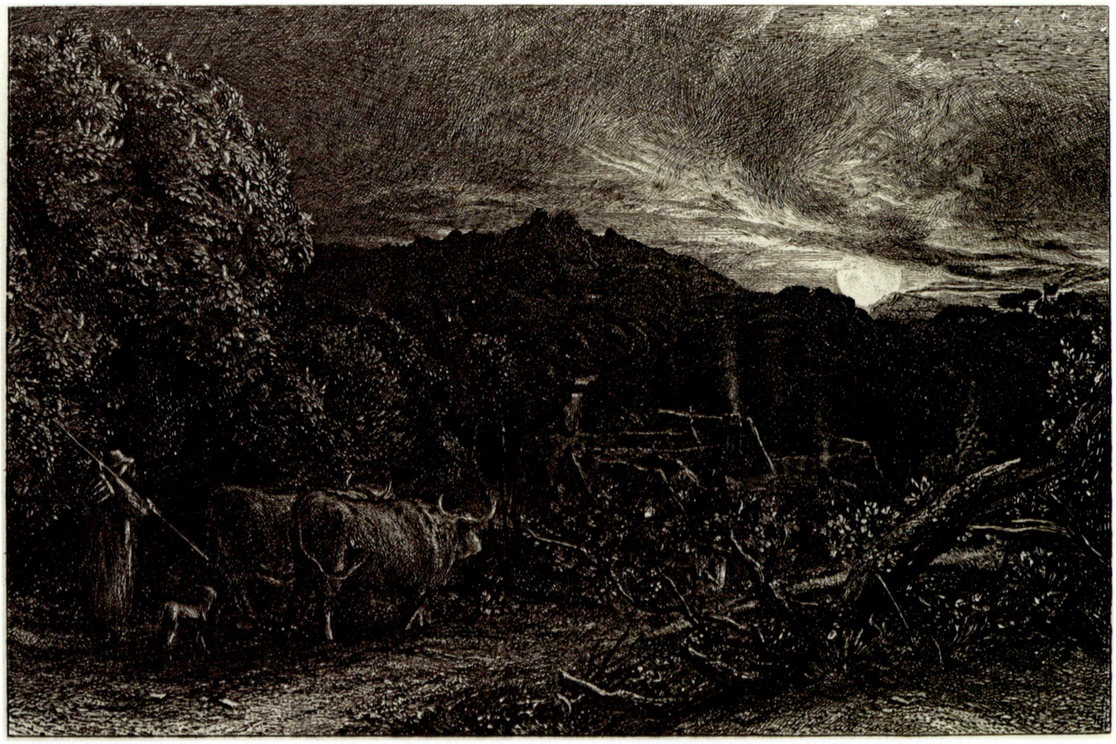

139c

other printers. A signed impression of the fourth state in the Metropolitan Museum of Art (gift of Theodore de Witt, 1923) is inscribed in another hand, 'At M$^{r}$ Haden's prep by Delatre', indicating that it was printed by the French etcher Auguste Delâtre on Seymour Haden's private press, possibly as early as late November or early December 1858 (see pp. 51–2), and almost certainly before March 1861 (*Letters*, p. 588). Annotations from August 1864 on the proof of the seventh state in the National Gallery of Art, Washington (cat. 139b), refer to a third printer, Martin, Jr., employed by Palmer following Gad's retirement. The Washington impression shows the design at a more advanced stage, surrounded by remarks to the printer concerning the clarity of the lines and the luminosity of the moon.

Palmer continued to develop the plate until 1865, when Joseph Cundall published the eighth and final state in *A Selection of Etchings by the Etching Club*. The results were impressive. As A.H. Palmer remarked of the design, 'the full moon seems to be racing through the clouds, as it appears to do in nature' (*Memoir*, p. 53). In the same year Palmer exhibited an impression (RA no. 876) – presumably similar to the one shown here (cat. 139c: Metropolitan Museum of Art) – entitled 'The Ploughman Homeward Plods His Weary Way'. That title – and its Latin alternative, *Tardus Bubulcus* – come from Thomas Gray's *Elegy Written in a Country Churchyard* (1751; V&A 1926, p. 78):

> The curfew tolls the knell of parting day,
> The lowing herd winds slowly o'er the lea,
> The plowman homeward plods his weary way,
> And leaves the world to darkness and to me.

Another title given to this plate, *The Herdsman*, drew A.H. Palmer's strong disapproval, although his father himself had used it (V&A 1926, p. 78; *Letters*, p. 1028). To avoid the controversy of *The Herdsman* – as well as the tongue-twisting complexity of its predecessors – F.L. Griggs proposed a new title, *The Weary Ploughman*, intended both to reaffirm the association with Gray's *Elegy* and to emphasize this etching's relationship to *The Early Ploughman* (cat. 141). It won A.H. Palmer's approval and is now commonly used (Alexander, p. 35).

The plate was destroyed, according to the artist's wishes, in about 1875, after A.H. Palmer discovered it in the hands of a publisher preparing to reissue it without his father's approval (V&A 1926, 195).

## 140

### *The Early Ploughman* or *The Morning Spread upon the Mountains*, begun before 1861

Etching on heavy cream wove paper, sheet 18.7 × 25.7 cm ($7\frac{3}{8} \times 10\frac{1}{8}$ in), plate 17.8 × 25.1 cm ($6\frac{7}{8} \times 9\frac{7}{8}$ in), image 13.1 × 19.7 cm ($5\frac{1}{4} \times 7\frac{3}{4}$ in), state 7 of 9 (Alexander's state 6 of 8)

Signed at lower right: *Samuel Palmer*; and inscribed at lower left: *finished state*

Lit: Alexander 9(vi); Lister E9(7)

Private collection, USA

Whereas the village of *The Weary Ploughman* (cat. 139) indicates a British setting, the tall cypress-like trees of *The Early Ploughman* evoke an Italian landscape. Here two men plough a narrow field before a ruined tower on a distant hill; a woman balancing a vessel on her head and carrying another in her hand pauses in her journey to the glistening river spanned by a simple bridge.

Palmer began this plate while living in Kensington and developed it intermittently for the rest of his life (*Memoir*, p. 18; *Letters*, p. 993). P.G. Hamerton published *The Early Ploughman* (then in its fourth state) in the first edition of *Etching and Etchers* (1868; V&A 1926, p. 79). (Delâtre – see p. 51 – also printed proofs of state 4/Alexander no. 9.) Palmer then re-bit the plate to intensify the contrasts of light and shade, and exhibited an impression of the seventh state printed by Frederick Goulding in 1873 (RA no. 1296); the title given at the Royal Academy, *The Morning Spread upon the Mountains*, had also been used during the previous decade (*Letters*, p. 875; V&A 1926, p. 79).

In November and December of that same year the artist's son (following a period of instruction by Goulding) began to reprint the plate. Using special ink and artificial printing techniques,

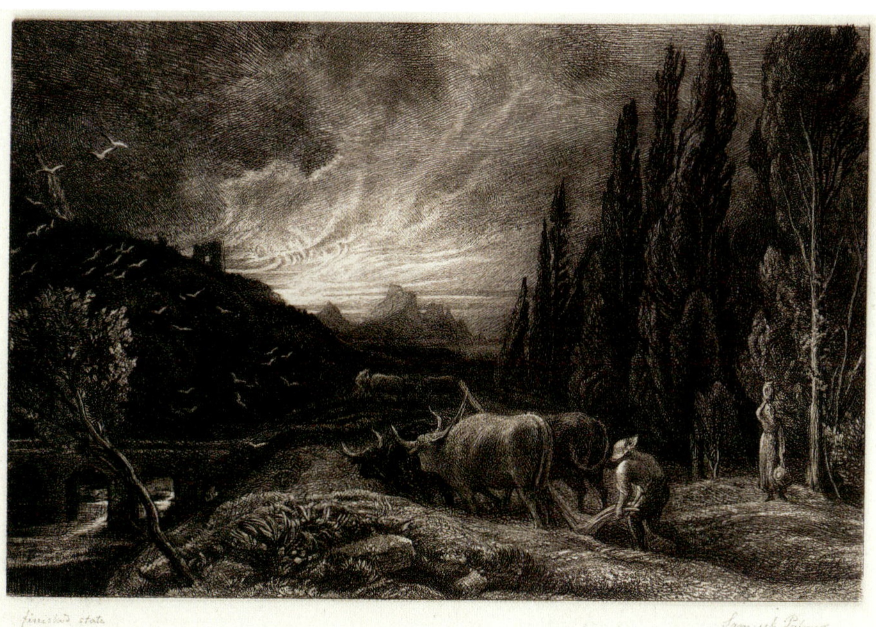

140

A.H. Palmer achieved 'an absolutely different standard than the old one' (V&A 1926, p. 79). From that 'practically worn out' plate the artist's son coaxed finer proofs than any previously known (Hardie 1913, p. 240). He sent two samples to Hamerton, prompting the author to exclaim, in the second edition of *Etching and Etchers* (1876): 'I always greatly admired this plate, but the full beauty of it was unsuspected until Mr. Palmer set up a printing-press in his own house' (V&A 1926, p. 79). This exquisite impression may be one of those remarkable prints, pulled on the private press, and inscribed (as is typical of this state) 'finished state'. In an attempt to make such effects permanent and unvarying – but to A.H. Palmer's regret – Palmer re-bit the plate in January 1880, creating an eighth (and final lifetime) state (*Letters*, p. 993).

Palmer depicted similar scenes many times: in a brown wash drawing squared in graphite (Lister 237), in three watercolour studies (Lister 610, 611 and another in the Morgan Library omitted from Lister), and in the watercolours and studies of *Lycidas* (Lister M7, M8) and *The Eastern Gate* (Lister M9, M10).

Following the posthumous reprinting of this plate by Short, Hardie and Griggs in 1926, the copper plate was cancelled and it is now in the Victoria and Albert Museum.

## 141

### Attributed to Samuel Palmer

*Two Men with Oxen Ploughing a Field*, undated

Monotype printed in brown ink on lightweight white wove paper, sheet 19.5 × 26.5 cm (7⅝ × 10⅜ in), plate 12.6 × 17.5 cm (5 × 6⅞ in)

Lit: Lister, with E9; Goldman 1991, no. 16

London, British Museum, 1929-4-16-17

Jane Richmond (née Gunning), the wife of George Richmond's youngest son John, sold this print at auction (Christie's, London, 3 March 1929, lot 66) as a work by Samuel Palmer. The Richmond family provenance lends weight to the historical attribution, and the present book and exhibition provide an opportunity to consider it further. The subject, certainly, is Palmer-esque. Within a dark landscape marked by trees, a jagged hill and what appear to be a wagon and possibly a provender trough, a ploughman drives his team across a field.

Although Palmer is not known to have made monotypes, the method – named for the single impression that the process typically yields – can be readily learned or even intuited by painters. To make the present example, the artist coated a metal plate (or perhaps a sheet of glass) with ink, then scratched out the lightest areas of the design using a sharp instrument (such as a pen) and lifted other passages of pigment with a brush, before finally pressing a sheet of paper against this surface to transfer the design onto the print. Thumbprints at the upper and lower right, and the reticulated surface of the ink at the upper left attest to this process.

The method has a long, but intermittent history (Becker). Giovanni Castiglione was its first great practitioner, and his methods became widely known in the nineteenth century. But Palmer is more likely to have learned of the technique from William Blake, whose large colour prints (begun *c.*1795) represent unusually sophisticated examples of the form (Hamlyn 2004, McManus and Townsend 2004, Townshend and Townsend 2004). Palmer might have attempted monotype at the beginning of his career, inspired by the example of Blake and by the printmaking activities of his fellow Ancients. Or he might also have attempted it later in life, in relation to his work as an etcher. The subsequent history of the medium is inextricably linked to that of the nineteenth-century European etching revival, and specifically to the expressive printing methods of Auguste Delâtre, the French master printer who pulled proofs of some of Palmer's etchings (Jauis 1980, pp. 13–18; Lochnan 1984, pp. 50–66).

Considering all these factors, it seems reasonable to retain this monotype's tentative attribution to Palmer until further evidence – or a better candidate for its authorship – should emerge.

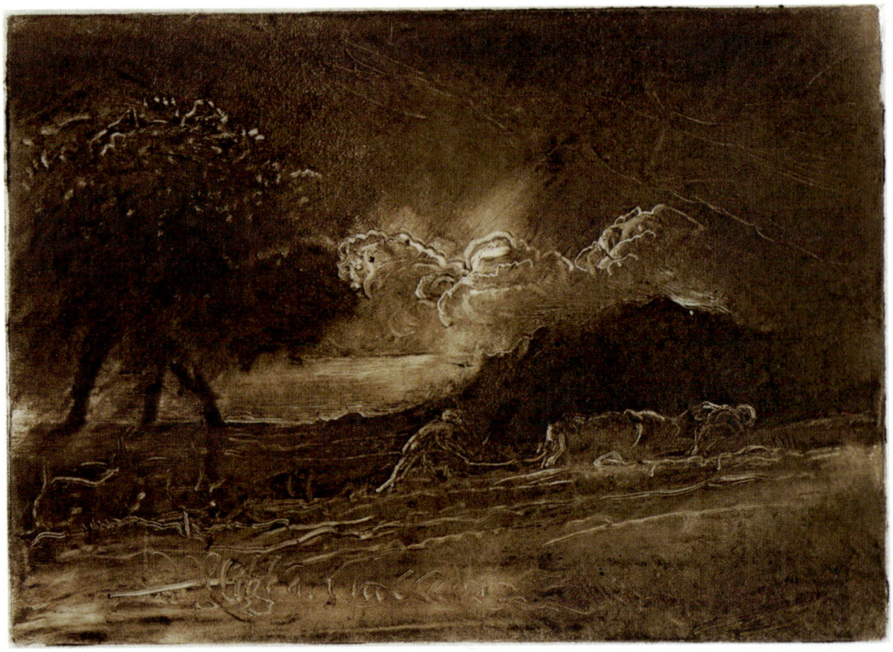

141

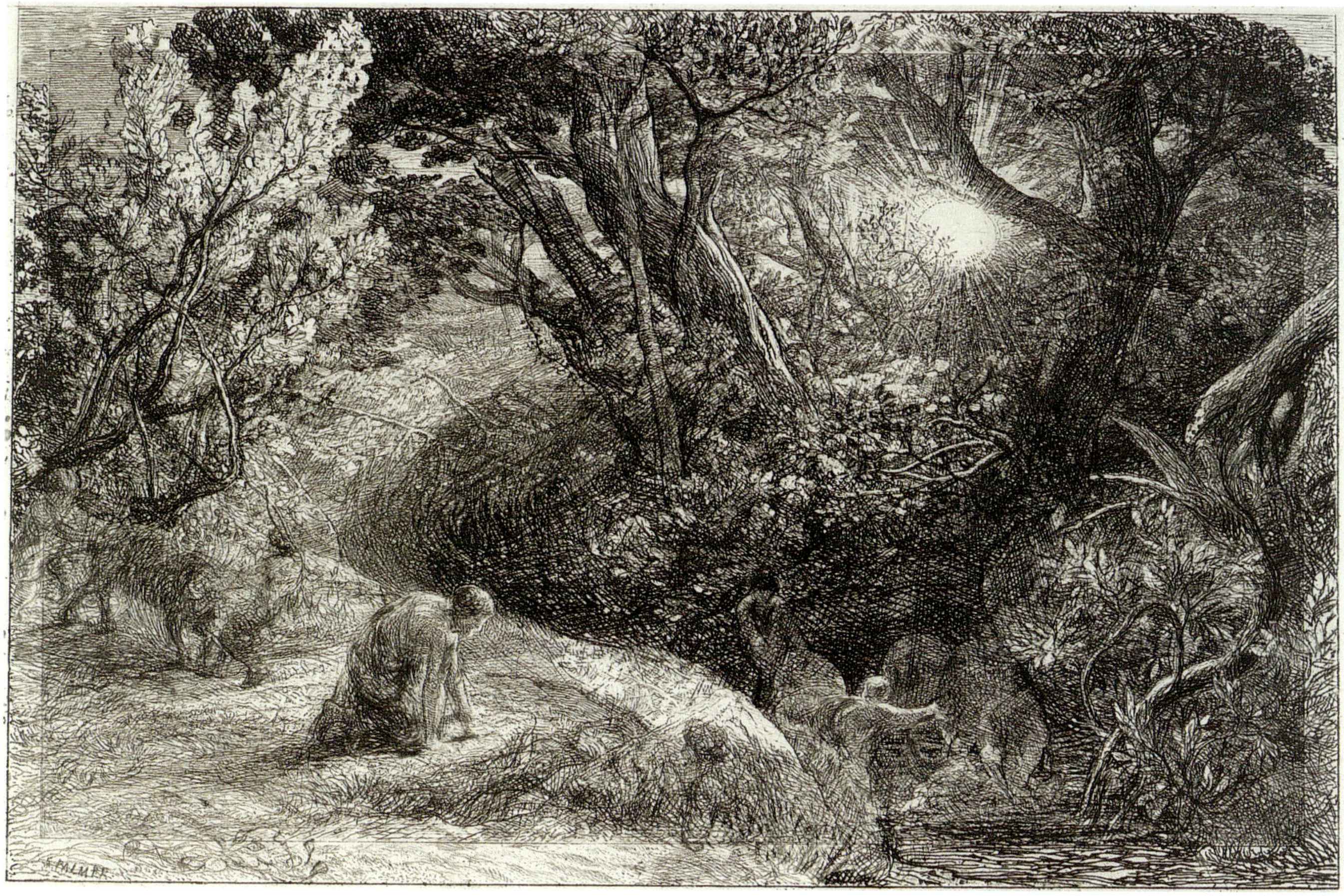

142

**142**

*The Morning of Life* or *A Leafy Dell* or *Work and Gossip* (formerly *Hercules and Cacus*), begun by 1861

Etching and engraving on chine collé, sheet 28 × 38.5 cm (11 × 15⅛ in), plate 18.1 × 25.4 cm (5¾ × 8½ in), image 13.6 × cm (5⅜ × 8½ in), state 7 of 7 (Alexander's state 6 of 6)

Signed within etching at lower left: *S. PALMER*; lettered in lower margin: *Samuel Palmer. The morning of life, 13.*

Lit: Alexander 10(vi); Lister E10(7)

Oxford, Ashmolean Museum, 1954.109

Palmer began this etching while he was living in Kensington (when Haden may have printed early proofs) and continued to develop it for many years (*Memoir*, p. 18). It originally depicted an episode from Book VIII of the *Aeneid* – Hercules pursuing the cattle-thief Cacus. No impressions of this state are known.

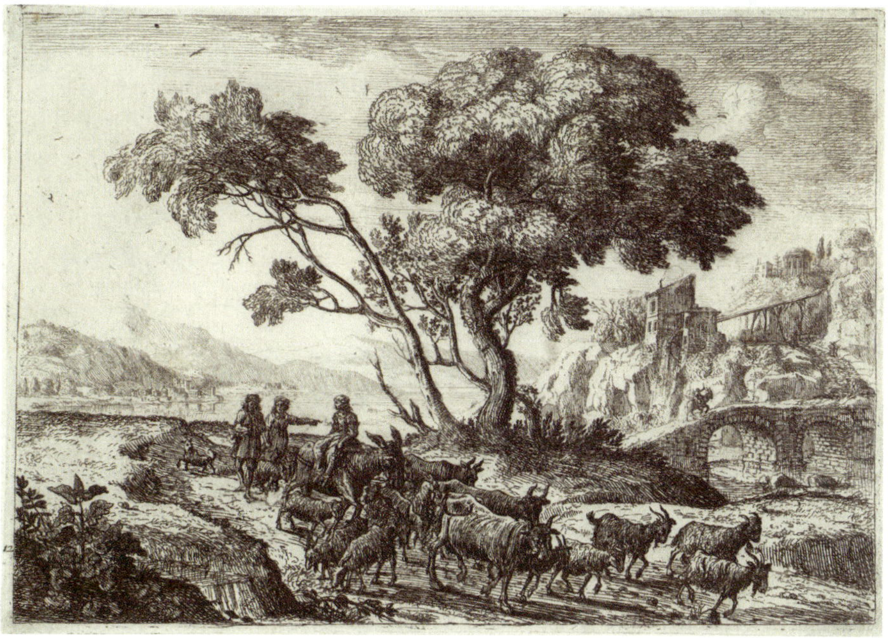

Fig. 30 Claude Lorraine, *The Departure for the Fields*, *c.*1638–41, etching, The Metropolitan Museum of Art.

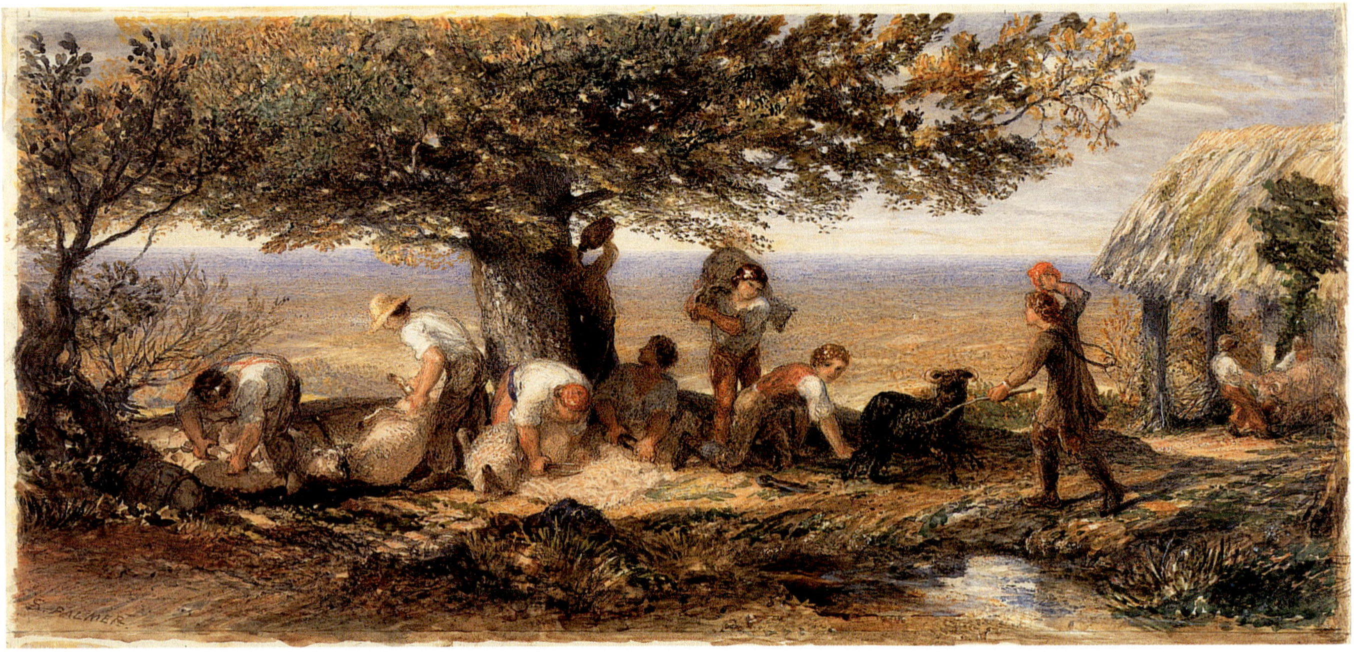


143

Unsatisfied with the result, the artist transformed the classical hero into a kneeling girl with a basket of apples, and the fleeing giant into a sheep washer. As Palmer later quipped, 'finding that I could no-how clip my poodle into lion-shape, I even let the hair grow, and christened him for the Art Union, *The Morning of Life*' (*Letters*, pp. 834–5). (He would also call this print 'Sheep-washing' and 'A Leafy Dell'.)

The dense woodland setting distinguishes this etching from Palmer's other prints and links it to the Milton watercolour, *The Dell of Comus* (1855), which features a similar composition: a foreground figure on the left, others amid trees on the right, and a bright source of light (Lister M3). The entwined, sharply angled trunks recall similar groups of trees etched by Claude in *Le Départ pour les champs* (*The Departure for the Fields*; fig. 30) and *Le Dessinateur* (*Coast Scene with an Artist*), both *c*.1638–41 (Mannocci 1988, nos 34, 36).

Different printers prepared the various states: Haden (Minutes, 9 June 1869; Pressly 1970, no. 13; The Metropolitan Museum of Art, Gift of Theodore de Witt, 1923), Delâtre (V&A 1926, 206), Martin, Jr. (V&A 1926, 207), and finally Frederick Goulding (Pressly 1970, no. 15; *A Vision Recaptured*, nos 10c, 10d), who printed the sixth and seventh (final) state (published as plate 13 in *Etchings for the Art Union of London by the Etching Club*, 1872). A.H. Palmer later railed against Goulding's 'savage wiping', which he believed had created impressions so 'awful' that they assaulted the viewer like 'slaps in the face', but the etcher himself tolerated the edition. Indeed, in 1873 Palmer exhibited an impression printed by Goulding (RA no. 1283; *Letters*, p. 875). The steel-coated copper plate was destroyed (*Letters*, p. 1028; *L&L*, p. 421).

## 143*

### *The Sheep Shearers*, 1863

Watercolour and gouache, over traces of graphite, 21.2 × 43.8 cm (8 7/16 × 17 1/4 in)

Signed at lower left: *S. PALMER*

Lit: Lister 615

Manchester City Galleries, 1917-30

This was exhibited at the Old Water-Colour Society summer exhibition in 1863 (238) with the following quotation:

> But who from England's olden time,
> Sent Jason's freight to every clime;
> With generous wealth and plenty blest,
> Our loom-built cities of the West?
> Poor shepherds shearing in a row,
> Upon some sunny upland brown.

The author of these somewhat convoluted lines has not been identified. There is a strong possibility that they could have been written by Palmer himself. Certainly, the sympathy for the 'poor shepherds shearing in a row' who produce the 'freight' that generates wealth for 'our loom-built cities' and travels to 'every clime' accords strongly with Palmer's adulation of the virtues of a traditional rural society and the wish to see this as the basis of national prosperity.

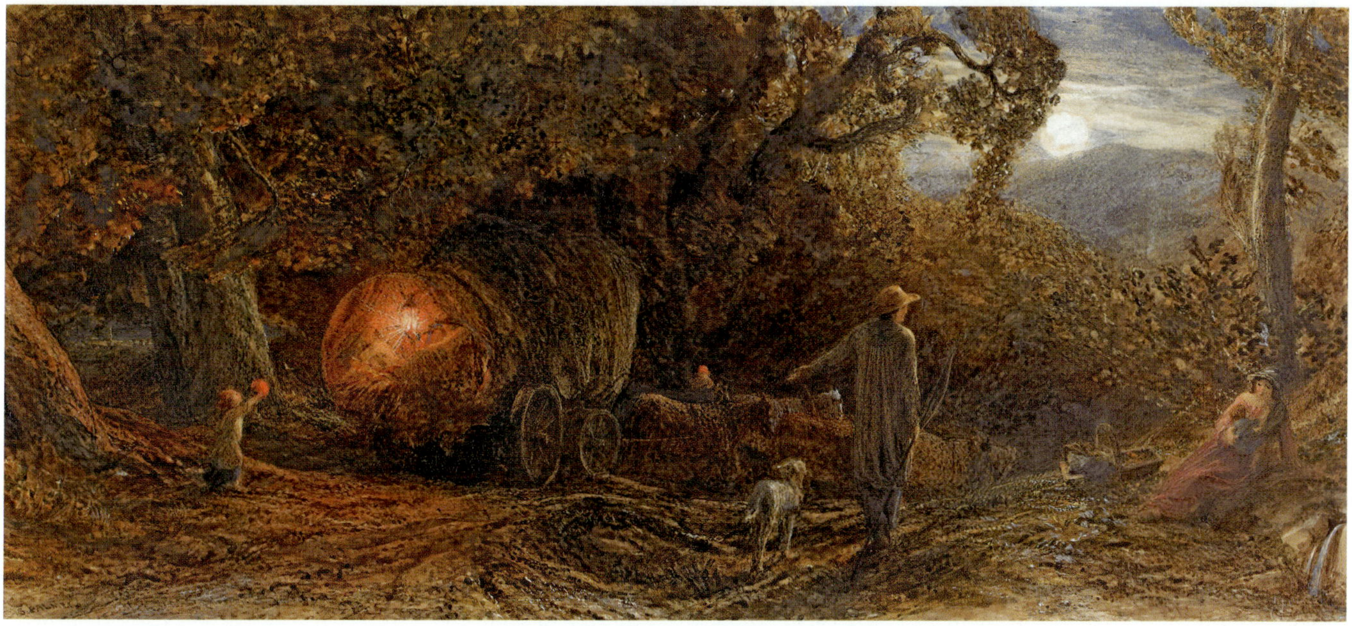

144

While the verse refers to the shepherds as 'poor', Palmer depicts no hardship in this scene. Instead he presents a profitable agricultural activity – the shearing of sheep – in a cheerful manner. Thematically, the picture is close to one of the greatest works of his later Shoreham years, *The Shearers* (cat. 88), but the treatment is very different. The more powerful early composition views the activities close up from inside a barn. The present picture by contrast has a more open aspect, being set on a ridge overlooking a valley. The format is that of the wide 'panorama' picture shape that Palmer first adopted for some of his Italian views in the early 1840s. Here he uses the form to spread out a lengthy narrative of people bringing sheep to be shorn and engaging in related activities. While a daytime scene, Palmer has managed to develop a vivid chiaroscuro in it by setting his figures in the shade of a spreading tree. The effect of sunlight filtered through the leaves of the tree is particularly brilliant. WV

## 144

## *A Wagoner Returning Home*, *c*.1865

Watercolour, gouache and graphite, 19.7 × 43.2 cm (7¾ × 17 in)

Signed at lower left in point of brush: *S. PALMER*

Lit: Lister 636, X15?

Simon and Gayle Jenkins

If Palmer's youthful work aspired to an epic style, and that of his early maturity, to the sublime, then his later mode could be described as pastoral. At each stage, the artist sought to improve mere nature, to create art that might rival Claude's: 'Ordinary landscapes remind us of what we see in the country; Claude's, of what we read in the greatest poets and of *their* perception of the country, thus raising our own towards the same level' (*Letters*, p. 912). Many of Palmer's later watercolours depict imaginary landscapes of the present type, featuring a panoramic view (often, as here, in the artist's 'little long' format), spectacular skies and an evocative narrative as universal as fable.

The timeless subject of the present work might have been painted by Thomas Gainsborough or written by the brothers Grimm: a man accompanied by a dog crosses a country lane to invite a sweet-faced young woman holding an infant to join his family in their covered wagon. This compassionate act might mark the beginning of a folk tale or the conclusion of a moralizing story in which a fallen woman is (or is not?) redeemed. A child runs merrily behind, raising a red ball above her head. The moon rises in the distance, illuminating the young mother's pink dress and contrasting with the softer glow of the lantern in the wagon. For Lister the close attention to foreground details suggested 'an almost Pre-Raphaelite emphasis' (Lister 599).

The protagonist – a man in long coat and straw hat accompanied by a loyal hound – appears with some regularity in Palmer's later work (Lister E1, E3, E4, E8, 547, 644, 645, 689, M12) giving alms, having his fortune told, embarking on a journey or (more often) coming home, and it is tempting to see in him an alter ego for the artist himself.

# 8. The Lonely Tower (*c.*1865–81)

*William Vaughan*

... the candle-light
From the far tower where Milton's
Platonist
Sat late, or Shelley's visionary prince:
The lonely light that Samuel Palmer
engraved
An image of mysterious wisdom won by
toil;

(W.B. Yeats, 'The Phases of the Moon', 1919)

The last two decades of Palmer's life were overshadowed by the most traumatic event in his life: the death of his son Thomas More Palmer on 11 July 1861. After that Palmer lived increasingly the life of a recluse. When the family moved to Furze Hill House, Redhill, in 1862, Palmer established his studio in the only suitable room, from which, to his distress, Leith Hill could be seen in the distance. As he indicated in his autobiographical letter (*Letters*, pp. 822–4), Leith Hill had a particular significance for him as it was close to the spot where Thomas More had died and above the small village of Abinger where he was buried and where Palmer hoped too to be buried one day (see cat. 151).

However tragic the personal circumstances surrounding Palmer's retreat to Furze Hill House, the move appears to have benefited him artistically. As with his move to Shoreham nearly forty years previously, seclusion seems to have encouraged the deepening of his own vision. This vision was different in kind to that of his early years. In the place of ecstasy and enthusiasm there was a more careful, meditative and richly laboured work. In his essay on Palmer F.G. Stephens contrasted these styles, likening the earlier one to Keats and the later to Tennyson (Stephens 1881, pp. 15–16). Like many of Tennyson's poems, the later watercolours and etchings certainly have a rich and tenebrous melancholy. As has been mentioned above (see p. 192), Stephens chose the term 'Dorian' – relating to the severe Greek Dorian mode of music – to characterize the sombre lyricism of Palmer's later style.

This last period of Palmer's career was also marked by growing critical success. While he was never regarded as a leading artist of the age, he was increasingly recognized – as is argued by Scott Wilcox in this book (pp. 43–6) – as an artist who produced a rare and fine kind of meditative idyllic landscape.

Palmer's change in critical fortunes was to some extent a reflection of the move away from realism in the wake of Pre-Raphaelitism and the Aesthetic movement. His own connections with the Pre-Raphaelites were strong. They began first through his contacts with Alexander Gilchrist, the author of the first substantial biography of William Blake. Palmer's first-hand accounts of Blake were one of the key features of the book and greatly influenced Gilchrist in his interpretation of Blake as an isolated visionary artist. It was at this period that Palmer gained the respect of Dante Gabriel Rossetti, who predicted a great future for Palmer's poetic form of landscape.

It was through a contact in the Pre-Raphaelite circle that Palmer gained the most substantial commission of his last years. This came from Leonard Rowe Valpy, the solicitor to John Ruskin, who offered Palmer the chance to develop a series of pictures on a theme of his own choice. Palmer took the opportunity to put into operation a scheme that he had been planning for some time to paint a cycle of landscapes based on Milton's early poems 'L'Allegro' and 'Il Penseroso'. This series formed his principal painting venture in his last years and remained uncompleted at the time of his death. Many of the Milton watercolours (see cats 145–53) are now regarded – together with the etchings related to them – as his greatest post-Shoreham achievements.

Palmer also had another major project in his last years, which developed to some extent out of his relationship with his dead son. For it was when discussing classical literature with Thomas More that he had first become enthused with the idea of making a translation of Virgil's *Eclogues*. He now carried out this task – with some advice from Calvert. While Palmer was aware of his limitations as a classical scholar it had been his hope that he would be able to communicate more of the 'pastoral essence' of Virgil than other modern translators had achieved (*L&L*, 155). However, when he showed the translation to the art critic P.G. Hamerton in 1872 the response was not altogether enthusiastic. He was advised only to publish it if it was accompanied by illustrations of his own. While initially disappointed with this advice, Palmer decided in the end to follow it. From this time until his death Palmer was engaged on designs for this project, aiming to produce a series of etchings as illustrations. These were only partially completed at his death, although his translation of Virgil was published subsequently in a limited edition with a mixture of etchings and facsimiles after preliminary designs in 1883 (see cat. 163).

Hamerton's advice was coloured by his admiration for Palmer's etchings. Palmer had already begun to gain respect as an etcher in the 1850s (see the previous section), but it was in his last years that he became best known for such work. His elaborate method contrasted strongly with the more sketch-like techniques practised by most revivers of etching in the period – inspired to a considerable degree by the example of

Whistler and French artists. Yet, while Palmer's method was condemned by some as a 'false' use of the medium, it did, like his watercolours, command immense respect for its integrity and depth of vision. Perhaps the most successful and admired of his etchings was the one that he made of his composition *The Lonely Tower* (cat. 161) in the last years of his life. This etching later inspired Yeats to write, in the poem cited at the beginning of this section, of the 'mysterious wisdom won by toil' that he found in Palmer's work.

On a personal level Palmer's last years witnessed a growing reconciliation with Hannah, from whom there had been some estrangement around 1860. Relations with John Linnell, however, never healed, and the two remained at loggerheads. The situation was exacerbated by the fact that Palmer was still to some extent financially dependent on Linnell, by far the more popular and financially successful painter of the two. Palmer continued to remain on close personal terms with surviving members of the Ancients, though group meetings became less frequent. His closest friend remained George Richmond, who was at his side when he died on 24 May 1881.

At the time of his death Palmer's critical reputation was higher than it had ever been. It is a sign of the respect in which he was held that a retrospective of his work was held later the same year in the Fine Art Society.

## The Milton series (cats 145–53)

The Milton series of watercolours occupied the last seventeen years of Palmer's life. The commission was given by the solicitor Leonard Rowe Valpy, who was a substantial connoisseur and collector in his own right, and occurred as a result of a purchase by Valpy of Palmer's now lost *Twilight – The Chapel by the Bridge* (Lister 618) from the 1863 winter exhibition of the Old Water-Colour Society. Valpy wanted Palmer to tone down the light in the chapel, which he found too glaring. Palmer complied, striking up a genial correspondence with Valpy in the process. Once the adjustment had been done, Valpy asked Palmer if he had anything on hand that 'specially affected his "inner sympathies"'. Palmer replied that he had begun to think of creating a series illustrating Milton's 'L'Allegro' and 'Il Penseroso' (1645), consisting of a dozen or so works 'half from one and half from the other poem'. According to A.H. Palmer (*L&L*, p. 150), a definite plan was agreed between painter and commissioner about April 1865. This involved the making of eight drawings (each *c.* 28 × 20 in / 71 × 51 cm) from 'L'Allegro' and 'Il Penseroso'.

The 'plan' was first reported by Palmer in a letter to Valpy dated September 1864 (*Letters*, p. 703). In this he paired subjects in the two poems to show 'opposites and varieties of colours and effects'. The pairings are given below, with extracts from Palmer's designations and titles of the works that eventually emerged from these proposed themes.

| | 'L'Allegro' | 'Il Penseroso' |
|---|---|---|
| 1 | 'Sunrise, Fine morning' (*The Eastern Gate*) | Grey morning. ' Grey moors' (*The Dripping Eaves*) |
| 2 | 'The upland Sentiment. Freedom. Merriment;' (not depicted) | 'The *inland* sentiment Deeply recessed. Cavern;' (*The Waters Murmuring*) |
| 3 | 'Wide expanse, melting into fairyland, etc.' (*The Prospect*) | 'Wide expanse of blank water … the solemn curfew.' (*The Curfew*) |
| 4 | '… the quintessence of the remote and romantic' (*A Towered City*) | 'Mysterious suggestion. More meant than meets the eye' (*The Lonely Tower*) |

In the end Palmer produced eight subjects, but they were unequally distributed between the two poems, with three from 'L'Allegro' and five from 'Il Penseroso'. In a highly perceptive essay on the series in *A Vision Recaptured* (pp. 33–47) Graham Reynolds suggests that Palmer may have retained the principle of pairing the works at the end by introducing *The Bellman* as a pendant to *The Lonely Tower* and shifting *The Prospect* to pair with *The Waters Murmuring*, and *A Towered City* with *The Curfew*.

Palmer did not complete the subjects in the order in which they appear in the poems. While most of the themes seem to have been sketched out in the mid-1860s, they were delivered in an apparently random order. They were all exhibited at the Old Water-Colour Society, in the following sequence:

1868 *A Towered City* (no. 93), *The Lonely Tower* (no. 16), *The Dripping Eaves* (no. 193)
1870 *The Curfew* (no. 97)
1877 *The Waters Murmuring* (no. 5)
1881 *The Prospect* (no. 18), *The Eastern Gate* (no. 56)
1882 *The Bellman* (no. 61)

*The Bellman* was not exhibited until after Palmer's death, as he did not consider it to have been fully finished.

The Valpy commission remained at the centre of Palmer's practice. However, the concern for Milton grew out of Palmer's lifelong obsession with the poet. Palmer was engaged in his later years with other subjects taken from Milton, as well as creating a large number of sketches and studies for the Valpy series.

Although Palmer had at first attempted an interior as one of the illustrations to 'Il Penseroso' (see cat. 145), the final series were entirely landscapes. This was appropriate given Palmer's expertise and the predominantly pastoral nature of both poems. However, the restriction did impose some limitations on the range of scenes that could be illustrated. Palmer was also concerned to preserve a sense of the narrator in his works, even if this figure is not actually represented. While originally intending to maintain an equal balance between the two poems, Palmer gave precedence in the end to the meditative 'Penseroso'. Furthermore, nocturnal and twilight effects predominate in his scenes from both, despite the fact that much of 'L'Allegro' describes daytime activities. Of the three 'L'Allegro' illustrations, two represent dawn (*The Eastern Gate* and *The Prospect*) and one twilight (*A Towered City*). The 'Penseroso' subjects are similarly crepuscular.

## 145*

### *First Sketch for 'Il Penseroso'*, 1864

Charcoal, 17 × 13.2 cm (6$^{11}/_{16}$ × 5$^{3}/_{16}$ in)

Inscribed on the verso in A.H. Palmer's hand: *The first sketch for an Il Penseroso subject / Which, in spite of his attempts, defeated S.P. totally / much to his sorrow*

Lit: Lister M17; *Letters*, p. 691

London, Victoria and Albert Museum, 1322-1925

This sketch appears to be an illustration to 'Il Penseroso', lines 79–82:

> Where glowing embers through the
> room
> Teach light to counterfeit a gloom,
> Far from all resort of mirth
> Save the cricket by the hearth.

It would seem, furthermore, to be one of the two companion pieces that Palmer reported that he was working on when accepting Valpy's commission in June 1864 (*Letters*, pp. 690–91). In that letter Palmer described the subject as follows:

> The student, in his country, old-fashioned room, meditating between the lights; the room dimly bronzed by the dying embers (warranted without *'RAYS'*) and a very cool, deep glimpse of landscape, and fragment of clouded moon seen through the lattice, just silvering the head and shoulders: the young wife in shade, spinning perhaps, on one side of the fireplace. Should I displease myself with it, the 'dying embers' may revive within my own fire-grate; if the contrary, it will give me much pleasure to show it you *by and bye.*

Since this free preliminary sketch is the only record of the composition it would seem that the work did indeed end up reviving the dying embers of Palmer's own grate. The interior setting was an unusual one for Palmer and this may have been why the result dissatisfied him. As a design, Palmer seems to have had some problems in bringing a view through the window of the night sky into close proximity with a fireplace. The work is also curious since it assumes that the student in Milton's 'Penseroso' is already married, a conceit that ill accords with the isolated tone of the poem.

The sketch is a fine example of the freedom with which Palmer recorded his first ideas as well as an interesting demonstration that Palmer did not assume, in the first place, that the Milton series would consist solely of landscapes.

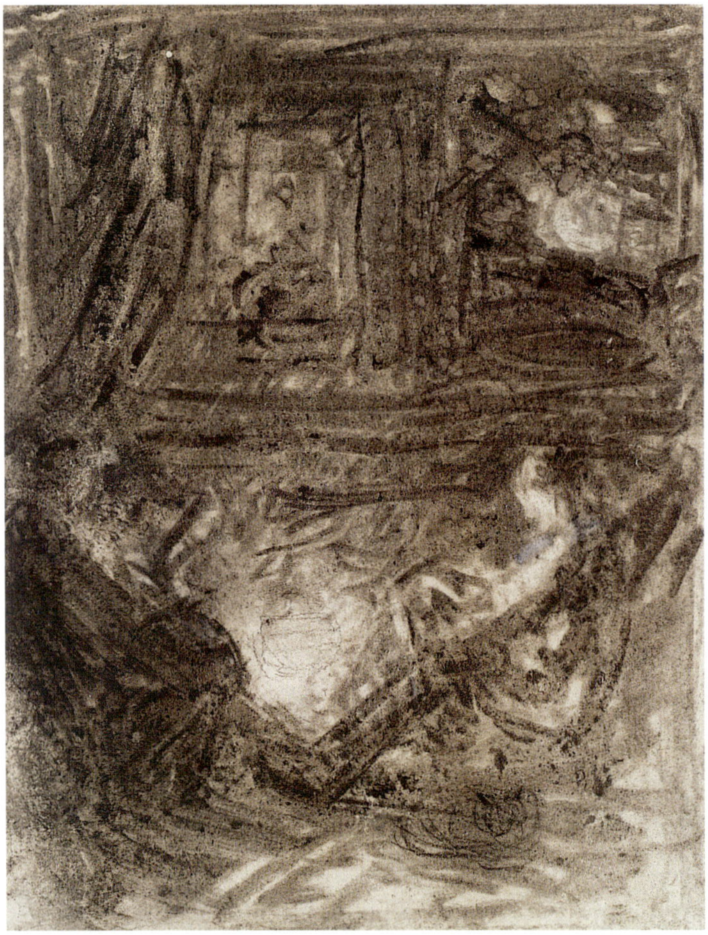

145

## 146

### *The Prospect*, 1881

Watercolour with gouache, 50 × 70.4 cm (19$^{3}/_{4}$ × 27$^{3}/_{4}$ in)

Lit: Fitzwilliam 1984, 61; Lister M12

Private collection

Thematically, this is the second in the Milton series, though it was not exhibited until Palmer's last exhibition at the Old Water-Colour Society in 1881, when it was shown at the same time as the first in the series, *The Eastern Gate*. Both were widely praised at the time, the critic F.G. Stephens describing them as 'epoch-making pictures'.

A label on the back (now separately preserved) has lines 69–80 from 'L'Allegro' on it:

> Straight mine eye hath caught new
> pleasures
> Whilst the landscape round it
> measures;
> Russet Lawns and fallows gray
> Where the nibbling flock do stray;
> Mountains on whose barren breast
> The labouring clouds do often rest;
> Meadows trim with daisies pied
> Shallow brooks and rivers wide.
> Towers and battlements it sees
> Bosom'd high on tufted trees,
> Where perhaps some beauty lies,
> The cynosure of neigh'bring eyes.

Lister quotes a letter from Palmer to Valpy about the painting:

> The other day I think the true 'vision' came of 'The Prospect'. It is a curious subject, for there seems no medium between a mappy Buckinghamshire treatment and a genial poetic swoon. If we can but cause the eye to shoot across the scene, we shall obtain a prospect whence 'new pleasures' may be caught, and these will be added to, by tempting due curiosity in due time into its recesses, and the hints of ancient habitation and present culture, without which a prospect may be very extensive, but very depressing. (*Letters*, p. 699 – undated.)

Palmer was still working on *The Prospect* in February 1881, some three months before he died. Writing to Valpy at that time he talks of being in bed,

> but with *The Prospect* on a table on my right, so that I could work upon it; and having had a splendid light (for a wonder), I *have* worked upon, and I think, finished the part I was most anxious about, namely, the little town by the blue river. So I hope all is safe, and, if so, it will be a wonder, for never man ran riot with a hobby as I have done here. I always, from a child, expected to see a great deal when I was taken to see a 'prospect'. (*Letters*, p. 1061.)

As Lister has commented, this watercolour – painted in vibrant colours like many of the Milton series – contains more of Italy than Britain in its distant scenery, although the foreground could be conceived of as British. Perhaps the notion of looking from Britain out to Italy appealed to Palmer, particularly at a time when he knew that his long-held ambition to return to Italy would now never be fulfilled. The combining of British and Italianate features also accords with Milton's classicizing view of the British countryside. As Lister also says, the picture is particularly rich in effects, which are often akin to those of oil. They show how he was continuously refining his painting technique right up to the end of his life, as can also be seen in such last works as the Huntington version of *The Lonely Tower* (see cat. 152).

According to the plan for the series that Palmer sent to Valpy in September 1864 (see p. 225), the subject of this painting was conceived as a counterpart to the line in 'Il Penseroso' that formed the basis of *The Curfew* (cat. 148). Although this scheme seems to have been altered by the time that he completed the present work, that comparison can still be perceived, the brightly coloured optimistic dawn landscape depicted here contrasting with the quiet and solemn evening view in *The Curfew*.

As with other pictures in the Milton series, Palmer preferred the tried and trusted London board (formerly known as Bristol board) as a support for his work rather than more modern papers. He complained in a letter to Richard Redgrave in 1865 that modern papers did not allow the 'full depth of colours' to be shown in the way that London board did. For an artist using watercolour as thickly as Palmer, this was a particularly important consideration.

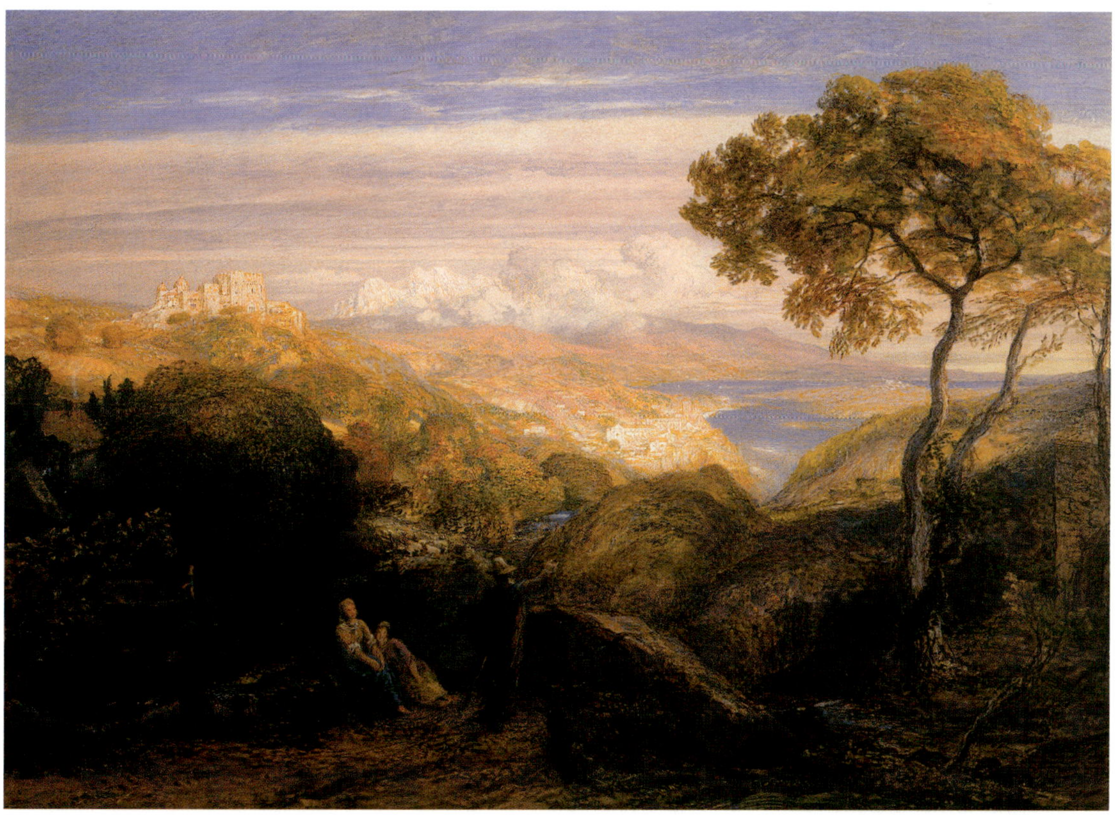

146

## 147

*The Waters Murmuring*, *c.*1880

Watercolour with gouache, 50.8 × 69.8 cm (20 × 27½ in)

Lit: *A Vision Recaptured*, pp. 75–6; Lister M27

ING Bank N.V., London Branch

This work was exhibited at the Old Water-Colour Society in 1877 with the following quotation from 'Il Penseroso':

> There in close covert by some brook,
> Where no profaner eye may look,
> Hide me from the day's garish eye,
> While the bee with honied thigh,
> That at her flowery work doth sing
> And the waters murmuring
> With such consort as they keep
> Entice the dewy-feathered sleep.

According to Reynolds in *A Vision Recaptured*, this work was conceived by Palmer as a pendant for *The Prospect*, providing a cool midday image to set against the bright midday described in 'L'Allegro'. It may be that this was the point that Palmer moved away from the initial scheme for the works laid out in his letter of 1864 to Valpy (see p. 224). There had been a gap of seven years since he had last exhibited a work from the series, and during that period Palmer had been evolving a new richness of effect.

Writing about this work to Valpy, Palmer commented: 'The "Waters Murmuring" will realize golden reflected light in chasmal hollows … I have for a long time been cultivating coolness in shadows, and that makes the light more gorgeous.'

Speaking of the subject, Palmer further said: 'The moment supposed is that immediately before the poet (in the covert) wakes; when the nymphs, sent by the genius of the wood, have just given a staccato tang, preluding the "sweet music" which he is to hear as he awakes.' (*Letters*, p. 697)

The main tree bears a resemblance to the study of oak trees made by Palmer *c.*1828 at Lullingstone (cat. 46). This seems highly appropriate since 'Il Penseroso' contains the phrase "monumental oak" that had so excited Palmer in his Shoreham days.

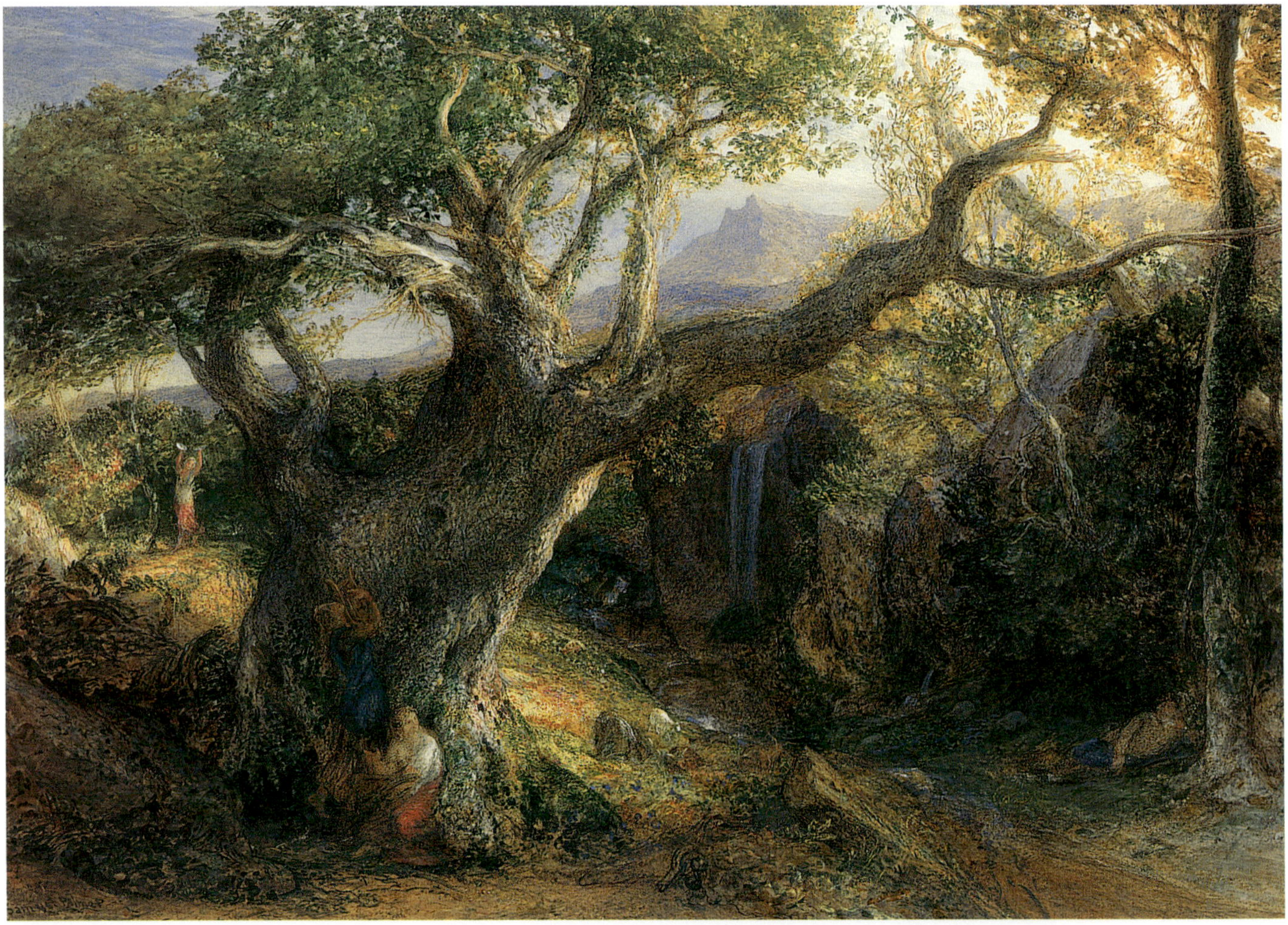

147

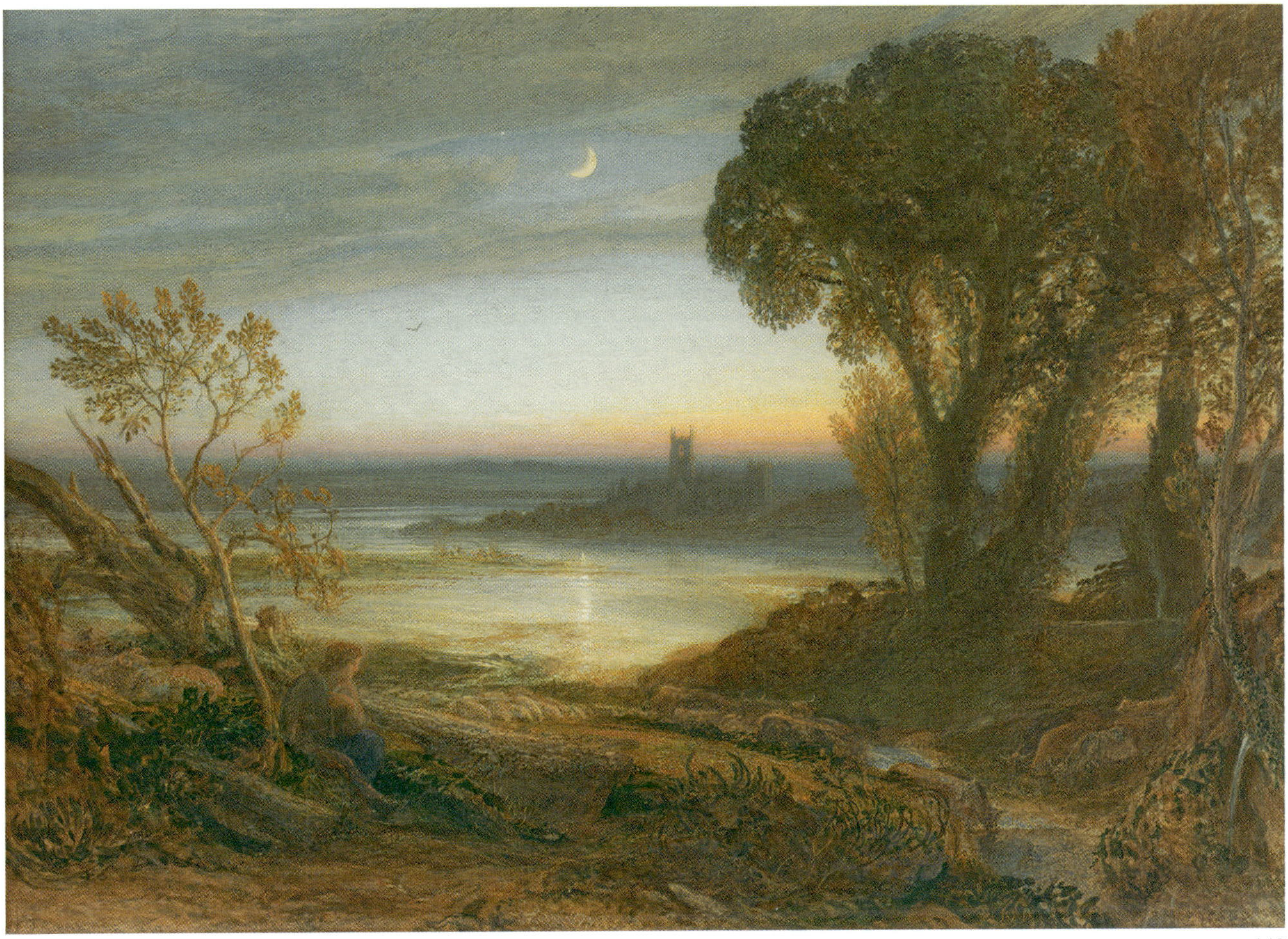

148

## 148

*The Curfew* or *The Wide Water'd Shore*, 1870

Watercolour and gouache on London board, 50 × 71.1 cm (19 11/16 × 28 in)

Signed and dated at lower left, point of brush: *S PALMER 1870*

Inscribed on verso at upper right in ink: *Other side prepared and ready*; at lower right: *The substance of the London Board / so much contributed to the Durability / that it should never be dampted* [sic] *behind / to get off* <*the*> *some of the papers, / an atrocity I know to have been once / committed with a view to making the / surface perfectly flat!!! SP.*

Lit: Lister M16

Amsterdam, Rijksmuseum, 1978:40

This picture was first exhibited under the title of *The Curfew* at the Old Water-Colour Society in 1870 (no. 97) accompanied by lines 73–7 from 'Il Penseroso':

> Oft on a plat of rising ground
> I heard the far-off curfew sound
> Over some wide water'd shore
> Swinging low with sullen roar.

Prior to exhibition, Palmer frequently referred to the work as *The Wide Water'd Shore*, particularly in letters to his patron Valpy. In his plan for the Milton series sent to Valpy in 1864 Palmer envisaged this subject as representing the 'solemn curfew' across a 'wide expanse of blank water' and forming a counterpart to the 'wide expanse melting into fairyland', which he planned to convey for the theme from 'L'Allegro' that later formed the subject for *The Prospect* (cat. 146).

Palmer seems to have been under some pressure from Valpy to complete the work, since he wrote pleading for more time and explaining the need to perfect it with:

> those tender breathings and bloom which, after all, are the 'seasoning as does it' … It is getting more and more, at every touch, of the solemn fusion belonging to the theme, and directly it reaches the point at which it is on even balance, and another touch may do harm instead of good, I will send it. (*Letters*, pp. 696–7, undated fragment.)

Palmer was also well aware that the lines from Milton that he quoted invoked a particular and refined effect of sound – the 'sullen roar' of the distant curfew bell across a level, quiet expanse. He felt that this was best achieved by the fine modulations of tone that he had brought into his picture: 'As painting cannot "roar", it can only, by a minute touch, indicate the curfew's solemn sound' (ibid.).

## 149*

### *A Towered City* or *The Haunted Stream*, *c*.1868

Brown wash with white body colour on card, 20.2 × 28.4 cm (17 15/16 × 11 3/16 in)

Squared in pencil

Inscribed with lengthy notes: see Lister

Lit: Lister M13

London, Victoria and Albert Museum, 1318-1925

As the squaring and notes would suggest, this is a study for cat. 150. While the overall composition is very similar, Palmer pays more attention in the study to the moon and to the relieving of the arch. The reduction of these, together with the adding of a 'purplish gloom' in the finished work served to throw greater focus on the 'Towred city'. Palmer reported the change in a letter of 6 November 1867 to Valpy (see cat. 150). It is perhaps for this reason that the title shifted from the earlier *Haunted Stream* to *A Towered City*.

## 150

### *A Towered City* or *The Haunted Stream*, 1868?

Watercolour and gouache with gum on London board, 51.1 × 70.8 cm (20 1/8 × 27 7/8 in)

Lit: Lister M14; *Letters*, pp. 701–2, 737, 743, 760, 764

Amsterdam, Rijksmuseum, 1978:39

This, *The Lonely Tower* (cat. 151) and *Dripping Eaves* (Lister M25) were the first of the Milton series to be exhibited, at the Old Water-Colour Society in 1868 (no. 93). It was accompanied by the following quotation from Milton's 'L'Allegro':

> Towred cities please us then,
> And the busie humm of men,
> Where throngs of Knights and Barons bold,
> In weeds of Peace high triumphs hold,
> With store of ladies whose bright eies
> Rain influence and judge the prise
> Of Wit, or Arms, while both contend
> To win her grace, whom all commend.
> Thus let *Hymen* oft appear
> In saffron robe, with Taper clear,
> And pomp, and feast, and revelry,
> With mask, and antique Pageantry,
> Such sights as youthful poets dream
> On summer eves by haunted stream.

Palmer has chosen the sequence of this quote to move us from the striking background image of the towered city, silhouetted against the setting sun (sanctioned by the end of day being signalled in the poem), through the middle ground, where the throng of knights and barons can be seen on the bridge, to the right foreground, where Hymen's rites are being celebrated in a forecourt. Below is the 'haunted stream' where Milton's poet would dream.

In his September 1864 schedule for Valpy Palmer described this subject (which he referred to most frequently as *Haunted Stream*) as follows: 'No. 4. The amber sky. Meant for the quintessence of the remote and romantic in the severe sense of the word. Day rather dreaming

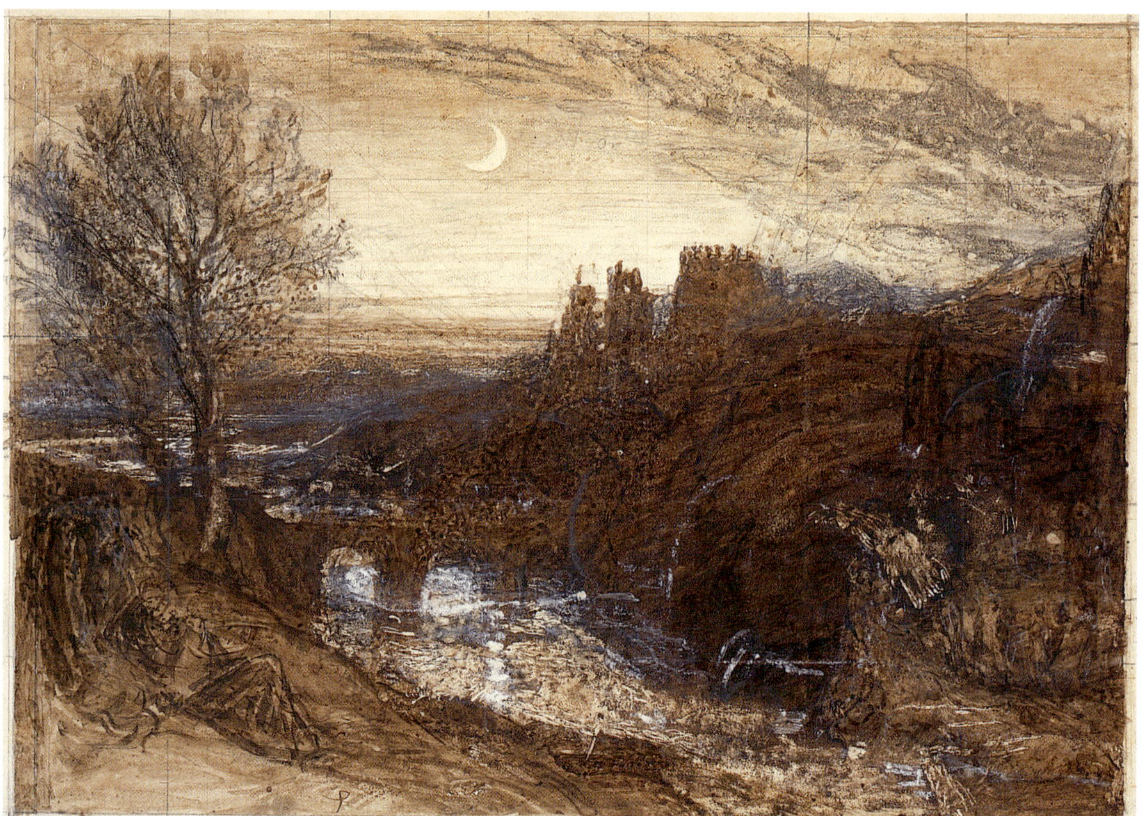

149

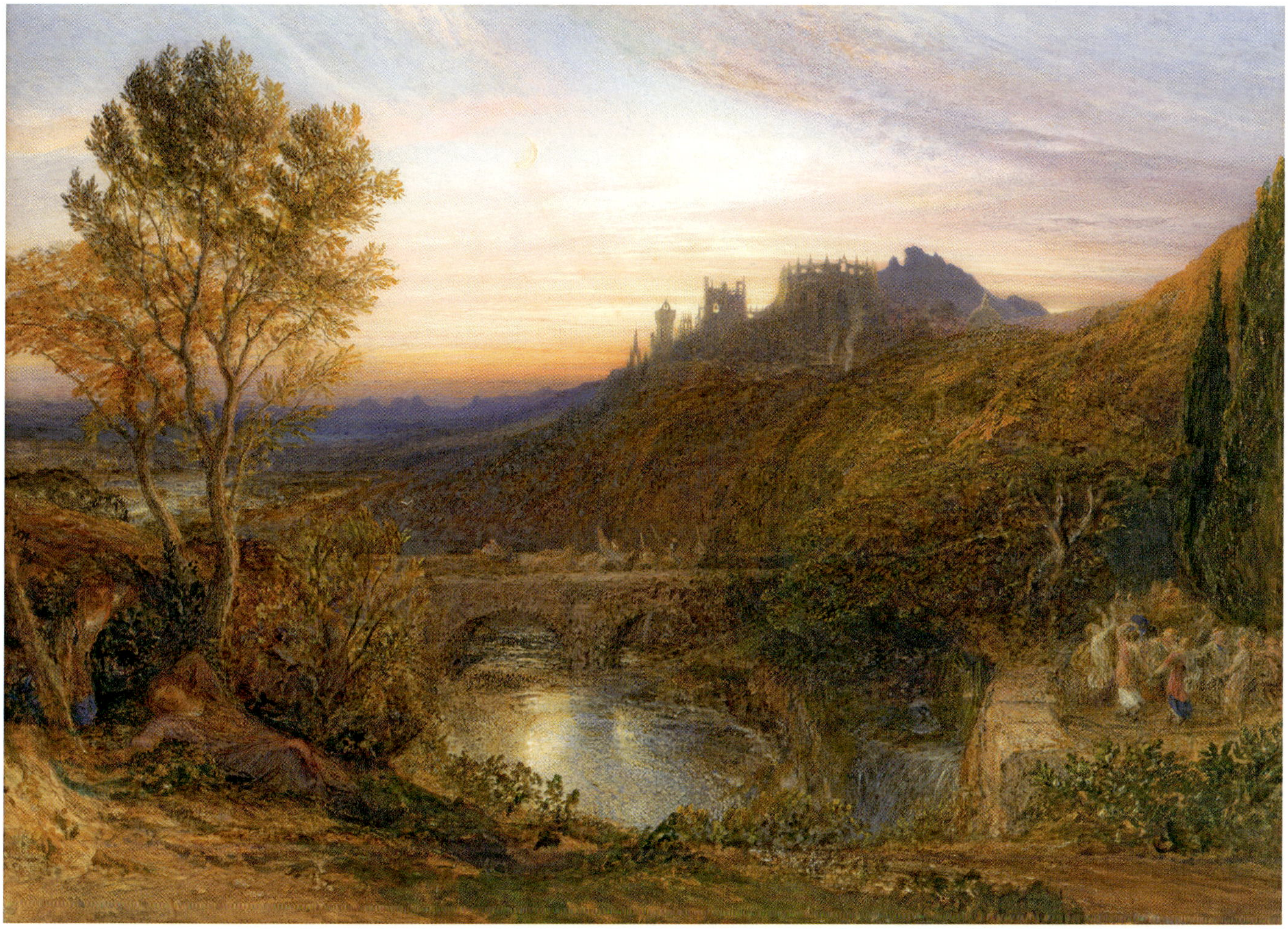

150

than dying.' Palmer had planned the composition as a counterpart to *The Lonely Tower*, and there are, indeed, ways in which their silhouettes seem to mirror each other. It is also striking that *The Lonely Tower* shows a waning moon, whereas here the moon is waxing. He characterized the *Lonely Tower* composition at the time as 'mysterious suggestion. More meant than meets the eye', something that may allude to his biographical interest in the scene (see entry for cat. 151) but also suggests that the night time of 'Il Penseroso' is deeper and more spiritual than the dreaming of 'L'Allegro'.

Palmer worked for a long time on the two together. In December 1865 he wrote to Valpy: 'The Pictures of *The Lonely Tower* and *Haunted Stream* have been in hand some time, and lately I have been at them *heart* and *soul*, wishing to get one or both ready for our summer show.' (*Letters*, p. 737). Despite this, neither picture was to be ready for exhibition for another three years. Palmer seems to have had particular trouble getting exactly the effect he desired. On 6 November 1867 he reported to Valpy that this had at last been achieved:

> Added to the result of our discussion on *The Stream,* I found out something after you left which has put it all in my power. I have worked on it a little to-day, most tenderly breaking those delicate crimson tones which, in the little sketch, depress the saffron to a focus, and merging the extreme distance, as in the sketch, to a more mysterious purplish gloom, and the result is that the city, which never pleased me, has sprung up and asserted itself (I fancy) as the poetic eye of the drawing. (*Letters*, p. 764.)

The emergence of the city as the 'poetic eye of the drawing' shifted focus away from *The Haunted Stream*, which had originally been the leitmotif of the work, and this is probably the reason why the title of the work changed from that to *A Towered City*.

Even at this point Palmer pleaded with Valpy for more time to complete the work, commenting: 'I had rather take time about *The Stream*, doing a little as I quite feel it, for the last subtleties are so much better done this way' (ibid.). The trouble taken with this work is evident in the heavy dotting and elaborate dappling techniques used.

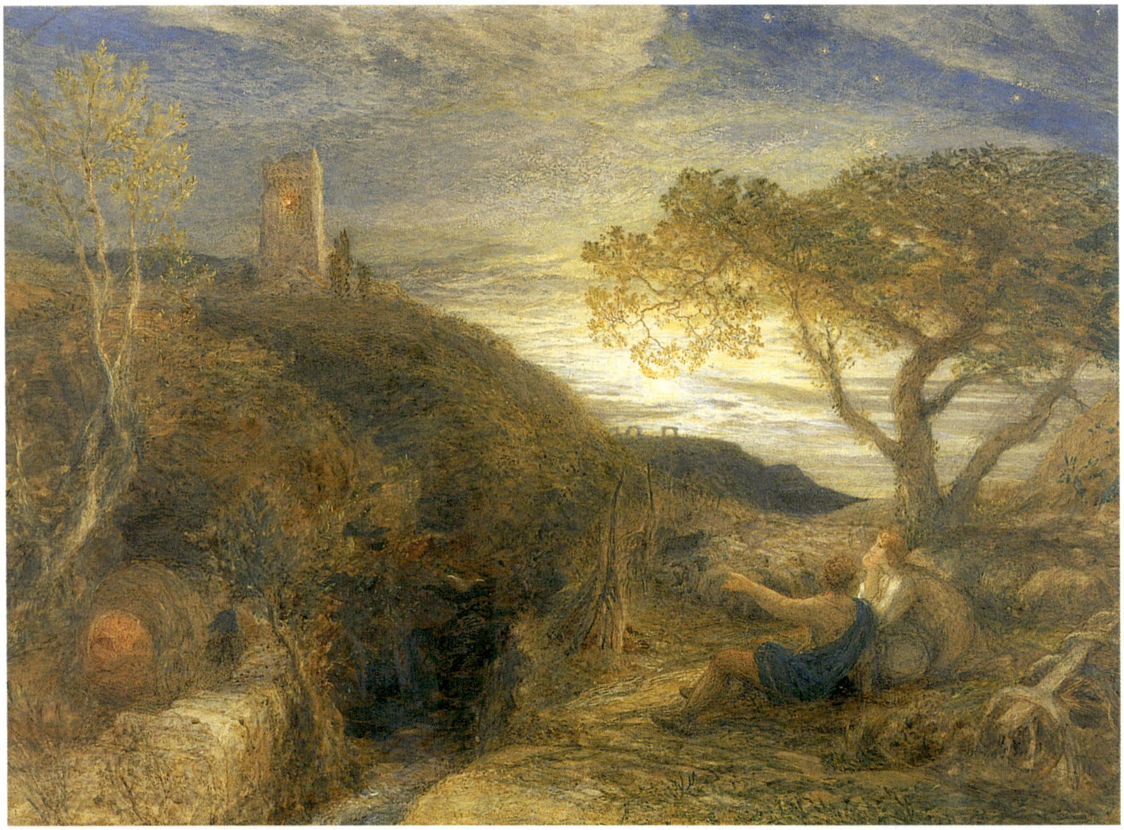

151

## 151*

*The Lonely Tower*, 1867–8

Watercolour and body colour, 51 × 70.5 cm ($20^{1}/_{16}$ × $27^{3}/_{4}$ in)

Lit: Irwin; Lister M22

New Haven, Yale Center for British Art, Paul Mellon Collection, B1977.14.147

This illustration – conceived by Palmer as the last in his Milton cycle – was among the first three to be exhibited, at the Old Water-Colour Society in 1868. It was shown with the following quotation from 'Il Penseroso' (lines 85–8):

> Or let my lamp at midnight hour,
> Be seen in some high lonely tower,
> Where I may oft outwatch the Bear,
> With thrice great Hermes.

As has been mentioned in the entry to cat. 150, Palmer originally conceived this subject as a counterpart to the *Towered City*, perceiving it as a more isolated and spiritual night to set against the sociably poetic and fantastic one of the earlier theme. He may still have had this concept of counterparts in mind when he first exhibited the two in 1868.

The *Lonely Tower* became the most potent image of Palmer's last period – though arguably this was more through the later etched version (see cat. 161) than from this earlier painting. However, this work is the largest and most elaborate presentation of the theme and the compositional arrangement is basically similar.

As with the *Towered City*, Palmer worked on this composition slowly over the years between 1864 and autumn 1867. A monochrome study of the subject now in Cincinnati Art Museum was marked by A.H. Palmer as being 'The first design for "The Lonely Tower"'. However, it is far more likely that the Cincinnati study was made in preparation for the later versions of the composition, the watercolour now in the Huntington Library (cat. 152) and the etched version (cat. 161), as it contains features that occur in those works but cannot be found in the present version (see cat. 152 for further details). Palmer brought the present composition to its conclusion in the autumn of 1867, at much the same time as he was finishing the *Towered City*. On 21 November 1867 he reported to Valpy:

> While I was touching on the sheep in *The Lonely Tower*, all of a sudden, I don't know why, the whole seemed to come as I intended it, so I packed it up in a paper and string to make it difficult to get at, lest I should spoil it. In this state, a few breathings, after we have had a final look at it, will be precious. (*L&L*, p. 151.)

As Irwin noted, the tower depicted is that of Leith Hill, near Dorking. This tower had a particular significance for Palmer as it was adjacent to High Ashes Farm, where his son Thomas More Palmer had died and where Palmer had lived, too, during his son's last weeks. Palmer could also see Leith Hill from his studio in Furze Hill House, Redhill (as he records in his autobiographical article in the *Portfolio* in 1871), while he painted this and other pictures in his later years. In a recent article (*Burlington Magazine*, September 2005) Vaughan and Barker argue that the picture contains many coded references to Thomas More. The waning moon is only visible in the early morning – the time when Thomas More died. The position of the constellation of stars – which shows the Bear in accordance with Milton's poem – was also that which could be observed on the day of Thomas More's death. This would strengthen the identification of the site as being based on Leith Hill as it rises above the Surrey landscape, rather than simply a use of the tower as a motif in itself (Vaughan and Barker).

In an undated fragment of a letter to Valpy Palmer speaks of the 'poetic loneliness' of the landscape, 'not the loneliness of the desert, but a secluded spot in a genial pastoral country, enriched also by antique relics, such as those so-called Druidic stones' (*Letters*, pp. 695–6). The stones are shown on the horizon, at the base of the hill. Such prehistoric remains can also be found at the base of Leith Hill. It need hardly be stressed how much Palmer himself identifies with Milton's lonely melancholic intellectual in his tower.

## 152

### *The Lonely Tower*, before 1881

Watercolour, 16.5 × 23.5 cm (6½ × 9¼ in)

Lit: Lister M23

San Marino, The Huntington Library, Art Collections, and Botanical Gardens 59.55.984, L.M23

This limpid and beautiful watercolour – a reworking of the composition first found in the large-scale watercolour for Valpy (cat. 151) – is probably one of the last, if not the very last, that Palmer executed. In *Life and Letters* A.H. Palmer describes how when Palmer was ill in bed in the last months of his life 'he continued his work, for a time, more effectively than I should have thought possible'. As well as completing *The Prospect* and other large watercolours he worked on 'small replicas of *The Bellman* and *The Lonely Tower*' (*L&L*, p. 166).

This version of the subject is almost identical to that of the etching (cat. 161), which Palmer had been working on in the later 1870s and had completed in 1879, and it seems most probable that this watercolour is based on the etched design rather than on the earlier watercolour. As in the etching, the composition here has become more focused and simple: the shepherd and his

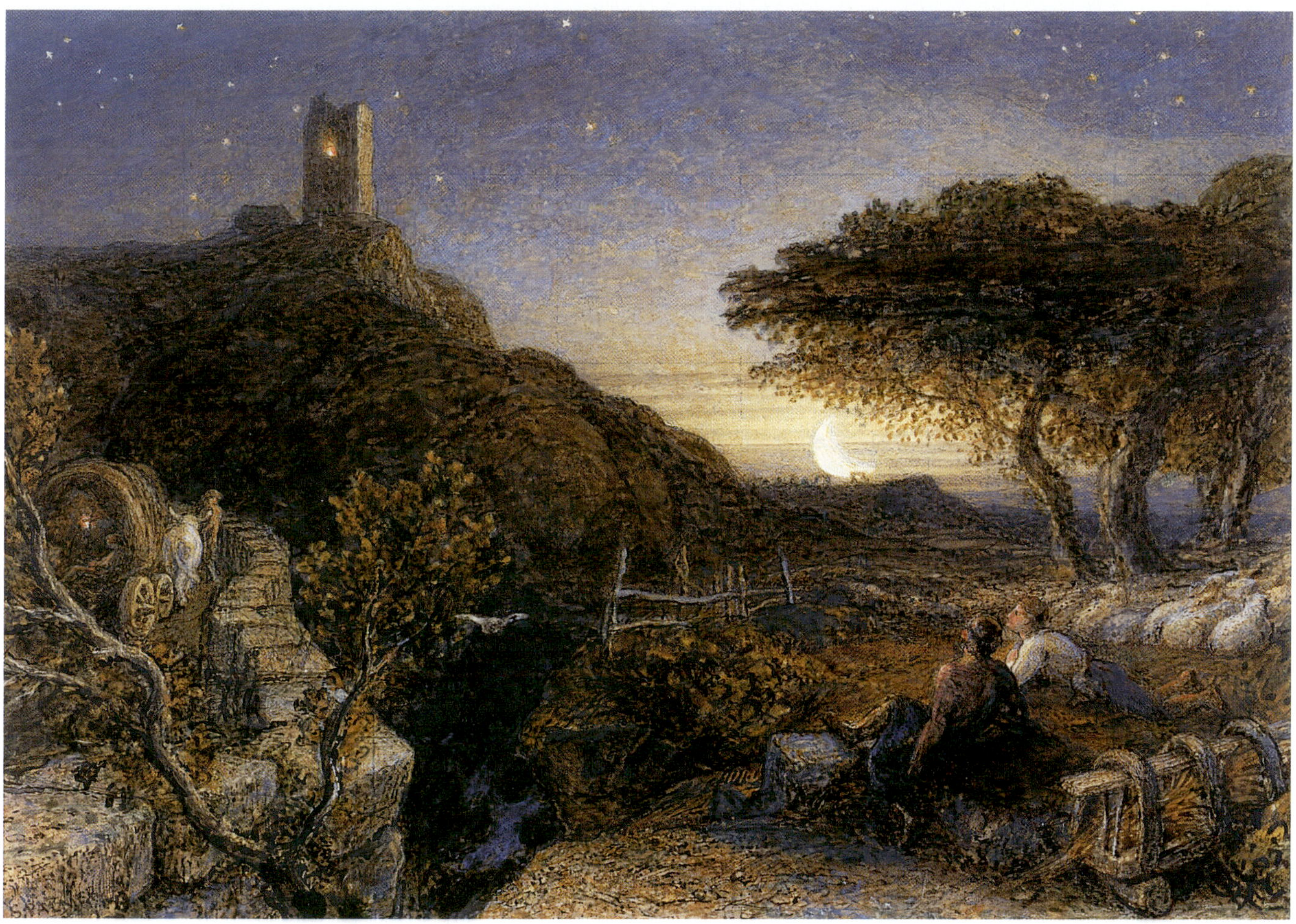

152

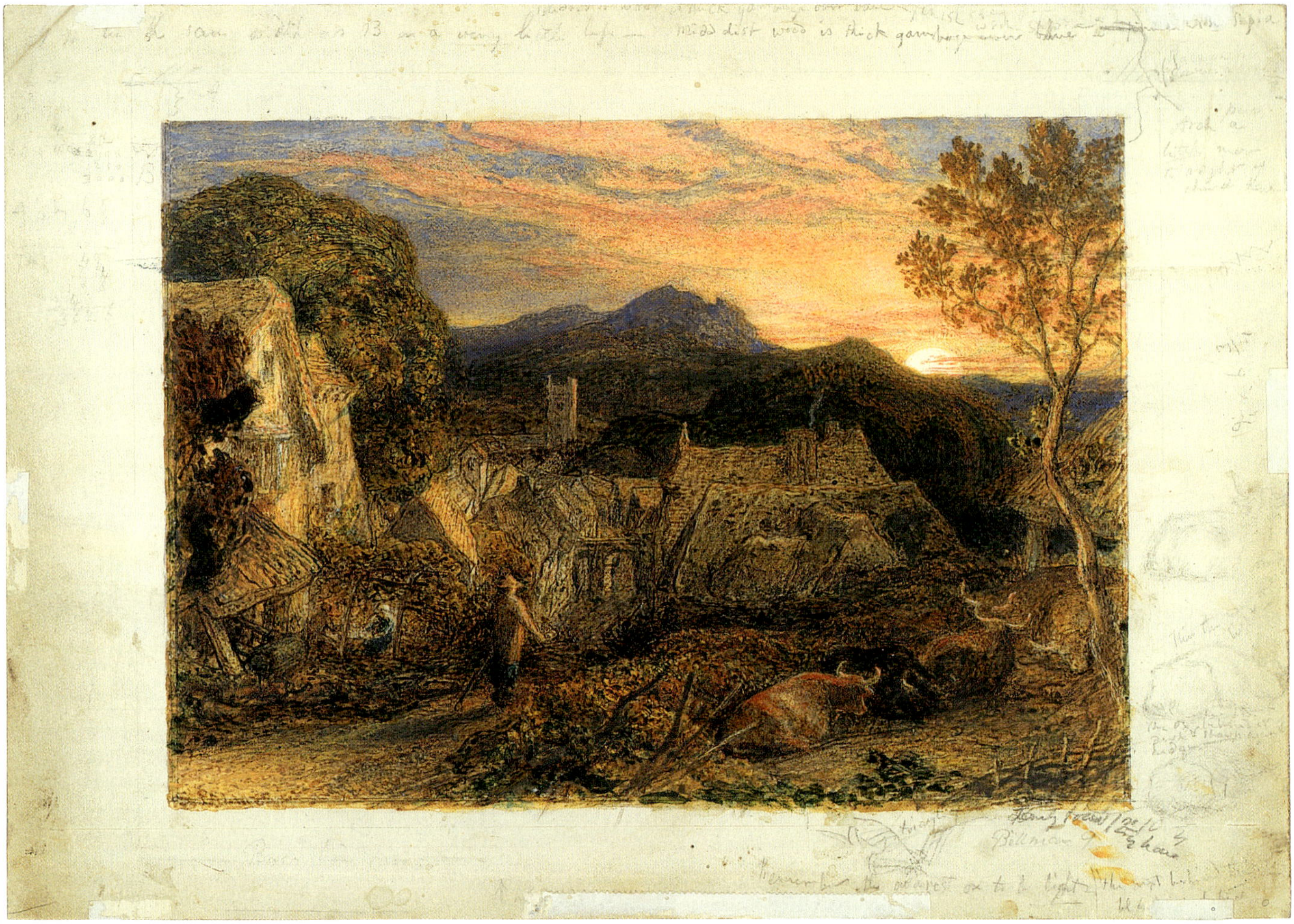

153

love concentrate in the later versions on the tower itself while in the earlier one they are looking around discursively. Greater attention is given to the tower, too, which is brought out in high dark relief against the sky.

Interestingly, both the etched version and this painting show the tower with a stair turret projecting, whereas the earlier version does not. As it happens, Leith Hill Tower had a turret added to it in the 1860s, a fact that Palmer must have been aware of since he could see Leith Hill from his studio window.

## 153

### *The Bellman*, before 1881

Watercolour,
image 17.2 × 23.9 cm ($6\frac{3}{4} \times 9\frac{3}{8}$ in),
sheet 22.5 × 23.9 cm ($8\frac{7}{8} \times 9\frac{3}{8}$ in)

Inscribed with lengthy notes: see Lister

Lit: Lister M19

Bedford, Trustees of the Cecil Higgins Art Gallery

This illustrates lines 83–4 from 'Il Penseroso', 'Or the bellman's drowsy charm, / to bless the door from nightly harm', which comes from the section of the poem where Milton is envisaging the activities signalling the coming of night. Palmer seems to have been particularly obsessed with this part of the poem since it provided subject matter for three other compositions either executed or planned for the series: *The Curfew* (cat. 148), *Glowing Embers* (see cat. 145) and *The Lonely Tower* (cat. 151). *The Bellman* was not in Palmer's scheme for the series as sent to Valpy in September 1864. However, it had already been mentioned as a companion piece to *Glowing Embers* in the first letter Palmer wrote to Valpy accepting the commission in June 1864 (*Letters*, pp. 690–91), when it would appear to have been thought of as a small vertical composition.

Palmer wrote to Valpy of the scene of the bellman walking through the street of a village: 'Here we enter seclusion without desolateness; where light enough remains to show the village sheltered in its wooded nest.' Palmer also told Valpy that he had 'almost exactly described the scene' in a letter to him giving an account of a Hereford village (*Letters*, pp. 699–700). However, it would seem that the main inspiration for the village was a remembered Shoreham. When writing to P.G. Hamerton about the engraved version, he said:

> I am very glad that you like my *Bellman* ... It is breaking out of village-fever long after contact – a dream of that genuine village where I mused away some of my best years, designing what nobody would care for, and contracting, among good books, a fastidious and unpopular taste. (*Letters*, p. 970.)

The situation of the village, folded between hills, certainly resembles that of Shoreham. Lister has seen in the middle distance some recollections of Devon and in the distant mountains 'memories of the Apennines'.

This version of the subject is probably a preliminary study for the large *Bellman* completed for Valpy in 1881 and now in the Chatsworth Collection. It may also have been used as a study for the etched version of the subject that Palmer completed in 1879 (see cat. 159). Although all three designs are close, this study and the etching are closer to each other than to the large watercolour. For example the cottage on the left has a hipped gable end in this work and the etching, whereas the one in the large watercolour does not. As is common with Palmer studies used for etchings (and larger pictures) the margins are full of notes – some illegible – recording desired changes in the transferred design. It seems likely, therefore, that this study predates both the etching and the large watercolour.

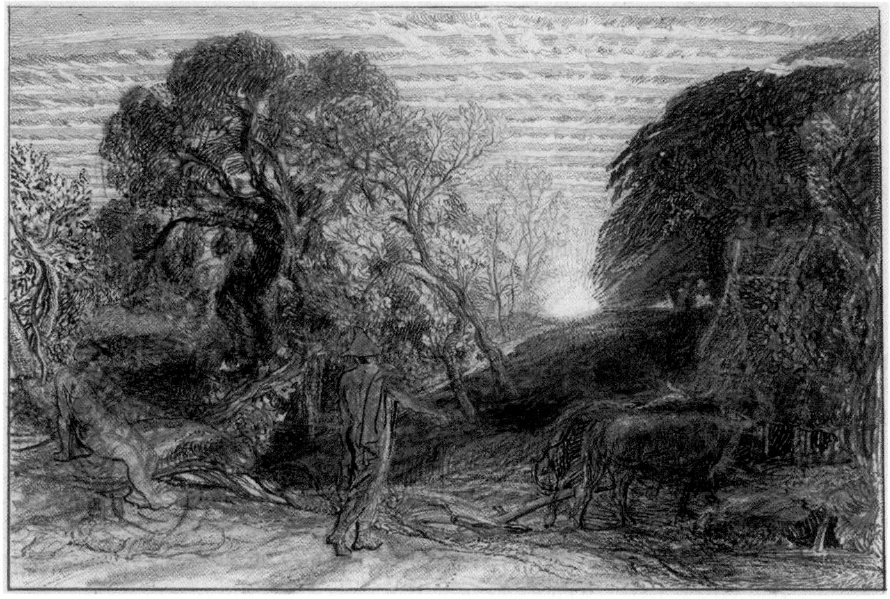

154

## 154

### *Eclogue I: 'O Fortunate Old Man!'*, *c*.1874

Graphite, black ink and gouache on card, 17.1 × 25.5 cm (6¾ × 10⅛ in)

Lit: Lister VI

London, British Museum, 1991.1109.22; bequeathed by Maude Wethered

Palmer began making designs for illustrations to Virgil's *Eclogues* after P.G. Hamerton had advised him only to publish his translation if he accompanied it with his own illustrations. Apart from his own lifelong fascination with Virgil – stimulated by his classicist friend Calvert and his own son Thomas More's expertise in Latin – Palmer had in mind the illustrations to *The Pastorals of Virgil* by Blake (cat. 19), which had been so important for opening his eyes to a poetic and visionary approach to landscape in his youth. When sending his text to Hamerton in the first place he had said:

> If Blake were alive and I could afford it, I would ask him to make a head-piece for each bucolic.
>
> How exquisitely he would have done it we know, seeing that perhaps the most intense gems of bucolic sentiment in the whole range of art are his little wood-cut illustrations to Phillips' *Pastorals* in Dr. Thornton's book. (*Letters*, p. 835.)

As this quote acknowledges, Blake did not illustrate Virgil in Dr Thornton's book, but one of Virgil's English imitators, Ambrose Philips. Perhaps there was a sense of trying to make good the omission.

Despite this, it must be admitted that – apart from occasional figurative quotations – Palmer's own Virgil illustrations bear little relationship to Blake's work, although they do have a more intimate scale than the Milton designs, perhaps because they are directly intended as book illustrations. Many of the designs are also characterized by the vividness so frequently evident in Palmer's first sketches. This one shows a combination of the use of fine pen lines (particularly in the representation of 'Margate mottle' in the sky, for example – see cats 116, 117) with graphite to mark out deep areas of shadow and to sketch out forms broadly in the foreground. Touches of body-colour white (gouache) highlight forms in the foreground, such as the backs of the cattle.

The present work illustrates the same passage as the painting *Tityrus* (cat. 157), yet its treatment is utterly different, in line with its smaller scale. Palmer uses his 'Margate mottle' for the sky as the unfortunate Meliboeus passes the fortunate Tityrus on his way into exile.

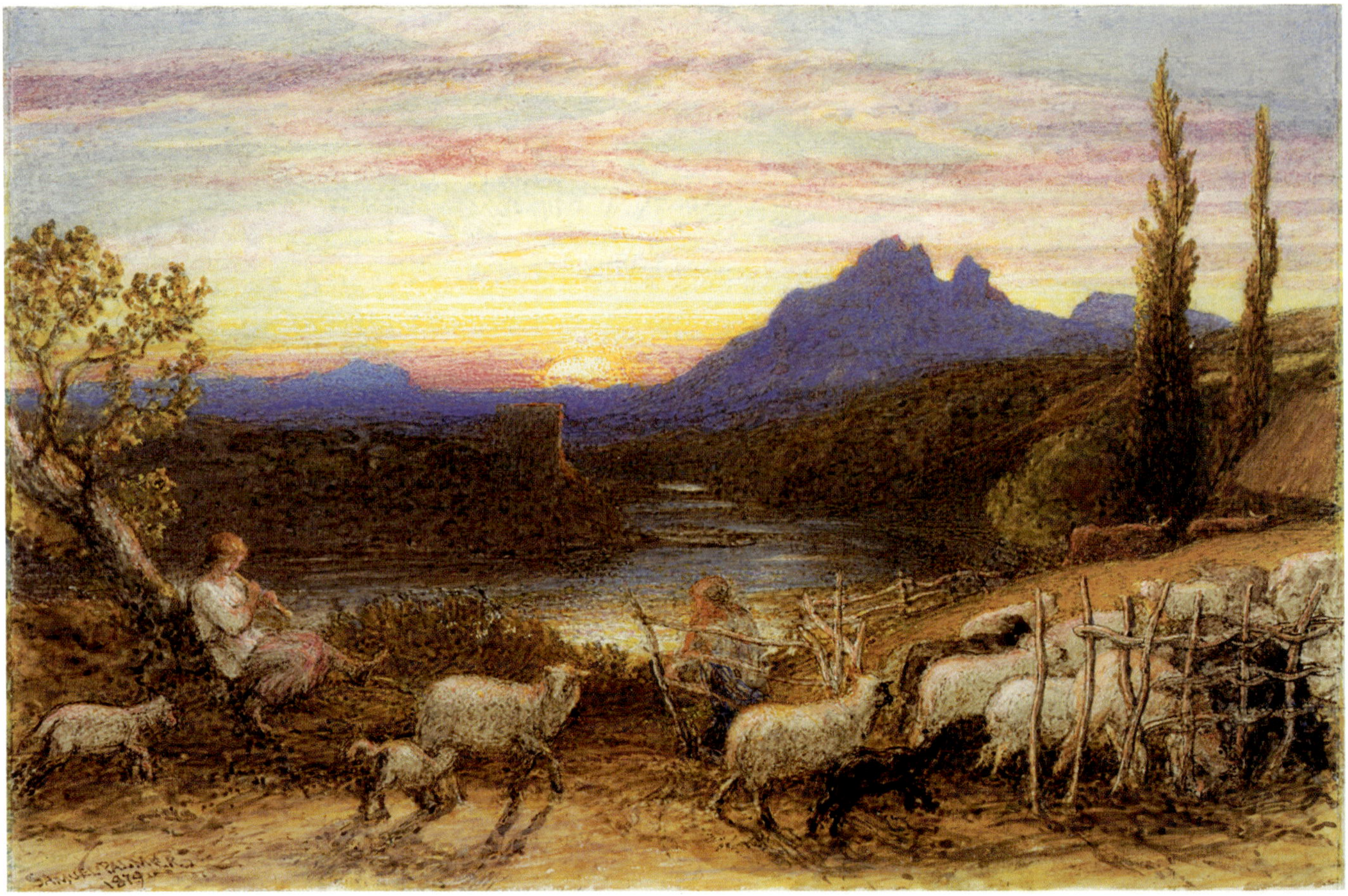

155

# 155*

*Study for Eclogue VI: 'Till Vesper Bade the Swain'*, 1879

Watercolour, 12.5 × 19.2 cm ($4\frac{15}{16} \times 7\frac{9}{16}$ in)

Lit: Lister VI4

London, Victoria and Albert Museum, 35-1919

This illustrates the lines from Virgil's Eclogue VI in Palmer's *English Version* (cat. 163): 'till Vesper bade the swain / number his flock and stall them from the dew, / and then from the reluctant skies withdrew.' A worked-up watercolour, it follows on from a pair of earlier studies, although one of these was described by A.H. Palmer as being 'the last unfinished work of S. Palmer' (V&A 1926, p. 51). It seems to have been conceived as a separate work and was exhibited at the Old Water-Colour Society in 1879 (no. 360) as *Going to the Fold*. It shows the idyllic style of Palmer's

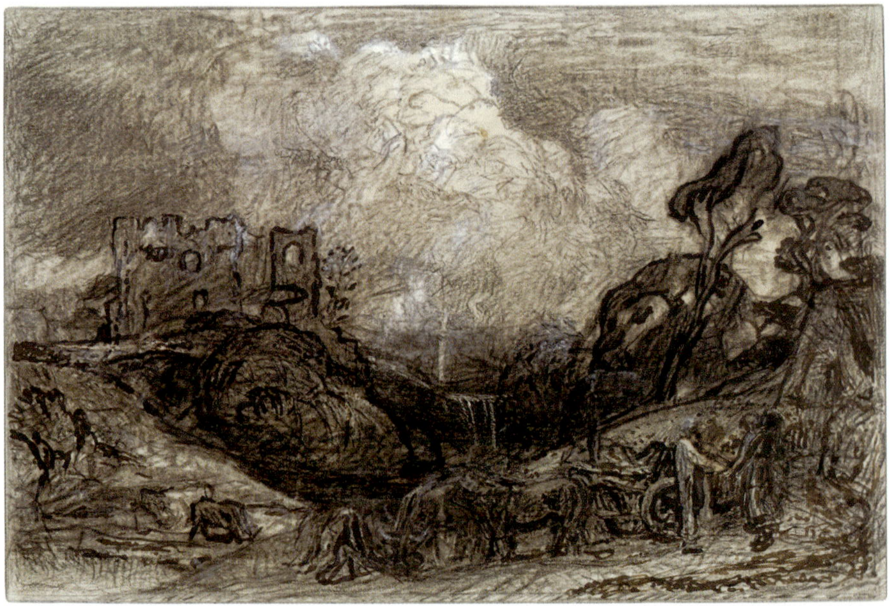

156

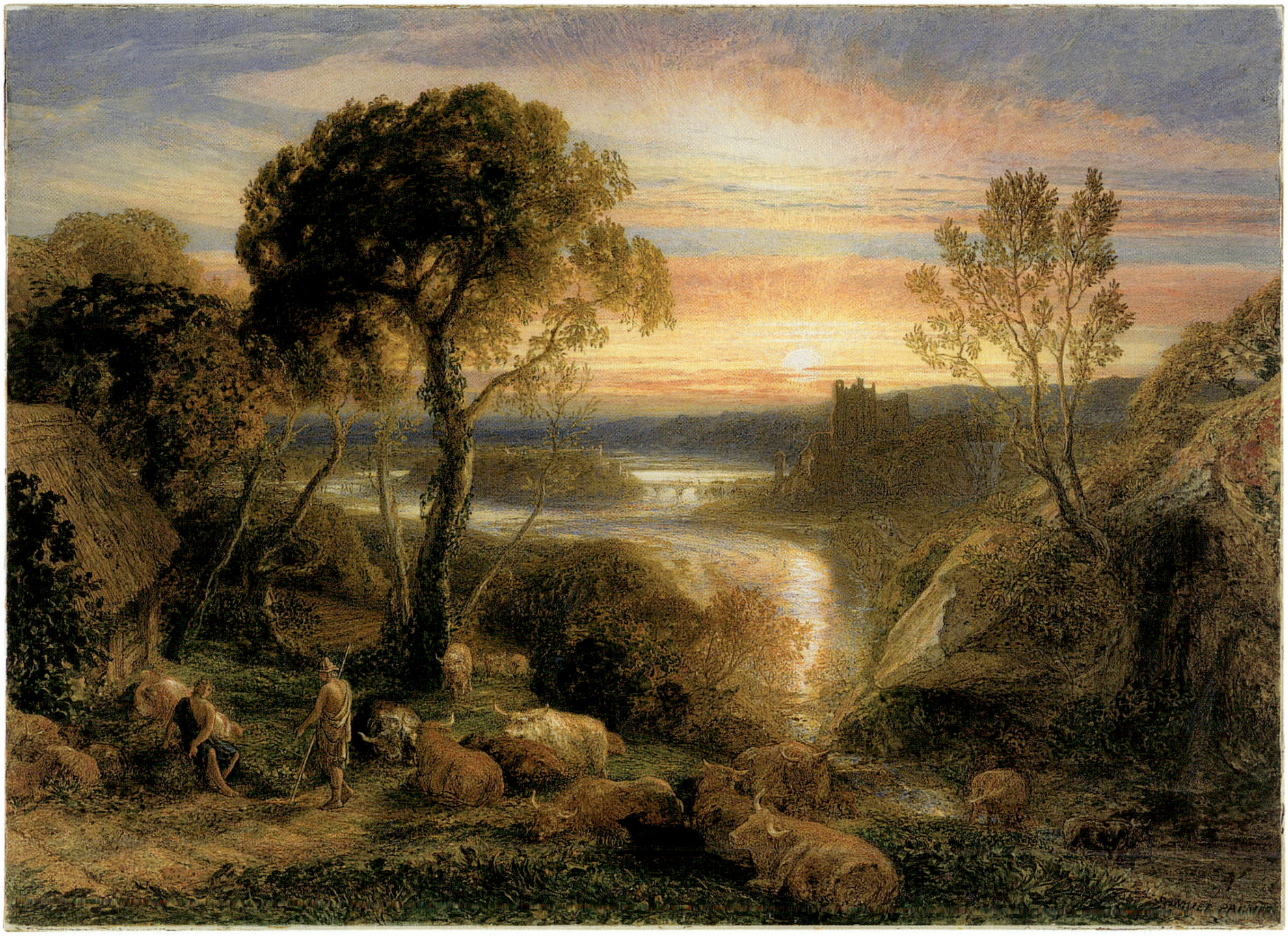

157

later years, typified by the swain who seems to be taking the task of numbering the flock very lightly.

## 156

*Eclogue III: 'Tis Gentle Phillis'*, c.1876

Black chalk and brown ink, heightened with white gouache, 10.2 × 15.2 cm (4 × 6 in)

Lit: Lister v8

London, British Museum, 1938.11-12-15

This illustrates the lines from Eclogue III in *An English Version* (cat. 163):

'Tis gentle Phillis I love best of all,
For when I left some tears began to fall;
'Adieu!' she cried, while her loose tresses fell
About me, 'Charming boy, a long farewell!'

This is one of four designs for the subject, and it may be the earliest. Unlike the other versions, this focuses less on the separating couple (seen in the right foreground) than on the surrounding landscape. However, the ruin and voluminous clouds seem to suggest the turmoil felt by the protagonists at their parting.

Like others in the series this design combines pen lines with the use of graphite to deepen tones and white to heighten lighter parts. It is one of the freest and most vigorous studies in the series. A different version (British Museum 1991-11-9-xx; Lister v7) was used as an illustration in *An English Version*.

## 157

*Tityrus Restored to his Patrimony*, c.1874

Watercolour and gouache, with touches of gum arabic on card laid down on paper, 50.2 × 69.9 cm (19¾ × 27½ in)

Signed at lower right with point of brush: *SAMUEL PALMER*

Lit: Lister v2; *Art Treasures* 1998, 242

Birmingham City Museums and Art Galleries, 279'05

Most of the works in the Virgil series were intended as studies for etchings and were therefore usually in monochrome, but this is one of the exceptions. It is a fully worked-up watercolour, comparable in scale and finish to those in the Milton series, and was exhibited at the Old Water-Colour Society in 1877.

The subject is taken from Virgil's Eclogue I and illustrates the dialogue between two farmers/shepherds, Meliboeus and Tityrus. Meliboeus is being driven off his land because he backed the wrong party. Tityrus, who backed Rome, has been allowed to regain his land. Meliboeus finds him lying under a spreading beech tree playing the pipe while his cattle roam freely yet safely. Palmer has chosen the moment when Meliboeus addresses Tityrus, acknowledging his good fortune, which in his translation reads as follows:

> O fortunate old man!
> These ancestral fields are yours again;
> And wide enough for you. Though naked stone,
> And marsh with slimy rush, abut upon
> The lowlands, yet your pregnant ewes shall try
> No unproved forage; neighbouring flocks, too nigh,
> Strike no contagion, nor infect the young;
> O fortunate, who now at last, among
> Known streams and sacred fountain-heads have found
> A shelter and a shade on your own ground.

The land behind is presumably Tityrus' patrimony, though it looks considerably more inviting than the 'bare stone and pools with muddy reeds' described by Virgil. As Lister has pointed out, the design owes a lot to Claude. It is considerably more elaborate than the drawing (Lister VI, private collection), which has more affinities with Blake's *Pastorals of Virgil* than with Claude. Both were included in the illustrated version of the *Eclogues*. The watercolour is in its original frame.

## 158

### *Classical River Scene*, *c*.1878

Watercolour and gouache on card, 23.1 × 35.2 cm ($9\frac{1}{8} \times 13\frac{7}{8}$ in)

Signed at lower right with point of brush: *S PALMER*

Lit: Lister 678

London, British Museum, 1958-7-12-360

Lister suggests that this may be the *River Banks at Even* exhibited at the Old Water-Colour Society in 1878 (no. 238). The work has the limpid quality evident in a number of Palmer's last water-colours, notably the Huntington version of *The Lonely Tower* (cat. 152).

It seems to be a perfect evocation of the concept of the 'idyll': a quiet, meditative representation of late evening with the sun having already set, leaving a purplish glow in the sky, and a sickle moon and the evening star in the clear sky above. There is a sense of the chill of

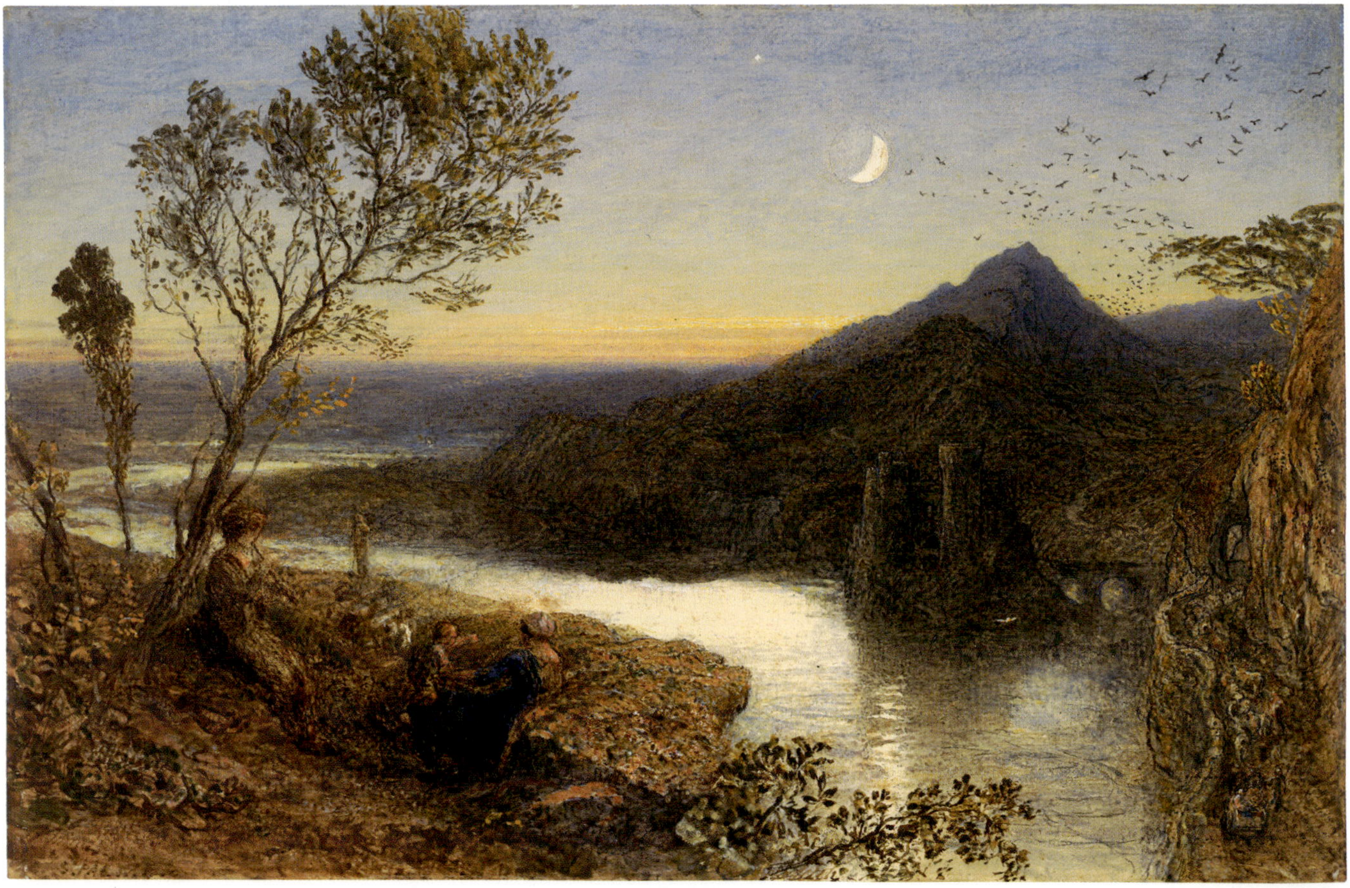

158

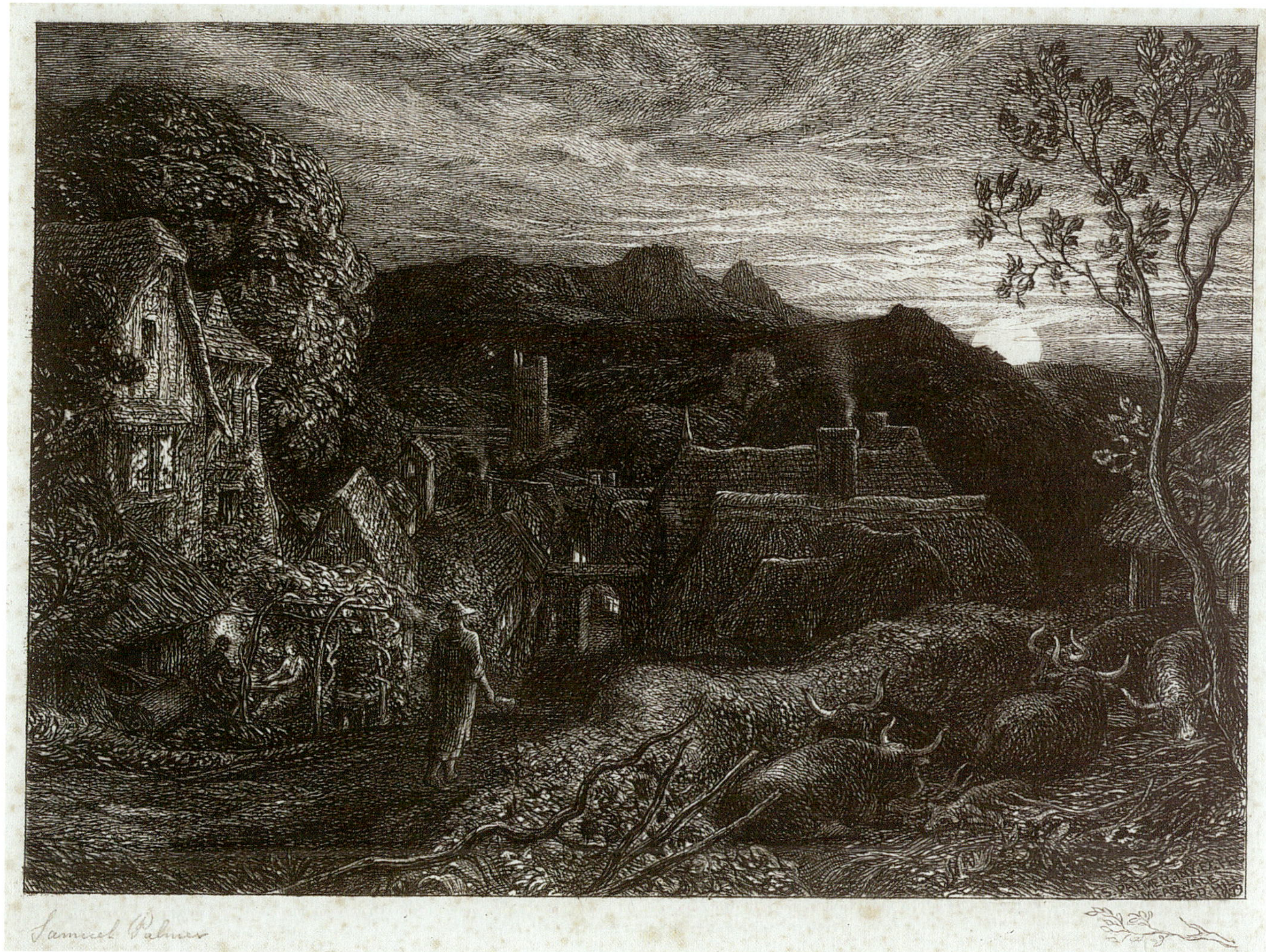

159

early autumn in the colours. Dark-coloured birds, probably rooks, are circling in the sky above the castle on the river. A single white bird flies across the river. In the foreground, on a promontory overlooking the river, there is a shepherd and his family. He pipes against a tree while his wife – in deep blue costume – tends the baby who gestures in excitement towards the middle ground, probably at the sight of the birds. Further off is a solitary figure. Lower down, on the other bank of the river, travellers are making their way along a narrow path in the direction of the castle.

The overall composition of the work has clear debts to classical landscape, in particular Claude. The theme and treatment are close to certain of the Milton subjects, in particular *A Towered City* (cat. 150) and *The Lonely Tower*. There is no evidence in this case, however, of Palmer illustrating a particular text.

## 159

### *The Bellman*, 1879

Etching printed in black ink on white wove paper, sheet 23.1 × 36.1 cm (9 1/8 × 14 1/4 in), plate 19 × 25.1 cm (7 1/2 × 9 7/8 in), image 16.7 × 23.3 cm (6 1/3 × 9 1/8 in), state 5 of 7

Signed in graphite at lower left: *Samuel Palmer*

Inscribed within etching at lower right: *S. PALMER. INV. ET. FEC / MEAD. VALE. RED HILL / 1879.*; remarque (tree branch) etched at lower right of margin

Lit: Alexander 11(v); Lister E11(5)

The University of Manchester, The Whitworth Art Gallery, P.1999.29; gift of Miss Ayuda Scott-Elliot

For commentary see cat. 160. EEB

## 160

### Cancelled plate for *The Bellman*, 1879

Steel-faced and cancelled copper plate, 19 × 25.1 cm (7 1/2 × 9 7/8 in)

Lit: Goldman 1991, no. 11b

London, British Museum, 1926-9-3-1; presented by A.H. Palmer, 1926

Soon after Palmer devised the plan to prepare eight large watercolours depicting subjects from Milton's 'L'Allegro' and 'Il Penseroso', he began

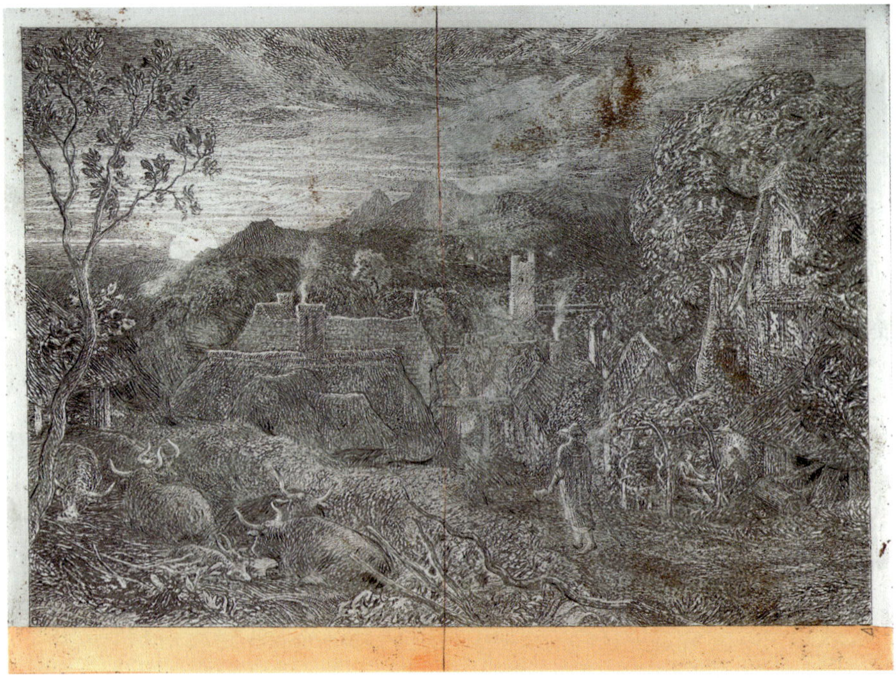

160

to contemplate the possibility of expanding the project to include prints (cats 159, 161; *L&L*, pp. 149–50). On 20 October 1864 Palmer described his inspiration to Leonard Rowe Valpy:

> The Etching dream came over me in this way. I am making my working sketches a quarter of the size of the drawings, and was surprised and not displeased to notice the variety – the difference of each from all the rest. I saw within, a set of highly-finished etchings the size of Turner's *Liber Studiorum*; and as finished as my moonlight with the cypresses; a set making a book – a compact block of work which I would fain hope might live when I am with the fallen leaves. (*Letters*, p. 12.)

The two large, exquisite etchings that Palmer completed for the project before his death – *The Bellman* and *The Lonely Tower* (cat. 161) – have, indeed, done much to ensure the immortality of his graphic art.

Palmer derived the composition of *The Bellman* from the large watercolour (Duke of Devonshire, Chatsworth; Lister M20) of the same name, which illustrates lines 83–4 from 'Il Penseroso' referring to the close of day: 'the bellman's drowsy charm, / To bless the door from nightly harm'. As the sun sinks behind the hills, a solitary man, bell in hand, makes his way past figures beneath an arbour and cattle beside a hedge towards a village marked by chimney smoke and a church spire, a view based on memories of Shoreham (see cat. 153).

Palmer seems to have prepared all six (lifetime) states of this print in the spring of 1879. Thirteen bitings, successive burnishings and other revisions transformed the once-smooth copper plate into a rich terrain of deep furrows and shallow incisions. The artist's son A.H. Palmer pulled working proofs on his first press at Furze Hill House and later printed proofs for sale on his large second press in London (V&A 1926, 212; *A Vision Recaptured*, p. 71). The etching was published by the Fine Art Society, London, in 1879. EEB

## 161

### *The Lonely Tower*, 1879

Etching on heavy tan wove paper, sheet 36.3 × 50 cm (14¼ × 19⅝ in), plate 18.9 × 25.2 cm (7½ × 10 in), image 16.5 × 23.3 cm (6⅝ × 9⅛ in), proof of state 4 of 7 (Alexander's state 4 of 6)

Signed at lower left of etching: *Sam.l Palmer.*; and at lower right in graphite: *S. Palmer.*

Inscribed at lower left in graphite in Samuel Palmer's hand: *Trial Proof*; and at upper left: *A- / 79*; in another hand at lower left: *Club A. Mr Goulding 18 March 1879 – slightly retroussé – Brown Ink*; and at lower right: *OJ. 35-*

Lit: Alexander 12(iv); Lister E12(4)

New York, The Metropolitan Museum of Art, Gift of Margaret Scolari Barr, 1986

*The Lonely Tower*, like its pendant *The Bellman* (cats 159, 160), corresponds to a large watercolour illustrating a subject from Milton (cat. 151). Unlike *The Bellman*, however, the etching of *The Lonely Tower* differs substantially from the related watercolour in various details – from the gestures of the figures and the profile of the distant tower to the inclusion of the crescent moon and the shapes of the trees. Palmer explored these changes in an intermediary brown wash drawing (Cincinnati Art Museum, Lister M21) similar in size to the etching and squared for transfer. (Lister orders these works differently, making the Cincinnati drawing preparatory to all other renditions of the subject.) The transformation of the sunset scene into a moonlit one received the praise of a critic reviewing the Fine Art Society exhibition of 1881: 'We much prefer Palmer's latest etchings to all his other productions. "The Lonely Tower" published in 1880, is a wonderful piece of work, far superior to the picture which it professes to interpret, & more intelligible in its harmony of various lights.' (Correspondence.)

The preparations for this etching, like those for *The Bellman*, seem to have taken place in 1879. A.H. Palmer recorded that his father bit the plate for *The Lonely Tower* no fewer than fourteen times (V&A

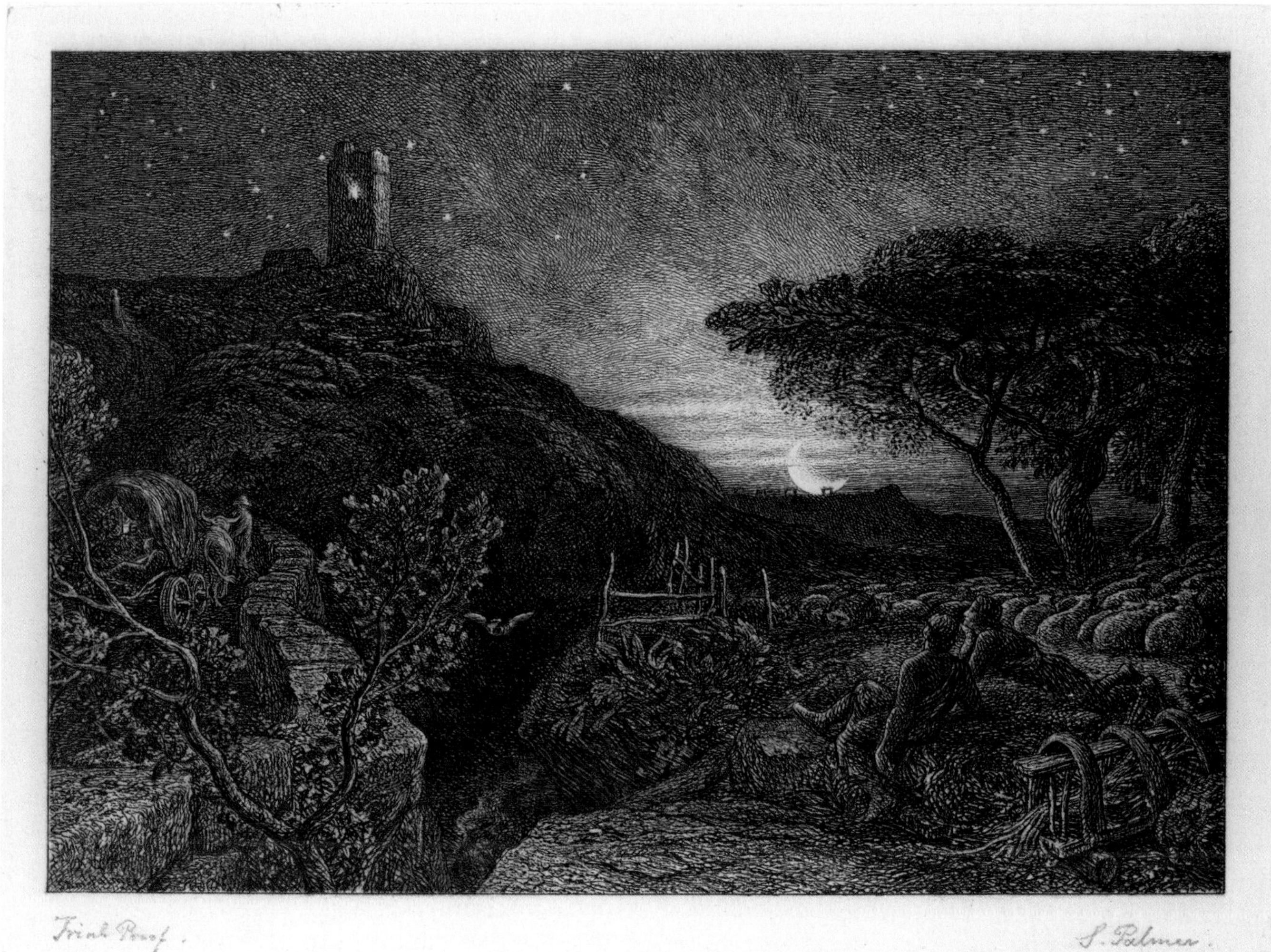


161

1926, p. 83). Of the seven states of this etching, the present (fourth) state yielded the finest impressions, perhaps – as R.G. Alexander speculated – because Palmer later reworked the plate to such an extent that it became difficult to print (Alexander, p. 49). The inscriptions in the margins of the present impression indicate that it was printed by Frederick Goulding and considered a model proof. Regrettably, however, this standard would not be followed. At the sight of *The Lonely Tower* as it appeared in R. Ansell's *Il Penseroso for the Etching Club* (1880) the artist lamented: 'the dear old Etching Club … has quite smashed *me*, by the way my Lonely Tower has been printed. Full directions were sent to the printer and a model proof, but in vain.' (*Letters*, p. 1046.)

Although Palmer stated that the plate had been destroyed, it remained in existence, was restored in the 1920s and was reprinted in 1952, 1962 and at another unspecified date (*Letters*, p. 1028; Lister E12). The cancelled plate is now in the collection of Mr David Gould. EEB

## 162

## *Opening the Fold* or *Early Morning*, 1880

Etching on buff wove paper, retouched with gouache, sheet 26 × 36.2 cm (10$\frac{1}{4}$ × 14$\frac{1}{4}$ in), plate 16.4 × 23.1 cm (6$\frac{3}{8}$ × 9$\frac{1}{8}$ in), image 16.2 × 23 cm (6$\frac{1}{2}$ × 9 in), state 3 of 8 with notations and corrections

Signed in etching at lower left: *S PALMER INV + FEC*

Inscribed in graphite at upper left in Samuel Palmer's hand: *Sky near olive / Figure opening / Beech Trees / Sheep*; at upper right: *CHARCOAL / double line in hat / distant rain [?] burnished / 3*; at lower left: *Private Press*; at lower left in another hand: *2670 / Hardie 13*; and at centre right in another hand: *Touched Proof / 1. R.S. / 6-0*; on verso: *Touched Proof / G.L. Winthrop*; Remarque (spray of harebells) in lower left margin

Lit: Alexander 13(iii); Lister E13(3)

New York, The Metropolitan Museum of Art, Gift of G.L. Winthrop, 1917

Samuel Palmer devoted decades of passionate labour to a secret literary project: preparing an English translation of Virgil's *Eclogues* intended to capture

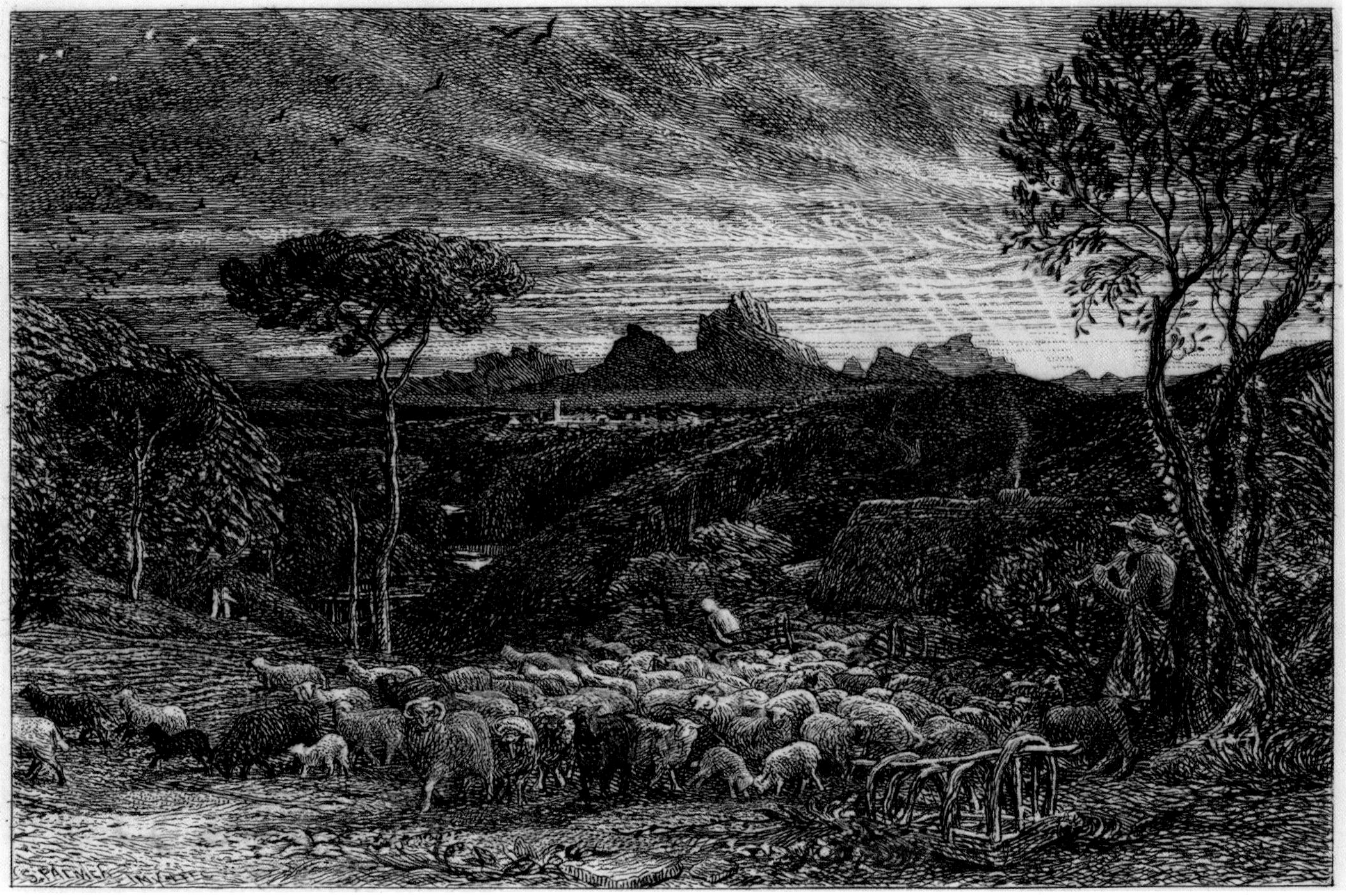

162

the 'pastoral essence' of the original Latin. By the time he finally broached the subject with a friend, the often-revised manuscript had become 'so interlined, erased, and cut about for the insertion of slips of new matter, that but little of the original remained' (*L&L*, p. 155). In January 1872 Palmer asked the successful author P.G. Hamerton (who had launched the innovative periodical the *Portfolio* in 1869) for publishing advice:

> If you would like to do so as an act of penance, I would annoy you with inquiries as to the best way of disposing of a completed verse translation of Virgil's *Eclogues* which, right or wrong, I am resolved (all being well) to print ... [my version] is a work done *con amore* in the superlative degree. (*Letters*, p. 835.)

Hamerton sensibly suggested that Palmer prepare illustrations for the work himself; he began the designs in August (*Letters*, p. 852) and in November reported to Hamerton:

> When you 'commanded' me to make illustrations I loathed the thought. But I took 'the disagreeable first', and now it is my all-engrossing study. They take a long time for the very reason that I am longing to see them done, and know that the shortest and only way is to aim at no mechanical finish and to put only touches of love. (*Letters*, p. 868.)

Sadly, Palmer would not live to see his beloved Virgil published (see cat. 163). Indeed, at the time of his death in 1881, Palmer had completed only this etching, *Opening the Fold*, which illustrates Eclogue VIII (lines 23–8):

> Scarce with her rosy fingers had the dawn
> From glimmering heaven the vale of night withdrawn,
> Or folded flocks were loose to browse anew
> O'er mountain thyme or trefoil wet with dew,
> When leaning sad an olive stem beside,
> These, his last numbers, hapless Damon plied.

*Opening the Fold* was published by the Fine Art Society, London, in 1880 and reprinted (in a later state) in the editions of the *Eclogues* published by the artist's son in 1883 and 1884. The plate was reprinted in 1926 by Sir Frank Short, Martin Hardie and F.L. Griggs, and then destroyed. Three drawings related to the design are known (Lister V16–V18).

EEB

## 163

### *An English Version of the Eclogues of Virgil by Samuel Palmer, with Illustrations by the Author*, Seeley and Company, 54 Fleet Street, London, 1883

Bound in vellum with gold lettering and design, 37.7 × 27.5 × 3.5 cm (14⅞ × 10⅞ × 1⅜ in), copy 79 in an edition of 135

Eclogue v: *The Cypress Grove* (between pp. 54 and 55) illustrated

Etching, plate 13.2 × 18.7 cm (5¼ × 7⅜ in), image 10 × 15.1 cm (4 × 6 in), state 1 of 4

Signed in etching at lower left: *S. PALMER*

Lit: Alexander 15(i); Lister B9(v), E15(I)

New York, The Metropolitan Museum of Art, Harris Brisbane Dick Fund, 1943

As discussed in the previous entry, Palmer spent many years preparing an English translation of the *Eclogues* of Virgil along with ten original etchings to illustrate the book, but died before the project was completed. The volume shown here, published in 1883, was finished by the artist's son. It contains only one etching completed by Palmer – *Opening the Fold* (Eclogue VIII, cat. 162). Four others – *The Homeward Star* (Eclogue I), *The Cypress Grove* (Eclogue V), *The Sepulchre* (Eclogue VIII) and *Moeris and Galatea* (Eclogue IX) – were begun by Palmer but finished by his son, who wrote in the Preface: 'It has been my aim to do ... just as much as would best fulfil what I knew to be his [Samuel Palmer's] intention, conveyed orally, or by the touched proofs and drawings – to do, in short, only what was absolutely necessary to render his meaning fully evident.' The nine remaining illustrations are facsimiles of Samuel Palmer's preparatory drawings (and alternative designs) for the remaining *Eclogues*, reproduced using the process of photo-etching.

Samuel Palmer seems to have brought the present plate to a highly developed stage before his death, as the etched signature suggests. (Mather's assertion that Palmer had completed the plates for Eclogues V and VIII cannot be sustained: Mather 1937; Pressly 1970, p. 35.) Palmer had certainly begun work on this etching by 1876, when he noted on the verso of its preparatory design (British Museum) the concentrations and lengths of the acid baths to which he had subjected the plate on 17 February, 22 March and 26 April (Lister V10). It illustrates Eclogue V, translated by Palmer to read:

> Untimely lost, and by a cruel death,
> The Nymphs their Daphnis mourn'd
> with falt'ring breath.
> O bowers of hazel, waters murmuring
> hoarse,
> Ye heard that mother's cry: she, the
> dear corse
> Embracing in a long, a last caress,
> Planets and gods rebuked as pitiless.

The smouldering volcano recalls Vesuvius, and the broad trees appear equally exotic. Lister identified them as Monterey cypresses, a type introduced to England from California in 1838 (Lister E15, p. 250 note 1). But given their general similarity to Palmer's *Old Cedar in the Botanic Garden, Chelsea* (cat. 130), and

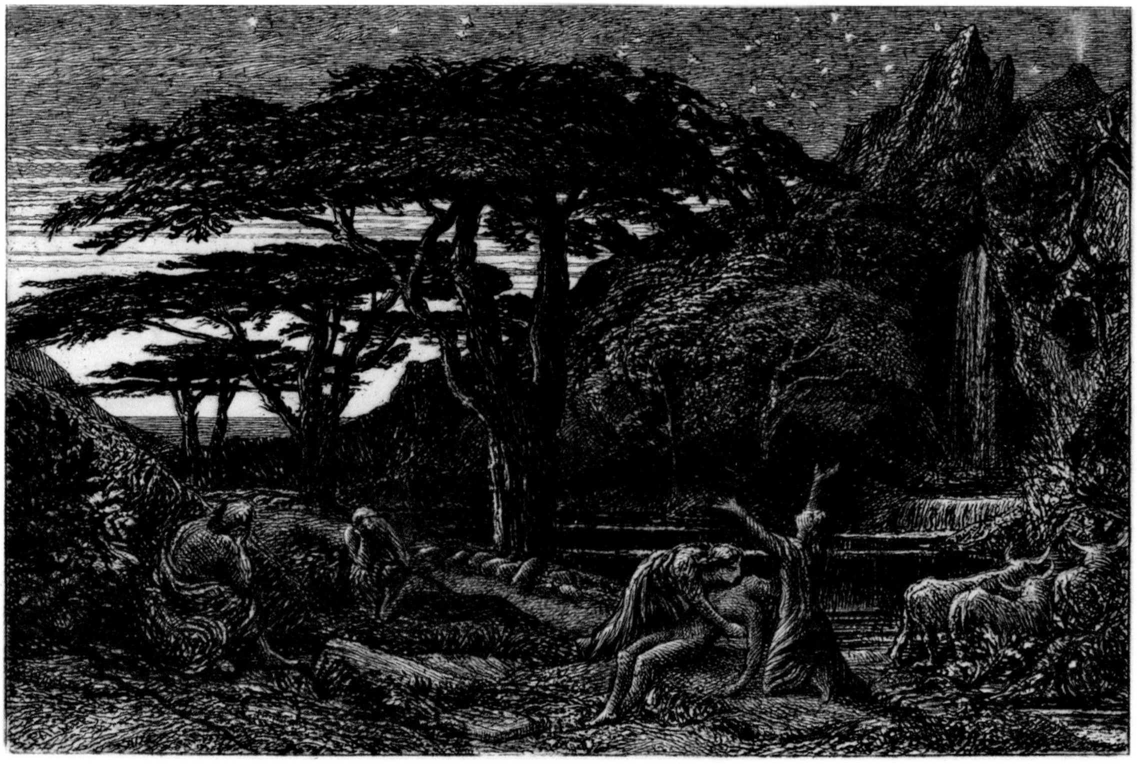

163

considering A.H. Palmer's reference to them as 'huge cedars' in the Preface, they seem more likely to represent ancient cedars, albeit somewhat altered by the artist's still-fertile imagination. The preparatory design and the cancelled copper plate for this etching are in the British Museum. EEB

## 164

### Charles West Cope (1811–90)

*Portrait of Samuel Palmer*, 1884

Etching on heavy off-white wove paper, sheet 31.5 × 20.9 cm ($12\frac{1}{2} \times 8\frac{1}{4}$ in), plate 19.7 × 14.5 cm ($7\frac{3}{4} \times 5\frac{11}{16}$ in)

Signed and dated in the etching at lower left: *CWC / 1884*

New York, The Metropolitan Museum of Art, A. Hyatt Mayor Purchase Fund, Marjorie Phelps Starr Bequest, 2003

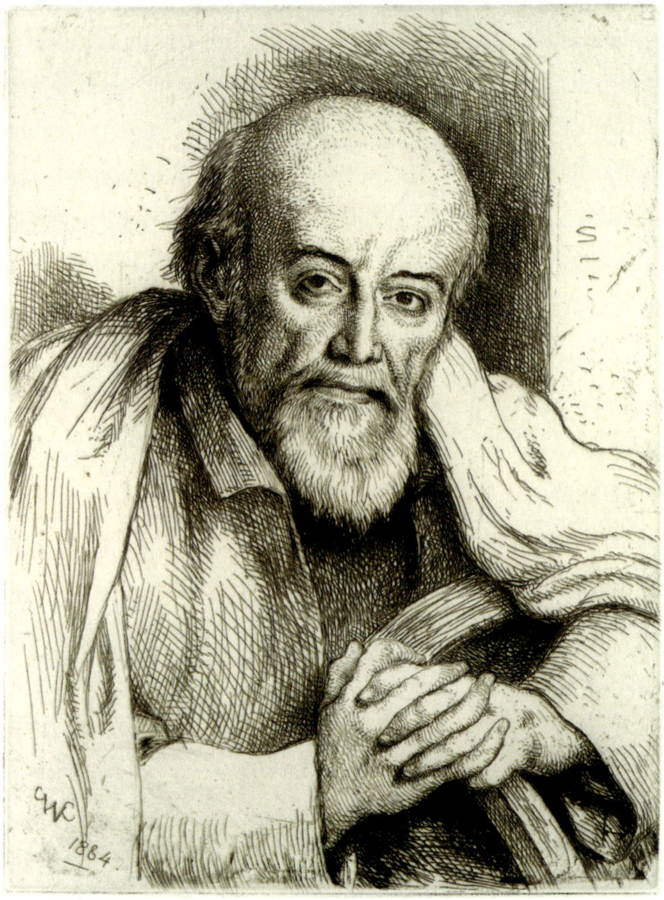

164

This sensitive portrait etching of Palmer by his friend Charles West Cope only recently came to light; no other impressions are known. It shows the bearded artist in half-length, clasping his hands before the back of a wooden chair. A pale tone of warm brown ink suffuses the design; brief strokes, dashes and dots describe the pensive face; cross-hatched lines indicate passages of shadow. The sitter meets the viewer's eyes with a calm even gaze, but his serpentine fingers seem barely to contain their agitation.

Cope – whom Palmer called his 'master in etching' (*Memoir*, p. 16) – may have made this print as part of a project undertaken by the Etching Club in November 1879 (Minutes, 10 November 1879): to prepare portraits and/or self-portraits of all its members etched on plates the size (approximately $9\frac{3}{4} \times 6\frac{3}{4}$ in) of those in Sir Anthony Van Dyck's *Iconography* (1645), a series of prints portraying approximately one hundred leading figures of the day (Mauquoy-Hendrickx 1956, Spicer 1994, Luitjen 1999).

The present plate is dated 1884, but Cope appears to have begun it in Palmer's lifetime. On 15 March 1880 Palmer wrote to Cope, apparently agreeing to his request to portray him. Palmer – then seventy-five and almost completely bald – referred playfully to his sitting for an etched portrait: 'All being well, I shall feel much honoured in submitting my scalp to your needle' (*Letters*, p. 997).

A graphite drawing (National Portrait Gallery, London) that can now be linked to this etching sheds light on Cope's work methods, indicating that he began the portrait by sketching his subject on paper (fig. 31). The sketch shows Palmer's head and shoulders the same size as the etching and in a closely similar pose, but in reverse. On the back of the lightweight sheet wide strokes of red chalk follow the design on the front, suggesting that Cope used it (like carbon paper) to transfer the basic outlines onto the etching plate. EEB

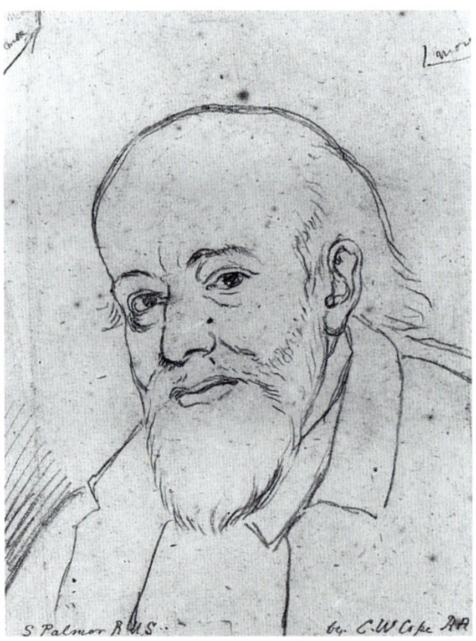

Fig. 31 Charles West Cope, *Portrait of Samuel Palmer*, graphite on tan wove paper, National Portrait Gallery, London, presented by the Misses F.M. and E. Redgrave, 1927.

# Bibliography


Abley
Mark Abley, *The Parting Light: Selected Writings of Samuel Palmer*, Manchester, 1985

Agnew's 2003
Susan Sloman, *Catalogue of Agnew's 130th Annual Exhibition of Watercolours & Drawings*, Thomas Agnew & Sons Ltd, London, March 2003

Agnew's 2004
Susan Sloman, *Catalogue of Agnew's 131st Annual Exhibition of Watercolours & Drawings*, Thomas Agnew & Sons Ltd, London, March 2004

Alexander
R.G. Alexander, *A Catalogue of the Etchings of Samuel Palmer*, The Print Collectors' Club, no. 16, London, 1937

Andrews 1964
Keith Andrews, *The Nazarenes: A Brotherhood of German Painters in Rome*, Oxford, 1964

Andrews 1989
Malcolm Andrews, *The Search for the Picturesque: Landscape Aesthetics and Tourism in Britain, 1760–1800*, Aldershot, 1989

*Art Treasures* 1998
*Art Treasures of England: The Regional Collections*, exh. cat., Royal Academy, London, 1998

Arts Council 1956
*Samuel Palmer and his Circle: The Shoreham Period*, exh. cat., Arts Council, London, 1956

Avery, Hardiman *et al.*
Kevin J. Avery, Tom Hardiman *et al.*, *The Grand Moving Panorama of Pilgrim's Progress*, exh. cat., Montclair Art Museum, Montclair, NJ, 1999

Barton and Tong 1995
Griselda Barton and Michael Tong, *Underriver: Samuel Palmer's Golden Valley*, Brasted Chart, Froglets, 1995

Becker
David P. Becker: 'Monotype', *The Grove Dictionary of Art Online*, Oxford University Press, <http://www.groveart.com>, accessed 23 September 2004

Bennett
Shelley M. Bennett, 'The Blake Followers in the Context of Contemporary English Art', in Gerald E. Bentley *et al.*, *Essays on the Blake Followers*, San Marino, CA, 1983, pp. 33–47

Bentley
Gerald E. Bentley, Jr., 'Blake and the Ancients: A Prophet with Honour among the Sons of God', in Gerald E. Bentley *et al.*, *Essays on the Blake Followers*, San Marino, CA, 1983, pp. 1–17

Berthoud 1982
Roger Berthoud, *Graham Sutherland: A Biography*, London, 1982

Bindman 1978
David Bindman, *The Complete Graphic Works of William Blake*, London, 1978

Bindman 1985
David Bindman, 'Samuel Palmer's *An Address to the Electors of West Kent*, 1832 Rediscovered', *Blake: An Illustrated Quarterly*, XIX/2 (1985), pp. 56–68

Binyon 1925
Laurence Binyon, *The Followers of William Blake*, London, 1925

Bowen 2000
John Bowen, 'Dickens and the Figures of "Pictures from Italy"', in *The Impact of Italy: The Grand Tour and Beyond*, ed. Clare Hornsby, London, 2000, pp. 197–217

Brown
David Blayney Brown, *Samuel Palmer 1805–81: Catalogue Raisonné of the Paintings and Drawings, and a Selection of Prints in the Ashmolean Museum*, Oxford, 1983

Bulwer-Lytton
Edward George Bulwer-Lytton, *The Last Days of Pompeii*, McLean, VA, 2002

Bunyan
John Bunyan, *The Pilgrim's Progress, with a New Introduction by Roger Lundin*, Signet Classic, New York, 2002

Butlin 1962
Martin Butlin, *Samuel Palmer's Sketchbook, 1824*, Clairvaux, 1962

Butlin 1981
Martin Butlin, *The Paintings and Drawings of William Blake*, 2 vols, New Haven and London, 1981

Butlin and Joll
Martin Butlin and Evelyn Joll, *The Paintings of J.M.W. Turner*, 2 vols, New Haven and London, 1984

Calvert
[Samuel Calvert], *A Memoir of Edward Calvert by his Third Son*, London, 1893

Chambers 1999
Emma Chambers, *An Indolent and Blundering Art? The Etching Revival and the Redefinition of Etching in England 1838–1892*, Aldershot, 1999

Collins 1848
W. Wilkie Collins, *The Life of William Collins, Esq. R.A., by his Son*, 2 vols, London, 1848

Cooke 1826
*Picturesque Views on the Southern Coast of England, from Drawings Made Principally by J.M.W. Turner, R.A. and Engraved by W.B. Cooke, George Cooke, and Other Eminent Engravers*, 2 vols, London, 1826

Corbett *et al.* 2002
D.P. Corbett, Y. Holt, F. Russell, eds, *The Geographies of Englishness: Landscape and the National Past 1880–1940*, New Haven & London, 2002, pp. 249–74

Correspondence
Correspondence between A.H. Palmer and Martin Hardie relating to Samuel Palmer, National Art Library, London, MSL/1953/2782, MSL/1962/1020

Cowling 1989
Mary Cowling, *The Artist as Anthropologist: The Representation of Type and Character in Victorian Art*, Cambridge and New York, 1989

Cox
David Cox, *A Treatise on Landscape Painting and Effect in Water Colours*, London, 1813

Crouan
Katharine Crouan, *John Linnell: A Centennial Exhibition*, exh. cat., Fitzwilliam Museum, Cambridge, 1982

Daniel 2004
Malcolm Daniel, '*On Nature's Invitation Do I Come*: Roger Fenton's Landscapes', in Gordon Baldwin, Malcolm Daniel, Sarah Greenough *et al.*, *All the Mighty World: The Photographs of Roger Fenton, 1852–1860*, exh. cat., National Gallery of Art, Washington, DC, pp. 32–53

Essick
Robert N. Essick, 'John Linnell, William Blake and the Printmaker's Craft', in Gerald E. Bentley *et al.*, *Essays on the Blake Followers*, San Marino, CA, 1983, pp. 18–32

*European*
*The European Magazine and London Review*, new series, vol. I, no. I, September 1825

Evans 2002
Mark Evans, 'Blake, Calvert – and Palmer? The Album of Alexander Constantine Ionides', *Burlington Magazine*, vol. 144, September 2002, pp. 539–49

Finch
Mrs E. Finch, *Memoirs of the Late Francis Oliver Finch*, London, 1865

Fitzgerald *Aeneid*
Virgil, *The Aeneid*, trans. Robert Fitzgerald, New York, 1983

Fitzgerald *Odyssey*
Homer, *The Odyssey*, trans. Robert Fitzgerald, New York, 1963

Fitzwilliam 1984
Raymond Lister, *Samuel Palmer and 'The Ancients'*, exh. cat., Fitzwilliam Museum, Cambridge, 1984

Fredericksen 2002
Andrea Fredericksen, 'The Etching Club of London: A Taste for Painters' Etchings', *Philadelphia Museum of Art Bulletin*, vol. 92, no. 388, Summer 2002

Fuseli
Henry Fuseli, *Lectures on Painting, Delivered at the Royal Academy*, London, 1801

Garton 1992
Robin Garton, ed., *British Printmakers, 1855–1955: A Century of Printmaking from the Etching Revival to St. Ives*, Aldershot, 1992

Gilchrist 1863
Alexander Gilchrist, *Life of William Blake, 'Pictor ignotus'. With Selections from his Poems and Other Writings, by the Late Alexander Gilchrist. Illustrated from Blake's Own Works, in Facsimilé by W.J. Linton, and in Photolithography; with a Few of Blake's Original Plates*, 2 vols, London and Cambridge, 1863

Gilchrist 1887
H.H. Gilchrist, *Anne Gilchrist: Her Life and Writings*, London 1887

Gilpin 1783
The Revd William Gilpin, *Observations on the River Wye, and Several Parts of South Wales, &c. Relative Chiefly to Picturesque Beauty; Made in the Summer of the Year 1770, by William Gilpin, M.A. Vicar of Boldre near Lymington*, London, 1783 [with a publication date of 1782]

Goldman 1991
Paul Goldman, *Samuel Palmer, Visionary Printmaker: A Loan Exhibition from the British Museum, Department of Prints and Drawings*, exh. cat., British Museum, London, 1991

Grant 1952
Colonel Maurice Harold Grant, *A Dictionary of British Etchers*, London, 1952

Graves 1906
Algernon Graves, *The Royal Academy of Arts: A Complete Dictionary of Contributors and their Work from its Formation in 1769 to 1904*, 8 vols, London, 1905–6

Graves 1908
Algernon Graves, *The British Institution, 1806–1867: A Complete Dictionary of Contributors and their Work from the Foundation of the Institution*, London, 1908

Grigson 1947
Geoffrey Grigson, *Samuel Palmer: The Visionary Years*, London, 1947

Grigson 1960
Geoffrey Grigson, *Samuel Palmer's Valley of Vision*, London, 1960

Hamerton 1868
Philip Gilbert Hamerton, *Etchers and Etching*, 1st edn, London, 1868

Hamerton 1872
Philip Gilbert Hamerton, 'Examples of Modern Etching: XI. Samuel Palmer – *Sunrise*', in *The Portfolio*, ed. Philip Gilbert Hamerton, London, 1872, pp. 161–2

Hamerton 1880
Philip Gilbert Hamerton, *Etching and Etchers*, 3rd edn, London, 1880

Hamlyn 2004
Robin Hamlyn, 'William Blake at Work: "Every thing which is in Harmony"', in Joyce H. Townsend, ed., *William Blake: The Painter at Work*, London, 2004, pp. 12–39

Hardie 1910
Martin Hardie, *Frederick Goulding: Master Printer of Copper Plates*, Stirling, 1910

Hardie 1913
Martin Hardie, 'The Etched Work of Samuel Palmer', *The Print Collector's Quarterly* 3/1, 1913, pp. 207–40

Hardie 1926–27
Martin Hardie, 'Samuel Palmer (1805–1881)', *Old Watercolour Society's Club* 4 (1926–27), pp. 25–50

Hardie 1928
Martin Hardie, *Samuel Palmer*, Print Collectors' Club, publication no. 7, London, 1928

Harrison
Colin Harrison, *Samuel Palmer*, Oxford, 1997

Harrison 1997
Colin Harrison, 'Treasures of the Ashmolean Museum', *Apollo*, vol. CXLV, no. 423 (May 1997), pp. 8–19

Herring
Sarah Herring, 'Samuel Palmer's Shoreham Drawings in Indian Ink', *Apollo*, CXLVIII, 441, November 1998, pp. 37–42

Hilton
Timothy Hilton, *The Pre-Raphaelites*, London, 1970

Hobsbawm and Rudé
E.J. Hobsbawm and George Rudé, *Captain Swing*, London, 1969

Holt 1982
Elizabeth Gilmore Holt, ed., *A Documentary History of Art, Volume II: Michelangelo and the Mannerists, the Baroque and the Eighteenth Century*, Princeton, NJ, 1982

Irwin
Helen Irwin 'Samuel Palmer: Poet of Light and Shade', *Apollo*, August 1981, pp.103–13

Jauis
E.P. Jauis, *The Painterly Print: Monotypes from the Seventeenth to the Twentieth Century*, exh. cat., The Metropolitan Museum of Art, New York, 1980

*Keats Letters*
*Letters of John Keats*, ed. Robert Gittings, Oxford, 1970

Kelly and Carr 1987
Franklin Kelly and Gerald L. Carr, *The Early Landscapes of Frederic Edwin Church, 1845–1854*, exh. cat., Amon Carter Museum, Fort Worth, Texas, 1987

Kelly *et al.* 1989
Franklin Kelly, with Stephen Jay Gould, James Anthony Ryan and Debora Rindge, *Frederic Edwin Church*, exh. cat., The National Gallery of Art, Washington, DC, 1989

Keynes 1977
Sir Geoffrey Keynes, *The Complete Portraiture of William and Catherine Blake*, London, 1977

Krill 1987
John Krill, *English Artists' Paper*, London, 1987

*L&L*
A.H. Palmer, *The Life and Letters of Samuel Palmer, Painter and Etcher*, London, 1892

Leger Galleries 1992
*Samuel Palmer: An Exhibition of Palmer's Works with a Leger Provenance to Celebrate a Century of Art Dealing*, introduction by Raymond Lister, Leger Galleries, London, 1992

*Letters*
*The Letters of Samuel Palmer*, ed. Raymond Lister, 2 vols, Oxford, 1974

Lewis
C. Day Lewis, *The Georgics of Virgil*, London, 1940

Libson 1990
Lowell Libson, 'Books in the Running Brooks', *Watercolours and Drawings*, vol. v, no. 1, 1990, p. 29

Linnell Autobiography
'Autobiography of John Linnell', Linnell Archive, Fitzwilliam Museum, Cambridge, Ms 32-3000

Linnell 1994
David Linnell, *Blake, Palmer, Linnell and Co.: The Life of John Linnell*, Lewes, 1994

Lister
Raymond Lister, *Catalogue Raisonné of the Works of Samuel Palmer*, Cambridge, 1988

Lister 1962
Raymond Lister, *Edward Calvert*, London, 1962

Lister 1972–73
Raymond Lister, 'Two Blake Drawings and a Letter from Samuel Palmer', *Blake Newsletter* VI, 1972–73, pp. 53–4, plates 1, 2

Lister 1974
Raymond Lister, *Samuel Palmer: A Biography*, London, 1974

Lister 1981
Raymond Lister, *George Richmond: A Critical Biography*, London, 1981

Lister 1985
Raymond Lister, *The Paintings of Samuel Palmer*, Cambridge, 1985

Lister 1987
Raymond Lister, *Samuel Palmer: His Life and Art*, Cambridge, 1987

Liversidge and Edwards 1996
Michael Liversidge and Catharine Edwards, eds, *Imagining Rome: British Artists and Rome in the Nineteenth Century*, exh. cat., Bristol City Museum and Art Gallery, 1996

Lochnan 1984
Katharine A. Lochnan, *The Etchings of James McNeill Whistler*, New Haven and London, 1984

Lord 1998
Peter Lord, *Clarence Whaite and the Welsh Art World: The Betws-y-coed Artists' Colony, 1844–1914*, Aberystwyth, 1998

Lord 2000
Peter Lord, 'Chapter 5: The Idea of Landscape' and 'Chapter 9: Building an Art World', in *The Visual Culture of Wales: Imaging the Nation*, Cardiff, 2000, pp. 129–66, 279–310

Lowry after Allom
J. Lowry after T. Allom, 'Ilfracombe Town & Harbour, Devonshire', steel engraving, in *Devon and Cornwall Illustrated, From Original Drawings by Thomas Allom, W.H. Bartlett &c. With Historical and Topographical Descriptions by J. Britton & E.W. Brayley*, London, 1832

Luitjen 1999
Ger Luitjen, 'The *Iconography*: Van Dyck's portrait in print', in Carl Depauw, *Anthony Van Dyck as a Printmaker*, New York, 1999, pp. 73–91

Lyles and Wilton 1993
Anne Lyles and Andrew Wilton, *The Great Age of British Watercolours, 1750–1880*, exh. cat., Royal Academy, London, 1993

McManus and Townsend 2004
Noa Cahaner McManus and Joyce H. Townsend, 'The Large Colour Prints: Methods and Materials', in Joyce H. Townsend, ed., *William Blake: The Painter at Work*, London, 2004, pp. 82–99

Malins
Edward Malins, *Samuel Palmer's Italian Honeymoon*, Oxford, 1968

Mannocci 1988
Lino Mannocci, *The Etchings of Claude Lorrain*, New Haven and London, 1988

Mather 1937
Frank Jewett Mather Jr., 'Samuel Palmer's Virgil Etchings', *The Print Collector's Quarterly* 24, October 1937, pp. 253–64

Mauquoy-Hendrickx 1956
Marie Mauquoy-Hendrickx, *L'Iconographie d'Antoine van Dyck: Catalogue raisonné*, 2 vols, Brussels, 1956

*Memoir*
*Samuel Palmer, a Memoir by A.H. Palmer. Also a Catalogue of his Works, Including Those Exhibited by The Fine Arts Society 1881, And An Account of the Milton Series of Drawings, by L.R. Valpy*, London, 1882

Minutes
'Minutes of the Etching Club of London', 6 vols, National Art Library, London, MSL/1912/1508-1512A, especially vol. 2 (Minutes, 1842–76)

Moir 1964
Esther Moir, *The Discovery of Britain: The English Tourists, 1540 to 1840*, London, 1964

Moore 1936
T. Sturge Moore, 'Samuel Palmer's Happiest Designs', *Apollo*, 1936, pp. 329–35

Morowitz and Vaughan
Laura Morowitz and William Vaughan (eds), *Artistic Brotherhoods in the Nineteenth Century*, Aldershot, 2000

Neve 1970
Christopher Neve, 'A Guilty Secret? Photography and Victorian Painting', *Country Life* (18 June 1970), pp. 1150–52

Norvig 1993
Gerda S. Norvig, *Dark Figures in the Desired Country: Blake's Illustrations to 'The Pilgrim's Progress'*, Berkeley and Los Angeles, 1993

Nugent 2002
Charles Nugent, *British Watercolours in The Whitworth Art Gallery, The University of Manchester: A Summary Catalogue of Drawings and Watercolours by Artists Born before 1880*, Manchester, 2002

Olson 1985
Roberta J.M. Olson, *Fire and Ice: A History of Comets in Art*, New York, 1985

Olson 1990
Roberta J.M. Olson, 'A water-colour by Samuel Palmer of Donati's Comet', *Burlington Magazine* 132/1052 (November 1990), pp. 795–6

Olson and Pasachoff 1998
Roberta J.M. Olson and Jay M. Pasachoff, *Fire in the Sky: Comets and Meteors, the Decisive Centuries, in British Art and Science*, Cambridge, 1998

Ormond
Richard Ormond, *Early Victorian Portraits*, London, 1973

Ormsby 2004
Brownyn Ormsby with Joyce H. Townsend, Brian Singer and John Dean, 'Blake's Use of Tempera in Context', in Joyce H. Townsend, ed., *William Blake: The Painter at Work*, London, 2004

Paley
Morton D. Paley, '"To Realize after a Sort the Imagery of Milton": Samuel Palmer's Designs for *L'Allegro* and *Il Penseroso*', in Gerald E. Bentley *et al.*, *Essays on the Blake Followers*, San Marino, CA, 1983, pp. 48–71

A.H. Palmer 1884
A.H. Palmer, 'The Story of an Imaginative Painter', *The Portfolio: An Artistic Periodical* 15 (1884), pp. 145–51

Paroissien 1973
Charles Dickens, *Pictures from Italy, with an Introduction and Notes by David Paroissien*, New York, 1973, pp. 247–9

Payne 1982
Christiana Payne, 'John Linnell and Samuel Palmer', *Burlington Magazine*, 124, no. 948 (March 1982), pp. 131–6

Payne 1993
Christiana Payne, *Toil and Plenty: Images of Agricultural Landscape in England, 1780–1890*, London and New Haven, 1993

Pennell 1925
Joseph Pennell, *Etchers and Etching*, 3rd edn, New York, 1925

Pointon 1978
Marcia Pointon, 'The Representation of Time in Painting: A Study of William Dyce's *Pegwell Bay: A Recollection of October 5th, 1858*', *Art History* 1/1 (March 1978), pp. 99–103

Pointon 1979
Marcia Pointon, *William Dyce, 1806–1864: A Critical Biography*, Oxford, 1979

Powell 1987
Cecilia Powell, *Turner in the South: Rome, Naples, Florence*, New Haven, 1987

Powell 1998
Cecilia Powell, *Italy in the Age of Turner: 'The Garden of the World'*, exh. cat., Dulwich Picture Gallery, London, 1998

Powers
Harold S. Powers, 'Dorian', *Grove Music Online*, ed. L. Macy, <http://www.grovemusic.com>, accessed 10 November 2004

Pressly 1969
William L. Pressly Jr., 'Samuel Palmer and the Pastoral Convention', in *Record of the Art Museum, Princeton University*, vol. XXVIII, no. 2, 1969, pp. 22–37

Pressly 1970
William L. Pressly Jr., *et al.*, 'Samuel Palmer, The Etching Dream, An Exhibition held January 6–February 7, 1971, The Art Museum, Princeton University', *Record of The Art Museum Princeton University*, vol. XXIX, no. 2 (1970)

Redgrave 1891
Frances Margaret Redgrave, *Richard Redgrave, C.B., R.A.: A Memoir, Compiled from His Diary*, London, 1891

*Richmond Papers*
A.M.W. Stirling, *The Richmond Papers, from the Correspondence and Manuscripts of George Richmond, R.A., and his Son Sir William Richmond, R.A, K.C.B.*, London, 1926

Robinson 1869
Henry Crabb Robinson, *Diary, Reminiscences, and Correspondence of Henry Crabb Robinson ... Selected and Edited by Thomas Sadler*, 2 vols, Boston, 1869

Roscoe 1836, 1844
Thomas Roscoe, *Wanderings and Excursions in North Wales. By Thomas Roscoe ... With Fifty Engravings, from Drawings by Cattermole, Cox, and Creswick ...*, London, 1836, 2nd edn, 1844

Rosenblum
Robert Rosenblum, *Modern Painting and the Northern Romantic Tradition: Friedrich to Rothko*, London, 1975

Ruskin 1846
John Ruskin, 'Of Truth', in *Modern Painters*, 5 vols, London, 3rd edn, 1846–60, vol. 1 (1846), part 2

Sickert 1915
Walter Sickert, 'The Future of Engraving', *Burlington Magazine*, vol. 27, no. 150 (September 1915), pp. 224–5, 228–31

Smith 2002
Greg Smith, *The Emergence of the Professional Watercolourist: Contentions and Alliances in the Artistic Domain, 1760–1824*, Ashgate, Aldershot and Burlington, VT, 2002

Sparrow 1926
Walter Shaw Sparrow, *A Book of British Etching From Francis Barlow to Francis Seymour Haden*, London, 1926

Spicer 1994
Joaneath A. Spicer, 'Anthony Van Dyck's Iconography: An Overview of its Preparation', *Studies in the History of Art* 46 (1994), 326–64

Stainton 1991
Lindsay Stainton, *Nature into Art: English Landscape Watercolours from the British Museum*, exh. cat., North Carolina Museum of Art, 1991

Stephens 1872
F.G. Stephens, 'Samuel Palmer', *The Portfolio*, ed. Philip Gilbert Hamerton, London, 1872, pp.162–9

Stephens 1881
F.G. Stephens, *Notes by Mr. F.G. Stephens on a Collection of Drawings, Paintings and Etchings by the Late Samuel Palmer*, London, 1881

Story 1892
Alfred T. Story, *Life of John Linnell*, 2 vols, London, 1892

Sutton 1863
Thomas Sutton, Esq., 'On Some of the Uses and Abuses of Photography', a paper read before the Photographic Society of Scotland, published in *The Photographic Journal, Being the Journal of the Photographic Society* [of London], vol. 8, no. 129 (15 January 1863), p. 204

Tassi n.d.
Roberto Tassi, *Graham Sutherland: Complete Graphic Work*, Barcelona, n.d.

Tillotson 1977
Kathleeen Mary Tillotson, ed., *The Letters of Charles Dickens, Volume Four: 1844–1846*, Oxford, 1977

*The Times* 1858
'Farewell to the Comet', from *Dickens's Household Words*, *The Times*, Friday, 29 October 1858, p. 10, col. A

Townshend and Townsend 2004
Piers Townshend and Joyce H. Townsend, 'The Conservation of a Large Colour Print: *Satan Exulting over Eve*' in Joyce H. Townsend, ed., *William Blake: The Painter at Work*, London, 2004, pp. 100–107

Twining 1893
Lousia Twining, *Recollections of Life and Work; Being the Autobiography of Louisa Twining*, London, 1893

V&A 1926
Martin Hardie and James Laver, with notes and introduction by A.H. Palmer, *Catalogue of an Exhibition of Drawings, Etchings & Woodcuts by Samuel Palmer and other Disciples of William Blake*, exh. cat., Victoria and Albert Museum, London, 1926

Vaughan 1979
William Vaughan, *German Romanticism and English Art*, New Haven and London, 1979

Vergo
Peter Vergo, 'Music and Art', *The Grove Dictionary of Art Online*, <http://www.groveart.com>, accessed 10 November 2004

*A Vision Recaptured*
*Samuel Palmer, A Vision Recaptured: The Complete Etchings and the Paintings for Milton and for Virgil*, Commemorative Handbook published on the occasion of the Samuel Palmer Exhibition at the Victoria and Albert Museum, London, 1978

Wedmore 1911
Frederick Wedmore, *Etchings*, London, 1911

White 1977
Christopher White, *English Landscape 1630–1850*, exh. cat., Yale Center for British Art, New Haven, 1977

White and Saynor
Macolm White and Joy Saynor, *Shoreham: A Village in Kent*, Shoreham, 1989

Wilcox
Timothy Wilcox, *Samuel Palmer*, London, 2005

Wilcox and Titterington 1984
Timothy Wilcox and Christopher Titterington, *William Turner of Oxford (1789–1862)*, exh. cat., Arts Council of Great Britain, London, 1984

Wildman 1991
Stephen Wildman, *British Watercolours from Birmingham*, exh. cat., Birmingham Museums and Art Gallery, 1991

Wilkinson 2002
Alan Wilkinson, ed., *Henry Moore: Writings and Conversations*, Aldershot, 2002

Willsdon 1988
Claire Annabella Willsdon, *Aspects of Mural Painting in London, 1890–1930*, Cambridge, 1988

Wilton 1977
Andrew Wilton, *British Watercolours 1750 to 1850*, Oxford, 1977

Wilton 1984
Andrew Wilton, *Turner in Wales*, Llandudno, Mostyn Art Gallery, 1984

Woof and Hebron 1998
Robert Woof and Stephen Hebron, *Towards 'Tintern Abbey': Bicentenary of "Lyrical Ballads", 1798*, Wordsworth Trust, 1998

Yeats
W.B. Yeats, *The Poems: A New Edition*, ed. Richard J. Finneran, London, 1983

Yorke 1988
Malcolm Yorke, *The Spirit of Place: Nine Neo-Romantic Artists and their Times*, London, 1988

Yorke 1990
Malcolm Yorke, *Keith Vaughan: His Life and Work*, London, 1990

# List of Lenders

Numbers refer to catalogue entries

**Public and Institutional Collections**

CANADA

Ottawa
  National Gallery of Canada: 46

THE NETHERLANDS

Amsterdam
  Rijksmuseum: 148, 150

UNITED KINGDOM

Bedford
  Cecil Higgins Art Gallery: 153
Birmingham
  Birmingham Museums and Art Gallery: 105a, 105b, 157
Cambridge
  The Fitzwilliam Museum, University of Cambridge: 20, 69, 97, 132, 136
London
  British Museum: 3, 4, 9a–e, 9g, 9i–t, 18, 19, 21, 23–7, 49, 51, 58–60, 62, 76, 121, 128b, 133, 134, 141, 154, 156, 158, 160
  ING Bank, N.V., London Branch: 147
  National Portrait Gallery: 54, 56
  Royal Academy of Arts: 111
  Tate: 17, 32, 35, 48, 53, 57, 75, 80, 94, 104
  Victoria and Albert Museum: 6, 9f, 9h, 16, 33, 36, 37, 39, 42, 55, 63, 64, 66, 106, 113, 115, 127, 145, 155
Maidstone
  Centre for Kentish Studies: 95
Manchester
  Manchester City Galleries: 87, 125, 137, 143
  The Whitworth Art Gallery, University of Manchester: 78, 123, 159
Oxford
  The Ashmolean Museum: 1, 10–15, 28, 31, 70–72, 74, 77, 82, 86, 91, 99, 116, 120, 122, 129, 131, 139a, 142, 149

UNITED STATES

New Haven, CT
  Yale Center for British Art, Paul Mellon Collection: 5, 7, 8, 30, 34, 38, 40, 41, 43, 45, 81, 83, 84, 92, 96, 100, 101, 102, 108, 126, 128a, 130, 151
New York, NY
  The Metropolitan Museum of Art: 44, 61, 98, 110, 118, 135c, 139c, 161–4
  The Pierpont Morgan Library: 47, 52, 65, 109
Princeton, NJ
  Princeton University Art Museum: 29, 119
Providence, RI
  Museum of Art, Rhode Island School of Design: 114
San Marino, CA
  The Huntington Library, Art Collections, and Botanical Gardens: 2, 50, 152
Washington, DC
  National Gallery of Art: 68, 139b
Wisconsin
  Chazen Museum of Art, University of Wisconsin-Madison: 107

**Private Collections**

AUSTRALIA

James Fairfax, AO: 89

UNITED KINGDOM

Simon and Gayle Jenkins: 144
Private Collection, Linnell family: 22, 112a, 112b
Private Collection (c/o Lowell Libson Ltd): 117
Private Collection (Lent Courtesy Richard Nathanson, London): 88
Three collectors who prefer to remain anonymous: 67, 138, 146

UNITED STATES

Collection of Gilbert and Ildiko Butler: 121
Richard L. Feigen: 90
Collection Michael and Judy Steinhart, New York: 85
Malcolm Wiener Collection: 103
Two collectors who prefer to remain anonymous: 73, 140; 93

# Contributors

ELIZABETH E. BARKER is Director of the Picker Art Gallery at Colgate University, Hamilton, NY. Her publications address British and American art of the eighteenth and nineteenth centuries.

DAVID BINDMAN is Durning Lawrence Professor of the History of Art at University College London. He is a leading expert on William Blake and has published on many aspects of the art and culture of the eighteenth and nineteenth centuries.

DAVID BLAYNEY BROWN is a Curator at Tate, responsible for the Turner Collection. He has published widely on Turner, Romanticism and British art.

ALEXANDRA GREATHEAD is Paper Conservator at the Ashmolean Museum, Oxford, specializing in works of art on paper with experience of working in both the UK and the USA.

COLIN HARRISON is the Assistant Keeper with special responsibility for British paintings and drawings in the Ashmolean Museum, Oxford. He is the author of numerous articles and exhibition catalogues on British and French art of the eighteenth and nineteenth centuries.

MARJORIE SHELLEY is Sherman Fairchild Conservator in Charge of Drawings and Prints Conservation at The Metropolitan Museum of Art, New York. She has lectured and published widely on artists' drawing materials from the sixteenth to the nineteenth centuries.

WILLIAM VAUGHAN is Professor Emeritus in the History of Art at Birkbeck College, University of London. He has published extensively on Romanticism and on British and German art of the eighteenth and nineteenth centuries.

SCOTT WILCOX is Curator of Prints and Drawings at the Yale Center for British Art, Yale University, New Haven, CT. He is an expert in British art of the eighteenth and nineteenth centuries and has published several studies on British watercolourists.

# Index of Works

Numbers refer to catalogue entries

# Index of Names

# Photographic Acknowledgements

Numbers refer to catalogue entries (apart from fig. numbers)


Aberdeen Art Gallery & Museum Collection: fig. 14
Ashmolean Museum, Oxford: 1, 10–15, 28, 31, 70–2, 74, 77, 82, 86, 91, 99, 116, 120, 122, 129, 131, 139a, 142, 149; figs 22, 23

Bildarchiv Preussischer Kulturbesitz: fig. 2
Birmingham Museums and Art Gallery: 105a, 105b, 157
British Museum: 3, 4, 9a–e, 9g, 9i–t, 18, 19, 21, 23–7, 49, 51, 58–60, 62, 76, 121, 128b, 133, 134, 141, 154, 156, 158, 160; figs 20, 21, 24, 27, 29

Cecil Higgins Art Gallery, Bedford, Trustees of: 153
Centre for Kentish Studies, Maidstone: 95
Chazen Museum of Art, University of Wisconsin-Madison: 107

Fitzwilliam Museum, University of Cambridge: 20, 69, 97, 132, 136

Alexandra Greathead: fig. 9

Huntington Library, Art Collections, and Botanical Gardens, San Marino, California: 2, 50, 152

ING Bank N.V., London Branch: 147

Manchester City Galleries: 87, 125, 137, 143
Metropolitan Museum of Art, New York: 44, 61, 98, 110, 118, 135c, 139c, 161–4; figs 1, 30

National Gallery of Art, Washington DC, copyright Board of Trustees: 68, 139b
National Gallery of Canada, Ottawa: 46
National Portrait Gallery, London: 54, 56; fig. 3

Paul Mellon Centre for British Art: fig. 29
Pierpont Morgan Library: 47, 52, 65, 109
Princeton University Art Museum: 29, 119

Rhode Island School of Design, Museum of Art, photo Erik Gould: 114

Rijksmuseum, Amsterdam: 148, 150
Royal Academy of Arts, London: 111

Marjorie Shelley: figs 10, 11, 12

Tate, London: 17, 32, 35, 48, 53, 57, 75, 80, 94, 104; figs 5, 7

V&A Images/Victoria and Albert Museum: 6, 9f, 9h, 16, 33, 36, 37, 39, 42, 55, 63, 64, 66, 106, 113, 115, 127, 145, 155

Whitworth Art Gallery, University of Manchester: 78, 123, 159

Yale Center for British Art, Paul Mellon Collection: 5, 7, 8, 30, 34, 38, 40, 41, 43, 45, 81, 83, 84, 92, 96, 100, 101, 102, 108, 126, 128a, 130, 151